D0520249

Special Edition

USING
WINDOWS NT
WORKSTATION 4.0

Special Edition

USING
WINDOWS NT
WORKSTATION 4.0

Written by Paul Sanna with

John Enck • Sam S.Gill • Kathy Ivens • Kevin Jones • Guy Robinson Kirkland • Michael Marchuck • Sue Mosher • Michael O'Mara • Sue Plumley • Michael D.Reilly • Gregory J. Root • Brian Underdahl

Special Edition Using Windows NT Workstation

Library of Congress Catalog No.: 96-67563

ISBN: 0-7897-0673-3

98 97   6 5 4

Interpretation of the printing code: the rightmost double-digit number is the year of the book's printing; the rightmost single-digit number, the number of the book's printing. For example, a printing code of 96-1 shows that the first printing of the book occurred in 1996.

Screen reproductions in this book were created using Collage Plus from Inner Media, Inc., Hollis, NH.

Credits

PRESIDENT
Roland Elgey

PUBLISHING DIRECTOR
Brad R. Koch

EDITORIAL SERVICES DIRECTOR
Elizabeth Keaffaber

MANAGING EDITOR
Michael Cunningham

DIRECTOR OF MARKETING
Lynn E. Zingraf

ACQUISITIONS MANAGER
Elizabeth A. South

PRODUCT DIRECTOR
Kevin Kloss

ASSISTANT PRODUCT MARKETING MANAGER
Christy Miller

TECHNICAL EDITORS
Bob Chronister
Don Doherty

PRODUCTION EDITOR
Thomas F. Hayes

EDITORS
Geneil Breeze
Lisa Gebken
Kate Givens
Sarah Rudy
Christy Prakel
Linda Seifert

TECHNICAL SPECIALIST
Nadeem Muhammed

ACQUISITIONS COORDINATOR
Tracy Williams

OPERATIONS COORDINATOR
Patty Brooks

EDITORIAL ASSISTANT
Carmen Krikorian

BOOK DESIGNER
Ruth Harvey

COVER IMAGE
Ken Davies/Masterfile

PRODUCTION TEAM
Marcia Brizendine
Jenny Earhart
Joan Evan
Bryan Flores
DiMonique Ford
Steph Mineart
Daryl Kessler
Darlena Murray
Staci Somers
Kelly Warner

INDEXERS
Ginny Bess

Composed in *Century Old Style* and *Franklin Gothic* by Que Corporation.

For my mother and father.

About the Authors

Paul Sanna has been using PCs for almost 10 years, and he has been using Windows NT since its first Beta program. Paul is a project manager in the development department of Hyperion Software, Stamford, CT, where he works on the company's line of client/server financial accounting software. He has coauthored three books on Windows 95: *Understanding Windows 95, Inside Windows 95* (New Riders), and *The Windows Installation and Configuration Handbook* (Que). Paul has a degree in English from Boston University and lives in Bethel, CT, with his wife, Andrea, his twin daughters, Rachel and Allison, and their new sister, Victoria. He can be reached on the Internet at **psanna@ix.netcom.com**.

John Enck is a data communications and networking specialist with over 15 years of hands-on experience. He is the author of numerous networking and computer-related books, and is a regular contributor to a variety of computer publications. John is currently a technical editor for *Windows NT Magazine*.

Sam S. Gill is vice president of DataWiz. Sam has a Ph.D. from the University of California, Berkeley. He is recognized in academic circles and in industry as an expert on client/server technology. Sam has written several articles on client/server topics, SQL Server, and application development methodologies and practices. He is a Microsoft Certified Trainer (MCT) for Visual Basic, SQL Server, Visual C++, Win32 API, Windows Operating Systems and Services Architecture (WOSSA), and the Microsoft Solution Development Discipline (SDD). Sam is involved in numerous Microsoft Beta programs and teaches state-of-the-art technology to audiences sponsored by Microsoft. He is also a full professor at San Francisco State University in the Business Analysis and Computer Systems department.

Sam has been involved in developing business applications for more than 35 years and has been focusing on the development of distributed computing applications for the last ten.

Kathy Ivens has been a computer consultant since 1984, and has authored and co-authored many books on computer subjects. She is a frequent contributor to national magazines, both writing articles and reviewing software. Before becoming an expert in computing, Ms. Ivens spent many years as a television producer, where she had fun producing sports and was mildly amused producing news and entertainment programs. Preceding that career was some professional time spent as a community organizer and also as a political consultant. She still doesn't know what she wants to be when she grows up.

Kevin Jones has worked in the computer industry for 15 years. He has worked at large corporations, IBM and Unisys, down to very small startups. He has worked on such flagship products as dBase III & IV, PC Tools for Windows, and Norton Navigator. Currently, he is a principal software engineer with the Peter Norton Division of Symantec Corp. Kevin, has been actively working with Windows 95 since October of 1993.

Rob Kirkland was, in previous lives, a banker then a lawyer. But Rob's fascination with computers and their endless uses drew him into computer consulting and training, which he has pursued full-time since 1988. Rob teaches classes in Novell Netware, Lotus Notes, Windows NT, communications software, numerous application programs, and hardware management. He also consults for many businesses that need to set up systems, design applications, or subdue unruly hardware or software. As a writer, Rob develops training manuals for his firm and has contributed to several Que books. Rob is a Certified Novell Engineer (CNE), a Microsoft Certified Product Specialist (MCPS) for Windows NT, and a Certified Lotus Notes Instructor (CLI). You can reach Rob on CompuServe at **74750,3360**, or on the Internet at **Rob_Kirkland.Rockey_&_Associates@Notes.Compuserve.com**. For information on courses, on-site training, training manuals, or consulting, contact Rob via e-mail.

Michael Marchuk has been involved with the computing industry for over 17 years. Michael currently manages the development research department for a mid-sized software development firm while consulting for small businesses and writing leading-edge books for Que Publishing. Along with his bachelor's degree in finance from the University of Illinois, he has received certification as a Netware CNE and a Compaq Advanced Systems Engineer.

Sue Mosher is an independent Windows consultant and has written about Windows networking, Microsoft Mail, Exchange, and Schedule+ for various newsletters and books. She is well known on the Windows support forums on CompuServe and the Microsoft Network, earning recognition as a Microsoft Most Valuable Professional. Before starting her own business, Slipstick Systems, she was a broadcast journalist and software developer for The Associated Press for 15 years. Her favorite previous job was as a progressive rock disc jockey.

Michael O'Mara is a freelance author and technical writer. Previously, he was a staff author with The Cobb Group where he wrote innumerable articles about leading computer software programs and served as Editor-in-Chief of several monthly software journals. He has coauthored or contributed to other Que books including *Using DOS, Using Windows 3.11, Special Edition Using CompuServe, Special Edition Using Windows 95, Special Edition Using Windows NT Workstation 3.51, 10 Minute Guide to Freelance Graphics 96 for Windows 95,* and *Using Your PC.* He can be reached at **76376.3441@compuserve.com**.

Sue Plumley has owned and operated her own business for eight years; Humble Opinions provides training, consulting, network installation, management, and maintenance to banking, education, medical, and industrial facilities. In addition, Sue has authored and coauthored over 50 books for Que Corporation and its sister imprints, including *10 Minute Guide to Lotus Notes, Special Edition Using Windows NT Workstation 3.51,* and *Easy Windows 95.*

Michael D. Reilly has 24 years of experience in computer data processing, including extensive experience on DEC's VAX series 780/785, SEL's 32/75, the CDC 3600, and Xerox 9300. He has been involved with personal computers since 1984. His background includes programming in Fortran and developing applications in Microsoft Access, Oracle, and Progress. He has worked on the VMS, UNIX, DOS, Windows, and Windows NT operating systems. Mike has held positions in management, research, software design and development, scientific data processing, computer sales and installation, training and support, and technical writing. In 1990, he co-founded Mount Vernon Data Systems, Inc., a consulting company that specializes in client/server database applications. He is a Microsoft Certified Trainer for Windows NT, and has coauthored two books on Microsoft Access. Mike has an M.A. degree in physics from Queens' College, Cambridge University. You can reach him on CompuServe at **72421,1336**.

Gregory J. Root is a project manager for a Fortune 400 corporation. Throughout his career he has administered and installed peer-to-peer and server-based networks, developed applications using FORTRAN and Visual Basic, and managed software development projects. He also has contributed to other Que publications such as *Windows 95 Connectivity, Killer Windows 95, the Windows 95 Installation and Configuration Handbook,* and *VBA Database Solutions.* He lives in Lake Hills, Illinois, with his beautiful wife and lifelong companion, Tracy.

Brian Underdahl is an author, independent consultant, and custom application developer based in Reno, Nevada. He's the author or coauthor of over 25 computer books, as well as numerous magazine articles. He has also acted as a product developer and as a technical editor on many other Que books. His e-mail address is **71505,1114** on CompuServe.

Acknowledgments

You wouldn't be reading this book if not for the support and assistance the following individuals provided to the author: Elizabeth South, Kevin Kloss, Tom Hayes, Diane Flaherty, Barrie Rysz, Emily James, Dave Morehead, the tremendous group of contributing authors, all of the production and editing folks at Que who never get the publicity they should, Dunkin Donuts (large black, please), and King Crimson.

We'd Like to Hear from You!

As part of our continuing effort to produce books of the highest possible quality, Que would like to hear your comments. To stay competitive, we *really* want you, as a computer book reader and user, to let us know what you like or dislike most about this book or other Que products.

You can mail comments, ideas, or suggestions for improving future editions to the address below, or send us a fax at (317) 581-4663. For the online inclined, Macmillan Computer Publishing has a forum on CompuServe (type **GO QUEBOOKS** at any prompt) through which our staff and authors are available for questions and comments. The address of our Internet site is **http://www.mcp.com** (World Wide Web).

In addition to exploring our forum, please feel free to contact me personally to discuss your opinions of this book: I'm **74201,1064** on CompuServe, and I'm **kkloss@que.mcp.com** on the Internet.

Thanks in advance—your comments will help us to continue publishing the best books available on computer topics in today's market.

Kevin Kloss
Product Director
Que Corporation
201 W. 103rd Street
Indianapolis, Indiana 46290
USA

N O T E Although we cannot provide general technical support, we're happy to help you resolve problems you encounter related to our books, disks, or other products. If you need such assistance, please contact our Tech Support department at 800-545-5914 ext. 3833.

To order other Que or Macmillan Computer Publishing books or products, please call our Customer Service department at 800-835-3202 ext. 666.

Contents at a Glance

Table of Contents

V | Networking with Windows NT

19 Understanding Windows NT Network Services 497

VI | Going Online with Windows NT Workstation

22 Installing and Configuring a Modem 593

23 Using Dial-Up Networking 615

Introduction

Thank you for taking a look at *Special Edition Using Windows NT Workstation 4.0*. We think this book offers a lot to people with both varying years and varying types of experience in Windows and PC software.

The aim of this book is to introduce you to Windows NT Workstation, as well as provide you with all of the information you'll ever need to configure and optimize the Windows NT Workstation system. At the same time, we're interested in teaching you how to take advantage of all of the features in Windows NT Workstation and make you as productive and efficient as possible.

So, what about Windows NT? With the release of version 4.0 of Windows NT, Microsoft has made the decision process for users choosing an operating system much more difficult than before. Hmm, Windows 95 or Windows NT? Since the release of Windows 95, the party-line has been Windows 95 for the home or small business user, and Windows NT as the high-powered, business-critical system.

The new version of Windows NT, however, supports much of the desired at-home features you may be looking for, such as multimedia and almost simple Internet support (plus the Windows 95 user interface), but the system has not lost any of its flexible, open, full 32-bit, secure, reliable, and fault-tolerant characteristics. The advice of this book—Windows NT. Read the book, for example, to find out how applications are shielded from each other, helping to ensure that one crashed program does not bring down the rest of the operating system, but also read to see how to connect to the Internet and browse the World Wide Web in minutes. ■

Who this Book is For

It's easy to say this book is for anyone who uses Windows NT Workstation, but this really is the case. If you are a help desk engineer, system or network administrator, or just the person who everyone in your department asks for help, you'll find this book up your alley. The book provides significant coverage of connectivity concepts, maintaining a workstation with multiple users both on the workstation and on the network, as well as loads of troubleshooting information.

If you are a home user of NT Workstation, you'll find information to help answer all of your questions. You'll find coverage of setting up new hardware, installing applications, and hints for finding more information about the system. The addition of Internet Explorer and almost simple access to the Internet in Windows NT makes the system a great choice for a family computer operating system, and you'll find all the help you need in the book

Lastly, as a corporate user, you'll also benefit from the coverage of network issues. You might also find beneficial the chapters covering management of the services and devices in the system, configuring memory and multitasking, optimizing your system, and protecting its data.

If you are a manager in an organization considering moving to NT Workstation, you'll find help in making your decision. Be sure to refer to the chapters describing NT Workstation's support for different networks, issues regarding installation, especially converting from existing Windows applications, and some of the positioning information that appears in Chapter 1.

What this Book Thinks You Know

This book assumes you've used Windows before, but coverage of the basics is provided in Chapter 3, "Working in Windows NT," and Appendix D, "A Review of the Windows NT GUI." Still, if you haven't used Windows before, you may want to consider reading a primer on Windows. Be sure you understand some of the Windows basics, like using a mouse and recognizing the graphical elements that appear on the Windows screen. This book also assumes you know some basic PC hardware and software concepts, such as what an operating system is, or what a hard drive or RAM is. An excellent source of this type of information is Que's *Upgrading and Repairing PCs*, by Scott Meuller.

Your NT Platform

Much of the development of this book and its focus is based on an x86-based system. This doesn't mean that the other platforms supported by NT are ignored. Whenever appropriate, issues specific to the PowerPC, DEC Alpha AXP, and MIPS R4000 are covered.

How to Use this Book

A discussion of how to use this book really is based on how the book is designed. Like other books in the Que's Special Edition series, *Special Edition Using Windows NT Workstation 4.0* is designed to provide useful, real-world information about the tasks you complete everyday. You won't find coverage of every feature in NT Workstation. You will find, however, detailed, informed instruction on the critical features and issues that determine your success in using the system.

Should you read this book from cover to cover? Why not? Do you have to? Certainly not. As you come across features and tasks in your everyday use of NT Workstation, open the book and find out what the author of the chapter had to say. Perhaps you've seen a reference in one of the computer periodicals to some NT feature. Use the index to track down the feature in this book and try putting the feature to work. Step-by-step procedures are included in many of the chapters. These procedures are generic, so even if you skim the rest of the material in the chapter, you can still gain some knowledge from following the how-to information. Perhaps you are about to start a project using one of the main features of NT Workstation, such as using TCP/IP; read the chapter covering the feature in this book to become fully prepared.

What's in this Book

This section gives you a quick preview of each of the chapters in this book. If you are looking for a particular piece of information or procedure, you can get an idea from this section as to where to find it. Use the Table of Contents and the Index as well to help you find a specific piece of information you're looking for.

Part I: Introducing Windows NT Workstation 4.0

Chapter 1, "Understanding Windows NT Workstation," positions Windows NT Workstation for you. You learn about the major features in Windows NT Workstation, and a comparison to Windows NT Server also is included.

Chapter 2, "Getting Started with NT Workstation 4.0," shows you how to progress from a powered-down computer to a system running Windows NT Workstation to which you are logged on. In this chapter, you learn how to logon to Windows NT Workstation, log off, change your password, and understand other start-up and shutdown procedures. In addition, you learn what happens when your computer boots up Windows NT and how to troubleshoot some typical startup problems.

Chapter 3, "Working in Windows NT," shows you to become productive using Windows. You're introduced to many of the new user interface features of Windows NT, including the Desktop and context menus, and how to complete common tasks in Windows NT.

Chapter 4, "Getting Help," shows you how to use all of the Help features in the latest version of Windows NT. You learn how to browse through the Table of Contents and the index, search for a word phrase in any help topic, as well as customize some elements of how Help behaves and appears.

Part II: Working with Windows NT

Chapter 5, "Printing and Setting Up Printers," covers everything you need to know about printing in Windows NT and setting up a printer.

Chapter 6, "Working with Folders and Files," explains how to work with Windows NT's file system of files and folders. Some of the terminology in version 4.0 of Windows NT is different from that of the previous version, as is the user interface. So, this chapter introduces you to these new terms and explains how to manage the files and directories.

Chapter 7, "Managing Disk Storage with the Disk Administrator," shows you how to work with Windows NT's tool for managing the hard disks on your computer. You learn how to create and delete partitions on your hard disks, and how to format them with either the FAT or NTFS file system.

Chapter 8, "Working with the Command Prompt," shows you how to work with a holdover from the days of DOS. Windows NT still supports some work at the command prompt—historically and affectionately known as the C-prompt—and this chapter shows you what commands you can use at the command prompt and how you use them.

Chapter 9, "Transporting Files with Briefcase," is an important stop for anyone running Windows NT on a mobile PC. The Briefcase applet helps users keep synchronized copies of documents they bring on the road or home with the central versions you keep in your main office. This chapter shows you how to create and use a briefcase.

Part III: Configuring Windows NT Workstation 4.0

Chapter 10, "Customizing the Windows NT Interface," shows you how to customize various elements of the Windows NT user interface. You find coverage in this chapter of desktop background, colors, fonts, mouse settings, the keyboard, screen savers, date and time formats, and regional settings.

Chapter 11, "Changing and Configuring Hardware," explains how to configure Windows NT to operate with new hardware you add to your system. Hardware covered in this chapter includes a mouse, keyboard, video adapter, your computer's serial ports, SCSI adapters, tape storage devices, and PC cards.

Chapter 12, "Managing Memory, Multitasking, and System Options," helps you configure your operating system, such as specifying memory options, multitasking behavior, startup options, and hardware profiles.

Chapter 13, "Configuring Windows NT Workstation for Multimedia," shows you how to configure Windows NT for audio and video. Many of today's most exciting applications, including the World Wide Web on the Internet, use video and sound clips. You learn how to add a multimedia device, configure it to work with Windows NT, and how to use the multimedia accessories built into Windows NT.

Chapter 14, "Managing System Services and Devices," helps you understand the special programs that support hardware and other peripherals. These programs are known as services and devices. This chapter helps you understand the difference between services and devices, how to start, stop, and pause services and devices, and more.

Chapter 15, "Securing Windows NT Workstation," explains to you the Windows NT system for protecting your system from unwanted access by others. You learn about user accounts, groups of users, security policies, and auditing user activity.

Chapter 16, "Managing the Boot Process," helps you understand and configure what occurs when Windows NT Workstation starts up. You learn how to customize the boot process via working with BOOT.INI file, and you learn how to set up Windows NT to boot with a choice of Windows NT and another operating system.

Part IV: Working with Applications

Chapter 17, "Working with Applications," helps you understand how to work with different types of applications in Windows NT. Windows 95 and Windows NT applications usually run without issue in Windows NT, but you can probably benefit from the details about configuring Windows NT to run finicky 16-bit applications, such as DOS and Windows 3.1 applications.

Chapter 18, "Using Windows NT Accessory Applications," helps you understand what accessories are available for Windows NT users.

Part V: Networking with Windows NT

Chapter 19, "Understanding Windows NT Network Services," provides detailed information about the different networks compatible with Windows NT. You learn general information about networks and connectivity, as well as the specifics about the different network operating systems and protocols you can use with Windows NT.

Chapter 20, "Configuring the Network at Your Workstation," provides you with step-by-step instruction on getting your Workstation to talk to a network. You find information on network adapters, protocols, and login scripts.

Chapter 21, "Managing Shared Resources," shows you how to control access to the resources on your system, including CD-ROM players, files, directories, and printers.

Part VI: Going Online with Windows NT Workstation 4.0

Chapter 22, "Installing and Configuring a Modem," explains how to add and configure a modem to Windows NT. You also learn about the new Unimodem support added to Windows NT.

Chapter 23, "Using Dial-Up Networking," gives you instruction in connecting Windows NT to remote networks, such as the Internet or the LAN used at your office.

Chapter 24, "Configuring TCP/IP," is a chapter for anyone who plans to use Windows NT Workstation to work with the Internet. TCP/IP is the network protocol of the Internet, and it also is used to communicate with certain types of other computer. This chapter explains TCP/IP concepts and explains how to configure it.

Chapter 25, "Using Windows NT with the Internet," explains the concepts and procedures for another of today's hottest topics—the Internet. This chapter provides you with an overview of the Internet, explains how to find an Internet Service Provider, how to set up Windows NT to connect to the Internet from either at home or the office, and then how to establish a connection to the Internet.

Chapter 26, "Using Internet Explorer, Internet Mail, and Internet News," shows you how to use three new Internet tools for Windows NT. Internet Explorer is a new World Wide Web browser. Internet Mail is a tool that lets you receive and send e-mail over the Internet. Internet News is a tool that helps you participate in UseNet discussions.

Chapter 27, "Using Peer Web Services," focuses on one of the hottest topics in the PC business—intranets. Windows NT Workstation includes features that let workstation systems act as Internet servers for other networked computers. This chapter shows you how to configure Peer Web Services and provide Internet service to other computers.

Chapter 28, "Configuring Windows Messaging Service," explains how to configure and use Exchange. This program lets you send and receive mail with a number of different mail providers, including the Internet and Microsoft Mail.

Chapter 29, "Using Windows Messaging," covers how to receive and send messages using Exchange Client. This chapter prepares you for exchanging messages with all of the mail providers you've configured exchange to work with.

Chapter 30, "Using HyperTerminal," explains how to connect to other online sources, *other* referring to non-Internet. A number of great online sources of information are available, such as computer bulletin boards, and this chapter explains how to configure HyperTerminal to connect and talk to these sources.

Part VII: Optimizing and Protecting Windows NT Workstation 4.0

Chapter 31, "Working with the Registry," can help the so-called power-user learn how to configure Windows NT Workstation systems using the system registry. The registry is a special database that stores information about your Windows NT system and the software you install in it.

Chapter 32, "Using the Event Viewer," gives you insight into one of the many powerful system administration tools built into NT Workstation. You learn what system events are recorded in the system log, as well as how to understand the information the event log presents you.

Chapter 33, "Optimizing Windows NT Workstation Performance," explains the factors that impact Windows NT Workstation's performance, the methods and tools to monitor performance of your system, and both strategies and tactics for maintaining and improving its performance.

Chapter 34, "Protecting Your Workstation and its Data," provides practical advice for protecting the most important resource on your NT Workstation—your data. Among the areas covered is use of a UPS, real-world advice for backing-up your system, and discussion about computer virus protection.

Chapter 35, "Using the Diagnostics Tool," shows you how to use an important tool that comes free with Windows NT. You learn how to get the information you need from the Diagnostics Tool, as well as how to understand some of the complicated data the tool provides you.

Part VIII: Appendixes

Appendix A, "Installing Windows NT Workstation," shows you how to plan and prepare for the installation of Windows NT, and then how to execute the steps to install the operating system. Because there a few strategic decisions you need to make about your system, so to run Windows NT, before you install, it's best to take a look at this appendix so you are prepared for the questions the install program asks you.

Appendix B, "Maintaining Windows NT with Service Packs." Microsoft uses service packs to maintain Windows NT Workstation (and Windows NT Server). These packs contain bug fixes and enhancements. This appendix explains where to find service packs and how to use them to fix bugs and enhance your system.

Appendix C, "Where to Get More Information." This appendix provides a road map to many other sources for information about NT Workstation.

Appendix D, "A Review of the Windows NT GUI," covers the basics of the graphical user interface used in Windows NT. If you've never used Windows before, this appendix is a good place to start.

Appendix E, "What's on the CD," provides you with a quick overview of the software found on the CD included with this book.

Conventions Used in this Book

The Windows interface presents an interesting challenge in trying to present written instruction about a graphical environment that keys off of pictures and colors. This section shows you some of the elements and conventions used in the book that help convey the topics about NT Workstation and Windows.

Special Elements

In this book you'll find a number of special graphical elements to call your attention to different kinds of information. For example, you 'll find boxes interspersed throughout the text in chapters pointing out useful tips and information relevant to the section of the chapter where they're located. Examples with descriptions of these elements follow in this section:

ON THE WEB

The "On the Web" reference points you to World Wide Web sites that are particular to the subject matter you are reading. Que's Web site is

http:\\www.mcp.com\que

N O T E A note provides you with information relevant to the topic where it is located but not critical to the mission of the chapter. ▪

 Tips are included in the book to provide time-saving, practical advice that probably is not covered in the documentation shipped with the product.

CAUTION

Wherever you risk losing data or harming your system, a caution like this one appears in the book. Be on the lookout for this type of element.

TROUBLESHOOTING

Does this book help me solve some of the odd, unexpected problems I run into when using NT Workstation? In each chapter, you'll find numerous examples of troublesome behavior that you may encounter in NT Workstation. These examples are found in their own Troubleshooting sections, and resolution of these problems is always included.

Lastly, you will find references to other parts of the book throughout each chapter. These cross-references point to relevant information in other chapters.

Typeface Conventions

Special typeface styles are used to indicate special text. These typeface conventions are described in the following table.

Typeface	Use
Italics	Italics are used to indicate new terminology, such as *client/server*. Italics also are used to express variables whose values you fill in, such as "copy the files to the USER*your name* directory."
Bold	Bold is used to represent text that you enter in the system.
Monospace	The monospace typeface is used to represent messages you see on the screen or information presented at the command prompt.
<u>U</u>nderscore	This effect is reserved for representing the keyboard accelerator for a command.

Introducing Windows NT Workstation 4.0

CHAPTER 1

Understanding Windows NT Workstation

by Paul Sanna

If you have never used Windows NT before, or if you are returning to NT after an absence, then this chapter is a good place to start. You'll learn about Windows NT Workstation's features and capabilities. From this chapter, you should develop an understanding of what to expect from Windows NT and what to expect of yourself using Windows. If you are an experienced Windows NT user, you may find this chapter helpful in putting into perspective Windows NT capabilities. You might have just a passing familiarity with a particular feature or function, but you're not sure how it could benefit you or how you might implement it. This chapter also can assist you. Although the book is dedicated to Windows NT Workstation, you find information about Windows NT Server here, as well. ▪

Understand the differences between Windows NT Workstation and Windows NT Server

Though closely related, there are a number of significant differences between the server and workstation versions of Windows NT. In this chapter, you learn the differences between the two flavors of the operating system.

Review Windows NT Workstation features

In the last section of this chapter, we'll take a look from 10,000 feet at Windows NT Workstation's features and strengths. You learn about NT Workstation network and security capabilities, as well as performance and scalability issues.

What is Windows NT?

Windows NT is Microsoft's high-end, high-performance, Windows-based operating system. The NT stands for *new technology*. Microsoft has positioned Windows NT as the operating system for the business, whereas Windows 95 is the operating system of the home. This section provides a quick review of Windows NT's features and capabilities. Many of these items are covered in detail later in this chapter.

Windows NT is a 32-bit, preemptive multitasking, multithreading operating system. As an operating system, Windows NT is the system that runs your computer. Windows NT's *multitasking* support generally means that you can do more than one thing at once while running Windows NT, such as recalculate a spreadsheet while you check the spelling of a document you've written using a word processing program. *Multithreading* means that some of the applications you run in Windows NT can do more than one task at once, such as performing complex calculations while letting you input more data.

Windows NT comes in two versions—*NT Workstation* and *NT Server*. NT Workstation is designed for powerful, mission-critical client operations. This means that if you perform work vital to your organization right at the computer on your desktop, then Windows NT Workstation probably is the operating system for you. This work could be software development, engineering, real-time transactions processing, or anything else.

NT Server is a a high-performance, scalable, secure network operating system (NOS) that works in multinetwork environments. What does this mean? Though we'll get into the details later in this chapter, Windows NT is one of the most secure commercial operating systems available. It meets the U.S. government qualifications for a C2 rating for operating systems. As for NT's scalability, as you increase the workload that you task NT Server with, you don't need to replace the machine, just increase its power via memory or storage enhancements—Windows NT's performance scales up as the capability of its platform increases. In addition to those features, your network server group could include one or more NT Server machines running alongside other servers running other NOSes, such as Novell NetWare or Banyan Vines.

With version 4.0, Windows NT features the now-familiar Windows 95 user interface (see fig. 1.1). This means that if you have experience running either Windows 95 or any of the new Windows 95 applications on version 3.51 of Windows NT or Windows 95, you should have no problem becoming productive in Windows NT right away.

FIG. 1.1
One of the key features of the newest version of Windows NT is use of the Windows 95 user interface.

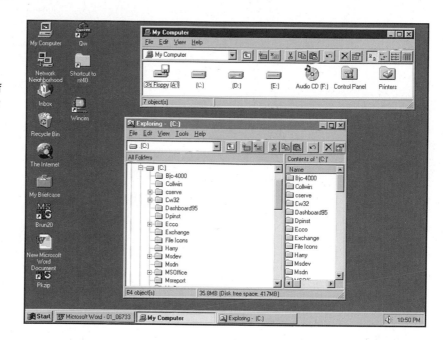

You can run numerous types of applications on Windows NT, such as DOS, Windows 95, Windows 3.x, and OS/2. This means that you do not have to give up your favorite applications you ran on other operating systems when you switch to Windows NT.

N O T E Windows NT also supports *POSIX* applications. POSIX stands for *Portable Operating System Interface* and is a set of standards defined by the IEEE (Institute of Electrical and Electronic Engineers) for promoting portability of applications across operating systems. Of the 12 POSIX standards, Windows NT supports POSIX.1 applications. This standard describes using a standard API (application programming interface) written in the C language. ■

Lastly, Windows NT runs on a number of top-performance systems, such as Pentium-based PCs, as well as RISC platforms, in addition to 386/486 machines. *RISC platforms* are computers that use a RISC chip. Users and organizations can run some of the fastest systems available, such as 200 MHz Pentium and RISC platforms, while sticking with the Windows NT operating system.

Comparing NT Workstation to NT Server

Windows NT includes the power, features, and flexibility to operate both as a client workstation on a network or as a network server operating system. Well, actually, you have to buy the correct product to get the features and tools you need. Table 1.1 outlines the differences between NT Server and NT Workstation.

Table 1.1   Features in NT Workstation versus NT Server

Item	NT Workstation	NT Server
Performance	Optimized for background tasks	Optimized for server and foreground
Remote Access Service sessions	1	256
Concurrent client connections	10 in; unlimited out	unlimited
Symmetric multiprocessors	2	32
Macintosh Services	No	Yes
Logon Validation and Customization	No	Yes
Disk Fault Tolerance	No	Yes

Windows NT Workstation Features and Capabilities

The following sections describe the critical features and capabilities of Windows NT. Detailed coverage of each topic is provided throughout the book. Consult the table of contents, index, or the cross-references in this book for more information.

Multiprocessor Support and Scalability

Multiprocessor support means that Windows NT supports the use of more than one processor on a computer running NT. Having more than one processor on a machine naturally results in performance advantages compared to machines with just one processor.

Windows NT provides support for computers with symmetric multiprocessor setups. You probably have seen the term *symmetric multiprocessing* many times, but you may not know what it means. Basically, symmetric multiprocessing support enables a single processor in a multiprocessor system to work on different tasks simultaneously, such as operating system work and application work. When the workload becomes too great, work is moved to the second processor, regardless of what the work is. This contrasts with *asymmetric multiprocessing*, in which the operating system always runs on one processor and applications on the other. Windows NT Server can support up to 32 CPUs; Windows NT Workstation supports a maximum of two.

This architecture in Windows NT makes scalability an automatic benefit. *Scalability* basically means that you do not have to choose a new operating system if you are unhappy with the performance of your system running Windows NT. The more CPU power you add to your system, the more work your system can handle at one time. This makes Windows NT a scalable system.

Scalability is also an import concept in client/server systems. For companies using client/server technology in the applications they run, they can dramatically increase the performance of the entire system by upgrading the server rather than each of the client workstations.

Multiplatform Support

Windows NT runs on a number of powerful desktop platforms. You can leverage the power of the newest Pentium chip from Intel, including the Pentium Pro, and you can run Windows NT on RISC-based platforms, such as MIPS R3000, R4000, as well as DEC Alpha AXP machines. The term *RISC* (*Reduced Instruction Set Computers*) refers to the type of processor chip installed on the computer. With a smaller set of instructions, these RISC chips naturally run faster than *CISC* (*Complex Instruction Set Computers*) chips found on 386/486/Pentium platforms. The drawback to RISC-based machines is that you need versions of your favorite applications that have been specially prepared to run on these platforms, but translators will become available that will let you run your applications on these platforms.

Multitasking and Multithreading

Windows NT truly lets you do more than one task at one time. Windows NT uses a preemptive multitasking scheme. Compared to the cooperative multitasking schemes used by Windows 95 and Windows 3.1, the scheme in NT really works. Rather than applications *cooperatively* releasing control of the CPU to other applications, NT's preemptive multitasking system lets the CPU manage its own time. The CPU pays attention to applications as it sees fit and according to the priorities defined by the system administrator. In Windows 3.1, what seemed like a simple task—such as copying a large set of files to a disk while continuing to work in a word processing application—actually was very frustrating. The CPU would spend all of its time copying the files, and your word processing application would run sluggishly, at best. With Windows NT, this simple example of multitasking is a reality.

▶ **See** "Working with Tasking and Priorities," **p. 307**

Security

The U.S. Department of Defense's National Security Agency developed and maintains sets of criteria that determine a particular software product's security level. Windows has been certified with a rating of C2, which is high but is still a few levels away from the highest rating. Here are the main criteria for a Level C2 rating:

- A user of the software owns resources on the computer—such as files—and the user establishes security access to those resources.

- Memory must be protected so that other processes running on the computer cannot read that memory while it is being used, and memory must be released immediately after it has been used.

- An audit trail must be established of the critical actions taken in the system by individual users (see fig. 1.2).

FIG. 1.2
Windows NT auditing options help it meet U.S. NCSC C2 level security.

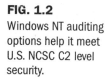
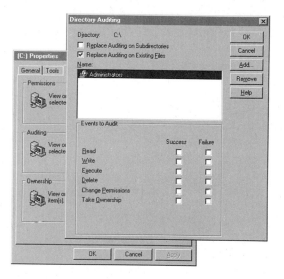

- Users must be able to uniquely identify themselves to the operating system, and this identity (via a user name and password) must be used to gain access to the system.

All of this means that Windows NT is a secure system. Unlike DOS and Windows 95, which provide no security against someone turning on a computer and accessing files, no file or directory or access to any resource on the computer, such as a CD player or printer, is available unless the user supplies a valid user ID and password. Also, when Windows NT is used in a network configuration in which users can let other networked users see files and directories on their systems, Windows NT offers the flexibility of securing individual files instead of entire directories or drives.

▶ **See** "Setting Access for Directories and Files," **p. 577**

Support for other Operating Systems

Windows NT can run on a computer with another operating system also installed. This gives the ability to *dual-boot*, that is, to choose the operating system that boots and then runs your computer when it first starts. Windows NT can peacefully co-exist on a computer that also runs DOS or Windows 95. While Windows NT runs applications made for those other operating systems, there may be some applications that run poorly or not at all in Windows NT. This may be a good reason why you should keep your existing operating system intact when installing Windows NT.

Support for Different File Systems

Windows NT has the capability of reading third-party file systems, such as FAT (the DOS file system). This makes sense considering you can run other operating systems on the same computer in addition to Windows NT. Although you lose much of Windows NT's file system (NTFS) capabilities by using other systems, you are not bound to an operating system by its file system. The following are overviews of the different file systems:

■ *NTFS*. NTFS is the Windows NT file system. NTFS supports file names 255 characters long. NTFS supports the Windows NT security system, so files and directories understand the access assigned to them. NTFS uses automatic recovery, so third-party file and disk recovery systems are not required. Because of the overhead associated with NTFS (the minimum partition size is 50M), you cannot format a floppy disk with NTFS. Also, NTFS supports unimaginably large files (larger than one billion gigabytes) and includes its own recovery capability so that other vendor's undelete and other file rescue tools are irrelevant in Windows NT.

■ *FAT*. FAT (*File Allocation Table*) is the old standby file system of the DOS operating system. File names can be eight characters in length with a three-character extension. A FAT primary partition must exist on ARC-compliant systems, like the RISC-platforms supported by Windows NT. The FAT system typically is categorized as efficient for small volumes of 200M or less.

New Windows 95 Interface

Starting with version 4.0, Windows NT takes advantage of the user interface introduced with Windows 95. Not just a different look and feel to the controls on the screen, the new user interface arrives with a number of time-saving features, such as wizards that automate the setting up of printers, modems, online communication, and other components. Here are some of the main points regarding the new interface:

■ The Start menu represents an improvement in helping alleviate new users confusion after they start Windows NT.

■ The taskbar running along the bottom the screen gives all users the quickest and most natural access to other applications they have running.

■ The focus on objects and documents intuitively points users more than ever towards the tasks and projects they are working on rather than on the tools and applications they use every day.

■ Shortcuts make it easy for users to set up their NT work environment however they choose. Users can place links to applications, tools, and documents everywhere, including on the Desktop and in any folder.

■ The Windows NT Explorer provides an easy-to-use hierarchical presentation of all the resources on a user's system. This makes it extremely easy to manage files, drives, folders, network resources, and attached hardware components, such as CD-ROM drives and printers.

Broad Network Support

Support for broad network connectivity is built into Windows NT. Any PC running Windows NT can act as a server or a client, which lends Windows NT easily into most workgroup computing schemes. Windows NT makes it easy to add drivers for new protocol stacks and network interface cards through both broad support and an easy-to-use interface for changing networking options (see fig. 1.3).

FIG. 1.3
Windows NT provides support for a wide range of network protocols.

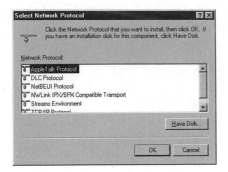

Windows NT is compatible with most vendors' network systems available today, including Novell NetWare, IBM LAN Server, Microsoft OS/2 LAN Manager, UNIX, Banyan Vines, DEC PATHWORKS (though it requires special redirector software), Microsoft Windows 95, and Microsoft Windows for Workgroups. The following five transport protocols are built-into Windows NT:

IPX/PSX	AppleTalk
TCP/IP	DLC
NBF (NetBEUI Frame Protocol)	

Windows NT also can serve in distributed application configurations with support for Sockets, NetBIOS, the Windows Network, and named pipes and mail slots.

▶ **See** "Configuring Windows NT Protocols and Services," **p. 506**

Internet Access

Windows NT makes it simple for a user to tap into the enormous resources of the Internet. With built-in TCP/IP and the new Internet Explorer version 3.0, all a user needs to start browsing through the World Wide Web is an Internet service provider (ISP) account.

Hardware Profiles

New with version 4.0 is the hardware profiles feature for Windows NT. This feature is aimed primarily at laptop computer users who also use their PCs at an office hooked to a network or a docking station. Using hardware profiles, a user can have one Windows NT configuration for times when they are away from the office and another profile for when they are at the office. Because different drivers are loaded depending on the location, and different NT services are required, it makes sense for the user to be able to choose how they want their system configured. The user sets up hardware profiles and then chooses which one to use as Windows NT boots.

Messaging and Mail

Windows NT includes a messaging system that enables the user to send and receive electronic mail (Exchange Client). An address book and messaging application helps users compose and review mail, and correspond with other e-mail-enabled users.

From Here...

In this chapter, you should have gained an understanding of Windows NT's capabilities and strengths. You probably also understand the difference between Windows NT Workstation and Windows NT Server. From this point, you should proceed by learning how to log on to Windows NT and how to work in Windows NT 4.0. With this foundation of understanding, you can refer to any part of the book and confidently put to use the concepts and procedures presented. For a better understanding of Windows NT, see the following chapters:

- Chapter 2, "Getting Started with NT Workstation 4.0."
- Chapter 3, "Working in Windows NT."
- Appendix D, "A Review of the Windows NT GUI."

Getting Started with NT Workstation 4.0

by Paul Sanna

Computer users tend to avoid two kinds of printed information about the software they use—information they perceive to be too basic, or information they perceive to be too difficult. The name of this chapter would suggest classifying the content in the former category. Whether you are experienced with the Windows interface or not, however, there are some basics you need to understand about NT Workstation, such as how to start and stop the system. This chapter is intended to teach you how to get in and out of NT Workstation, how to handle some basic password maintenance, and how to handle some troubleshooting. ■

Understand the Windows NT startup process

This chapter covers what occurs during the boot process for a computer running Windows NT workstation, as well as what the user does during the startup process.

What to do if you have problems at startup

In this chapter, you learn how to troubleshoot a handful of problems, such as if you forget your password, or if your system will not boot at all.

How to change your password

Windows NT requires users to log on with a user name and a password. This chapter shows you how to supply this information when the system starts, as well as to change your password.

How to halt operations in Windows NT Workstation

To halt operations in Windows NT Workstation, you can log off, lock the workstation, or power-down your entire system. This chapter will show you how to complete each.

Starting NT Workstation

For Windows 3.x users, the startup process for Windows NT Workstation probably will seem very different than what you are used to seeing. When you start your computer running NT Workstation, you are starting both the operating system (DOS) and the pleasant, familiar graphical interface with which to work (Windows). Where you previously started your computer, watched DOS initialize, perhaps logged on to a network, and then typed **WIN** to start Windows, most of the functions now have been integrated in a single startup of, and logon to, Windows NT. This is also the case with Windows 95, which also happens to package a graphical user interface into an operating system. We'll take a look in this section at the process for starting up NT Workstation, including what processes occur in your computer, what appears on-screen, and how to get access to NT Workstation.

What Happens When Your System Boots Up

While you can't change the order of the events that occur when Windows NT starts, or really modify what functions are carried out in each, it's helpful to know what is happening as your Workstation boots.

The following events occur when a computer running NT Workstation starts:

1. When you turn on your computer, the system's diagnostics, also known as *POST* (for *Power-On Self Test*), checks to make sure the system is in working order. Next, the system's BIOS takes over to initialize interrupts, memory, and hardware on the system. Finally, the BIOS checks the boot drive's boot record to determine how to start the operating system for the computer.

N O T E   BIOS stands for Basic Input/Output Services. A PC's BIOS provides the primary services a computer needs to run, including launching any operating system installed, such as Windows NT. BIOS is typically built in to a computer in ROM (read-only memory) so there's no chance for a system's BIOS to become corrupted or overwritten. ■

You'll see a number of things on-screen, including version and copyright information about your system's BIOS, the memory on your system queuing up, and probably a prompt to run setup on your system.

2. A menu of operating system options is presented to you.

   After you select an operating system (or if one is chosen for you when you do not select one in time), Windows NT informs you that a program named NTDETECT.COM is checking the hardware on your system. NTDTECT.COM takes inventory of the hardware on your system, such as video cards, ports, and so on. This information is used to help Windows NT configure your system during startup.

3. After Windows NT does a quick inspection of your system, you are given a chance to start NT Workstation with the configuration that was used the last time the system started properly. This configuration is known as the Last Known Good configuration. You are only given a short amount of time to specify the Last Known Good configuration.

4. If you did not choose to revert back to a working configuration, you are next given a chance to choose a configuration to use with your computer (only if you have established multiple configurations beforehand). Like Last Known Good in step 3, if you do not make a selection from the Hardware Profile menu in the predetermined amount of time, the default configuration is chosen for you.

   After passing the Hardware Profile menu, your screen appears black and eventually blue. During these periods, NT Workstation is loading drivers and starting services. While the screen is blue, you can see the version of NT Workstation running, how many processors NT Workstation has installed on your PC, how much memory, and the build number of your version of NT Workstation.

Part I
Ch 2

N O T E During installation of Windows NT, you were given the option of converting the existing file system on your computer to NTFS, which is Windows NT's file system. If DOS was already installed on your computer, you may have wanted to convert the FAT file system to NTFS. (If IBM OS/2 was already installed with the HPFS file system, you would have been forced to reformat the drive because NT does not recognize HPFS.) If you chose to convert your file system at startup, the blue screen messages described in step 3 also include information about the file system conversion. You see information about the disk whose file system is being converted, and then the conversion begins. The system probably restarts, so you may have to repeat the steps described earlier in this section. ■

5. Your indication that the startup sequence is over is the appearance of the NT Workstation logo. After the logo appears, you are invited to log on to the system.

Defining the Build Number

The build number roughly indicates how many times the entire NT Workstation program code was compiled during its development up to its release. Because every software development company is different, it's difficult to tell what the build number means relative to the build numbers you may be aware of in other products. For example, a build number of 1,057 doesn't necessarily mean it took Microsoft more than 1,000 tries to get NT right, nor is it easy to tell if 1,000 tries is a reasonable amount.

▶ **See** "Logging On to NT Workstation," **p. 30**

▶ **See** "Using Last Known Good," **p. 33**

Choosing an Operating System

Your first chance to participate in the startup of NT Workstation occurs just after your system's BIOS has initialized the system. You are presented with a menu of operating systems you can use to boot the system, for example:

```
Windows NT Workstation Version 4.0
Windows NT Workstation Version 4.0 (VGA)
Windows NT Workstation Version 3.51
Windows NT Workstation Version 3.51 (VGA)
MS-DOS
```

In addition to NT Workstation, you may see one alternative operating system, and that operating system can be only MS-DOS or Windows 95. If NT Workstation was installed on a PC that already had an operating system, the person who handled the installation had the option of retaining the original operating system.

N O T E If you use any one of the commercially available boot managers, you can have as many operating systems installed on your computer as you please, such as Linux, IBM OS/2, DOS, Windows 95, or multiple NTs. ▪

Choosing an operating system to load is simply a matter of using the up and down cursor keys to make a selection and then pressing Enter. If you do not choose an operating system within an allotted time, the default operating system is loaded. A timer appears on-screen showing you how long you have to make a selection, but you can stop the timer by moving the selection to any operating system on the menu.

▶ **See** "Understanding Your Operating System Options," **p. 1030**

▶ **See** "Customizing the Boot Process," **p. 412**

Choosing a Hardware Profile

If you are a user of a portable computer, you probably will end up using the Hardware Profiles feature in Windows NT. Most laptop computer users use their PCs in two distinct places—a central or home base location, and some remote location.

Typically, your system's working configuration is different at those locations. At the home base location, your system probably is attached to a network, and it also may be loaded into a docking station that may have installed other components, such as a CD-ROM player, an additional hard drive, and possibly a network adapter of its own, different from the one installed on your PC. At the remote location, perhaps a hotel room, you may have no external connections, except for perhaps a modem connection and a local printer connected to the LPT 1 port. Though a laptop computer makes this dual-work-location scheme convenient, managing these different configurations can be extremely difficult:

■ Some systems will not boot if the computer cannot resolve differences between how it expects a system to be configured and the system is actually set up.

■ If your system does boot, you must manually reconfigure the system.

Windows 95 was the first of recent operating systems to allow a user to define different hardware configurations and select one at startup. Starting with version 4.0, Windows NT now offers the same capability. Here's how it works:

■ You must create Hardware Profile first in Windows NT. This is done in three places—through the System, Services, and Devices icons in the control panel. You create the hardware profiles that appear on the menu through the System icon, and then define the profile in Service and Devices.

> **N O T E**   Keep in mind that you do not define any new hardware profiles, the Hardware
> Profile/Configuration Recovery menu will not appear, and after you choose an
> operating system, the boot process brings you immediately to the Last Known Good
> menu.   ▪

▪ After the Last Known Good menu appears, the Hardware Profile/Configuration Recovery menu appears. While there is a lot of verbiage on the screen, you really have just two choices:

> Using the up and down arrow keys, choose a hardware profile from the menu, which may look similar to this one, and press Enter:
>
> ```
> Docking Station Configuration
> Portable Configuration
> ```
>
> or
>
> Press L to switch to the Last Known Good configuration. You also have the option of pressing F3 to reboot the system. If you do not choose a hardware profile within an allotted time, the default operating system is loaded. A timer appears on-screen showing you how long you have to make a selection, but you can stop the timer by moving the selection to any hardware profile on the menu.

 T I P   You can specify the time that Windows NT waits for you to select a hardware profile
before selecting the default. You set this time through the System icon in the Control
Panel folder.

▶ **See** "Managing System Services," **p. 362**

Logging On to NT Workstation

You must log on to NT Workstation in order to access any part of the system. Unlike Windows, in which you could access functionality in the interface without logging on to the network, you must supply logon information first in NT Workstation.

You initiate the logon process by pressing Ctrl+Alt+Del. You are prompted to do so in the Welcome dialog box (see fig. 2.1), which appears immediately after the NT Workstation logo appears.

FIG. 2.1
Press Ctrl+Alt+Del to
initiate the logon
sequence when NT
Workstation starts.

After you press Ctrl+Alt+Del as part of the startup of NT Workstation, you are
presented with another dialog box titled Welcome (see fig. 2.2). You supply a user
name, account source, and password in this dialog box in order to log on to NT
Workstation.

FIG. 2.2
You log on to NT
Workstation by
supplying a name, a
password, and the
source of the logon.

N O T E DOS users may be surprised at the use of the Ctrl+Alt+Del key combination
used in NT to start the logon process. In fact, Ctrl+Alt+Del can be used from
anywhere in NT Workstation to initiate logon, logoff, and other chores. Use of the
Ctrl+Alt+Del combination helps shut out applications intent on breaking into NT
Workstation. ▨

You must supply the following information to log on:

- *Username.* The user name is the label that identifies you to NT Workstation,
  and it is used publicly in many places in NT Workstation. You either supplied
  this name when you installed NT Workstation, or it was provided to you by
  your network administrator.

- *Source for Account.* This is either a domain on your NT Server network, or
  the computer name of the Workstation you are attempting to log in to.

- *Password.* The password is the secret key that truly identifies you as the
  person specified by the user name. The password is case-sensitive (if your
  password is secretword and you enter SECRETWORD, you will be denied access),
  and it can be 1 to 14 characters in length.

N O T E If you're the person setting up Windows NT on a workstation, you will be asked to supply a password for the Administrator account, which is the first and most powerful account in the system. At installation, you're also given the opportunity to add other accounts (including password). You must also make sure the NT password is in keeping with any passwords required by the network to which NT is attached.

If you were not the person who set up Windows NT on the workstation you'll be using, you'll need to know whether an account has been set up for you, and, if so, what the password is. If no account has been set up for you, someone (such as your network administrator) will at least provide you some access to Windows NT, perhaps giving you the password to an already established guest account.

N O T E In order to log on to NT Workstation, you supply a user name and a password. The combination of these two pieces of information is known as a *login*. The combination of a user's login and all of the information about that login's rights and privileges both on the workstation and any domains to which the login belongs is known as an *account*. A login has a *source*, which is the location where the login was created. The source could be the local machine where you are trying to log on, or it could be a domain if the workstation is part of a NT server network.

Troubleshooting the Startup Process

Table 2.1 lists some common, usually easy-to-address problems that you may encounter at startup of Windows NT Workstation. The sections following the table provide you with even more detailed advice for troubleshooting startup problems.

Table 2.1   Common Problems at Startup

Problem	Resolution
Can't remember password	Unless you have recorded your password somewhere, it cannot be retrieved except from your memory. Your system administrator must supply you with a new logon.
Incorrect password message	Passwords are case-sensitive; be sure you are supplying the correct password. Be sure your account on the workstation is

Problem	Resolution
	valid; check with a system administrator. Or, another user has locked the workstation, so you must supply that user's logon to unlock.
`Couldn't find NTLDR` message	The critical file in starting NT Workstation is deleted or corrupted. Copy the NTLDR.COM file to the root directory of the boot drive from the I386\NTLDR directory on the installed CD, or from installation disk No. 2, enter the following command: **expand ntldt.$** *boot drive*:**\ntldr,** where *boot drive* is the letter of the drive from which NT Workstation boots.
`Non-system or disk error` message	A disk probably is in the floppy drive. Remove the disk and press any key. If there is no disk in the floppy drive, you may have hard disk troubles. See "Repairing Your System" later in this chapter.

Using Last Known Good

If you are like most NT users, you will tinker with the configuration of your system at some point. This tinkering may be as trivial as changing the shape of the cursor, or it may be as significant as making drastic changes to the Registry database. If your tinkering happens to make your system unusable, Windows NT provides you with a life preserver.

As your computer running NT Workstation starts up, you can revert back to the configuration that was in place the last time the system started successfully. This is helpful if changes you've made to the configuration make it impossible for NT Workstation to start. How do you know if you've made catastrophic changes? Typically, after you've modified the workstation's configuration, NT asks you to restart the system in order for the modifications to take effect. As the system attempts to restart, NT informs you that it can no longer run.

Here's how this system works. Every time NT Workstation starts, it determines whether it loaded successfully or not. If the system loads properly, it compares the current configuration to the configuration it regards as the *Last Known Good* configuration. These configurations are stored in the Registry database. If they are different, the Last Known Good configuration is updated with the current configuration. If you specify using the Last Known Good configuration (or NT Workstation makes the determination), the Last Known Good configuration from the Registry is used as the current configuration. Windows NT also automatically tries to use the Last Known Good configuration if it detects that it will not be able to load successfully.

To use Last Known Good, follow these steps:

1. Just after you choose an operating system to load, this message appears:

   ```
   Press SpaceBar NOW to invoke the Last Known Good menu
   ```

   To use the Last Known Good menu, press the spacebar while the message appears on your screen. This menu appears:

   ```
   Use Current Startup Configuration
   Use Last Known Good Configuration
   Restart Computer
   ```

2. If you are sure you want to revert to the Last Known Good configuration, use the up and down cursor keys to select that choice from the menu and then press Enter. If you want to try the current configuration, choose Use Current Startup Configuration. To reboot the computer, choose Restart Computer.

Repairing Your System

You may find that you are unable to start your system, even by using the Last Known Good configuration. If this is the case, you probably will have to use the Microsoft-recommended process for repairing your NT Workstation. The Repair process addresses the following problems:

- *Corrupt or missing system files.* If critical files on your system become deleted or corrupt, the Repair process can restore them.

- *Improper configuration.* Configuration information is stored in the Registry database. If the current configuration settings make it impossible for the system to start, the Repair process can restore previous Registry settings.

- *Improper environment variables.* Improper environment variables can cause your system to become unusable. The Repair process can restore the proper environment variables.

- *Boot sector problems.* On x86 computers, the Repair process can salvage a damaged boot sector. The Repair process also can restore the original boot configuration if you have changed it.

The Repair process uses information that is stored both on your workstation and on the Emergency Repair disk created when NT Workstation was installed. The Repair process is launched from the NT Workstation setup program, so you must have access to the installation floppy disks or CD-ROM, or the network setup program in order to run Repair.

To repair your NT Workstation, follow these steps:

1. Start the NT Workstation setup program.

2. When Setup asks you whether to install Windows NT or repair files on your system, type **R** to repair.

3. Follow the on-screen instructions to repair your system. This may involve using the Emergency Repair disk or inserting floppy disks (if you used the disk as installation media), so be prepared.

N O T E The Emergency Repair Disk is a special disk created at startup that contains the information required to rescue your Windows NT from an otherwise unusable or even unbootable state. Windows NT may enter this state as a result of a system crash (rarely) or of a faulty hardware or software installation or configuration. While you cannot boot Windows NT from the Emergency Repair Disk, the disk contains files that can restore critical Windows NT files. You would use the boot disk either supplied with Windows NT or created during installation to start Windows NT in an emergency condition. ▨

▶ **See** "Installing Windows NT Workstation," **p. 1025**

Updating the Repair Information

Your NT Workstation changes as you add hardware and reconfigure software options. You should always maintain the latest repair information so that you can return to normal operation in the shortest amount of time in case you need to restore an earlier, working configuration.

The repair information on your hard drive is stored in the Repair subdirectory off of your main Windows NT directory. NT Workstation includes a utility that updates the repair information on your hard disk and invites you to create an Emergency Repair disk. The disk is used as a backup to the repair information stored on your hard drive.

To update repair information, follow these steps.

1. Open the Start menu and choose Run.

2. Type **RDISK** in the Open edit box and then choose OK or press Enter. The dialog box shown in figure 2.3 appears.

FIG. 2.3
You can update the information used to repair your workstation using the Repair Disk Utility.

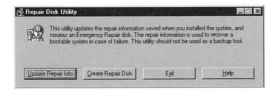

3. To update the repair information stored on your hard drive, choose Update Repair Info. To create a new Emergency Repair disk, choose Create Repair Disk. If you choose Update Repair Info, you are also prompted to create the Emergency Repair disk; if you want to update the repair information in two places, choose the Update Repair Info option.

> **CAUTION**
>
> You should only update your repair information if your system appears to be running properly. If you update your repair information while your configuration is faulty, you may have problems using the repair process in an emergency.

Halting Operations in NT Workstation

NT Workstation provides a number of options for halting operations. You can specify that the workstation be halted so the computer can be turned off, or you can temporarily lock the workstation so no other user has access to it until you unlock it. The method you choose to halt operations in NT Workstation is dependent upon your requirements. Table 2.2 shows you some of the ways you can stop operations in NT Workstation.

Table 2.2   Options for Halting NT Workstation

Option	Description
Logoff	Logs the current user off of the system, but leaves NT Workstation running so another user can log on.
Shutdown	Terminates NT Workstation so that the computer can be turned off.
Lock	Freezes the system until the user who locked the workstation unlocks it by supplying a valid password.

You access these options from the Windows NT Security dialog box (see fig. 2.4). To display the dialog box, regardless of where you are in NT Workstation, press Ctrl+Alt+Del.

FIG. 2.4

You manage a number of Workstation options via the Windows NT Security dialog box.

The following sections provide details on the various options for halting Windows NT.

Logging Off

The logoff option is convenient if a number of users will be using the same computer running NT Workstation. After one user has completed work on the system, he or she can log off but still leave the system running for another user to log on. If a number of users use a common computer running NT Workstation, each user should habitually log off of the system after each completes work. This is done to protect any sensitive files, directories, and other resources that only a user's login gives them access to.

To log off of NT Workstation, follow these steps:

1. Choose File, Logoff from Program Manager; or press Ctrl+Alt+Del to display the Windows NT Security dialog box. Choose Logoff. The Logoff Windows NT dialog box (see fig. 2.5) appears.

FIG. 2.5
You get one chance to cancel logging off of NT Workstation.

2. Confirm your decision to log off by choosing OK. If you choose Cancel, you return to the Windows NT Security dialog box.

N O T E   If a Windows NT service, such as Remote Access Server, is running when you log off, this service will continue to run. If you prefer the service not to run while you are logged off, shut down the service prior to logging off. ■

Shutting Down

The shutdown command is used to prepare NT Workstation for the computer to be turned off or restarted. When you issue the command to shut down NT Workstation, you specify whether or not you want the system to be restarted immediately. If you choose restart, the computer's POST and BIOS initialization begins after NT Workstation is closed down. You might do this to force changes you've made to the system configuration, such as through the System icon in Control Panel, to take effect. If you do not specify restart, NT Workstation informs when you can power-down the system.

To shut down NT Workstation, follow these steps:

1. Open the Start menu and then choose Sh<u>u</u>tdown; or press Ctrl+Alt+Del to display the Windows NT Security dialog box. Choose <u>S</u>hutdown. The dialog box shown in figure 2.6 appears.

FIG. 2.6
You can specify that NT Workstation shuts down or that the system reboots.

2. To shutdown NT Workstation in order to power down the computer, click the <u>S</u>hutdown option button. To specify that the system immediately reboot, click the Shutdown and <u>R</u>estart option button.

3. Choose OK.

4. If you did not choose to restart, NT Workstation notifies you that it is saving data to disk (see fig. 2.7) in preparation for powering down the computer. When that operation is complete, NT Workstation notifies you that it is OK to turn off your system (see fig. 2.8).

FIG. 2.7
NT warns you that it may not be safe to turn off your computer immediately after issuing the Shutdown command.

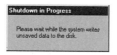

FIG. 2.8
NT alerts you when it is OK to power-down your computer.

CAUTION

Always wait for NT Workstation to tell you it is safe to power-down your computer before doing so. NT Workstation keeps a lot of important data in different parts of memory while the system is running, and the operating system needs a chance to return the data back to physical storage space before the system is shut down.

Locking the Workstation

Locking the workstation is a handy option in what seems like a complicated but really a typical scenario: A user will be away from their NT Workstation for a period of time, there is sensitive information either on the computer or on a network to which the computer is logged on, and the user prefers not to log off. Such a user can lock the workstation, thus preventing any other user from accessing the system without the proper password. When the user is ready to resume work, the user supplies the password associated with the logon to unlock the workstation.

To lock NT Workstation, follow these steps:

1. Press Ctrl+Alt+Del to display the Windows NT Security dialog box.

2. Choose Lock Workstation. The dialog box shown in figure 2.9 appears.

FIG. 2.9
An NT Workstation can be unlocked only by supplying the password for the account currently logged on to the system.

Changing Your Password

Windows NT's security features include an option that lets the system administrator require users to change their passwords at the specific intervals. This is done to help enforce security in the system. Should someone learn your password, the damage they could do is minimized by the fact that the password is good only for a certain period of time. As the deadline for changing your password approaches, you'll probably see a message reminding you to change your password.

On some networks, such as the Microsoft Windows Network, you also can change your password in NT Workstation *without* the help of a network administrator. You change your password in the Change Password dialog box, which you access from the Windows NT Security dialog box.

Part

I

Ch

2

The Change Password dialog box makes it easy to change any password for any account a user has access to, because you can specify the user name and login source that you want to work with.

To change your password, follow these steps:

1. Press Ctrl+Alt+Del to display the Windows NT Security dialog box.

2. Choose Change Password. The Change Password dialog box appears (see fig. 2.10).

FIG. 2.10
You can change the password for any account you have access to in the Change Password dialog box.

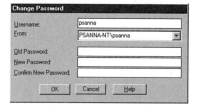

3. For the account whose password you want to change, enter the user name in the Username box and select the login's source from the From drop-down list. Remember, the source could be the name of the local machine where you are working, or it could be a domain on the NT Server network to which the workstation is attached.

4. Enter the current password for the login in the Old Password edit box.

5. Enter the new password for the login in the New Password edit box.

6. Re-enter the new password for the login in the Confirm New Password edit box.

7. Choose OK, or press Enter.

From Here...

With the information in this chapter, you should now be able to log on to and shut down Windows NT Workstation. You should also be familiar with what occurs as Windows NT boots up, as well as how to troubleshoot some common problems. Refer to the following chapters for related information:

- Chapter 15, "Securing Windows NT Workstation."
- Chapter 16, "Managing the Boot Process."
- Chapter 34, "Protecting Your Workstation and its Data."

Working in Windows NT

by Paul Sanna

At this point, you've learned something about version 4.0 of Windows NT and you've probably logged onto the system. You've probably also figured out that version 4.0 of Windows NT features the user interface introduced with Windows 95. This user interface represents more than just a different appearance of the buttons and controls on the screen, however. There are new methods for completing old tasks, and, again compared to the previous version of Windows NT, many of the tools and applications have been moved to different locations and organized with different elements. Where Chapter 1 provided you with a general review of Windows NT capabilities, this chapter provides you with the details, shows you how to access the features, and shows what the features look like so you recognize them.

Understand and work at the Desktop

This chapter will help you understand the concept of the Desktop and how it helps you get your work done quickly. You'll learn how to add applications to the Desktop as well as place other items on the Desktop, such as folders, documents, and shortcuts.

Work with the Start menu and taskbar

The Start menu and taskbar gives you easy access to applications. You'll learn in this chapter how to work with and customize the Start menu.

Understand and work with shortcuts

Shortcuts help you access applications, folders, files, printers, and more from anywhere in Windows NT. You'll learn in this chapter how to create shortcuts.

Work with Windows NT Tools

Windows NT provides a number of tools and applications to help you work, such as those to help you see the files and folders on your system or connect to the network. These tools also help you complete common tasks, such as recover deleted files.

Windows NT version 4.0 incorporates the user interface introduced in Windows 95. For Windows 3 users, the new user interface changes how you complete many basic operations. Some operations have been simplified, some are simply different, and just a few are more complicated. These operations range from copying a file to a disk to organizing your Desktop to enhance your productivity. This chapter is intended to show you how to work every day in Windows NT. Rather than focus on the features of Windows NT 4.0, you'll find explanations in this chapter of how to complete your everyday work, from seeing Network resources to recovering a deleted file. ■

Working at the Desktop

The most prominent component of the Windows NT user interface is the Desktop. Windows NT uses the concept of the *desktop* to organize and present documents and applications you work with. The Desktop in Windows NT is much like the real desktop in your office at work or at home.

Look at your desktop now. You probably will find items you work with often, such as a file folder containing information for a project you're working on, different tools, such as letter opener, and probably your phone or fax machine. Your Desktop in Windows NT can contain the same types of items. You can place a folder on the desktop that stores documents you are working with, such as letters to the IRS. This enables you to quickly open the document rather than having to open the application associated with the document first. Also, you can keep a tool right on your desktop, such as your e-mail reader, giving you quick access to mail you send and mail sent to you.

The Desktop is the place where you'll initiate most of your tasks in Windows NT. Here are some of tasks you'll certainly start from the Desktop:

- Launch applications
- Receive and send e-mail
- Create folders
- Add and configure printers
- Change the background color of the Desktop
- Connect to a network resource

Recognizing Desktop Items

You work at the Desktop by selecting, moving, adding, and launching items on the Desktop. Figure 3.1 shows some of the main Desktop elements. Following the figure is a brief explanation of those elements.

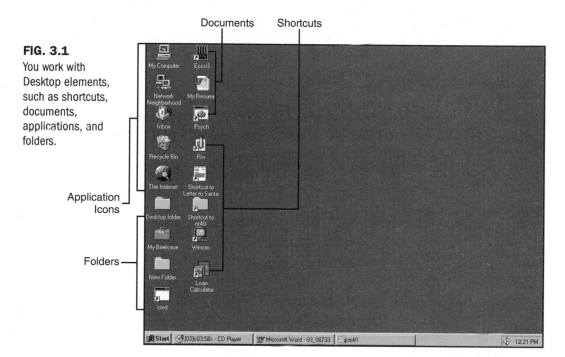

FIG. 3.1
You work with Desktop elements, such as shortcuts, documents, applications, and folders.

Part I

Ch

3

Application Icons   An application icon is a visual element that represents some application or program you run in Windows NT. The application might be one that you personally installed, or it might be one of the utilities shipped with Windows NT Workstation, such as My Computer or Internet Explorer. The application represented by the icon could be stored on your hard drive, or it could be installed on a network drive to which your computer is connected. When you select the icon, you are launching the file that is associated with the icon.

▶ **See** "Presenting the Windows NT Interface," **p. 1056**

Documents   A document can appear on the Desktop. The document can be a memo, a spreadsheet, a computer-aided design (CAD) drawing, or any other document you create or use with an application. Placing a document directly on the Desktop means you can open the document with the application associated with it just by selecting the document; you don't have to start the application and then open the document. When you select a document, such as a spreadsheet file, the program associated with the document is automatically opened. Windows NT understands what application to associate with a document by the document's type.

▶ **See** "Understanding File Properties," **p. 181**

Shortcuts   A shortcut is a special Windows NT element. A shortcut can point to another application, such as a word processing application, a document or spreadsheet, a folder on some drive either installed on your computer or one that you can access via a network. When you select a shortcut, you are actually selecting the element that the shortcut points to. Shortcuts let you access other applications and documents from anywhere in Windows NT rather than just the location where the application, folder, or drive exists.

Folders   Folders are the basic storage containers in NT Workstation. If you have worked with prior versions of Windows NT, or with Windows 3.1 or DOS, you'll probably recognize folders as directories. Folders are used throughout Windows NT to store files and other folders.

Folders also can appear on the Desktop. You might keep a folder on the Desktop storing documents related to a project you are working on. This makes it easy to see all of the documents related to the project, and having the folder on the Desktop makes the documents easy to access. When you select a folder, it is opened, and the contents of the folder are displayed. Figures 3.2, 3.3, and 3.4 show some of the uses for folders.

▶ **See** "Working with Folders and Files," **p. 159**

Opening Desktop Objects

While you can place a number of different objects on the Desktop, the methods you can use to open these objets are the same. To open an object that appears on the Desktop, do one of the following:

- Double-click the object
- Right-click the object and then choose Open from the Context menu
- Move the selection to the folder and then press Enter.

FIG. 3.2
Folders can contain
folders, and those
folders can contain
folders, and so on.

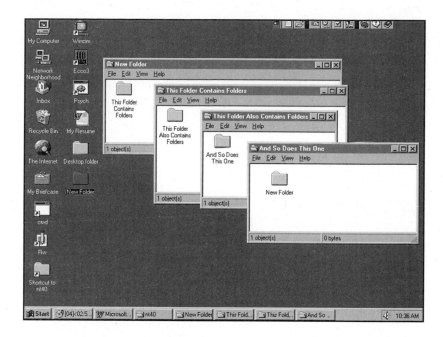

FIG. 3.3
A folder can contain
many Windows NT
objects, such as
shortcuts, applica-
tions, and docu-
ments.

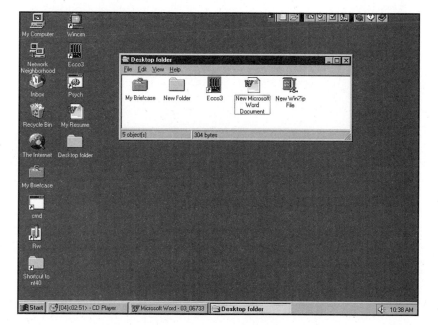

Part
I

Ch
3

FIG. 3.4
You can view the
contents of folders as
small icons, large
icons, as a list, or
with many details
about each content.

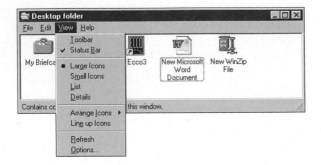

You'll see a different result when you open an object depending on the type of object you've selected.

- When you open a folder, a typical folder window opens with the contents of the folder displayed.

- When you open a document, the application associated with the document is launched with the document loaded.

- When you open a shortcut, the object referenced by the shortcut is opened, such as a folder, document, or application.

- When you open an application, the application is launched.

Arranging Items on the Desktop

You may find that you want to arrange the appearance of items on the Desktop. This certainly may be the case after you've added items to the Desktop or after you've moved items, either accidentally or intentionally. Windows NT enables you to organize the items on the Desktop in a number of different ways, including by sorting the items according to their name, type, size, and date. You can also tell Windows NT to automatically arrange the items that appear on the Desktop whenever you move, delete, or add an item.

To arrange items on the Desktop, follow these steps:

1. Right-click anywhere on the Desktop (but not on the taskbar or any item that appears on the Desktop). The menu shown in figure 3.5 appears.

FIG. 3.5
You right-click the
Desktop when you
want to arrange the
items that appear on
the Desktop.

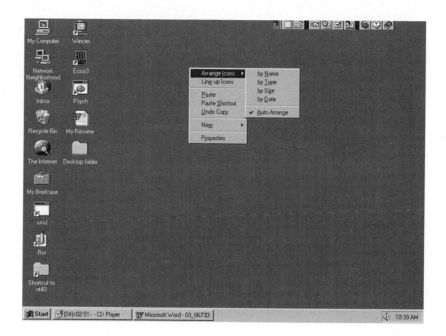

2. To line-up the items that appear on the Desktop so they appear in uniform rows and columns, choose Line up Icons. To have Windows NT automatically line-up items on the Desktop whenever you move, delete, or add items, choose Arrange Icons, and then choose Auto Arrange. A check will appear on the menu after you select Auto Arrange.

3. To organize the items according to their name, size, date, or time, or to specify that items automatically be lined-up, move the mouse pointer over the Arrange Icons choice (see fig. 3.6).

4. To sort the items by date (newest first), choose by Date. To Sort the items by size (smallest first), choose by Size. To sort the items by name, choose by Name. To group items of the same type, choose by Type. Based on your selection, the items will appear sorted in columns.

Understanding the Desktop

In order to really understand the relationship between items you see on the Desktop and the Desktop, you need to understand a bit about the Desktop itself. The Desktop is actually a folder. Any items included in the DESKTOP folder appear on the Desktop. For example, if the Desktop shows shortcuts to three applications, these shortcuts appear in the DESKTOP folder.

FIG. 3.6

You can arrange items on the Desktop according to name, size, type, and date, and you can also have Windows NT automatically organize the Desktop.

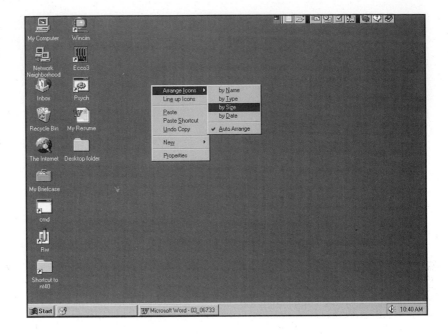

Each user in Windows NT has his own Desktop folder. Items a user adds to the Desktop are stored in his own Desktop folder. When a user is logged into NT, changes he makes to the Desktop affect the Desktop folder that appears in his personal Desktop folder. This folder is located in the *SystemRoot*\PROFILES*user name* folder, where *SystemRoot* is the directory where Windows NT 4.0 is installed and *user name* is the account name for the user (see fig. 3.7). Keep in mind that no Desktop folder appears until the user modifies the basic Desktop installed with NT. There is also a folder named ALL Users under Profiles. This folder is used to store settings that should be available to all users.

N O T E A number of other folders are used to store user-specific information. In the user's folder in the *SystemRoot*\PROFILES folder, there also are folders for storing user settings for the Start Menu, Favorite settings, and the list recently opened documents, and more. ▪

FIG. 3.7
The Desktop is
actually a user-
specific folder that
contains all of the
items a user sees on
the Desktop.

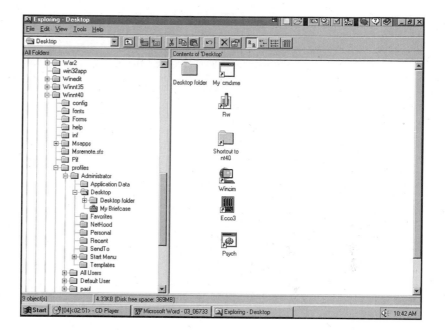

Adding Items to the Desktop

When Windows NT is installed on your computer, a few items are loaded automatically onto the Desktop, such as My Computer, Recycle Bin, and Inbox. You probably will want to add additional items to the Desktop so you have quick access to them. Here's how to add different objects to the Desktop:

■ *Applications.* Use Windows NT Explorer to move the application from the directory where it was installed to either the user's or the All User's Desktop folder.

Doing so can be tricky, however, because usually it is not enough simply to move the file that launches an application to a different location in order to launch the application from that new location. You have to be sure Windows NT can find any other files required for the application to run, which usually means having the applications' original folder being included in NT's PATH.

You may have better luck simply creating a shortcut to the application.

- *Shortcuts.* Create a shortcut to the element you want. Refer to "Working with Shortcuts" section later in this chapter for help.

- *Documents.* Use Windows NT Explorer to move the document to the appropriate DESKTOP folder.

  ▶ **See** "Working with Windows NT Explorer," **p. 163**

- *Folder.* Open the appropriate user's DESKTOP folder using Windows NT Explorer or My Computer and then create a new folder in the DESKTOP folder. Alternatively, right-click the Desktop, and choose New, Folder to create a folder.

N O T E Keep in mind that the user logged in at the time when changes are made to the system will be the only user to see the changes moving forward unless the changes are moved to the ALL USER's folder. ▪

Removing Items from the Desktop

If you find you no longer want an item to appear on the Desktop, you can do one of two things:

- Move the item to a new location.
- Delete the item. You can delete the item by either selecting it and pressing Del, or by dragging the item to the Recycle Bin. Refer to the section, "Deleting (and Recovering) Items Using the Recycle Bin" later in this chapter for help in understanding what happens when you delete a Windows NT element.

Working with the Start Menu

The Start menu may be the most significant enhancement to the Windows NT interface. From the Start menu, you launch most tasks and applications in Windows NT. While you can access certain programs from the Desktop, including from shortcuts, and from the taskbar, you'll often access applications, utilities, and documents from the Start menu.

To open the Start menu, click the Start button on the left end of the taskbar. The Start menu appears, as shown in figure 3.8.

FIG. 3.8
The Start menu appears when you press the Start button on the taskbar.

In this section, we'll take a quick tour of the options found on the Start menu. Later on in this section, you'll learn how to customize the Start menu by adding and removing choices.

Working with Start Menu Choices

Before describing the options on the Start menu, you should learn a little bit about how the Start menu works. The Start menu behaves differently than any of the menus in previous versions of Windows NT or in Windows 3.x.

Here's the basic difference. You don't have to click or press Enter over a menu choice to see its selections. In the Windows NT Start menu, the choices under a menu appear automatically after leaving the highlight over a selection for a second or two. To try this on your own, do the following:

1. Click the Start button.
2. Move the mouse cursor up until it rests over the Programs menu choice. Do not click. You'll notice that after a second or two, the Programs menu appears. (You can click immediately, however, and the Programs menu will appear.)

N O T E Most Windows NT menus work in the same manner as the Start menu. This includes the Context menus, which appear when you right-click over objects in Windows NT.

Understanding the Programs Menu

The Programs menu on the Start menu is where you'll find choices for most of the applications and utilities you'll launch in Windows NT. When applications are installed into Windows NT, most likely a choice for the application will be loaded onto the Programs menu. Windows NT accessory applications also are found on the Programs menu. Lastly, you'll notice that as the Programs menu fills, additional panes of choices are created (see fig. 3.9).

FIG. 3.9
From the Programs menu you can find choices for many of the applications installed on your system.

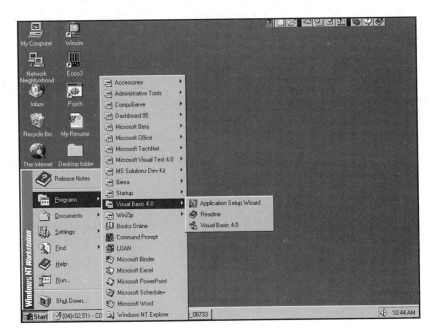

Understanding the Documents Menu

From the Start menu, you can directly open any of the last 15 documents you worked on (see fig. 3.10). These documents can be word processing documents, spreadsheets, technical drawings, or any other document whose application is properly registered with Windows NT. In order for Windows NT to remember a document on the menu, the application must be one that registered itself properly with Windows NT when it was installed. Given this, you may find that some of the documents you worked with recently might not appear on the menu.

By choosing one of the documents shown on the Documents menu, you launch the application and open the document you want to work with in one step.

FIG. 3.10
You can quickly open any of the last 15 documents you've worked on without first launching an application.

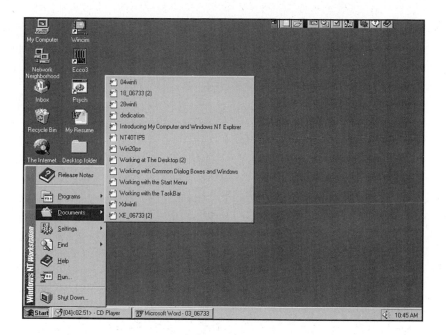

NOTE You may find that you want to clear the contents of the Documents menu. To do so, right-click anywhere on the taskbar and then choose Properties from the Context menu that appears. Next, choose the Start Menu Programs tab. Choose the Clear button to erase all entries on the Documents window. ■

Control Panel

The Control Panel folder contains a number of mini-applications, also known as applets, that help you configure and monitor your system running Windows NT. You can access the Control Panel immediately from the Start menu by opening the Start menu and then choosing Settings, Control Panel. Here is a list of some of the tools you can find in the Control Panel.

- ■ *Add/Remove Programs Wizard.* Automates installation and removal of applications and Windows NT components.
- ■ *Network.* Configures all network hardware and software. Allows you to add services and protocols, such as TCP/IP. Netware, and Remote Access Service.

Part
I

Ch
3

■ *Regional Settings.* Configures your system based on your geographical location and local customs.

■ *Modems.* Helps you install and configure your modem.

The Control Panel is actually a special type of folder. As you learned earlier, folders can contain different types of objects. The Control Panel folder contains applets. An applet is a mini-application. The Control Panel applets are used to configure Windows NT and the hardware installed on your system. Figure 3.11 shows the Control Panel folder. Because of different computer configurations for both hardware and software installed, it is likely your Control Panel may differ slightly from the one shown in the figure.

FIG. 3.11
The Control Panel folder contains applets that you use to configure the hardware and software on your system.

Setting Up Printers

Printer maintenance is also available directly from the Start menu. Open the Start menu and choose Settings and you'll find choices for Control Panel, the taskbar, and the Printers folder (see fig. 3.12).

FIG. 3.12
You add, remove, and configure printers from the Printers folder.

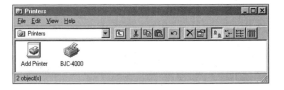

From the Printers folder, you can view information about any Printers installed on your system, as well start the program that walks you through the steps of adding a new printer (see fig. 3.13).

FIG. 3.13
Windows NT walks you through each of the steps required to add a new printer to your configuration.

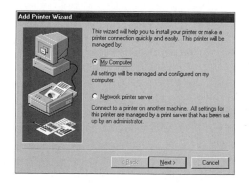

Understanding the Taskbar

You can customize the behavior of the taskbar, including the options that appear on the Start menu. When you open the Start menu and choose Settings, Taskbar, the dialog box shown in figure 3.14 appears. This is where you make changes to the taskbar.

FIG. 3.14
You can control how the taskbar behaves, such as specifying that it can never be obscured by any running application.

Finding Files, Folders, and Computers

Windows NT provides a convenient method for finding files and folders anywhere on your computer or on the network to which your computer is attached. You can also search for other computers connected to your network using the same utility.

Part

I

Ch

3

Open the Start menu and then choose Find, Files or Folders or Computers, depending on what you want (see figs. 3.15 and 3.16). Enter the name of the file, folder, or computer you're looking for and then press Enter. For more information about the file finding capabilities of Windows NT, especially the Advanced capabilities. refer to Chapter 6, "Working with Folders and Files."

FIG. 3.15
You can search for files and folders located on your computer or on the network.

FIG. 3.16
You can search by name for other computers attached to the network.

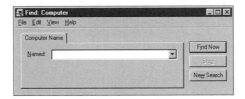

Help!

You needn't travel far in Windows NT to get help. Open the Start menu and choose Help, and the dialog box shown in figure 3.17 appears. From the Help Topics dialog box, you can browse through the table of contents for Windows NT Help, review an index for the information you're looking for, or take advantage of powerful word search capabilities.

▶ **See** "Getting Help," **p. 226**

Running Programs from the Start Menu

The Start menu gives you the capability to launch applications and programs without the need for an application icon or a shortcut. The programs can be applications, such as Microsoft Word for Windows, batch files, etc. When you choose Run from the Start menu, you enter the name (and location) of the application you want to run and choose OK to launch it. You can even browse through all of the drives and folders accessible from your computer to identify the program you want to run. For help in browsing, refer to the "Browsing Through Your System" section later in this chapter. The Run dialog box is shown in figure 3.18.

FIG. 3.17
Help is available directly from the Start menu.

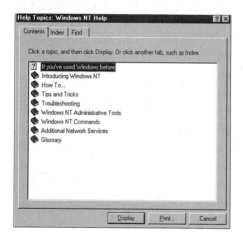

FIG. 3.18
You can launch any program from the Start menu.

Customizing the Start Menu

Windows NT lets you customize the Start menu by adding and removing choices. As you learned earlier in the section on the Windows NT Desktop, many of the elements you see in Windows NT that store other elements, such as the Desktop and menus, actually are folders. This holds true for the Start menu. The Start menu is a special folder that happens to be represented as a menu. Given this, it not hard to figure out that you modify the Start menu by modifying contents of the Start menu folder and the folders that it contains.

Windows NT provides two methods for customizing the Start menu, a basic method and an advanced method. The advanced method leverages your knowledge that the Start menu is actually a folder. The advanced method uses the

Windows NT Explorer to help you create and move shortcuts among the different folders that make up the Start menu. The basic method provides wizard-like step-by-step instruction for adding items to the Start menu. Here is a review of those steps:

1. Right-click the taskbar but not on a button for a running application.

2. Choose Properties from the Context menu. The Taskbar Properties dialog box appears (see fig. 3.19).

FIG. 3.19
You use the Taskbar Properties dialog box to modify the Start menu.

3. Choose the Start Menu Programs tab.

4. Choose the Add button. The Create Shortcut dialog box appears (see fig. 3.20).

FIG. 3.20
When you add a choice to the Start menu, Windows NT walks you through the steps for creating a shortcut.

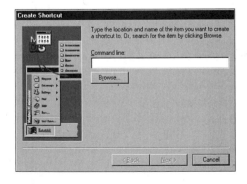

5. In the Command line edit box, enter the filename and location of the program that should be run when the menu choice you're setting up is selected. For example, if you are adding Netscape Navigator to the Start menu, you might enter C:\PROGRAMS\NETSCAPE\NETSCAPE.EXE. You can Browse through your system to select the file by choosing the Browse button. Don't worry right now about which folder in the Start menu the choice will appear; you'll get to specify that soon. Choose Next. The Select Program Folder dialog box appears (see fig. 3.21).

FIG. 3.21
When you add a choice to the Start menu, you choose where in the Start menu tree the choice appears. You can add folders to the tree, as well.

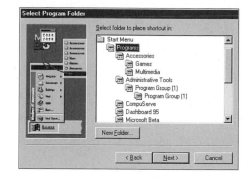

6. If you want the new menu choice to appear in a pre-existing folder, select the folder by clicking on it and then choose Next. The new selection will appear as a choice on the menu folder you selected.

If you want to add a new branch to the Start menu to show your new selection, select the folder where the new menu will appear and then choose New Folder. Enter the name of the new folder and then choose Next.

7. Enter the caption that will appear on Start menu for your new selection. Next, choose Finish, and from the taskbar Properties dialog box, choose OK.

Removing Items from the Start Menu   In addition to adding items to the Start menu, you can also remove individual menu selections or entire branches from the menu tree. To remove items from the Start menu, follow these steps:

1. Right-click the taskbar but not on a button for a running application.

2. Choose Properties from the Context menu.

3. Choose the Start Menu Programs tab.

4. Choose the Remove button.

5. Choose the branch or item to be removed. You can expand the tree to any selection or branch on a lower level of the Start menu tree by clicking on the + button.

6. Choose Remove, and then verify the operation by choosing Yes in the Confirmation dialog box.

7. Choose Close and then choose OK.

Seeing Small Icons on the Start Menu

If you compare figures 3.22 and 3.23, you should notice just one difference. The Start menu in figure 3.22 displays in a font smaller than in figure 3.23, and the icons displayed also are smaller. This option helps you see more of the Desktop, but it means that the Start menu is slightly more difficult to read.

FIG. 3.22
The Start Menu in this figure is shown in the default size.

FIG. 3.23
The Start menu in this figure is shown with the small icons option selected.

To specify the use of small text and graphics on the Start menu, do the following:

1. Right-click anywhere on the taskbar except on a button for a running application.

2. Choose Properties from the Context menu.

3. Choose the Show small icons in Start menu check box.

Working with the Taskbar

One of the most useful parts of the Windows NT user interface is the taskbar. Usually located the bottom of the screen, the taskbar shows you all of the applications you have running at any time. These applications are represented by buttons on the taskbar, allowing you to quickly switch among them.

In addition to displaying the applications you have running, the taskbar also displays the clock. The clock panel also is home to any special visual elements displayed by different applications. An example of this is the speaker symbol that appears next to the time when an audio device is running (see fig. 3.24).

FIG. 3.24
The taskbar gives you access to all applications you have running, the Start menu, as well as information about your system.

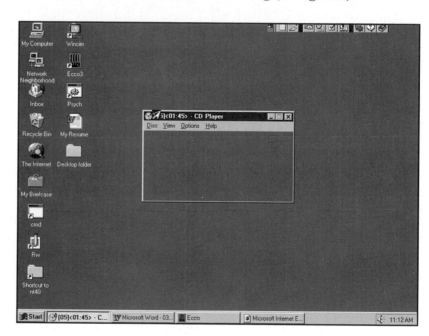

Switching Programs with the Taskbar

When an application is started, a button representing the application appears on the taskbar. When you start more than one application, the size of the buttons decrease in order to show all of them on the taskbar (see fig. 3.25).

FIG. 3.25
As applications are launched, buttons representing them appear on the taskbar.

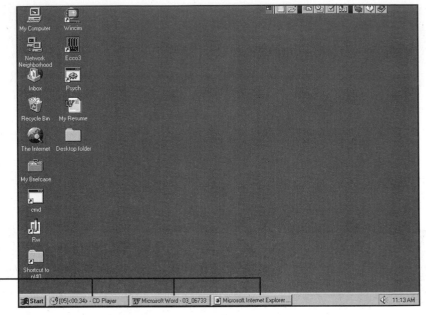

Click a button on the taskbar to switch to an application

The taskbar usually sits on top of the application you are working with. This makes it easy to quickly switch to another application. To switch to another application that appears on the taskbar, click the its button.

Moving the Taskbar

The taskbar appears on any of the four edges of the screen. When Windows NT is installed, the taskbar appears on the bottom edge of the screen. The taskbar remains on the bottom of the screen until you move it. You can move the taskbar to the left, right, or top edge of the screen, or return it to the bottom (see fig. 3.26). To move the taskbar, click any clear area of the taskbar (including the clock area), and then drag it in the direction of the edge you want to move it to. Release the taskbar when it appears in the location.

Customizing the Taskbar

Windows NT provides a few options for customizing how the taskbar appears and behaves. For example, you can specify that the taskbar is hidden from view until you use it. This option is useful if there is information on the bottom of your applications' window that is obscured by the taskbar when it is displayed.

FIG. 3.26

The taskbar can be moved to any of the four edges of the screen, such as the right-hand edge of the screen.

Part I

Ch 3

To customize how the taskbar behaves, follow these steps:

1. Right-click any clear area of the taskbar, such as in between application buttons, or even on the clock.

2. Choose Properties from the Context menu. The Taskbar Properties dialog box appears (see fig. 3.27).

FIG. 3.27

The Taskbar Properties dialog box is where you customize how the taskbar behaves.

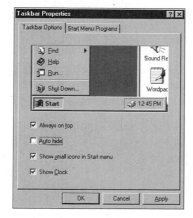

3. To specify that the taskbar always appears above any application running, including full-screen Windows applications, choose the Always on top check box. Otherwise, the taskbar will remain in the background, and you'll have to minimize or restore a full-screen application in order to access it.

4. To hide the taskbar until you need to use it, choose the Auto hide check box. With this option selected, the taskbar remains hidden until you move your mouse pointer over its location.

5. To hide the clock on the taskbar, clear the Show Clock check box. Doing so will give you more room on the taskbar for application buttons.

6. Choose OK.

Working with Task Manager

To help you manage multiple applications you may have running, Windows NT provides you with the Task Manager. These applications might be software you have acquired, such as Microsoft Excel, or Windows NT applications, such as the Control Panel. The Task Manager gives you control over all of the applications running, making it easy for you to close them down, minimize them, switch between them, arrange them on the screen, or simply to see all of them listed in one location. The Task Manager also shows information about different processes running on your computer. Windows NT always is running a number of different processes at one time, and it is likely an application you're running has generated a few processes. Seeing what processes are running is helpful even after the application associated with this process has been shut down, and you can learn how Windows NT works by viewing the different processes it maintains to keep the operating system working (see fig. 3.28).

There are two ways to make the Task Manager appear:

- Press Ctrl+Alt+Del and then choose Task List from the Windows NT Security dialog box.

- Right-click the taskbar and then choose Task Manager from the Context menu.

FIG. 3.28
The Task Manager
helps you manage
any applications or
Windows NT tools you
have running.

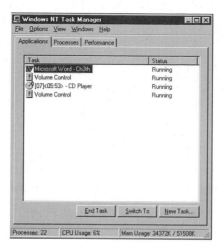

The next three sections describe the options available from each of three tabs in
Task Manager.

Applications

The Applications tab in Task Manager helps you manage the different applications
running in Windows NT. You can shutdown an application, switch to another running application, or a launch new one. To end an application or switch to it, choose
the application in the Task list and then choose either End Task or Switch To. To
start a new application, choose the New Task button or File, New Task from the
menu and then enter the name of the file you want launched and choose Enter.

 TIP To select any item in a list, such as a task from the Active Task in the Task Manager dialog
box, do one of the following: click the task using the mouse, or press Tab until the
highlight moves to the list, and the use the up and down arrow keys to select an item.

Processes

The Processes tab (see fig. 3.29) lists for you the different processes running in
Windows NT, as well as different data for each process. For any process, you can
see how long it has been running, how much memory it is using, and other data.
You can specify what data appears by choosing View, Select Columns from the

menu and then by making selections from the dialog box that appears (see fig. 3.30). Lastly, by choosing the process in the list and choosing the End Process button, you can shut down a running process.

CAUTION

You should exercise caution in shutting down a process. You could cause an abrupt halt in Windows NT or in the application associated with the process.

FIG. 3.29

You can view all of the processes running on your Windows NT system.

FIG. 3.30

You can specify which data appears for each process running on your system.

Performance

The Performance tab (see fig. 3.31) shows you how Windows NT and your computer running NT is performing. You can observe the percentage that the CPU is being tasked, how much memory is being used, and more. Options under the View menu helps you control how often the data that appears on the Performance tab is updated, whether a graph appears for each CPU on your system (if you are running a multiprocessor system), as well as performance statistics for the NT kernel appears.

FIG. 3.31

The Task Manager displays performance statistics for your computer running Windows NT.

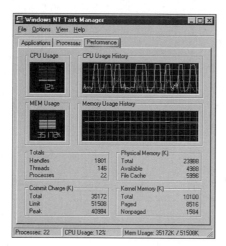

Introducing My Computer

My Computer (see fig. 3.32) provides handy access to all of the resources on your computer. These resources can be drives, floppy and fixed, printers, CD-ROM drives, and important system folders, such as Control Panel and Printers. Once you can see these resources, you can manage them, such as copying and moving files from location to another, installing a printer, changing system settings, or launch an application loaded on a CD-ROM. My Computer happens to be a special type of folder in Windows NT. As such, you manage the objects you see in the My Computer folder as you would any other folder. For more information on managing folders, refer to Chapter 6, "Working with Folders and Files." That chapter also provides detailed coverage of My Computer.

Part

I

Ch

3

FIG. 3.32
My Computer gives you access to the different files and folders on your computer in a folder view.

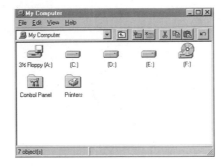

▶ **See** "Using My Computer," **p. 176**

Introducing Windows NT Explorer

The Windows NT Explorer (see fig. 3.33) is a tool that gives you a hierarchical view of all the resources accessible from your computer, including network resources. From Windows NT Explorer, you can open, copy, move, rename, delete files and folders, connect to network resources, and more. The Windows NT Explorer is the last choice on the Programs menu. Detailed coverage of Windows NT explorer is found in Chapter 6, "Working with Folders and Files."

▶ **See** "Working with Windows NT Explorer," **p. 163**

FIG. 3.33
Windows NT Explorer lets you view and manage all of the resources on your computer.

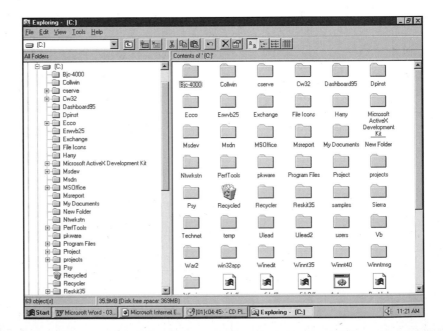

Introducing Network Neighborhood

If you installed the network when you installed Windows NT, you'll find an icon for Network Neighborhood on your Desktop. Network Neighborhood gives you access to the network resources your computer is attached to. These resources include file servers, print servers, other workgroup members, and other network assets. Network Neighborhood, like My Computer and Recycle Bin, is a special folder. As such, you work with the Network Neighborhood folder as you would any other folder, such as sorting objects in the folder, hiding or showing the toolbar, etc. When you open Network Neighborhood, you see all of the computers that belong to the same workgroup as you, as well as a special icon labeled Entire Network that gives you access to the rest of your network.

▶ **See** "Working with Folders and Files," **p. 159**

Part

I

Ch

3

Mapping to Network Resources

From Network Neighborhood, you can attach to and map drive letters to different network resources. When you open the entire Network folder, you see the different types of LAN networks services installed on your system. After choosing the network service you want to use, you see all of the servers on your network. When you open a server, you can map to any of its folders.

Seeing Shared Resources

Users on the Microsoft Windows Network belong to a workgroup or domain. Members can share resources on their computer with other members of their domain or workgroup, such as directories on their physical drives, CD-ROM drives, or even printers. From the Network Neighborhood folder, you see all of the members of your domain or workgroup. Members are displayed in the Network Neighborhood folder as computer icons with the name of the computer as a caption. For more information on connecting to other computers in your workgroup or domain or for sharing resources on your computer with other members, refer to Chapter 21, "Managing Shared Resources."

Browsing Through Your System

Oftentimes in Windows NT, you're asked to specify a file that exists already on your system to help complete some task. For example, when you create a shortcut in Windows NT, you must specify the file that is run when the shortcut is selected. If you know the exact name and location of the file, such as C:\PROGRAM FILES\NETSCAPE\PROGRAM\NETSCAPE.EXE, you enter that information in the dialog box supplied.

If you don't know the exact location of a file you need to specify, or if you do not want to enter the location and name of the file manually, you can browse through the system to help specify the file. The Browse dialog box is the standard dialog box you use in Windows NT to browse through the system. A button with the caption *Browse* usually appears next to the edit box where you would enter the name and location of the file. Choosing the Browse button makes the Browse dialog box appear.

Figure 3.34 shows how to use the Browse dialog box.

FIG. 3.34
The browse dialog box helps you look through your system to specify a file or folder or other item.

Click here to choose a different drive or Desktop folder

You can open these directories to specify a file

Enter the name of the file here

Click here to see details about objects in the dialog box

Click here to back up one directory

Working with Applications

Most likely, you'll spend a majority of your time in Windows NT working with applications. No, we're not talking about Windows NT Explorer, My Computer, or Solitaire. Rather, we're referring to the Microsoft Excel, Lotus Notes, Adobe AutoCad, and Borland Delphi applications you'll install and run in Windows NT. This section will show you to how to install and run applications in Windows NT. For detailed information about installing and running applications in Windows NT, including coverage of DOS, Windows 3.x, and Windows 95 applications, refer to Chapter 17, "Working with Applications."

Installing Applications with the Add/Remove Programs Applet

Windows NT provides a tool to use for installing and uninstalling programs on your computer. In most cases, using the Add/Remove Programs applet (see fig. 3.35) removes some of the guesswork associated with installing new software. For example, rather than having to search the distribution media for the file that launches the installation, the Add/Remove Programs applet does the searching for you. Once found, the Applet launches installation of the software. In addition, for Windows 95 applications and some Windows NT applications, information about the program being installed is logged into the Registry database, which, using the Add/Remove Programs applet, helps you reliably and completely uninstall an application when you no longer want it loaded on your system. You can find the Add/Remove Programs applet in the Control Panel folder.

Part

I

Ch

3

FIG. 3.35
The Add/Remove Programs applet automates many of the steps in installing new applications.

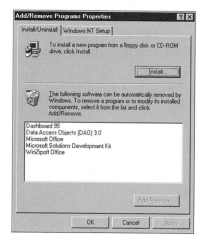

▶ **See** "Installing Applications," **p. 424**

Starting Applications

Once an application has been installed onto your system, you can launch the application and begin to use it. Depending on the application, following installation, a new choice may appear on the Start menu or on the Programs menu, which is accessible from the Start menu, or a new shortcut may appear on the Desktop. There are a number of methods for starting applications in Windows NT:

- *Start Menu*. Open the Start menu and then choose the application, or open the Start menu, choose Programs and then choose the application.

- *Desktop Shortcut*. Double-click a shortcut to the application, or right-click the shortcut and then choose Open from the Context menu.

- *Document Launch*. Locate a document related to the application you want to open in My Computer or Windows NT Explorer. Double-click the document, or right-click the document and then choose Open from the Context menu.

- *Run*. If you know the name of the file that launches the application, all you have to do is supply it (plus its location) in the Run dialog box. Open the Start menu and choose Run. Enter the name and location of the file that launches your application in the Open edit box and then press Enter. You can search graphically for the file by choosing the Browse button.

- *Choose Executable*. If you know the file that launches the application, all you have to do is select that file. For example, the file Winword.exe launched Word for Windows 95. You can select that file from My Computer or Windows NT Explorer. Once you see the file, double-click its name, or move the selection to the file and press Enter. Also, you can click the file and then right-click. Next choose Open from the Context menu that appears.

Switching between Applications

There are a number of different methods you can use to switch to another running application:

- Click the application on the taskbar.

- Press Alt+Tab and then hold Alt to display a dialog showing all running applications. Press Tab until the application you want to switch to is selected and then release Alt+Tab.

- Press Ctrl+Alt+Delete to display the Windows NT Security dialog box and then choose Task List. From the Task Manager dialog box, either double-click the application you want to switch to, or select it and then choose Switch To.

TIP To display the Task Manager using the mouse, right-click anywhere on the taskbar and then choose Task Manager from the Context menu that appears.

■ If the application you want to switch to is partially onscreen by another application, click any part of the window housing the desired application to bring it to the foreground.

Shutting Down a Halted Application

It is not uncommon for an application to stop responding. The usual symptoms of an application that has been abnormally halted is that it no longer responds to keyboard or mouse input, and generally no activity seems to be occurring with the application. It's usually a good idea to shut down an application. Depending on the application, you may be able to restart it immediately after shutting down. Also, Windows NT may not let you use exit until the errant application has been closed down. Windows NT provides a method for shutting down a halted application.

To shut down a halted application, follow these steps.

1. Press Ctrl+Alt+Del. The Windows NT Security dialog box appears.

2. Choose Task Manager. The Task Manager dialog box appears. Choose the Applications tab (see fig. 3.36).

3. Click the application you want to terminate in the list of applications and then choose End Task. If the application was running properly, at least in Windows NT's perception, the application will be closed down. If the application does not immediately disappear from the list, click its name and then choose End Task again. Windows NT will give you the opportunity to wait a short while for the application to start responding again.

4. If you want to wait 5 more seconds for the application to become responsive again, choose Wait from the dialog box that appears. To cancel shutting down the application, choose Cancel. To immediately terminate the application, choose End Task.

Part

I

Ch

3

FIG. 3.36
You can see the list of all running applications by choosing Task List from the Windows NT security dialog box.

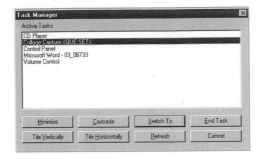

Working at the DOS Prompt

Windows NT gives you the flexibility to work at the command prompt. You can perform file and folder maintenance, connect to network resources, and launch applications from the command prompt. You access the command prompt from the Programs menu. You can work in full-screen mode at the command prompt or in a window. A toolbar is available from the command prompt to speed-up common tasks, and you can customize the color and size of the text shown in the command prompt.

▶ **See** "Understanding the Command Prompt," **p. 212**

Understanding the Context Menu

One of the most useful features of the Windows NT interface is the Context menu. The Context menu is a special menu that appears when you right-click most objects in Windows NT. The real benefit of the Context menu is that it only shows choices relevant to the object you've selected. For example, when you right-click a filename in Windows NT, the Context menu displays choices such as Rename, Print, and Quick View, all appropriate actions you would take on a file. When you right-click the Recycle Bin, the Context menu displays choices such as Open, Explore, and Empty Recycle Bin, all relevant operations for the Recycle Bin (see fig. 3.37).

 TIP Throughout this book, you'll be asked to right-click here and right-click there. As you work in Windows NT Workstation, experiment by right-clicking on any object you're working with. You may find quick access to a task or menu choice you need.

FIG. 3.37
When you right-click most objects in Windows NT, the Context menu appears. The Context menu for a file differs from the Context menu for the Recycle Bin.

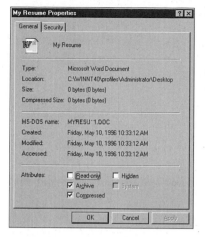

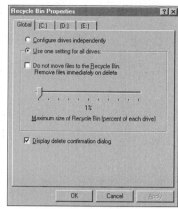

Part I

Ch 3

Seeing Information About Any Object with Property Sheets

While the Context menu for any object you click in Windows NT displays choices relevant to the object, you'll find the Properties choice on almost every Context menu you display. When you choose Properties, a dialog box displaying one or more property sheets for the object you choose appears (see fig. 3.38).

FIG. 3.38
A Property dialog box displays property sheets for the objects you choose, which display information and settings you can usually change.

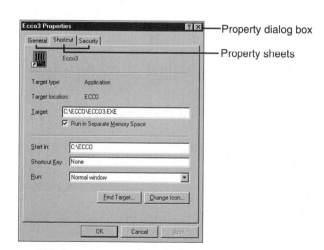

Property dialog box

Property sheets

Available for most objects, property sheets display useful information about whichever you object you've selected. Figures 3.39, 3.40, and 3.41 show examples of different property sheets used in Windows NT.

FIG. 3.39
The property sheet(s) for a DOS application are extensive because of the support required to run one of the apps.

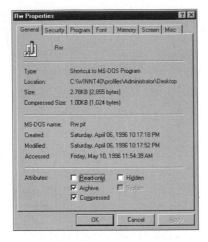

FIG. 3.40
The Inbox property shows the settings you change to configure Windows NT's email system.

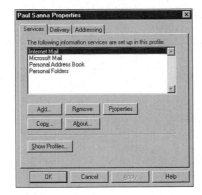

FIG. 3.41
The property sheet for a document includes just informational fields, as well as options to secure the document.

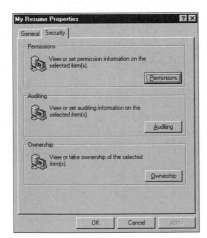

Working with Shortcuts

A shortcut is a special Windows NT element that points to an *another* element, such as an application, document, or folder. When you select a shortcut, you are actually selecting the element that the shortcut points to. Shortcuts provide you with quick access to any folder, document, or application from anywhere in Windows NT, such as the Desktop or other folders. You can create as many shortcuts as you need, and you can create multiple shortcuts to the same application wherever you want one. Figure 3.42 shows the different types of shortcuts you can create.

FIG. 3.42
Shortcuts point to applications, folders, or documents.

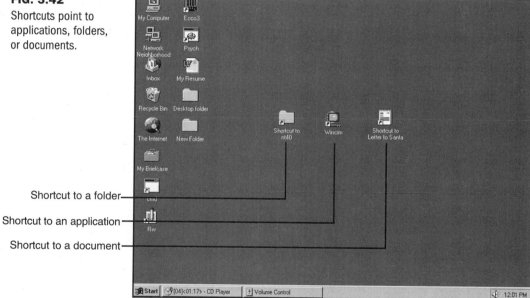

Shortcut to a folder
Shortcut to an application
Shortcut to a document

Part
I

Ch
3

Here are the steps to create a shortcut:

1. Open the folder in which you want to create the shortcut. To create a folder on the Desktop, be sure some part of the Desktop is visible on the screen.

2. Right-click. The Context menu appears.

3. Choose New and then Shortcut. The Create Shortcut dialog box appears (see fig. 3.43).

FIG. 3.43

You supply the name of the application that runs or the folder that is opened when the shortcut is selected.

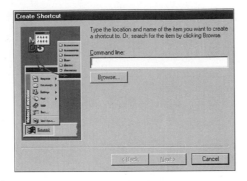

4. In the <u>C</u>ommand line edit box, enter the name of the item that you want to create a shortcut to. If the item is an application you want to start with the shortcut, enter the path to the file that starts the application and the name of the file (including extension), such as C:\PROGRAMS\NETSCAPE\NETSCAPE.EXE. If the item is a folder, enter the path to the folder and the name of the folder, such as C:\PROJECTS\GOODBOOK\QUE_NT40.

 When you are specifying the name of the folder to open or file to run with the shortcut, you don't have to type a single character. Choose the Browse button to poke through your system to specify the file. For help in browsing through your system and using the Browse dialog box, refer to the "Working with Common Dialog Boxes and Windows" section later in this chapter.

5. After entering the name of application or folder, choose the <u>N</u>ext button. A dialog box with the caption, "Select a Title for the Program" appears (see fig. 3.44).

FIG. 3.44

You can enter any caption you like for the shortcut.

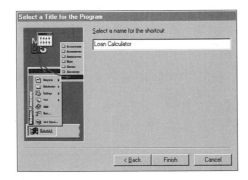

6. In the edit box supplied, enter the text you want to appear below the shortcut icon. Windows NT allows you to use 260 alphanumeric characters.

7. If the file you selected has an icon associated with it, a button with the caption Finish appears at the bottom of the dialog box (all folders automatically use the file folder icon). Choose the Finish button, and a shortcut will appear on the screen. If Windows NT does not detect an icon associated with the file you specified in the shortcut, a button with the caption Next should appear at the bottom of the dialog box. Choose the Next button to continue.

8. If you chose the Next button, the dialog box shown in figure 3.45 appears. Click the icon you want to use for the shortcut and then choose Finish. The shortcut you've created will appear on the screen. If you do not like any of the icon choices presented, choose any icon for now and follow the instructions presented in the next section to change it.

Part

I

Ch

3

FIG. 3.45
Windows NT provides you with a set of icons to choose from.

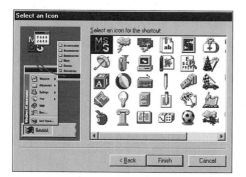

Selecting an Icon for the Shortcut Many files have embedded at least one icon that becomes visible when the file appears in a folder or on the Desktop or is referenced by a shortcut. Other files refer to icons stored in other files. For example, many of the files used in Windows NT use icons stored in the file SHELL32.DLL, found in the SYSTEM32 directory in the main Windows NT directory. Files that do not contain icons or reference others are assigned default icons by Windows NT. If you do not like the icon associated with a shortcut you've created, you can choose another icon that may be embedded in the file referenced in the shortcut, or you can choose an icon found in any other file on your system, as well as one from the default set of icons that ships with Windows NT.

To change the icon associated with a shortcut, follow these steps:

1. Right-click the shortcut and then choose Properties from the Context menu.

2. Choose the Shortcut tab.

3. Choose the Change Icon button. The dialog box shown in figure 3.46 appears.

FIG. 3.46
Windows NT provides you with a set of icons to choose from if your application doesn't have icons of its own or you don't like those provided.

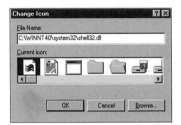

4. The dialog box contains a list box that scrolls horizontally. This list box shows icons contained in the file associated with the shortcut. If no icons are included in that file, Windows NT displays its default set of icons from the file SHELL32.DLL. Use the scroll bars to view all of the icons contained in the file.

5. To choose one of the default icons, click the icon in the list box and then choose OK.

6. To choose an icon from another file, enter the name of the file containing the icon you want to select in the File Name edit box and press Enter. Click the Browse button to scan through all the drive's directories for other files containing icons. If you select a file that contains icons, they appear in the list box. Click the icon in the list box and choose OK.

7. Choose OK to save the icon selection you've made and to close the Properties dialog box.

TIP There is a quick way to create a shortcut without marching through all of the steps described above. Find the item for which you want to create a shortcut. This could be an application, folder, document, whatever. Right-click the item and then choose Copy from the Context menu. Go to the location where you want to create the shortcut, such as the Desktop, and right-click. Choose Paste Shortcut from the Context menu.

Was that fast enough? Here's an even faster method: Open the folder containing the item for which you want to create the shortcut. Be sure you can see the location where you want the shortcut created. Right-click the item, and while holding the right mouse button down, drag the item to the shortcut location. Release the object when you reach the location, and then choose Create Shortcut(s) Here from the popup menu that appears.

Deleting (and Recovering) Items Using the Recycle Bin

When you delete items in Windows NT, such as files, folders, and shortcuts, these items are moved to the Recycle Bin. This allows you to recover objects you accidentally deleted. When the Recycle Bin become full, you must empty it. Once you have emptied the Recycle Bin, it is impossible to recover a file you deleted previously.

The Recycle Bin appears as a trash can on the Desktop, but is actually a special type of folder. You can view the contents of the Recycle Bin by opening the Recycle Bin object from the Desktop. When you open the Recycle Bin, you see its contents displayed in a window (see fig. 3.47).

Emptying the Recycle Bin

Objects stored in the Recycle Bin do not claim as much space as before they were deleted, but they do take up space nonetheless. When you empty the Recycle Bin, you claim space used by the Recycle Bin to store a fragment of the object in the bin. This fragment is all Windows NT and the Recycle Bin need to recover your file.

FIG. 3.47
The Recycle Bin is actually a folder, and you can use any of the standard folder options for displaying the items in the Recycle Bin folder.

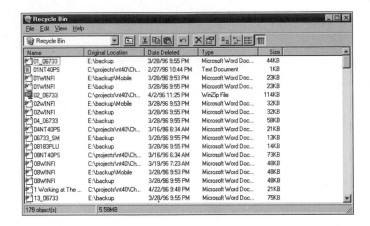

You will be prompted to empty the Recycle Bin when it's filled, or you might empty it before you are warned. You can also selectively delete items from the Recycle Bin without emptying the entire Recycle Bin.

There are two ways to empty the Recycle Bin:

- Right-click the Recycle Bin and then choose Empty Recycle Bin from the Context menu.

- Open the Recycle Bin and then choose File, Empty Recycle Bin (see fig. 3.48).

FIG. 3.48
You can empty the Recycle Bin folder from the Desktop or from the folder.

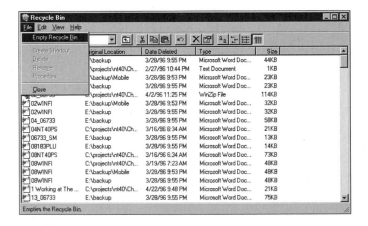

Selectively Deleting Items from the Recycle Bin   Rather than empty the Recycle Bin and permanently deleting every item in the Recycle Bin, you can selectively choose which item(s) in the Recycle Bin to delete and then delete them. This is useful if your Recycle Bin becomes full, but you do not want to delete every item in it. To selectively delete item(s) from the Recycle Bin, follow these steps:

1. Open the Recycle Bin folder. You can do this by selecting the Recycle Bin from the Desktop or by choosing the Recycle Bin folder using Windows NT explorer or My Computer.

2. Select the items you want to delete.

   ▶ **See** "Working with Windows NT Controls" **p. 1080**

3. Right-click and then choose <u>D</u>elete from the Context menu, or choose <u>F</u>ile, <u>D</u>elete from the menu.

 You can see information about any item in the Recycle Bin. This is could be helpful if you are unsure whether to delete an item. Select the item and then choose <u>F</u>ile, <u>P</u>roperties to find information about the item.

Customizing the Recycle Bin

There are a few options you can use to customize how the Recycle Bin works. For example, if you have more than one physical drive on your local PC, you can specify how much room the Recycle Bin claims on a per-drive basis before you are prompted to empty the trash. You can also specify a single setting that applies to all drives on your computer. You manage the Recycle Bin's properties from the Recycle Bin property sheet (see fig. 3.49).

FIG. 3.49
You can manage Recycle Bin Properties, such as how much room is allotted to the Recycle Bin on each drive, or if deleted items are stored in the Recycle Bin.

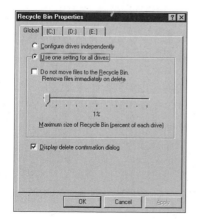

To modify how the Recycle Bin operates, follow these steps.

1. Right-click the Recycle Bin on the Desktop and then choose Properties from the Context menu.

2. To specify that the Recycle Bin is not used and all files be permanently deleted, choose the Do not move files to the Recycle Bin check box and then choose OK. To use the Recycle Bin to manage deleted items and to continue configuring Recycle Bin, move to the next step.

3. To specify settings for all drives, choose the Use one setting for all drives radio button. To make individual choices for each drive on your system, choose the Configure drives independently radio button. If you chose to configure drives independently, repeat the next two steps in this procedure for each drive on your system. Choose a drive by clicking on its tab in the Recycle Bin Properties dialog box.

4. Drag the slider that appears in the middle of the dialog to specify the percentage of your hard drive capacity you want the Recycle Bin to claim before you are forced to empty it.

5. To specify that you are asked for confirmation before deleting files and other items, choose the Display the delete confirmation dialog check box.

N O T E If you specified that the deleted items not move to the Recycle Bin, you cannot disable confirmation for deleting an item. ▪

6. To save the changes you've made to Recycle Bin and to close the dialog box, choose OK. To save changes but continue working in the dialog, choose Apply. To cancel work you've done with Recycle Bin, choose Cancel.

Recovering Deleted Items

One of the main features of the Recycle Bin is the ability to restore previously deleted items. Here's how to do it:

1. Open Recycle Bin.

2. Select the items you want to recover. Take note of the information shown in the Original Location column of the folder (only available if the folder is set to Details View). This is the location where the item will be restored.

> ▶ **See** "Working with Windows NT Controls" **p. 1080**

3. Choose <u>F</u>ile, <u>R</u>estore, or right-click and choose <u>R</u>estore from the Context menu. Having done so, you'll find the item(s) you selected to restore will disappear from the Recycle Bin folder and appear in the location from which it was originally deleted.

From Here...

After reading this chapter, you should have an understanding of how to complete most of your common tasks in Windows NT. With this basis, you should be able to complete any project in Windows NT, increase your productivity, work with most new applications you might run in Windows NT, and, perhaps most importantly, be able to complete any of the tasks or procedures described in the following chapters in this book. Here a few more chapters in this book that can provide you with more of the same type of information.

- Chapter 1, "Understanding Windows NT Workstation."
- Chapter 2, "Getting Started with NT Workstation 4.0."
- Chapter 4, "Getting Help."
- Chapter 10, "Customizing the Windows NT Interface."
- Chapter 16, "Managing the Boot Process."
- Chapter 20, "Configuring the Network at Your Workstation."
- Chapter 35, "Using the Diagnostics Tool."

Getting Help

by Sue Mosher

Where do you go when you have questions about Windows NT 4.0? Most of the information you need is in the online Help system. Help has been enhanced to include full-text searching, incorporate improved links among various Windows Help files, and to the configuration tools in Control Panel. In many cases, getting in and out of Help is much faster now. ■

How to use the new Help option on the Start menu

This chapter tells you how to use the online Help system, including new features for NT 4.0.

Get quick help in application dialog boxes

Most of time, you'll be looking for help on a particular function. Help gives you quick pop-ups and detailed explanations.

Browse and search for information with the Contents, Index, and Find tabs

New tools for navigating Help let you find topics in a hierarchy, like a table of contents, with keywords, or by searching the entire text of the Help file.

Understand procedural Help topics

Many Help topics are now oriented toward giving you a step-by-step procedure for the most common tasks.

Change the way Help looks on your system

You can control whether Help stays on top of other windows and set the size of the font used in Help.

Asking for Help

Where you turn for help depends on what kind of question you're trying to answer, whether it pertains to a particular dialog box or accessory or the operating system as a whole.

For example, if you want to know the valid entries for a field on a dialog box, then press F1 or use the What's This Help we'll describe a little later. But, if you're looking for details on NT networking or setting up multimedia devices, go to the Start menu.

▶ **See** "Exploring Help's New Look," **p. 93**

Launching Help from the Windows NT Start Menu

To start the main Help system for NT, choose Start, <u>H</u>elp, as shown in figure 4.1.

FIG. 4.1
Use the Help choice on the Start menu to access information about the NT operating system and its accessories.

The Help Topics: Windows NT Help dialog box appears, open to the Contents tab. As shown in figure 4.2, you'll see a series of books, each of which represents a collection of Help topics or other books.

To expand the contents of a book icon, double-click it or press the + key on your numeric keypad. Keep going in the same fashion until you see a list of actual Help topics, represented by document icons with a question mark. To display any topic, either double-click it or select it, then press Enter.

To close one of the opened books, double-click it or press + on your numeric keypad.

TIP To close Help, press Esc.

FIG. 4.2
The structure of the Contents tab corresponds to the table of contents you would expect to find in a user's manual.

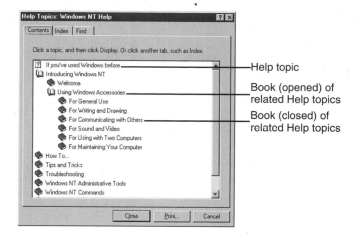

The other tabs, Find and Index, give you ways to search for particular topics, not just browse the hierarchy. Index corresponds to the index in the back of a book, with keywords chosen by the author of the Help system. Find gives you full-text search capability; you can look for any word or phrase that appears anywhere in the Help system. We'll get into the details of using the Index and Find tabs later. But first let's look at how you'll access Help within an application.

Starting Help within an Application

You're going to see a big change in the way Help works within many newer applications designed for Windows NT 4.0. You can get information about particular buttons and fields more quickly, but finding out how a program works may take you a little longer than before. At the dialog box level, the Help system is often oriented toward telling you "what's this" button or box, rather than explaining the purpose of the dialog box as a whole.

In this section, we'll show you how to get quick help about a dialog box, then go back to the application for more details.

Getting Pop-Up Help in a Dialog Box   If you've been using Windows for a while, it's likely that one of the first function keys you learned was F1, the universal Help key. You came to depend on it to provide information about the function you were currently working with. Programmers call this *context-sensitive* help.

Part
I

Ch
4

One of the big improvements to context-sensitive help in NT 4.0 is the ability to pop up a Help window right over your application, without launching the full Windows Help application.

Figure 4.3 shows what happens when you press F1 in a dialog box that's been equipped with this type of help. To close the Help pop-up, press any key or click anywhere on the dialog box.

FIG. 4.3
Context-sensitive help for an application dialog box appears over the application, rather than in a separate window.

On many dialog boxes, there are two other ways (besides pressing F1) to access this context-sensitive help. You can right-click a field, button, or other control, then pick <u>W</u>hat's This from the context menu that pops up. Or, you can click the question mark button on the title bar, then click any dialog box element to get pop-up information about it.

 TIP   To print a pop-up topic, right-click it and choose <u>P</u>rint Topic.

N O T E   Not all applications' Help systems use pop-ups this way. Instead of a pop-up about a particular field on a dialog box, some will open a full Help topic containing information about the entire dialog box or application. In a programming application, you're likely to get a Help topic on the particular command you're working with. In some other applications, you'll get the Contents tab or a Contents topic. ■

Help Menu   Where do you go for general information about an application or the purpose of a dialog box, rather than a particular field on that dialog box? Look on the application's <u>H</u>elp menu. You'll see at least one Help Topics choice, possibly more. Exchange, for example, has a Help Topics selection for each information service installed, as you can see in figure 4.4.

FIG. 4.4
For general informa-
tion about how an
application works,
look on the Help
menu.

When you access Help through the Help menu, you can choose whether to use the Contents, Index, or Find tab to look for a topic. In the next section, you learn what each of those tabs does and when you might want to use each one.

Exploring Help's New Look

Even older Help files get a new look under NT 4.0. While only Help files designed for NT 4.0 have a Contents tab (refer to fig. 4.2), all Help files have Index and Find tabs. In this section, you learn how you can use all three of these tabs to find what you need in Help. You also see some of the new styles, like procedural topics and troubleshooters, for presenting information in Help files.

Contents Tab

The Contents tab in figure 4.2 uses a book and document metaphor to present a hierarchical view of the Help system. In many cases, several Help files (documents) are combined into one system (book). A special contents file, using a CNT extension, defines what individual Help files will be combined into the Help system.

N O T E Files with the HLP extension contain the Help topics, but they're only part of the Help system. Windows NT 4.0 and most new 32-bit programs also install CNT or contents files. A GID (general index) file will be created on-the-fly the first time you use a HLP file. (You'll briefly see a message, `Preparing Help file for first-time use`.) Also, the first time you use the Find tab, indexes to support the full-text search function are generated with FTS and FTG extensions. When you switch to the Find tab, you see a message `Loading Word List` while these files are being accessed. ■

Part
I

Ch
4

One useful feature of this new Contents tab is that it lets you print an entire "book" with a single command. To do this, click the open or closed book icon whose topics you want to print, and then choose Print. Make any changes you need on the Print dialog box, and then choose OK.

Index Tab

Whether to use the Index tab or the full-text search function of the Find tab is often a matter of personal preference. The Index tab lets you pick from the topics that the Help author thought were important, like the index in the back of the book. The Find tab, on the other hand, allows you to perform a search of the entire text of the Help system.

Notice in figure 4.5 how the Index tab is structured with topics and indented subtopics to let you browse related subjects. For example, under Access Control, you'll see several topics related to passwords.

FIG. 4.5

The Index tab uses a keyword index to guide you to the most important concepts and procedures.

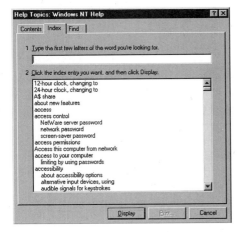

If you're looking for general information on a function, the Index tab is your quickest option. To use the Index, enter your topic of interest in the box labeled Type the First Few Letters of the Word You're Looking For. The index, which is in alphabetical order, automatically scrolls to the first keyword that matches the first letters of the topic you typed. Select a topic, and then choose Display. If only one topic matches the keyword you've chosen, Help takes you directly to it. If more than one topic fits, you'll see a Topics Found dialog box like that in figure 4.6. Select the topic you want, and then choose Display again.

FIG. 4.6
When an Index tab keyword refers to more than one topic, Help pops up a list of topics for you to choose from.

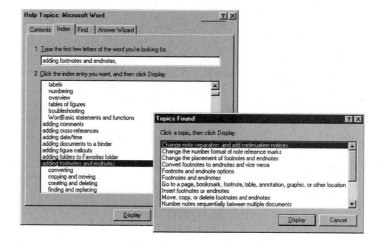

Find Tab

The full-text search capabilities of the Find tab can be fine-tuned to the way you like to search and the amount of space you can afford to devote to the Find tab's index files.

The first time you use the Find tab, the Find Setup Wizard appears, giving you a choice of three configurations:

■ Minimize Database Size

■ Maximize Search Capabilities

■ Customize Search Capabilities

As you might expect, there is a trade-off between keeping the size of the index file small and having the most powerful search tools available. What kind of trade-off? Let's take Microsoft Word as an example.

The Word Help system consists of four files, WINWORD.HLP, QWINWORD.HLP, WRDBASIC.HLP, and WKEYWORD.HLP, which total 3,258K. Generating the minimum Find tab index results in index files (FTS and FTG) totaling 1,933K. However, if you choose to maximize search capabilities, the index files grow to 4,929K—250 percent larger!

Part
I

Ch
4

Obviously, the size of the index files is a concern if your hard drive space is limited. A larger index also means that Help takes a few seconds longer to load when you're using the Find tab.

A good approach is to start with <u>M</u>inimize Database Size, then move to either custom or maximum search capabilities if you discover that you're not able to easily find the information you need. To change your search index settings at any time, open Help to the Find tab, and then choose <u>R</u>ebuild. This restarts the Find Setup Wizard.

Generating the Minimum or Maximum Index   If you decide to start with the <u>M</u>inimum Database Size or Ma<u>x</u>imize Search Capabilities, make your choice on the Find Setup Wizard, choose <u>N</u>ext, and then Finish. You'll see a message `Creating Word List`, and then you'll be presented with the Find dialog box where you can begin your search.

▶ **See** "Searching with the Find Tab," **p. 98**

Customizing the Find Index   If you want to customize the Find options, then go to the Find Setup Wizard, and choose <u>C</u>ustomize Search Options, <u>N</u>ext. You'll be presented with a series of dialog boxes where you can decide exactly how you want the Find tab to behave. The next few sections discuss each of those options.

Help Files to be Included   Help for most applications and for NT is a complex system, not just a single file. In many cases, the Find index draws on the resources of several Help files. On the first customizing screen of the Find Setup Wizard, you can select which ones to add to your full-text search index.

The default selects all files intended for this particular Help system. To deselect a file, excluding it from the Find tab index, hold down the Ctrl key while you click that file.

When might you want to exclude a file? Say, you're setting up a workstation for a user who will have no network administration duties. You might, therefore, want to exclude the User Manager for Domains Help and the User Profile Help, as shown in figure 4.7.

When you've made your selections, choose <u>N</u>ext.

FIG. 4.7
If you use the Find
Setup Wizard to
customize the full-
search text index, you
can choose what files
to include.

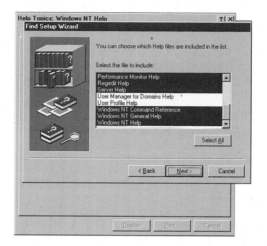

Untitled Topics   Your next choice in the Find Setup Wizard is between Include
Untitled Topics and Ignore Untitled Topics, the latter being the default.

Untitled topics generally include "What's This" Help pop-ups that duplicate information explained more comprehensively in other topics, so it's best to ignore those
untitled topics.

When you've decided what to do about untitled topics, choose Next to continue.

Phrase Searching   On the next Find Setup Wizard dialog box, you're asked to
choose between Include Phrase Searching and Don't Include Phrase Searching.
This is one of the most important options for the Find tab.

Phrase searching lets you look for a particular combination of words, in order. For
example, you could search for the precise phrase "user profile." However, if you
choose not to include phrase searching, you would be limited to searching for
"user" and "profile" both appearing anywhere in the same topic—a much broader
search.

Another advantage of choosing phrase searching is that it allows you to search for
all words with similar roots. For example, you can search for "justify" and also get
topics containing "justified" and "justifies."

The trade-off here is that phrase searching results in a larger set of index files. If
hard drive space is at a premium, you'll probably want to disable phrase searching.

Part

I

Ch

4

After making your choice on phrase searching, choose Next. If you chose not to use phrase searching, then this will be the last pane of the Find Setup Wizard, so choose Finish to build the indexes. If you are going to use phrase searching, you'll have two more choices to make.

Display Matching Phrases The next choice on the Find Setup Wizard governs not how you search, but what the Find tab does while you're searching.

The Find tab can operate dynamically, displaying matching phrases as you type in your search words. This can often make it easier for you to find what you're looking for. If you want to try using the Find tab this way, choose Display Matching Phrases.

On the other hand, on a sluggish computer or very large Help system, the dynamic matching could slow you down. In that case, choose Don't Display Matching Phrases.

 T I P The Display Matching Phrases setting, like all the others in the Find Setup Wizard, is specific to only the current Help system. You may want to display matching phrases with some Help systems, but not others.

When you've decided what to do about displaying matching phrases, choose Next.

Similarity Searches The last pane of the Find Setup Wizard asks about similarity searches. This is the ability to perform a search, and then select one or more topics and use them as the basis for a second search. You're asking Help to look for topics that are similar to the one(s) you've marked. As you can imagine, it works best on large Help systems with lots of different topics to search.

To enable similarity searches, choose Support Similarity Searches. If you'd rather not allow this type of search, choose Don't Support Similarity Searches.

After you've made your choice here, choose Next, and then Finish to build the FTG and FTS full-text search word lists for use with the Find tab.

Searching with the Find Tab Once you've run the Find Setup Wizard, you're ready for your first search. Here's how to perform a simple search:

1. Enter the word(s) you want to search for in the box labeled Type the Word(s) You Want to Find.

2. If you want, select just some of the words in the box labeled Select Some Matching Words to Narrow Your Search. This step can usually be skipped, since you'll probably want topics containing all the words that appear in this box.

3. Select a topic in the box labeled Click a Topic, then Click Display.

4. Click Display to view the selected topic.

Figure 4.8 shows the result of a search for the word "justify" in the Microsoft Word Help system, accessed by choosing Help, Microsoft Word Help Topics. At the bottom of the dialog box, you can see the number of topics containing "justify" or one of several variants, including "justified."

FIG. 4.8
The Find tab is used for searching the full text of the Help system.

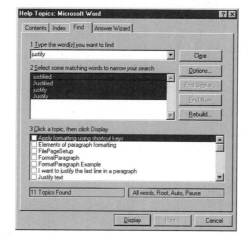

Using the Find Options   At the bottom right of the dialog box, the current options for the Find tab are shown. To change any of these options, choose Options from the Find tab, and then make the appropriate change on the Find Options dialog box shown in figure 4.9. Table 4.1 shows the possible values for these settings.

FIG. 4.9

The scope of your full-text search is controlled by the settings on the Find Options dialog box.

Table 4.1 Settings for the Find Tab

Option	Description
Search for what?	
All words	All the words you typed in any order
One+ words	At least one of the words you typed
Phrase	The words you typed in exact order
Show words that...	
Begin	Begin with the characters you type
Containing	Contain the characters you type
Ending	End with the characters you type
Matching	Match the characters you type
Root	Have the same root
Begin searching when?	
Manual	After you click the Find Now button
Auto	Immediately after each keystroke
Pause	Wait for a pause before searching

Notice that the options for phrase searching (The Words You Typed in Exact Order) and for searching for words with the same root are not be available if you chose the Minimize Database Size option on the Find Setup Wizard or if you chose Customize Search Capabilities, but decided not to use phrase searching.

Sometimes a simple search gives you more topics than you care to browse. To narrow a search, you might try these techniques:

- Add another word to the box labeled Type the Word(s) You Want to Find, if you're using an All Words search.
- Switch from a One+ Words search to an All Words or Phrase search.
- Switch from a Root, Begin, Ending, or Containing search to a Matching search.
- Choose Files on the Find Options dialog box to display a list of the files that make up the current Help system, then select only a few to use in the search.

Try either of these strategies if you didn't find the topic you need and you want to broaden your search:

- Switch from a Matching search to a Root, Begin, Ending, or Containing search.
- Switch from an All Words search to a One+ Words search.

Another way to broaden a search, assuming you enabled phrase-searching in the Find Setup Wizard, is to select one or more topics in the Find tab, and then choose Find Similar. In figure 4.10, you can see the results of searching for "registry," selecting the topic, "Accessing the Registry in a Remote Computer," and then using Find Similar to display a list of possibly related topics. We can now select a topic from this new list, and then choose Display to view it.

TROUBLESHOOTING

When I click the Find tab in the Help Topics dialog box, I get an error message `Unable to display the Find tab. (177).` **How can I fix that?** This problem is usually the result of a corrupted or old GID (general index) or FTS or FTG (full-text search) file. The solution is to delete the bad file, which will then be rebuilt the next time you use

continues

Part

I

Ch

4

continued

Help. However, because a Help system may consist of a number of separate files, it's not easy to know which GID or FTS is at fault.

If it's the Help for an application that's giving you this error, look in the application directory to see if it stores its Help files there. If so, then delete all the GID, FTS, and FTG files.

▶ **See** "Finding Files and Folders," **p. 173**

FIG. 4.10
With phrase-searching enabled, you can select one or more topics to use in finding others that cover similar information.

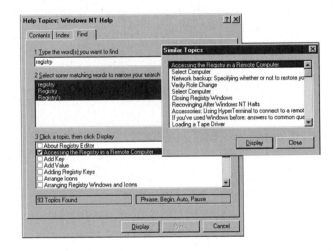

If you're working with the NT Help system or with an application that stores its Help files outside the application directory, your best bet is to use Start, Find and search for *.GID, *.FTS, and *.FTG files in the \Windows folder, including all subfolders. (While most Help files will be in \Windows\Help, NT also stores some in \Windows\System32.) First, try deleting those that, by their filenames, seem most likely to be associated with your application. If that doesn't work, then delete all the *.GID, *.FTS, and *.FTG files.

TROUBLESHOOTING

I cleaned out my \Windows\Help folder, leaving only the HLP files, but now I don't see a Contents tab, only the Index and Find tabs. How can I get the Contents tab back? While the data for the Index and Find tabs can be rebuilt if you delete their associated GID, FTS, and FTG files, the information for the Contents tab cannot. It's contained in a CNT file.

To restore the Contents tab, you'll need to recover the CNT file from the Recycle Bin or, if it can't be found there, reinstall the application.

Notice that older Windows programs will probably only have the Index and Find tabs, not a Contents tab.

▶ **See** "Deleting (and Recovering) Items Using the Recycle Bin," **p. 83**

Procedural Topics

Based on testing and user feedback, Microsoft has made a major shift in the way Help is written. The emphasis now is on telling you how to perform the functions that you're most likely to use, without spending much time explaining why those features work the way they do. These "procedural" topics are by far the most common type of topic in the newer Help files.

Figure 4.11 is an example from the Help file for HyperTerminal. It gives you five numbered steps for changing your modem port settings, plus a couple of tips. If you want to know more about modem settings, you can click the small Related Topics button at the bottom of the topic or choose Help Topics and use the Contents, Index, or Find tab.

FIG. 4.11

Procedural topics give you numbered steps to follow and often add tips and links to related topics.

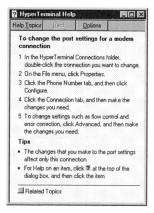

Part

I

Ch

4

Procedural windows usually have no menus. Even the use of buttons at the top is optional, though you usually see at least these three buttons:

Help Topics	Returns to the Contents, Index, and Find Tabs
Back	Returns to the previously accessed Help topic
Options	Choices for customizing Help, copying, printing, and annotations

If you don't see an Options button, you can right-click the Help topic and get a menu of options, as shown in figure 4.12.

FIG. 4.12
To print, copy, annotate, or customize Help, right-click the topic to get a context-sensitive menu.

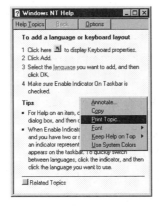

Troubleshooters

Another new type of Help topic is the troubleshooter (see fig. 4.13). On these topics, you'll find several buttons next to statements that describe typical problems. Pick the statement that most closely matches your problem, and then click the button next to it. This takes you to another Help topic that either asks more questions or provides you with steps for fixing the problem.

FIG. 4.13
Look for troubleshooter topics that will walk you through the steps needed to solve a problem.

Shortcuts, Related Topics, and other Links

You're probably familiar with Help's system of defining links to other topics with an underline, usually green, for different topics and a dotted underline, also usually green, for pop-up topics like definitions. The cursor will change from an arrow to a pointing hand as you pass over these links and over icons and other pictures that also contain links.

 TIP To move through all the links on a particular Help topic, press the Tab key repeatedly.

Shortcut and Related Topics buttons are two types of links that you'll see increasingly used in the newer Help files.

The shortcut is a common feature of both troubleshooters and procedural topics, usually represented with a button with an arrow on it, as you can see in figure 4.14. In this example, clicking that button launches the Control Panel. You also may see shortcuts to launch entire applications or take you to World Wide Web sites or Microsoft Network interest areas.

FIG. 4.14
This procedural topic includes a shortcut to start the Control Panel Modem.

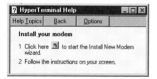

In figure 4.11, you saw a topic with a Related Topics button. Another example is shown in figure 4.15. When you click the Related Topics button, a new list of topics appears in the Related Topics dialog box. You can select a topic, and then choose Display to view it. Or you can choose Cancel to return to the current topic.

 TIP Because these related topics are based on keywords chosen by the author of the Help system, they're likely to stick to the subject at hand. Try Related Topics (if available) first, before choosing Help Topics to get more information from the Contents, Index, or Find tab.

FIG. 4.15
You can use a
Related Topics button
to quickly locate
other Help topics that
might be of interest.

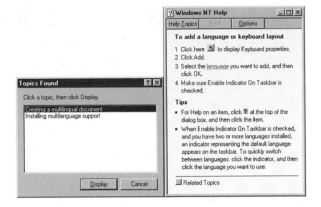

Customizing Windows Help

Help under NT 4.0 offers some new ways to make Help look and work the way you want it to, while retaining the capability to add content to Help systems with annotations and, in some cases bookmarks.

Help Window Settings

Because most of the topics you're likely to see will be procedural topics, without menus, we'll discuss how to change the Help window settings using the right-click context menu, which is always available. However, notice that these options also may be available from a menu or an Options button.

To change whether or not the Help topic stays on top of other Windows, follow these steps:

1. Right-click the topic, then choose Keep Help on Top.

2. Choose Default (whatever the Help file is set for), On Top, or Not On Top.

To change the size of the font used to display the Help topic, follow these steps:

1. Right-click the topic, and then choose Font.

2. Choose Small, Normal, or Large.

N O T E You cannot change the display font, only the size. If the Help file was written with a font that is not available on your system, a similar font will be substituted. ▪

If the author of the Help system used custom colors to indicate jumps and pop-ups, you can switch back to the usual green for those links by taking these steps:

1. Right-click the topic.

2. Choose Use System Colors.

3. Choose Yes when you're asked whether you want to close Help so the change can take effect.

The change will take affect the next time you start Help. This also changes the background color of the Help window to white.

Annotations

Just as you might add sticky notes to the margins of a favorite book, you can add your own comments to any Help file. For example, you might make reference to where additional information can be found or to an exception to the procedure described in the topic. These notes are called *annotations*.

Add an annotation to a Help topic by following these steps:

1. Right-click the topic.

2. Choose Annotate.

3. Enter your notes.

4. Choose Save to save the annotation.

A topic with an annotation has a paper clip icon next to the title. Click the paper clip to display the annotation.

Bookmarks

One Windows Help feature that many users find useful is the ability to keep a list of favorite or frequently referenced topics in a Help file. This makes it easy to find your way back to information that was particularly useful.

Part
I

Ch
4

However, because of the way changes in the new Windows Help system are implemented in many Help files, you often will not be able to use bookmarks. (Particularly with procedural topics, the author of the Help system must make a conscious decision to include bookmarking capability. It isn't available automatically.) Unfortunately, Microsoft omitted bookmarking from most of its Help systems for Windows NT and the new 32-bit Windows applications.

Usually, you'll be able to bookmark only those topics that have a menu, not those with only buttons at the top. For Help topics with menus, choose Bookmark, Define to add new bookmarks. To use an existing bookmark to go straight to a particular topic, choose Bookmark, and then pick the bookmark from the numbered topics on the menu.

Reusing Help Information

The new Help system makes it easier than ever to copy all or part of a Help topic for use in another application and to print out a single topic or an entire group of topics.

Copying Help Topics

To copy an entire topic, follow these steps:

1. Right-click the topic.
2. Choose Copy from the pop-up menu.

   Or, you can simply press Ctrl+C.

To copy part of a topic, follow these steps:

1. Use the mouse to select the text you want to copy.
2. Right-click the topic.
3. Choose Copy from the pop-up menu.

   Or, after you've highlighted the text, press Ctrl+C.

Once you've copied the text, you can use Ctrl+V to paste it into any other Windows document.

Printing Help Topics

There are two ways to print from Help, depending on whether you need a single topic or want to print out a group of related topics.

To print just the current Help topic, do this:

1. Right-click the topic.
2. Choose Print Topic from the pop-up menu.
3. On the Print dialog box, change the printer if you need to, select the number of copies, then choose OK.

To print a group of topics listed under a book title in the Contents tab, follow these steps:

1. Select the book whose topics you want to print. It can be either open or closed.
2. Choose Print.
3. On the Print dialog box, change the printer if you need to, select the number of copies, then choose OK.

You also can print a single topic from the Contents tab using the same method.

From Here...

In this chapter, you've learned several ways to use the new Help system in Windows NT 4.0. Since user documentation is increasingly being provided in this online format—with only a small printed manual, if any—it's important to know how to get around in Help. Here are some other chapters you might like to check out as you learn to use NT:

- Chapter 2, "Getting Started with NT Workstation 4.0," helps you understand the mouse, which Help uses to navigate jumps and to pop up the context menu that lets you copy, print, and annotate Help topics.

- Chapter 3, "Working in Windows NT," shows you how the Start menu works, that being one of the ways to launch Help.

- Chapter 5, "Printing and Setting Up Printers," tells you how to get your printed output set just right.

Working with Windows NT

Printing and Setting Up Printers

by Rob Kirkland

Windows NT comes in two flavors—Server and Workstation. Many of NT's printing features, while available in both versions, are really useful only in NT Server. For example, because NT Workstation only permits 10 remote computers to connect to it at one time, it is not a suitable candidate for a print server in any but the smallest local area network. Accordingly, this chapter focuses on those Windows NT printing features that are most useful to a user of Windows NT Workstation. ∎

Set up and configure printers

You can connect a printer to your own computer, connect a printer to another computer on your network, or connect a printer directly to the network cable.

Manage printers and print queues

From one workstation you can manage all the print servers, printers, and print queues on a network.

Manage printer security

Define who gets access to each printer and the degree of access. You can audit printing activity to find out who is using each print device, how much usage each print device gets, when people use printers, and whether people are succeeding or failing in their printing efforts.

Advanced printer setup techniques

Speed up the printing process. Delay long print jobs to the middle of the night. Jump high-priority print jobs to the head of the line. Set up forms-based printing. Discover the multiple uses of separator pages.

Understanding the Windows NT Printing Process

In Windows NT, the operating system manages printing so that applications do not have to. Windows applications merely direct printer output to a Windows-defined printer. The printer driver, which is part of Windows itself, properly formats the output and sends it to the printer.

This is the beauty of printing under Windows. You tell Windows what brand and model of printer you have, and it installs the appropriate drivers. Thereafter, in all of your Windows applications, the only available formatting capabilities are those the printer can deliver. If you later acquire a new, more capable printer, your applications will be able to format to that printer's capacity. You only have to install the appropriate printer driver, and you only have to do it once per printer. All of your Windows applications will just go along with whatever you do.

Another important feature of Windows NT printing is its built-in networking capabilities. You can give people using other computers permission to send print jobs to your printer, and you can send your print jobs to other people's printers. You can control and print on printers that are connected directly to the network.

Some Definitions

To understand printing in Windows NT, it helps to know that NT defines certain terms differently than other operating systems. NT uses the terms defined in the following sections.

Printers and Print Devices   To you and me, a printer is a peripheral component that plugs into the back of a computer and puts text and pictures on paper—a laser printer or an inkjet printer. But to NT, this is a *print device*. To NT, a *printer* is a logical representation of the physical print device. That is, the software is the printer; the hardware is the print device.

Print Queues   When you print in a multitasking operating system such as Windows, or across a network, your print job goes to a print queue; then the system sends the job to the print device. In earlier network operating systems, you had to specify which print queue you were printing to. In NT, users specify which printer, not which queue. It's a semantic difference, but it represents that much less for the average user to learn about the arcane inner workings of the computer.

Spooling   When you print a file in NT, you write it to disk (converting it, along the way, to a form that the print device can understand); then you send that disk file to the print device. That is, you send it to the Spooler, which *spools* it to a *spool file* in the print queue, where it waits until the Spooler can *de-spool* it to the print device.

Network-Interface Printers   Most of us think of a printer as being connected to and receiving print jobs from a computer. Network-interface printers, however, can connect directly to a network cable via their own internal or external network adapter. The most widespread such printers are Hewlett-Packard LaserJets connected via JetDirect adapters. Also, Apple LaserWriters have built-in AppleTalk ports.

Print Server   A *print server* is any computer that shares one or more printers with other computers. Windows NT Server and Workstation, Windows for Workgroups, and Windows 95 all act as print servers, as can file servers running under LAN Manager, LAN Server, Novell NetWare, UNIX, and other network operating systems. Because Windows NT Workstation only permits 10 simultaneous connections from other computers, it is not a good choice to act as a print server in any but a small network.

Windows NT and Networks

While a computer running Windows NT Workstation could very well operate in isolation, the reality is that, increasingly, business computers are being interconnected to each other in local area networks (LANs). Windows NT was designed from the outset to interact with other computers on local area networks, and this includes the printing function. When connected to a network, it is a simple matter to share one's printer with others on the network and to connect to others' shared printers. Printing to remote printers across the network is virtually transparent to the user, who simply chooses from a list of printers, any or all of which may be accessible only across the network.

Part

II

Ch

5

The Printers folder and [printername] windows

The printing process starts with the Printers folder. As shown in figure 5.1, you can locate this folder in a number of places:

- In the Settings menu, in the Start menu
- In the Control Panel
- In the Explorer window, under My Computer
- In the My Computer icon on the desktop

You also can put a shortcut to it anywhere that suits you.

FIG. 5.1
Can you find the Printers folder in this screen shot? Hint: It appears four times.

Printers folder icon——

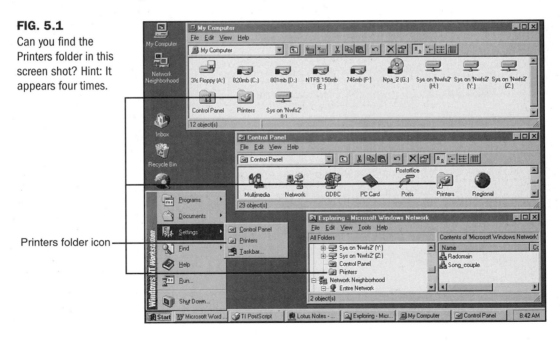

The Printers folder, shown in figure 5.2, contains an icon for the Add Printer Wizard that allows you to install new printers and connect to network printers. It also contains icons for all the printers you have installed or connected to. You can tell the network status of a printer by its icon. A local, non-shared printer appears as a simple picture of a printer. A local, shared printer appears to be held out by a hand. A remote printer to which you have established a connection appears to be connected to a network cable. In the Printers folder you can:

- Install and connect to printers using the Add Printer Wizard
- Share installed printers
- Access installed printers to monitor and manage them
- Remove printers

FIG. 5.2

The Printers folder contains the Add Printer Wizard and icons for all defined printers.

Add Printer wizard   Local, shared printer

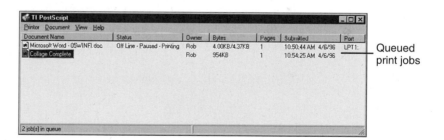

Local, non-shared printer   Remote printer

Each printer icon opens into a separate window, named for that printer (see fig. 5.3). In a printer window you can:

- Configure and share the printer
- Monitor and manage print jobs

FIG. 5.3

This printer window indicates that the printer called TI PostScript has two print jobs pending. It displays the source, status, and owner of each print job, among other things.

Queued print jobs

Part
II

Ch
5

CAUTION

This chapter refers to the *Printers folder* and *printer windows*. Don't confuse them. The *Printers folder* contains icons for all printers defined in your system. Each printer icon opens into a window named with the name of the printer, hence referred to in this chapter as a *printer window*.

Setting Up Printing on Your Computer

Before you can do any printing, you must set up the process. Because Windows NT computers usually connect to a local area network, printing from NT may mean printing to a local printer, printing to a printer attached to another computer, or printing to a network-connected printer. The processes of setting up for each type of printing are slightly different. But they all begin with the Add Printer Wizard in the Printers folder. The Add Printer Wizard walks you through the steps of defining a new printer.

 TIP In the following procedures, NT may have to install a printer driver. Be prepared. Know the path where the Windows NT distribution files are located. They may be on floppy disks, a CD-ROM, or in a directory on a file server. If the files are on a file server, you may have to be logged in as an administrator to access them.

Printers Attached to Your Own Computer

If a printer is attached to one of the physical ports on your computer (for example, LPT1 or COM1), you may follow these steps to define it in NT:

1. In the Printers folder, run the Add Printer Wizard by double-clicking it or by selecting it and pressing Enter or by selecting and choosing File, Open. The first screen of the Add Printer Wizard appears, as shown in figure 5.4.

FIG. 5.4
Choose between installing a local printer or connecting to a remote printer in the first screen of the Add Printer Wizard.

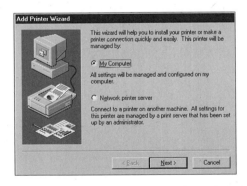

2. Choose My Computer, then choose Next. The second screen of the Add Printer Wizard appears, as shown in figure 5.5.

FIG. 5.5

In this screen, choose your printer's port.

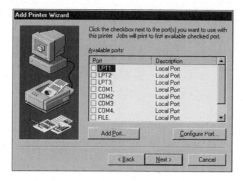

3. Place a check mark in the check box next to the port to which your printer attaches. For a printer connected directly to your computer, choose one of the hardware port names. Most modern printers connect to the parallel port, and most modern computers only have one parallel port, so you will almost always choose LPT1. Click Next; the screen in figure 5.6 appears.

FIG. 5.6

Choose your printer's Manufacturer and Model in the third screen of the Add Printer Wizard.

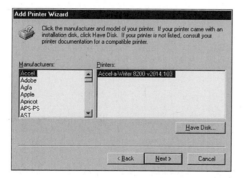

Part

II

Ch

5

4. Choose the manufacturer and model of your printer. If your printer's manufacturer or model name does not appear in the lists, check your printer documentation. It may include a disk with the appropriate information on it, in which case you may press the Have Disk button. Or it may tell you what printer it emulates, in which case you may choose the emulated printer from the lists. Choose Next to move to the fourth screen of the Add Printer Wizard.

If Windows NT does not provide a driver for your printer, check the printer manual to see if it emulates another brand of printer. Most non-PostScript laser printers emulate Hewlett-Packard LaserJets. PostScript printers almost always work with Apple LaserWriter drivers. Dot-matrix printers (remember them?) emulate Epson or IBM dot-matrix printers. And most inkjet printers emulate Hewlett-Packard DeskJets. Most daisy-wheel printers...well, maybe you should start thinking about retiring your daisy-wheel printer.

5. The screen that appears at this point depends on whether you have previously defined a printer that uses the same driver as the one you are defining now. If you have not, you see the "printer name" screen, as shown in figure 5.8. If you have, you see the screen in figure 5.7, in which you tell the wizard whether to keep the existing driver or replace it. After you make that choice, you go to the screen in figure 5.8.

FIG. 5.7

In this screen, tell the wizard whether to keep the existing printer driver or replace it.

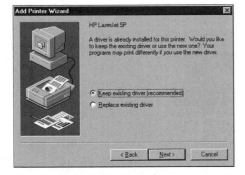

FIG. 5.8

In this screen, enter a name for your printer and specify whether it will be the default printer.

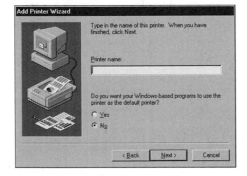

6. Type a name for the printer in the Printer Name text box. The name can be 32 characters long and can include spaces and non-alphabetical characters. If you share this printer with other users (see next step), other *NT users* will know the printer by this name when they connect to it, so make it descriptive, such as *Rob's HP LaserJet IIp*. Choose Next. The screen in figure 5.9 appears.

FIG. 5.9
You may choose to share your printer in this screen of the Add Printer Wizard.

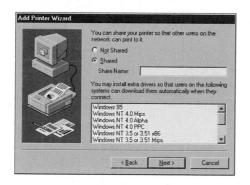

7. If you want to let other users print on your printer, choose Shared, then enter a Share Name for your printer. Non-NT users see this name when viewing shared printers, so again make it descriptive. If you will be sharing with DOS users, the Share Name should be no longer than 12 characters and should not include spaces. If you will be sharing with users of Windows 95 or other versions or platforms of Windows NT, you may select those systems from the list in the bottom half of the screen. When those users connect to your shared printer, the appropriate drivers will download to their machines automatically. Click Next. The screen in figure 5.10 appears.

8. Choose whether or not to print a test page, then click Finish. It is a good idea to print a test page to verify that you have made all the right choices.

What happens next depends on whether a driver has already been installed on your computer for the printer you are creating. If so, then your new printer's Printer Properties dialog box appears. If not, NT prompts you for the location of the driver. Enter the path and click OK, then follow the prompts. Windows installs the driver files and updates the Registry. Then NT displays all or part of your printer's Printer Properties dialog box.

FIG. 5.10
You may choose to print a test page in the last screen of the Add Printer Wizard.

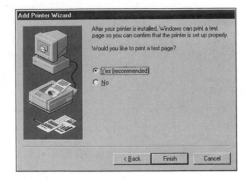

In the Printer Properties dialog box, you can set up certain printer defaults, such as the amount of printer RAM, the contents of any paper trays, and the identity of any font cartridge or downloaded soft fonts. The actual choices in this dialog box will vary, depending on your printer's capabilities. When you choose OK, NT completes the printer installation process by adding a new printer icon to the Printers folder and printing a test page, if you ordered one.

NT asks if the test page printed correctly. If you answer No, the Print Troubleshooter appears. The Print Troubleshooter presents you with a series of choices aimed at helping you discover the reason printing did not take place as expected. Depending on your answers, it will suggest courses of actions for you to take. If you let it, the Print Troubleshooter will methodically take you through all the possible causes of printer malfunctioning that might be caused by improper setup or configuration of the printer (see fig. 5.11).

Any time you experience problems with printing, such as failure to print, improper printing, or unusual slowness of printing, you can bring up the Print Troubleshooter to help you investigate the problem methodically. Choose Help in the Start menu, then Troubleshooting, then "If you have trouble printing." Then follow the prompts.

FIG. 5.11
If your printer fails to print properly, you can use the Print Troubleshooter to uncover the cause and correct the problem.

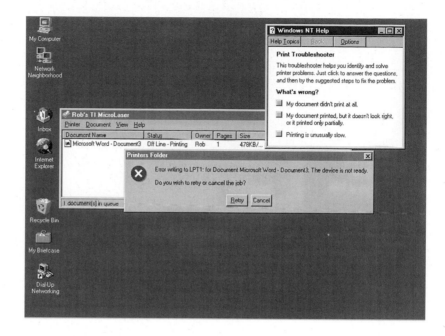

Printers Attached to Another Computer

If a printer is attached to another computer on the network, setting up printing is a simple, two-part process. The owner of the remote printer must share it with you. Then you must connect to it. The owner shares the printer either during the installation process or at any time afterward. You connect to it either by using the Add Printer Wizard or by finding the printer icon in the Network Neighborhood or Explorer window, selecting it, and choosing File, Install in the menu.

Sharing a Local Printer   If the printer has not been installed yet on the host computer, install it there by following the steps in the section "Printers Attached to Your Own Computer" earlier in this chapter. If the printer *has* been installed, and the host computer runs Windows NT 4.0, follow these steps on that computer:

1. In the Printers folder, select the icon of the printer to be shared.

2. Choose File, Properties. The [*printername*] Printer Properties dialog box appears. It has several tabbed pages of choices you can make.

Part

II

Ch

5

3. Choose the Sharing tab. The Sharing page appears (see fig. 5.12).

4. Choose Sharing. Enter a share name for the printer. Computers running operating systems other than Windows NT see this name when they browse for shared printers. Other NT computers see the printer name.

FIG. 5.12
Set up printer shares under the Sharing tab in the Printer Properties dialog box.

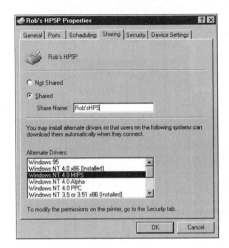

5. Optionally, in the bottom half of the Sharing page, select operating systems for which you want to install alternate printer drivers. You only need to select any of these if you anticipate that people using other computers with these operating systems will want to connect to your computer in the future. If you want to skip this step, you can always do it later. Or, if you never do it, the users will simply have to install their drivers manually at connect time.

6. Optionally, choose the Security tab, then choose Permissions. For most printers you need not change the default permissions. See "Printer Security" later in this chapter for more information about this page.

7. Click OK to close the Printer Properties dialog box.

The printer icon will now appear to be held out by a hand. The printer will now appear in other users' browse lists.

TIP   If any Windows 3.x or MS-DOS based clients will be connecting to this printer, the share name should use only letters and numbers, no spaces, no illegal DOS characters, and be 12 characters or less in length.

Connecting to a Shared Printer   You can connect to shared printers in either of two ways. First, in the Printers Folder, you can run the Add Printer Wizard. Second, in either the Explorer or Network Neighborhood, you can browse the network until you find the computer to which the desired printer is attached.

When you find the computer in Network Neighborhood, opening a window into it will show all of its shared resources, including printers. If you select the icon for the desired printer, you can then click File, Install to run the Add Printer Wizard. Or you can right-click the icon to open the shortcut menu, where you can click Install to run the Add Printer Wizard. For example, in figure 5.13, I double-clicked the Network Neighborhood icon to open the Network Neighborhood window. An icon for a computer called Ace appeared in that window. I double-clicked the Ace icon to open the Ace window, in which Ace's shared resources appeared, including a printer called HP. I right-clicked the HP icon to open the shortcut menu, and selected Install. Choosing Install will run the Add Printer Wizard.

FIG. 5.13
In Network Neighborhood, connect to a remote shared printer by selecting its icon, then choosing Install from the File menu or the shortcut menu.

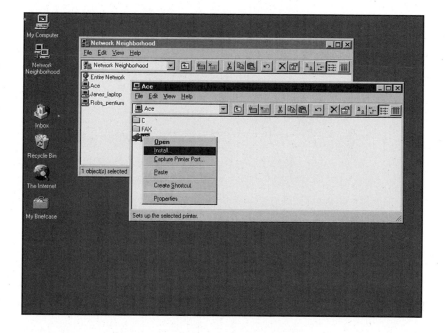

Part

II

Ch

5

Alternately, in Windows Explorer, you see the target computer in the left-hand pane of the window. Selecting the target computer displays its shared resources, including printers, in the right-hand pane. You can select the desired printer on the right-hand side, then choose File, Install to run the Add Printer Wizard. Or you can right-click the printer icon to open the shortcut menu, then choose Install. For example, in figure 5.14, Ace's shared printer HP is selected and about to be installed.

FIG. 5.14
In Windows Explorer, connect to a remote shared printer by selecting its icon, then choosing Install from the File menu or the shortcut menu.

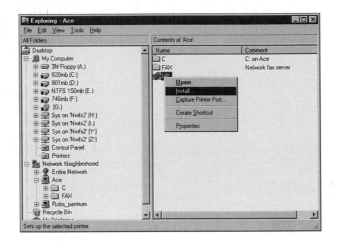

When the Add Printer Wizard starts, you see the same screen you saw previously in figure 5.4 when installing a local printer. Last time you chose My Computer. This time choose Network printer server, then choose Next. The Connect to Printer dialog box appears.

Your goal in the Connect to Printer dialog box, shown in figure 5.15, is to enter a printer share name in the Printer text box. When you have done so, click OK. If you know the share name, you may type it using the following format:

\\computername\sharename

> **N O T E** Windows NT uses the *Universal Naming Convention (UNC)* to refer to shared resources. UNC names of shared resources in Windows are formatted as follows:
>
> *computername**sharename*

If you do not know the printer share name, you may browse for and select it in the Shared Printers list. The Shared Printers list is organized as a hierarchical tree. The topmost level of the tree lists networks. If the network is a Microsoft network, the second level lists domains or workgroups, while the third level lists computers or locally shared printers, and the fourth level lists each remote computer's shared printers.

If the network is a non-Microsoft network, the levels may be organized differently. For example, figure 5.15 shows a Novell network in which the second level shows a NetWare Directory Services tree and a file server; the third level shows a print queue.

FIG. 5.15
Shared printers appear in a hierarchical tree.

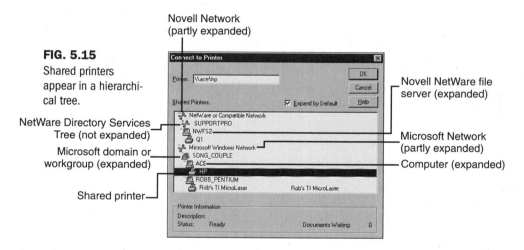

Novell Network (partly expanded)

Novell NetWare file server (expanded)

NetWare Directory Services Tree (not expanded)

Microsoft Network (partly expanded)

Microsoft domain or workgroup (expanded)

Computer (expanded)

Shared printer

If a listing has a plus sign next to it, there are subordinate levels below it, but it is collapsed and they are invisible. Double-click the listing to expand it and expose the first subordinate level. Or select it and press the gray plus key (+). To display all subordinate levels, select it and press the gray asterisk key (*).

An expanded listing or one with no subordinates has a minus sign next to it. Double-click an expanded listing to collapse it. Or select it and press the gray minus key (-).

To choose a printer in this list, expand the network that it is in. If it's in a Microsoft network, expand the domain or workgroup, then the computer. Select the shared printer. Information about the selected item appears in the Printer Information area of the dialog box. Its UNC name appears in the Printer box. Click OK to connect to it.

Part
II

Ch
5

In a Novell network, expand the file server, then select a print queue. Its UNC appears in the <u>P</u>rinter box. Click OK to connect to it.

When you click OK, your computer completes the connection to the remote printer. One of the following scenarios occurs:

- ■ *Printer driver is already installed.* If your computer already has a driver for the new printer installed, the Device Options page of the Printer Properties dialog box appears. Make any desired changes, then choose OK.

- ■ *Printer driver installs automatically.* If your computer does not have the driver installed, and the computer hosting the printer is another NT computer or a Windows 95 computer, and it has a printer driver installed that your version of NT can use, the host computer downloads that printer driver into your computer. You may notice that it takes some time before a new printer window appears, during which time your disk drive seems to be working overtime.

- ■ *You must install the printer driver manually.* Under certain circumstances, you may have to select a printer driver manually. If so, a dialog box appears, prompting you to select the correct driver from the list of standard printer drivers. Select a driver, and then choose OK. You only have to select a driver manually if two conditions arise: your computer does not already have the correct driver installed, and either the computer hosting the shared printer is *not* running Windows NT or Windows 95, or it *is* running NT or 95 but it does not have the correct printer driver for your computer.

  This might be the case if, for example, your computer is based on an Intel processor but the host computer is based on a non-Intel processor, such as the Alpha processor by Digital Equipment Corporation. Some printer drivers are not compatible across hardware platforms, and the host computer may have a version of the driver for its own platform but not for yours. Thus, NT would prompt you to load a driver manually.

  You may then be prompted to enter the path of the Windows NT distribution files. Upon your doing so correctly, NT installs the drivers.

All three scenarios end with the display of the Device Options page of the Printer Setup dialog box for the new printer. Make any desired changes in it, and choose OK.

A new icon representing your new printer appears in the Printers folder. The connection process is now complete, and you should now be able to print to that printer. Run a test print to be sure.

Printers Connected Directly to the Network

Most of us are accustomed to thinking of printers as connecting directly to a port on a computer. However, a popular way to set up printers on local area networks is to use a network interface that connects them directly to the network cable. This eliminates all sorts of hassles associated with connecting a shared printer to a computer. For example, it becomes unnecessary to keep a computer running solely so that people may access its attached printer.

Before any computer can print to a network-connected print device, at least one computer must become its print server by choosing My Computer in the Add Printer Wizard when installing it (but more than one computer can do so, if desired). Thereafter, any other computer on the network can print to the network-connected printer merely by connecting to the first computer's printer. Thus, there are two ways to set up printing to a network-connected print device:

- Become its print server by choosing My Computer in the Add Printer Wizard
- Connect to another computer's representation of it by choosing Network Printer Server in the Add Printer Wizard

Part
II

Ch
5

CAUTION

Only one computer should act as a print server to a network-connected printer. That is, only one computer should choose My Computer in the Add Printer Wizard. All others should choose Network Printer Server in the Add Printer Wizard and send print jobs to it via its print server. While it is possible for multiple computers to choose My Computer, and thus to print directly to the print device represented by the printer, only one computer at a time will be able to establish a communication session with the print device. Until that session ends, all other computers will be refused access to the printer. The effect is that it will be unpredictable when the print device will become available to a given print server.

The most common method of connecting printers to the network is via Hewlett-Packard's JetDirect adapters. The adapter may be internal—installed in a slot in the printer, with a network cable connector projecting out the back of the printer. Or it may be external, a small box with a network cable connector and one or more external printer ports that connects to the printer via a printer cable.

The JetDirect adapter is an extra-cost item which you would normally buy from the same seller as the printer; the seller may then install it in the printer for you and, perhaps, install the printer on your network for you. Or, you could buy the adapter separately—say, for an existing printer that you intend to move from a workstation to a direct network connection.

N O T E   JetDirect is a brand name of Hewlett-Packard, and the JetDirect adapter is a Hewlett-Packard product. However, there are other brands of adapters that work similarly. Hewlett-Packard's adapters are neither the only ones available nor the only good ones. If for any reason—price, features, superstition—you prefer another brand over the JetDirect, don't let me influence you one way or the other. The instructions that follow have not been tested with any particular brand of adapter, but describe the general process necessary to set up an adapter of the JetDirect type.

Another common printer-to-network connection, seen primarily in Apple Macintosh networks, is via an AppleTalk adapter. Most PostScript printers include one as a standard feature. It may be an extra-cost add-on for some brands or models.

To communicate with each other on the network, two devices must use the same transport protocols. Computers on local area networks typically communicate using Microsoft/IBM NetBEUI, Novell IPX/SPX, or TCP/IP. Apple computers usually use AppleTalk.

JetDirect adapters, on the other hand, use Data Link Control (DLC). Since PCs don't use DLC to communicate with each other, it is almost always necessary to install DLC on a computer before it can communicate with a JetDirect-connected printer. In fact, in Windows NT, Hewlett-Packard network ports don't even show up in the list of available ports until you first install the DLC protocol.

Installing the DLC Protocol   You install the DLC protocol by running the Network option of the Control Panel. In the Network dialog box that appears:

1. Click the Protocols tab. The protocols page will appear.

2. If DLC is not listed, click Add. The Select Network Protocol dialog box will appear.

3. Choose DLC Protocol from the list of software choices. Then click OK.

4. If prompted to do so, enter the path of the NT installation directory and click OK. NT will install the DLC protocol.

5. Restart the computer for the change to take effect. A prompt will appear offering to restart your computer for you.

Creating a JetDirect-Connected Printer   You define a JetDirect-connected printer the same way as any other printer, except in one respect: Instead of choosing a hardware port in the Ports screen of the Add Printer Wizard, you choose Add Port and choose Hewlett-Packard Network Port from the list. Before starting the printer creation process, however, you must take care of some preliminaries:

- Install the JetDirect adapter in the printer (or, if the adapter is external, connect the printer to it).

- Connect the printer to the network.

- Print out a test page or a configuration plot. Your printer documentation will instruct you how to do this. You need the information on this sheet, in particular the network address of the JetDirect adapter, later in the creation process.

- Make sure the printer is turned on and is online.

When these preliminaries are complete, create the printer as follows:

1. In the Printers folder, start the Add Printer Wizard.

2. Choose My Computer in the first screen of the Add Printer Wizard. Choose Next. The Ports screen appears.

3. In the Ports screen, choose the Add Port button. The Printer Ports dialog box appears.

N O T E   You can also add a port independently of creating a new printer. To do so, choose File, Server Properties in the Printers folder. The Print Server Properties dialog box appears. In the Forms page, choose the Add Port button, then follow the directions in steps 4 through 8. ■

Part
II

Ch
5

4. If you previously installed the DLC protocol, as described in the previous section, an entry appears for Hewlett-Packard Network Port. Select it, and click OK (see fig. 5.16).

FIG. 5.16

Hewlett-Packard Network Port appears in the Print Destinations dialog box only if you previously installed the DLC transport protocol in the Control Panel.

5. The Add Hewlett-Packard Network Peripheral Port dialog box appears (see fig. 5.17). You must complete two of the fields; the others are for fine-tuning communication between the printer and computer, and you may ignore them for now.

6. Enter a name for the port in the Name box. The name should indicate that this is a network connection, not a connection internal to the computer—something like **NET01** or **JETDIRECT01**. Spaces are legal, but some applications may not be able to work with a port name that includes spaces, so leave them out. Don't end the name with a colon (:).

FIG. 5.17

In the Add Hewlett-Packard Network Peripheral Port dialog box, enter the name and network address of the JetDirect-connected printer.

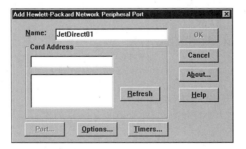

7. Enter the network address of the JetDirect adapter in the Card Address field. This is a 12-digit number. Get it from the test page or configuration plot you printed out earlier.

8. Click OK. If the OK button is grayed out, it is because you entered the name or the network address incorrectly; correct the error so the button will become available. You return to the Printer Ports dialog box. Choose Close to continue.

9. You return to the Ports screen of the Add Printer Wizard. There you will discover that your newly added port now appears. Select it and choose <u>N</u>ext to continue.

10. Complete the remaining screens in the Add Printer Wizard, then click Finished.

You may be prompted to enter the path where the Windows NT distribution files are located. You also have a chance to make changes in a Printer Properties dialog box for the new printer. When you complete these steps, a new icon appears in the Printers folder for the newly created printer. Send a print job to it to make sure everything works.

Printer Configuration

The owner of a printer—that is, the person who defined it in the first place, or any-one who later took ownership of it—can define default printer settings and default document printing characteristics. So can members of the Administrators and Power Users groups. Later, when a user connects to that printer, the user can change those defaults as they apply to that user. At print time, the user can change the settings as they apply to the document being printed.

The tools for configuring printers are in the Printer Properties dialog box. The tools for setting the printing characteristics of a document are in the Document Properties dialog boxes. The Add Printer Wizard presents the Printer Properties dialog box to you as the last step of installing a new, local printer. It presents only one page of it, the Device Options page, if you are connecting to a remote printer. You can usually accept the defaults and just click OK to close it. The Add Printer Wizard does not open the Document Defaults dialog box for you. If you need to set unusual document defaults, you must open the dialog box yourself after closing the Printer Properties dialog box.

Part

II

Ch

5

Displaying the Printer Properties Dialog Box If you need to go back later and reconfigure a printer, you may display the Printer Properties dialog box in any of three ways:

- Right-click a printer icon to display the shortcut menu, and then choose Properties

- In the Printers folder, select a printer, and then choose File, Properties

- In a printer window (opened by double-clicking a printer icon), choose Printer, Properties

The Printer Properties dialog box appears (see fig. 5.18).

FIG. 5.18
Configure printer characteristics in the Printer Properties dialog box.

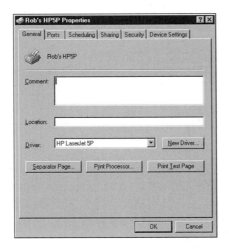

The Printer Properties dialog box has six tabbed pages, some of which you first encountered in the Add Printer Wizard. You click a tab to work in a specific page. The six pages and their functions are:

- *General.* Enter descriptive information about the printer. Change the driver. Set the separator page or print processor. Print a test page.

- *Ports.* Reset the printer port. Add or delete a port. Configure a port.

- *Scheduling.* Define times of day when the printer is in service. Define printer priority. Define spooling characteristics.

- *Sharing.* Share the printer. Revoke a share. Rename a share. Install alternate printer drivers that users of Windows 95, older versions of Windows NT, and

Windows NT for other processor platforms can download automatically when they connect to your shared printer.

■ *Security*. Set printer permissions, auditing, and ownership.

■ *Device Settings*. Set device-specific characteristics, such as the contents of paper trays, amount of installed printer memory, installed font cartridges and soft fonts, certain graphics printing characteristics, plotter pen characteristics, and time-out values. The contents of this page vary and depend on the capabilities of the selected printer.

Setting Device-Specific Options on the Device Options Page   If you need to change the default printer settings when setting up a new printer, you will probably be looking at the Device Options page of the Printer Properties dialog box. (When setting up a remote printer, this is the only page you will have access to.) The Device Options page is divided into top and bottom halves (see fig. 5.19). The top half consists of a series of options listed in outline format; that is, some of the options are grouped within general categories. Each line consists of either a category or an option. Each option line includes its name, followed by its setting enclosed in corner brackets. When you select an option, its possible settings appear on the bottom half of the page.

FIG. 5.19
The Device Settings page of the Printer Properties dialog box lists options in the top half. The bottom half shows the possible settings of the selected option.

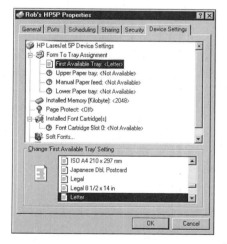

Generally, you select an option in the top half of the page, then select its setting in the bottom half. When you have set each option you want to set, click OK to close the dialog box.

CAUTION

Make sure the amount of printer memory in the Printer Setup dialog box matches the amount of memory that's actually installed in the print device. If it exceeds the amount of actual memory, the computer sends more data to the printer than it can accommodate. The printer locks up as a result and stops printing. You have to reset it or restart it. But if it locks up again, you will get nowhere with your print job—or your day.

Alternatively, if the amount of memory in the Printer Setup dialog box is less than the amount of memory actually installed in the print device, the excess memory goes unused, and printing generally takes longer.

If you are not sure how much memory is installed in the print device, print out a printer test page. It should indicate the amount of installed memory. If it does not, check your printer manual.

TROUBLESHOOTING

How can I find out how much memory my printer has?   To find out how much memory your printer actually has, print out a printer test page, following the instructions in the owner's guide that came with the printer.

Setting default document properties   To set default document printing properties, you may display the Document Properties dialog box. In the Printers folder, double-click the printer to open its printer window. Then, in the printer window, choose Printer, Document Defaults. The [printername] Default Document Properties dialog box opens (see fig. 5.20). It has two tabbed pages, with the following functions:

- *Page Setup*. Set defaults for paper size, paper source, number of copies, and print orientation (portrait, landscape, or rotated landscape).
- *Advanced*. Set defaults for all of the above items as well as for certain graphics printing characteristics and any other options that the subject printer offers, such as PostScript or plotter features.

FIG. 5.20

The Document Properties dialog box as it appears when invoked from the Printers menu in a printer window to set document defaults or when invoked from within an application to set up a specific document for printing.

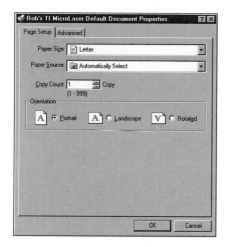

Changing Document Printing Properties at Print Time   At print time you may change the document defaults from within most Windows applications. Typically, there will be a choice on the File menu called something like Printer Setup, or there will be a button in the Print dialog box. You see the same dialog box as the one shown in figure 5.20. The changes you make will be temporary, affecting only the document you are about to print.

Changing document printing properties in queued print jobs   Even after sending a document to the print queue, you can view some document settings and change others. Go to the printer window (by double-clicking the printer icon), where the pending print jobs will be listed. Select a print job, then choose Document, Properties. The [*documentname*] Properties dialog box appears. It is basically the same dialog box as the [*printername*] Properties dialog box previously discussed, except it has a third page, called General, which includes information about how the job was set up for printing, its size, owner, submission date and time, priority, and scheduling information (see fig. 5.21).

Part

II

Ch

5

FIG. 5.21

The [documentname] Properties dialog box as invoked for a document in the print queue. It has a third page, General, that includes information about the file in the queue.

Setting a Default Printer

If more than one printer appears in the Print Manager, you have to decide which will be the default printer. The default printer is the one your Windows applications print to if you do not specify otherwise at print time. If you do not choose a default printer, the first one you install is the default.

You set the default printer in the Printers Folder or in an open printer window. In the Printers folder, select a printer, then choose File, Set as Default. In an open printer window, choose Printer, Set as Default Printer. If, when you open either menu, a check mark appears next to Set as Default (or Set as Default Printer), then that printer is already the default.

There are two ways to tell which is the default printer:

■ Open the Printers folder, then select each printer in turn and open the File menu. When the default printer is selected, a check mark appears next to the Set as Default entry.

■ Open any application. Choose File, Print. The name of the default printer appears at the top of the Print dialog box.

Updating a Printer Driver

Someday you may have to update a printer driver. You may turn up a bug in the one you are using now. The printer manufacturer or Microsoft may release a better one. If updated drivers exist, you can obtain them from various sources, which are listed in the back of the Hardware Compatibility List included with your copy of Windows NT.

After downloading the updated driver, you should look for a README.TXT, README.WRI, or README.DOC file that's included with it. That file tells you how to install the updated driver.

In general, the README file will instruct you to display the General page of the Printer Properties dialog box, click the New Driver button, choose the Have Disk button, then specify the path to the new driver file. The driver loads automatically.

Printing

Once printing is properly set up, your involvement in the printing process is minimal. Basically, you print from within your applications by choosing File, Print. Make any changes you want in the Print dialog box—you probably won't want to make *any* changes—then choose OK. Your document prints. Occasionally you might have to use the Printer window to adjust a printer or queue setting, or to deal with a print failure. But mostly printing takes care of itself.

In this release of NT, there is a new method available for printing—drag-and-drop. You can drag an icon representing your file over to and drop it on top of an icon representing the printer. This signals NT to open the document in the application, instruct the application to format the document for printing and send the print output to Windows, then close the application. You don't have to do all that manually as in previous releases.

Part of the reason printing in Windows NT is so effortless is that, behind the scenes, it is a rather complex process. To put it simply, clients send print jobs to the Spooler, which in turn sends the jobs to print devices. The clients in this case include application programs and remote workstations. The Spooler consists of several components, including the router, local and remote print providers, print processors, and print monitors.

The router receives a print job from a client, then delivers it to the appropriate print provider. (That would be the local print provider if the target print device is defined locally, or a remote print provider if the target print device is remote.) The remote print provider delivers the print job to the appropriate remote computer. The local print provider manages the print job while it remains in the print queue, hands it off to a print processor if the print job needs modification before being printed, and hands it off to a print provider for actual printing.

The details of the printing process could fill a book and are of great interest to a certain type of person—programmers mostly—but are well beyond the scope of this chapter.

Managing Printer and Print Job Settings

Once printing is working, you should rarely have to change anything. If you do, you do so in the Printer Properties and Document Properties dialog boxes. You may have to update printer drivers, modify and remove printers, or manage the print queue or specific documents waiting in the queue. You can also manage remote printers and manage printer security if you have the appropriate rights.

Managing the Print Queue

Inevitably, you will send print jobs to a printer by mistake. If it's a long print job, you will want to remove it from the queue so as not to tie up the printer and waste paper. Or a printer will malfunction, and print jobs will accumulate in the printer's print queue, waiting to be printed. These print jobs grow stale as people give up on them ever being printed and reprint the document to some other printer. These jobs need to be removed from the print queue. Or a job will need to be bumped to the top of the queue, because there is a rush job on it. Or a job will be paused, then have to be resumed or restarted.

You do all these things in the [printername] window. When you send a print job to a printer, it appears as a row of information in that printer's window until it finishes printing. The job starts at the bottom of the list, works its way to the top. Then, after printing takes place successfully, the job disappears from the list entirely. During the print job's tenure in the print queue, [*printername*] window reports on its progress. You know this because the words Spooling and Printing succeed each other in the Status column as the print job arrives from the client application, then proceeds to the print device.

If you pause a printer, the word Paused appears in its window title. If you pause a document, the word Paused appears in its Status column.

If you need to move a document in the queue, you simply drag it with the mouse. If you need to remove a job from the queue, you can select the job, then press the Delete key. If you need to resize a column of information about a print job, you can drag the column divider at the top of the printer window. All other actions are performed via the <u>D</u>ocument menu.

TROUBLESHOOTING

My printer does not print at all.   Verify that the job or the printer has not been paused. Verify that the print device is turned on, is connected to the network or computer, and is online (that is, make sure that its Ready light is on). Print a test page to verify that the print device is functioning correctly. Test the printer cable by trying it out on another printer. Verify that the port is working correctly by connecting a loopback connector to it and running diagnostics or by connecting another printer to it. If the hardware seems to be working correctly, print to another port (for example, to FILE). If the job prints, then the print monitor for the failing port may be corrupt.

Remote Administration

If you have the appropriate permissions, NT lets you administer remote printers. That is, you can change the settings in the Printer Properties and Document Properties dialog boxes, as well as manipulate print queues. In a domain, members of the Administrators, Server Operators, and Print Operators groups have sufficient permissions. In a workgroup, members of the Administrators and Power Users groups have sufficient permissions.

To administer a remote printer, locate the icon for that printer either in the Printers folder or in a Network Neighborhood or Explorer window. From the icon you can display the Printer Properties dialog box. Or you can double-click the icon to open a printer window. From the printer window you can open the Printer Properties and Document Properties dialog boxes and manipulate the print queue.

Printer Security

Windows NT security features extend to the print function and can be found on the Security page of the Printer Properties dialog box. Here you can change the actions people can perform by choosing Permissions; you can audit the usage of printers by choosing Auditing, and you can see who owns an object and can even assume ownership by choosing Ownership.

Printer Ownership   The owner of a printer automatically has Full Access permissions for that printer. Initially, the printer's owner is the person who created it. You might want to change the owner if, for example, you get a promotion and take over a new computer as a result.

You can change the ownership of a printer by clicking the Ownership button on the Security page of the Printer Properties dialog box. The Owner dialog box appears, showing the identity of the owner of the selected printer. Click Take Ownership to become the new owner.

Setting Printer Permissions   If you will be sharing printers or if multiple users will be logging into your computer under their own names, you can secure printers by setting permissions on them. What a given person can do with the printer and with documents waiting to be printed depends on the permissions they have with respect to each printer.

You set permissions for each printer separately. The permissions that you can set include Full Control, Manage Documents, Print, and No Access. You can assign these permissions to individual users or to groups, in which case they apply to every member of the group. Table 5.1 enumerates the actions that each permission activates.

Table 5.1   Printer Permissions and Actions

Permission	Permitted Actions
No Access	The holder of this permission is locked out of the printer entirely and cannot print to the printer or control the printer or print queue in any way.
Print	The holder can print documents and pause, resume, restart, and delete his or her own documents.

Permission	Permitted Actions
Manage Documents	The holder can change settings of documents in the queue and can pause, resume, restart, and remove documents in the queue. The holder *cannot* add documents to the queue (that is, cannot print a document).
Full Control	The holder can take all available actions with respect to both documents and printers.

These permissions are cumulative, except that No Access overrides all the others. Say that you belong to two groups: one called "Print Users" with the Print permission to printer X and the other called "Print Queue Managers" with the Manage Documents permission to printer X. Because of your membership in those groups, you hold both the Print and Manage Documents permissions. They are cumulative. But then say you are added to a group called "Outlaws" with the No Access permission. Now you lose all other permissions because No Access overrides the others.

Table 5.2 shows the groups that exist at the time you install NT, with the following default printer permissions.

Table 5.2 Default Printer Permissions

Group	Permission
Administrators	Full Control
Power Users	Full Control
Everyone	Print
CREATOR OWNER	Full Control

Everyone and CREATOR OWNER are not groups in the same sense as the others. They don't appear in the list of groups in User Manager. You can't create or remove them. The system maintains them for special purposes and they only show up externally in places like the Printer Permissions dialog box.

All users are automatically members of Everyone. It provides a handy way to assign permissions to anyone using the resource.

CREATOR OWNER includes, for a given print job or printer, only the user who created or now owns that print job or printer. Its effect is to allow the creator (or subsequent owner) of a print job or printer to control his or her creation.

You can add other groups and give them permissions as follows:

1. Open the Printer Properties dialog box of the printer. Choose the Security page.

2. Click Permissions. The Printer Permissions dialog box appears, as shown in figure 5.22. The Printer Permissions dialog box indicates the name of the printer and its owner, lists all users and groups that have been granted permissions to it, and shows the type of access each has.

FIG. 5.22
Monitor and change a user's or group's power to manage printers and print queues in the Printer Permissions dialog box.

3. To change the type of access granted to a user or group, select the user or group in the Name box, then choose a permission in the Type of Access drop-down list. Choose OK.

4. To add another user or group to the list, click the Add button. The Add Users and Groups dialog box appears (see fig. 5.23). The Add Users and Groups dialog box contains two lists:

The Names box shows either all groups or all users in a selected domain or on a selected computer.

The Add Names box, initially empty, shows all users or groups that you intend to add to the list of permitted users and groups in the previous dialog box.

FIG. 5.23
Pick additional users
or groups from the
list in the Add Users
and Groups dialog
box.

5. The Names list initially shows only groups. If you want to see users, too, click the Show Users button.

6. If the group or user you want to add still does not appear in the Names list, you may need to display another list. Choose another domain or computer from the List Names From drop-down list.

TIP The List Names From drop-down list shows domains if you are a member of a domain maintained by Windows NT Server or Advanced Server or LAN Manager computers. It shows computers if you are in a workgroup.

7. Select the desired user or group in the Names box, and then click Add. The name now appears in the Add Names box. The added user or group has the default permission of Print. Change it, if you want, in the Type of Access drop-down list.

8. When you have added the desired names, choose OK. You will be returned to the Printer Permissions dialog box, and the new names will appear in the Name list. Choose OK again to accept the new settings.

Auditing Printer Usage   One nice feature of Windows NT is that it permits you to track usage of resources. If you are responsible for administering a group of printers and need to balance the load among them, or if you are trying to track down the cause of printing problems, the printer auditing feature might be just the tool for you.

Part
II

Ch
5

To audit printer usage, you must first enable auditing of file and object access in User Manager. Then, in the Printer Properties dialog box, you specify what groups, users, and types of events to track. Thereafter, occurrences of audited events are recorded in a file which you can review in Event Viewer.

 TIP Before you can audit any print events, you must enable auditing of File and Object Access in User Manager.

To specify what users, groups, and events to audit, click the Auditing button on the Security page of the Printer Properties dialog box. The Printer Auditing dialog box appears (see fig. 5.24).

FIG. 5.24
Set up tracking of printer usage in the Printer Auditing dialog box.

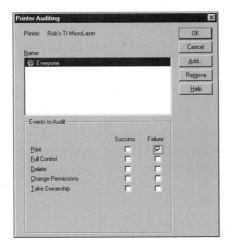

The Printer Auditing dialog box indicates which printer is being audited, whose actions are being audited, and what actions are being tracked. If you want to add a user or group, click Add. If you want to remove a user or group, select it and click Remove.

Clicking Add displays the Add Users and Groups dialog box described in the previous section. In the Add Users and Groups dialog box, you can browse lists of users and groups and select the ones whose actions you want to audit.

The events which can be tracked include successes and failures in the following categories:

■ *Print.* Records attempts to send print jobs to the printer.

■ *Full Control.* Records attempts to change job settings for documents; attempts to pause, restart, move and delete documents in the queue; attempts to share a printer; and attempts to change printer properties.

■ *Delete.* Records attempts to remove printers.

■ *Change Permissions.* Records attempts to change printer permissions.

■ *Take Ownership.* Records attempts to take ownership of a printer.

▶ **See** "Using the Event Viewer," **p. 927**

Advanced Printer Setup Techniques

Now that you have the basics of printing under control, you might want to fine-tune your printer setups. Windows NT provides a series of tools for this purpose. Among other things you can do:

■ Speed up the printing process

■ Define multiple printers that print to the same print device

■ Define separator pages

Three Ways to Speed Up the Printing Process

You can define the speed of the printing process in two ways: how fast it takes a print job to get out of your application program; and how fast it takes the print job to get out of the printer. That is, you may be in a hurry to get back to work in the program that is sending the print job, so you can send even more stuff to the printer and get out from under the teetering pile of to-do items that threatens to bury your evening. Or you may be in a hurry to get the paper out of the printer so you can meet that filing deadline.

Unfortunately, the general rule is that you cannot have both kinds of speed. It is a trade-off. Either you can tie up your program longer and send the print job directly to the print device; do not pass Spooler, do not collect $200. Or you can spit the job out of the program real quickly, then wait your turn in the print queue. (Actually, you *can* have both kinds of speed. Just buy a faster printer. But that solution is really beyond the scope of this discussion. Sorry.)

The way NT printing works, by default, is that your application converts your file into a series of characters that the print device will interpret properly to generate the properly formatted page of text and graphics that you are looking for. The application sends this print image file to the Spooler, which stores it in the print queue. When the print job reaches the top of the queue, and the print device becomes available, the Spooler sends the print job to the print device, feeding the job to the print device as fast as the print device can accept it. If, when the print job arrives in the print queue, there are no jobs ahead of it and the print device is idle, NT will start sending the print job to the print device as soon as it has one full page of output. This is a change from earlier versions of NT, which did not send page one to the print device until the last page had arrived in the print queue. There are three ways to manipulate this process that might speed it up in one way or another.

Bypass the Spooler   First, if a print device is local and not shared, you can bypass the Spooler and print queue entirely, and have the application program send the print job directly to the port to which the print device is attached. This eliminates some of the processing inherent in having a "middleman" process, the Spooler, mediating between the application program and the port. The first page will reach the printer sooner; therefore, the last page will probably reach the printer sooner, and your document will be on its way out the door sooner.

The drawbacks of this are that your application program will be tied up talking to the printer until the last page is sent to it. Because the printer is always the bottleneck in the printing process, this represents a big slowdown in the time it takes before you can use the program again. Also, you will not be able to send any print jobs from other programs while the first print job is still in progress. Since you have elected to bypass the Spooler, there is no print queue for the jobs to wait in.

You can set up direct printing in the Scheduling page of the Printer Properties dialog box. There you can choose Print Directly to the Printer.

Enhanced Metafile Spooling   The second way to speed up printing is to enable enhanced metafile (EMF) spooling. And you can only do this if the program you are printing from and the print device you are printing to both support it. (You can assume that any program written specifically for Windows NT or Windows 95 will support EMF spooling.) In this process, your program does not generate a printer-ready file, but rather a metafile, that is, a file that is only partially processed for printing. Your program hands the metafile off to the Spooler, which will finish the conversion of it to a printer-ready file, then send it to the printer.

By only partially processing the file, your program gets to hand the file off a lot sooner than if it had to do all the processing. The program might be able to hand the file off in as little as half the time it might otherwise have taken. The benefit to you is that your program is ready that much sooner for you to start working in it again. You benefit even more if the print device is remote, because your Spooler will send the metafile to the print server. The print server will finish converting the file. The background processing, which would otherwise take processor cycles away from you and your foreground-processing application program, takes place on the print server instead of your computer.

The downside here is that not all programs can generate metafiles. In those cases you have to disable metafile spooling. You can, however, do that from within the application program for benefit of that program only. All other programs can continue to send metafiles to the Spooler.

To enable metafile spooling, display the Document Defaults dialog box (by choosing Printer, Document Defaults in the printer window). In the Advanced page, select Metafile Spooling in the top half of the page, enable it in the bottom half of the page, and then click OK to close the dialog box (see fig. 5.25).

To disable metafile spooling for one program, run the program, and choose File, Printer Setup in the menu. If there is no such entry, and there is no other obviously printing-related entry in the File menu, then choose File, Print, and look for a Printer Setup button or something similar. You will know when you have found the right combination because the Document Defaults dialog box will appear. There, in the Advanced page, you can disable metafile spooling just for the program you are in. Click OK.

FIG. 5.25
Metafile spooling is selected in the top half of the page. It has been enabled in the bottom half of the page.

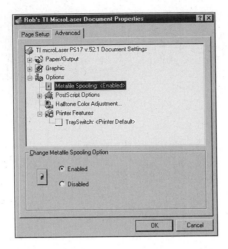

Start Printing After the Last Page Has Been Spooled   The third way to speed up printing is probably more relevant for a high-volume print server than for your workstation. It involves changing the default of sending a job to the printer as soon as one page is available to be printed. Instead, you tell it to use the pre-4.0 method of holding the print job until the last page is ready to be printed. That way, the print device isn't tied up by a job until the job is fully print ready.

The benefit here is that the print device will never be idled by a complex print job in which the print device is ready to print page n but the application program is still trying to figure out how best to convert a complex, on-screen graphic image into the correct stream of ones and zeros that the printer will receive. You don't have print jobs held up in the queue, waiting for a job that has started printing but is now stalled.

The drawback here is that your print jobs, especially long ones, will seem to take forever to start printing. Also, on a lightly used printer, the print device might be sitting there idle when it could perfectly well be printing out the first pages of the print job while the application program is still sending the last pages to the print queue. As I said before, this trick is really only useful for heavily used, shared printers that frequently have multiple jobs waiting in the print queue; don't bother with it for a lightly used printer.

To cause print jobs to start printing only after the whole print job has been spooled, go to the Scheduling page of the Printer Properties dialog box. Choose Spool Print Jobs so Program Finishes Printing Faster and Start Printing After Last Page is Spooled.

Multiple Printers, One Print Device

Windows NT permits you to define multiple printers that actually refer to a single print device. You might wonder why you would want to do this. Here are some scenarios.

Scenario 1: High-Priority Print Jobs   Your computer has a shared laser printer attached. Because it has higher resolution than the other laser printers in the office, it is very popular. You find that your print jobs don't get printed soon enough because of all the other jobs that are queued up; therefore, you'd like to bump your print jobs to the top of the queue. You could go into the [printername] window and do just that if you have Full Control access to the printer. You just drag your print job up to the top of the list. Or you could change its priority in the [documentname] Properties dialog box.

Here's a better way. Define a second printer with a higher priority than the one everyone else uses. Don't share the second printer. Whenever you need a printout fast, print to the second printer. Because it is higher priority than the first, all of its print jobs will print out before any print jobs in the first printer's queue.

How to Define a High-Priority Printer   In the Printers folder, create a new printer. In the Add Printer Wizard, enter the same driver and port as for the original printer, but enter a different printer name. At the end, when the Printer Properties dialog box appears, display the Scheduling page (see fig. 5.26).

Change this printer's priority by dragging the slider in the Priority field or by pressing Alt+P then the right or left arrow key. You can set any number from 1 to 99, where 1 is the lowest priority and the default. So, if you set your new printer at 2, it will have higher priority than the original (assuming that printer's priority was never changed from the default of 1). Save your new printer by choosing OK in each dialog box.

Part
II

Ch
5

FIG. 5.26
Printer priority has
been set to 2 on the
Scheduling page of
the Printer Properties
dialog box.

Scenario 2: Long Documents Are Tying Up the Printer From time to time, you print large documents with lots of graphics in them. You know from experience that these jobs tie up the office's one shared printer, and that your coworkers grumble when you hog the printer for so long.

One solution to this problem would be to print the job in the middle of the night. You can do that in two ways (not including hanging around until everyone leaves). Either you can send the job to the print queue then set it to wait until the middle of the night before it prints. Or you can define a printer that *only* prints in the middle of the night.

How to Delay a Single Print Job Until the Middle of the Night

1. Before sending your print job to the printer, pause the printer. Do this in the Printers folder by right-clicking the printer icon and choosing Pause Printing, in the Printers folder by selecting the printer, then choosing File, Pause Printing, or in the printer window by choosing Printer, Pause Printing.

2. Print the document from within your application or by dragging its icon and dropping it on the printer icon.

3. Set a time range for the print job. Do this in the printer window. Select the print job, which should now appear in the printer window, then choose Document, Properties. The Document Properties dialog box appears.

4. In the Schedule field, choose Only From, then specify a time range during which the print job may be printed. Say, for example, 9:00 PM to 6:00 AM. Click OK.

5. Resume the printer. Choose Printer, Resume.

CAUTION

Don't forget to resume the printer after changing the document. Nothing prints until you do.

How to Set Up a Printer that only Prints in the Middle of the Night Do this if you are going to make a habit of delaying print jobs to the middle of the night. Use the Add Printers Wizard to create a second printer that describes the same print device that you are tying up now with your long print jobs. Give it a different name but keep the same driver and port as the original printer.

When the Printer Properties dialog box appears, display the Scheduling page. Change the Available field from Always to From and enter a time range during off-hours. Click OK.

From now on, send long print jobs to this printer. They will sit in the print queue until the Available From time arrives. Then your job starts printing automatically.

Using Forms

If you have a departmental printer that has multiple paper trays, earlier versions of Windows permitted you to specify which tray a print job should pull paper from. If you happened to know which tray had what paper in it, that was fine. If not, then you had to walk over to the printer and check.

Windows NT eliminates the user's need to know what paper is in which tray by allowing users to specify which form to print on rather than which tray to pull paper from.

The administrator of a multi-tray printer can specify which trays contain that paper as part of the printer setup. You do this in the Device Setup page of a printer's Properties dialog box. The Device Setup page for a multi-tray printer looks similar to the one shown in figure 5.27.

Part
II

Ch
5

FIG. 5.27
Here we have
assigned the custom
form "Redline legal
stationery" to one
tray.

The Form To Tray Assignment section shows what form is assigned to each paper tray. To change any assignment, click a paper tray in the top section of the page, then click a form in the bottom section of the page. The selected form will appear next to the selected tray in the top section of the page. Newly assigned forms are red in color; existing assignments are blue.

TIP   If a form does not appear in the list of forms, it may be too large or too small for the printer. For example, 11 × 17 forms will not appear for a printer that can only print forms 10 inches wide.

The list of available forms has many paper and envelope sizes, but they all have rather generic descriptions. If you can't find a paper size you need, or you want to customize your form descriptions (for example, Letterhead, Preprinted envelope), you may define new forms. To do so, return to the Printers folder and choose File, Server Properties. The Print Server Properties dialog box appears, displaying the Forms page (see fig. 5.28).

The Forms page displays a list of all defined forms, and a description of the selected form. The description includes the name of the form, its paper size, and its print area margins. You may redefine a form or define an entirely new one. You may reset the paper size and printing area of an existing form. If you choose to create a new form, you get to name it. To define a new form, check the Create a New Form check box. When you finish defining a form, click the Save Form button.

FIG. 5.28
Here we define a
custom form called
"Redline legal
stationery."

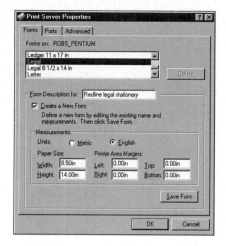

Separator Pages

A *separator page* is a page that precedes a print job and physically separates it from the preceding print job. The traditional purpose of separator pages has been to identify the owner of each print job. When a lot of users are sharing a single printer, this can be a useful feature.

Windows NT separator pages can serve another function. If your printer has both PostScript and PCL printing capabilities, you can use the separator page to force the printer into the proper mode for your print job. That way, you do not have to worry that the printer will be expecting a PCL print job when you are about to send it a PostScript print job. NT separator pages can serve this function because they are actually separate files that get printed in between each print job, and they can contain printer commands.

NT provides three default separator page files, and you can create your own if you don't like the ones that come with NT. The files that NT provides are located in the SYSTEM32 subdirectory of your Windows NT PROGRAM directory:

SYSPRINT.SEP — Prints a page before each document, and is compatible with PostScript printers only.

PCL.SEP — Forces a dual-language printer into PCL mode. Does not print out an actual page.

PSCRIPT.SEP — Forces a dual-language printer into PostScript mode. Does not print out an actual page.

Part
II

Ch
5

Separator pages, at least the ones that actually print out a page, do use paper. Most people do not like them for that reason and turn off the feature if they can. Windows NT separator pages are disabled by default. To enable the feature, go to the General page of a printer's Properties dialog box and click the Separator Page button.

The Separator Page dialog box appears. There you can enter the file name of a separator page, if you know it; or, you can click the Browse button. This opens another dialog box, also named Separator Page, but which is really the standard file browsing dialog box you see when you choose File, Open or File, Save As. The dialog box opens to the SYSTEM32 directory, and the available separator pages are listed there. Choose one from the list and click OK three times to close all the dialog boxes.

TROUBLESHOOTING

How do I troubleshoot printing problems? When troubleshooting printing problems, it may help to turn on logging of spooling events. To do so, choose File, Server Properties. The Print Server Properties dialog box appears. In the Advanced page, enable logging of Spooler error, warning, and information events. Use the Event Viewer in the Programs, Administrative Tools (Common) menu to view the logged events.

Also, you can open the Print Troubleshooter to help you investigate the problem methodically. Choose Start, Help, choose Troubleshooting in the Help Topics window, then choose If You Have Trouble Printing. Follow the prompts that appear.

My printer experiences frequent memory errors. Make sure the amount of installed printer memory in the Device Settings page of your printer's Properties dialog box matches the amount of memory actually installed in the print device. If Windows NT assumes there is more memory than the printer actually has, it sends more data to the printer than it can accommodate. This produces a memory error condition in the printer and halts printing entirely until the condition is cleared.

My printer produces incorrect output. Possible causes of incorrect output include an incorrect or misconfigured driver for the print device. Review the General, Ports, and Device Settings pages of your printer's Properties dialog box to verify that the driver matches the print device, and that it is correctly configured.

Also, a corrupted document or bugs in the program producing the output could cause printing errors. Try printing another document or printing from another program.

I want to turn off network popups notifying me that jobs have finished printing. In the Registry, find the key HKEY_LOCAL_MACHINE\SYSTEM\CurrentControlSet\Control\Print\Providers. Add the value **NetPopup** with type **REG_DWORD** and value equal to zero.

I've tried everything and printing still doesn't work correctly. When all else fails, read the documentation that came with Windows NT. In particular, don't forget the Release Notes. There are lots of printing tips in the Release Notes, many of them highlighting quirky problems that occur only in one brand or model of printer.

From Here...

This chapter taught you how to install and configure your printers. For more information, see the following chapters:

- Chapter 6, "Working with Folders and Files."
- Chapter 33, "Optimizing Windows NT Workstation Performance."

Part
II

Ch
5

Working with Folders and Files

by Kathy Ivens

A file system is a scheme for storing and keeping track of files. Different file systems use different methods for storing files on a hard drive, finding and fetching those files when they are needed, and keeping information about the files. In fact, the kind of information stored about files differs depending on the file system you install. When you install Windows NT 4.0 you have a choice of two file systems, FAT or NTFS. ■

Learning about file systems, especially NTFS

A file system allows you to store and track files. In an NTFS system, the information about a file is stored with the file.

Finding files and folders

Learn how wildcards allow you to search for virtually any file name in your system.

Understanding file properties

Learn how to use property boxes to find out all the latest information about your files.

Understanding FAT

The FAT file system uses a File Allocation Table (hence the name FAT) to track files. The File Allocation Table is like an index or table of contents, tracking the location of the files on your disk. It is made up of links that hold information on the blocks of data that make up a file. Sometimes these blocks aren't contiguous, and the table keeps track of the location of the parts of the file, starting with the first allocation unit, then tracking the next allocation unit, and continuing this through the last allocation unit used by the file.

The data blocks that hold files (or parts of files) are allocated in clusters of 512 bytes or a multiple of 512 bytes, depending upon the size of the hard drive or the partition. The FAT cannot handle more than 16 bits of information to track clusters, so the maximum number of clusters that can exist is 65535. If the size of the cluster is 512 bytes, and the maximum number of clusters is 65535, that means the maximum total disk size that the FAT can track is 33553920 (about 33M). And, in fact, early versions of DOS forced users to partition hard drives into logical drives of no more than 33M each. Today, however, large disks are supported by changing the size of the clusters. The math is quite simple—you just divide the size of the disk by 65535 to get the cluster size. It's all automatically done by the operating system when the disk is formatted.

In a FAT system, the directory information includes file names, file attributes, file sizes, last modification time, last modification date, and the starting allocation unit. This starting allocation unit is really a pointer to an entry in the File Allocation Table.

As files are created, deleted, or modified, and new files are created (and deleted and modified), they get fragmented (split among multiple blocks). The system has to create additional pointers to the allocation units, which are called chains.

So, as a disk becomes full and fragmented, two elements come together to cause a slowdown in the system:

- The File Allocation Table becomes very large and there is a lot of information the system has to wade through to find the information it needs in order to fetch a file.

- The number of steps in the chains gets larger and, since each step in the chain has to be traversed, it takes longer to put together the parts of the file from their individual blocks.

Defragmenting the drive puts the files back into contiguous blocks (but then the whole process starts over again).

The filenaming convention for FAT file systems was originally designed to be 8.3—a file name of no more than 8 characters, an extension of no more than 3 characters. However, Windows NT, like Windows 95, is programmed to accept long file names. That means you can use up to 155 characters in a file name, and even include multiple periods. You could have a file named "my.report.to.the.committee."

The advantage of using FAT is its compatibility to DOS and Windows programs.

Understanding NTFS

An NTFS file system doesn't have any form of an allocation table that uses pointers or chains to find files or store other information about files (attributes, modification dates, and so on). In NTFS the information about a file is stored with the file itself.

In fact, it's not only the modification dates, size, file name, and all the other FAT-like characteristics that are stored with the file and treated as attributes; so is the data. It's all one object.

NOTE For those who are familiar with HPFS, this is one of the major differences between these two non-FAT file systems. HPFS keeps extended attributes separate from the data, although attached to the file. ■

In addition, NTFS has an attribute for permissions available for each file. This means you can have a security system that works right down to the file level.

File names in an NTFS system can have up to 255 characters and you can have as many periods in the name as you wish (since the period does not indicate a separator between the file name and the extension, as it does in FAT). You could name a file my.letter.to.mom.about.money. And, the system will automatically create short DOS-compatible file names for those software applications that can't handle the long file names.

NTFS systems maintain a Master File Table (MFT). This is a special file that keeps information about the files on the disk. Without going into great detail about all the technical aspects of the MFT, it's worthwhile to point out a few items of interest:

Part
II

Ch

6

- The MFT creates several redundant items within itself so that, if any part of the file is damaged, it can recover itself.

- The MFT stores information about some of its own contents in the boot sector, and then mirrors the boot sector and places the duplicate in the logical center of the volume (the theory being that if the boot sector—which sits on the edge of the volume—is damaged, it may not automatically follow that information in the center of the volume is damaged).

- The MFT also contains a log file record, which can be used to recover files.

 TIP You can't format a floppy disk as anything but FAT, but the FORMAT command in an NTFS system includes parameters that will let you format disks with a FAT file system.

Deciding on a File System

When you install Windows NT 4.0 you can choose either file system. And, you can convert from FAT to NTFS if you decide on FAT and then change your mind.

There are two scenarios in which you must choose a FAT file system:

- You plan to have multiple operating systems (DOS, Windows 3.x, Windows 95, OS/2, or any combination) and want the partition to be accessible to all of them.

- You have applications that rely on the FAT file system.

- You spend most of your work day in an application that makes large sequential writes to files. The FAT file system is faster than NTFS for such writes.

Choose NTFS when its features provide desirable effects such as:

- Advanced file security features.

- Excellent performance when working in an application that generates many random-access disk reads and writes.

- The ability to create striped or mirrored volume sets using multiple hard disks.

- Storing files larger than FAT-formatted disks can support (FAT is limited to file and partition sizes of 2^32 bytes).

Understanding How Files and Folders Work Together

If you have a background in DOS and understand the concepts of path, directory, and subdirectory, everything is still the same. Except, those concepts have been implemented as objects. In Windows NT, directory objects are called folders.

An object is a representation of an item created by a user or by the operating system (a file or a folder) or a system resource (a drive or a peripheral).

Folders are container objects. They can contain other folders, files, or a combination of both. The desktop itself is a folder and fits the definition of being a container. It contains various folders (which in turn contain objects which may be folders, files, or resources). The one difference between the desktop and all the other folders in your NT system is that you can't close the desktop folder.

Working with Windows NT Explorer

The best way to picture your system as a group of objects is to launch Windows NT Explorer. There are two ways to do this:

- Choose <u>P</u>rograms from the Start menu, then choose Windows NT Explorer.
- Right-click the My Computer folder, then choose <u>E</u>xplore from the menu.

When Explorer opens, it displays objects representing your system (see fig. 6.1).

FIG. 6.1
Explorer displays a
bird's eye view of your
system.

Menu bar

Folders pane

Status bar
(shows used
and remaining
bytes)

Toolbar

Contents pane

Part
II

Ch
6

Understanding Explorer's Views

The view Explorer presents is hierarchical. Like a hierarchical outline, it formats the view so that the display of each object is indented to indicate its level in the hierarchy.

For example, notice that in Figure 6.1 the local drives (A, C, and D) and network drive (F) are equally indented under My Computer. The folders on Drive C are indented under the drive's object.

The computer itself, represented by My Computer, is indented under the Desktop, as are other resources such as Network Neighborhood, My Briefcase, and Recycle Bin.

To make it all even clearer, there's a dotted line, representing the hierarchy and the levels (indentations), that extends vertically from each level, with horizontal offshoots for each lower level.

Some other things to notice about the display are:

- Control Panel and Printers are NT folders that appear on the same level as the drives.
- Even though the view appears to be a view of the Desktop, if you have created any Desktop shortcuts they don't appear in this view, not even in the Contents pane (they do appear in the Contents pane if you highlight the Desktop Object).
- If you've created any folders on the Desktop they will display on the same level as the drives and system (the folder named My Stuff in fig. 6.1 is an example).

Changing the View

There are two changes you can make to the way Explorer displays your system:

- You can go deeper into the hierarchy in the Folders pane.
- You can totally change the way the objects in the Contents pane are displayed.

In the Folders pane, any folder that has a plus sign (+) next to it contains additional folders. Click the plus sign to display them.

In the Contents pane, the default view shows all the contents as a vertical list, with folders first, then the files (all in alphabetical order). You can change the way the Contents pane displays, using these other choices from the Toolbar or the <u>V</u>iew menu:

- Large Icons, as seen in figure 6.2
- Small Icons, as seen in figure 6.3
- Details, as seen in figure 6.4

FIG. 6.2
Large icons display in horizontal rows, alphabetically from left to right.

FIG. 6.3
Small icons display in horizontal rows, alphabetically from left to right.

FIG. 6.4
The Details view reveals more information about the objects.

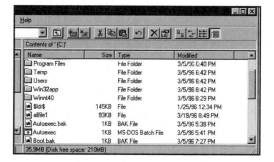

You can change the width of the two panes by positioning your pointer over the bar between them until the pointer changes to a vertical line with two bars. Then drag the separator bar in either direction (depending on which pane you want to widen).

Moving Around in Explorer

If you used File Manager in Windows, you'll find that while the basic approach is the same, Explorer is much more efficient when you want to navigate through your system.

Part
II

Ch
6

■ Highlighting (single-clicking) a folder in the Folder pane causes the contents of the folder to be displayed in the Contents pane.

■ Instead of double-clicking a folder in the Folders pane to display or hide the subfolders, you can use the plus and minus keys that are to the left of the folder. If old habits die hard, don't worry; double-clicking works too.

■ To see the contents of any subfolder, including one that's displayed in the Contents pane (you don't have to click the plus sign of the parent folder), right-click it and choose Explore. The contents of that folder are displayed in the Contents pane.

TIP Whenever the view in Explorer changes, the current top of the hierarchy is displayed in the title bar.

■ When you use the plus or minus keys, it is not the same as highlighting the folder. Therefore, the objects in the Contents panel don't change to reflect the folder you're expanding or contracting.

That last point is extremely important and makes moving objects much faster and easier. It means that the left and right panes are really independent entities. You can view the contents of one folder, then move to another folder and expand its subfolders, and Contents Pane doesn't change—it still displays the contents of the first folder. This makes moving files around much faster and easier.

N O T E If you do need two windows to copy files between folders or drives, you'll have to open another copy of Explorer. Unlike File Manager, Explorer does not have a facility for opening a second child window. When the second copy of Explorer launches, right-click the taskbar and choose Tile Horizontally to have easy access to both windows.

Create a Desktop Shortcut to Explorer

The first thing you should do, once you've discovered Explorer and its power, is put a shortcut to it on your desktop. Here are the easy steps:

1. Open Explorer and highlight the directory where Windows NT resides.

2. Find the Explorer object and drag it to the desktop.

That's all it takes. An icon named Shortcut to Explorer resides on the desktop and you can double-click it whenever you need to use Explorer.

 TIP Windows NT 4.0 is intelligent enough to know that when you drag an executable file to the desktop you want to make a shortcut. If you drag any other file type to the desktop, you've moved it.

Choosing what You Want to See

By default, Explorer does not display hidden files or folders (although on the status bar it tells you how many exist in the current folder).

You can change the selection of file types you see by choosing Options from the View menu. This brings up the Options dialog box with the View tab in the foreground (see fig. 6.5).

FIG. 6.5
You can decide for yourself which file types you want to view when you're using Explorer.

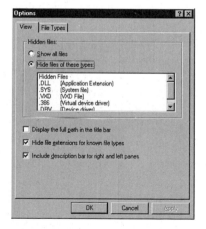

- Choose Show all files to see every file in the Contents pane. This is a toggle selection with the choice to Hide files of these types, which includes all hidden and system files.

  It's not a bad idea to leave the default selection alone and hide all those system files, since it means you won't accidentally delete or move them.

- You can choose to Display the full path in the title bar (instead of the default "Exploring - Foldername\Filename").

- You can choose to Hide file extensions for known file types. This makes the display less cluttered. The known file types are displayed on the File Types tab of the dialog box. You can delete any of the entries or add entries for file types you use when you create data files.

- Choose Display compressed files and folders with alternate color to recognize those elements easily. This is an available option if you are using NTFS, which permits the compression of individual files and folders.

- Deselect Include description bar (by default this choice is selected) if you want to get rid of the bar on top of the panes that reminds you what you're looking at.

File Manipulation with Explorer

Once the Explorer window is open, there are a host of chores you can perform within the program.

Dragging Files and Folders   You can drag files and folders around the Explorer window to copy or move them.

- Dragging with the left mouse button moves the item.

- Dragging with the right mouse button lets you move or copy the item (or create a shortcut). When you drop the item, a menu of choices appears (see fig. 6.6).

FIG. 6.6
Using the right mouse button to drag an item lets you choose what you want to do with it.

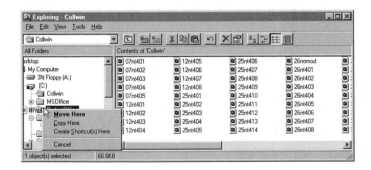

TIP If you're dragging an item and change your mind, press the Esc key while you're still holding down the mouse button. The drag operation will end.

Selecting Items

There are some shortcuts for selecting items in the Explorer window:

- To select multiple items, hold down the Ctrl key after you select the first item. Otherwise, clicking the second item deselects the first item.

- To select multiple contiguous items that are in a column display, select the first item, move to the last item, and select it while holding down the Shift key. All the items in between the first and last are selected.

- To select all the items, use Ctrl+A instead of using Edit, Select All, from the menu bar.

Right-clicking an Item

Clicking an item with the right mouse button displays a menu of choices. The choices vary depending on the type of item.

Figures 6.7 through 6.9 show some of the right-click menus available.

FIG. 6.7
The right-click menu options for a folder.

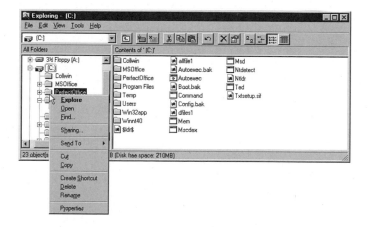

Part

II

Ch

6

FIG. 6.8
The right-click menu options for an executable file.

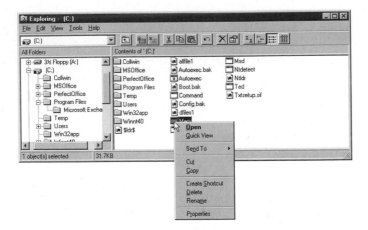

FIG. 6.9
The right-click menu options for a data file.

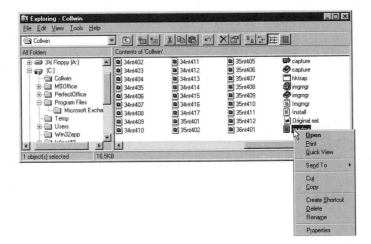

All right-click menus have some options in common:

- Open, which means different things to different file types. An executable file is launched, a data file is opened into an associated application (which is automatically launched into order to accomplish this), and a folder is displayed in a window.

- Send To, which moves the item to one of the choices in the submenu that displays when you choose Send To. By default, the choices are Drive A and My Briefcase, but you can place additional targets on the submenu (see the section on tricks and tips later in this chapter).

- Cut, which removes the item from its current location. Once that step is performed you can move to another location (folder) and right-click. Paste will appear as a choice on the menu and you can Paste the item into the target location.
- Copy, which places a copy in a target location using the Paste command.

 T I P The Clipboard (Cut/Paste and Copy/Paste combination) is used in Explorer to move and copy items. This is different from File Manager, which, when you choose Move or Copy, opens a dialog box so you can enter the target location.

- Create Shortcut, which creates a shortcut icon for the item. The shortcut is placed in the current location and you can drag it to the appropriate folder or the Desktop.
- Delete, which removes the file and sends it to the Recycle Bin.
- Rename, which allows you to change the name of the item.
- Properties, which displays the properties for the item. Those properties vary depending on the item type.

The other right-click menu items are specific to the type of item:

- Folders and peripherals permit Sharing.
- You can Explore a folder (open a window that displays icons for all the items in the folder).
- You can Print data files.
- Quick View is a way to preview a file without launching a software application. There are a number of viewers available for this feature and you can add more (from your original Windows NT media or by getting viewers from Microsoft). If a viewer is not available for a specific file, the Quick View option will not appear on the menu.
- Find is an option on the menu for folders, and it opens a Find dialog box so you can set criteria for a search. More information about using Find is found later in this chapter.

Sorting the View

You can sort the items in the Contents pane by name, date, type, or size. Choose Arrange Icons from the View menu to choose the sort scheme.

If the Contents pane is in Details view you can sort on any of the column headings by clicking the column name. Clicking again reverses the sort (ascending to descending).

Customizing the Send To Command

By default, Explorer offers two choices when you choose Send To from the menu that appears after you right-click an item. You can add choices by placing items in the Send To folder.

Adding to the Send To menu is convenient if you find that you frequently perform the same actions on files. Perhaps you gather data files to put into a specific folder for backup or for copying to another computer on the network. Or, you move files to a folder in order to compress them. Having the folder on the Send To list saves a couple of keystrokes.

The way to add items to the Send To menu is to place items into your Send To folder. Windows NT 4.0 has a Send To folder for each user profile. That way, as each user logs onto the workstation, the Send To choices are customized for that user. As an example, suppose you want to add a folder for zipping files to the Send To menu choices. To do this, follow these steps:

1. Find your Send To folder and then click the plus signs for the folders and subfolders above Send To, so that the Send To folder is visible in the Folders pane.

 TIP   To find your Send To folder, follow the path \WINNT\PROFILES\USER, where WINNT is the name of the folder where your Windows NT 4.0 software was installed, and USER is your user name.

2. Select the parent folder of the folder that you use to hold files that you want to compress together, which puts the folder you need into the Contents pane.
3. Scroll the Folders pane until your Send To folder is visible and accessible—in fact, put them as close to each other as possible.

4. Right drag the compressed files folder to your Send To folder in the Folder pane. When you drop it on the folder, choose Create Shortcut Here.

Now, when you right-click an item and choose Send To, the folder for compressing files will be on the menu.

Finding Files and Folders

You can search your system to find a file or a folder by choosing Find from the Start menu, then choosing Files or Folders from the submenu.

If you're working in Explorer, you can choose Find from the Tools menu, then Files or Folders from the submenu (or by choosing Find from the menu displayed when you right-click a folder).

Either way, the Find dialog box appears (see fig. 6.10).

 TIP The Find submenu also offers an option to find a Computer, which opens a dialog box into which you enter the name of a computer. The system searches your network to locate that computer.

FIG. 6.10
Use the Find dialog box to locate items on your system.

■ If you opened Find from Explorer, the program assumes you want to start your search from the folder that was highlighted at the time you invoked the Find program. You can change that by modifying the entry in the Look in box.

■ Select Include subfolders to search from the current level down.

■ Enter the name of the file or folder you want to search for in the Named box. You can use wildcards (see the following section on wildcards).

Part
II

Ch

6

- You can move to the Date Modified tab to narrow the search to specific date ranges.

- You can use the Advanced tab to narrow the criteria by asking for files of a certain type, files that are larger or smaller than a specified size, or for files that contain a specified string of text.

When you have specified all the criteria, choose Find Now to begin the search.

When the matching files or folders are located, they are listed (see fig. 6.11).

FIG. 6.11

I asked Find to locate all the executable files in the current folder that started with the letters PA— note that the title bar displays my search criteria.

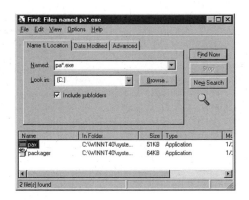

If no files were located, or too many files were located and you want to change or narrow the criteria, choose New Search to clear the current values and enter new ones.

Understanding Wildcards

Wildcards are special characters that indicate to the system that you'll accept any character or series of characters in place of the wildcard. This helps you search for files and folders when you either don't know an exact name, or you don't want to bother entering an entire name.

There are two wildcards available, an asterisk (*) and a question mark (?). They return different results.

Using an Asterisk as a Wildcard

An asterisk (*) indicates you will accept any number of characters in place of the asterisk.

For example, in the Find exercise above, I entered **pa*.exe** in the <u>N</u>amed box of the Find dialog box. This meant I would accept any file that had a name starting with pa, regardless of the length of the file name. I also indicated that I would only accept files with an extension of .exe. Files named PAX.EXE and PACKAGER.EXE were located as a result of this wildcard entry.

If the entry had been **pa*.***, indicating I would accept any extension, I might have been offered the existing two files plus files named PARTY.TXT, PAX.DLL, PACKAGER.HLP, and so on.

Indicating *.* means all file names of any length, and all extensions. Essentially, that means all files.

Using a Question Mark as a Wildcard

A question mark (?) indicates you'll accept any individual character at the same exact place in the file name that you entered the question mark.

For example, in the above exercise an entry of **pa?.exe** would have returned only PAX.EXE, because I indicated that I wanted only files with one character after the pa.

- If the criteria had been **pa??????.exe**, only PACKAGER.EXE would have been returned.
- A request for **pa????.exe** would have found no matching entries.
- A request for Smith?.doc would return Smith0, Smith1, and so on through Smith9, but not Smith10 (but Smith* would produce all files that start with Smith, regardless of the number of characters after Smith).
- A request for Sm?th would return Smith or Smyth.

Using My Computer

Some of the tasks you can perform in Explorer also can be accomplished in My Computer. This handy icon that is placed on the Desktop during installation of Windows NT 4.0 can be used to explore your system.

When you open My Computer, you see icons representing the very top of the hierarchy of your system (see fig. 6.12).

FIG. 6.12
All the drives in your system (including network drives) and folders holding important system resources are shown in the My Computer window.

My Computer displays all the same elements as Explorer, but instead of working in a hierarchical display, you navigate through each layer of the hierarchy one folder at a time.

Double-click the icon for Drive C and the top layer of the hierarchy displays in a new window (see fig. 6.13).

FIG. 6.13
Each time you move down the hierarchy, a new window opens.

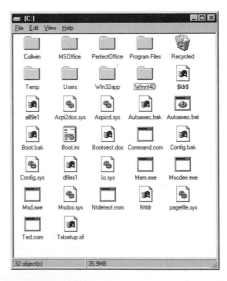

- As you open (double-click) each folder, the contents are displayed in a new window.

- If you right-click any object in one of these windows, the menu that displays contains the same items as the menu you saw in Explorer.

- If you choose Explore after right-clicking a folder, Windows NT Explorer launches with the contents of that folder in the Contents pane.

 TIP If you don't feel like hunting for Explorer (and you didn't put a shortcut for it on the desktop), move to any folder and double-click it as if you were going to open it, *but* hold down the shift key. You get Explorer. This even works if you pick My Computer as the folder to click.

Tips and Tricks for Using My Computer

One of the problems with using My Computer is that as you open folders to move down through the tree, you end up with a lot of folders cluttering up your desktop.

You can change the way the system opens folders by following these steps:

1. Open any folder and choose Options from the View menu of the folder window. The Options dialog box is displayed with the Folder tab in the foreground (see fig. 6.14).

FIG. 6.14
You can decide whether you want multiple folder windows or instant replacement of folder windows as you open folders.

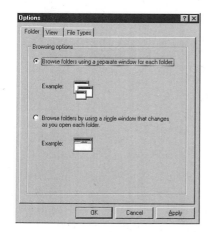

2. By default, Browse folders using a separate window is selected. Select Browse folders using a single window to have each folder window you open replace the previous one.

Once you've made this change, any subfolder you open will replace its parent.

If you prefer the default of opening multiple windows (perhaps you frequently move or copy files or subfolders between folders, or perhaps you like to keep track of the path you're taking), you can force the folder replacement method on an event by event basis:

- Hold down the Ctrl key as you double-click a folder in a window. The new window that opens to display this new folder replaces the parent folder.

If you've been opening folders without replacing each one with the next, you can end up with a lot of open windows before you finish working your way through the system. When you want to go back to work on an application, you have to close all those windows. You don't have to click the X (the close button on the upper right of the window), one at a time, for each window:

- Hold down the Shift key while you click the X of the last folder (the youngest grandchild in your family tree). All the folders will close.

If you do want to close all the windows one at a time, maybe to get to the middle of the family tree, there's a quick way to do it:

- Instead of moving the mouse to the X and clicking, hit the backspace key. It closes down folders, one at a time, starting with the bottom of the tree, working back to the parent.

Using My Computer to Put the Desktop on the Taskbar

There have been many occasions when I've had my screen filled with application software and want to use Explorer or go to a command prompt. I have shortcuts on my Desktop for both of those objects, but I can't see (or get to) my Desktop. My Desktop also has a folder with diversions (okay, games) for those times that I'm bored (or have a spell of writer's block). I don't want to close down applications to find the Desktop. I'm too impatient to move through the Start menu, land on Programs, and slide my mouse down through all the programs, just to open a command prompt or Explorer. And most of the stuff in my games folder I didn't even bother to add to the Start menu.

The trick is to make the Desktop a button on the taskbar, so you can single-click that button and have access to everything on the Desktop.

You can accomplish this with My Computer by following these steps:

1. Open My Computer, then choose Toolbar from the View menu to display the toolbar (see fig. 6.15).

FIG. 6.15
When you add the toolbar, the folder window looks a little like an application window.

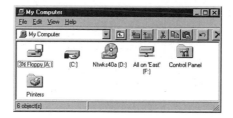

2. Click the arrow to the right of the drop-down box (which displays My Computer), then click the Up arrow to move one level higher. You will see the Desktop.

 TIP Don't use the yellow Up One Level button on the toolbar to move up to the Desktop. You'll receive a message saying you're at the top level. You are at the top level of My Computer; it's just that everything, including My Computer is really on the Desktop. Only the arrow next to the dropdown list box can get you there.

3. Select Desktop. The window changes into a miniature version of your Desktop (see fig. 6.16).

4. Minimize this new Desktop folder, which places a Desktop button on the taskbar.

Now, whenever you need to get to anything on the Desktop, click the button and select whatever you need. When you're finished, minimize it again. Don't close it or you'll have to go through all those steps again.

Part
II

Ch

6

FIG. 6.16
The Desktop is now a folder window.

Here's the best part—don't ever close that button. When you're ready to shut down your computer, close down all the applications that have buttons on the taskbar, but don't close the Desktop button.

When you reboot, it'll be there.

Creating Folders

You should be creating folders quite frequently—to organize your data, your software, and any other categories of files you have on your system. Folders make everything easier to manage.

You can create a folder from almost anywhere in Windows NT. The folder is put into the same location as you are when you create it, but you can move it anywhere.

 You can even create a folder from the command line. Remember, a folder is a directory. The same MS-DOS command that's worked since version 2.0 (version 1 didn't support directories) still works: **MD \path.**

- Create a folder in an open folder by choosing Ne<u>w</u> from the <u>F</u>ile menu, then choosing <u>F</u>older.
- Right-click any blank spot in any folder window, then choose Ne<u>w</u>, <u>F</u>older.

CAUTION
You cannot use either of those methods with My Computer, although you can with any of the folders that open when you open (double-click) a drive from My Computer.

■ To create a folder on the Desktop, right-click any blank space on the Desktop, then choose New, Folder.

■ To create a folder in Explorer, highlight the parent folder (which can be the Drive if you want the new folder on the root directory), then choose New, Folder from the File menu.

When you create a new folder, an icon appears and the text New Folder is below the icon. The text has a box around it, indicating it is in edit mode. Enter the real name for the folder, then press Enter or click a blank spot in the folder (or Desktop).

 If the folder isn't in the proper location you can use Explorer to move it. You can also use Explorer to move files (and other folders) into your new folder.

Understanding File Properties

All the objects in Explorer (which means all the objects in your system) have properties. Properties differ depending upon the object type.

You can view the properties of any object by right-clicking it and choosing Properties. If the object is in a window (a folder window or Explorer), you can highlight the object, then choose Properties.

 When you are using Explorer with the default view of not showing file extensions, it is sometimes difficult to ascertain exactly what a file is or what it might do. Taking a quick look at the file's properties is often helpful.

Some of the objects with properties you might need to know about, or want to change, are discussed in this section.

Folder Properties   The information available in the Folder Properties dialog box includes:

■ Number of bytes in the folder (the accumulated bytes of all subfolders and files).

■ Number of files and number of subfolders contained in the folder.

Part
II

Ch
6

- The MS-DOS name of the folder (automatically shortened if the folder has a long name).
- The creation date.
- The folder's Attributes.
- Sharing information—if the folder is marked as shared, the share name, user limits, and permissions information is available for configuration.

Data File Properties   The Properties dialog box for data files includes:

- The location (folder).
- The size.
- The MS-DOS name.
- The creation date.
- The last modification date.
- The last access date.
- The attributes (you can select Read Only or Hidden).

Windows Program Files   Executable files for programs written for Windows have the following properties displayed:

- The location (folder).
- The size.
- The MS-DOS name.
- The creation date.
- The last modification date.
- The last access date.
- The attributes (you can select Read Only or Hidden).
- The Version tab displays detailed information about the program's version (see fig. 6.17).

DOS Program Files   The Properties for DOS applications and utilities are more complicated than other file types. This is because these programs run in a virtual DOS machine. Each program may have different needs, especially for the way it uses memory.

FIG. 6.17
Detailed information about a Windows program's version and history is often available from the Properties information.

It's possible to invent an environment for one DOS program and a totally different environment for another DOS program, even though they're both running on the same computer. Each program thinks it has your computer to itself. It even thinks it has your computer's hardware and peripherals to itself.

Generally it's a good idea to try a DOS program with the defaults on the Properties page. If there are memory errors (the message "not enough memory" is usually a strong hint) or other untoward behavior, you can experiment with changing the values on the Memory tab of the Properties dialog box (see fig. 6.18).

FIG. 6.18
You can manipulate the environment for DOS programs with the Memory tab of the Properties dialog box.

Part
II

Ch
6

You can also control the screen, the fonts, and the program window through the Properties dialog box.

All the information and manipulation available through Explorer and the file and folder handling features of Windows NT 4.0 make it easier to control and customize your system.

From Here...

This chapter discussed files and folders. You learned about file systems and Windows NT 4.0 features for manipulating files and folders. For further information, see the following chapters:

- Chapter 7, "Managing Disk Storage with the Disk Administrator."
- Chapter 10, "Customizing the Windows NT Interface."

Managing Disk Storage with the Disk Administrator

by Sue Plumley

When you first installed the Windows NT Workstation software, you chose how to partition the hard disk. Windows NT supplies a tool, the Disk Administrator, that you can use to make changes to your hard disk partitions now that you've used NT for a while, and to make changes to the partitions of any hard disks attached to your computer.

You might want to change partitions if, for example, an original partition was not large enough to hold all the files you wanted to store on it. You may also need to partition a new hard disk you've added to your computer since installing Windows NT Workstation. You perform partitioning tasks plus create volumes, logical drives, and more, with the Disk Administrator. ■

Learn to create, format, and secure partitions

This chapter shows you how to create primary and extended partitions and logical drives. You also learn how to format them so you can manage your hard drives and their respective file systems.

Learn to create, extend, and delete volume sets

A volume set helps you make use of bits and pieces of free space on two or more drives. This chapter shows you how to create volume sets to improve the performance of your drives.

Create and delete stripe sets

Stripe sets are similar to volume sets but have the advantage of increasing disk drive efficiency even more than a volume set. If the free space available fits the bill, you can create stripe sets across your drives.

Customize the Disk Administrator

Learn to modify the colors and patterns used in the Disk Administrator interface to make the screen more comfortable to view and more interesting to work with.

Understanding the Disk Administrator

The Disk Administrator is a graphical tool you can use to organize and manage the hard disks on your computer. There are many tasks you can perform with the Disk Administrator, including the following:

- Create and delete partitions (partitions are separate areas, or divisions, of the hard disk)
- Format and label volumes (volumes are fixed amounts of hard disk storage space labeled with a name)
- Create and delete volumes
- Get information about disks, including partition sizes, free space available, and so on
- Change drive-letter assignments for hard disk volumes and CD-ROM drives
- Create and delete stripe sets

Using the Disk Administrator Screen

When you open the Disk Administrator, it reads the hard disks on your computer and creates a graphic representation of each disk. In this representation, the Disk Administrator reports the size of the disk, the file system, volume name, partitions, and free space.

Figure 7.1 shows the Disk Administrator with information displayed about three hard disks and a CD-ROM drive.

Table 7.1 describes the elements of the Disk Administrator window.

Table 7.1 Disk Administrator Elements

Element	Description
Toolbar	Provides shortcut buttons to view the drives in disk or volume view, and to view properties of selected volumes.
Disk bars	Each bar is a graphical representation of one hard disk attached to the computer; the disk bar includes the drive number, volume label, file system, and size of the disk.

Element	Description
Legend	Each color and label in the legend describes a possible component of the hard disk.
Status bar	Displays information about a partition when you select it, including size, file system, drive letter, and so on.
Volume name	A name, or label, assigned to volumes on the hard drive.
Drive letter	The drive letter assigned to the drive.
File system	Describes the file system: FAT or NTFS.
Disk size	Gives the size of the drive in megabytes.

FIG. 7.1

The Disk Administrator enables you to manage your computer's hard drives.

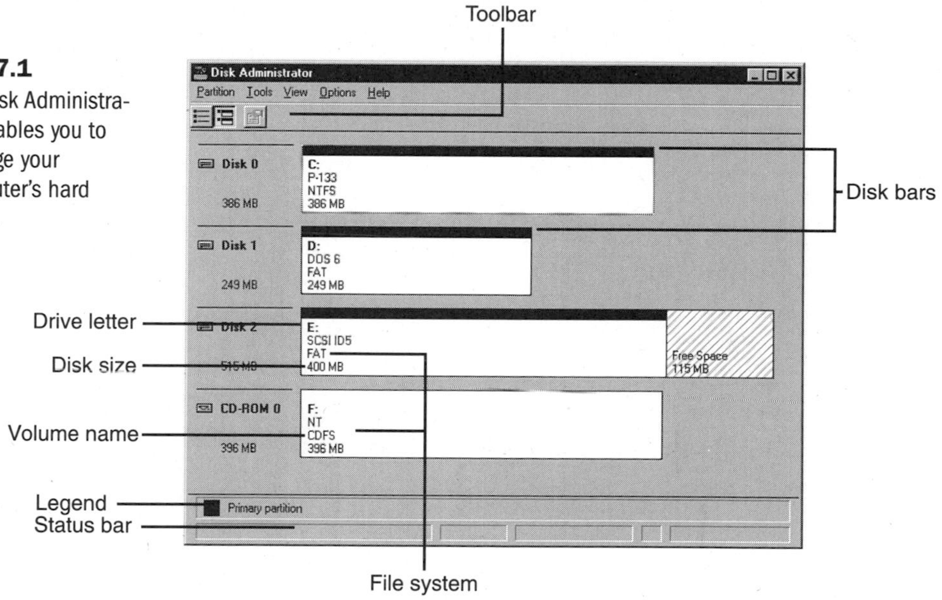

TIP To display or hide the status bar, tool bar, and/or legend, choose Options and then Status Bar, Tool Bar, and/or Legend.

Starting and Quitting the Disk Administrator

To start the Disk Administrator, you must be a member of the Administrators group. Choose the Start button, Programs, Administrative Tools, and Disk Administrator.

Part

II

Ch

7

The first time you start the Disk Administrator, a message box appears asking if you want to mark a signature on the primary disk; choose Yes to continue. This will not alter your disk or data in any way and if you do not mark the disk signature, which identifies your drive, you cannot use the disk in Disk Administrator.

To quit the Disk Administrator, choose Partition, Exit, or double-click the Disk Administrator's Control menu button.

If you've made changes to the disk configuration, the Disk Administrator asks if you want to save the changes. You can choose Yes to save the changes, No to cancel the changes, or Cancel to return to the Disk Administrator. If you choose to save the configuration changes, the Disk Administrator displays a message when the disks have been updated. Depending on the change, choose OK to close the message box or choose Restart to restart the computer to make the changes take effect.

Viewing the Disk Administrator

You can view the disks in the Disk Administrator in Volumes view, Disk view, or in detail through the Properties view. This chapter uses the Disk view to work with partitions, volumes, and stripe sets (refer to fig. 7.1).

You might prefer to view the disks on your computer in Volume view, however. Volume view presents the disk information in a different way (see fig. 7.2). View the drive letter (volume), volume label (name), drive size, free space, percent free, file format, and so on. The Volume view is handy when you have many drives attached to your computer and find it hard to view them all in Disk view.

To change views to Volume view, click the Volumes View button. To change the view back to Disk view, click the Disk View button.

You might want to use Property view to look at any one disk at a time. In Property view, you see the same information as in Volume and Disk view, presented a bit differently (see fig. 7.3). In addition to viewing the label, file system, free space, and so on, you can format a drive from Properties view as well.

To view a drive's properties, select the drive and choose the Volume Properties button on the Disk Administrator toolbar. To return to the previous view, choose OK in the Volume Properties sheet.

FIG. 7.2
View free space, size, file system, and more using the Volume view in Disk Administrator.

Volumes view—

Disk view—

Volume Properties—

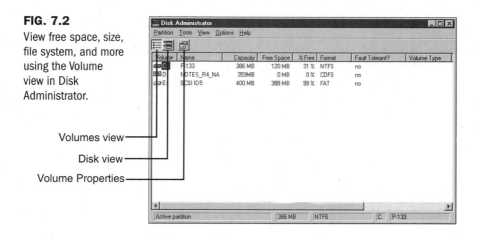

FIG. 7.3
You can view drive properties in the Volume Properties sheet.

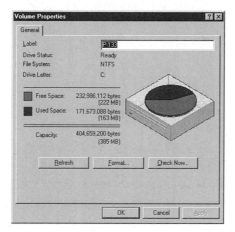

Working with Partitions

When setting up partitions on your hard disk, you can choose the file system each partition will contain. If you formatted your drive upon installation to use only the Windows NT Workstation operating system, for example, then your hard disk has a single partition formatted with NTFS (New Technology File System).

Part
II

Ch
7

If you installed Windows NT Workstation and preserved your existing system and files, you have at least two partitions—one containing Windows NT files and one containing FAT (File Allocation Table) files. FAT systems are used for the DOS operating system.

> **CAUTION**
>
> The active system partition, usually found on Disk 0/Active Partition (often drive C), contains hardware-specific files needed to load the operating system. The operating system searches drive C when you start your computer for certain files needed to get the system up and running. Do not try to delete or change the active system partition.

You can modify these partitions by changing their sizes, formatting them, securing each partition (on RISC platforms), creating new partitions, deleting partitions, and so on. You use the Disk Administrator to help you manage partitions.

▶ **See** "Installing Windows NT Workstation," **p. 1025**

Configuring a New Hard Disk

After physically installing a new hard disk, you can view it in the Disk Administrator and use the Disk Administrator's tools to add partitions to that drive. Disk 2 in figure 7.1 represents a new hard disk; all you see is free space. *Free space* is unused and unformatted space on a hard disk.

You can use the Disk Administrator to configure the hard disk in any of the following ways:

- Create a single primary partition; a *primary partition* is a part of the disk that can be used by an operating system.
- Create up to four partitions, any or all of which can be primary partitions.
- Create an extended partition with any number of logical drives, depending on the size of the partition; an *extended partition* can be used to hold *logical drives*, or subpartitions. Only one extended partition may exist on a physical disk.

You might create an extended partition with several logical drives when you want to create, for example, a DOS partition on a 4G hard disk. A DOS partition is limited to 2G, and without the logical drives, there would be 2G of disk space you couldn't use.

The following sections describe how to create partitions, logical drives, and volumes.

TROUBLESHOOTING

I installed a hard disk that I once used with MS-DOS 6.2 to my NT Workstation, but the Disk Administrator doesn't recognize the free space on the disk. What should I do? If you used the MS-DOS 6.2 Undelete Sentry feature to free space on the disk, Windows NT can't see the free space; instead, it sees the stored deleted files that the Sentry feature creates and reports the space as FAT partition. You can format the disk and then try again.

I'm using a SCSI hard disk, and I formatted the disk for DOS FAT. The hard drive appears to be the wrong size; what can I do? DOS is limited to see a 1,024 cylinder count. Some SCSI and IDE hard disks contain 1,048 or more. Newer computers take care of this problem when an IDE drive is involved and many SCSI controllers automatically perform an extended translation of size; some do not. The only solution here is to use another allocation besides FAT; you could try NTFS to format that drive, for example.

Creating Partitions

You can create a primary or extended partition on a hard disk by following the previously outlined guidelines. Use the Disk Administrator to create partitions. You must be logged on as a member of the Administrator's group in order to use the Disk Administrator.

Primary   To create a primary partition, follow these steps:

1. In the Disk Administrator, select the area of free space on the disk you want to configure; an outline appears around the free space area.

Part

II

Ch

7

2. Choose Partition, Create. The Create Primary Partition dialog box appears (see fig. 7.4).

FIG. 7.4

The Create Primary Partition dialog box defines the current amount of the free space and the minimum and maximum size for a partition.

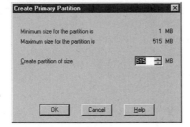

3. In Create Partition of Size, enter the size—in megabytes—you want to assign to the partition. You can, alternatively, use the spinner arrows to indicate the size of the partition.

4. Choose OK to create the partition. Figure 7.5 shows a disk that's had a 400M partition created.

FIG. 7.5

The new partition appears as a primary partition on the new disk.

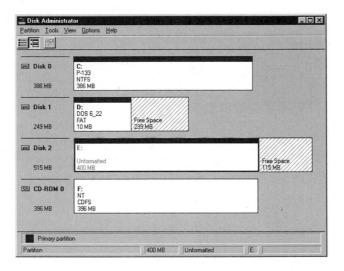

TIP   Before you can use the new partition, you must format it, as described in the next section.

Extended   To create an extended partition, follow these steps:

1. In the Disk Administrator, select the free space you want to partition.

2. Choose Partition, Create Extended. The Create Extended Partition dialog box appears (see fig. 7.6).

3. In Create Partition of Size, enter the size of the extended partition.

4. Choose OK to close the dialog box. The extended partition looks no different than the free space area of the drive.

FIG. 7.6
The Create Extended Partition dialog box displays the minimum and maximum size you can create an extended partition.

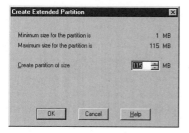

Logical Drives   To create a logical drive in an extended partition, follow these steps:

1. In the Disk Administrator, select the area of unformatted extended partition.

2. Choose Partition, Create. The Create Logical Drive dialog box appears and looks similar to the Create Partition dialog box.

3. In Create Logical Drive of Size, enter the size you want to apply to the logical drive.

4. Choose OK. Figure 7.7 shows a disk partitioned into one primary partition (E) and two logical drives (F and G).

TROUBLESHOOTING

I tried to create a logical drive out of some free space on my disk, but the Create Partition dialog box appeared instead of the Create Logical Drive dialog box. What did I do wrong? You're selecting free space instead of an extended partition. You must designate the free space as an extended partition before you can create logical drives on it. Select the free space and choose Partition, Create Extended. You can only create a logical drive on an extended partition.

Part

II

Ch

7

FIG. 7.7
The logical drives are designated by a different color on the legend and along the top of the partition, on the disk bar.

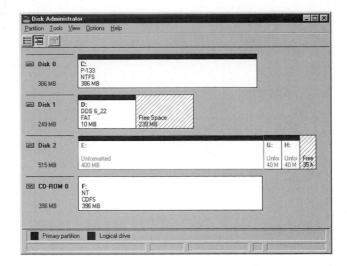

Formatting Partitions

Just like you would format a floppy disk for use before saving files to it, you must format each individual partition or logical drive for use as well. You must specify the file system you want to use with each partition, and you can choose to add a volume label, or name, to the partition to describe its contents.

Before you can format a partition, however, you must commit to the changes you have made. Committing to the changes you make in the Disk Administrator is similar to choosing OK in a dialog box. If you do not commit to the changes, the changes are canceled; if you do commit to changes, the changes are saved.

To commit to changes, choose Partition, Commit Changes Now. The Confirm dialog box appears; choose Yes to save the changes, No to cancel the changes, or Cancel to return to the Disk Administrator without saving the changes (see fig. 7.8).

FIG. 7.8
Choose to save the changes you've made to the disk.

When the changes are saved, the Disk Administrator displays a dialog box telling you the disks were updated successfully. Choose OK to close the message box.

To format a partition or logical drive, follow these steps:

1. Select the partition or logical drive and choose Tools, Format. The Formatting dialog box appears (see fig. 7.9).

FIG. 7.9

Choose a file system and a label to assign to the partition.

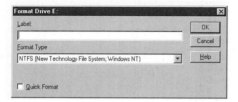

2. In the Format Type drop-down list, choose the file system you want to use for the partition.

3. In the Label text box, enter a volume name for the partition following these guidelines:

   No more than 16 characters, letters, and/or numbers.

   Limit the use of symbols such as the asterisk, question mark, period, comma, colon, or other symbols used in naming files or as switches or wildcards.

4. Optionally, choose Quick Format if you do not want to scan the partition for bad sectors and mark them as bad during the formatting process.

 TIP Even though the Quick Format option is faster than not using this option, it's still dangerous; unmarked bad sectors can be used for data storage, program files, and so on.

5. Choose OK to begin formatting. The Disk Administrator displays a Confirm dialog box. Choose Yes to format the partition or No to cancel the command.

6. When complete, the Disk Administrator displays the Format Complete dialog box that tells you how much disk space was available and how much was formatted (see fig. 7.10).

7. Choose OK to close the dialog box. The label, file system, and size of the formatted partition appear in the Disk Administrator. Figure 7.11 shows the primary partition and two logical drives formatted.

Part

II

Ch

7

FIG. 7.10
The Format Complete
message tells you
how much space is
available on the
partition.

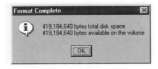

FIG. 7.11
Formatted partitions
and logical drives are
ready for use.

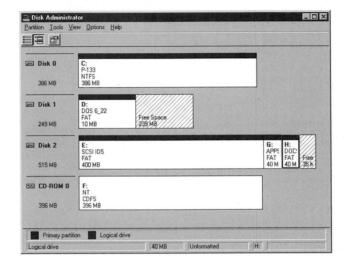

N O T E To help you choose a file system, FAT (File Allocation Table) partitions support
file names of 11 characters maximum (8 plus an optional 3-letter extension).
A volume can be as large as 2G in size.

The NTFS (New Technology File System) is accessible only under Windows NT. File names
can be 256 characters long, and the volume size is limited to 8G.

Activating a Partition

The system partition is the partition that contains the startup and system files, as
well as boot partitions, needed to load the operating system. The system partition
must be marked as *active* to identify it to the computer as containing files needed
for startup. There can be only one active system partition at a time, and this partition must be located on Disk 0, Active Partition, most usually drive C.

You can create and mark any system partition meeting the previous criteria as active; therefore, you indicate to your computer to use that partition to start the computer. Changing the active system partition lets you change operating systems.

To mark a system partition as active, follow these steps:

1. In the Disk Administrator, select the primary partition you want to make active.

2. Choose Partition, Mark Active. The Disk Administrator displays a message confirming your choice. Choose OK to close the message.

3. Close the Disk Administrator and shut down Windows NT. When you restart your system, the selected system partition controls the operating system that starts your computer.

TROUBLESHOOTING

The Mark Active command is not available to me. What can I do to make it available?
The Mark Active command is not available if the partition you chose is not a primary partition. You can make any primary partition active so be careful that the partition you choose has the operating system startup files needed to start the operating system.

Deleting Partitions or Logical Drives

You can delete a partition, volume, or logical drive in the Disk Administrator. When you delete a partition or logical drive, the area reverts to free space; you'll have to create a new partition and format the space before you can use it again.

CAUTION

Make sure all data is backed up or copied from the partition, volume, or logical drive before you delete it, because you'll lose all of your data.

 Windows will not allow you to delete the partition or volume containing the files needed to run Windows NT.

Part
II

Ch
7

To delete a partition, volume, or logical drive, follow these steps:

1. In Disk Administrator, select the partition, volume, or logical drive to be deleted.

2. Choose Partition, Delete. The Disk Administrator displays a confirmation message.

3. Choose Yes to delete or No to cancel the command. If you choose to delete, the space becomes free space again.

TROUBLESHOOTING

I deleted a logical drive, and now I want it back. Is it too late? No, not if you have not committed to the changes. To restore the deleted logical drive and/or partitions, choose Partition, Exit. The Disk Administrator displays the Confirm message box asking if you want to save the changes you've made to the disk configurations. Choose No to close without saving the changes. Naturally, no other changes made since you last committed changes will be saved either.

Changing Labels

You can change the label of any partition or logical drive using the Disk Administrator. You might, for example, change the files or programs stored on a logical drive or change the size and use of a partition and then want to make the label more descriptive of the changes.

To change a label, follow these steps:

1. In the Disk Administrator, select the partition or logical drive.

2. Choose Tools, Set Volume Label. The Set Volume Label dialog box appears (see fig. 7.12).

FIG. 7.12
Rename a partition or logical drive to identify it over the network, for example.

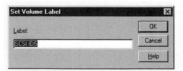

3. Enter the new label in the Label text box and choose OK to apply the new label.

Changing Drive Letters

You also can assign new drive letters to any partition or logical drive. The letters A and B are reserved for floppy drives; C is generally the active system partition. Any other drives, partitions, and logical drives can be assigned drive letters from the remaining letters in the alphabet. You cannot assign more than 24 drive letters.

To change the drive letter, follow these steps:

1. In the Disk Administrator, select the partition or logical drive you want to change.
2. Choose Tools, Drive Letter. The Assign Drive Letter dialog box appears (see fig. 7.13).

FIG. 7.13
Select a drive letter to assign the partition from the drop-down list of available letters.

3. Choose either Assign Drive Letter and select a letter from the list; or choose Do Not Assign a Drive Letter to use only the Volume label as an identifier.
4. Choose OK to close the dialog box.

> **CAUTION**
>
> Be careful when assigning drive letters, because many programs may need specific drives to run, locate program files, set environment variables, save and access files, and so on.

 TROUBLESHOOTING

NT keeps changing my CD-ROM drive letter. Is there any way I can set the drive letter so it doesn't change, say when I open a new network drive? Yes. In the Disk Administrator, choose Tools, CD-ROM Drive Letters; a list of attached drives appears. Select the CD-ROM drive whose letter you want to assign and choose the letter to assign it. Choose OK.

Working with Volume Sets

You can create partitions and logical drives on any hard disk by following the guideline previously presented and using the Disk Administrator. Sometimes, however, you might have bits and pieces of free space left on two or more drives—none large enough to use as a partition but still enough free space that you don't want to waste it. You can collect the free space from several disks together and incorporate it into a volume set.

A *volume set* can be one partition or a collection of partitions that are formatted for use by a file system. A volume is often assigned a drive letter, although it can be assigned a label, or name, instead. You usually use a volume to help organize directories and files.

Creating a Volume Set

You may improve performance by using volume sets, because using volume sets balances reading and writing tasks over several drives.

To create a volume set, follow these steps:

1. In the Disk Administrator, select two or more areas of free space on available hard disks by choosing the first free space area, holding the Ctrl key, and choosing the next free space area.

 You can use up to 32 hard disks to gather free space for volume sets.

2. Choose Partition, Create Volume Set. The Create Volume Set dialog box appears (see fig. 7.14).

FIG. 7.14
Combine several areas of free space to make a larger volume set.

3. In the <u>C</u>reate Volume Set of Total Size text box, the Disk Administrator displays the amount of selected free space. You can change the number, if you want.

N O T E   If you choose to use less free space than is available, the Disk Administrator divides the free space equally among the selected areas. ▪

4. Choose OK to close the dialog box. The free space is labeled with a new drive letter, and the color band across the top matches the color for Volume Set in the legend (see fig. 7.15).

FIG. 7.15
Drive D is a volume set made up of two different free space areas.

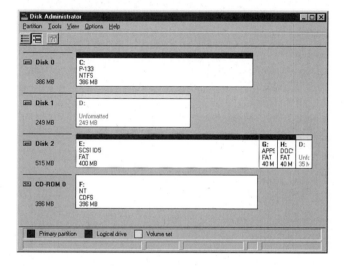

 TROUBLESHOOTING

I created a volume set from some free space in two disks, but now I can't get my MS-DOS system to recognize the space. What am I doing wrong? If you're using a dual boot computer, the MS-DOS partition cannot recognize any volume sets created by Windows NT because MS-DOS doesn't have volume-set functionality. That space is lost to you as far as MS-DOS is concerned unless you want to change it back to a partition using the FAT file system. You can, however, use the volume set in Windows NT.

Part
II

Ch

7

Extending a Volume Set

You can add free space to an existing NTFS volume or add free space to an existing volume set as the space becomes available.

To extend a volume set, follow these steps:

1. In the Disk Administrator, select the existing volume or volume set and the free space you want to add.

2. Choose Partition, Extend Volume Set. The Extend Volume Set dialog box appears (see fig. 7.16).

FIG. 7.16
Confirm the size of
the volume set.

3. In the Create Volume Set of Total Size box, accept the size or lower the total megabytes, if you want.

4. Choose OK to close the dialog box and extend the volume set. The Disk Administrator displays a message to restart your computer to put the changes into effect. Choose Restart.

Deleting a Volume Set

You can delete a volume set so that the space becomes free space again, at any time. Make sure you back up any data you want to keep before deleting a volume set.

To delete a volume set, follow these steps:

1. In the Disk Administrator, select the volume set to be deleted.

2. Choose Partition, Delete. A confirmation message appears.

3. Choose Yes to delete the volume set.

Working with Stripe Sets

Stripe sets are similar to volume sets in that they use combined free space from two to 32 different disks into one volume you can use to store directories and files. The difference between stripe sets and volume sets is that stripe sets each must be located on a different disk and the free space areas in stripe sets each must be about the same size.

In a volume set, the data is written to the first area on the first disk, then continued to the next disk, and the next, and so on, and then read in that same pattern. In a stripe set, the data is written across disks in a stripe to disk one, disk two, disk three, and then start over to disk one again. The advantage of the stripe set is that input/output commands can be issued at the same time and throughput is increased; this is true for both SCSI and EIDE drives. The only problem is that with EIDE, the number of drives that can be used is limited.

Creating a Stripe Set

Create a stripe set to increase the efficiency of your disk drives. The Disk Administrator averages the sizes of the free space areas and divides it to make each area about the same size.

To create a stripe set, follow these steps:

1. In the Disk Administrator, select two or more areas of free space, each on a separate physical disk. Hold the Ctrl key while clicking on each area to select multiple areas of free space.

2. Choose Partition, Create Stripe Set. The Create Stripe Set dialog box appears; the dialog box looks similar to the Create Volume Set dialog box.

3. In the Create Stripe Set of Total Size text box, the total size of the stripe set is listed. You can change the size if you want.

4. Choose OK, and the Disk Administrator creates the stripe set from the selected areas of free space. The new stripe set is labeled with a drive letter, and the bar across the top is the same color as the color designated in the legend. You must format the striped set before you can use it.

Part

II

Ch

Deleting a Stripe Set

You can delete a stripe set in the Disk Administrator; however, make sure you back up all data saved in the stripe set area before deleting the volume.

To delete a stripe set, follow these steps:

1. In the Disk Administrator, select the stripe set you want to delete.
2. Choose Partition, Delete. The Disk Administrator displays a confirmation dialog box.
3. Choose Yes to delete the stripe set.

Customizing the Disk Administrator

You can customize the colors and patterns used in the Disk Administrator to make the graphical interface more comfortable or interesting for you to work with. Additionally, you can customize how the partition sizes appear. You also will find the status bar and legend helpful when viewing partitions and logical drives in the Disk Administrator.

Using the Status Bar and Legend

The status bar displays information about the selected disk, partition, or logical drive. Because it's important to select the right disk and partition before changing or modifying it, use the status bar to confirm your selection before performing actions in the Disk Administrator. Figure 7.17 shows the information about the selected disk—Disk 0—in the status bar.

The legend displays colors and/or patterns that identify the various partitions, logical drives, volume sets, and so on in your drives.

To show or hide the status bar and/or legend, choose Options and then Status Bar and/or Legend.

FIG. 7.17
Use the status bar to confirm information about the selected disk.

Disk selected

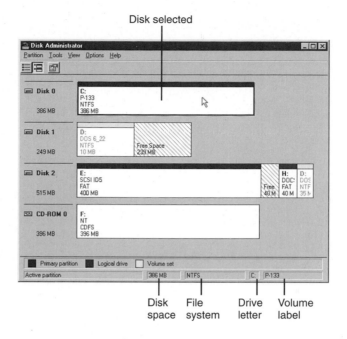

Disk space   File system   Drive letter   Volume label

Changing Colors and Patterns

You can change the colors and patterns used in the legend to suit your tastes or your monitor. If, for example, your monitor doesn't display the various colors well, choose patterns to represent volume sets, partitions, and other elements in the disks.

To change colors and patterns, follow these steps:

1. In the Disk Administrator, choose Options, Colors and Patterns. The Colors and Patterns dialog box appears (see fig. 7.18).

FIG. 7.18
Select any pattern or color to represent elements in the legend.

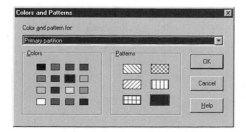

Part
II

Ch
7

2. In Color and Pattern For, choose the element you want to change from the drop-down list.

3. In the Colors box, choose the color you want to represent that element.

4. In the Patterns box, choose the pattern to represent the selected element.

 TIP The default pattern for all elements is solid.

5. Repeat steps 2 through 4 for each element you want to change.

6. Choose OK to close the dialog box.

Changing Regions

The region display refers to the display of the size of partitions in the Disk Administrator. You can change to display the regions on each disk based on their relative size or to size all regions equally. The default choice is to let the Disk Administrator control the displayed size.

To change the region display, follow these steps:

1. In the Disk Administrator, choose Options, Region Display. The Region Display Options dialog box appears (see fig. 7.19).

FIG. 7.19
Choose to change the relative display size of each disk.

2. In the For Disk drop-down list, choose the disk you want to change the settings for: Disk 0, Disk 1, Disk 2, and so on, or choose All Disks.

3. Choose from one of the three options to apply to the selected disk:

Size Regions Based on Actual Size. Displays the regions within the selected disk based on its relative size.

Size All Regions Equally. Sizes all regions the same.

Let Disk Administrator Decide How to Size Regions. Default selection.

4. Click the Reset All button to return all settings back to the default choices.

5. Choose OK to close the dialog box.

Saving and Restoring Disk Configuration

The disk configuration information includes assigned drive letters, stripe sets, volume sets, logical drives, and so on. After setting up this information in the Disk Administrator, you can save your disk configurations to floppy disk and then restore the configurations at any time using the Save and Restore commands in the Disk Administrator. Additionally, you can search for specific disk configuration information and use that configuration to overwrite the existing configuration.

Saving Disk Configuration

You can save the disk configuration to a floppy disk from the Windows NT Registry, but the information does not include any changes made during the current session.

To save disk configuration, follow these steps:

1. In the Disk Administrator, choose Partition, Configuration, Save. The Insert Disk dialog box appears (see fig. 7.20).

FIG. 7.20

Insert a disk to save the disk configuration.

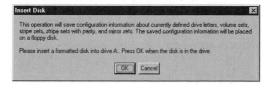

2. Insert a disk and choose OK to save the configuration to the floppy disk.

3. The Disk Administrator displays a message telling you the disk configuration information was saved successfully. Choose OK to close the dialog box.

Part
II

Ch
7

Searching for Disk Configurations

When you search for disk configurations, the Disk Administrator searches through other installed versions of Windows NT, and you can select from a list and overwrite the current settings. Be careful when using this feature, because you lose all settings in your Disk Administrator as well as new settings made in the current session.

To search for disk configuration information on the floppy disk, follow these steps:

1. In the Disk Administrator, choose Partition, Configuration, Search. The Confirm dialog box appears (see fig. 7.21).

FIG. 7.21
Be careful when searching for other NT installations.

2. To continue, choose Yes. The Disk Administrator displays a list of other Windows NT installations registered on your workstation, if any.

3. Select an installation from the disk and choose OK.

4. The Disk Administrator restarts your computer, and the new changes take effect.

Restoring Disk Configuration

You restore a disk configuration from disk to change settings that have been modified back to the original settings you recorded. All current settings are overwritten by the settings on the floppy disk.

To restore a configuration, follow these steps:

1. In the Disk Administrator, choose Partition, Configuration, Restore. The Confirm dialog box appears; this dialog box looks similar to the Confirm dialog box displayed when searching for configurations.

2. Choose <u>Y</u>es to confirm the restoration. You are prompted for a floppy disk containing the configuration information.

3. Insert the disk containing the information and choose OK. The Disk Administrator copies the files and restarts your computer.

From Here...

In this chapter, you learned how to manage disk storage using the Disk Administrator. The following are some additional chapters you might want to read:

- Chapter 11, "Changing and Configuring Hardware," shows you how to install and configure new hardware, such as a mouse, a keyboard, serial ports, SCSI adapters, and tape drives.

- Chapter 12, "Managing Memory, Multitasking, and System Options," covers memory management and environment variables.

- Chapter 35, "Using the Diagnostics Tool," covers how to view information about your CPU, BIOS, memory, drives, system services, and so on.

Part
II

Ch
7

Working with the Command Prompt

by Sue Plumley

Windows NT Workstation is an operating system based on a graphical interface; that is, Windows NT uses images and icons to represent programs, tasks, and procedures you work with every day. As a graphical interface, Windows NT is easy to use, navigate, and control.

Many people, however, prefer working at a command prompt to working in a graphical interface, especially when performing certain tasks such as administering the network resources. The Windows NT command prompt window offers the flexibility of MS-DOS plus many of the advantages of Windows NT. ■

Learn to use the command prompt window

Windows NT includes a command prompt window that enables you to load DOS programs and use DOS commands. This chapter shows you how to use the command prompt window, how to customize the window, and more.

Use commands to query the system

Learn to use the appropriate syntax, switches, and parameters with NT commands so you can find out more about your system and perform various tasks and procedures.

Run DOS applications from the command prompt

You can install and run DOS programs from the command prompt window. Additionally, you can manipulate NT windows and DOS windows to help you complete your work.

Customize the command prompt window

For comfort and ease in working, you can change font sizes, colors, and other elements of the command prompt window.

Understanding the Command Prompt

At first look, the command prompt window seems like any MS-DOS prompt you've ever used and indeed, it does work similarly. The commands you use in the Windows NT command prompt window are similar to those you use in MS-DOS; in fact, you can use almost all of the MS-DOS commands you used in MS-DOS version 6.x except for some of the newer utilities, such as memmaker and defrag. In addition, Windows NT has included some new commands and some special Windows NT commands.

Use the Windows NT command prompt window to perform the following tasks:

- *Start programs.* You can enter the executable file name of any Windows NT, Windows 3.1, MS-DOS, or POSIX-compliant program to start that program at the command prompt.

- *Enter and execute any supported commands.* You can issue Windows NT commands in addition to many MS-DOS, Windows 3.1, or POSIX commands.

- *Administer network resources.* Connect to the network and use network resources through the command prompt.

 TIP You can cut and paste information between applications running from the command prompt using the Windows NT Clipboard.

To start and quit a command prompt window, follow these steps:

1. To start a command prompt window, from the Desktop click the Start button and choose Programs, Command Prompt. The command prompt window appears (see fig. 8.1).

2. To quit the command prompt, type **exit** at the prompt and press Enter; alternatively, you can double-click the Control Menu button or click the Close (X) button.

N O T E If you have a program open in the command prompt window, you must exit the program before quitting the command prompt so you don't lose any unsaved data or configurations. To exit a program, you normally choose File, Exit or Quit; see the program's documentation for more information. ▪

FIG. 8.1
The Windows NT command prompt looks and acts like a MS-DOS command prompt.

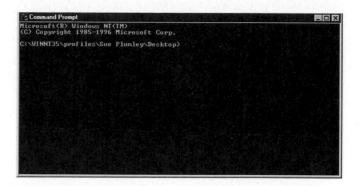

You can open more than one command prompt window at a time; you might want to use one window to run a program, another window to issue commands, and yet another window to use network resources, for example. To open multiple command prompt windows, choose Start, Programs, Command Prompt for each window you want to open.

When you open a program within a command prompt window, the window's title changes to include that program's name.

See "Customizing All Command Prompt Windows," **p. 220**

TROUBLESHOOTING

I tried to open a program in a command prompt window, and the title of the window changed to Frozen. **What should I do?** If the application is not responding and Frozen appears in the title bar, then close the command prompt window by clicking the window's Close button. The Windows NT Security dialog box appears. Choose the Task List button and select the application's name from the list of Active Tasks. Choose the End Task button to close the application, in which case you'll lose any unsaved data. Choose Cancel to return to the open window and application.

Customizing the Command Prompt Window

You can customize certain properties of the command prompt window to individualize the look of the window and make it more comfortable to work in. You can customize the window mode, fonts, screen size and position, and the colors used in the window. In addition to customizing the current command prompt window, you can customize the same properties for all command prompt windows.

To modify the current command prompt window, click the Control menu button, Properties. The Command Prompt Properties dialog box appears (see fig. 8.2). The name of the current window appears in the quotation marks in the Properties dialog box; command prompt is the default name.

FIG. 8.2
Use the Properties dialog box to customize general and specific settings for the command prompt window.

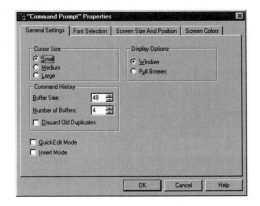

To change any of the options in the Properties dialog box, select the appropriate tab and choose the options as described in the following sections.

When you finish changing any properties in the Properties dialog box, you choose OK to close the dialog box. The Apply Properties to Shortcut dialog box appears offering two options: Apply Properties to Current Window Only and Modify Shortcut which Started this Window. If you choose the first option, the changes you make apply only to the current command prompt window. If you choose the second option, the changes you make apply each time you open the command prompt window using the shortcut that the window was originally opened from (in this case, the Command Prompt command on the Program menu).

Changing General Settings

The General Settings for the command prompt window includes setting the cursor size, command history, edit mode, and the windows mode. Table 8.1 describes the options in the General Settings tab of the Properties dialog box.

Table 8.1   General Settings Options

Area	Option	Description
Cursor Size	Small Medium Large	Select the size you want to apply to the cursor in the command prompt window
Command History	Buffer Size	Enter a value to designate the size of the buffer (temporary storage area created for each program that accepts buffered input)
	Number of Buffers	Specify the number of buffers to create
	Discard Old Duplicates	Deletes duplicate commands
Quick Edit Mode		Enables you to use the mouse for cut and paste operations within the command prompt window
Insert Mode		When selected, the text you type inserts at the cursor; not selected means text that's typed replaces existing type
Display Options	Window	Displays the command prompt in a window you can resize using the window borders
	Full Screen	Displays the command prompt full screen showing no Control menu, title bar, scroll bars, or window border

 TIP   To toggle between Window and Full-Screen mode, press Alt+Enter.

Modifying Font Selection

The Font Selection tab of the Properties dialog box controls the font (typeface) and size for use in the command prompt window as well as the terminal font you use. Again, the selections you make in this tab only apply to those windows using the same title as the current window. Figure 8.3 shows the Font Selection tab of the Command Prompt Properties dialog box.

FIG. 8.3
Change fonts to make it more comfortable to read the text and commands in the command prompt window.

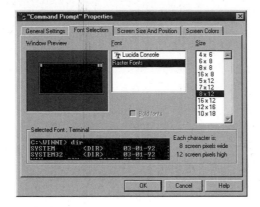

Table 8.2 describes the options in the Font Selection tab of the Properties dialog box.

Table 8.2 Font Selection Options

Area	Option	Description
Window Preview		Displays the size of the window needed to accommodate your font choices
Font		Choose the font you want to use in the window
Size		Choose the size font you want to use in the window
Bold Fonts		Choose to make the fonts on-screen bold, if this option is available
Select Font	Terminal	Displays examples of your font selections

Part

II

Ch

8

TIP You can change the window size even if it does change with the new font or font size in the Screen Size and Position tab.

TROUBLESHOOTING

I'm having a hard time reading the text in my command prompt window; the text looks distorted. You may have changed the font size to one that is hard to read with other changes, such as screen size and screen colors; or you may have a problem between your configuration changes and your display settings. Rather than change the display settings in the Control Panel, open the Command Prompt Properties dialog box and make changes, one at a time, to the font, screen colors, and screen size until you fix the problem.

If you still have problems, go back to the defaults for all of the settings in the Properties dialog box. The defaults are as follows: Font Raster Fonts, Size 8 × 12, screen colors black background with gray letters (192 for each color: Red, Green, and Blue), screen buffer size is Width 80 and Height 25, window size is 80 × 25.

It is best to not change your display settings in the Control Panel because you could really cause a problem with your screen. However, if you must change the display, refer to your monitor's documentation and make sure you test the settings before accepting them.

Altering Screen Size and Position

You can change the window size and position or the screen buffer size. The font and size of the screen type you use determines the screen buffer size. If the window is smaller than the screen buffer size settings, scroll bars appear in the current window. Also you can't resize a window larger than the area set by the screen buffer settings.

Figure 8.4 shows the Screen Size and Position tab of the Command Prompt Properties dialog box.

Table 8.3 describes the options in the Screen Size and Position tab of the Properties dialog box.

FIG. 8.4
Set properties to
control the screen
size and position in
the Properties dialog
box.

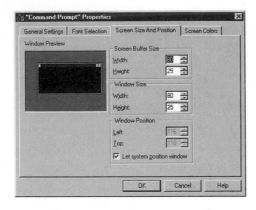

Table 8.3 Screen Size and Position Options

Area	Option	Description
Screen Buffer Size	Width	Set the width of the screen buffer from 1 to 9999 characters in width
	Height	Set the height of the screen buffer from 1 to 9999 lines in height
Window Size	Width	Set the width of the screen buffer from 1 to 9999 characters in width
	Height	Set the height of the screen buffer from 1 to 9999 lines in height
Window Position	Left	Enter a value to move the window around on the desktop; values closer to 0 move the screen to the left and values closer to 600 move the screen to the right
	Top	Enter a value to move the window to the top or bottom of the screen; values closer to 0 move the screen to the top and values closer to 400 move the screen to the bottom of the desktop
	Let System Position Windows	Check this option to let Windows NT position the window when you open it

TROUBLESHOOTING

My computer is slower since I changed Screen Size And Position settings. What can I do to fix it? Your computer memory may be taxed due to a large buffer size or a large number of buffers in the General Settings tab; a buffer is reserved in memory. Change the size and the amount of buffers to see if there's any change in your computer's speed and memory.

Changing Screen Colors

You can choose a color for the text and for the background of the command prompt window. Choose colors that make it easier for you to work in the character-based interface using the Screen Colors tab.

Figure 8.5 shows the Screen Colors tab of the Properties dialog box.

FIG. 8.5
Change the colors to give your eyes a rest when using a command prompt window.

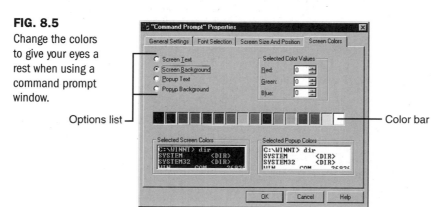

Options list

Color bar

To change screen colors, choose the text or background you want to change from the options list. Select a color from the color bar or enter values in the Selected Color Values text boxes. Zeros in all three boxes make black. If you enter **255** in the Red box, for example, and leave zeros in the other two boxes, the resulting color would be a bright red. Enter different values in the boxes to create your own colors.

Table 8.4 describes the options in the Screen Colors tab of the Properties dialog box.

Pop-up windows are small character-based windows, such as the Command History window, that present additional information or options related to the command prompt window.

Table 8.4   Screen Colors Options

Area	Option	Description
Options	Screen Text	Select to change colors on screen text
	Screen Background	Select to change background color
	Popup Text	Select to change the color of the pop-up window's text
	Popup Background	Select to change the color of the pop-up window's background
Color bar		Select a color to apply to the selected option
Selected Color Values	Red Green Blue	Enter a value between 0 and 255 to create your own color
Selected Screen Colors		Displays the colors you've chosen for the background and text colors of the screen
Selected Popup Colors		Displays the colors you've chosen for the background and text colors of the pop-up screen

Customizing All Command Prompt Windows

You can customize any one command prompt window by making changes in the window's Properties dialog box as shown in the previous sections. You also can make changes that will apply to all future command prompt windows you open. You can modify General settings, font, screen size and position, and screen colors for all prompt windows just like you do for one.

To customize all future command prompt windows, follow these steps:

1. From the Desktop, choose Start, Settings, Control Panel.
2. In the Control Panel, double-click the MS-DOS Console icon. The Console Windows Properties dialog box appears and looks exactly like the current Command Prompt Properties dialog box.
3. Using the options from tables 8.1, 8.2, 8.3, and 8.4, change General Settings, Font Selection, Screen Size and Position, and/or Screen Colors.
4. To close the dialog box, choose OK.

Using Programs at the Command Prompt

You can install and run programs at the command prompt just as you would in MS-DOS. You can run a program in a window or maximize the command prompt window to run the program full-screen. Additionally, you can copy and paste items between programs running in the command prompt window and between programs in the command prompt window and Windows NT windows.

Starting a Program at the Command Prompt

You can start most programs at the command prompt by typing in the name of the program. You may first need to change to the directory in which the program resides before you can start the program. Additionally, sometimes the command to start a program is a shortened form of the name or simply its initials.

The following directions also work for running batch files; *batch files* are unformatted text files that contain several commands that run one after another to perform specific tasks. Batch files, or programs, usually have a BAT or CMD filename extension; typing the file name (with or without the extension) at the command prompt starts the batch program.

Additionally, you can install programs using the following directions. An installation file usually has an EXE, COM, or BAT extension and works the same way as other program files. Look for an INSTALL or SETUP file to install software programs.

To start a program in the command prompt window, follow these steps:

1. In the command prompt window, type **cd** *directoryname*. CD changes the directory to the name of the directory that holds the program.

 TIP If you don't know the directory name, type **dir *.** at the C:\ prompt to list only directories.

2. At the directory prompt, type the name of the program. If you're not sure of the program name, type **dir *.exe** and press Enter. This lists the executable program files. Executable program files start the program when you type the file name (with or without the three-letter extension).

 TIP If you do not see any EXE files, try looking for BAT or COM files.

When you run a program from the command prompt in this manner, the command prompt window is not available for other use until you exit the program. You can, alternatively, start a program from a command prompt and retain the use of the command prompt window by typing **start** and the name of the program's executable file. The program starts, but you can still use the window for entering commands and so on.

Copying and Pasting

When you want to copy and paste information from one program to another, whether one or both programs are running in the command prompt window, you can use the Windows NT Clipboard.

To copy and paste information from a program in a command prompt window, follow these steps:

1. Select the command prompt's Control menu and choose Edit, Mark.
2. Select the information using the methods described in the application's documentation.
3. Select the command prompt window's Control menu and choose Edit, Copy.
4. Switch to the window in which you want to paste the information using the taskbar.

5. Position the insertion point.

6. If you're in a command prompt window, click the window's Control menu button and choose Edit, Paste.

    If you're in a Windows NT window, choose Edit, Paste.

Using Command Prompt Commands

Using commands, you can list directories, copy data, delete files, copy disks, display shared resources on the network, start a network service, copy directory trees, and much, much more. You can use most MS-DOS 6.x commands and any of the Windows NT commands at the prompt. You can even connect to a UNIX system computer using TCP/IP utilities.

A *command* is the name of a file that contains instructions for the computer. When you choose File, Open in a Windows application, for example, you've issued a command, and Windows carries it out. You're doing the same thing at the command prompt; however, you're entering the entire command that Windows would normally fill in for you.

 TIP Command file names usually end in one of the following extensions—EXE, BAT, or COM.

Understanding Syntax

The first part of issuing a command is the command name, naturally. But there are other possible elements you can add to complete the command: file name(s), path, or other descriptors. Some commands require nothing but the command name, while others may require additional information.

When entering a command, and all of its various required elements, you must use a particular order, or *syntax*, that the operating system (OS) will understand. If you do not enter a command and its parts correctly, the OS responds with

```
The name specified is not recognized as an internal or external
command, operable program or batch file
```

The following sections describe the elements of a command and the proper syntax for using commands.

Command Name   The command name always comes first. You can type the name in uppercase, lowercase, or a combination of the two; the OS doesn't recognize case. You do not have to type the three-letter extension to the command name. You must, however, enter the correct spelling of the command. Since many commands are limited to eight letters or less, the spelling may seem cryptic.

Some examples of commands are: dir, path, ver and cls. Dir lists the directory, path sets a path to a specific file, ver lists the version number of the operating system, and cls clears the screen of all previous commands and results.

TIP If you get a message from the OS that it doesn't recognize the name as a command, try carefully typing it again; typographical errors are the most common problems with entering commands.

Command Symbols   There are command symbols you often use in conjunction with a command and other elements. Table 8.5 lists those command symbols.

Table 8.5   Command Symbols

Symbol	Description
> (greater than)	Redirects output
< (less than)	Redirects input
>> (two greater than signs)	Appends redirected output to existing data
¦ (pipe or vertical bar)	Pipes output
|| (two pipes)	Runs the command after the symbol if the command before the symbol fails
& (ampersand)	Separates multiple commands on the command line
&& (two ampersands)	Runs the command after the symbol if the command before the symbol is successful
() (parens)	Groups commands

Symbol	Description
^ (caret)	Enables command symbols as text
; or , (semicolon or comma)	Separates parameters

Examples of the use of a command symbol in a command include

```
dir ¦more and path ;. Dir ¦more
```

lists a directory one screen at a time, and

```
Path ;
```

clears all search path settings so the search is only in the current directory.

Parameters   A *parameter* is additional information that defines the item you want the OS to act on. A parameter may be one or more files, a directory, or other element. Often, you add two or more parameters to a command line; for example, to copy a file to a directory, you need the file name and the directory name, both of which are parameters.

Examples of parameters in a command line are as follows:

```
copy sales01.doc a:\quarter1
del letter01.doc
```

Copy sales01.doc a:\quarter1 consists of the command—copy—and two parameters: the file name followed by the directory. The result of this command is the file SALES01.DOC is copied to the QUARTER1 directory. Del letter01.doc tells the OS to delete (del) the file LETTER01.DOC. The file name is the parameter.

Switches   A *switch* modifies how the command performs a task; for example, you can add a switch to the dir command that lists the directory in several columns so you can see the contents on-screen at the same time. A switch is either a forward slash (/) or a hyphen (-) and follows the command and any parameters. A switch is always followed by a letter, word, or number.

TIP   You can use more than one switch at a time; simply separate the switches with a space.

Examples of commands using switches are as follows:

```
dir /w
dir /w /s /o
```

Dir /w lists the directory in several columns so you can see the entire directory on-screen at the same time. Dir /w /s lists the directory wide and displays all subdirectories.

Values   Values determine how a switch works. A value can be a colon (:) or an equal sign (=) and is followed by a word, letter, or number. A value is not separated from the switch by a space.

Examples of values used in a command are as follows:

```
format b: /f:720
convert c: /fs:ntfs
```

Format b: /f:720 formats the B drive to a specific size disk. convert c: /fs:ntfs converts the C drive volume to the NT File System.

TROUBLESHOOTING

I can never remember the switches for even the most common commands. Can I hurt anything if I accidentally issue a command using the wrong switch? Yes. Be very careful when using switches, values, and parameters. Some commands have as many as twenty switches, so entering the wrong one could result in an action you do not want. If ever you're in doubt about which switch to use, use the command reference help feature at the command prompt: commandname /?; for example, type format /? for help on formatting disks.

If you need to repeat a command immediately, press F3 to direct the OS to type the command for you.

Getting Help

You can get help in the command prompt window when you're having trouble with a command. Additionally, you can use the Windows NT help feature for help with using the command prompt.

Figure 8.6 shows the command prompt screen after the command `help` was entered. Table 8.6 describes the common help commands.

FIG. 8.6

Use the command prompt help feature to find out more about commands.

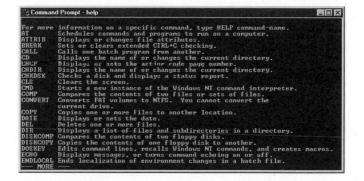

```
Command Prompt - help                                    _ □ ×
For more information on a specific command, type HELP command-name.
AT        Schedules commands and programs to run on a computer.
ATTRIB    Displays or changes file attributes.
BREAK     Sets or clears extended CTRL+C checking.
CALL      Calls one batch program from another.
CD        Displays the name of or changes the current directory.
CHCP      Displays or sets the active code page number.
CHDIR     Displays the name of or changes the current directory.
CHKDSK    Checks a disk and displays a status report.
CLS       Clears the screen.
CMD       Starts a new instance of the Windows NT command interpreter.
COMP      Compares the contents of two files or sets of files.
CONVERT   Converts FAT volumes to NTFS.  You cannot convert the
          current drive.
COPY      Copies one or more files to another location.
DATE      Displays or sets the date.
DEL       Deletes one or more files.
DIR       Displays a list of files and subdirectories in a directory.
DISKCOMP  Compares the contents of two floppy disks.
DISKCOPY  Copies the contents of one floppy disk to another.
DOSKEY    Edits command lines, recalls Windows NT commands, and creates macros.
ECHO      Displays messages, or turns command echoing on or off.
ENDLOCAL  Ends localization of environment changes in a batch file.
--- MORE ---
```

Table 8.6   Help Commands

Command and Syntax	Description
`help`	Lists the native system commands with a brief description of each, one screen at a time
`help command`	Lists help for the command you enter, including syntax, switches, parameters, and so on
`net help`	Lists names of network commands
`net help command`	Lists help for the network command you enter, including syntax, parameters, switches, and so on
`command /?`	Lists syntax for specified command

Using Common Native Commands

Native commands refer to those commands used with the 32-bit operating system, including many of the MS-DOS commands you may be familiar with.

Table 8.7 lists some common native commands with a brief description.

Table 8.7   Native Commands

Command	Description
attrib	Displays or changes a file's or directory's attributes, such as read-only, hidden, archive, and so on
cd	Changes directory, or displays the name of the current directory
chkdsk	Checks a disk for errors, bad clusters, and so on, and then displays a report of the results
cls	Clears the screen of previous commands and results, leaving only the current prompt
comp	Compares the contents of two files and displays a report when finished
copy	Copies file(s) from one disk or directory to another
date	Displays the date or lets you set the date
del	Deletes file(s)
dir	Lists files and subdirectories in the current directory
find	Searches for a text string in a file or files
format	Formats a disk; if size is unspecified, it format to the drive size
help	Displays a list of the commands and a brief description of each
md	Makes, or creates, a directory
more	Displays information on-screen, one screen at a time
net computer	Adds computers to the Windows NT Server domains
net file	Displays the names of all open shared files on a server
net group	Adds, displays, or modifies global groups on Windows NT Server
net helpmsg	Displays help about a network error message
net share	Creates, deletes, or displays shared resources
net statistics	Displays the statistics log
net view	Displays a list of servers or shared server resources
path	Displays or sets a search path for executable files

Command	Description
pause	Pauses a batch file in the middle of the processing
print	Prints a text file
recover	Recovers any salvageable information from a bad disk
ren	Renames a file or files
rd	Removes a directory
sort	Sorts input
start	Starts a separate command prompt window
time	Displays or sets the system time
type	Displays the contents of a text file
xcopy	Copies files and directory trees quickly by reading data into memory and then copying to the destination

Using Common Subsystem Commands

Subsystem commands are older 16-bit commands included to maintain MS-DOS compatibility. Table 8.8 lists some of the more common subsystem commands.

Table 8.8 Subsystem Commands

Command	Description
edit	Starts the MS-DOS Editor in which you can create and modify text files
edlin	Starts Edlin, a line-oriented text editor
expand	Expands compressed file(s)
loadhigh	Loads a program into upper memory
mem	Displays a screen showing used and free memory in the MS-DOS subsystem
share	Starts the share program

Using Common Configuration Commands

Configuration commands enable you to configure the MS-DOS subsystem and affect only the MS-DOS subsystem. Many configuration commands are included only for compatibility and have little or no use for Windows NT Workstation because Windows NT uses its own set of commands. Configuration commands are not available at the command prompt but are useful in configuration files, such as an AUTOEXEC.BAT.

Table 8.9 shows some common examples for configuration commands.

Table 8.9 Configuration Commands

Command	Description
device	Loads a device driver into memory
devicehigh	Loads a device driver into high memory
dosonly	Allows only MS-DOS-based applications to start from the command.com prompt
install	Loads a memory resident program into memory

Using Common TCP/IP Commands

Use *TCP/IP commands* to communicate with hosts such as UNIX. You must have the TCP/IP network protocol installed to use these utilities. Table 8.10 describes some common TCP/IP commands.

Table 8.10 TCP/IP Commands

Command	Description
finger	Shows information about remote system users
ftp	Transfers files to and from an FTP service node
hostname	Displays the current host's name
netstat	Displays current TCP/IP connections and protocol statistics
ping	Verifies remote host connection

Command	Description
rcp	Copies files between computers
rsh	Runs commands on remote hosts
tftp	Transfers files to and from an FTP service node

Using the Command History

The *command history* is a pop-up box from the command prompt window that lists the commands you've recently used. You can quickly display the command history, select one of the commands, and easily reissue the command by selecting it and pressing Enter.

The command history can store up to fifty commands but you can change the buffer to hold more commands, if you want. The larger the buffer, however, the more memory the command history uses.

To use the command history, follow these steps:

1. In the command prompt window, press F7 to display the Command History window (see fig. 8.7).

FIG. 8.7
The Command History window displays the last 50 commands you've entered in the command prompt window.

2. Use the arrow keys to select the command you want to repeat, and then press Enter. The command appears at the command prompt and is executed.

If you issue the same command several times, the command history records that command each time. You can choose the Discard Old Duplicates check box in the Properties dialog box to eliminate repeated commands.

From Here...

In this chapter, you learned to use the command prompt window to query your system and to run DOS applications. The following are a few more chapters you might want to take a look at:

- Chapter 16, "Managing the Boot Process," describes how to configure a dual boot with DOS, how to customize Start files, and how to configure hardware profiles.

- Chapter 17, "Working with Applications," shows you how to install and configure DOS applications in Windows NT.

- Chapter 34, "Protecting Your Workstation and its Data," explains how to back up your system, protect against viruses, and update your emergency repair disk.

Transporting Files with Briefcase

by Michael D. Reilly

Briefcase is a utility that updates, synchronizes, and tracks files on different computers to ensure that the files remain identical. Introduced in Windows 95, Briefcase goes beyond the normal file matching found in a previous generation of synchronization programs, which allowed you to pick—or automatically selected for you—the most current version of a file. Software such as Laplink and Fastlynx or utility packages such as Norton Commander and PC Tools used to set the standards, but could only compare file sizes and time stamps. Briefcase has the capability to notify applications that they must synchronize files. When the application has the ability to resolve conflicts between multiple versions of a file, Briefcase becomes a very powerful tool for keeping your files up-to-date. ■

Getting the most out of your Briefcase

Briefcase was designed with the portable computer user in mind. This chapter explains how to benefit most from using Briefcase.

Utilizing Briefcase

Unlike with Windows 95, Briefcase is automatically installed with Windows NT. This section explains how to create folders and files with Briefcase.

Working with Access 95

Access is one of the many applications that replicate Briefcase files. This section details how to convert files between applications.

Understanding Briefcase

Briefcase is a tool for the user who needs to work on a file on more than one computer. A mobile worker with a portable computer and a desktop computer could use Briefcase to keep files synchronized. Anyone who needs to take files home and load them on a home computer can use Briefcase to ensure that the latest versions of the files are on both computers. It is important to keep in mind that Briefcase was intended for use by one person with two computers. It was not designed for synchronizing data files between multiple members of a workgroup. Nevertheless, it can be used to keep simple databases synchronized, as you see later in this chapter. As more applications support merging or reconciliation of different versions of the data, Briefcase expands its role and becomes more useful.

The Benefits of Briefcase

Briefcase was designed with the portable computer user in mind. If everyone were connected to the network all the time, a simpler solution would be possible. Multiple computers could connect to the same set of files, stored on one of the computers, and the latest version of the file would be available to everyone. Then the only worry would be two users opening the same file simultaneously. With databases, even that is not a concern any more, thanks to record locking.

Synchronizing Laptop Computers and Desktop Computers   The reality is that not everyone is connected to the network all the time. Some employees, such as sales staff, may only connect once a day, or less. Others may connect during the day, and then take their portable computers home at night. Another group may work on a desktop computer at the office, then go home and fire up another computer so that they can continue working on the data. In each case, the challenge is the same—to ensure that changes made on one computer appear on the other. A second requirement is that when changes are made on both computers, the user is aware of the potential conflict, and can either reconcile the changes, or select the correct version of the file.

Briefcase is a good way to meet the requirements of these users, especially in the situation where a desktop computer and a portable computer must be synchronized. When the same person uses both computers, the assumption is that changes are made on only one computer at a time. Therefore any changed files can be copied to the other computer without any concerns about reconciliation. Newer portable computers that have Plug and Play docking stations can automatically start Briefcase when they are reconnected, so that file synchronization immediately takes place.

The Briefcase feature was introduced in Windows 95, so it makes sense to have the desktop computer running Windows NT 4.0, and the portable computer running Windows 95. The Briefcase works with no problems between these two operating systems, but it is not backward compatible with Windows NT 3.51 or Windows 3.1. Of course, you will have an even better solution if the portable computer is also running Windows NT 4.0.

Part
II
Ch
9

Replicating Simple Databases   Contact and sales databases are exactly the type of database people like to have on their portable computers. But for corporate productivity, the information in these databases should be available to all. You can do this by building a central database on a server, using an application such as Access 95. Then copies of the database are kept in Briefcases on each portable computer. When the mobile users connect in, they update the server database with the changes. Access supports briefcase replication, so that only records that have been changed are updated—the entire database file is not replaced. The result is that several users can make changes to the same master copy of the database. Access also supports reconciliation, so that the database administrator or the user can decide what record should be kept or discarded when there is a conflict.

Database replication with Briefcase works best when each user is responsible for a set of data, and there is no overlap. For example, members of a sales force may each cover a different territory with different customers. There will be little risk of conflicting changes, and the corporate server will contain a master copy of the data for use by accounting, marketing, etc. This master copy could also be useful if something happens to the copy on the portable computer.

The preferred design for these replicable databases is to split the data from the application, which is easy to do in Access 95. The application resides on the portable computer, and works with a replica of the data file. When the portable computer connects to the network, the data records are compared for changes.

Programming Considerations

In order to allow the Briefcase replication to work, some changes have been made to the OLE specification, and several new APIs have been introduced to allow programmers to take advantage of the Briefcase functionality.

OLE 2.1 Changes

Windows NT 4.0 and Windows 95 incorporate an updated version of the OLE specification, version 2.1. There are some additional features used by OLE 2.1 that are used in Briefcase replication. These include:

- Reconciling the contents of the Briefcase. This feature works with OLE enabled applications such as Access 95 to determine where there are conflicts, and provides a mechanism for the resolution of the conflicts.

- Tracking the contents of the Briefcase. A replica set is identified by a unique value, called a *GUID* (*Globally Unique ID*) that is a 128-bit hexadecimal number. Each item in the replica set has the same GUID, which is generated by Windows NT.

New APIs and DLLs

To encourage application developers to use the Briefcase feature, Microsoft has supplied the AddObjectToBriefcase( ) API. The API copies the physical data for the document to the Briefcase, and also updates the control information associated with the Briefcase. Control information is kept in two hidden files within the Briefcase. The Briefcase Database file contains the date, time, size, status, and location of the original file for each file in the database. This information is updated when the file is synchronized. The DESKTOP.INI file contains OLE registration information. You cannot see this file in the Briefcase even if you turn on the Show Hidden Files menu option. This is to prevent the files from being accidentally deleted. (You can see them if you use the dir /a:h command from the Windows NT command prompt.)

Other files that are used by briefcase include the following DLLs:

- SYNCENG.DLL, which checks to see if the files match.
- SYNCUI.DLL, which is the user interface for the Briefcase.
- LINKINFO.DLL, which tracks the files to be updated, and converts paths to UNC names or volume names depending on the location of the Briefcase.

Binding Reconciliation Handlers

The ReconcileObject( ) API is used to reconcile two different copies of an object. The actual updating is done by calling a reconciliation handler. A *reconciliation handler* is a set of methods used to reconcile changes made to the various replicas of an original document. The reconciliation handler may simply replace the older version of a file with the newer, or it may list the conflicts and provide a mechanism for resolving them. Any application can provide its own reconciliation handler, in which case, it must register this handler so that it can be called by the application to act upon the appropriate object. Each file type is associated with a specific file extension, and these associations are stored in the registry. Briefcase then can use the file type to look up the reconciler that is registered for that application.

Working with Briefcase

Briefcase is installed automatically when you install Windows NT 4.0. This differs from Windows 95, where the Briefcase was an option, or was installed as part of the portable computer setup. Briefcase appears as one of the default icons on the desktop. The first time you open Briefcase, a welcome message appears on the screen, as shown in figure 9.1. This message does not show up again, so take a moment to review it.

 TIP The welcome message shows up again if you build a new briefcase, or log on as a different user, and open the Briefcase for the first time.

FIG. 9.1
The Briefcase
Introductory dialog
box contains some
useful information
about the Briefcase.

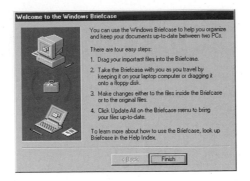

Creating a New Briefcase Folder

You can create a new Briefcase folder if you have deleted the original, or if you wish to have multiple Briefcase folders. The easiest way to create a new Briefcase is to click with the secondary mouse button on a blank area on the desktop. The desktop's shortcut menu opens, and when you select the New option, one of the choices listed is Briefcase, which will create a new Briefcase on the Desktop. Figure 9.2 shows these dialog boxes.

FIG. 9.2
Adding a new
Briefcase can be
done from the
desktop with just a
couple of mouse
clicks.

The new Briefcase icon is automatically labeled New Briefcase, but you can rename it by the normal Windows NT 4.0 method of clicking with the secondary mouse button on the icon, then selecting the Rename option. If you create another new Briefcase without renaming the first, the second icon will be labeled New Briefcase (2).

Clicking the Briefcase icon with the secondary mouse button allows you to open the Properties dialog box for the Briefcase, as shown in figure 9.3.

If you check in the Explorer, you will find the Briefcase at this location, winnt_root%\PROFILES\%username%\DESKTOP, (%winnt_root% is the path to your Windows NT 4.0 installation, and %username% is the name used to identify the user profile) assuming that the Explorer has the Show All Files option set in the View, Options menu. This option has to be turned on, as the Briefcase would normally be a hidden folder.

FIG. 9.3
The Briefcase
Properties dialog box
shows when the
Briefcase was
created, and its
location.

Copying Files to the Briefcase

There are several methods you can use to copy files into the Briefcase. The number of approaches can be confusing at first. For now, let's look at placing files in a briefcase on a desktop computer. Then let's move the Briefcase files to another computer, perhaps a portable computer. Finally, let's look at how to move files on one computer into a briefcase on another computer.

The first method for placing files in a Briefcase uses the following steps:

1. Open Explorer and find the file which you want to move into the Briefcase.
2. Highlight the file, and then click the right mouse button.
3. From the pop-up dialog box that appears, select Send To, then My Briefcase, as shown in figure 9.4.
4. Minimize Explorer, and open the Briefcase to verify that the file is there.

Notice that this method is restricted to sending the file to the folder called My Briefcase. Even if you have multiple Briefcase folders, the pop-up box only looks for one called My Briefcase. If you do not have a folder called My Briefcase, Windows NT searches for a folder called My Briefcase, and asks if it should use whatever it finds, even if that briefcase belongs to a different account.

FIG. 9.4
You can move files
into the Briefcase
using the pop-up
menu for the file in
the Explorer window.

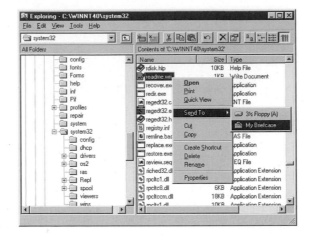

The second method is more direct, but requires more care in arranging the desktop:

1. Open Explorer and find the file that you want to move into the Briefcase.

2. Arrange the windows on your desktop so you can see both the Explorer with the file highlighted and the Briefcase icon, as shown in figure 9.5.

3. Drag the file from the first copy of Explorer and drop it on the Briefcase.

FIG. 9.5
You can move files
into the Briefcase
by dragging them
from Explorer and
dropping them on
the Briefcase icon.

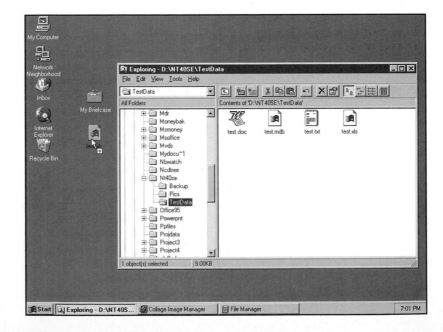

The third method requires that you open two copies of Explorer:

1. Open Explorer and find the file that you want to move into the Briefcase.

2. Open a second copy of Explorer, and locate the Briefcase folder, as shown in figure 9.6.

FIG. 9.6
You cannot open two windows within Explorer, but you can open two copies of Explorer at the same time.

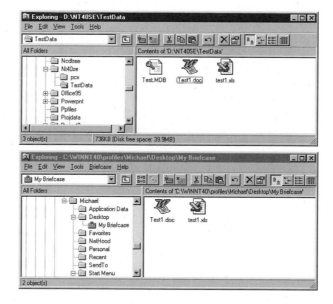

3. Drag the file from the first copy of Explorer and drop it on the Briefcase shown in the second copy of Explorer.

This method also allows you to move the file to any Briefcase folder on the desktop, not just the one labeled My Briefcase. Just make sure that you have the correct Briefcase showing in the second Explorer window, or your file could show up in someone else's Briefcase when they log on.

An alternative approach starts at the My Computer folder instead of using Explorer:

1. Open the My Computer folders as needed to find the file you want to move into the Briefcase.

2. Arrange the windows on your desktop so that you can see both the folder containing the file, and the Briefcase icon.

3. Drag the file from the folder and drop it on the Briefcase, as shown in figure 9.7.

FIG. 9.7
You can move files into the Briefcase by dragging them from their file folders and dropping them on the Briefcase.

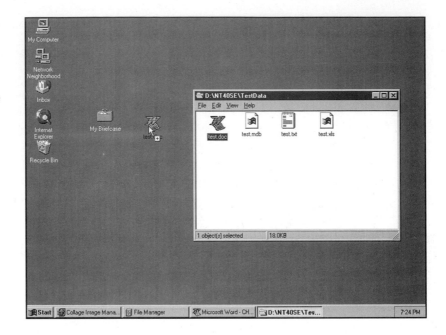

This method also allows you to move the file to any Briefcase folder on the desktop.

You can, of course, combine any of the three methods. So you could drag a file from a folder and drop it on a Briefcase folder open in another window, or drop it on a Briefcase listing in an Explorer window. You can drag and drop from Explorer to a folder containing the Briefcase. The only rule is that you need to be able to see the file and the destination in order for the drag and drop to work.

Moving the Briefcase to a Different Computer

The point of using Briefcase is to be able to take the Briefcase and the files it contains, and move them to a different computer. The options include moving the Briefcase across the network, or transferring it using floppy disks.

TIP You should make sure that the clocks are synchronized on the various computers, so that when you look at the update information, you are not confused about which file is the most recent.

Network or Direct Connect   Moving the files across the network is obviously the preferred method. It is faster, and more reliable than trusting your data to floppy disks. When your files are of any significant size, it is the only way to go. The procedure for moving the Briefcase is similar to the technique used to get the files into the Briefcase.

1. Open the Explorer, or the Network Neighborhood, and locate the target computer.

2. Arrange the windows on your desktop so that you can see both the Explorer or Network Neighborhood window, with the disk drive on the target computer visible, and the Briefcase icon on your desktop.

3. Drag the Briefcase from your desktop and drop it on the target computer, as shown in figure 9.8.

FIG. 9.8
When you move the Briefcase to the target computer, it shows up as just another folder in the Explorer.

Notice that the Briefcase disappears from your desktop because it was moved to the target computer. This is as it should be—there should only be one Briefcase on one computer of the pair. You should not have a Briefcase on both computers at the same time, or you will run into problems.

The previous instructions did not specify where to drop the icon on the target computer. If you simply drop it on the disk drive icon, then a folder appears for the Briefcase within the folder for that disk drive on the target computer. You can work on the files in that Briefcase folder, or you can drag it onto the desktop, and work on the files from there.

Windows NT 4.0 does not offer the Direct Cable Connection software from Windows 95, which allows you to connect to another computer via a serial or parallel cable. But you can use RAS (Remote Access Service) to connect the two computers with a null-modem serial cable. When configuring RAS, just select Null Modem instead of a specific modem.

▶ **See** "Using Remote Access Service," **p. 629**

Using Floppy Disks   If your second computer is not connected to the network, or perhaps is at a different location, then you can use floppy disks to transfer the Briefcase from one machine to another. The limitation is that you can only put as many files in the Briefcase as fit on one floppy disk. If you try to copy a Briefcase to a floppy disk, and the Briefcase file is too large, you see an error message. There is currently no mechanism in Briefcase to split the files between floppies. Hopefully this will appear in a future upgrade, or perhaps will become less of a problem with the 100M floppy disk drives being introduced by several manufacturers, notably Compaq, with the support of 3M.

The technique for transferring Briefcase data with floppy disks is simple:

1. Copy the files to the Briefcase on the originating computer.
2. Move the Briefcase to the floppy disk by dragging and dropping it.
3. Take the floppy disk to the target computer, drag the Briefcase from the floppy disk, and drop it on the desktop, as shown in figure 9.9. Notice that the Briefcase icon is now in the floppy disk folder, and no longer on the desktop.

FIG. 9.9
Transferring files with floppy disks is a convenient way to take work home from the office—perhaps too convenient!

You can now work on the files on the target computer, or on the original. When you are finished, reverse the process and move the Briefcase back to the originating computer. Now you are ready to synchronize the data on the originating computer with the files from the second computer. You can, if you wish, modify step 3 so the Briefcase remains on the floppy disk and is never actually transferred to the hard disk on the target computer.

Checking File Status within Briefcase

Checking the status of files in the Briefcase can be done by clicking the Briefcase icon or folder, which then opens the Briefcase window. The file status is shown, and you can quickly see what files need updating, as illustrated in figure 9.10.

If you want more information about a file in the Briefcase, select it and then click the secondary mouse button. From the shortcut menu, select Properties, and a tabbed dialog box will open, as shown in figure 9.11.

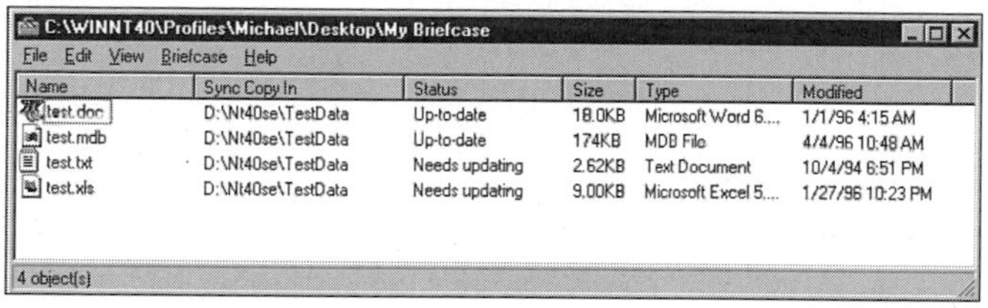

FIG. 9.10
The Briefcase window shows the contents of the Briefcase and the status of each of the files.

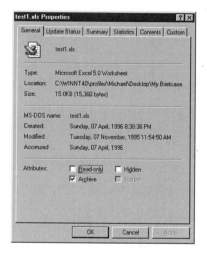

FIG. 9.11
Selecting the Properties option from the shortcut menu associated with a Briefcase file opens this tabbed dialog box.

The contents of the Properties dialog box will vary depending on the type of file. And if you are using the NTFS file system, there will be an additional tab, the Security Tab. In this example, the Update Status tab shows the status of the file, but also has the option to find the original file. Selecting this option opens a new window, similar to an Explorer window, with the original file highlighted, as you can see in figure 9.12.

Updating Files and Synchronization

An easier way to see what files must be updated is to select the Briefcase, Update All menu option. This produces a list, as shown in figure 9.13, of the files that need updating, and includes information about which files have been modified, and which do not exist in one or other of the directories. When you have multiple directories in the Briefcase, you can check each one of them for files that have changed.

FIG. 9.12
The Update Status tab allows you to locate the original file.

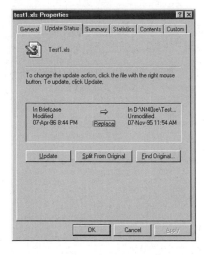

FIG. 9.13
This window shows which files need to be updated, and which version is the latest.

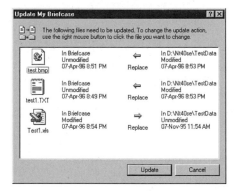

Now that you have the list of files to be updated, you can accept the list, and let Briefcase perform the update. However, if you want to change some items in the list, you can do so at this point. Right-click the item and a shortcut menu shows a list of available alternative actions (see fig. 9.14).

Preventing a File from Synchronizing   Perhaps there will be times when you do want to keep two versions of a file, and then merge them later. If you wish to prevent a file from synchronizing, select either the original or the copy in the update window, and right-click to bring up the list of update options. Choose the Skip option, and the file will not be updated.

FIG. 9.14

You can reverse the direction of the update if you want to discard the changes and restore the original file.

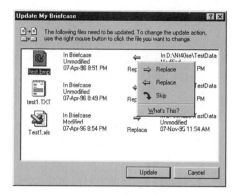

Splitting Files from Briefcase   Sometimes you may wish to drop a file permanently from the Briefcase replication process, and make it a stand-alone file. To do so, use the Briefcase\ Split From Original menu option. The file remains in the Briefcase folder, but is shown as an orphan file as seen in figure 9.15.

FIG. 9.15

Splitting a file from the original results in an orphan file.

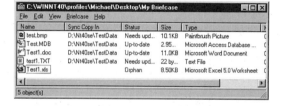

You may then want to copy the file to another folder so that it does not cause confusion by appearing in the Briefcase window.

Adding Files to an Existing Briefcase

You have moved the Briefcase to the second computer, and now you decide that you want to add some more files to it. You could move it back to the original computer, add the files, and then send it back to the target computer. But if you are connected via a network, it is possible to just drag the files from the first computer and drop them directly on the Briefcase on the other computer. Again, the only requirement is that you can see both the file and the destination for the drag-and-drop process to work. This applies even when using floppy disks; there is no need to move the Briefcase back to the first computer, when you can drop the additional files on the Briefcase on the floppy disk.

Briefcase and Access 95 Databases

Access 95 is just one of the applications that support, or will support, Briefcase replication. It is used as an example here because it goes a step beyond the simpler word processing and spreadsheet applications. When used with applications that fully support reconciliation, Briefcase generates what is known as a design master. Then replicas are made of this design master in multiple Briefcases. The design master and the replicas form a replica set. Changes can be made to the data in the replicas, but not to the design.

Whenever a file with an MDB extension is dragged into the Briefcase, the Briefcase calls its reconciler code to convert the Access database to a replicable format. The converted file at the original location is known as the Design Master. A replica of the Master MDB file is placed in the Briefcase.

The conversion is performed as follows:

1. To build the replica set, open the Windows 95 Explorer, drag the database file from there, and drop it on the Briefcase. A message will appear, stating that the file will be converted into a member of a replica set (see fig. 9.16). Choose Yes to continue.

FIG. 9.16
The Briefcase requests confirmation to convert the database to a replica set, because the process is not reversible.

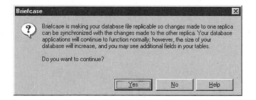

2. Briefcase then offers to create a backup copy of your original database for you. This is a good idea, because the conversion process adds tables, fields, and properties that configure the database as a Design Master. Choose Yes to continue.

3. You must then specify where you will want to make changes to the design of your database. Figure 9.17 shows the options. The best choice is the original file, not in the Briefcase replica. You want users to be able to update the data but not to make changes to the structure.

FIG. 9.17

The Briefcase asks you for the Design Master location—the only place where the changes can be made to the database.

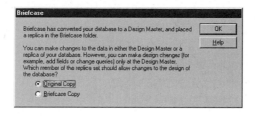

4. Minimize Explorer and open My Briefcase. You will see your replica in the Briefcase list. Currently it is synchronized with the original.

If you open the replica database and open a table in design mode, Access shows that this is a replicated table. Now close the copy of the database from the Briefcase. If you open the Properties dialog box, you see that the Briefcase copy has been modified, because Access always updates the date stamp when you open and close an MDB file, not because you have made changes (see fig. 9.18). Do not synchronize the two copies yet.

FIG. 9.18

The Briefcase copy is most recent, so it is the suggested master copy for the update process.

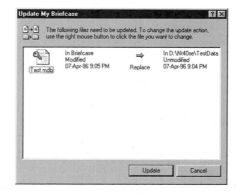

Now move the Briefcase to another computer. To see how replication works, make changes to the database data entries on both computers. (If you are experimenting on one computer, the description here still applies—just skip the step about moving the Briefcase). Then open the Briefcase, and look at the files that need updating, as shown in figure 9.19.

Because you changed both files, a simple replacement will not work. Now you see the merge option is available. As before, you can change the operation from a merge to a replace in one direction or the other, choosing one version of the replica set to write over the other.

FIG. 9.19
In the Update My Briefcase window, both copies have changed, so you will want to merge the changes.

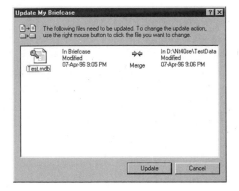

The biggest problem with replication is designing a scheme to handle conflicting updates. In the simplest case, different users changed different records, and so the changes can all be accepted as valid. Now suppose that the same data has been changed by two or more people. Then it is a question of which one takes precedence, as only one value can be correct. But what if different data has been changed within the same record?

Say one salesperson changed a contact's telephone number, and someone else changed the name of the contact person. Are both changes valid? Fortunately, briefcase does include a method for resolving conflicts. When Briefcase replication finds two records that have been changed, but the changes are different, it uses the following logic:

- Compare the two records for change status.
- Whichever record has been changed the most times becomes the master record and is used to update all the other records.
- Changes from the other records are placed in a log file for conflict resolution.

Each record has a version number. Whenever the data in a record is changed, the version number is incremented. If the record at one replica has been changed once and the same record at the second replica has been changed three times, then the record at the second replica has a higher version number than the record at the first replica. The reconciler compares the version numbers for the same record, and assumes that the version that has changed the most is the more correct of the two versions. The method of taking whichever record has been changed the most reduces the number of entries in the error file. If user 1 has changed the record four times, and user 2 only once, then it is better to resolve the conflict on the single change from user 2.

The conflict will not necessarily show up at the Design Master—it shows up at whatever copy has the record which is in conflict. When you open the copy of the database with the conflict, you are notified of the problem, as shown in figure 9.20.

FIG. 9.20
Notification of conflicting records.

You can then go to the Resolve Replication Conflicts dialog box, which shows the table with the conflicting records, as shown in figure 9.21. The record is shown with the table fields side by side.

FIG. 9.21
The Resolve Replication Conflicts dialog box shows that the Project Name is different, and you must decide which is correct.

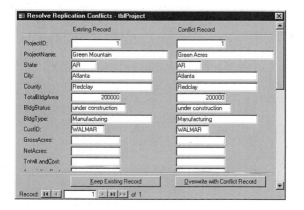

You have the option of specifying which set of changes to accept—the set that was accepted, or the conflicting data. You can accept either set, and it will be written to your local database as a change. Once you accept one set or the other, you should replicate this change by running the briefcase replication again. And that is where a danger lies.

As we mentioned, the conflicts can appear at the user replica database. The changes have been written at the Design Master already. Now the user decides that his or her changes were correct, and resolves the conflict by selecting the changes again, overriding what was sent from the Design Master. This change is written at the user's local replica. When the user does a synchronization again, the user's database shows the changes since the last synchronization. The Master

Design database shows no changes. Therefore the synchronization assumes that the user's changes should be accepted, and this time, they write over the data with which they were in conflict.

For this reason alone, many DBAs will not want to use the Briefcase replication on a shared database. It leaves too much control in the hands of the user, especially in the area of conflict resolution.

Copying the Briefcase to Multiple Systems

Suppose you want to make copies of the database for several computers, and tie them back to the original Design Master. To do so, follow these steps:

1. Make the first Briefcase copy as described earlier.

2. Copy and paste the Briefcase to your desktop as many times as you have target computers. The copies will be labeled Copy (*n*) of My Briefcase, as shown in figure 9.22, but you can rename them to keep track of what's going on. Perhaps you could name each copy after the target computer it is bound for.

FIG. 9.22
Multiple copies of the Briefcase are ready to move to the target computers.

3. Drag and drop each briefcase to the appropriate target computer.

Now when you open one of the Briefcase folders on any of the remote computers, you can check the status and, if necessary, update the copy. If either the local copy or the Design Master has changed, the status in the Briefcase indicates that the replica set needs updating. In this way, you can keep several copies of the database synchronized with the original, and therefore with each other.

From Here...

This chapter covered how replication works within Windows NT 4.0. We discussed how to copy files to the Briefcase, and how to move the Briefcase to another computer. We looked at determining the status of the files, and synchronizing updated files. Finally, we used Access 95 as an example of an application that supports reconciliation. For more information, you may want to jump to the following chapters:

- Chapter 18, "Using Windows NT Accessory Applications," for more information on Windows NT and Windows 95 applications.
- Chapter 23, "Using Dial-Up Networking," to see how to replicate and synchronize data using the RAS features of Windows NT.

Part
II

Ch
9

Configuring Windows NT Workstation 4.0

CHAPTER 10

Customizing the Windows NT Interface

by Michael O'Mara

One of the great things about Windows NT is that you can customize the interface to suit your preferences. In Chapter 3, "Working in Windows NT," you discovered that you can rearrange the furniture on your desktop by moving icons and customizing the taskbar. But that's just the beginning. You can redecorate your desktop with colors and wallpaper and customize the mouse pointer and other interface elements. ■

Customize your desktop with backgrounds, colors, and screen savers

Learn to change the appearance of your Windows NT desktop by changing color schemes, desktop backgrounds, and setting up a screen saver.

Set the date and time

Discover how to set your computer's clock and even configure it to adjust for daylight savings time automatically.

Change regional settings

You can configure Windows NT to display numbers and currency symbols appropriate for your country or region.

Configure your keyboard and mouse

Learn to customize the keyboard and mouse operations, and choose a different set of mouse pointers using Control Panel settings.

Select sounds for Windows events

Take charge of the sounds Windows NT plays to alert you of opening windows, error messages, and the like.

Customizing the Desktop

Everyone has different preferences when it comes to the colors in their surroundings. You may have limited options for selecting or changing the colors of the walls in your office. However, you can change the appearance of your Windows NT working environment very easily. You can change colors, patterns, and wallpaper on your desktop in just seconds.

Display

You'll find the desktop redecoration controls in the Display Properties dialog box shown in figure 10.1. You can open the Display Properties dialog box by clicking the Start button in the taskbar, pointing to Settings and choosing Control Panel. When NT opens the Control Panel dialog box, double-click the Display icon to open the Display Properties dialog box.

 TIP   There's a much faster way to open the Display Properties dialog box. Just right-click the desktop and choose Properties from the pop-up menu.

FIG. 10.1
The Display Properties dialog box is where you customize your desktop.

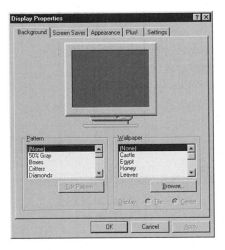

Changing the Desktop Background

The first tab of the Display Properties dialog box lets you control the appearance of the desktop background. You can add a pattern to the solid-color background or you can display a bitmap image—like hanging a picture or wallpaper on your office wall.

Applying a Pattern   Patterns are created by overlaying the background color with black dots. NT starts with a small pattern template and repeats the pattern to cover the entire desktop background. The result is a "textured" background instead of a simple, solid color.

To apply a pattern to your desktop, simply select one of the standard patterns from the Pattern list box. The thumbnail monitor at the top of the dialog box will show you a preview of the effect. If you like the pattern, click the Apply button to apply it to your desktop. After selecting a pattern, you can continue to work in the Display Properties dialog box to adjust other desktop settings, or you can click the OK button to close the dialog box.

If you're the ambitious type, you can try your hand at creating or modifying your own patterns. First, select an existing pattern as a starting point, then click the Edit Pattern button to open the Pattern Editor dialog box shown in figure 10.2. You can edit the pattern in the window on the left. Clicking the mouse on a spot in the pattern will toggle that pixel on or off (black or transparent). The right panel previews the effect of repeating your pattern across the desktop. When you achieve the desired result, give your new pattern a name by typing something appropriate into the Name text box. Click Add to add your new pattern to the list back in the Display Properties dialog box. Click Done to close the Pattern Editor dialog box. Now, you can select and use your newly edited pattern just like any other desktop pattern.

Part
III

Ch
10

FIG. 10.2
Create your own patterns in the Pattern Editor dialog box.

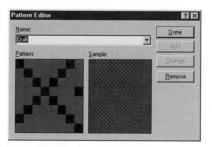

Hanging Wallpaper   If you want a more elaborate background, you can choose to display Windows wallpaper—a bitmap image that covers all, or part, of the desktop background. You can display a single image, centered on the background, or have NT repeat the image to cover the entire desktop.

To add wallpaper to your desktop, simply select an image from the Wallpaper list box on the Background tab of the Display Properties dialog box (refer to fig. 10.1). As with patterns, the thumbnail monitor shows a preview of your selection.

By default, the image is centered on the desktop. However, most of the standard wallpaper supplied with Windows NT are small images that are designed to be tiled (multiple copies displayed side-by-side to cover the desktop) much like ceramic tiles cover a floor or counter top. So, you'll probably want to click the Tile radio button to tile the wallpaper image. A few of the larger images look good centered; in fact, some wallpaper images will fill the entire desktop when centered. The trick is to match the size of the image to the display resolution of your monitor.

If you like the looks of the wallpaper in the preview, click the Apply button to display the wallpaper on your full desktop. Figure 10.3 shows an example of wallpaper centered on the desktop.

FIG. 10.3
Choose one of the standard Windows wallpaper images or try your own images.

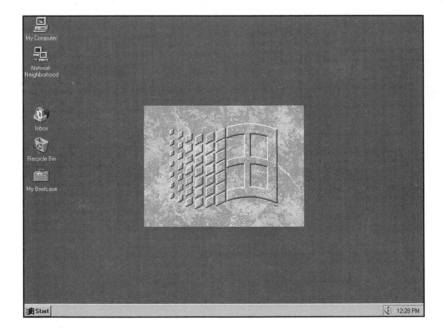

> **T I P** You're not restricted to the standard wallpaper images supplied with Windows NT. You can use a any bitmap image that is in the BMP file format. (You can create BMP files with the Paint program and with many other graphics programs.) Use the Browse button below the Wallpaper list box to select BMP files located anywhere on your system for use as wallpaper.

Configuring a Screen Saver

Screen savers started out as a way to prevent damage to a computer monitor caused by a static image remaining on the screen too long. They also help protect your work from prying eyes by removing it from the screen if you stop work for a few minutes. Modern computer monitors are less susceptible to "burn in" from an image remaining on-screen too long, but screen savers remain popular—perhaps because the dancing images of a screen saver are just more fun than the boring desktop. Windows NT includes an assortment of screen savers for your visual distraction. After a predetermined period of inactivity, the screen saver will replace the image of your desktop with moving lines or shapes. When you're ready to return to work, simply move your mouse or press any key on your keyboard to deactivate the screen saver and return your on-screen desktop to its normal condition.

> **CAUTION**
>
> Occasionally, screen savers may conflict with another application and cause crashes or erratic behavior. If you experience problems with an application, try disabling your screen saver to see if it helps clear up the problem.

Pick a Screen Saver   You can select a screen saver in the same Display Properties dialog box you use to adjust the other desktop display settings. Click the Screen Saver tab to bring up the screen saver options as shown in figure 10.4.

Part

III

Ch

10

FIG. 10.4
When your desktop isn't busy, you can display the screen saver selected here.

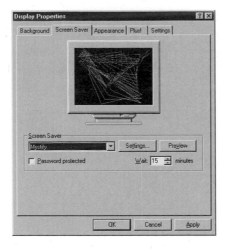

To activate a screen saver, select a screen saver module from the Screen Saver drop-down list box. The thumbnail monitor shows a preview of the screen saver effect. If you want to see what the full-scale screen saver looks like, click Preview. To turn the screen saver off and return to the Display Properties dialog box, press any key or move the mouse.

Adjusting Screen Saver Settings   Many of the screen savers allow you to fine tune the settings that control details such as how many objects appear on the screen and their colors. To adjust the settings, click the Settings button to open a dialog box similar to the Mystify Setup dialog box shown in figure 11.5. The specific settings for each screen saver module will vary somewhat depending on the design of that module. After you adjust the settings, click OK to close the dialog box.

There's one more major adjustment you need to make to control the behavior of the screen saver. That is how long NT will wait after your last keystroke or mouse movement before activating the screen saver. You can adjust the length of the delay by changing the value in the Wait number box. You can type in a number or increase or decrease the number by clicking on the small up and down arrow buttons in the number box. To enable the screen saver, click Apply. Of course, the screen saver will not appear immediately; it will not be activated until your keyboard and mouse remain inactive for the period of time you designated in the wait setting.

FIG. 10.5
This dialog box lets
you control just how
mystifying the Mystify
screen saver will be.

Using Password Protection   If you're really paranoid about hiding the data on
your screen, you can add password protection to the screen saver. Once the screen
saver is activated, you must enter a password to disable the screen saver and
return to your previous screen. Simply moving the mouse or pressing a key isn't
enough. A password protected screen saver is not a strong form of security, but it's
sufficient to discourage casual snooping.

By default, NT doesn't require a password to deactivate a screen saver. If you want
to add password protection, click the Password Protected check box to activate the
option and click Apply to record the change in your desktop settings.

To deactivate a screen saver with password protection, press a key on the keyboard or move your mouse. NT displays a small message box stating that the
workstation is locked. Press Ctrl+Alt+Del to open the Workstation Locked dialog
box where you can enter your user name and password. You use the same user
name and password you use to log onto NT in the first place. (See Chapter 15,
"Securing Windows NT Workstation," for more information on setting up a user
account and what to do if you forget your password.) Enter the password and click
OK to regain access to your NT desktop.

 There is a short delay between the time the screen saver appears and the time the
password protection takes effect. If you move the mouse during the first few seconds that
the screen saver is on-screen, you can return to your desktop without having to enter your
password. This comes in handy in those cases when the screen saver kicks in when you
have just paused to think or grab a sip of coffee.

Changing Colors

Windows NT lets you exercise your flair for color to redecorate your desktop according to your whim. You can control the color of the desktop background and

also the colors and fonts NT uses for windows and dialog boxes. Your desktop color schemes can be as conservative, or as garish, as you want.

You control the desktop colors with the settings on the Appearance tab of the Display Properties dialog box (see fig. 10.6). The top part of the dialog box is a preview window that identifies the items you can control and previews the color selections you make with the settings in the lower half of the dialog box.

FIG. 10.6

The Appearance tab of the Display Properties dialog box lets you change desktop colors from drab to dynamic.

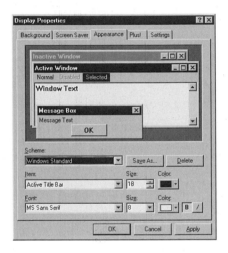

Select a Color Scheme   There are a lot of items on the desktop you can color. To make it easier to change colors, Windows lets you save and select sets of colors called *color schemes*. NT comes with several pre-configured color schemes.

To try one of the standard color schemes, select a color scheme name from the Scheme drop-down list box. NT shows the effect of the newly selected scheme in the preview area. If you like the effect, click Apply to repaint your desktop with the new colors. Otherwise, you can just keep trying other color schemes to until you find one you like.

Applying Custom Colors   Selecting a color scheme affects all of the desktop elements at once. But you also can control colors on an item-by-item basis. For instance, you can adjust the color of the active title bar or the text in the menu bar without changing other colors. You can use this detailed color control to fine tune an existing color scheme or to develop your own color combinations.

To adjust the color of an individual desktop item, first select the item you want to recolor. You can select an item by selecting its name from the Item drop-down list box or by simply clicking on the item in the preview area. Once you select the item, you can adjust its size (if appropriate) and color. To adjust the item's size, change the value in the Size box by typing in a new number or by clicking on the up and down arrows in the Size box. To change the item's color, click the down-arrow button in the Color box. This opens a small color palette as shown in figure 10.7. To select one of the standard colors from the color palette, just click the color sample you want to use. You'll see the effect of your choice in the preview area immediately.

FIG. 10.7
This small color palette gives quick access to commonly used colors.

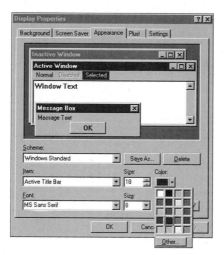

If none of the standard colors appeal to you, click Other in the color palette. This opens a much larger Color dialog box as shown in figure 10.8. The dialog box includes a larger selection of basic colors plus the ability to mix custom colors. You can select any of the basic colors by just clicking on a color swatch.

If you want to mix a custom color, start by clicking the color in the large color spectrum box in the right half of the Color dialog box. The color appears in the Color box below the spectrum. You can adjust the brightness of the color by dragging the slider up or down the brightness column to the right of the color spectrum. You also can adjust the color-by-the-numbers using either the Hue, Saturation, Luminance or Red, Green, Blue color models. The number boxes below the color spectrum show the values for the currently selected color. Simply type a new number into the appropriate box to modify the color. Once you define a custom color, you can use it by clicking OK. If you want the color to be available for future use, you can add it to the color palette in the Color dialog box. To do so, click Add to Custom Colors before you close the dialog box. The color appears in the next available spot in the Custom Colors area below the Basic Colors palette.

FIG. 10.8
This dialog box gives you access to the full rainbow of colors.

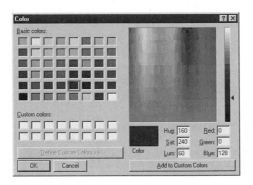

Changing Desktop Fonts

You not only can change the colors of the windows that appear on your system, you can change the fonts Windows will use in title bars, menus, and dialog boxes. Changing the font is very similar to changing the color of an item. First you select the item (such as the Active Title Bar), then you can change the characteristics of the text that will appear in that desktop item.

Choose the font you want to use for the selected item by selecting it from the Font drop-down list box. You can choose any of the listed fonts, including TrueType fonts, but it's a good idea to stick with system fonts such as MS Sans Serif. After you select the font, you can select a text size from the Size drop-down list box. Selecting the text color is the same as selecting the item color. You also can make the text bold or italic by clicking the B and / buttons.

Saving a Color Scheme

Once you have created a color scheme you like, you can save it for future use. Saving a color scheme will save all of the color and font settings currently shown in the preview area and add the new color scheme to the list in the Scheme drop-down list box. Once you save a custom color scheme, you'll be able to select it in the future just like it was one of the pre-configured color schemes that came with Windows NT.

To save a color scheme, click the Save As button to open the Save Scheme dialog box shown in figure 10.9. Type a name for your color scheme and click OK. That's all there is to it. Later, if you decide you don't want the saved color scheme in the Scheme list after all, you can remove it by selecting it from the Scheme drop-down list box and then clicking Delete.

▶ **See** "Configuring Your Video Display," **p. 284**

FIG. 10.9
You can name and save the color schemes you create.

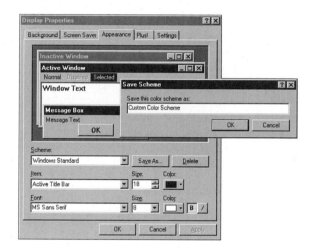

Part
III

Ch
10

Plus! Settings

Now that Windows NT shares the same interface with Windows 95, it also seems to be able to share at least some of the Windows Plus! package additions. You can't install the Plus! Package intended for Windows 95 on an NT system. However, we've observed that upgrading to NT on a machine containing Windows 95 with the Plus! Package already installed adds another tab to the Display Properties dialog box. The Plus! tab enables you to change the desktop icons for items such as My Computer and the Recycle Bin. You can also elect to use larger icons, show window contents while dragging, smooth the edges of screen fonts, show icons using all possible colors, and stretch undersized wallpaper images to fill the screen. See the Windows Plus! documentation for more information on how to use these, and other, Plus! package features. But, be forewarned, this isn't a recommended configuration and could cause some conflicts.

Keeping Track of the Date and Time

Windows NT is smart enough to help you keep track of the correct date and time. In fact, having the correct date and time available is essential for the operation of some programs. Generally, you can set the date and time once and then forget it. However, if you travel with a notebook computer, you may need to reset the system time more often as you travel.

 When it comes time to set your computer's clock, open the Start menu, and choose Settings, Control Panel. Then double-click the Date/Time icon to open the Date/Time Properties dialog box shown in figure 10.10.

FIG. 10.10
Set your computer's clock and calendar from the Date/Time Properties dialog box.

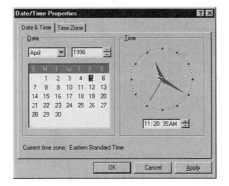

Setting the Date and Time

Setting the date is simple. Just select the month in the drop-down list box and adjust the year setting by clicking on the up- or down-arrow buttons in the year number box. To set the correct day, click the date in the calendar box.

Setting the time is just as easy. The large analog clock displays the time. You change the time setting by using the number box below the clock. You can highlight a number (hour, minute, second, or AM/PM) and change it by typing in a new number or clicking on the up- or down-arrow buttons to increase or decrease the value. Click the Apply button for your changes to take effect.

Time Zones

Windows NT not only needs to know the correct local time, the system needs to know what time zone it is in. This information is important for e-mail programs and other applications that must convert time stamps on files and messages from other areas to the correct local time.

In the Date/Time Properties dialog box, click the Time Zone tab to display the options shown in figure 10.11. Select your time zone from the drop-down list box above the map. The map will scroll to show the local time zone in the center of the dialog box.

FIG. 10.11
NT can even keep track of daylight savings time.

If you are in an area that changes to daylight savings time, make sure the check box below the map is checked. This will instruct Windows NT to adjust its clock automatically for the changes between standard and daylight savings time each spring and fall. It's really nice not to have to make those changes manually.

Click OK to close the Date/Time Properties dialog box and record your date and time settings.

Changing Regional Settings

Windows NT lets you customize the way it formats and displays numbers, currency, and dates to conform with the conventions of various countries or regions. For instance, you can specify whether to use a comma or a period to separate thousands in a number and whether the day or the month should appear first in a date. Many word processors and other programs will refer to Windows regional settings for this format information.

Part
III

Ch
10

If you stay in the United States and don't correspond with other countries, you may never need to adjust any of the regional settings. However, for those with international interests, NT's regional settings provide for quick access to the formatting and alternate keyboard layouts you will need for other locales.

Regional
Settings

To open the Regional Settings Properties dialog box (see fig. 10.12), open the Start menu and choose Settings, Control Panel, and then double-click the Regional Settings icon.

FIG. 10.12
The Regional Settings Properties dialog box.

Specifying Your Locale

The first step in specifying regional settings for Windows NT is to select your locale from the drop-down list box above the map. (The map is just for decoration. You can't select a locale by clicking on a location on the map.) Once you select a locale, Windows will update the number, currency, time, and date settings to conform to the formatting conventions in that region. You can override Windows default settings for the locale by adjusting the settings on the other tabs in the Regional Settings Properties dialog box.

Number Formats

To review or change the settings for number display, click the Number tab to display the options shown in figure 10.13. You can change the settings by selecting an option and typing in a new value or selecting a value from the drop-down list box for that option. The Appearance Samples at the top of the dialog box will show the result of your changes.

FIG. 10.13
Control how NT displays numbers.

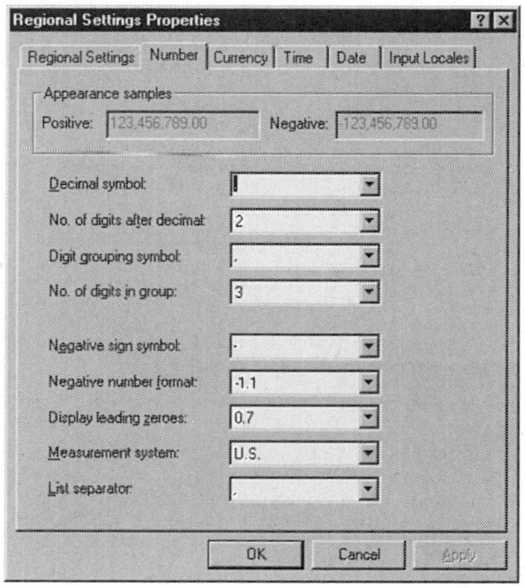

Currency Formats

Click the Currency tab to display the options shown in figure 10.14 for your review or editing. Again, you can change the settings by typing in a new value or making a selection from the drop-down list boxes.

FIG. 10.14
Customize NT's currency displays.

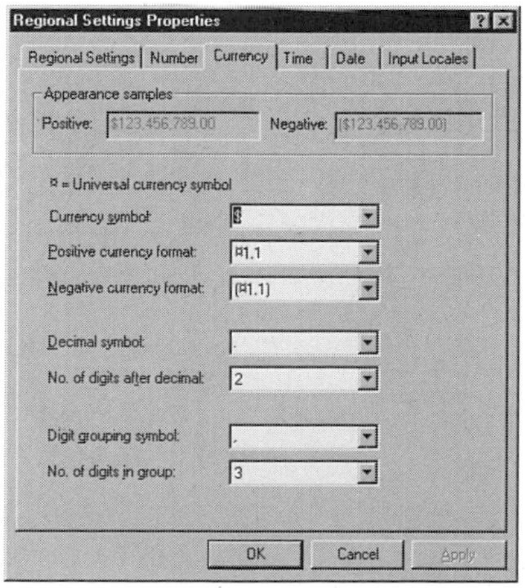

Time Formats

To change the way Windows NT formats time displays, click the Time tab in the Regional Settings Properties dialog box. As you adjust the settings shown in figure 10.15, you won't have the option of typing in values of your own choosing. You must select from the options on the drop-down list box for each setting. The Time Style settings are particularly cryptic but you'll be able to find the correct setting with just a little experimentation. You can keep trying different Time Style settings and observing the results in the Time Sample box until you find the one you like.

FIG. 10.15
Tell NT how to format
time displays.

Date Formats

Click the Date tab to display the options shown in figure 10.16. You can specify both a short date format and a long date format. The sample boxes show how your dates will appear. Change the date format by making selections from the drop-down list boxes.

FIG. 10.16
Make sure NT
displays dates in the
proper format.

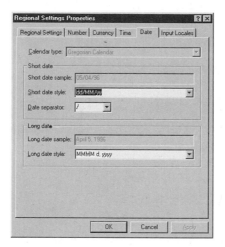

Switching Input Locales

If you use settings for more than one locale, you can configure Windows NT to
enable you to switch back and forth between different regional settings easily and
conveniently. Click the Input Locales tab to display the options shown in figure
10.17, which allow you to set up multiple input locales and switch between them.

FIG. 10.17
You can install
regional settings for
more than one locale.

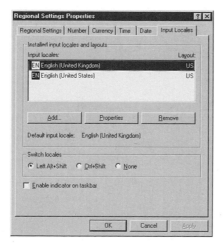

Part
III

Ch
10

The Input Locales list starts out with your default locale listed. You can add additional locales as needed. Just click the Add button to open the Add Input Locale dialog box as shown in figure 10.18. Select the locale you want to add from the Input Locale drop-down list box. When you click OK, NT closes the Add Input Locale dialog box and adds the new locale to the Input Locales list. You can select and input the locale to use by clicking on it in the Input Locales list. Select a locale and click the Properties button to open a dialog box where you can change the keyboard layout that Windows will use when you select the locale.

FIG. 10.18
Select a locale to
add to the list of
regional settings.

The other options on the Input Locales tab allow you to select a hot key for switching between input locales (of course you can always return to the Regional Settings Properties dialog box to change locale settings), and enable an input locale indicator that will cause a small box to appear next to the clock in the taskbar showing which input locale is currently active.

After adjusting the regional settings, click Apply to activate your changes. Or, simply click OK to do the same thing and also close the dialog box.

Configuring How the Keyboard Works

Is your keyboard too touchy? Do you inadvertently repeat characters because you held a key down for a fraction of a second too long? If so, you may need to adjust the Keyboard Properties settings.

To open the Keyboard Properties dialog box (see fig. 10.19), open the Start menu, and choose Settings, Control Panel, and then double-click the Keyboard icon.

FIG. 10.19

Make your keyboard match the speed of your fingers.

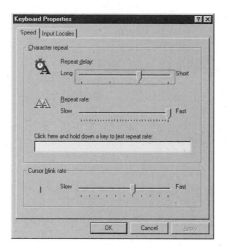

The dialog box's Speed tab is where you can fix the problem with repeating characters. First, adjust the Repeat Delay setting by dragging the pointer left or right. This setting controls how long you must hold a key down before it begins repeating multiple characters. The Repeat Rate setting is also a slider you can drag left or right. It controls how fast characters will spew forth when you press and hold a key on your keyboard. After adjusting the settings, click in the text box and hold down a key to test the new settings.

Although it's not a keyboard setting as such, you'll also find the Cursor Blink Rate setting in this dialog box. It's another slider you can drag left or right to make the on-screen cursor blink slower or faster. There's a sample cursor just to the left of the slider to preview the changes you make in the setting.

The Keyboard Properties dialog box includes an Input Locales tab (see fig. 10.20) that mirrors the one in the Regional Settings Properties dialog box. You can use it to switch keyboard layouts and formatting to work with different languages just like you can use its counterpart in the Regional Settings Properties dialog box. The settings are duplicated here for convenience.

After adjusting the keyboard settings, click Apply to apply the new settings to your system. Clicking OK applies the setting changes and also closes the dialog box.

FIG. 10.20
Activate language-specific keyboard layouts by selecting an input locale.

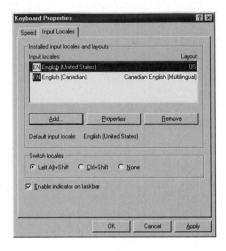

Customizing How the Mouse Operates

Mouse

Windows NT's mouse settings can help you tame the rodent and train it to do your bidding. To adjust the mouse settings, open the Control Panel window (click the Start button in the taskbar, point to Settings, and choose Control Panel), and double-click the Mouse icon. This will open the Mouse Properties dialog box shown in figure 10.21.

FIG. 10.21
Southpaws, reverse your mouse buttons here.

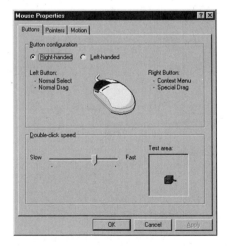

Adjusting Button Behavior

The options on the Buttons tab enable you to adjust the button configuration and double-click speed. By default the mouse is configured for use in your right hand. The left mouse button is the main button for clicking and dragging because it naturally falls under your index finger when you grasp the mouse with your right hand. However, you can select the Left handed option to reverse the button assignments so that the right mouse button becomes the main button thus making it easier to use the mouse in your left hand.

The Double-click Speed option is a slider. Drag the pointer to the left if you have trouble clicking the mouse button fast enough for the system to recognize the action as a double-click. Drag the pointer to the right if you're having trouble with the system mistakenly interpreting separate clicks as a double-click. After moving the slider, you can test the new setting by double-clicking on the jack-in-the-box in the Test Area.

Part

III

Ch

10

Picking Pointers

Click the Pointers tab of the Mouse Properties dialog box (see fig. 10.22) to customize the mouse pointers. Windows NT includes several alternate sets of mouse pointers. Some pointers are designed to be easier to see. Some are just for fun. You can choose a different set of mouse pointers by selecting an item from the Scheme drop-down list box. The pointers in the scheme will appear in the scrolling list in the middle of the dialog box. You can scroll down the list to see all the various pointers included in the selected scheme.

You can even change individual pointers by selecting the pointer you want to change, clicking on the Browse button, and choosing a different cursor file to substitute for the selected pointer. After you modify a pointer scheme by substituting different pointer shapes, you can save your new set of pointers as a named scheme. Just click Save Address, enter a name in the resulting dialog box, and click OK. NT will add your scheme to the list in the Scheme drop-down list box. In the future you can load your favorite set of pointers by selecting the saved scheme.

FIG. 10.22
Even the humble mouse pointer can get a new look.

Modifying Mouse Motion

You can control the way the on-screen pointer moves in response to mouse movements with the settings on the Motion tab (see fig. 10.23). Dragging the Pointer Speed slider to the right (toward Fast) makes the mouse pointer more sensitive. In other words, a small movement of the mouse creates a large, fast movement of the on-screen pointer. The pointer will be quick and responsive, but perhaps too jumpy. Dragging the slider in the other direction means that you will have to move the mouse farther for a given amount of on-screen pointer movement. That makes fine detail work easier, but if you move the slider too far to the Slow side, the pointer will seem sluggish.

The Pointer Trail option is intended for use with the LCD screens commonly found on notebook computer. The mouse pointer often disappears from view on such screens when you move the mouse quickly. If the Show Pointer Trails option is checked, to Windows will display a series of afterimages showing the track of the mouse pointer. This can make it easier to keep track of the mouse pointer even if the active pointer itself isn't visible while it's moving. To you can adjust the length of the trail the pointer will lead behind by adjusting the Pointer Trail slider.

After changing the mouse settings, click the Apply button to apply the changes to your system. Alternatively, clicking the OK button will apply the settings and also close the Mouse Properties dialog box.

FIG. 10.23
Control mouse speed
and improve its
visibility with trails.

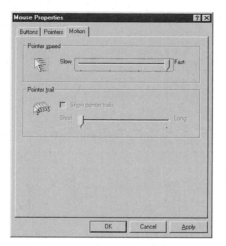

Configuring How Sound Is Used

If you have a sound card installed, Windows NT can use various sounds to alert
you when certain Windows events take place. You don't have to settle for a simple
beep from your PC speaker. You can hear a lively tune when Windows starts, a
piano chord to accompany the appearance of a dialog box, and a different tune
when Windows exits. You can pick the sounds Windows will use for each of these
sounds—and many more.

Sounds
To adjust the Windows sound settings, open the Sounds Properties dialog box
(see fig. 10.24) by double-clicking the Sounds icon in the Control Panel window.

FIG. 10.24
Take control of
Windows' burps,
beeps, and bleeps.

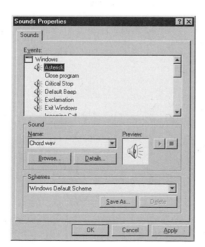

Associating Sounds with Windows Events

The Events box in the top half of the dialog box contains a scrolling list of events to which you can assign individual sounds. A speaker symbol beside an item in the list indicates that there is a sound associated with that event. When you select an item in the Events list, the name of the sound file associated with the highlighted event appears in the Name box. You can preview the sound by clicking on the right-pointing arrow button beside the Preview box. (Use the button with the square box on it to stop playback of a long sound file.)

 If you'd prefer that Windows *not* play a sound when a particular event occurs, select the event in the Events list and then select **(None)** from the Name drop-down list box. This will disable sound playback for the event.

If you want to select a different sound to be associated with the highlighted event, just select a different sound file from the Name drop-down list box. However, you're not restricted to the sound files that initially appear on the list. Indeed, you can use any appropriate sound file on your system. To select a sound file stored in a different folder, click the Browse button to open a standard Browse dialog box that you can use to locate the file you want. Once you locate the file, select it and click the Browse dialog box's OK button to close the dialog box and associate the sound file with the event.

 Some programs add their own events to the Events list. Once an event is on the list, you can change the sound associated with that event just as you can for other Windows events.

Saving and Selecting Sound Schemes

Windows lets you save a set of sounds and their associations with Windows events as a sound scheme. Then, when you want to change sound settings, you don't have to change each event individually. Instead, you can simply select the name of the sound scheme you want to use (select the name of the scheme from the Schemes drop-down list box) to change all of the sound associations to those saved in the scheme.

Once you have assembled a set of sounds that you like, you can save those settings as a sound scheme. The procedure is essentially the same as saving desktop color schemes. Just click the Save As button to open a dialog box, and you can type in a name for your sound scheme. When you click the OK button to close the dialog box, NT will save your current sound scheme settings and add its name to the list in the Schemes box. You can delete an unneeded sound scheme from the list by first selecting it and then clicking on the Delete key.

After completing your sound selections, click the Apply button to make them effective and click the OK button to close the Sounds Properties dialog box.

From Here...

This chapter has covered the ways you can customize Windows NT by changing the desktop colors, configuring screen savers, adjusting regional settings, controlling the behavior of your keyboard and mouse, and even selecting the sounds Windows will make when certain events occur. However, there are many other ways to customize Windows NT. In fact, that is a large part of what this book is about—making Windows NT function and behave the way you want it to.

- See Chapter 3, "Working in Windows NT," for more information on moving desktop icons and the taskbar.
- Chapter 8, "Working with the Command Prompt," gives you more information about changing the appearance of the MS-DOS window.
- Chapter 11, "Changing and Configuring Hardware," describes how to customize the way Windows NT works with your video display and other peripherals.
- See Chapter 13, "Configuring Windows NT Workstation for Multimedia," for more information on changing multimedia settings.

Changing and Configuring Hardware

by Kathy Ivens

One of the basic tenets of computing is that things change so fast that keeping up is next to impossible. New and more powerful hardware is introduced almost daily, and the best part is that prices keep coming down.

When you upgrade your equipment, to get it to work properly in NT 4.0, you have to install the appropriate drivers so that NT can manipulate the equipment. ■

Changing and configuring your video display

Video controllers keep getting more powerful and less expensive. When you upgrade your video hardware, you have to reconfigure your NT system.

Configuring serial ports

Getting the power out of all the communications software that comes with NT requires careful configuration of the hardware. Whether you're adding ports or configuring their use, there's no room for error in the settings.

Adding a tape backup device

Windows NT supports a variety of tape devices, and they have to be installed correctly to be recognized and to function properly. Then, you can use the built-in NT software, giving you a choice in addition to the drive's proprietary application.

Configuring a PC Card

PC Cards (PCMCIA cards) provide a host of hardware services, especially for portable computers, and Windows NT will recognize the slot and support the peripheral after you configure it properly.

Configuring Your Video Display

Upgrading video is one of the more popular exercises for computer users. As graphical applications become more powerful, the additional resources available in modern video adapters become more necessary. Even if you aren't purchasing a new video controller, you may decide to change the settings for the current one to take advantage of features you haven't been using.

ON THE WEB

You can find video driver updates from Microsoft at

> **http://www.microsoft.com/kb/bussys/winnt/**

Changing the Video Driver

If your video adapter dies or you decide you want to spring for a video adapter with RAM, speed, or some other new and better features, you have to tell Windows NT about it. Installing a new video adapter into your NT system is a straightforward process, which you perform after you physically install the adapter.

 T I P   Before adding a new video card, it is always a good idea to boot into NT with the standard VGA driver rather than the one that has already been installed. NT does not always graciously allow new cards to be installed.

If you're installing a new adapter, follow these steps:

1. Choose Settings from the Start menu, then choose Control Panel (or open My Computer, then open Control Panel).

2. Double-click the Display icon to bring up the Display Properties dialog box. Click the Settings tab to move to the Settings page.

3. Choose Change Display Type to see the Display Type dialog box (see fig. 11.1), which shows information about your current adapter.

4. Click Change to bring up the Select Device dialog box (see fig 11.2).

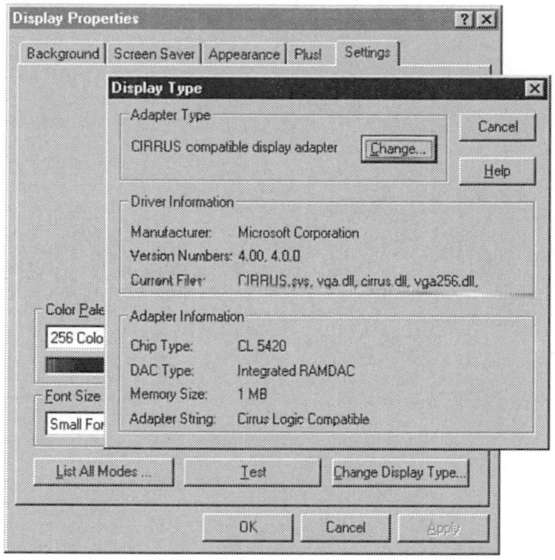

FIG. 11.1

Use the Display Type dialog box to view your video adapter settings or to begin the installation of another adapter.

FIG. 11.2

Use the Select Device dialog box to install the drivers for a video adapter.

5. Highlight the model and choose Install to begin the installation.

6. If your new adapter model isn't listed, you need drivers from the manufacturer. (These disks usually come with the adapter, but if you didn't find any in the box, you can call the manufacturer to obtain them). Choose Other from the Select Device dialog box and follow the easy instructions for inserting the disks.

Detect, one of the choices on this dialog box, is not quite as automatic or simple as other detection features in Windows NT. If you choose this option, drivers for every supported adapter will be copied to your drive. Then, you will have to reboot and begin the detection process. This choice should probably only be invoked if you don't know exactly which adapter is in your computer (either you don't want to open the computer or there's no clear marking on the card indicating the model), and you assume it's supported.

CAUTION

Before you purchase a new video adapter or change the settings for one, make sure your changes are compatible with your monitor. Check the documentation for the monitor and/or call the manufacturer. You can damage a monitor by setting incorrect options for video.

Changing Display Settings

The settings available for configuration (whether you are installing a new video adapter or changing the settings for the current one) are the following:

- Number of colors that appear
- Resolution
- Refresh rate
- Size of the fonts on your desktop window

To change the video settings:

1. Go to the Settings tab of the Display Properties dialog box (see fig. 11.3).

FIG. 11.3
Making changes in your video settings should be a cautious maneuver—the system provides a way to test your new settings before finalizing them.

You can configure your display settings individually in the Display Properties dialog box, as described here.

Or, as a shortcut, click List All Modes. A list of combinations (colors, resolution, and refresh rate) appears, and you can highlight the combination you want and click OK (see fig. 11.4).

FIG. 11.4

All the permutations and combinations of settings that are valid for your adapter are displayed—pick the one you want.

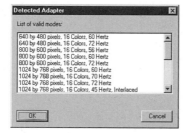

The following sections describe the individual options and settings you can specify in the Display Properties dialog box.

Changing the Color Palette   Choose Color Palette to change the number of colors you can display. The list of choices is limited by the capabilities of your adapter.

Changing the Resolution   Choose Desktop Area to select the number of pixels used in your display. Move the slider bar to the right to increase the number of pixels (the numbers change as the slider progresses). The higher the number of pixels, the higher the resolution. This choice is actually a specification of the size of the visible screen area you use for your display. A larger desktop area makes everything look smaller on your screen, which makes it easier to fit multiple windows on-screen.

Depending on the memory capabilities of your adapter, you may find that specifying a higher resolution may require you to reduce the number of colors (or vice versa). Or, you might want to investigate whether it is possible to add memory to your video adapter.

Changing the Font Size   You can change the size of the fonts that appear on your screen with the Font Size option. For most adapters, there are only two choices—small or large. Other adapters may offer typeface choices.

Setting the Refresh Rate   Choose Refresh Frequency to specify the *refresh rate*, the rate at which your screen is redrawn. The higher the frequency, the less flicker you see on-screen. *Flicker* is that annoying state in which the display on your

Part

III

Ch

11

screen seems unable to stay still. You must choose a refresh rate that is consistent with the capabilities of your monitor, which change depending on the resolution you selected (the higher the resolution, the more complicated the refresh process). When in doubt, choose a low refresh rate. Actually, for many adapters, the only choice available is Use Hardware Default Setting, which means that Windows NT figures out the correct rate.

N O T E Actually, flicker is a function of more than just the refresh frequency you choose in your display settings (the frequency rate is really the number of times per second a screen is refreshed).

Your monitor specifications also control the flicker. Monitors are available with two refresh capabilities (these terms describe the manner in which the screen is refreshed, rather than the rate):

- Interlaced monitors refresh by redrawing the odd-numbered lines, then return to the top of the screen to redraw the even-numbered lines.

- Non-interlaced monitors redraw every line with each refresh pass. This is a bit more complicated (and non-interlaced monitors are a bit more expensive), but it reduces flicker. If you are doing a lot of graphical work, the extra money is probably worthwhile, but if you spend almost all your time looking at text with occasional graphics (such as word processing), it probably isn't necessary to insist on a non-interlaced monitor.

Screens are refreshed from the top down, with the lines redrawn starting at the top and repainting each line.

And, you will always see flicker if you aren't looking at a monitor straight-on. Peripheral vision always produces flicker.

Testing the New Settings

Before you press OK, you should click Test to make sure everything works. Your screen goes black for a second, and then a display of colors at the specified resolution flies across your screen. Each color is labeled (if something labeled red looks yellow, something's wrong). A few seconds later, you are asked if everything looks correct and proper. If it does, choose Yes. If it doesn't, choose No and go back to the dialog box and start again.

Once you confirm that the new settings work properly, you need to shut down and restart your computer to have the settings take effect.

Configuring Ports

You can add and configure serial ports so that each port works correctly with the peripheral attached to it. Most desktop computers come with two serial ports, called *COM1* and *COM2*. Internal devices that use serial port standards (internal modems, fax cards, and so on) use COM3 through COM256. Windows NT supports as many as 256 serial ports, although it's highly unlikely you'll use anywhere near that number.

To add a serial port or to specify serial port settings:

1. Choose Settings from the Start menu, then choose Control Panel (or open My Computer, then open the Control Panel).

2. Double-click the Ports icon to see the Ports dialog box which lists the currently installed serial ports.

Adding Ports

To add a serial port to your system, first install the hardware into your computer, and then do the following:

1. In the Ports dialog box, click Add, which displays the dialog box seen in figure 11.5.

FIG. 11.5
To add a new serial port, you must configure its hardware settings.

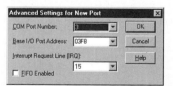

2. The system displays the next available COM number, and you must assign the Base I/O Port Address and Interrupt Request line (IRQ). Windows NT usually detects the value of these items properly, but if you know you've physically set the new port for different values, open the list and choose the correct setting.

3. If your computer or new serial port card is equipped with on-chip buffering or a UART serial chip, you can select FIFO Enabled to allow the port to manipulate the memory buffering of incoming data. Some UART chips have buffering built in, and it's probably a good idea to enable this box so that if buffering is available, NT will take advantage of it.

4. Choose OK when you are finished with this dialog box. A message displays telling you that your new settings will not take effect until you restart Windows. You can restart from that message dialog box (choose Yes) or opt to wait (choose No) before performing a shutdown manually.

 Sometimes, after you configure a port, the Event Viewer reports that user settings are being used instead of the default values. As long as everything is working properly, you don't have to worry about that report; it's an informational message that doesn't really affect the port's reliability.

Resolving Interrupt Conflicts

One of the most frustrating things about adding bells and whistles and equipment to your computer is that you frequently end up with conflicts on IRQ settings. Each device in your computer needs to occupy a specific, unique interrupt setting.

Sometimes that isn't easy, because some devices permit you to choose between a small number of IRQ choices. I've seen tape backup controllers that only offered IRQ 3 through 6, and network interface cards that had the same limited choices. With these limitations, you can end up with more devices than you have interrupts for.

One way to avoid conflicts is to purchase devices that have a range of choices for IRQ settings. Many of these permit you to configure the device through software instead of moving dip switches and jumpers. Once you can move a device's IRQ, you have more flexibility and can handle more devices on your computer.

Even before you add peripherals, devices in your computer are already occupying IRQs. There are 15 IRQs available. Table 11.1 lists the standard device/IRQ settings.

Table 11.1 Standard Device/IRQ Settings

IRQ	Device
0	Timer
1	Keyboard
2	Cascade (handles other IRQs above IRQ 8)
3	COM2 (and COM4 if installed)
4	COM1 (and COM3 if installed)
5	LPT2
6	Floppy controller
7	LPT1
8	Clock
13	Math coprocessor
14	IDE Controller

Part

III

Ch

11

CAUTION

IRQ 10 through 12 and IRQ 15 are generally available (unless you have a PS2 mouse port, which uses IRQ 12), although if you install a second controller for a hard disk instead of adding a second disk to your current controller (cabled to a SCSI controller, added as a slave to the first disk for IDE controllers), it will probably use IRQ 15. IRQ 9 is usually not used (although it can be used as a specific IRQ for ISA in a PCI machine).

Technically, while two things cannot occupy the same IRQ, I've made it work and so have lots of other users. In fact, if you have more than two serial ports, you already have a conflict. The trick is to avoid conflicts for hardware that gets used simultaneously.

You can, however, share IRQ settings between multiple serial ports, making sure that you don't simultaneously use two serial devices that are attached to ports sharing the IRQ. If you have two modems, attaching them to different serial ports that share an IRQ is probably okay, especially if they share the same telephone line. Even if they don't, it just means you can't be dialing out to two places at the same time.

If you aren't using both serial ports (maybe you have a mouse that attaches to a mouse port and the only serial device you have is a modem), you can disable one of them and free up the IRQ for another device. Disabling a port usually requires more than removing the port from your Windows NT system via a dialog box. You might also have to enter the CMOS Setup program for your computer and disable the port. Check the documentation for your computer.

Removing Ports

If you've changed the configuration of your computer and removed any serial ports, click Delete in the Ports dialog box. You are asked to confirm the deletion by clicking OK in the next dialog box. You must have administrative rights to delete a port.

Configuring Ports

You can set the configuration of serial ports to control the way information is moved between your computer and the port, and between the port and any device attached to it.

The communications settings you establish determine the way information is moved from your computer to a device attached to the port. Many of the choices are quite technical in nature and are related to the specific peripheral attached to the port, as well as the way that peripheral is used. You can usually get some guidance from the documentation that came with the peripheral. And, for modem communications, the host machine you're dialing into requires specific settings, so you need to gather that information before configuring the ports.

 TIP Most of the software applications that interact with serial ports (for example, communications/fax programs) have their own setup programs to specify port configuration options. These settings prevail when you use the application, even if they are not the same as the settings that are established through the Windows NT Port Settings options.

To establish communications settings for a serial port:

1. Select the port you want to configure and choose Settings to bring up the Settings dialog box (see fig. 11.6).

FIG. 11.6

The communications settings for a serial port should be configured to optimize the peripheral that's attached to the port.

2. Select and change the appropriate settings:

Choose Baud Rate to select a speed for the transfer of data. Printers generally operate happily with a speed of 9,600; modems should be configured for the speed at which the modem is rated, or higher.

CAUTION

If you're setting up a port that has a modem attached to it, avoid the Baud Rate setting of 14,400, even if your modem is rated at 14,400. Using the 14,400 setting can cause problems in the modem's performance. The modem may hang up when connecting, not recognize a connection, or exhibit some other bizarre behavior.

If you have a 14,400 modem, set the port's speed for 19,200. In fact, it never does any harm to set the port for a higher speed than the modem's certification. Sometimes, it speeds up modem communications.

Part
III

Ch
11

Choose Data Bits to specify the number of data bits you want to use for characters. Almost always, characters are transmitted in 7 data bits or 8 data bits.

Choose Parity to select the method for error checking. Almost always, you need None or Even Parity.

Choose Stop Bits to specify the number of bits in the time interval between characters that are being transmitted. Almost always, the choice should be 1.

Choose Flow Control to select the way you want to control data flow. You can choose None to specify no control of the flow of data. The standard for software control is Xon/Xoff. If the device attached to the port has built-in data flow controls, select Hardware.

For more detailed information on these choices, see Chapter 22, "Installing and Configuring a Modem."

Installing and Configuring a New SCSI Adapter

There are a number of devices that can run from a SCSI adapter. In fact, in my own computer I have the following SCSI peripherals, all attached to one SCSI card:

- Hard drive
- Tape backup system
- CD-ROM

There are several steps involved in the installation of SCSI devices:

- Physically install the SCSI adapter
- Physically install the devices and attach them to the adapter
- Set terminations, IRQ, and so on (see the specific adapter and device instructions)
- Run the setup software that came with the adapter to tell the SCSI adapter which devices are attached to its ports
- Install the drivers for the adapter and device(s) into Windows NT Workstation

If your SCSI devices are already installed in your computer, Windows NT Workstation will usually detect them during the installation of the operating system.

However, if you're adding a SCSI adapter to your installed Windows NT system, you need to tell the operating system about it to have it recognized:

1. Choose Settings from the Start menu, then choose Control Panel (or open My Computer, then open Control Panel).

2. Double-click the SCSI Adapters icon to open it.

3. Click Add. Then find the name of your device in the list of supported devices (see fig. 11.7).

4. Click Install to begin the installation process of putting the drivers into your system.

5. Insert your Windows NT disks as prompted. If you have the CD-ROM version of Windows NT Workstation, be sure the disc is in the CD-ROM drive.

FIG. 11.7
To install SCSI
services, choose a
driver from the list
of SCSI adapters
supported by
Windows NT
Workstation.

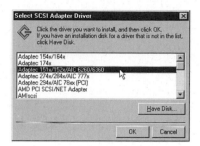

If your SCSI adapter isn't listed, you will have to use the manufacturer's disks to install it. If the SCSI adapter kit didn't come with a disk of drivers, you need to contact the manufacturer to get them (you may be able to download them, because most manufacturers have a BBS or CompuServe section for drivers). Make sure the drivers are for Windows NT 4.0.

Follow the previous steps to install a SCSI device driver, and then do the following:

1. Instead of selecting a device name from the list of supported SCSI devices, choose Have Disk.

2. Specify a location for the drivers (see fig. 11.8) and choose OK.

FIG. 11.8
Designate a location
for the driver, either a
disk or the path to
the directory where a
downloaded driver
resides.

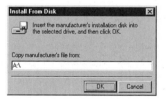

Shut Down the Computer

When you finish the installation procedure, a message appears informing you that to have the new driver take effect, you must restart Windows. The dialog box includes an offer to take care of that chore for you, which you should take advantage of.

 If you have any programs open, before you let NT shut down the system, right-click the program buttons on the taskbar and choose Close.

Part

III

Ch

11

Configuring a PC Card

If you are going to add a PC card (formerly called PCMCIA), you have to tell Windows NT about it.

If you have PC Card sockets (even if they're empty), when you double-click the PC Card icon in the Control Panel, you see the PC Card Devices dialog box (see fig. 11.9). If Windows NT can't find PC Card sockets, an error message displays (telling you there is no PC Card service on this computer).

FIG. 11.9
The fact that the PC Card dialog box displays means that Windows NT has found the PC Card socket(s) and will let you install and configure a PC Card.

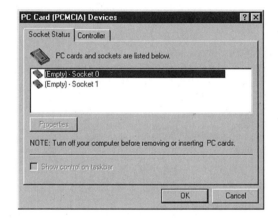

> **CAUTION**
>
> Before physically installing a PC Card, shut down and turn off your computer.

After a PC Card is inserted in a socket, opening the PC Card icon in the Control Panel should reflect the installation (see fig. 11.10). The PC Card should be listed in the correct socket. If it's not, you should turn off the computer and check to see that you inserted the card correctly. Make sure the contacts are meeting properly and firmly.

Any configuration options that have to be set will vary depending on the type of PC Card. Highlight the card and choose Properties to begin. Whether the card is a modem, a network adapter, or some other type of peripheral, there will be hardware settings to enter or confirm (see fig. 11.11).

FIG. 11.10
When Windows NT checks the PC Card sockets, it should find the device you inserted.

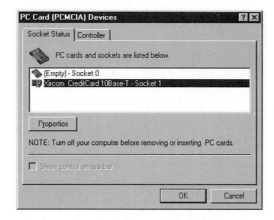

FIG. 11.11
The hardware configuration for this PC Card adapter requires all the information you would need to install a regular bus adapter.

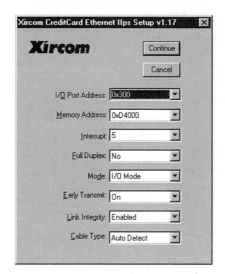

You may have to shut down and restart your computer before the new settings will take effect.

From Here...

Configuring new or upgraded hardware is an enormously important part of using a hardware protected operating system like Windows NT 4.0. For information about related topics, see the following chapter:

■ Chapter 14, "Managing System Services and Devices," covers the way devices are loaded and used in Windows NT.

CHAPTER 12

Managing Memory, Multitasking, and System Options

by Paul Sanna

One of the advantages Windows NT has over non-graphical user interface operating systems is the ease with which you can manage complex options for the entire operating system. Rather than having to identify and then input arcane commands and difficult syntax to manage options such as memory management and startup configurations, Windows NT enables you to just point and click. This isn't to suggest, however, that Windows NT has a less than robust set of system options. Directly from a dialog box, you can control the size of virtual memory swap files, multitasking priorities, and more. This chapter presents these types of options to you, explaining their significance and then providing you with advice for configuring them. ■

Understand memory and memory management

This chapter explains how Windows NT uses memory and describes NT Workstation's memory requirements.

Understand multitasking and change multitasking priorities

In this chapter, you learn about the multitasking scheme used in Windows NT.

Understand and customize environment variables

Windows NT maintains both environment variables used by all applications and all users, as well as environment variables unique to each user. This chapter explains how environment variables are used.

Configure NT Workstation for crash conditions

It is, unfortunately, likely that Windows NT Workstation will crash at some point during your use of it. This chapter helps you understand and configure the options (built into the system) that help diagnose why the system crashed, as well as control the system's behavior following a crash.

Managing Memory in NT Workstation

You can optimize your system performance with memory management. (Don't worry, not all memory problems are solved by acquiring more memory.) In this section, you learn how to manage the memory you already have in NT Workstation. This section starts with a brief overview of how memory is managed internally in NT Workstation 4.0. Following the overview, practical instruction and guidance are given for changing the memory configuration of your NT Workstation. This section also provides hints for when you may need to manage the memory in your NT Workstation.

Understanding Memory in NT Workstation

The available memory resources are comprised of the RAM installed on your system plus some amount of your hard disk space. The memory in NT Workstation is managed by the Virtual Memory Manager (VMM). The VMM works in a triage mode, identifying requirements for memory among applications and processes, and dispensing the memory to the applications as it sees fit.

When an application or a process starts in NT Workstation, it is provided with its own memory space. Each application or process started in NT Workstation believes it has 2G of memory to work with. In addition, Windows NT uses an additional 2G for system files and drivers. You probably don't have 4G of RAM on your system, much less 4G available for *each* process you start on your system. The VMM uses a virtual pagefile to help simulate 4G for each process. The virtual pagefile lets NT Workstation use more memory than is physically available on the system.

A *virtual pagefile* is a special file on your hard drive used by the VMM. The VMM uses the pagefile to store data that applications and processes require to be present in memory but is not being used at a particular instant. As applications and NT Workstation demand more memory, data present in memory is swapped to the pagefile, and data required by an application is swapped back to RAM. The advantage of this system is that you can make more memory available to your applications. The disadvantage is that application speed can be affected by the overhead associated with accessing data directly from your hard disk.

N O T E The virtual pagefile is an actual file on your system named PAGEFILE.SYS. You can find this file in the root directory of every partition where you use a pagefile. ■

NT Workstation maintains a minimum and maximum size of the pagefile. It expands the size of the pagefile as needed within the boundaries defined by you. Managing the size of that pagefile is the primary function of managing memory in NT Workstation.

If you have more than one hard drive on your computer, you can dramatically enhance the performance of your system. You can do this by creating a pagefile on each hard drive on your system. The VMM can use pagefiles simultaneously, perhaps reading to one pagefile while writing to another. Later in this section, you learn how to create a pagefile. This is useful if you want to create another pagefile on a second partition or hard drive.

CAUTION

When creating pagefiles, don't confuse hard drives with partitions. You shouldn't create pagefiles on multiple partitions on the same hard drive. This setup degrades system performance significantly because when Windows NT writes to these pagefiles, the disk arm of the hard drive is forced to swing back and forth across the disk rather than being able to stay in the general area of the single page file.

N O T E The VMM passes memory between RAM and the pagefile in blocks. The blocks of data are known as *pages*. Depending on your processor, the size of these pages is different. On Intel x86 and MIPS platforms, the size of a page is 4,096 bytes. On a DEC Alpha platform, the size of a page is 8,192 bytes. ■

Part
III

Ch
12

Configuring Memory in Windows NT

You view and manage the memory configuration on your NT Workstation from the Virtual Memory dialog box (see fig. 12.1). The dialog box shows you the dimensions of each pagefile on your system (don't forget, you can have one pagefile on each hard drive or partition), as well as the total dimensions of all virtual memory on your system. Table 12.1 explains the information contained in the dialog box.

FIG. 12.1

The Virtual Memory dialog box shows you information about all the virtual memory on your PC.

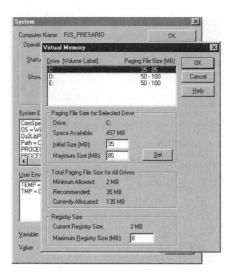

Table 12.1   Information in the Virtual Memory Dialog Box

Item	Description
Drive	Indicates for which drive, or partition, pagefile data appears.
Space Available	Total space available on the current drive.
Initial Size	The size of the pagefile when NT Workstation starts.
Maximum Size	The maximum size the pagefile will expand to as the VMM pages add data to it.
Minimum Allowed	The smallest allowable size for a pagefile.
Recommended	The recommended initial size for all pagefiles on all drives and partitions (usually calculated by adding 11 to your total physical RAM).
Currently Allocated	The total size of all pagefiles on all drives and partitions.
Current Registry Size	Current amount of RAM allocated to the Registry.
Maximum Registry Size	Determines the maximum amount of memory that can be allotted to the Registry.

Understanding When Memory Management Is Required   It may not be clear to you when your NT Workstation system needs memory management. The following are three signs that your memory configuration may not be optimal:

■ You receive the Not enough memory message when you start an application or switch between running applications (see figs. 12.2 and 12.3).

FIG. 12.2
The appearance of this message from an application is a clear sign that you may have to engage in memory management.

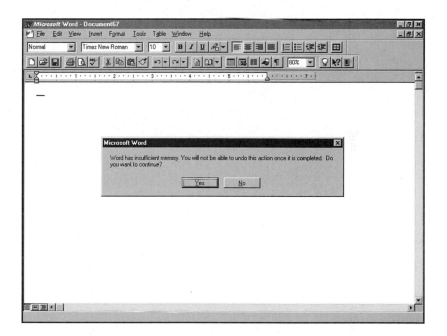

FIG. 12.3
This message from NT Workstation clearly informs you that you have to tangle with memory management.

■ You observe sluggish behavior in your applications, such as delays in displaying all the elements of an application's screen.

■ You observe significant hard drive activity (such as the hard drive's status light flickering or hearing the hard drive working) when you are not specifically accessing the hard drive.

Calculating Memory Requirements   Before configuring the pagefile in NT Workstation, you should understand NT Workstation's memory requirements and how total memory is calculated.

When NT Workstation is installed, an *initial pagefile size* is determined. After the size of the file is determined, NT Workstation attempts to create the file. The size of the file is based on the following equation:

initial pagefile size = physical RAM + 11M

So, if you have 24M RAM on your system, NT Workstation tries to create a pagefile of 35M.

NT Workstation also must determine a *maximum size* for the pagefile. This dimension is approximately twice the value of the initial size of the pagefile.

In addition to the pagefile size, you should also be concerned with the amount of *working memory* NT Workstation has available. NT Workstation needs at least 22M of working memory. Working memory is the sum of physical RAM plus the size of the pagefile. To recognize if you have enough working memory, you need to know at least the amount of RAM installed on your system.

working memory = physical RAM + pagefile size

This calculation isn't completely accurate, however, because NT Workstation keeps 10M of your total physical RAM for its own use. You should subtract 10M from the physical RAM total in calculating working memory:

working memory = (physical RAM − 10M) + pagefile size

So, let's use the example again of a system with 24M of RAM. Subtract the 10M Windows NT requires from total RAM and 14M is the result. Knowing that the minimum working memory total is 22M means that a pagefile size of 8M is required:

$(24 - 10) + 8 = 22$

To conclude, regardless of the minimum pagefile size and minimum working memory calculations described here, there are two important things to keep in mind:

■ NT Workstation has a minimum requirement for a 2M pagefile size. Even if the amount of RAM on your system determines that you do not need a pagefile, you must still specify a minimum pagefile size of 2M.

■ You'll probably need more than a minimally sized pagefile if you plan to run more than one application at once. Consider doubling or even tripling the initial pagefile size in determining the maximum size of the pagefile.

▶ **See** "Optimizing Windows NT Performance," **p. 943**

Guidelines for Memory Management   Before reviewing the steps for changing your computer's memory configuration, here are some guidelines and advice to help you manage the memory of your NT system.

■ *Configure Windows NT for at least 40M of working memory.* Though Windows NT requires 22M of working memory, the optimum value is 40M. Subtract 10 from the total RAM installed on your system, and then subtract that number from 40. That number should be the initial size of your pagefile.

■ *Monitor the size of your pagefile.* Make it a habit to check the size of your pagefile at the end of the day. You can use Explorer to do this. If you find that the file is consistently sized at a level greater than the setting for the initial pagefile size, then you may want to change that setting to the size to which the pagefile usually grows. For example, if the initial size of your pagefile is 40M, but you observe its size usually between 50-55M, change the initial setting to 55M. This way, Windows NT doesn't have to do the work of expanding the size of the file as your requirements for memory grow beyond that of the previous initial setting.

■ *Make the maximum pagefile setting as large as possible.* Don't be modest about the maximum size of the pagefile. Use a setting two to three times the size of the initial pagefile size or more. Windows NT will only expand the size of the pagefile when it needs to, so you are not using valuable hard drive space unless you need to. This way, you can avoid the Insufficient Memory Error during a complex operation.

■ *You may need more RAM or a larger hard drive.* After you have attempted the different methods for managing memory described in this section, you may

Part

III

Ch

12

conclude you need more RAM or hard drive space. If you cannot provide the appropriate initial pagefile size or provide Windows NT with enough working memory, you may need to increase RAM or provide more hard disk space.

Changing the Memory Configuration   To change the size of the pagefile or create a new pagefile on another drive or partition, follow these steps:

1. Open the Start menu, and then choose Settings, Control Panel.
2. Choose the System applet, and then choose the Performance tab.
3. Choose the Change button in the Virtual Memory section. The Virtual Memory dialog box appears (refer to fig. 12.1).
4. Select from the Drive list the drive or partition whose pagefile you want to modify or create.
5. Specify an initial and maximum size for the pagefile in the Initial Size (M) and Maximum Size (M) edit boxes. Use the guidelines specified in the preceding section to help you determine the values.
6. Choose OK. Windows NT must restart the computer for the changes you made to virtual memory to take effect. After choosing OK, you are prompted, in a dialog box, to let Windows NT restart your system immediately so the changes take effect, or you can tell Windows NT not to restart the computer.

TROUBLESHOOTING

When I start Windows NT, I see an error message telling me I have limited virtual memory. Then the System dialog box appears. Actually, NT Workstation might display any number of messages, all similar to the one described here, if you are running low on virtual memory. In any case, the message is telling you that you need to create some space on your hard drive to increase the size of your pagefile. If you specify an initial size of your pagefile that is below the recommended amount, NT Workstation creates a temporary pagefile to assist with memory. NT Workstation displays the message each time you boot until the temporary file is no longer needed. You might also see a similar error message if you do not have sufficient room to create the pagefile even if you have specified a sufficient initial parameter.

Working with Tasking and Priorities

In the previous section, you learned about how memory is used in Windows NT Workstation and how to configure memory for best performance. Proper memory management helps your system run smoother, especially when you run more than one application at once. One of the features of NT Workstation is *multitasking*. This feature allows you to run multiple applications and processes at once. You might say that multitasking also was a feature of earlier versions of Windows. This is true, but the multitasking capabilities of Windows NT are far superior than those of Windows 3.1 and Windows for Workgroups. This section looks at multitasking as well as how you can specify tasking priorities in NT Workstation. This feature lets you specify which applications have a higher priority when more than one application is running.

Understanding Multitasking

The most important point to keep in mind about multitasking is that use of the CPU is the real issue. All applications need to use the CPU to process, so when more than one application is run at once, access to the CPU is the critical point. The differences between the multitasking schemes used by Windows 3.1 and Windows NT are related to CPU usage.

Cooperative Multitasking   Windows 3.1 (including Windows for Workgroups) uses a multitasking scheme known as *cooperative multitasking*, which mean that all applications must cooperate for smooth multitasking to occur. Unfortunately, applications are written by humans, and sometimes humans aren't cooperative, so cooperative multitasking doesn't always work. Cooperative multitasking is based on the premise that applications borrow CPU time for short bursts before relinquishing control to other applications. But not all applications do a good job of freeing up CPU control. Some applications tie up the CPU for longer than acceptable periods of time, and some applications never relinquish control of the CPU. Some applications demonstrate these uncooperative characteristics out of bad design; some, like very CPU-intensive applications, have no choice.

Part
III

Ch
12

Preemptive Multitasking   Windows NT uses *preemptive multitasking* to manage multiple applications. In this scheme, the CPU cycles through all the processes running to make sure that each gets a chance to run. As you learn in the next section, some processes get more attention from the CPU than others. What's important to understand with this scheme, however, is that the chances are remote for a single application to tie up the CPU.

Understanding Priorities

All processes in NT Workstation 4.0 are assigned a priority when they start. This priority is expressed in a value from 1 to 31. The standard priority has a value of seven. A process' priority determines how much attention from the CPU the process gets. In the earlier discussion about preemptive multitasking, you learned that the CPU cycles through all the applications running and gives each some time to process. An application with a higher priority gets more attention from the CPU than another application. At the same time, the CPU pays just enough attention to the application with a lower priority to keep it running.

Starting Applications at a Specific Priority

You can start an application at a specific priority. Keep in mind that only 32-bit applications can start at a priority higher than Normal (7). To start an application at a specific priority, you must launch the application from the command line using the START command. You start an application at a specific priority by providing the priority class (low, normal, high, real-time) on the command line with the START command.

▶ **See** "Using Command Prompt Commands," **p. 223**

To start an application at a specific priority, follow these steps:

1. Open the Start menu and then choose <u>P</u>rograms, Command Prompt.

2. Type the command **START */priority_class application*** where *application* is the name of the application to run, and *priority class* is the class of priority at which you want the application started. Use one of the following priority classes:

Priority Class	Priority Value
Low	4
Normal	7
High	13
RealTime	24

3. Press Enter. The application named on the START command line is launched at the priority specified.

Specifying Multitasking Priorities

There is no doubt that you will run more than one application at one time in NT Workstation. You probably will want the application that appears in the active window on your screen to have the highest priority—that is, have the most attention paid to it by the CPU. When you switch to another application, you then probably want that application to have the highest priority. This is the default behavior in NT Workstation—but NT Workstation lets you change that behavior.

You can customize the relative priority levels for foreground and background processes in NT Workstation. A *foreground* process is one that runs in the active window in Windows NT. A *background* process is any process that is running that is not contained in the active window. By switching windows, you change the priority a process receives depending on whether the process is in the active window. You can specify that foreground and background processes have the same priority level, or you can specify that a foreground process has a priority two levels higher than any background process. You can also choose a condition in the middle.

To change the multitasking priorities, follow these steps:

1. Open the Start menu, and then choose Settings, Control Panel.

2. Choose the System applet, and then choose the Performance tab (see fig. 12.4).

3. To optimize the performance of applications running in the foreground, move the slider all the way to the right to maximum. To generate slightly better performance of applications in the foreground, move the slider to the middle position. To see comparable performance of foreground and background applications, move the slider all the way to the left to None.

Part III

Ch 12

FIG. 12.4

You can customize the relative priority classes assigned to foreground and background applications.

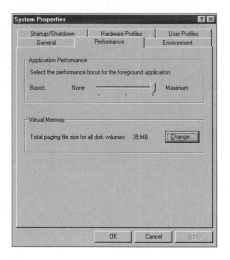

The following table provides details about each of the three Performance settings:

Option	Description
Best Foreground	Foreground applications have a priority of 9 while background processes have a priority of 7. This option is useful if the application you are working on is CPU-intensive, such as a spreadsheet doing large calculations, and you are not interested in the performance of any other application you may have running.
Foreground More Responsive	Foreground applications have a priority of one level higher than next highest background applications. This option is useful if you are working on an application in the active window, but you still want another application you have running, such as a sort of a database or a print of a document, to continue smoothly (though you know its

Option	Description
	performance will not be equal to that of the application you're working on).
Foreground and Background Equal	Foreground and Background applications have the same priority levels. Use this option if you are interested in the same performance of all applications you have running. This option is useful if you are truly working on a number of applications—constantly switching from one to another—but you do not want processing of an application you have just switched from to slow.

N O T E The tasking priorities you set in the Tasking dialog box affect only applications that have a base priority class of Normal. Any application with a specific priority class of Low, High, or RealTime is unaffected by the setting in the Tasking dialog box. Applications have their priority class established programmatically. This means that when the application was written, a priority class was built into the software. ■

Part
III

Ch
12

NT Workstation and Crash Conditions

Probably no software system in use today is totally bug-free, and NT Workstation is no exception. Bugs in NT Workstation can range from minor to fatal. When NT Workstation runs into a fatal condition—that is, a condition in which the system crashes—the consequences are severe. Compared to crashing a spreadsheet program or a game, when NT workstation crashes, your PC's operating system has been shut down and is unusable until it is restarted.

The polite term used by NT Workstation to describe a crash is *STOP condition*. When NT Workstation crashes, your screen appears blue, and an error message is displayed informing you of the STOP condition. There can be any number of reasons why NT Workstation would crash, and as a user or administrator of NT Workstation, you should be interested in understanding why the crash occurs (especially if it occurs frequently), what you can do to prevent a crash, and how to get your system up-and-running quickly after a crash. NT Workstation provides functionality to help achieve those goals. Fortunately, because of the protection Windows NT provides for each of its internal subsystems, you should rarely encounter a Windows NT Workstation stop condition.

Preparing NT Workstation for a STOP Condition

You can specify how NT Workstation reacts when a STOP condition occurs. This reaction could take the form of writing information to a special log file that describes the state of NT Workstation when the STOP condition occurs. The reaction also could involve sending a message to administrators of the system. You specify what happens in NT Workstation when a STOP condition occurs in the Recovery box (see fig. 12.5).

FIG. 12.5
You specify in the Startup/Shutdown property sheet how NT Workstation responds when a STOP condition occurs.

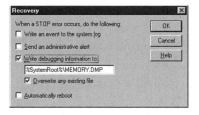

The different options you can specify for responding to a STOP condition are as follows:

■ *Record STOP event in event log.* You can record the event that caused the STOP condition in the system event log. The log stores the time of the event, as well as details about the event, such as a description and the system services and files involved. You can view all events recorded in the event log in the Event Viewer utility, which is available in the Administrative Tools program group.

▶ **See** "Viewing a Log," **p. 930**

■ *Send a message to administrators*. At a STOP condition, you can specify that users belonging to the Administrators group be sent an alert that a particular workstation has crashed. The Alerter service must be started in order for the automatic message to be sent to members of the Administrators group.

▶ **See** "Managing System Services and Devices," **p. 361**

■ *Write debugging information*. Probably the most important task to complete after your NT Workstation has crashed is determining how to prevent the STOP condition from occurring again. This may not be easy because the crash may have been a result of a unique sequence of events that may be difficult to reproduce. Regardless, a key to preventing a recurring crash is to understand why the crash occurred. NT Workstation can provide help in determining why the crash occurred. You can specify that a file be created when NT Workstation crashes that shows the contents of system memory. This information could be critical in determining why NT Workstation crashed. The file could point the finger at an irresponsible application, hardware device, device driver, or a particular process. You can specify that this file be created, as well as the name and location of the file.

■ *Reboot*. You can specify that NT Workstation automatically reboots after a STOP condition. This option is especially beneficial if a workstation shares important resources, such as printers or directories with other networked users. With this option turned on, those resources are available immediately after the crash rather than when the system is eventually manually rebooted. Selecting this option has two drawbacks:

- It is not immediately obvious that a Workstation has crashed if it immediately reboots on recovery.

- Less information is logged in the event log about what happened during a crash condition than is displayed on the screen, so you might want to copy some of this information down, which you will not be able to do if the system automatically reboots.

Part

III

Ch

12

To configure recovery options for NT Workstation after a crash, follow these steps:

1. Open the Start menu, and then choose Settings, Control Panel.

2. Choose the System applet, and then choose the Startup/Shutdown tab.

3. To write information to the system log about the event that preceded the STOP condition, click the Write an Event to the System Log check box. Otherwise, be sure that the check box is clear.

4. To send a message to users with Administrator rights when the workstation crashes, click the Send an Administrative Alert check box. Otherwise, be sure that the check box is clear.

5. To dump the contents of system memory to a file when NT Workstation crashes, check the Write Debugging Information To check box. If the name of the log file that appears in the edit box is satisfactory, move on to the next step. Otherwise, enter a name for the file in the edit box. You can precede the name of the file with the directory location where you would like the file created.

N O T E By default, NT Workstation proposes `%SystemRoot%\MEMORY.DMP` as the name and location of the file created for debugging purposes when NT Workstation crashes. The first portion of the name and location, `%SystemRoot%`, is an environment variable whose value is the root directory where NT Workstation files are installed. If NT Workstation is installed in a directory on your C drive named WINDOWS, then `%SystemRoot%MEMORY.DMP` equals C:\WINDOWS\MEMORY.DMP. ■

If you specify debugging information to be written to a file, when NT Workstation starts again after a crash, it attempts to create a file with the name specified in the edit box in the Recovery dialog box. If a file by that name already exists, NT Workstation deletes the original file only if the Overwrite Any Existing File check box is selected. Otherwise, a debugging file is created.

6. To specify that NT Workstation automatically reboots after a STOP condition, select the Automatically Reboot check box. Otherwise, to leave NT Workstation in its crashed state, be sure the check box is clear.

7. Choose OK.

Understanding what to do after NT Crashes

There are a few steps you should follow after Windows NT crashes. Though the chances are slim that NT will encounter a STOP condition, there are certainly a few things you can do after the crash to help debug the problem and prevent it from happening again:

- *Check the event log.* Review the event log for information as to why the crash occurred. The latest event shown in the log most likely is related to the crash.

  ▶ **See** "Viewing a Log," **p. 930**

- *Copy the memory dump file somewhere safe.* Be sure to specify the option to create a file dump of memory and other data when NT crashes. If NT crashes, copy the file (`%SystemRoot%\MEMORY.DMP`) to a safe location just in case the support engineers require the file. You can review the file yourself, if you choose. Use any text editor like Notepad to do so.

- *Try to reproduce the problem.* If you are truly interested in understanding why the crash occurs, you may want to reproduce the crash. Simply repeat the tasks and steps you completed, if this is possible, just before Windows NT crashed. If Windows NT crashes again, congratulations, you may have found a new career in software quality control. Record the steps that caused Windows NT to crash and report the problem to Microsoft.

Working with Environment Variables

Environment variables are pieces of data used by the operating system of a PC or by applications that run on it. The variables store information about the PC that helps applications and operating systems run properly on differently configured PCs. Environment variables make it easy for applications or operating systems to look at a common location for important information about the platform they are running on. Examples of environment variables include TEMP, which defines the name of the directory where temporary files are stored, and PROMPT, which defines the appearance of the command prompt.

Every environment variable has a label. The label helps NT Workstation and applications refer to its value. For example, the TEMP environment variable might have the value C:\TEMP. Even the PATH statement is an environment variable. Figure 12.6 shows all the environment variables in use on the computer that was used to write this chapter. Table 12.2 explains what the environment variables illustrated in the figure are used for.

FIG. 12.6
Environment variables can store different types of data, such as directory information or logical names of devices.

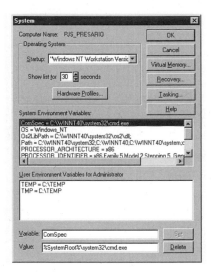

Table 12.2   Examples of Environment Variables

Item	Description
Path	Specifies the directories Windows NT searches to find files.
Prompt	Determines the format of the prompt that appears in the command prompt window.
Windows NT Directory	Specifies the main directory for Windows NT.
Type of Processor	Specifies the type of CPU installed on your computer.

Understanding Environment Variables in Windows NT Workstation

NT uses environment variables just as DOS does. Using environment variables retains compatibility for NT with legacy Windows and DOS applications. Windows NT uses three different types of environment variables:

- System
- User
- AUTOEXEC.BAT

The following three sections describe each type of environment variable used in NT Workstation.

System Environment Variables   System environment variables define information used by the NT operating system, such as the directory where Windows NT files are stored or the class of processor(s) installed on your computer. The PATH environment variable is also a system type variable. The values for system environment variables are the same regardless of the user logged on to the system. You never have to worry about whether a system variable has a value; each system environment variable gets assigned its value when the system starts up. Any application running under Windows NT can use a system environment variable if the application needs the information stored in the variable. A typical use is by login scripts, which is a special set of commands that are executed when you log on to certain networks.

User Environment Variables   User environment variables are stored for each login for the workstation. If you happen to log in to the same workstation on different occasions using a different login name and password, the user environment variables would be different. User environment variables store information for applications you run, such as working directories, or special pieces of data. Typically, software compilers require a number of environment variables to be able to create software program files.

AUTOEXEC.BAT Environment Variables   Windows NT Workstation maintains environment variables in AUTOEXEC.BAT to retain compatibility with DOS and Windows applications that store information in environment variables that appear in the file. Variables specified in AUTOEXEC.BAT are used only by applications that access that file.

N O T E The path Windows NT Workstation uses to find files and applications is based on the value of the path environment variable. The value of the Path variable starts with any path statement defined as a system environment variable. The user path environment variable is appended to the system, and the path from AUTOEXEC.BAT is added last. For example, let's say that the system environment variable for path is %SystemRoot%\system32;%SystemRoot%;C:\MSDEV\BIN, and the user environment variable for path is C:\SQL;C:\TEMP, the path statement in AUTOEXEC.BAT is C:\FUN, and Windows NT is install in a directory on your C-drive named WINNT40. Your path statement would be used as follows:

C:\WINNT40\system32;C:\WINNT40;C:\MSDEV\BIN;C:\SQL;C:\TEMP;
C:\FUN ■

Viewing and Modifying Environment Variables

You can see all the system environment variables and user environment variables in the System Properties dialog box (see fig. 12.7). The two list boxes store as many of each type of environment variables as are in use, and if more than seven of either type exist, scroll bars appear in the list boxes to help you navigate through the list. In the working area below the list boxes, you modify the values of the variables.

To display environment variables, follow these steps.

1. Open the Start menu, and then choose Settings, Control Panel.
2. Choose the System applet, and then choose the Environment tab.
3. Select the environment variable from either the System or User list boxes that appear in the middle of the dialog box. Notice that when you select any variable in either of the two lists, the label of the variable appears in the Variable edit box located at the bottom of the dialog box, and the current value of the variables appears in the Value edit box.

FIG. 12.7

The System Properties dialog box displays system and user environment variables and their values.

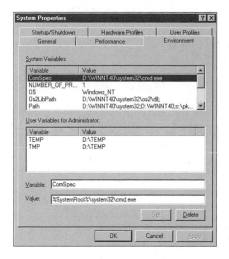

 There is an easy way to see the current value of all environment variables in use on your NT Workstation. Start the system prompt by opening the Start menu and choosing Programs, Command Prompt. Next, type **SET** and press Enter. All current environment variables and their values will appear on the screen. If the list is particularly long and the first variables scroll off the screen, use the |MORE parameter after SET to display environment variables one screen at a time.

N O T E The order in which environment variables are initialized is important to understand. System environment variables are set first, but they can be overridden by identically named user environment variables. AUTOEXEC.BAT variables are set last, but they never override variable values set at the system or user level. This is the rule for all environment variables except for path-type variables. ■

Part
III

Ch
12

Depending on the type of environment variable, you may be able to change the value of a variable, delete a variable, or add a new one. If your login belongs to the Administrators group, you can change the value of an existing system variable, add a new system variable, or delete one.

Unlike system environment variables, you can add and delete user environment variables at will, as well as change the values of existing variables. As for AUTOEXEC.BAT environment variables, you add, edit, and delete environment variables directly in the file. You can use the EDIT utility at the command prompt to make your changes.

TIP   You can use the SYSEDIT utility to modify AUTOEXEC.BAT. This utility originated in Windows 3.x and it is also part of Windows NT Workstation. The utility provides a handy interface for viewing and editing the four files critical to the configuration of a computer running Windows 3.x: CONFIG.SYS, AUTOEXEC.BAT, WIN.INI, and SYSTEM.INI. To start SYSEDIT, open the Start menu and choose <u>R</u>un. Next, in the Run dialog box that appears, enter **%SystemRoot%\SYSTEM32\SYSEDIT.EXE** and then choose OK. SYSEDIT works like NOTEPAD; you use Cut, Copy, and Paste to edit the files.

To modify the value of a system or user environment variable, follow these steps:

1. Open the Start menu, and then choose <u>S</u>ettings, <u>C</u>ontrol Panel.

2. Choose the System applet, and then choose the Environment tab.

3. Select the environment variable to modify from either the <u>S</u>ystem Variables list or the <u>U</u>ser Variables list. The caption above the User Variables list shows the name of the user for which the variables will be applied.

4. The label of the variable that you chose in step 3 appears in the <u>V</u>ariable edit box, and the current value of the variable appears in the V<u>a</u>lue edit box (refer to fig. 12.7).

5. Edit the text that appears in the V<u>a</u>lue edit box. Next choose S<u>e</u>t and then OK. The environment variable is set with the new value.

To add a new user environment variable, follow these steps:

1. Open the Start menu, and then choose <u>S</u>ettings, <u>C</u>ontrol Panel.

2. Choose the System applet, and then choose the Environment tab.

3. Select any environment variable from the <u>U</u>ser Variables list. The name and value of the variable you select appear in the <u>V</u>ariable and V<u>a</u>lue edit boxes that appear at the bottom of the dialog box.

4. Edit the contents of those dialog boxes so that they show the name for your new variable and its value.

5. Choose S<u>e</u>t and then OK.

Specifying the Default Operating System

As you may have figured out by this time, you can run another operating system on your computer in addition to Windows NT, such as Windows 95 or DOS. These other operating systems do not come with NT Workstation; you have to acquire and install them yourself. When you have more than one operating system loaded on your computer, you can choose which operating system NT Workstation should load by default. This can be useful if you know you will be working with a specific operating system over a period of time and you would like that operating system automatically loaded when you start the computer.

N O T E After you have installed Windows NT on a computer with another operating system, when the computer boots, Windows NT is always the first operating system listed on the boot menu. The content and order of items in the boot menu is determined by a special file named BOOT.INI. ■

To specify the default operating system on your computer, follow these steps:

1. Open the Start menu, and then choose Settings, Control Panel.
2. Choose the System applet, and then choose the Startup/Shutdown tab.
3. From the Startup drop-down list, select the operating system you want to start by default.
4. You can also specify how long Windows NT Workstation should wait at boot time for you to select an operating system before it loads the default operating system. Enter the time in seconds (maximum of 999 seconds) in the Show List for n Seconds scroll list.
5. Choose OK to save changes.

Part
III

Ch
12

From Here...

By now, you've learned about Windows NT's memory requirements and how to configure memory (including hard drive space, how Windows NT manages more than one application running at one time, and how to configure environment variables). In addition, you've picked up information on how to prepare NT for a system crash. In all, you probably have learned much about some of the more complicated parts of the NT Workstation system.

The following chapters can probably provide with more of the same type of information:

- Chapter 1, "Understanding Windows NT Workstation"
- Chapter 16, "Managing the Boot Process"
- Chapter 32, "Using the Event Viewer"
- Chapter 33, "Optimizing Windows NT Workstation Performance"

CHAPTER 13

Configuring Windows NT Workstation for Multimedia

by Gregory J Root

Windows NT 4.0 brings many improvements to the interface and usability of the entire operating system. You'll soon discover that the multimedia capabilities of Windows NT were not left untouched. Configuring any multimedia aspect of Windows NT has become much easier. From just two control panels, you'll be able to add, configure, and remove multimedia devices. Windows NT also provides several multimedia accessories. These accessories allow you to listen to your favorite audio CDs, record audio, or play any type of multimedia file.

Understanding multimedia drivers in Windows NT

Before diving into the configuration of Windows NT multimedia, an understanding of multimedia drivers will make the configuration process much more simple.

Adding a multimedia device

Learn how to install a multimedia device into your system case and select the correct software driver. Find out how to protect yourself and your investment in the new hardware.

Learn how to configure your multimedia devices

When you add new hardware into your system, you may need to go back and change settings for existing hardware. Learn areas to watch out for when working with hard drives.

Changing multimedia settings

You can customize how multimedia files are played on your computer. Learn tips to make sound enhance your office setting, not overpower it.

Understanding Multimedia and Drivers

Before diving into using multimedia in Windows NT, a basic understanding of what multimedia is will help you understand your options when it comes time to add or configure your multimedia devices. Knowing how Plug and Play hardware interacts with Windows NT will also be extremely useful. Also knowing how to find what resource settings the multimedia devices are using will come in handy when trying to troubleshoot problems.

New Features in Windows NT 4.0

Even though not many technical multimedia features have been added to Windows NT 4.0, existing capabilities are now grouped together more logically. But what happened to some of the hot new multimedia capabilities that everyone is talking about? Some have already been added to Windows NT; others are yet to come. The next few sections cover the most popular topics.

Video for Windows   The latest Video for Windows 1.1 was introduced in Windows NT 3.5 and provides true 32-bit throughput for displaying and hearing video clips. You get better full-screen video performance from these changes.

Also, the Volume Control on the taskbar works in conjunction with a video being played. In previous versions, you had to stop the video, adjust the sound to a new level, and restart the video. Speaking of sound, the new version of the Audio Compression Manager provides better audio performance because it uses less memory.

Display Control Interface   The Display Control Interface (DCI) was introduced in Windows NT 3.51. The DCI is important because it greatly improves video playback quality and speed. By using a display driver that supports DCI, programs are allowed to send information directly to the video card rather than first into RAM and then the video card. This also directly affects the performance of Video for Windows.

▶ **See** "Configuring Your Video Display," **p. 284**

MIDI   Although MIDI has been a part of Windows NT, certain performance improvements were made in Windows NT 3.51. These enhancements allow you to listen to more complex MIDI files without notes dropping out in the middle of playback. In Windows NT 4.0, the interface for configuring MIDI has been improved. See also "MIDI Settings" later in this chapter.

Joysticks Unfortunately, native support for joysticks has not yet been added to Windows NT. Until this is added, you will have to continue to use the drivers provided by your joystick manufacturer. Alternately, most games provide direct access to the joystick.

Plug and Play

Plug and Play is a new computer BIOS specification that allows you to install new hardware without having to configure jumpers for I/O, DMA, and IRQ settings. This removes the usual hassle of trying to find available IRQ, I/O, and DMA settings among the ones being used by other devices and cards in your system. After the computer is turned on, the operating system senses the new hardware, sets the correct configuration parameters, and installs the appropriate driver.

Plug and Play has been around for about two years. It is becoming more and more popular every day. In fact, most new model multimedia cards come with Plug and Play support. Windows NT does not yet support the Plug and Play BIOS standard. Therefore, it will not be able to support Plug and Play devices directly. You'll need to configure a new device with a software setup utility that comes with it. This utility could be a DOS-based or Windows-based application. In either case, you must run the utility and manually set the configuration parameters. Then you can install the Windows NT drivers for the new device.

Understanding MCI Devices

Windows NT's Media Control Interface (MCI) is a layer that sits between the hardware devices (such as sound cards and CD-ROM drives) and the software programs (such as the CD Player accessory). The MCI layer exists to make multimedia applications not depend on specific drivers and resource settings to work. MCI lays out several major device types, including waveaudio (from WAV files), digital video (from AVI files), CD Audio (from CDs), vcr (from a video tape recorder), and laserdisc (from laser disc players).

Each hardware manufacturer creates a driver that complies with the MCI specification. These drivers specify the type of MCI device and its capabilities. Figure

Part
III

Ch
13

13.1 lists the MCI drivers that come with Windows NT. You can pick out the MCI devices by the MCI prefix or (Media Control) suffix.

FIG. 13.1
Windows NT comes
with a default set of
MCI devices.

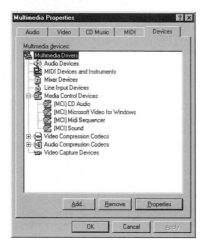

If you don't see a device you need (like a VCR or laser disc player), you can contact your hardware manufacturer for the latest drivers. Most manufacturers have forums on CompuServe or Web sites on the Internet. Use your favorite search engine on the Internet to find them.

Understanding Audio and Video Codecs

A *codec* is an algorithm to handle the *co*mpression and *dec*ompression of audio and video data. The codec improves the capability to transfer large amounts of multimedia data across a smaller bandwidth. Take for example a Video for Windows clip. A 320 x 240 pixel video playing at 15 frames per second would require transfer of 3 megabytes of data each second. The difficulty is that the typical CD-ROM player can't transfer more than 1.2 megabytes of data each second. Therefore, the data needs to be stored in a compressed (smaller) format and then uncompressed in memory after it has been transferred off the CD-ROM.

Windows NT Diagnostics and Multimedia

Typically when adding new hardware to your computer, the most difficult task is finding available settings for the IRQ, I/O address, and DMA channel. The

Windows NT Diagnostics program greatly assists you in this task. You can quickly determine what resource settings have already been used. The choices for your new device are shown clearly.

N O T E Until Plug and Play BIOS support is added to Windows NT, finding available settings will continue to require changing jumpers or running separate configuration utilities. When Windows NT supports Plug and Play BIOS, all you'll need to do is change a few settings on a dialog box, without removing the device from the computer! ■

To start the Windows NT Diagnostics program, select from the Start menu, Programs, Administrative Tools (Common), Windows NT Diagnostics. The Windows NT Diagnostics dialog box appears (see fig. 13.2).

FIG. 13.2
The Windows NT Diagnostics application provides complete information on every aspect of your system.

N O T E See also Chapter 33, "Using the Diagnostics Tool," for full details on the rest of the pages in the Windows NT Diagnostics application. ■

Viewing Resource Usage with Windows NT Diagnostics

The Windows NT Diagnostics program can tell you a lot about your computer. When dealing with multimedia, the Resources page provides the most relevant information. For example, to find out what other devices are using a particular IRQ setting, select the Resources page and click the IRQ button. As listed in Figure

13.3, each used IRQ shows the Device using the IRQ, the Bus it resides on, and which Type of bus (usually ISA or PCI).

 T I P You can sort the list by clicking the column name. For example, to sort the IRQ list by device name, click the Device column heading. To sort it in reverse, click the Device column heading one more time.

FIG. 13.3
The Resources page shows IRQ settings already in use by other devices.

Knowing ahead of time which devices use which I/O ports can also speed up the installation of a new device in your computer. An I/O port (also known as an *I/O address*) is a location in memory that allows the operating system to send and receive data to the device.

Used Input/Output (I/O) ports can also be displayed using the Windows NT Diagnostics application. Click the I/O Port button at the bottom of the Resources page (see fig. 13.4). For each device listed, the Address Range, the Bus it resides on, and the Type of bus are displayed.

Direct Memory Access (DMA) channels are also shown by the diagnostics program. DMA channels provide a way for programs to directly access the memory on a peripheral without requiring any time from the CPU. Sound cards usually require at least one DMA channel.

To view which DMA channels are in use, click the DMA button at the bottom of the Resource page (see fig. 13.5).

FIG. 13.4
Clicking the I/O Port button on the Resources page shows I/O address ranges in use by other devices.

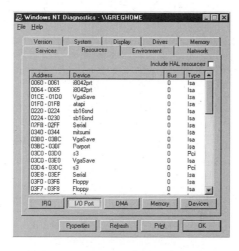

FIG. 13.5
Knowing about used DMA channels helps when setting up a sound card.

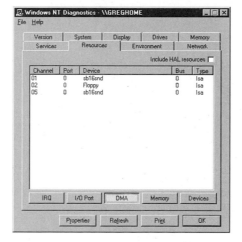

Upper memory ranges in use by devices can also affect your installation of a new multimedia card. The operating system uses the memory range to transfer large amounts of data back and forth with the device.

Click the Memory button in the lower portion of the Resources page to view which memory ranges are in use (see fig. 13.6). Shown for each Address range are the Devices using the address, the Bus, and the bus Type on which the devices reside. If you are installing a video capture card, this information comes in handy.

Printing a hard copy of the resources used by the devices in your computer will greatly assist you when a new device needs to be installed in the computer. You then can compare the choices on the new device with the settings shown not to be in use on the report. To print a report, perform the following steps:

1. Click Print in the Windows NT Diagnostics dialog box. The Create Report dialog box appears, as shown in figure 13.7.

FIG. 13.6

Memory ranges in use are displayed by clicking Memory on the Resources page.

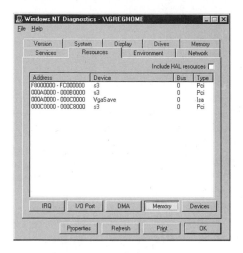

FIG. 13.7

Having a printout of the used resources can assist you to install a new device when the computer is turned off.

2. Make the report contain information on just the current tab. You can do this by selecting the Current tab radio button in the Scope group box.

3. To conserve paper, only a Summary Detail Level is needed to obtain the used resources.

4. Choose the Default Printer as the destination for your report. You can choose a File or the Clipboard as the destination of your report, but you need to turn off your computer to install the new device, so a hard copy is needed.

Adding a Multimedia Device

Two major steps outline the installation of a new multimedia device in your computer. First, you must install the hardware into your system case. Take certain precautions while performing this task to prevent damage to your new hardware and prevent injury to yourself. After the hardware is installed, you must tell Windows NT how to communicate with the new device by specifying the driver to use. The next few sections lead you through these steps.

Installing the Hardware

Before you begin installing the hardware, try to obtain the following list of tools. These tools can usually be found in a small "PC toolkit" sold at most computer stores for about $30:

Small Phillips screwdriver
Small flat-blade screwdriver
3/16-inch hex-nut driver
1/4-inch hex-nut driver
Needle-nosed pliers
Tweezers
Claw-type parts grabber

The screwdrivers and hex-nut drivers are used to open the computer's case and install the multimedia device. The needle-nosed pliers come in handy to move jumpers around on any adapter card that comes with your device. No matter how hard you try when installing the device, you'll probably drop a screw or jumper inside the computer case. Use the tweezers and claw grabber to reach for them in places where your fingers don't fit.

Part
III

Ch
13

> **CAUTION**
>
> You might be considering using a cordless hand drill rather than a screwdriver. Do *not* use one. It is very easy to strip a screw or mounting hole.

After you've gathered the necessary tools, you're ready to install your multimedia device.

You install your device just like you would install any other adapter, such as a modem or network card. This is a four-step process:

1. Identify hardware settings.
2. Remove the system unit cover.
3. Install the multimedia device.
4. Replace the system unit cover.

You'll want to use the steps presented in this chapter. They include important safety precautions to protect you and your investment in your computer.

Determining Hardware Settings   If your multimedia device is a Plug and Play compliant card, you need to use the software configuration utility that came with it. Windows NT doesn't support the Plug and Play BIOS, yet. Follow the manufacturer's instructions on how to change the settings.

If your multimedia device isn't Plug and Play compliant, you need to manually configure some settings for the computer to find it. You must identify the base I/O address (or I/O port), Interrupt ReQuest channel (IRQ), and base RAM address. Most computers usually have certain settings available. Use the steps earlier in this chapter in "Viewing Resource Usage with Windows NT Diagnostics" to obtain a printout of the specific settings available on your computer. Compare these to the settings that can be used by the multimedia device as identified in the manufacturer's documentation. Write down an available setting for each.

If you haven't yet installed Windows NT, then use table 13.1 to determine an available base I/O address, table 13.2 for a free IRQ setting, and table 13.3 for an available base RAM address.

Table 13.1   Base I/O Addresses Commonly Taken by Other Devices

I/O Address Range	Standard Usage
000-0FF	Unavailable for use by devices
1F0-1F7	Hard disk controller
200-207	Gameport joystick
220-22F	Sound card
240-24F	Sound card
2F8-2FF	Communications port (COM2)

I/O Address Range	Standard Usage
330-33F	MIDI adapter (sometimes part of sound card)
376-376	Hard disk controller
378-37A	Printer port (LPT1)
3B0-3DF	Display adapter
3F0-3F7	Floppy disk controller
3F8-3FF	Communications port (COM1)
4D0-4D1	PCI bus
CF8-CFA	PCI bus

Table 13.2   IRQ Lines Commonly Used by Other Devices in Your System

IRQ	Standard Usage
0	System timer
1	Keyboard
2	Programmable interrupt controller
3	Communications port (COM2)
4	Communications port (COM1)
5	Printer port (LPT2)
6	Floppy disk controller
7	Printer port (LPT1)
8	Real-time clock
9	Used by IRQ2
10	Usually available (sometimes a sound card)
11	Usually available
12	PS/2 port mouse
13	Numeric data processor (math coprocessor)
14	Hard disk controller
15	Usually available

Part
III

Ch
13

Table 13.3 Common RAM Addresses in Use by Other Devices	
RAM Address Range	Standard Usage
0A0000-0C7FFF	Video adapter RAM
0E8000-0EBFFF	PCI bus

Finally, you need to configure the multimedia device to use these settings. If your device is an older style, you may need to move jumpers on the device to specific settings. Consult your manufacturer's manual for these settings.

Removing the System Unit Cover   After you've determined the hardware settings for your new multimedia device, you're ready to open up the system unit cover. This exposes the expansion slots and drive bays in which you'll install any cards or CD-ROM drives, respectively.

To remove the system unit cover:

1. Gather your tools and multimedia devices at the computer and situate yourself in a comfortable position. Don't shuffle your feet around while you work because it causes static electricity.

CAUTION

Static electricity is one of the leading causes of damage to electronic components. So when you begin working on the computer, try not to move around too much. Avoid plastic, vinyl, Styrofoam, and fur in the work area. Consider buying a disposable grounding wrist strap for under five dollars at your local electronics store.

2. Shut down the computer, turn off the power, and touch a metal part of the system unit case to discharge any static electricity you may have built up. Now, unplug the power cord from the back of the system unit.

If you purchased a disposable grounding wrist strap or have a reusable model, now is the time to properly ground yourself. Follow the manufacturer's instructions on how to apply it and attach it to a valid ground source.

3. Turn the system unit around so that you're facing the rear of the unit. Locate the five to seven screws around the border of the case that hold the system unit cover in place.

NOTE Computer systems come in a wide variety of configurations. You may not have screws holding the system unit cover in place. Be sure to consult the documentation that came with your system. ▪

4. Use the 1/4-inch hex-nut driver to remove the cover screws.

5. Slide the cover off the system unit until it stops. Certain models slide forward, but others slide backward. Many models don't slide open all the way.

CAUTION

Don't pound or sharply strike the system unit cover. You may damage the hard drive inside the computer.

 TIP If the case won't move very easily, work your way around the back edge of the case using a flat-head screwdriver to gently pry it open. Once you've started the case moving a little bit, you should be able to slide it open until it stops.

6. Lift up the front of the cover and remove it from the chassis.

You're now ready to install the multimedia device in an available expansion slot or drive bay.

Installing the Multimedia Device To install a multimedia card in the computer, you need to locate an available expansion slot on the motherboard. Most computers' motherboards are arranged similarly. However, you need to know what type of slot your multimedia card requires.

Most multimedia cards today require either an ISA or PCI expansion slot on the motherboard. The packaging in which the card arrived should clearly state which type it is. However, if the packaging or documentation is unclear, here is an easy way to tell the difference. A PCI card has a two-part connector on its edge approximately 4 1/8 inches long. An ISA card has a two-part connector as well, but its connector is longer at 5 5/16 inches. The slot in which you insert the card matches these dimensions.

Part
III

Ch
13

To install the card, follow these steps:

1. Using the appropriate screwdriver, remove the blank metal bracket from the back side of the system unit at the expansion slot you expect to use. Set the screw aside to be replaced in a few steps.

2. Carefully remove the card from its anti-static bag.

CAUTION

When you work with the card, handle it only by the metal bracket or edges. Try not to touch the connector that plugs into the expansion slot or any of the circuits or chips on the card.

3. Slowly press the card into the expansion slot (PCI or ISA).

You may need to press in on the bottom of the metal bracket so that it doesn't get stuck on the case. You may also need to wiggle the card from front to back a little bit to make it go into the slot. However, don't tilt the card side-ways. If you do, it may break the electrical connections inside the board, rendering it unusable.

4. To secure the card's metal bracket to the system case, replace the screw you removed in step 1 of this section.

CAUTION

Don't over-tighten the screw. If you strip the mounting hole threads, any other card you install won't be securely fastened. When you feel resistance, give it only another half-turn.

If you're installing a CD-ROM drive, follow these additional steps:

1. Using the flat-head screwdriver, remove the blank plate covering the front opening from which the CD-ROM drive will protrude.

2. Carefully remove the CD-ROM drive from its anti-static bag.

3. Slowly slide the CD-ROM drive into the empty drive bay.

4. To secure the CD-ROM drive to the system case, use the screws provided with the CD-ROM drive.

You're now ready to replace the system cover. If you had to rearrange jumpers on the multimedia card to different settings from the factory defaults, this is your last chance to write down the resource settings for base I/O address, IRQ, and base RAM address. You need them when you install the software driver.

Replacing the System Unit Cover   Now that the multimedia device is installed, you're ready to close everything up. Replacing the cover is practically the reverse of removing it. To replace the system unit cover, follow these steps:

1. Gently set the cover on the chassis. Make sure that the guide rails on the inside edges of the cover are properly seated.

2. Slide the cover back onto the system unit until it stops. Certain models slide forward, but others slide backward.

   If the cover doesn't seem to close all the way, don't force it closed. Open the cover slightly and check around all the edges. Make sure that all the tabs line up with their intended slots and that no cable connectors from inside the computer are getting caught.

3. Use the 1/4-inch hex-nut driver to replace the cover screws.

4. Replace the power cord into the back of the system unit.

 T I P   If you are using a grounding strap, you can safely remove it from the grounding source at this point.

N O T E   Don't forget to plug in the audio output of the CD-ROM drive to the AUX or Line In on your sound card. See the manufacturer's instructions for details. ■

Specifying the Driver

The driver makes the link between the multimedia device and the operating system. To install *kernel drivers* (drivers that access hardware), you must be logged on to the computer as a member of the Administrators group. The drivers you install will be available to all users.

The procedure to specify the sound card driver is different from the procedure for a CD-ROM drive. To specify the sound card driver, you'll use the Multimedia control panel. For a CD-ROM drive, you'll use the SCSI Adapters control panel. The next two sections lead you through the process.

Part
III

Ch
13

Specifying a Sound Card Driver   Each sound card has its own unique driver. However, the process to specify a sound card driver is almost the same for all types. To specify the sound card driver, follow these steps:

1. Open the Multimedia control panel. Select the Devices page on the Multimedia Properties dialog box, as shown in figure 13.8.

2. From the Devices page, click Add. A List of Drivers appears (see fig. 13.9).

FIG. 13.8

The Devices page of the Multimedia Properties dialog box enables you to Add a new device driver.

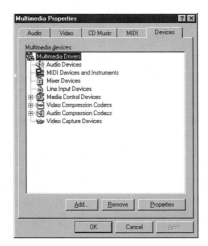

FIG. 13.9

Select the sound card type from the List of Drivers.

3. Select the name of your sound card in the List of Drivers, for example, a Sound Blaster 16 card. If your sound card isn't listed or you have an updated driver, choose Unlisted or Updated Driver at the top of the list, and you will be prompted for the location containing the driver.

4. You then are asked to insert the Windows NT CD-ROM (see fig. 13.10). In the dialog box of figure 13.10, you should enter the drive letter of the CD-ROM and the CPU type of your computer. Valid CPU types are I386, ALPHA, MIPS, and PPC. For example, if your computer is an IBM PC clone and your CD-ROM drive is F:, you would enter: **F:\I386**.

N O T E   The I386 directory is also used for 486, Pentium, and Pentium Pro class CPUs. The I386 is the generic name for them all. ■

CAUTION

Be sure you are using the latest drivers from your sound card manufacturer. If you don't, a newer Plug and Play sound card may not function correctly under Windows NT.

FIG. 13.10
Enter the location of the driver files for your sound card.

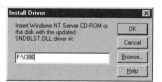

5. After the necessary files are copied to your Windows NT installation, a dialog box appears that is specific to the sound card you are installing. Typically, you are asked to select the base I/O Address first (see fig. 13.11). Click Continue.

FIG. 13.11
Select the I/O Address.

Part III
Ch 13

6. Enter the rest of the parameters as necessary to complete the installation. These were the values you wrote down when you installed the sound card in the system case or when you ran the configuration utility.

   In the Sound Blaster 16 example and most other sound cards (see fig. 13.12), you also need to enter the Interrupt (IRQ), a DMA channel (the Sound Blaster 16 has two), and an MPU401 I/O Address to play MIDI files on the sound card.

FIG. 13.12
Select the rest of the settings for the sound card.

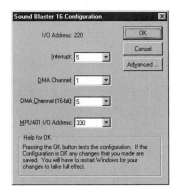

7. Click OK to complete the installation of the driver. When prompted, click Restart Now to start using your sound card. Your sound card won't work until you do.

If you also installed a CD-ROM drive when you installed the sound card, now would be a good time to specify its driver, too. When prompted to restart the computer, instead click Don't Restart Now. Use the next section to specify the CD-ROM driver.

Specifying a CD-ROM Driver   No matter what brand or make of CD-ROM drive you purchased—or if the CD-ROM drive was not detected when you installed Windows NT—the procedure for specifying the CD-ROM driver is the same. To identify which driver you want to use, follow these steps:

1. Open the SCSI Adapters control panel. Select the Drivers page on the SCSI Adapters control panel, as shown in figure 13.13.

2. To add a new CD-ROM driver, click Add. The Select SCSI Adapter dialog box appears as shown in figure 13.14. Select the make and model of your CD-ROM interface card.

FIG. 13.13
The Drivers page of the SCSI Adapters control panel enables you to Add a new CD-ROM driver.

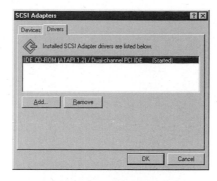

FIG. 13.14
Select the make and model of the CD-ROM interface card from the list.

 If you can't find your CD-ROM driver in the list and you don't have a disk from the CD-ROM drive manufacturer, be sure to read the README.TXT file on the Windows NT CD-ROM in the \DRVLIB\STORAGE\RETIRED\CPU directory. It gives instructions on how to install a driver for retired drivers that won't be supported beyond this release of Windows NT. The CPU in the directory path stands for the type of processor of your computer. The valid choices are ALPHA, MIPS, and I386.

3. Usually, you need to restart the computer to access the CD-ROM drive. When prompted, click OK to restart the computer and complete the driver installation. When your computer restarts, you can access audio or data CD-ROMs.

Multiple Hardware Configurations

Sometimes, you won't need to access your multimedia devices. A docking station with multimedia capabilities is a prime example. By not loading the drivers for the sound card and the CD-ROM drive, Windows NT can boot much faster. By default, Windows NT repeatedly attempts to connect to devices that aren't available just in

Part
III

Ch

13

case they weren't quite ready the first time. However, in the case of a docking station, the devices don't even exist. So by creating a second hardware configuration, you skip the startup of the multimedia drivers.

To create a new hardware configuration, follow these steps:

1. Open the System control panel and select the Hardware Profiles tab, as shown in figure 13.15.

FIG. 13.15
Select the Hardware
Profiles tab to start
creating a new
profile.

2. The current hardware profiles are listed under the Available Hardware Profiles (see fig. 13.16). To create a new profile, select one from the list that will be the model for the new profile.

FIG. 13.16
Select a hardware
profile to model your
new profile after and
click Copy to create
the new profile.

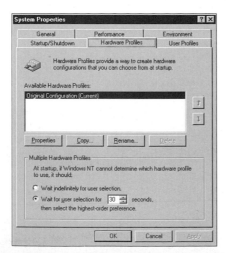

3. Click Copy. Type in a new name for the profile in the To edit box shown in figure 13.17.

FIG. 13.17
Create a descriptive name for your new hardware configuration.

TIP Like the example, use a descriptive name to identify how this hardware configuration is different from the other configurations. Don't name it **Hardware Configuration #2** or something similar.

4. Click the three OK buttons to save your changes.

You're not quite finished. Now you need to specify which devices don't belong to the new hardware configuration. To do this, you need to access the control panels and use these steps:

1. Open the Devices control panel. Select the device name you don't want to be included in the hardware configuration.

TIP If you aren't sure what the device name is, see "Viewing Resource Usage with Windows NT Diagnostics" previously in this chapter to identify its name.

2. Click the HW Profiles button shown in figure 13.18.

FIG. 13.18
Select the device to exclude from the configuration and click HW Profiles.

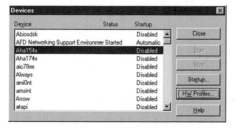

3. From the Device dialog box (see fig. 13.19), select from the list the profile name you just created. Click Disable to remove the device from the configuration. Click Enable to add the device to the hardware configuration.

FIG. 13.19
Click <u>D</u>isable to
remove the device
from or <u>E</u>nable to add
the device to the
configuration.

4. Click OK to save your changes. If you have another device to remove, go
   back to step 3. Otherwise, you're finished.

The next time you start your computer, you are presented with a menu listing the
defined hardware configurations. In the example in this chapter, if you've un-
docked your computer, you would select the No Multimedia configuration. However, if you are starting your laptop and it has been docked, you would select the
Original Configuration option on startup.

N O T E The section "Managing the Boot Process" in Chapter 16 gives more details on
managing multiple hardware configurations. ▨

Configuring Multimedia Devices

The Multimedia control panel gives you quick access to the resource settings of
sound cards and MCI devices. The SCSI Adapters control panel allows you to view
and change the resource settings of your CD-ROM drive and adapter card. You
may want to change the configuration of a multimedia device already in your system because you are about to add another device that may conflict.

To get to the SCSI Adapters control panel, do the following:

1. Open the Start menu and choose <u>S</u>ettings, <u>C</u>ontrol Panel.

2. Double-click the SCSI Adapters icon to display the control panel (see fig.
   13.20).

From here, you can view information about your CD-ROM drive. You also can add
a new CD-ROM drive or remove an existing one.

FIG. 13.20
CD-ROM drive information can be viewed and changed from the SCSI Adapters control panel.

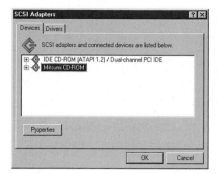

To get to the Multimedia control panel, do the following:

1. Open the Start menu and choose Settings, Control Panel.
2. Double-click the Multimedia icon to display the control panel.

   You can view many different aspects of multimedia on your computer. However, you need to get to the resource information on the Devices page as seen in figure 13.21.

FIG. 13.21
Select the Devices page to view information about the sound card resources.

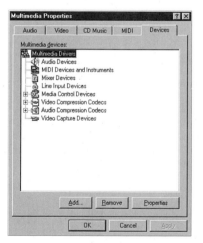

Part
III

Ch
13

The following section shows you how to change the settings of either your CD-ROM drive or your sound card.

Changing Resource Settings of Multimedia Devices

Changing which resources are used by a multimedia device involves more than just changing a few settings on a dialog box. You must first find out which settings are available for use. Previously in this chapter, the section "Viewing Resource Usage with Windows NT Diagnostics" describes how to generate a report on all the used resource settings.

Changing Settings for a CD-ROM Drive   To change a CD-ROM drive's resource settings, the SCSI Adapters control panel is used. To make changes (to a Mitsumi CD-ROM drive, in the following example), follow these steps:

> **CAUTION**
>
> Your hard drive's drivers and resource settings are also located in this control panel. Be sure you've properly identified which SCSI adapter has your CD-ROM attached before proceeding with any changes. You could accidentally change your hard drive's parameters.

1. Open the SCSI Adapters control panel. The SCSI Adapters control panel appears similar to figure 13.21.

2. From the list, select the SCSI adapter to which your CD-ROM drive is attached—for example, the Mitsumi CD-ROM.

3. Click Properties to view the CD-ROM's properties dialog box.

4. Click the Resources page to view the resources being used by the CD-ROM. You see a dialog box similar to the Mitsumi CD-ROM properties sheet shown in figure 13.22. Select the Resource Type you want to change.

FIG. 13.22
You can change the resource settings of the selected CD-ROM in the Resources page of the properties sheet.

5. In the Change Settings dialog box, you can change the current setting to a new value. Depending on which Resource Type you choose, a different dialog box appears. When you're finished making the change, click OK.

N O T E If the Change Settings button is disabled as in the example, then the settings for this CD-ROM cannot be changed. ▧

6. You are prompted to restart your computer for the changes to take effect. Click Yes to finish the changes.

Changing Settings for a Sound Card   To change a sound card's resource settings, the Multimedia control panel is used. To make changes (to a Sound Blaster 16 card, for example), follow these steps:

1. Open the Multimedia control panel. The Multimedia control panel appears similar to figure 13.21.

2. Select the Devices page on the Multimedia control panel. Double-click the Audio Devices to display the installed sound cards.

 If you double-click and get the Audio Devices Properties sheet, check to see if a plus sign is in front of the Audio Devices line. If a plus sign isn't there, a sound card hasn't been installed. See the section "Adding a Multimedia Device" earlier in this chapter.

3. Select the name of your sound card. In this example, select Creative Labs Sound Blaster 1.X, Pro, 16.

4. Click Properties to view the sound card's properties sheet. Then, click Settings on the properties sheet to start changing the settings. The next few dialog boxes are different depending on your sound card. In this example, you first need to confirm the I/O Address (see fig. 13.23).

5. To access the rest of the Sound Blaster 16 card's settings, click Continue. You see a dialog box similar to the Sound Blaster 16 Configuration dialog box shown in figure 13.24. Make the changes necessary to the configuration.

6. When you're finished making the changes, click OK.

7. You are prompted to restart your computer for the changes to take effect. Click Yes to finish the changes.

Part

III

Ch

13

FIG. 13.23
For a Sound Blaster 16 card, confirm the I/O Address first.

FIG. 13.24
You can change the resource settings of the Sound Blaster 16 card in its configuration dialog box.

If you find that changing the settings didn't resolve your problem, maybe you are using the wrong driver. To learn how to change the driver for your multimedia device, read the next section.

Changing the Driver

In some cases, you need to change the driver of your multimedia device. You might need to do this because you received an upgraded driver. Or, you might have accidentally installed the wrong driver. In any case, the next two sections lead you through changing drivers for a CD-ROM drive and a sound card.

ON THE WEB

You can get updated drivers from Creative Lab's WWW site:

http://www.creativelabs.com

If you have a Media Vision sound card, try their site at:

http://www.mediavis.com

Compaq sound card drivers are available at:

http://www.compaq.com

Changing a CD-ROM Driver   Changing the CD-ROM driver is a simple two-part process. You must remove the existing driver and then install the new one. The following steps show you how:

1. Access the SCSI Adapters control panel and select the Drivers page, as shown in figure 13.13.

CAUTION

Your hard drive's drivers and resource settings are also located in this control panel. Be sure you've properly identified which SCSI adapter has your CD-ROM attached before proceeding with any changes. You could accidentally delete your hard drive's driver.

2. Highlight the name of the driver you want to remove. Click Remove to take out the driver.

3. Click OK to save your change. You must reboot your computer before you can specify a new driver.

4. When your computer has rebooted, reopen the SCSI Adapters control panel. Click the Drivers page again.

5. To specify a new driver, follow the instructions under "Specifying a CD-ROM Driver" previously in this chapter.

Changing a Sound Card Driver   Changing a sound card driver is a simple two-part process. You must remove the existing driver and then install the new one. The following steps show you how:

1. Open the Multimedia control panel. The Multimedia control panel appears similar to figure 13.21.

2. Select the Devices page on the Multimedia control panel. Select Audio Devices from the Multimedia devices list and click Properties to display the installed sound cards.

TIP   If you double-click and nothing happens, check to see if a plus sign is in front of the Audio Devices line. If a plus sign isn't there, a sound card hasn't been installed. See "Adding a Multimedia Device" earlier in this chapter.

Part
III

Ch
13

3. Highlight the name of the sound card you want to remove. Click Remove to take out the driver.

4. Click OK to save your change. You must reboot your computer before you can specify a new driver.

5. When your computer has rebooted, reopen the Multimedia control panel. Click the Devices page again.

6. To specify a new driver, follow the instructions under "Specifying a Sound Card Driver" previously in this chapter.

Changing Multimedia Settings

While working with your multimedia devices, you may want to customize or change the way multimedia files work on your machine. For example, you may want to adjust the recording quality for audio or make Video for Windows files play back on the entire screen. The next sections steps you through how to make these changes.

Audio Settings

While listening to audio clips or audio CD-ROMs, you might have noticed that the volume was too low. Or, you might want to decrease the recording quality of the audio clips you are making because they are taking up too much hard drive space. In either of these cases, you'll want to change the audio settings of your sound card.

You can change the audio playback settings by following these steps:

1. Open the Multimedia control panel. Click the Audio page if it isn't already open (see fig. 13.25).

2. To adjust the playback volume, move the Volume slider to the left to lower the volume or to the right to make the volume higher.

3. If you have more than one sound card in your computer, select which one is the Preferred Device. You want to make this selection especially if a certain software package supports specific sound cards.

FIG. 13.25

The Audio page of the Multimedia control panel gives access to many different settings.

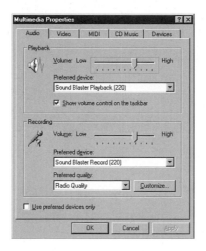

 T I P If you haven't already done so, check Show Volume Control on the taskbar. Then, you won't have to keep coming back to the Multimedia control panel to turn down the volume every time the phone rings.

You can change the audio recording settings by following these steps:

1. To adjust the overall recording volume, move the Volume slider to the left to lower the input volume or to the right to amplify the incoming sound and make the recording level high.

2. To change which device will be tried first to record audio, change the Preferred Device drop-down list to the desired sound card.

3. To change the quality of the recordings you'll make, change the Recording Quality to the level desired. Remember, the higher the recording quality, the more hard drive space is used. If the clip is recorded at a lower quality, the same duration of the sound clip takes up much less disk space.

4. To make a custom recording quality, click Customize. If you don't want to create a custom quality, skip to step 7.

5. In the Customize dialog box (see fig. 13.26), select the desired Format (also known as the codec) and Attributes.

6. Click Save As and enter a name for the new quality. Click OK to use this quality setting.

Part

III

Ch

13

FIG. 3.26
You can customize the recording quality with a Format and its Attributes.

7. If a certain application requires that you use the devices you've previously specified for playback and recording, check Use Preferred Devices Only at the bottom of the Multimedia Properties sheet.

8. When complete, click OK to save your changes and close the Multimedia Properties dialog box.

If you want to make other multimedia changes, don't click OK. Instead, the next several sections show you how to change the Video, MIDI, and CD Music settings.

Video Settings

While watching a video clip, you may have noticed that the picture was too small and you couldn't see it. Or it may have been too big and many of the frames were skipped, or it was really grainy. You may want to consider changing the video playback properties of your computer.

You can change the video playback settings by following these steps:

1. Open the Multimedia control panel. Click the Video page if it isn't already open (see fig. 13.27).

2. Choose how big the playback window will be by selecting the portion of the window size in the drop-down combo box.

3. You may also opt to play back the video full-screen by selecting Full Screen.

4. When complete, click OK to save your changes and close the Multimedia Properties sheet.

If you want to make other multimedia changes, don't click OK. Instead, the next two sections show you how to change the MIDI and CD Music settings.

FIG. 13.27
The Video page of the Multimedia control panel gives access to the playback size of the video clip.

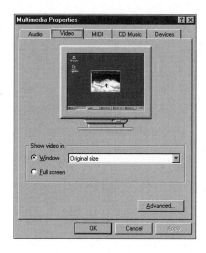

MIDI Settings

The capability to plug in a MIDI instrument into a MIDI port on a sound card is commonplace among most sound cards on the market today. You can easily add a MIDI device to your system. You can also easily change the settings after you've installed it.

Setting Up a MIDI Instrument   To set up a MIDI instrument, follow these steps:

1. Plug the instrument into the sound card's MIDI port.

2. Open the Multimedia control panel. Click the MIDI page if it isn't already open (see fig. 13.28).

FIG. 13.28
Configure the new MIDI instrument using the MIDI page of the Multimedia Properties sheet.

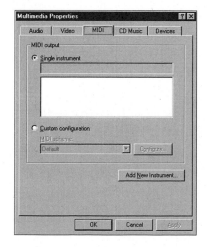

Part
III

Ch
13

3. Click Add New Instrument.

4. Follow the instructions on the screen to install the instrument.

5. Choose Single Instrument on the MIDI page.

6. Select the instrument you just installed and click OK to save your changes and close the Multimedia Properties sheet.

Your new MIDI instrument is now ready to go.

Changing MIDI Settings   You can redirect where the MIDI data is routed. To change where it is sent, follow these steps:

1. Open the Multimedia control panel. Click the MIDI page if it isn't already open (refer to fig. 13.28).

2. Choose to send the MIDI output to a Single Instrument or to a Custom Configuration.

CAUTION

You can choose Custom configuration. However, unless you have experience with MIDI, you may make your computer unable to play MIDI files and put yourself in a situation where it will take a while to restore the settings back to normal.

3. When complete, click OK to save your changes and close the Multimedia Properties sheet.

If you want to make other multimedia changes, don't click OK. Instead, the next section shows you how to change the CD Music settings.

CD Settings

When you have more than one CD-ROM drive connected to your computer, you might want to visit the CD Music page of the Multimedia properties sheet. You might also want to see the page if you can control the volume of the headphone plug on your CD-ROM player via software. To change these settings, perform the following steps:

1. Open the Multimedia control panel. Click the CD Music page if it isn't already open (see fig. 13.29).

FIG. 13.29
Change which CD-ROM to listen to or adjust the head-phone volume on the CD Music page.

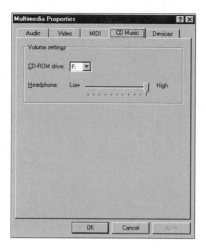

2. To change which CD-ROM you'll be listening to, select a new CD-ROM drive letter.

3. If your CD-ROM drive supports it, you can also choose to adjust the playback Headphone Volume while you're listening to the disc. To lower the volume, drag the slider to the left. To raise the volume, drag the slider to the right. If this control is disabled, your CD-ROM doesn't support changing the head-phone volume through software.

Now that you've adjusted the multimedia settings of Windows NT, it's time to inter-act with some multimedia clips. The next section steps you through how to use the multimedia accessories.

Using the Multimedia Accessories

Windows NT has some useful sound accessories related to the recording and play-ing of sound, either from audio CDs or specially recorded files.

Sound Recorder is a good introduction to digital recording, using a microphone that plugs into your sound card. This feature enables you to make recorded files that you can edit and mix into other sound files.

CD Player enables you to play audio CDs from your CD-ROM drive while you are working in other applications. CD Player offers many of the controls found in stand-alone audio CD players for your home and operates in much the same way. In addition, CD Player enables you to edit your play list that corresponds to the audio CD being played, playing the tracks in the order you want.

Using the Sound Recorder

The Sound Recorder accessory provides a good introduction to the world of digital recording. Using Sound Recorder, you can record sound files to your hard drive to include in multimedia presentations or to attach to documents for distribution among colleagues. You can even e-mail the file across your local area network or out over the Internet. Sound Recorder does not have the advanced features of high-end digital recorders, but it does provide for most users' needs.

To access Sound Recorder:

1. Open the Start menu and choose <u>P</u>rograms, Accessories.

2. Choose Multimedia.

3. Choose Sound Recorder to open the Sound Recorder dialog box (see fig. 13.30).

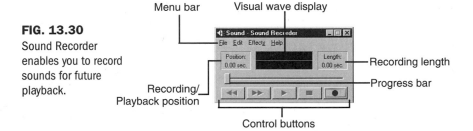

FIG. 13.30
Sound Recorder enables you to record sounds for future playback.

The *menu bar* lists the menus that are discussed briefly here. *Recording/Playback position* represents the current position in the audio file, whereas *Length* tells you the complete length of the file in seconds. The *Visual wave display* offers a visual demonstration of the audio file, and the *progress bar* indicates how far along in the file you are. Finally, the *control buttons* control such operations as fast forward and rewind, as in a regular tape recorder.

To record a sound, follow these steps:

1. Click the Record button on the far right and speak into the microphone.

2. When finished, click the Stop button.

3. When you have the sound recorded the way you want, choose File, Save and enter a name for your new recording.

Using the CD Player

The CD Player enables you to play audio CDs in the background while you are working in other applications. To access the CD Player, follow these steps:

1. Open the Start menu and choose Programs, Accessories.

2. Choose Multimedia.

3. Choose CD Player to open the CD Player dialog box (see fig. 13.31).

 T I P Also, you can simply place an audio CD into your CD player and the CD Player accessory will automatically launch.

Menu bar

FIG. 13.31
The CD Player allows you to play audio CDs and edit play lists just like a regular CD player as part of your home audio system.

Time indicator
Artist name
CD title
Current track

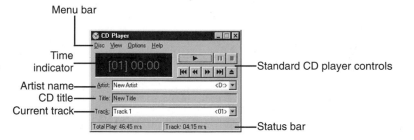

Standard CD player controls

Status bar

CD Player includes a number of advanced functions that you access from the menu bar such as Random Order, Continuous Play, and the capability to edit the play list.

To edit the play list and the name of the artist, title, and track names, follow these steps:

1. Choose Disc, Edit Play List.

2. Change the data in the fields as desired. If you want to change the play list, use the Add, Remove, Clear All, and Reset buttons.

3. When complete, click OK to save your changes. Your changes are saved permanently. Even if you put in this CD a month from now, the settings you just made will be used again.

To adjust the playback volume of the audio CD:

1. Choose View, Volume Control. The Volume Control dialog box appears similar to figure 13.32.

FIG. 13.32
In addition to controlling volume, you can also set WAV and MIDI file volumes via the Volume Control option in the View menu.

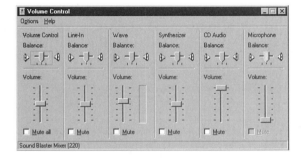

2. Change the CD Audio slider up and down until the volume is adjusted correctly.

3. If adjusting the volume control didn't seem to make a difference, try changing the CD Audio slider on the right. It may have been turned down too low.

4. When complete, close the dialog box to save your changes.

From Here...

In this chapter, you learned about some of the new multimedia features in Windows NT 4.0. You learned how to view what other devices are using resource settings via the Windows NT Diagnostics program. You learned how to install a multimedia device, specify its driver, and change its resource settings. You also learned a little bit about how to change multimedia settings and use the multimedia accessories. For more information on related topics, you might want to review the following chapters:

■ Chapter 11, "Changing and Configuring Hardware," shows you how to install other pieces of hardware.

- Chapter 35, "Using the Diagnostics Tool," shows you in detail how to use the Windows NT Diagnostics application mentioned in this chapter.
- Appendix C, "Where to Get More Information," gives you a starting point for more information if you can't find what you are looking for on Windows NT multimedia.

CHAPTER 14

Managing System Services and Devices

by Michael Marchuk

Windows NT is a wonderfully modular operating system which allows you to configure what services and devices are available at any one time. With this functionality, you also run the risk of building a house of cards. If one service or device fails, any other dependent service also will fail. These chapter helps you learn about these devices and services which in many cases run behind the scenes. ∎

System services

This section helps you understand what makes up a system service and a system device.

Making system services work

You learn how to install and remove system services and devices and control the way that a service or device starts up when Windows NT boots.

Dealing with problems

Learn how to troubleshoot system service and system device problems.

Managing System Services

A system service is a portion of the operating system which is required for certain functions to occur. For example, one system service is the Spooler service. The Spooler service allows print jobs to be accepted from an application and passed on to the printer when the printer is ready. Without the Spooler service, your computer would hold up your application while it was printing.

System services build upon the base operating system, currently installed hardware devices, and other system services. Figure 14.1 shows how system services can fit within the Windows NT operating system environment.

FIG. 14.1
System services build upon the base operating system and even other services to provide new functionality.

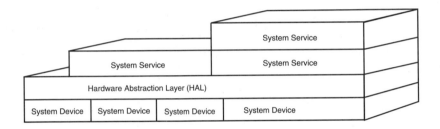

Understanding System Services

System services also provide network connectivity, error detection, security, and other basic operating system functions. Table 14.1 shows the default system services and their functions within Windows NT.

Table 14.1   Default Systems Services within Windows NT

System Service	Description
Alerter	Provides notification to selected users or computers when administrative alerts such as service failures occur. The Alerter service is used by the Server service and requires the Messenger service to operate.
ClipBook Server	Allows remote Clipbook Viewers on other computers to see pages stored in the local Clipbook.

System Service	Description
Computer Browser	Keeps track of other computers on the network and provides the information to applications when needed. Explorer and Network Neighborhood use the Computer Browser service.
Directory Replicator	Replicates directories, and the files in those directories, between computers on a network. This is typically used when administrators set up fault-tolerant environments locally or when a local copy of a remote server would increase the performance of accessing files.
Event Log	Stores application, security, and system events in the event logs. The Event Log viewer allows you to see events stored by the Event Log service.
Messenger	Sends and receives messages sent by administrators or by the Alerter service.
Net Logon	Maintains the security features such as user logons and domain security. The Net Logon service also provides the mechanism by which security files are synchronized between servers within a domain.
Network DDE	Provides a network transport for DDE (dynamic data exchange) conversations and provides security for the DDE conversations. Applications such as Word and Excel make use of the Network DDE service when sharing information through DDE across a network.
Network DDE DSDM	The DDE Share Database Manager (DSDM) handles the management of multiple DDE conversations. It is used by the Network DDE service.

continues

Part
III

Ch
14

Table 14.1 Continued

System Service	Description
NT LM Security Support Provider	Provides Windows NT security for RPC applications that use transports other than LAN Manager named pipes. This service is used mainly by older database server applications.
Plug and Play	The Plug and Play service manages the interface between Windows NT and any Plug and Play hardware you have installed in your system. Your system must also have Plug and Play BIOS support in order to make use of this technology.
Remote Procedure Call (RPC) Locator	The RPC Locator service handles the directory of distributed applications such as database servers. An RPC application will use the RPC Locator to register its availability. The RPC Locator is also used by the clients to find distributed RPC server applications which are compatible.
Remote Procedure Call (RPC) Service	The RPC Service provides the communication function for the RPC Locator and other RPC services.
Schedule	The at command uses the Schedule service to run applications at specified times and dates.
Server	The Server service manages file and print services for users connected to the local computer. It also manages Named Pipe sharing and RPC support functions. When the Server service fails, the computer cannot be accessed from users on the network.

System Service	Description
Spooler	Provides print job spooling services. When a print job is sent to a printer, the Spooler service queues it up behind any earlier print jobs waiting to be sent to the printer. When the print job is ready for printing, the Spooler service manages the flow of data from the print queue to the printer.
UPS	Manages the functions of an uninterruptible power supply connected to the computer. The UPS service will handle communication between the UPS hardware and the UPS controller service on the computer. When the power goes out, the UPS service sends a message to the UPS controller service which manages the timing of the outage and handles any system shutdown functions.
Workstation	The Workstation service manages network connections, drive letter mappings, printer connections, and other local application interactions with the network. Explorer uses the Workstation service.

Without system services, your computer would not have much of its functionality, especially when considering the network functions that many of the system services handle.

In addition to the default system services, there are many other services which can be loaded and unloaded to provide various functions within the Windows NT operating system. For instance, you may purchase software for performing backups at scheduled intervals, which is run as a system service. When you install the backup software, the system service for the scheduling function may be automatically installed into your system services list. You may even download a shareware application off of the Internet which provides Telnet Server services. This system service may be automatically installed or you may have to install the service manually. The next section describes the installation and removal process for system services.

Installing and Removing System Services

Most software packages that contain a system service module will automatically install the service within Windows NT. However, there may be times when the system service needs to be manually installed or removed when you have discontinued use of the product.

In these cases, you'll need to understand how to install and remove the system services from your Windows NT configuration. A system service registers itself as "available" when it is installed. Like a camper who packs a flashlight in the backpack, the service is ready to be started at any time. This installation and registration process is handled by the system service which is being installed. Typically, the service will have a command to accomplish the following tasks:

- Install the service and register its availability
- Start the service
- Stop the service
- Remove the service from the system

The system services which are manually installed will almost always have some sort of documentation which explains the exact syntax of the command necessary to accomplish one of these tasks. For example, if you had a system service that provided an electronic mail post office that was called POSTMAN.EXE, you might have to manually install the service as shown by the command in figure 14.2.

This manual installation is usually due to a lackluster or even non-existent installation program for the service. However, it is possible that the system service is installed manually for debugging or other reasons. More frequently, the removal command is used to eliminate an older service application or one which is no longer being used. A remove command looks similar to the installation command which was shown earlier. Figure 14.3 shows the command line function which removes the example POSTMAN e-mail service.

FIG. 14.2
The example POSTMAN e-mail service is manually installed with the *install* command line parameter.

FIG. 14.3
The example POSTMAN e-mail service is manually removed with the *remove* command line parameter.

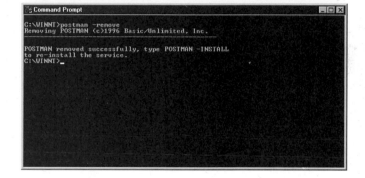

Starting and stopping the service may also be performed through the command line, however, you may want to make use of the Control Panel application which manages the startup and shutdown functions for all system services. The Services Control Panel applet handles these functions and is explained in the next section.

Controlling System Service Startup

The Services dialog box, shown in figure 14.4 allows you to start, stop, pause, and control the automatic startup of system services. Additionally, you can see the status of all services installed on your system through the Services applet.

Since system services are like a flashlight in a camper's backpack, they may or may not be in use at all times. Typically, you will install a service to provide some desired functionality. Since you want that functionality, that service will have to be running. However, there may be times when you know that the service is not going to be used. Like the camper's flashlight, you can shut off the service, yet keep it available for use later on when conditions change.

Part
III

Ch
14

FIG. 14.4

The Services dialog box manages the system services installed on your computer.

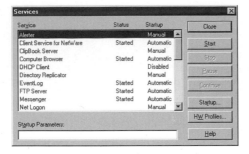

You must be logged in to Windows NT as a user which is part of the Administrators group to manage the startup of system services. ▨

You may need to stop a system service due to a hardware failure or for security purposes. If you are running Windows NT on your portable computer which is not attached to the network, you might want to disable the FTP service since no one can access your computer over the network. To disable a service, like the FTP service, follow these steps:

1. Select the service that you want to stop from the list box in the Services dialog box.

2. Press the Stop button. Services displays a dialog box like the one shown in figure 14.5, which lets you know that it is trying to shut down the service.

FIG. 14.5

The Service Control dialog box initiates the shutdown of a service when you press the Stop button.

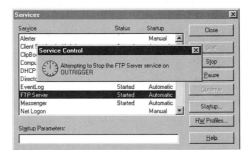

Once the service has been successfully stopped, the status within the Services list box will be blank for that service as shown in figure 14.6 where the FTP service is no longer running.

FIG. 14.6
Once the FTP service
has been stopped,
the status within the
Services dialog box
changes to a blank.

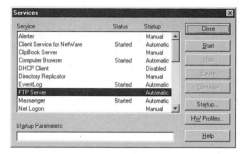

There may be times, though, when stopping the service is too abrupt. For example, you may be using your Windows NT system on the network with users accessing the FTP service. Instead of stopping the service, which cuts off all of the user's currently transferring files, you could pause the service, which lets current users finish up what they're doing but prevents new users from attaching. As soon as the current users log off of your FTP service, they will not be able to get back on until you continue the service. To pause the FTP service, you would:

1. Select the FTP service from the Services Control Panel applet list box.

2. Press the Pause button. This will prevent new users from logging on to your FTP service. Figure 14.7 shows the FTP service in the paused state.

FIG. 14.7
The FTP service is
paused, only allowing
current users to
continue their
transactions.

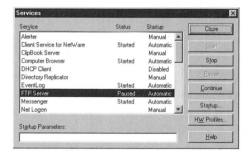

To resume a paused service, you would:

1. Select the FTP service from the Services list box.

2. Press the Continue button. This will restart the FTP service and allow new users to access your system.

Part
III

Ch
14

But sometimes the process of starting and stopping a service needs to be automated. You may not want to have to start the FTP service manually each time you start your computer. To instruct Windows NT to automatically start a service when it boots, follow these steps:

1. Select the service you want to automatically run during boot time from within the Services Control Panel applet list box.

2. Press the Startup button. This will display the dialog box shown in figure 14.8.

FIG. 14.8
The Service startup dialog box allows you to manage the initialization of a system service during boot time.

3. To instruct Windows NT to start the service during boot time, select the Automatic option from the Startup Type section.

4. If you want to have the service logged on with limited rights to the system, you can choose a user ID and password which you've setup with the appropriate rights. If you have not setup a particular account for a service, then choose the System Account option from the Log On As section.

CAUTION
Make sure you know what your system service is doing when you load it on your system. If you assign System Account privileges to a service which has been written by a hacker, you may cause great damage to your system. Most system services will provide only the functionality that they say, but like viruses, not every application is a friendly one.

5. Press the OK button to finalize your selection.

NOTE   Most services will assume that they will be logged in as the System Account and have access to all resources. If you decide to manage your services using user accounts with specific permissions, make sure that you consult the software vendor to see what the service needs to access. ■

The Manual and Disabled startup options provide you with additional flexibility over how a service is initialized. For example, if your Windows NT system was providing FTP services only occasionally, you may want to set this startup option to Manual. This will prevent access to your system via FTP when you don't want it, and will save memory by not running a service that you don't need.

The Disabled function prevents you or another service from accidentally starting the service. For example, you might want to disable a network backup agent if you don't want your system automatically backed up while it is connected to the network. If a backup scheduler service tried to start the network backup agent service, it would return a message indicating that the service has been disabled rather than automatically starting the backup agent.

Managing System Devices

System devices require far less attention than system services after they are installed. Since hardware changes far less frequently than software on your computer, these system devices can be installed and go unnoticed for years.

However, to ensure that your system is running at peak efficiency when you install Windows NT, you should verify that the correct system devices have been installed on your system. This section will cover the details that you need to verify when managing system devices within Windows NT.

▶ **See** "Configuring a PC Card," **p. 296**

Understanding System Devices

System devices, like system services, are operating system modules which provide functionality. However, system devices are communication modules or drivers that are linked very closely to the hardware to which the system device driver is communicating. For example, your mouse uses a system device driver to communicate between the mouse hardware and the operating system. The mouse system device driver takes hardware signals and provides operating system events. When you move the mouse, the hardware relays signals back to the device driver which interprets them and passes on an operating system event. Windows NT then uses that event to position the mouse cursor on the screen based on the data received by the mouse system device driver. Figure 14.9 depicts the interaction between the mouse hardware and Windows NT.

FIG. 14.9

The mouse system device driver handles the interpretation of hardware signals into operating system events.

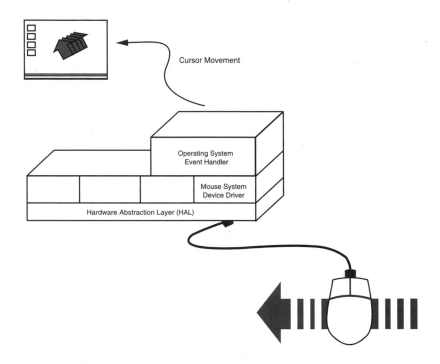

Cursor Movement

Operating System
Event Handler

Mouse System
Device Driver

Hardware Abstraction Layer (HAL)

Generally speaking, the system device driver will be one of the lowest levels of software components within the operating system. Figure 14.10 shows how the system device fits in with the Hardware Abstraction Layer (HAL) and system services.

System devices include all of the following types of drivers:

- Video Cards
- Multimedia/Audio Cards
- Keyboard/Mouse

FIG. 14.10

The system device builds a platform on top of the hardware so that the Windows NT Hardware Abstraction Layer can manage the system services without knowing about the details of the hardware.

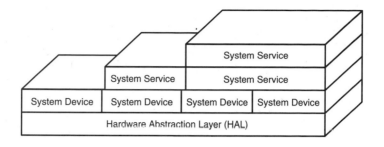

- Diskette Drives
- IDE Hard Drives
- CD-ROM Drives
- SCSI Controllers
- PCMCIA Controllers
- Network Interface Cards
- NTFS and FAT File Systems

Since system devices are so critical to the operation of your computer within Windows NT, let's take a look at how you can install or remove system devices safely.

Installing and Removing System Devices

Most hardware is configured using one of the Control Panel device managers. For example, to modify your computer's video display, you would most likely use the Display applet from within the Control Panel rather than the Devices applet. While you can modify the video system device driver through the Devices applet, the Display applet provides a more intuitive and automated way to make the change. Additionally, the Display applet will allow you to test the various options available for the video display system device.

N O T E PCMCIA devices, also known as PC Card devices, use the PC Card (PCMCIA) device driver to manage the drivers used for each specific card you install. The first time you install a PC Card in your system, you need to open the PC Card (PCMCIA) applet to install the specific driver for that PC Card. ▪

Part
III

Ch

Table 14.2 outlines the various hardware components and the proper installation or management tool within Windows NT. You should use these methods of managing the respective system devices before you attempt to make any changes within the Devices applet in the Control Panel.

Table 14.2   System Device Installation Methods

System Hardware	Proper Management Tool
Video display	Display applet
SCSI Adapter	SCSI Adapters applet
Multimedia/Sound Board	Multimedia applet
PCMCIA Devices	PC Card (PCMCIA) applet
Network Interface Cards	Network applet
CD-ROM drives	SCSI Adapters applet
NTFS/FAT File Systems	Drive Manager application within the Administrative Tools Start menu folder
Disk/IDE drives	Devices applet

Although the management tools vary for the different types of system devices, you can still manage all system devices from within the Devices applet in the Control Panel. Figure 14.11 shows the Devices dialog box containing the list of the system device drivers that are either installed or available for installation off of the Windows NT CD-ROM.

Within the list box in the Devices dialog box, you can see the current status of a particular driver. A system device driver is typically installed and running at all times, however, you may encounter the situation when a system device driver is not running due to hardware failure or incorrect I/O or memory settings.

As an example, let's assume you've purchased a new 6X speed IDE CD-ROM drive to replace your older 2X speed Mitsumi CD-ROM. You'll have to both add the new CD-ROM device driver and remove the old one using the SCSI Adapters applet in the Control Panel. Figure 14.12 shows the SCSI Adapter applet.

FIG. 14.11

All system devices can be managed from within the Devices applet in the Control Panel.

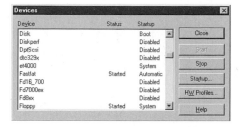

FIG. 14.12

The SCSI Adapters applet can be used to install new SCSI Adapter device drivers or drivers for other storage device interface hardware such as proprietary CD-ROM interfaces or disk arrays.

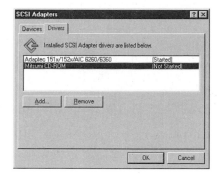

To add a new CD-ROM device driver, you can follow these steps:

1. Either before you remove your old CD-ROM drive or with another computer, copy the system device driver from the CD-ROM to a floppy disk. Since we are swapping CD-ROM drives, we won't be able to load the CD-ROM device drivers directly from the Windows NT CD-ROM.

2. Open up the Control Panel and run the SCSI Adapters applet.

3. Choose the Drivers property sheet and press the Add button.

4. Select the appropriate driver from the list of known drivers or insert the floppy disk which contains the Windows NT device driver supplied by the manufacturer and press the Have Disk button.

5. Click on the OK button. Windows NT will now ask you where to find the device driver which matches the device you are trying to install. Choose the disk drive that contains the system device driver you copied in step 1.

Part
III

Ch
14

TIP You may be caught in a bind when installing a CD-ROM device because you won't have the Windows NT CD-ROM from which to copy the appropriate drivers. If you have enough additional hard drive space (about 100 megabytes) you may want to copy the entire /I386 (or whatever processor you are running) directory to your local hard drive. Since device driver names may not make any sense (SPARROW.SYS = Adaptec SCSI Device Driver) you may not know exactly which driver to copy in step 1. With the entire Windows NT installation on the local hard drive, you won't need to know the file name of the driver.

6. You will have to reboot Windows NT after you have made changes to your system device list.

Removing a system device is much easier than installing one. For example, if you were removing the Mitsumi CD-ROM device driver, you would:

1. Open up the Control Panel and run the SCSI Adapters applet.

2. Select the appropriate device driver from the list.

3. Press the Remove button and confirm that you want to remove the device driver. You will have to reboot Windows NT for the changes to take effect.

If you do not know which device driver to remove from your computer, you can check the System Event Log which contains details about device failures. Figure 14.13 shows the System Event Log which depicts the failure of the Mitsumi system device.

FIG. 14.13
The System Event Log is a good place to check for the name of the system device driver that has failed when you remove a piece of hardware.

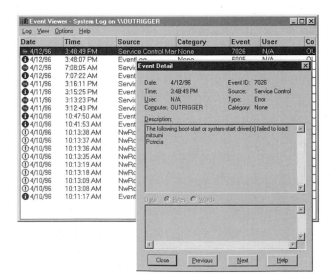

▶ **See** "Viewing a Log," **p. 930**

Controlling System Devices

The Devices dialog box allows you to manage not only which device drivers are loaded on your system, but also when they are loaded during the boot process. For example, most storage management hardware such as disk drives, IDE hard drives, and CD-ROM drives will be loaded as the operating system boots. To manage when a system device driver is loaded, follow these steps:

1. Open the Devices applet within the Control Panel.

2. Select the system device driver that you want to manage.

3. Press the Startup button. This will display the dialog box like the one shown in figure 14.14.

FIG. 14.14
The Device startup dialog box lets you control when a system device driver is loaded.

4. You can choose any of the options shown in figure 14.14; however, you should have instructions from your manufacturer that will let you know the proper selection. Do not change this option unless you have been given instructions by the vendor!

5. Press the OK button to save the changes. You will have to reboot before the new options are recognized by Windows NT.

> **CAUTION**
>
> Although you can make changes to the system device drivers in this way, it is suggested that you get explicit instructions from your hardware vendor before altering the operation of any system device driver.

Part
III

Ch
14

If you want to verify a system device driver's settings, you can load the Windows NT Diagnostic Tool. This is helpful when you have installed the correct system device driver, yet Windows NT generates an error when you attempt to load the device. Figure 14.15 depicts the Windows NT Diagnostic Tool dialog box showing the system devices loaded on the computer.

FIG. 14.15

The Windows NT Diagnostic Tool is helpful when troubleshooting your system device driver installation problems.

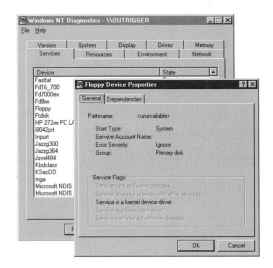

▶ **See** "System Resources and Devices," **p. 1014**

From Here...

In this chapter, you learned what a system service and a system device are and how Windows NT uses them. You learned how to install, remove, and configure both system services and devices, and how to verify that your system devices are set up properly.

Other chapters you may want to explore include:

- Chapter 7, "Managing Disk Storage with the Disk Administrator."
- Chapter 11, "Changing and Configuring Hardware."
- Chapter 31, "Working with the Registry."
- Chapter 32, "Using the Event Viewer."
- Chapter 35, "Using the Diagnostics Tool."

CHAPTER 15

Securing Windows NT Workstation

by Sue Plumley

Members of a network depend on the server, and often other computers on the network, to share files, directories, printers, and other resources; however, it's important to apply limitations and security practices over the network so that everyone has some level of separation and data safety. Windows NT Workstation provides assistance in that area by way of the User Manager.

The User Manager is a tool for administering computer security. With the User Manager, you can supervise who can access your computer and, specifically, which resources they can access. You first create accounts for each individual who will access your computer and then you assign security rights. Normally, the system administrator uses the User Manager to assign security rights, but you also can use the feature to govern rights on your own computer. ∎

Add and modify user accounts

The NT User Manager makes editing and managing the users who access your computer easy.

Assign user rights to groups

Use NT's built-in groups to grant access to the users and groups that use your computer.

Add and modify groups

Create specialized groups to suit your way of working; assign those groups rights and permissions to your resources.

Manage security policies

Control user passwords, track security breaches, and manage user rights as they apply to your computer.

Working with Accounts

The user accounts describe pertinent information about each person who works on Windows NT Workstation, including his or her name, password, and permission rights. Windows NT provides some built-in accounts, but you can also add accounts and modify any user account with the User Manager.

In addition to specifying a user's full name—first, last, and initial, if you want—you specify a *user name* for each user. A user name is an alias or nickname that represents the user on the network and within the workstation. You can accept the default user names assigned by Windows NT, or you can assign your own.

 T I P If you assign your own user names, you might find it easier to organize and manage the user accounts on your workstation.

Defining Terms

The User Manager helps you to create and assign user accounts, groups, and security policies that govern your workstation. A *user account* is a collection of information that defines the user of one workstation to Windows NT, including user name, password, group membership, and a list of rights. *Rights* authorize the user to perform specific tasks over the entire system, whereas *permissions* authorize the user to utilize a specific object, such as a printer, file, or directory.

A *group* is an account that contains a collection of users, or members, who share the same or similar rights. Often, with the use of the term *group*, you hear the terms *domain* and *workgroup*. A *domain* is a group of computers sharing a common security policy, and similarly, a *workgroup* is a collection of computers grouped on a network so that they are easy to find and reference. Generally, you share printers and directories with the users in your workgroup. Workgroups and domains refer to those workstations attached to a Windows network, such as Windows NT Server.

Security policies are rights and permissions that regulate which users can use which resources. Only those drives formatted with Windows NT file system (NTFS) can take full advantage of Windows NT security.

Understanding the User Manager

The User Manager is a tool for creating and modifying the individuals and groups that can use the workstation. You can use the User Manager to organize, manage, and control those allowed to connect to and use your computer.

Gaining Access to the User Manager   As with other Administrative tools, only certain groups can use the User Manager. For security purposes, Windows NT creates certain built-in groups, and each is designated certain rights. For more information about groups, see "Working with Groups" later in this chapter.

Following is a list of groups permitted to use the User Manager and a description of the extent of their use with this feature:

- *Administrators*. Administrators can perform all User Manager functions.
- *Power Users*. Power Users can create user accounts and groups, and delete and modify those user accounts and groups, as well as add and remove users from the Power Users, Users, and Guests groups.
- *Users*. A user can create groups and modify and delete those groups; a user can also grant user account memberships in those groups.

Opening and Closing User Manager   You can open the User Manager no matter which group you're a member of. However, depending on the group to which you belong, some features and commands may be unavailable to you (grayed out).

To open the User Manager, follow these steps:

1. Choose Start, Programs, Administrative Tools, User Manager. The User Manager window appears, as shown in figure 15.1.

 TIP   Choose Options, Save Settings on Exit before quitting the User Manager to retain the window size and position for the next time you open the Manager.

2. To close the User Manager when you are finished, choose User, Exit; alternatively, press Alt+F4.

Using Built-in Accounts   Windows NT Workstation creates three user accounts you can use in the User Manager. Any of these accounts can be renamed, but not deleted. All the built-in groups appear in the User Manager from which you can choose.

FIG. 15.1

The User Manager window displays a list of users and a list of groups.

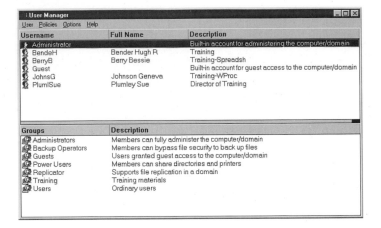

The following is a brief description of each of the built-in user accounts:

- *Administrator.* As a member of the Administrators group, this user account has all rights and permissions pertaining to the workstation and network. The administrator can modify, create, or delete user and group accounts in the User Manager, as well as control tasks and procedures such as printing, backups, modifying the operating system software, updating device drivers, and more. Members of the Administrators group supervise and control the entire network.

- *Guest.* As a member of the Guests group, a guest can create files, delete those files, and read any files that the guest is permitted to access by the administrator. Usually, a guest is an occasional user who has limited access to resources.

- *Initial User.* The primary person using the workstation is the initial user and is also a member of the Administrators group when dealing with his or her own workstation, and thereby can fully control the workstation.

N O T E   Your membership to a specific group, including the Initial User group, is decided and entered during installation of the Windows NT Workstation software. Additionally, the system administrator can designate you as a member of any group he or she chooses. ▨

TROUBLESHOOTING

Why is there no Initial User in my User Manager? If, during installation, your computer was added to a domain used in the Windows NT Server network, then the Initial User account isn't created. Instead of the initial user, you log on using an account from the domain.

If you're not a member of a domain, then you may be a member of a workgroup instead, which also disables the use of the initial user.

Alternatively, if the workstation was not configured for network use during installation, the Initial User account was not created. See your system administrator for more information.

Adding a New User Account

You can add new user accounts to accommodate supplementary workstations or people. Additionally, you can modify existing user accounts.

When adding and modifying user accounts, you must follow several guidelines. For example, when you name a new account (Username) or when you rename an existing account, you must follow the naming guidelines.

When naming the new user account, you must follow these guidelines:

- Use no more than 20 characters (letters and/or numbers); the names you use are case sensitive.

- The name must be unique.

- You cannot use the following (but you can use spaces):

  " \ / [ ] : ; | = + , * ? < >

 Because Windows NT sorts user accounts by the user names, be consistent in the way you name new accounts; for example, you might use the first five letters of the last name followed by the first initial.

In addition to the name and password, there are a few other specifications you may need to know; setting the user's profile is optional. To set the user's profile, you need to know the following information:

■ *Logon script name and path.* The logon script identifies certain information about the user to the network and runs each time the user connects to the network. The file is usually a batch file or an executable program file that uses the extension BAT, EXE, or CMD. To specify a logon script for a new user, you must know the path to the script file, usually C:\SYSTEM32\REPL\IMPORT\SCRIPTS.

■ *Home directory.* The home directory is located on the workstation and is shared by (made available to) certain groups for backup and administrative purposes; the home directory is where a user's saved files are usually stored. The home directory can be located on the workstation or on a shared network directory. On the workstation, the home directory is usually \USERS\DEFAULT. If the home directory is located on the shared network drive, ask your system administrator for the path.

You may also want to assign the new user to other groups besides the Users group. For more information, see the section "Working with Groups" later in this chapter.

Creating Accounts   Create a new account to add users to the workstation, group, and/or network. You can create a new user from scratch, or you can copy a user account and change only the specific data, such as user name and password, for example.

To create a new user, follow these steps:

1. In the User Manager, choose User, New User. The New User dialog box appears (see fig. 15.2).

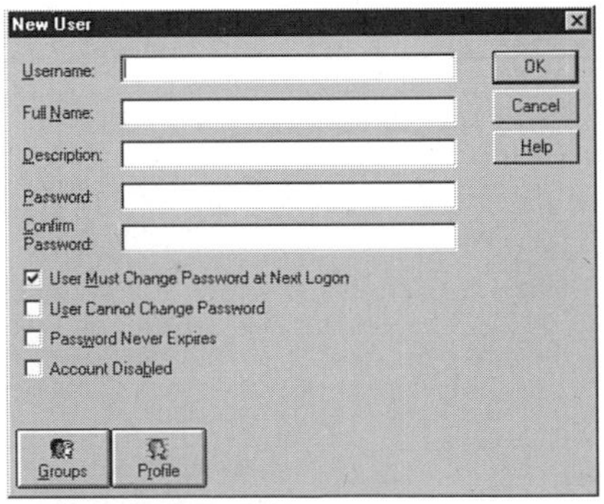

FIG. 15.2
Define a new user by a user name, full name, and other information in the New User dialog box.

Part

III

Ch

15

2. In the Username text box, enter the identifying name of the user.

3. In Full Name, enter the full name of the user, following a standard you set for all users   last name followed by the first name, for example.

4. In Description, optionally enter a word or phrase describing the user.

5. In Password, enter a password no longer than 14 characters; the password is case sensitive. Enter the same password in the Confirm Password text box.

6. Select from the following options:

User Must Change Password at Next Logon. Prevents the user from logging on until he or she enters a new password and confirms it.

User Cannot Change Password. Prevents the user from changing the password; good for guest accounts.

Password Never Expires. Prevents the password from expiring so that the user can always access the account.

Account Disabled. Prevents further use of the account unless or until you enable the account at a later date.

7. Click Groups to assign a group other than or in addition to the Users group to the new user. Figure 15.3 shows the Group Memberships dialog box.

To add a group membership, select the group from the Not Member Of list and choose Add; to remove the user from a group, select the group in the Member Of list and choose Remove. Choose OK to close the dialog box. For more information about groups, see "Working with Groups" later in this chapter.

FIG. 15.3
Select the groups you want to assign the new user.

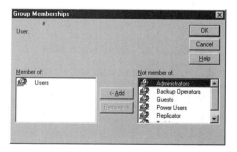

8. Choose Profile. The User Environment Profile dialog box appears (see fig. 15.4).

FIG. 15.4
Use the User
Environment Profile
dialog box to assign
a logon script.

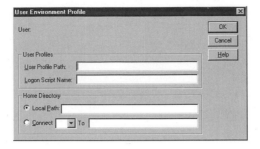

In the Logon Script Name text box, enter the path and file name of the logon script to be used.

In the Home Directory area, either choose the Local Path text box to enter the user's home directory on the workstation or choose the Connect text box and enter the shared network drive. Then in the To text box, enter the path of the home directory on the network drive. Choose OK to close the dialog box.

9. Choose OK to close the New User dialog box that adds the new user to the list.

TROUBLESHOOTING

In the User Manager, my user name is preceded by another name. Should I use this other name in front of the new users I add? If you see a domain or a computer name in front of the user name in the User Manager, that signifies your workstation is a member of a Windows NT Server domain. Yes, use the domain or computer name in front of the user name when adding new users. Additionally, sometimes the Full Name is preceded by the domain or computer name as well.

To copy an existing user account, select the user account from the list in the User Manager and choose User, Copy. In the Copy Of dialog box, change the user account as described in the previous instructions and choose OK.

Modifying Accounts   You can modify one user account or several accounts at one time. Generally, the items in the User Properties dialog box are the same as the ones in the New User dialog box: Full Name, Password, Description, and so on.

To modify a user account, follow these steps:

1. In the User Manager, select the user you want to modify and choose <u>U</u>ser, <u>P</u>roperties. The User Properties dialog box appears (see fig. 15.5).

FIG. 15.5

Change a user name, password, or other option in the User Properties dialog box.

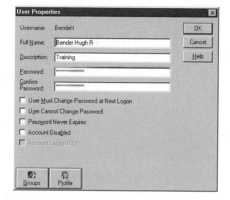

 T I P To open the User Properties dialog box, double-click any user on the list in the User Manager.

2. Using the descriptions listed in the previous section, "Creating Accounts," make any changes to the Full <u>N</u>ame, <u>D</u>escription, <u>P</u>assword, and other options listed in the dialog box.

3. You can make changes to the additional option Account Loc<u>k</u>ed Out. If the account is locked out, because of too many unsuccessful logon attempts for example, you can clear the check box to unlock the account. You cannot lock the account using this check box. The check box is unavailable if the account is not locked out.

 T I P The <u>P</u>assword text box not only displays asterisks instead of the actual password for security purposes, but it also displays the wrong number of characters in the password.

4. Choose OK to close the dialog box and accept any modifications you made.

To make the same change in several user accounts at one time, follow these steps:

1. In the User Manager window, select two or more accounts by selecting the first account, then pressing and holding down Ctrl, and selecting the other accounts.

2. Choose Uuser, Pproperties. The User Properties dialog box appears (see fig. 15.6).

FIG. 15.6
Modify more than
one user account at a
time to save time.

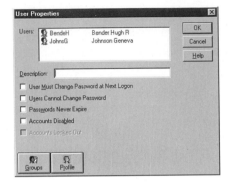

3. Make the changes by following the steps in the previous section, "Creating Accounts."

4. Choose OK to close the dialog box.

Managing User Accounts

You can also manage selected user accounts by deleting an account, renaming the user account, or disabling the account. You also can perform management tasks on either one user account or on several selected accounts.

Deleting User Accounts   When you delete a user account, you remove the account and the account's data from the workstation. You can delete just one account or select several accounts to delete all at one time.

 You might want to disable (by choosing Uuser, Pproperties) an account for a week or two before deleting it, just to make sure that you really want to erase the account.

> **CAUTION**
> When you delete a user account, you cannot recover it; not only will you lose all information about the user, you'll also lose all rights assigned to that user.

To delete one or more user accounts, follow these steps:

1. In the User Manager window, select one or more user accounts.

2. Choose <u>U</u>ser, <u>D</u>elete or press the Delete key. The User Manager confirmation message dialog box appears (see fig. 15.7).

FIG. 15.7
Read the warning carefully before deleting unrecoverable user accounts.

3. Choose OK to delete the user account.

Renaming Accounts   You can assign a new name to the user name of any user in the list. Make sure that you use the same guidelines as described earlier in the section "Creating Accounts."

To rename a user account, follow these steps:

1. Select the user in the User Manager window.

2. Choose <u>U</u>ser, <u>R</u>ename. The Rename dialog box appears (see fig. 15.8).

FIG. 15.8
Change the user name to reorganize or clarify the user.

3. In the <u>C</u>hange To text box, enter the new name and then choose OK to close the dialog box.

Working with Groups

A *group* is a collection of user accounts, and all user accounts, or members within a group, are permitted the same rights and permissions. There are several reasons to collect users within a group; most important is the ease of administrative procedures. It's much easier and takes less time to assign a group a set of rights than it is to assign each individual user rights and permissions. It's also easier to manage a group: changing or deleting permissions, for example. Additionally, managing resources—such as shared printers, directories, and files—through groups seems effortless.

Understanding Groups

The users within a group usually work within the same department—such as accounting, training, sales, and so on—or the same agency or office. Group memberships govern much of what the user can do on the network and within the workstation. The group is granted rights to directories, files, printers, and other resources; the member of the group is permitted those same rights and permissions.

A user can be a member of one or more groups. A user who is a member of more than one group possesses all rights and permissions from all the groups to which he or she is a member.

Windows NT Workstation includes *local groups*, groups used and managed only for one workstation. Those users working at a computer connected to a Novell network, for example, would only use local groups within one workstation. If, however, the workstation is a member of the Windows NT Server network and a member of a domain, then more groups than just the local groups are available.

A Windows NT Workstation can contain its own user accounts, and user accounts and global groups from its own domain and from trusted domains. *Global groups* are groups that can access their own domain, servers and workstations of the domain, and trusted domains. *Trusted domains* are different domains linked together for users to share and access other resources.

When Windows NT displays a group name and domain, it presents it in the following format: *domain_name\group_name* or *computer_name\group_name* in the User Manager window. If, for example, the domain is Training and the group is Database, the name would be displayed as TRAINING\DATABASE. Other groups in that domain might be displayed as TRAINING\SPREADSHT and TRAINING\WORDPROC.

Using Built-in Groups

Windows NT Workstation provides several built-in groups, each with its own set of permissions and built-in capabilities. The built-in groups might be all you need to efficiently organize your workstation.

Rights and Abilities   *Rights* refers to everyday use of the workstation and its files. *Abilities* refers to the management and administration for the computer.

The following is a list of common rights:

- Log on to the computer
- Manage the security and auditing log
- Change system time
- Back up and restore files and directories
- Load and unload device drivers
- Shut down the system

The following is a list of common abilities:

- Create and manage user accounts
- Create and manage local groups
- Assign user rights
- Format the computer's hard disk
- Create common groups
- Share and stop sharing directories and printers

Group Descriptions   Following is a brief description of the built-in user groups provided with Windows NT Workstation:

- *Administrators.* The most powerful group on the workstation, the Administrators have control over all rights and abilities within the workstation. A domain Administrators group member is also an administrator over the workstation.

> **TIP**   The Initial User, if created during installation, is a member of the Administrators group.

- *Power Users.* The Power Users group has some administrative abilities and rights. The Power Users group rights include logging on locally, accessing the workstation from the network, changing system time, and shutting down the system. This group's abilities include creating and managing any user accounts and local groups that this member creates, locking the computer, sharing directories, and stopping the sharing of directories and printers.

■ *Users*. Users perform common tasks on the workstation, including logging on and shutting down the system and creating and managing local groups. Members of the domain's Users group also have normal user access to the workstation.

 T I P New user accounts added to the workstation are automatically added to the Users group.

■ *Guests*. Guests are occasional visitors to the workstation and have limited rights. Guests' only right is to log on locally to a workstation. A guest has no abilities unless you grant them.

■ *Backup Operators*. The Backup Operators group backs up and restores files and directories for all workstations and therefore has certain rights and abilities associated with the job. Rights include logging on locally, shutting down the system, and backing up and restoring files and directories. The only automatic ability for a Backup Operators member is to keep the local profile for each workstation.

■ *Replicator*. The Replicator group enables the members to log on to a workstation's Replicator Service only. *Replication* is the process of copying master files and directories from the server to the workstation to guarantee identical files and directories on multiple computers.

■ *Special*. Special groups are created by the system for specific purposes; Special groups aren't listed in the User Manager window.

TROUBLESHOOTING

I don't want the domain administrator to have control over my workstation; is there anything I can do? Yes, you can remove the Domain Admins global group from the workstation's Administrators group. See the section "Deleting Groups" later in this chapter.

Can I stop members of the Domain Users group from accessing my workstation? Yes, remove the Domain Users global group from the workstation's Users group. See the section "Deleting Groups" later in this chapter.

Adding Groups

You can add new local groups to your workstation, if the built-in groups do not supply what you need in terms of security and flexibility.

To add a new local group, follow these steps:

1. In the User Manager window, select the user accounts you want to include as initial members of the new group. Alternatively, you can select any group, and all user accounts will be added to the new group.

2. Choose <u>U</u>ser, New <u>L</u>ocal Group. The New Local Group dialog box appears (see fig. 15.9).

FIG. 15.9

Create new local groups to use on the workstation.

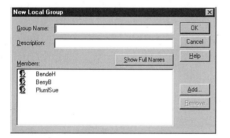

3. In the <u>G</u>roup Name text box, enter the name to apply to the new group. The name must follow these guidelines:

   The name must be unique—not like any other group or user name of the workstation.

   The name cannot contain these characters:

   " \ / : ; | = + * ? < >

   You can use upper- and lowercase characters as well as numbers and spaces in the name.

 TIP You cannot rename a built-in group.

---

4. In the <u>D</u>escription text box, enter text that briefly characterizes the group.

5. Choose <u>S</u>how Full Names to list the full names of any user accounts in the <u>M</u>embers list box. Initially, only user names are listed; it may take quite some time for Windows NT to list all full names in the group.

6. Choose <u>A</u>dd to add users and/or groups to the new group. Figure 15.10 shows the Add Users and Groups dialog box.

FIG. 15.10

Add users and groups to the new local group.

7. In the <u>L</u>ist Names From drop-down list, choose the workstation and/or domain name.

8. In the list of <u>N</u>ames, all user accounts of the selected computer or domain appear. Select one or more names and then choose <u>A</u>dd. Those names appear in the Add Names list box.

 TIP You also can type names directly into the A<u>d</u>d Names list box; separate multiple names with semicolons.

9. Optionally, you can add names to the group by doing the following:

To view and select the members of any group, select the group in the <u>N</u>ames list and then choose <u>M</u>embers.

To search for a specific group or user, choose <u>S</u>earch. In the Find Account dialog box, enter the name of the user or group and choose <u>S</u>earch. Select the user or group name, when found, and choose <u>A</u>dd.

10. Choose OK to add the users and groups to the new group.

 TIP Instead of creating a new group from scratch, you can copy an existing local group and then modify its members. Select the group in the User Manager window; choose <u>U</u>ser, <u>C</u>opy; then, define the new group as described in the preceding steps.

After you create the new group, you can assign rights to the group as a whole. If you copied a group, you also copied the rights assigned to that group. For more information about rights, see "Managing the User Rights Policy" later in this chapter.

Modifying Groups

You can modify any new or existing group to add or remove members. You use the Local Group Properties dialog box, which is similar to the Add Users and Groups dialog box, to modify the members of a group. To modify a group, follow these steps:

1. In the User Manager Group window, select the group you want to modify.

2. Choose User, Properties. The Local Group Properties dialog box appears (see fig. 15.11).

FIG. 15.11
Modify the selected group using the Local Group Properties dialog box.

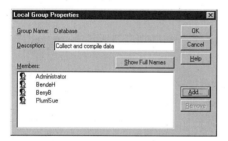

3. Make any changes to the description and members as described in the preceding section, "Adding Groups."

4. Choose OK to close the dialog box.

N O T E To remove a user or a group from the selected group, select the member from the Members list and then click Remove. ▨

Deleting Groups

You can delete any group that was created in the User Manager windows; however, you cannot delete built-in groups provided by Windows NT. When you delete a group, you cannot recover it, so be careful when deleting groups.

To delete a group, follow these steps:

1. In the User Manager Group window, select the group to be deleted.

2. Choose <u>U</u>ser, <u>D</u>elete; alternatively, press the Delete key.

3. The User Manager confirmation message box appears. To delete the group, choose OK.

Managing Security Policies

Security policies control the various safeguards on the workstation to ensure that only those with legitimate passwords and permission can access the workstation and its contents. Additionally, security policies enable you to record violations of security and other problems in a log so that you can appropriately supervise the workstation.

When setting security policies, you must be logged on as a member of the Administrators group. You can access and manage three types of security policies in the User Manager window:

- *Account.* The account policy governs how passwords are used by user accounts and controls the computers account lockout policy.

- *Audit.* The audit policy controls which event types are recorded in the Security log of the Event Viewer so that you can effectively watch and manage security breaches.

    ▶ **See** "Viewing a Log," **p. 930**

- *User Rights.* User rights refer to permissions assigned to groups and user accounts for your computer.

Managing the Account Policy

The account policy governs the use of passwords by all user accounts. You can modify time limits, character length, and other options on a password in the account policy, and you can set options for the account lockout. The *account lockout* is a feature that prevents a user from logging on to the workstation after a specific number of incorrect logon attempts. For more information, see "Adding a New User Account" earlier in this chapter.

The locked account remains locked until the administrator unlocks it in the User Properties dialog box.

To manage the account policy, follow these steps:

1. In the User Manager dialog box, choose Policies, Account. The Account Policy dialog box appears (see fig. 15.12).

FIG. 15.12
Set options for password limits in the Account Policy dialog box.

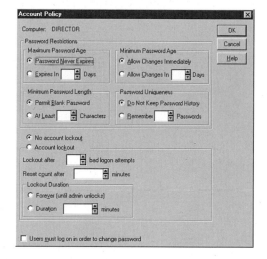

2. In the Password Restrictions area of the dialog box, set the following options for the password:

Maximum Password Age. Choose the amount of time a password can be used before the system requires the user to change it; choose either Password Never Expires or Expires In and set the number of days the password will be good for.

Minimum Password Age. Choose an option to set the amount of time a password must be used before the user can change it; choose either Allow Changes Immediately or enter a value between 1 and 999 days in the Allow Changes In text box.

Minimum Password Length. Enter the fewest characters (1 to 14) a password can contain in the At Least text box or choose Permit Blank Password.

Password Uniqueness. Enter the number of new passwords a user must use before an older password can be reinstated. Enter a number (1 to 8) in the Remember text box or select Do Not Keep Password History.

3. In the Account Lockout area, choose from the following:

   No Account Lockout. User can make unlimited incorrect logon attempts without being locked out.

   Account Lockout. User can only make a specified number of incorrect logon attempts before being locked out of the system; the user then must see the system administrator to get back into the system.

4. If you choose Account Lockout, choose from the following options in the Account Lockout area:

   Lockout After n *Bad Logon Attempts.* Enter the number of incorrect logons allowed before lockout in the text box.

   Reset Count After n *Minutes.* Enter the maximum number of minutes (1 to 99999) that come to pass between any two incorrect logon attempts for lockout to take place.

   Lockout Duration. Choose Forever to lock out the user until the administrator unlocks the system or Duration to set a number of minutes (from 1 to 99999) that the lockout remains before automatically unlocking.

5. Select the option Users Must Log On In Order To Change Password to require users to log on before they can change the password.

6. Choose OK to close the dialog box and accept changes.

TROUBLESHOOTING

It seems like anyone in the domain can log on to my workstation at any time. Can't I protect my workstation? If you're having trouble with too many users accessing your workstation, you should modify the account policy of your computer. Changing a few of the options discussed previously will help. The most effective option to change in this case is the Maximum Password Age. Change the option to Expires In 1 Day to limit everyone who has access; then reassign passwords to only those people you want to have access to your workstation.

Managing the Users Rights Policy

User rights refer to the ability of the user to perform tasks or actions to the entire system. A member of the Administrators group, for example, has the right to log on to a workstation and view all files and directories. If, however, the user has set permissions to exclude the administrator from viewing the files and directories, the user's permissions prevent the administrator from doing so.

There are many layers of user rights you can manage, from basic logging on to advanced programming rights. Following is a list of the basic user rights you can manage:

- *Access this computer from network.* Enables you to go through the network to attach to the computer.
- *Back up files and directories.* Enables you to back up files and directories, even on files and directories with set permissions.
- *Change the system time.* Enables you to set the internal computer clock.
- *Force shutdown from a remote system.* Not currently working; this right will be used in later versions of Windows NT Workstation.
- *Load and unload device drivers.* Enables you to install and remove device drivers.
- *Log on locally.* Log on to the computer at the computer's keyboard.
- *Manage Auditing and Security log.* Enables you to specify the types of file, directory, and other resource access to audit in the Security log.
- *Restore files and directories.* Enables you to restore files and directories from backups, even on files and directories with set permissions.
- *Shut down the system.* Shuts down Windows NT.
- *Take ownership of files or other objects.* Enables you to take ownership of files, directories, and other objects. Ownership belongs only to the person who creates the file or directory, unless granted this right.

No matter the type of rights you're dealing with, you can manage user rights as follows:

1. In the User Manager window, choose Policies, User Rights. The User Rights Policy dialog box appears (see fig. 15.13).

FIG. 15.13

Manage rights to authorize users to perform tasks over the system.

2. In the Right drop-down list, select the right you want to apply. The Grant To list shows the groups that are granted the selected rights.

3. To remove a group from the list, select the group and choose Remove.

4. To add a group to the list, choose Add, and the Add Users and Groups dialog box appears (see fig. 15.14). Select the groups you want to add and then choose Add. Choose OK to return to the User Rights Policy dialog box.

FIG. 15.14

Add groups to the Grant Rights list from the Add Users and Groups dialog box.

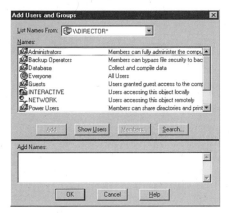

5. To display advanced user rights, click the Show Advanced User Rights check box.

6. Choose OK when you're finished assigning rights.

TROUBLESHOOTING

I've changed some of the advanced rights for the Users group, but I'm really not sure what I changed. Is there anything I can do? Advanced user rights generally apply to programmers writing applications for Windows NT. You should not grant those rights to the Users group, or to most groups really. If you want to remove advanced, or any, rights from a group, open the User Rights Policy dialog box and select the right. If you're unsure of the right you assigned, start at the beginning and select one on the list. When you select a right, the list of users granted the right appears in the Grant To list box. When you see the Users group appear on one of the advanced rights, you can then remove the Users group from the Grant To box.

Managing the Audit Policy

Windows NT Workstation includes a feature called the Event Viewer, which records user activities in various logs for you to view. One log in particular, the Security log, lists actions related to the user rights and any problems, or events, occurring with user's actions. You can specify which user's actions the Security log records by managing the audit policy in the User Manager.

▶ **See** "Viewing a Log," **p. 930**

▶ **See** "Viewing a Log," **p. 930**

Following is a list of the events you can choose to be audited:

- *Logon and logoff.* Monitors users logging on and off the workstation and the network.

- *File and object access.* Sets a specific file or object, such as a printer, for auditing.

- *Use of user rights.* Logs user's use of rights.

- *User and group management.* Logs creation, change, or deletion of user accounts or groups, password changes, renaming, disabling, or enabling of user accounts.

- *Security policy changes.* Records when a change is made to user rights or audit policies.

- *Restart, shutdown, and system.* Records system restarting or shutdown, and events that affect system security.

■ *Process tracking.* Tracks events such as program activation, indirect object access, and process exit.

> **CAUTION**
>
> The size of the Security log is limited, so you'll want to choose the events to monitor carefully. Each event takes up disk space as well. You can define the size of the Security log in the Event Viewer.

To manage the audit policy, follow these steps:

1. In the User Manager window, choose Policies, Audit. The Audit Policy dialog box appears (see fig. 15.15).

FIG. 15.15

Choose which events to audit in the Security log.

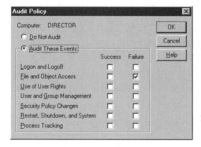

2. Choose one of the following:

   Do Not Audit. Audits and records no security events.

   Audit These Events. Audits and records the events you select in the Audit These Events area.

3. If you choose Audit These Events, select the events you want to audit and record from the previous descriptions. Choose the Success check box to log successful completion of tasks or the Failure check box to record unsuccessful attempts of tasks.

4. Choose OK to close the dialog box.

 Choose only to record failed events to target problems and not use too much hard disk space by recording all successful events.

From Here...

In this chapter, you learned to use the User Manager to add and manage user accounts; modify, add, and delete groups; and manage security policies. For related information, see these chapters:

- Chapter 19, "Understanding Windows NT Network Services," explains basic networking with NT Workstation as a client.

- Chapter 20, "Configuring the Network at Your Workstation," shows you how to choose networking services, protocols, adapters, and so on to use your workstation with your network.

- Chapter 32, "Using the Event Viewer," shows you how to view the Security log, Auditing log, and the System log.

CHAPTER 16

Managing the Boot Process

by Michael O'Mara

When you turn on your computer, the system doesn't instantly spring to life with the Windows NT environment appearing in the blink of an eye. Instead, the system embarks on a boot process consisting of several steps. Most of those steps happen automatically, outside your direct control. However, there are some parts of the boot process that you *can* control, ranging from choosing what operating system to load to displaying troubleshooting information about the boot process. That's what this chapter is all about. ■

Dual-booting Windows NT or another operating system

Windows NT's boot options menu enables you to choose between NT and another operating system when you boot your machine.

How Windows NT uses traditional startup files

NT no longer needs traditional startup files such as AUTOEXEC.BAT and WIN.INI, but it can still use some of the information those files contain.

Changing boot options from the Control Panel

You can change some basic boot options from the comfort of your Control Panel.

Editing the BOOT.INI file

For more detailed control over the boot options of an Intel-based computer, you can edit the BOOT.INI file.

Using Hardware Profiles

Switching hardware configurations is no problem if you use Hardware Profiles as part of your boot process to tell NT which configuration you're using.

What Happens During the Boot Process?

The boot process begins with the hardware bootup and self-diagnostics. Windows NT plays no part in the process until your computer starts to load the operating system from the hard disk. When you installed Windows NT, it configured your system's boot record to run the NT boot loader (a program called NTLDR). It's when the boot loader takes over that things start to get interesting. The following steps summarize the Windows NT boot process:

1. As your system starts to boot up, the OS Loader notation appears on-screen as the boot loader refers to the BOOT.INI file for a list of operating systems. If you've configured your system to dual-boot between different operating systems, the boot loader presents the list of options on the boot options menu. If, however, you're not dual-booting, the boot loader skips displaying the boot options menu and goes directly to step 3.

2. You can choose one of the operating systems from the list or allow the boot loader to run the default selection after waiting a specified amount of time.

   If you choose another operating system from the menu, that operating system will load normally. Otherwise, the boot loader continues the Windows NT boot process with the following steps.

3. The boot loader runs NTDETECT to determine what components are installed in your computer system.

4. The OS Loader notation appears on-screen again briefly. If you press the space bar, the boot loader pauses the boot process and displays the Hardware Profile/Configuration Recovery menu, allowing you to choose a hardware configuration or the Last Known Good configuration. This feature is invaluable when you make configuration changes that unexpectedly prevent Windows NT from starting successfully.

5. The blue screen appears as the low-level components of Windows NT load.

6. Windows NT then refers to the Registry, initializes drivers, and starts services based on the information stored there.

7. The high-level Windows NT components load.

8. The Windows NT logo screen appears along with the Welcome dialog box. At this point, you can press Ctrl+Alt+Delete and log on to the system.

9. Windows NT opens your user account, installs your user profile, and performs network logons. You're ready to work in Windows NT.

   ▶ **See** "Using Last Known Good," **p. 33**

   ▶ **See** "Logging on to NT Workstation," **p. 30**

   ▶ **See** "Working with Accounts," **p. 380**

Part

III

Ch

16

N O T E   This sequence describes the Windows NT boot process on an 80×86-based system configured to dual-boot between Windows NT and a previous operating system. The process may vary slightly on other systems. For instance, the boot options menu can be configured not to appear, and RISC-based systems store boot information in non-volatile RAM instead of in the BOOT.INI file. ▪

As Windows NT loads, it does so by using configuration settings determined during or modified since installation. (Those installation and configuration issues are covered in other chapters.) The options that are specific to the boot process itself have to do with the choices presented on the boot options menu. In addition, if you run Windows NT on an 80×86-based system, you can edit the BOOT.INI file to activate some options to assist in troubleshooting your system.

Choosing Your Operating System

The most important feature of the boot loader is that it allows you to have two (or more) operating systems (or configurations) installed on your system and to choose which one you want to run when you boot the machine.

When you turn on the computer, the boot loader checks the contents of the BOOT.INI file and uses the information from the file to display the boot options menu shown in figure 16.1. When you install Windows NT, the options are created to give you a choice of running either NT or your previous operating system. The third option—Windows NT [VGA mode]—allows you to override the display settings and run Windows NT in plain VGA mode. This option is handy for troubleshooting display configuration problems. Later, you can edit the BOOT.INI file to tweak the options.

▶ **See** "Choosing an Operating System," **p. 28**

FIG. 16.1
The boot options
menu enables you to
choose operating
systems.

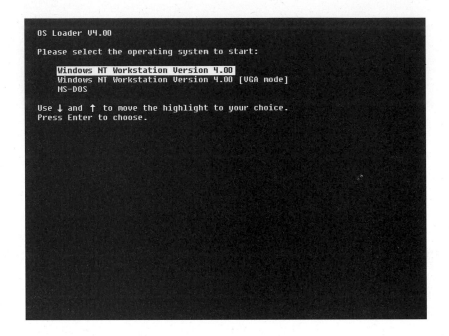

```
OS Loader V4.00

Please select the operating system to start:

    Windows NT Workstation Version 4.00
    Windows NT Workstation Version 4.00 [VGA mode]
    MS-DOS

Use ↓ and ↑ to move the highlight to your choice.
Press Enter to choose.
```

To use the boot options menu, simply press the up- or down-arrow keys to high-light the name of the operating system you want to run. Then press Enter to make your choice and begin loading the operating system. If you don't make a choice within a predetermined amount of time (the default is 30 seconds), the boot loader loads the default operating system. Later in this chapter, you learn to use the Windows NT Control Panel to change the default operating system and the length of time the boot options menu remains on-screen before invoking the default selection.

> **TIP** The boot options menu doesn't appear if it's configured to select the default operating system immediately. To display the menu, use the Control Panel or edit the BOOT.INI file to increase the timeout value to allow time for the boot options menu to appear.

Dual-Booting with DOS and Windows 3.1   To add Windows NT to a system running MS-DOS or DOS and Windows 3.1, simply run setup normally. Windows NT setup will install the system and automatically configure it to dual-boot between your previous operating system and Windows NT. Just be sure you choose the option to install NT into a separate directory instead of "upgrading" your old Windows installation.

▶ **See** "Installing Windows NT Workstation," **p. 1025**

To run MS-DOS, simply choose MS-DOS (rather than one of the Windows NT options) from the boot options menu. After DOS is running, you can start Windows 3.1.

Dual-Booting with Windows 95   You can install Windows NT and Windows 95 on the same system and dual-boot between them. However, installing both systems on the same system is a little different than installing Windows NT and Windows 3.11 on the same system. Unlike Windows 3.11, which runs on top of MS-DOS, Windows 95 is a complete operating system, and it even has its own dual-boot capability to let you choose Windows 95 or the previous (old MS-DOS) operating system.

If you plan to keep your other operating system, you can't install Windows NT and Windows 95 in the same directory because installing either operating system over the other will overwrite critical files. As a result, you can't "upgrade" Windows 95 to Windows NT or vice versa if you plan to dual-boot between them. You must install the new operating system in a different directory and set up all your options and applications from scratch.

To add Windows NT to a system running Windows 95, simply run Setup normally (starting it from Windows 95) and choose to install NT in a directory different from your existing Windows 95 system. Windows NT Setup installs the system and automatically configures it to dual-boot between Windows 95 and Windows NT.

To run Windows 95, choose Microsoft Windows (instead of one of the Windows NT options) from the boot options menu. If you installed Windows 95 over a previous MS-DOS system, you can run DOS by choosing Microsoft Windows from the boot options menu and then pressing F4 to bring up the Windows 95 boot options. You can then choose to run your previous (MS-DOS) operating system.

Adding Windows 95 to a system that is already running Windows NT is only slightly more complicated:

1. Reboot your system and choose to run DOS rather than Windows NT.
2. Install Windows 95 from the MS-DOS operating system.

When you reboot the computer, the Windows NT boot options menu should appear. Choosing the MS-DOS option will run Windows 95 because Windows 95 has now replaced the MS-DOS operating system.

Part

III

Ch

16

Later, you can edit the BOOT.INI file so the name of the option that appears in the boot options menu reflects the change in operating systems.

Dual-Booting with OS/2   You can also install Windows NT on a system running OS/2. Just as it does when you install NT on a DOS or Windows 95 system, Windows NT Setup installs the system and automatically configures it to dual-boot between the previous operating system and Windows NT. OS/2 appears as an option in the boot options menu. Simply choose that option to run OS/2 instead of Windows NT.

Working with the Startup Files

You're probably accustomed to working with a variety of startup files containing system configuration information. The MS-DOS operating system has its AUTOEXEC.BAT and CONFIG.SYS files. The WIN.INI and SYSTEM.INI files (among others) contain configuration information for Windows 3.1.

Windows NT doesn't store system configuration information in any of these files; but it doesn't completely ignore them either.

AUTOEXEC.BAT and CONFIG.SYS   At system startup, Windows NT scans the AUTOEXEC.BAT and CONFIG.SYS files and transfers any PATH, PROMPT, and SET commands to its own environment variables. Windows NT ignores any other entries in these DOS configuration files. It won't start applications or initialize drivers based on commands in the AUTOEXEC.BAT or CONFIG.SYS files.

If you need to run an application automatically every time you start your computer, don't add a command to run the application to the AUTOEXEC.BAT file. Instead, add a shortcut for the application to the Start menu's STARTUP folder. For most device drivers, use the Services applet in the Control Panel to define the service and set its startup type. You can install and configure other drivers with other Control Panel applets.

▶ **See** "Adding Ports," **p. 289**
▶ **See** "Managing System Services and Devices," **p. 361**

You might expect that Windows NT would use the AUTOEXEC.BAT and CONFIG.SYS files to provide configuration information for the MS-DOS based programs you run. However, that isn't the case. The configuration for the DOS virtual machines that Windows NT creates when you run DOS programs comes from special files created for that purpose (AUTOEXEC.NT and CONFIG.NT) and from the programs' property sheet.

▶ **See** "Configuring DOS and Win 16 Applications To Run in Windows NT," **p. 439**

WIN.INI and SYSTEM.INI   Unlike previous versions of Windows, Windows NT doesn't use the WIN.INI and SYSTEM.INI files for storing configuration information. That information is now stored in the Registry. If you install Windows NT as an upgrade to Windows 3.1, the installation program will copy settings from your existing WIN.INI, SYSTEM.INI, CONTROL.INI, PROGMAN.INI, and WINFILE.INI files into the Windows NT Registry automatically.

▶ **See** "Understanding the Registry," **p. 894**

Although Windows NT doesn't rely on the WIN.INI and SYSTEM.INI files for configuration information, it continues to maintain the files for backward compatibility with older 16-bit Windows applications—applications that expect to find those files and to be able to store application configuration information there.

BOOT.INI   When it comes to system startup files, Windows NT's BOOT.INI file is the new kid on the block. This file contains the boot loader settings with such details as the location of the operating system files.

The BOOT.INI file is created during your Windows NT installation, and it's stored in the root directory of the system partition of the main hard drive. (The BOOT.INI file is used for 80×86-based systems only. RISC-based systems store boot information in non-volatile RAM instead of a file.) Like most system initialization files, BOOT.INI is a text file, and you can edit it with any text editor.

> **CAUTION**
>
> Don't delete or move the file BOOTSECT.DOS. It contains the address of the boot record for your alternate operating system. (The file has the same name, even if your alternate operating system isn't MS-DOS.) If the boot loader can't find this file in the root directory of the system partition on your main hard drive, you won't be able to boot your alternate operating system.

Customizing the Boot Process

Your basic boot options are defined when you install Windows NT. For example, the installation program automatically configures your system to dual-boot between Windows NT and the operating system you were running when you installed NT. By default, when you boot your system, the boot options menu appears for 30 seconds. If you don't make a selection within that time, the boot loader loads the default operating system—Windows NT.

You're not stuck with those choices, however. You can modify the behavior of the boot options menu with the Windows NT Control Panel, and you can exercise still more control over the boot process by editing the BOOT.INI file.

Changing Boot Options from Control Panel

Typically, the only changes you need to make in the boot options menu are to specify which of the available operating system choices will be the default, and how long the boot options menu will remain onscreen before the boot loader begins loading that default operating system. You can adjust both options easily by using the Windows NT Control Panel.

To adjust the boot option settings, open the Control Panel and double-click the System icon. This opens the System dialog box, as shown in figure 16.2. The boot options are found on the Startup/Shutdown tab.

First select a default operating system. The setting in the Startup field determines which of the available operating systems will be loaded if you don't make a selection from the boot options menu within the allotted time. You can choose from the options available in the drop-down list box. These options are determined when you install Windows NT, depending on what the previous operating system was.

Next, set the timeout value for the boot options menu. The value in the Show List For field specifies how long the boot options menu will remain onscreen, awaiting your choice, before the boot loader starts the default operating system. The acceptable range of values is 0–999 seconds.

FIG. 16.2
The most important
boot options are
controlled from the
System dialog box.

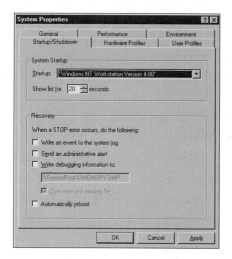

 Setting the timeout value to zero causes the boot loader to start the default operating system immediately without waiting for any user input. This effectively disables the boot options menu, preventing it from appearing onscreen. Later, if you want the boot options menu to appear, simply increase the timeout value and then reboot.

Editing the BOOT.INI file

When you make changes in the boot options, the settings are stored in the BOOT.INI file. The BOOT.INI file is stored in the root directory of your system partition of the main hard drive. You can adjust the most common boot options from the Control Panel, but you can also change those settings, and others, by editing the BOOT.INI file directly.

N O T E 80×86-based systems use the BOOT.INI file. RISC-based systems, on the other hand, store the boot information in non-volatile RAM. ▪

A typical BOOT.INI file might look like Listing 16.1.

Listing 16.1   A Typical BOOT.INI File for a Windows NT or MS-DOS System

```
[boot loader]
timeout=30
default= multi(0)disk(0)rdisk(1)partition(1)\WINNT4

[operating systems]
multi(0)disk(0)rdisk(1)partition(1)\WINNT4=
➥"Windows NT Workstation Version 4.00"
multi(0)disk(0)rdisk(1)partition(1)\WINNT4=
➥"Windows NT Workstation Version 4.00 [VGA mode]" /basevideo /sos
C:\="MS-DOS"
```

The two lines in the `[boot loader]` section correspond to the options you can set in the Control Panel—the timeout and the default operating system, respectively. The `[operating systems]` section defines what operating system options are available. Each line corresponds to an option in the boot options menu.

The first portion of each line in the `[operating systems]` section defines the location of the operating system files. (The lines beginning with `multi` or `scsi` describe the location of the Windows NT operating system.) You shouldn't need to edit this information. The portion of each line enclosed in quotes is the descriptive text that appears in the boot options menu. You can edit this text to suit your preferences.

CAUTION

Be very careful when editing the BOOT.INI file. Errors in the file (such as an incorrect location in one of the `multi` lines) could cause Windows NT to fail to boot. Before editing the BOOT.INI file, be sure that you have a good backup of the file and an Emergency Repair Disk on hand.

One change you can make in the BOOT.INI file is to rearrange the order of the lines under the `[operating system]` heading to change the order of the items in the boot options menu. For instance, if you want `MS-DOS` to appear at the top of the list, you can use a text editor to edit the BOOT.INI file so that the line `C:\="MS-DOS"` is the first line following the `[operating systems]` heading.

Changing the Timeout and Default Operating System   Making changes in the `[boot loader]` section of the BOOT.INI file has the same effect as changing the corresponding settings in the Control Panel. The `timeout=` setting is simply a numerical value in seconds.

Part
III

Ch
16

TIP You can set the boot options menu to wait indefinitely for your choice by changing the timeout value to -1. You must make this change by editing the BOOT.INI file, because the System dialog box in the Control Panel accepts only values between 0–999 seconds.

The `default=` setting determines which option from the `[operating systems]` section will take effect if you don't make a choice from the boot option within the allotted time. If you make a change in this setting, be sure to cut and paste the exact text for the option you want from the `[operating systems]` heading to avoid typos. (You can omit the text in quotes. That's for your benefit; boot loader doesn't need it.)

Changing the Name of the Alternate Operating System

One change you might want to make is to alter the name of one or more operating system options that appear in the boot options menu. Remember that the items under the `[operating systems]` heading in the BOOT.INI file correspond to the numbered options in the boot options menu, and the portion of each item enclosed in double quotes is what will appear in the on-screen menu.

You can change the text of the menu entry by editing the corresponding line in the BOOT.INI file.

For example, if you add Windows NT to a system that previously ran Windows 3.11 and configure it to dual-boot, the previous operating system option in the boot options menu appears as Microsoft Windows. If you subsequently upgrade Windows 3.11 to Windows 95, you'll want to update the boot options menu to reflect the change. To make the menu item appear as a more descriptive Windows 95, edit the BOOT.INI file so that the `c:\="Microsoft Windows"` line under the `[operating systems]` heading reads `c:\="Windows 95"`.

Getting Debugging Information During Bootup

If you need to troubleshoot the boot process, you can instruct the boot loader and Windows NT to provide information about the boot process to aid in debugging boot problems. To enable this extra boot process reporting, edit the BOOT.INI file to add one or more of the switches in the following table to the end of the operating system's line in the `[operating systems]` section of the file. The data will be sent to a COM port, where you can route it to another machine for analysis.

Switch	Description
/NODEBUG	Turns debugging off (this is the default).
/DEBUG	Enables debug reporting.
/DEBUGPORT=COMx	Specifies the COM port for debug output.
/BAUDRATE=nnnnn	Specifies the baud rate for the debug data being sent to the COM port.
/CRASHDEBUG	Used for remote debugging via modem. It allows access to stack pages following a fatal error.
/SOS	Displays the names of drivers as they load during setup.
/NoSerialMice=COMx,COMy	Disables detection of a serial mouse on the specified COM port or ports.

Testing Windows NT Performance with Less Memory   You can fool Windows NT into thinking you have less memory than is actually available.

Normally, you want Windows to use all available memory. However, there might be times when you want to test the performance of Windows NT or an NT application with less memory. In that case, you can add a switch to the end of a line in the [operating systems] section of the BOOT.INI file to restrict Windows NT to a limited amount of memory.

The format for the switch is

/MAXMEM=*n*

where *n* is the amount of memory you want to test. The value can be less than the amount of physical memory available, but must be at least the 8M required by Windows NT for proper operation.

In Listing 16.2, for example, the second option in the [operating systems] section forces Windows NT to run on only 8M of RAM; the first option runs the same version of the operating system using the full complement of installed RAM.

**Listing 16.2   The /MAXMEM Switch Forces Windows NT to Use Only
a Limited Amount of RAM**

```
[boot loader]
timeout=30
default= multi(0)disk(0)rdisk(1)partition(1)\WINNT4

[operating systems]
multi(0)disk(0)rdisk(1)partition(1)\WINNT4=
➥"Windows NT Workstation Version 4.00"
multi(0)disk(0)rdisk(1)partition(1)\WINNT4=
➥"Windows NT Workstation Version 4.00 8Mb" /MAXMEM=8
multi(0)disk(0)rdisk(1)partition(1)\WINNT4=
➥"Windows NT Workstation Version 4.00 [VGA mode]" /basevideo /sos
C:\="MS-DOS"
```

Part
III

Ch
16

Using Hardware Profiles

One of your options during the boot process is to select a Hardware Profile. A *Hardware Profile* is basically a record of a particular system configuration—a list of the devices and device drivers. When you install NT, the system creates a Hardware Profile called Original Configuration. As you add and remove devices and drivers, NT updates the Hardware Profile for you. For most people, the only Hardware Profiles they need are the Original Configuration profile and, perhaps, the Last Known Good configuration.

However, you can create and maintain multiple Hardware Profiles if needed. This feature is a boon to hardware test technicians, but it's more likely to be employed by notebook computer users. You might create one Hardware Profile for your notebook computer alone and another profile for your notebook computer connected to its docking station, complete with network connection and auxiliary devices.

Managing Hardware Profiles

In order to choose a Hardware Profile, you need to have more than one profile to choose from. To begin creating an additional Hardware Profile, double-click the System icon in the Control Panel to open the System dialog box shown earlier in figure 16.2. Click the Hardware Profiles tab to display the options shown in figure 16.3.

FIG. 16.3

You can create Hardware Profiles in this dialog box.

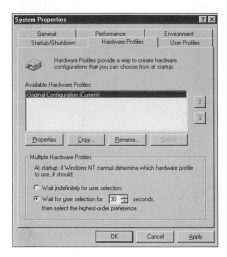

You create a new Hardware Profile by copying an existing profile. By default, the current profile (Original Configuration) is highlighted, but you can select another profile to copy if you want.

After you select the profile to copy, simply click the Copy button to open the Copy Profile dialog box (see fig. 16.4).

FIG. 16.4

Name your new Hardware Profiles in this dialog box.

Enter a name for your new profile and click the OK button to add the Hardware Profile to the list in the Hardware Profile tab of the System Properties dialog box.

Next, you can select the new profile and click the Properties button to open the New Configuration Properties dialog box shown in figure 16.5. If you're configuring a portable computer, check the appropriate options pertaining to docking and then click the OK button. Once you add a profile to the list, it will be available for selection from the Hardware Profiles/Configuration Recovery menu the next time you boot your system.

FIG. 16.5
NT needs to know
if your portable
computer is docked.

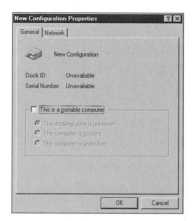

After you define multiple Hardware Profiles, you can use the other settings in the Hardware Profiles tab to tell NT what configuration to use as its default. The default configuration is the one that appears at the top of the Available Hardware Profiles list. To change a profile's position in the list, select it and click the up- or down-arrow buttons to move the profile up or down in the list. The options in the Multiple Hardware Profiles section at the bottom of the dialog box let you define how long NT will wait for you to make a selection from the Hardware Profiles/Configuration Recovery menu during a system boot. After you finish adjusting options in the Hardware Profiles, click the OK button to close the Hardware Profiles dialog box, and then close the System dialog box.

So far, your new Hardware Profile is just a duplicate of an existing Hardware Profile. You use the Devices and Services applets from the Control Panel to control the configuration of each Hardware Profile, enabling and disabling specific devices and drivers.

▶ **See** "Managing System Services," **p. 362**
▶ **See** "Managing System Devices," **p. 371**

Choosing a Hardware Profile at Startup

After you have defined multiple Hardware Profiles, choosing a profile during system boot is easy. After you select NT as your operating system from the boot menu, the OS Loader screen appears, and you can press the space bar to bring up the Hardware Profile/Configuration Recovery menu. This menu operates in much the same way as the boot options menu. The available Hardware Profiles are listed in the same order they appeared in the Hardware Profiles dialog box. You can use the up- or down-arrow keys to highlight a selection and then press the Enter key to select the highlighted Hardware Profile. If you don't make a selection within the allotted time (usually 30 seconds), NT will use the default Hardware Profile unless you opted to have NT wait indefinitely.

Of course, if you don't open the Hardware Profile/Configuration Recovery menu during the boot process, NT uses the default Hardware Profile. You don't have to bother with making a Hardware Profile selection unless you want to boot your system using a different configuration.

From Here...

This chapter has covered the principal options you can choose during system boot and how to set up the menus that provide those choices. Check out these other chapters for more details on configuring the various options.

- Chapter 2, "Getting Started with NT Workstation 4.0," offers details on the Last Known Good feature.
- Chapter 14, "Managing System Services and Devices," covers system configuration options affecting Hardware Profiles.
- Chapter 15, "Securing Windows NT Workstation," provides information on setting up user accounts and security.
- Appendix A, "Installing Windows NT Workstation," details the installation process and how to create a dual-boot system.

Working with Applications

CHAPTER 17

Working with Applications

by Paul Sanna

Soon after installing Windows NT Workstation, you're ready to start loading and running applications in your new NT environment. Some of these may be older applications you've had for awhile, including character-based DOS programs and Windows 3.*x* applications, and some may be newer Windows NT-specific or Windows 95 versions of programs. Luckily, you should have few problems installing and running any applications you've used with previous versions of Windows, including Windows 3.*x*, Windows NT, and Windows 95. Windows NT provides broad support for many types of applications. In Windows NT, separate internal subsystems support running older DOS and Windows applications, and 32-bit applications built for Windows NT and Windows 95 naturally run well in NT Workstation. Getting these applications installed and running smoothly is not automatic, however. There are special issues related to each type of application you plan to run in Windows NT. This chapter

Learn about applications you can run in Windows NT

You can run a number of types of applications in Windows NT. In this chapter, you learn which types of applications are compatible with Windows NT and what their distinguishing features are.

Install applications in Windows NT

You learn how to install applications in Windows NT. You learn how to prepare for installing into Windows NT, as well as how to use the new Add/Remove Programs utility in the Control Panel.

Run DOS and Win16 applications in Windows NT

Applications built for the DOS operating systems, including those built specifically for Windows 3.*x*, sometimes require special attention when they run in Windows NT. This chapter shows you how to run these types of applications.

Run Windows 95 applications in Windows NT

Applications built for Windows 95 can run in Windows NT. You learn how to install and configure these types of applications.

shows how to install and run applications in Windows NT. You learn how to install applications, the special settings required to make older applications run in Windows NT, and the unique aspects of new Windows NT and Windows 95 applications. ■

Identifying Application Types

Four types of applications are discussed in this chapter. Before diving into information on installing and running these applications, you should understand what applications this chapter deals with:

■ *Windows 95 applications*. These are 32-bit applications built specifically for Windows 95. Many of these types of applications run without issue in Windows NT, and most show the official Microsoft Windows 95 logo on their packaging. These applications cannot run in Window 3.*x* without the use of the Win32s kit from Microsoft.

■ *Windows NT applications*. These are 32-bit programs built just for Windows NT. There are fewer of these applications than any of the other three types covered in this section. These applications also can run only in Windows NT and usually in Windows 95.

■ *DOS applications*. This set of 16-bit applications is those that do not run in Windows except using the Windows command prompt. These are the character-based applications that existed before Windows, though many of them have been developed since Windows.

■ *Windows 3*.x *Applications*. These 16-bit applications also are known as Win16 applications because they were built with the Win16 software development kit. This group of applications refers to those built for Windows 3.0, 3.1, 3.11, and Windows for Workgroups.

Installing Applications

Most software these days is shipped with an accompanying installation program, a small program whose sole function is to get the software installed and configured on your PC. Generally, the more sophisticated the application that you are installing, the more sophisticated the installation program will be. There certainly are exceptions to this rule, however. Installation programs vary from product to product in regard to their flexibility, friendliness, and capability to cope with problems that occur during the installation. However, most, if not all, applications you acquire provide you with some form of installation instructions.

The process of installing application programs is almost always the same for DOS, Windows 3.*x*, Windows NT, and Windows 95 programs. The process usually involves running a program located on the first disk of the installation set. Often the program is called INSTALL or SETUP and has an extension of EXE, COM, CMD, or BAT. To be sure of what program launches installation, read the installation instructions first. After this program is located and launched, an intelligent process then takes over to guide you through the rest of the installation. Starting with version 4.0, a special utility, the Add/Remove Programs applet, handles many chores associated with installing applications. Using the Add/Remove Programs applet is covered later in this section.

Installation Methods

The method a company or software developer uses to deliver software to the consumer also affects the installation process. Software can be made available commercially, such as through a retail store or mail order, or software can be free or tested on a try-before-you-buy basis. The next few sections look at the installation issues related both to commercial software and shareware/freeware.

Commercial Software   Most software you purchase will be commercial applications, which include printed or CD-based manuals, floppy disks or CD-ROM for installation, and perhaps a toll free number for technical support and assistance. Because this software arrives to you in a ready-to-install format, all you have to do is follow the included installation procedure to get the software loaded on your system.

Shareware and Freeware   Although buying software from a store is one way to get new applications, it is by no means the only way. Making software available electronically via online services or the Internet has become the method of choice for distributing other types of software such as *freeware* (software you pay nothing for), *shareware* (software you are normally allowed to evaluate for a certain period of time before you are required to pay for it), demonstration/evaluation versions of software, and even some commercial software applications. Electronic distribution normally means using a modem to dial an online service, such as a public or private bulletin-board system (BBS), the Internet, or a commercial online service such as CompuServe, America Online, Prodigy, or The Microsoft Network.

 http://www.mcp.com/que/software   You can find shareware, freeware, and other useful information in Que's software library.

When software is downloaded, it is usually comprised of a single compressed file (or *archive*) that contains within it the files that together make up the application. The files are reduced to a fraction of their original size and combined together using a data-compression utility, such as PKWare's PKZIP. Compressing the files in this way makes distribution both simpler (one file versus many) and faster.

> **CAUTION**
>
> It is possible for the software you download to contain *viruses* (programs attached to other programs that cause damage to your data). It is highly recommended that you acquire some form of anti-virus software and scan all files you download prior to running them. Some utilities are even capable of scanning files still contained within archives before they are uncompressed.

Handling Self-Extracting Compressed Files   A useful variant of the standard compressed file (such as ZIP) is a *self-extracting compressed file*. This type of file is a compressed, archive file that has been converted into a stand-alone executable file. This means that the compressed file knows how to *unpack* itself; it does not need the compression utility that created it. These files end in an EXE extension rather than in ZIP (or other archive format) extension and can be launched by simply typing the first part of the name before the EXE and pressing Enter as if you were starting a program. The decompression begins automatically after you press Enter, and the files in the archive are created in the current directory.

Often, when a self-extracting file is unpacked, a collection of setup files appears on your system. You may then have to run a setup program that was extracted from an archive file. Indications that this is the case occur after you have extracted the file: you haven't noticed any installation program launched on your system, and of the files created in the directory where you extracted the file, you find one named similar to SETUP.EXE or INSTALL.EXE. Again, documentation provided with the program, such as in a READ.ME or SETUP.TXT file or a file similarly named, should provide you help.

> **CAUTION**
>
> Before launching a self-extracting archive file, be sure the file is located in the directory where you want the files to be created. Also, be sure that no files are in the directory that might be overwritten by identically named files in the archive. Many self-extracting files will not ask for confirmation before overwriting an existing file with the same name as a file extracted from the archive.

Part
IV

Ch
17

AutoRun Compact Discs   Starting with version 4.0, Windows NT has a new feature for working with compact discs (CDs) called *AutoRun*. This feature automatically launches the application associated with a CD as soon as you load the CD into the computer. For example, when you load the Microsoft Office for Windows 95 CD into a system running Windows NT, the Setup dialog box automatically appears without you having touched a key or clicked the mouse. You might notice that the CD supplied with this book is AutoRun enabled.

N O T E   If you were to load an audio CD into a computer running Windows NT 4.0, the CD Player applet would start automatically, playing the first selection on the CD (see fig. 17.1). ■

FIG. 17.1
The CD Player applet is launched as soon as you load an audio CD into the CD drive.

Preparing for Installation

If you want to maximize the success of your software installation, there are a few steps you can take beforehand. These steps help ensure a smooth installation and help prevent any nasty surprises. These steps are, by no means, necessary, but they will help you get the most from your new software and your NT system in general:

1. Verify ahead of time that you have sufficient RAM (memory) and hard disk space for the application you are running. Check the application's documentation or call the company to find out if your system is adequate for the new software.

2. If you have an NT-compatible hard disk defragmentation utility, consider using it to optimize the speed and organization of data on your hard disk.

> **CAUTION**
>
> If you are running dual-boot NT/DOS with a FAT partition and are using long file names, do not use a standard DOS or Windows 3.x disk defragmenter unless you are sure that it supports long file names—otherwise, damage to the files or the disk's file allocation table may result.

3. Make backup copies of the NT Registry and the WIN.INI, SYSTEM.INI, AUTOEXEC.NT, and CONFIG.NT files. The Registry contains all of NT's configuration information, and the INI files are used for backward-compatibility with earlier Windows versions. The NT files are used to configure the command prompt environment and set environment variables. Any of these files can be modified by the installation routine, and it is therefore good practice to have a preinstallation backup copy of each.

   ▶ **See** "Understanding the Registry," **p. 894**

Note that the NT Backup program or a similar NT backup program must be used to back up the Registry.

Using Add/Remove Programs to Install Applications

The easiest method for installing a new application in Windows NT is to use the Add/Remove Programs applet. The Add/Remove Programs applet takes some of the guesswork out of installing applications. For Windows 95 and Windows NT applications, it provides a central location for uninstalling applications.

N O T E Windows 95 and Windows NT applications behave differently during installation than DOS and Windows 3.x applications. For the sake of this note, consider applications built for Windows 95 and Windows NT no differently. When these types of applications are installed into Windows NT, they register themselves with the system. This helps them run better with Windows NT, helps them use common components built into Windows NT more easily, and significantly reduces the hassle of uninstalling them. Only Windows 95 and Windows NT applications have this feature, which is why only those types of applications appear in the Add/Remove Programs dialog box. A thorough discussion of Windows NT and Windows 95 applications appears at the end of this chapter. ■

To use Add/Remove Programs to install an application, follow these steps:

1. Open the Start menu and then choose Settings, Control Panel. The Control Panel folder appears (see fig. 17.2).

FIG. 17.2
The Add/Remove Programs icon is found in the Control Panel folder.

Add/Remove Programs

2. Start Add/Remove Programs (see fig. 17.3).

3. Choose Install. The dialog box shown in figure 17.4 appears.

4. Insert the disk containing the setup program for the application you want to install. For applications with multiple installation disks, the setup disk is usually the first. If the application is delivered on CD, load the disc into the CD drive on the computer.

5. Choose Next. Windows NT now searches your system for a program it recognizes as being used for setup. It first looks through disks in floppy drives and then through a CD if one is loaded in your CD drive.

FIG. 17.3

The Add/Remove Programs applet walks you through the installation and removal of applications, as well as of Windows NT components.

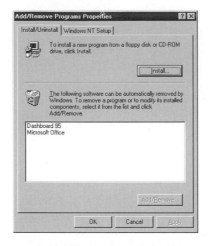

FIG. 17.4

The Add/Remove Programs applet gives you the opportunity to load the distribution media for the application you want to install.

6. If the Wizard finds a setup program, it displays the program name and location in an edit box prompting you for confirmation (see fig. 17.5). If the program the Wizard finds is correct, choose Finish. If the Wizard cannot find a setup program, or the program the Wizard finds is incorrect, supply the correct name and location of the setup program in the Command line for installation program edit box. Alternatively, instead of typing the command via keyboard, choose Browse to search for the application graphically. Choose Finish.

FIG. 17.5

Windows NT attempts to locate the file that starts installation of your new application.

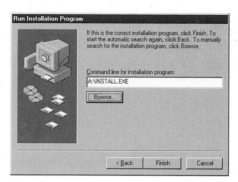

Add/Remove Programs launches the setup program you indicate. When complete, the Wizard will close, but the Control Panel folder still will be open. Regardless, you are ready to run the application you just installed. Depending on the application, one or more of the following describes the state of the your system:

- Windows NT is telling you it must temporarily shut down to properly finish installing the application. Windows NT will automatically restart after doing so. You may also defer the shutdown and subsequent restart (Windows NT will ask you), but the application you've installed will not run properly until the system is restarted.

- A shortcut appears on the desktop for the application you just installed.

- A choice appears on the Start menu—or on one of the menus that appear on the Start menu—for the application you just installed.

- A special utility or graphical element, such as the Microsoft Office for Windows 95 shortcut toolbar, appears on the desktop, related to the application you just installed (see fig. 17.6).

Part

IV

Ch

17

FIG. 17.6
The Microsoft Office
shortcut bar (at the
top of the screen)
provides a useful
interface for
launching applica-
tions quickly.

Microsoft Office
shortcut bar

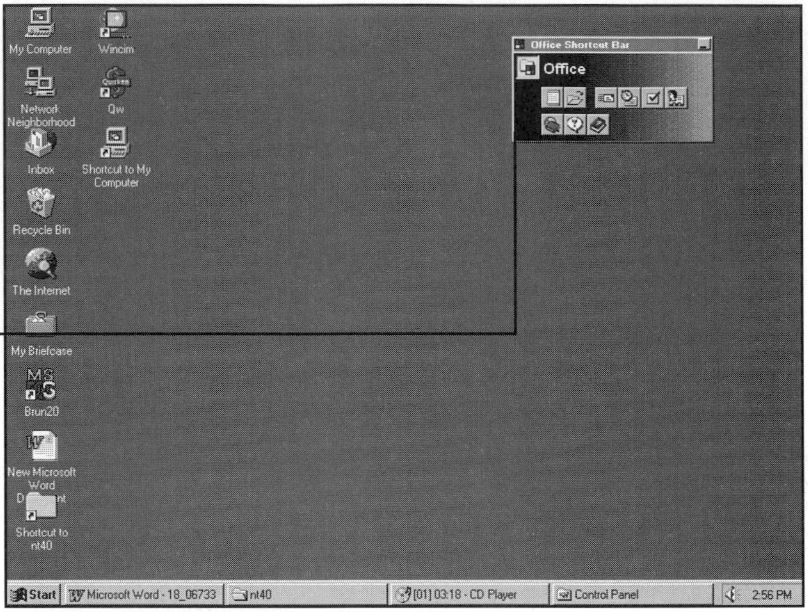

Installing Applications from the Desktop

You can install an application directly from the desktop.

The process of installing software from the desktop is started by launching the main setup program accompanying the application. To do this, you need to know the drive and directory where the program is located, along with the program's file name. Check the documentation for the specific file name required to launch the setup program. Often, if a set of disks is used as the distribution media, Disk 1 indicates the file to run.

To install an application from the desktop, follow these steps:

1. Open the Start menu and then choose <u>R</u>un (see fig. 17.7).

2. In the <u>O</u>pen edit box, enter the full path and name of the setup program. Alternatively, instead of typing the command via keyboard, choose <u>B</u>rowse to search for the application graphically.

3. When the correct file name is entered, click OK or press Enter to start the installation. If other Win16 applications are running while you are installing the new Win16 application, you may want to check the Run In Separate

<u>M</u>emory Space option so that the installation program does not monopolize use of the processor. The application's install program now starts.

FIG. 17.7
You can launch installation of an application via the Run dialog box off the Start menu.

N O T E Like installing an application from the desktop, you can also install an application from Windows NT Explorer or My Computer. The prerequisite is that you must know the name and location of the program that launches installation of the application. Open the drive and folder that contains the installation program, and then choose the program as you would any other application. For instruction on the use of My Computer and Windows NT Explorer, turn to Chapter 3, "Working in Windows NT." ■

Removing Applications

It is likely that you will want to remove an application from your NT Workstation at some point. In the case of Windows NT and Windows 95 applications, this is an easy task, handled mainly by the Add/Remove Programs wizard. For DOS and Windows 3.x applications, the challenge of removing all traces of a no-longer-useful application while leaving Windows NT in good working condition is much tougher.

Removing Windows 3.x and DOS Applications

Uninstalling DOS and especially Win16 applications can be difficult, considering the mayhem some of these types of applications cause during installation. These applications make a habit of affecting critical system files such as AUTOEXEC.BAT, CONFIG.SYS, SYSTEM.INI, and WIN.INI. In addition, these types of applications sometimes install older versions of critical common library files into the System subdirectory of the main Windows directory. Following are three strategies to help manage the safe removal of Windows 3.x and DOS applications from your Windows NT system:

■ *Check SYSTEM.INI/WIN.INI.* Search these files for any occurrence of the application you are about to remove or the directory where it is installed. If any other application is using the directory or any of the other files in it, it may be unwise to delete the directory. As much as these INI files are not used by Windows NT, their use is supported to run older Windows 3.*x* and DOS applications. You can find these files in the SYSTEM subdirectory beneath the main Windows NT directory.

■ *Preserve common DLLs.* Do not delete any files that the application you are deleting may have installed in any Windows NT directory. These files might be used by other applications and deleting them could cause the other applications to stop working. Although these files are tough to identify, they may support common technologies that are used by many applications, or provide services to many different applications, such as special controls. The documentation shipped with your application probably can tell you what files were installed and where during installation of the application.

■ *Rename the Directory First.* Even if you feel confident that deleting the directory where the Windows 3.*x* or DOS application is installed will not cause problems, don't do so yet. Instead, first rename the directory where the application is installed, restart the system, and then check to see if the system, including other Win16 applications, is in working order. If all seems well, only then, delete the directory.

Removing Windows NT and Windows 95 Applications

Your chances for a successful uninstallation increase significantly when you are working with a Windows 95 or Windows NT application, compared to removing an older 16-bit application. Most new 32-bit applications include built-in support for uninstallation. In fact, a requirement for Windows 95 applications to qualify for the official Windows 95 logo is to provide easy uninstallation support. This means that a Windows 95 application must load the critical information necessary to uninstall an application into the system registry during installation. Any application that can be removed by using Windows NT's built-in support for uninstallation appears in the Add/Remove Programs Wizard.

To remove an application using the Add/Remove Programs Wizard, follow these steps:

1. Open the Start menu and then choose Settings, Control Panel. The Control Panel folder appears.

2. Start the Add/Remove Programs Wizard.

3. Click the name of the application that you want to remove from the list box that appears in the bottom half of the dialog box (see fig. 17.8).

FIG. 17.8
Select from a list which applications you want removed from Windows NT. Only applications that register themselves with Windows NT when they are installed can be reliably uninstalled by NT.

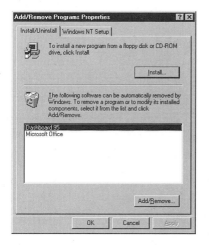

4. Choose Remove/Add. The application's uninstallation program now starts. Some applications, such as Microsoft Office, use a common utility to uninstall, add components, or completely reinstall. If this is the case, choose the uninstall option. Also, you may be asked to provide the original installation media, so you may want to have it handy.

Understanding How DOS and Win16 Applications Work with Windows NT

The first set of applications examined in this chapter is DOS and Win16 applications. In this section, you learn how NT Workstation supports DOS and Windows 3.*x* applications. You also learn about the architecture of the subsystem that supports running DOS and Win16 applications, as well as how NT Workstation creates the proper environment for those applications. With this understanding, you are better prepared to troubleshoot problems with these types of applications.

Part
IV

Ch
17

A Quick Word About the Architecture

When a DOS or Win16 application starts in NT Workstation, the application thinks it is running in the DOS operating system. Actually, the application is running in what NT calls a *virtual DOS machine* (VDM). A VDM is a virtual process that simulates the DOS environment for any DOS or Win16 application running in it. Any services requested by the applications are brokered by the VDM to virtual device drivers and other service providers, which pass requests on to the real NT drivers or other systems in NT.

When a VDM is created for a Win16 application, however, a level of complexity is added. The standard VDM is insufficient to support Win16 applications, as these applications rely on services provided by the Windows system. NT Workstation uses a system known as *WOW (Win16 on Win32)* to translate requests from Win16 applications to the appropriate provider in NT. These services range from user interface painting to memory management.

The VDM is a stable environment for DOS applications. Each DOS application launched in NT Workstation runs in its own VDM. This contrasts to how Win16 applications are treated. All Win16 applications run in one VDM. After one Win16 application is loaded, the WOW VDM is started, and all subsequent Win16 applications are run in that VDM. This design can lead to problems if you run a volatile Win16 application; if one Win16 application crashes, it could bring down the entire VDM along with all Win16 applications running in it. You have the option of running a Win16 application in its own memory space. This is a memory-expensive operation, and this topic is covered later in the chapter.

Understanding the Environment for DOS and Win16 Applications

The most critical factor in determining whether a 16-bit application can run is environment. The correct drivers must be loaded (and in the correct order), pathing must be correct, and a handful of other settings have to be in place. Windows NT provides broad control over the environment in which you run Win16 and DOS applications. For example, support is provided by a number of virtual device drivers, so there is little for you to do to tune the environment. Five elements contribute to the stable, consistent VDM environment:

- AUTOEXEC.BAT and CONFIG.SYS
- AUTOEXEC.NT and CONFIG.NT
- INI file settings and the Registry
- Device drivers
- Property sheets for DOS applications

You take a look at each of these elements in the following sections.

AUTOEXEC.BAT and CONFIG.SYS   For those NT enthusiasts with short memories, AUTOEXEC.BAT and CONFIG.SYS are the two main files DOS uses to configure a PC running the DOS operating system. When NT Workstation is started, environment variables and path information are retrieved from AUTOEXEC.BAT. Any commands that load device drivers are started, and any other processes are ignored—CONFIG.SYS also is ignored.

AUTOEXEC.NT and CONFIG.NT   The AUTOEXEC.NT and CONFIG.NT files are much like their AUTOEXEC.BAT and CONFIG.SYS cousins from the DOS operating system in NT Workstation. AUTOEXEC.NT and CONFIG.NT are used to configure the environment for all applications, including those that run from the command prompt like DOS applications. Any commands issued in either of those two files—such as loading a driver or starting a memory-resident program—occur for all applications you launch from the command prompt.

AUTOEXEC.NT and CONFIG.NT typically are located in the SYSTEM32 subdirectory of the main NT directory. You can view or edit the contents of the files using the Edit utility from the command prompt.

To view or edit the contents of AUTOEXEC.NT and CONFIG.NT, follow these steps:

1. Open the Start menu and choose Programs, Run.
2. From the Run dialog box, enter **Notepad** *name of file* and press Enter. The Notepad utility then starts with the file you specified open for viewing (see fig. 17.9).

Part

IV

Ch

17

FIG. 17.9

You can view and edit the AUTOEXEC.NT and CONFIG.NT files using the Windows NT editor.

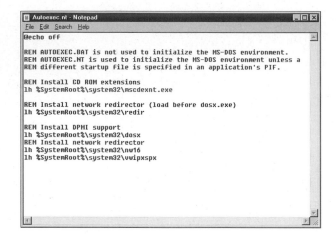

```
Autoexec.nt - Notepad
File  Edit  Search  Help
@echo off

REM AUTOEXEC.BAT is not used to initialize the MS-DOS environment.
REM AUTOEXEC.NT is used to initialize the MS-DOS environment unless a
REM different startup file is specified in an application's PIF.

REM Install CD ROM extensions
lh %SystemRoot%\system32\mscdexnt.exe

REM Install network redirector (load before dosx.exe)
lh %SystemRoot%\system32\redir

REM Install DPMI support
lh %SystemRoot%\system32\dosx
REM Install network redirector
lh %SystemRoot%\system32\nw16
lh %SystemRoot%\system32\vwipxspx
```

3. If you make any changes to the file, choose <u>F</u>ile, <u>S</u>ave. When you are through working with the file, choose <u>F</u>ile, E<u>x</u>it.

4. From the command prompt window, enter **EXIT** and press Enter.

INI File Settings   INI files are used in Windows 3.*x* to supply initialization information to Windows and to applications that run in Windows. One of the top complaints about the use of INI files is that you would often have to look through a number of them to find all the information about Windows or an application. Windows NT uses a centralized database to store information that Windows houses in INI files.

If NT Workstation is installed over an existing Windows system, then much of the information stored in WIN.INI, SYSTEM.INI, CONTROL.INI, and so on, is written to the NT Registry. Win16 applications requesting information from those files now has it supplied out of the Registry. You still find a number of INI files in the NT directory, however, for maintaining compatibility with other Win16 applications you run and install in NT Workstation.

Device Drivers   An NT-compatible device driver must be supplied for applications to work with specific pieces of hardware. NT Workstation includes a number of hardware and virtual device drivers, and requests made by DOS and Win16 applications can be mapped to an appropriate driver if it is available.

N O T E Any attempt by an application to access a piece of hardware directly results in the application being halted. When this occurs, a message box appears on the screen informing you what occurred and that the application is being shut down. ■

Property Sheets for DOS and Win16 Applications Property sheets are an important part of the user interface in Windows NT 4.0, including for running DOS and Win16 applications. You use property sheets to tell Windows NT how to interact with you and your applications. Property sheets are used to specify how DOS and Win16 applications operate in Windows NT. You specify how a DOS application uses memory, and what batch file should be run with the DOS application. And, for Win16 applications, you specify settings such as security, whether the application should run in a separate memory space, and more. If you have not modified a property sheet for an application, default settings are used to control it.

Configuring DOS and Win16 Applications to Run in Windows NT

Most 16-bit applications require special care and feeding when running in Windows environments, especially DOS applications. As the user, you must provide Windows NT with a great deal of information about your application to ensure that it runs smoothly. The more finicky your application is about its environment, the more you will have to tune the settings Windows NT uses to run it. As such, Windows NT provides great control over how you configure your application to run in Windows NT, and conversely, you have great flexibility in configuring Windows NT to run your 16-bit applications.

Understanding DOS Application Property Sheets and Shortcuts

You specify the settings Windows NT needs to run a DOS or Win16 application in the property sheets associated with each application you run in Windows NT. You do not work directly with the property sheet for the application, however. Instead, you create a shortcut to the application and work with the shortcut's property sheets. A shortcut stores the information Windows NT needs to properly run a

DOS application. The shortcut points to the executable file that launches the application. This executable file is the one whose name you type at the command prompt when you want to launch the application. When you want to launch the application with the settings you created, you launch the shortcut (see fig. 17.10).

FIG. 17.10
You create a shortcut to run a 16-bit application, which contains all the information Windows NT needs to run the application.

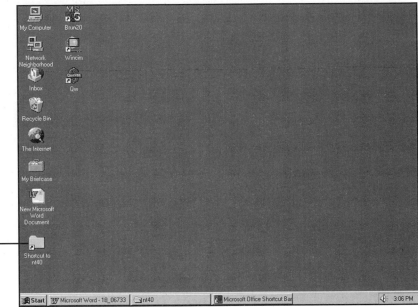

A shortcut is used to launch a DOS or Win16 application.

Creating the Shortcut for 16-bit Applications

There are two ways to create the shortcut for a DOS application: automatic and manual.

Method 1—Automatic

1. Using Windows NT Explorer or My Computer, open the folder where the DOS application is for which you want to create a shortcut.

2. Right-click the file that executes the application. The context menu appears.

3. Choose Properties from the menu. The Property Sheet dialog box appears.

4. Change any setting on any of the property sheets. As a suggestion, to minimize the chance of doing something harmful to the shortcut, clear the Compressed check box at the bottom of the General property sheet.

5. Choose OK. The Property dialog box closes. A shortcut appears in the folder where you were working (see fig. 17.11).

FIG. 17.11
A shortcut is automatically created when you edit the properties of a DOS application.

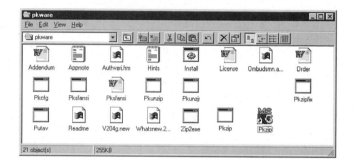

6. Move the shortcut you created to any location in Windows NT from which you want to launch the application, such as the desktop.

Method 2—Manual

1. Move to the location from which you want to launch the DOS application, such as the desktop, or a folder shown on the Start menu.

2. Create a shortcut that points to the file that executes the DOS application.

   ▶ **See** "Working with Shortcuts," **p. 79**

3. After the shortcut is created, right-click it to display the Context menu.

4. Choose Properties. The Property Sheet dialog box appears. Change other properties for the DOS application, including the icon, by displaying the property sheets for the shortcut the same way you did for the application in steps 2 and 3.

5. Choose OK to save changes you made on any of the property sheets. To save the changes you've made without closing the property sheet dialog box, choose Apply.

Working with the Property Sheets for DOS Applications

After a shortcut is created for a DOS application, you can change settings on the property sheets for the shortcuts to help the DOS application run. Seven property sheets are associated with any DOS application (see fig. 17.12). Collectively, the

Part
IV

Ch
17

property sheets for each type of application are presented in a property sheet dialog box.

FIG. 17.12
Seven property sheets are used to control how DOS applications interact with Windows NT.

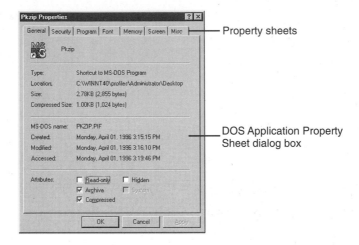

Property sheets

DOS Application Property Sheet dialog box

To change the properties for a DOS application, follow these steps:

1. Right-click the shortcut to the DOS application.

2. Choose Properties from the Context menu that appears.

3. Make changes to any of the settings on the seven property sheets. To have changes you make take effect without closing the property sheet, choose Apply. To save changes and close the property sheet, choose OK. To close the property sheet with no changes taking effect, choose Cancel.

General Properties

The first property sheet displayed for a DOS application is the General property sheet (see fig. 17.13). The General property sheet is used mainly to display information about the application and the shortcut. The only settings on the property sheet you can change are the file system attributes for the application that the shortcut is pointing to. The following is a quick review of the information presented on the General property sheet:

■ The first set of information describes information about the shortcut, not the application. It shows the location of the shortcut, as well as its size.

- The second set of information describes more information about the shortcut. You see the name of the file that stores information shown in the property sheets (a file with an extension of PIF for *program information file*). You can also see when the information shown on the property sheets was created, last viewed, and last changed.

- You can change the attributes of the shortcut file by checking or clearing any of the options in the Attributes section of the property sheet.

FIG. 17.13
The General property sheet shows information about the shortcut.

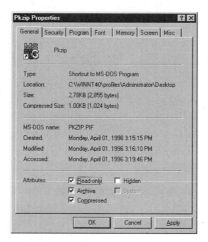

Security Properties

The Security property sheet (see fig. 17.14) helps you control access to the shortcut for other users of the system you're working on. The Security property sheet appears only if the shortcut is located on a drive formatted with NTFS. From the Security property sheet, you can control which users have what types of access to the shortcut and how Windows NT stores information about when the shortcut is used, accessed, or edited; and, you can take ownership of the shortcut. For more information about security in Windows NT, refer to Chapter 15, "Securing Windows NT Workstation."

 TIP The Security property sheet is useful if more than one user will be working at the NT Workstation. To restrict users from changing settings you create in the shortcut for the DOS application, you should secure the shortcut.

FIG. 17.14
You set up security to
the shortcut from the
Security property
sheet.

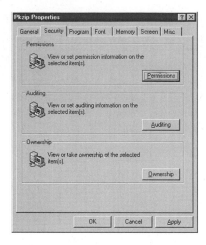

Program Properties

In the Program property sheet (see fig. 17.15), you specify the most critical information about the DOS application, such as the executable file run for the shortcut, its working directory, and configuration files that should be used with the DOS application. The following section describes the information you supply on the Program property sheet.

FIG. 17.15
The most critical
information about the
DOS application is
specified on the
Program property
sheet, such as the
name of the file
executed with the
shortcut and special
configuration files
used with the
application.

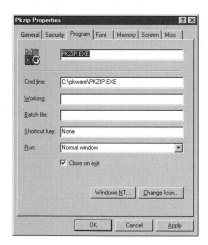

Command Line   You specify the program file name of the application you want to run, including its location, in the Cmd Line edit box. For example, to run the QUE.BAT file, which is located in the PUBS directory on your C drive, you would specify C:\PUBS\QUE.BAT. Also, be sure to include any command-line parameters that normally appear after the program file name.

Working Directory   You can specify the directory that is current for the application when it starts in the Working edit box. This is useful if you want the application set to the directory where you keep the working files for the application. Specify the full directory name and path in the Working edit box.

Batch File   You can specify a batch file that runs immediately before the DOS application associated with the shortcut. Specify the name of the file in the Batch File edit box, including its location and any command-line parameters.

Shortcut Key   You can specify a shortcut key combination that automatically switches you to the application's window, regardless of where you are in NT Workstation. If the application is not running, the shortcut key launches the shortcut. The application shortcut key combination must include Ctrl or Alt. It can include both. Examples of valid application shortcut key combinations are Alt+9, Ctrl+F5, and Ctrl+Alt+Q. You set the application shortcut key combination by clicking in the Shortcut Key edit box and pressing the key combination.

Window State   From the Run drop-down list, you choose whether the application is launched in a minimized, maximized, or normal window.

Close Window   The Close On Exit option specifies that the window housing the DOS application closes as soon as the application completes. This option is more useful when it is turned off. There may be a DOS application that you run in which you are interested in the data that appears on-screen. With this option cleared, you can see the data before the window closes.

Custom Startup Files   You define the DOS application's environment by pointing to the AUTOEXEC and CONFIG files that contain the settings and commands for your DOS application. The default setting for AUTOEXEC and CONFIG are AUTOEXEC.NT and CONFIG.NT. Because you probably will have unique settings for each DOS application, you should create a custom version of each file for use with every DOS application you use in Windows NT. Here is how to create custom versions of the files:

1. Make a copy of AUTOEXEC.NT and CONFIG.NT to use as templates. Name the copies whatever you like. Because the AUTOEXEC and CONFIG names are so recognizable, you should use the extension part of the name to specify what DOS application the files work with. For example, to use CONFIG and AUTOEXEC to store settings about a pop-up clock you use in a command prompt window, you might call the files AUTOEXEC.CLK and CONFIG.CLK. Use File Manager or the command prompt to copy the files.

2. Configure the files with settings for the DOS application you're working with.

3. From the Program property sheet for the DOS application's shortcut, choose Windows <u>N</u>T. The Windows NT PIF Settings dialog box appears (see fig. 17.16).

FIG. 17.16

You can specify custom initialization files for each DOS application you run in Windows NT.

4. Enter the name and location of the file in the appropriate edit boxes.

5. Choose OK.

Changing the Icon for a Shortcut   When a shortcut is created for the DOS application, the basic MS-DOS icon is assigned to the shortcut. You can customize the shortcut by assigning it the icon of your choice. Icons are usually provided with most applications, but you can also use an icon from another application. For example, you can use the icon for Lotus 1-2-3 for Windows with the program item for Microsoft Excel for Windows. Typically, icons are stored in one of the program files associated with an application, such as files with extensions like EXE, DLL, and COM. It doesn't matter what icon you use to represent your application; the icon has no effect on the application at all. It makes sense, though, to choose an icon that helps you recognize the application that runs when you click the icon.

 A treasure trove of icons is shipped with Windows NT in the file MORICONS.DLL. You can find more than 150 icons in that file, which is located in the SYSTEM32 subdirectory of the main Windows NT directory. In addition, you can find icon libraries either sold commercially or available for downloading from most online services.

To change a shortcut's icon, follow these steps:

1. From the Program property sheet for the DOS application's shortcut, choose <u>C</u>hange Icon. The Change Icon dialog box appears (see fig. 17.17). The dialog box contains a list box that scrolls horizontally. This list box shows icons contained in the file associated with the program item. If no icons are included in that file, Windows NT displays icons from Program Manager (PIFMGR.DLL). Use the scroll bars to view all the icons contained in the file.

FIG. 17.17
You can select from a collection of stock icons an icon to use with your new shortcut.

Part
IV

Ch
17

2. To choose one of the icons contained in the list, click the icon in the list box and then choose OK.

3. To choose an icon from another file, enter the name of the file containing the icon you want to select in the <u>F</u>ile Name edit box and press Enter. Click <u>B</u>rowse to scan through all the directories for other files containing icons. If you select a file that does not contain an icon, you see the message shown in figure 17.18. If you select a file that contains icons, the icons appear in the list box. Click the icon in the list box and choose OK.

FIG. 17.18
Windows NT informs you if you choose a file that does not contain icons.

Font Properties

The Font property sheet is the place where you control what type of fonts are used with your DOS application and how large the type is (see fig. 17.19). After making a font type or size selection, you can preview how your screen will appear in the two mini-windows at the bottom of the dialog box.

FIG. 17.19

You control the type of fonts and their size used by DOS applications from the Fonts property sheet.

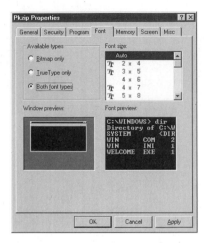

Memory Properties

NT Workstation can simulate and provide both expanded and extended memory to DOS applications that need it. The documentation that shipped with your application can tell how much and what type of memory your application needs. Following are details about the four sections of information presented in the Memory property sheet (see fig. 17.20):

- *Conventional.* In the two drop-down lists in this section, you specify how much conventional memory should be available to the DOS application when it starts, as well as the initial size of the command interpreter environment for the application. You can also specify that the DOS application run in Protected mode. This is helpful because it protects the rest of the Windows NT from an errant DOS application.

- *Expanded (EMD).* Windows NT can make expanded memory available to a DOS application that needs it. You can specify the maximum amount to allot to the application, specify that no expanded memory be allotted, or set the amount to Automatic, in which case there is no limit, and Windows NT makes available as much expanded memory as the application requires.

N O T E *Expanded memory* is a special memory that can either be provided to applications via a piece of hardware or simulated by the operating system or other software. ■

■ *Extended (XMS)*. Windows NT can make extended memory available to a DOS application that needs it. You can specify the maximum amount to allot to the application, specify that no extended memory be allotted, or set the amount to Automatic, in which case there is no limit, and Windows NT makes available as much extended memory as the application requires. You can also specify that the DOS application use the High Memory area.

N O T E Extended memory is the memory that exists after the 1M boundary for memory addressable by 286 and 386 computers. Most later applications built for DOS and Windows 3.*x* use extended memory. High Memory is the first 64K of extended memory, and it is typically used for drivers. ■

■ *Protected Mode*. Windows NT can make protected mode memory available to a DOS application that needs it. You can specify the maximum amount to allot to the application, specify that no protected mode memory be allotted, or set the amount to Automatic, in which there is no limit, and Windows NT makes available as much protected mode memory as the application requires. You can also specify that the DOS application use the High Memory area (between the 640K and 1M address space).

FIG. 17.20
You can specify how much memory and of what type is available to a DOS application.

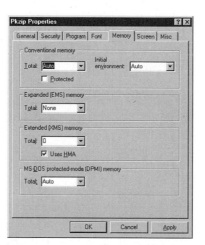

Screen Properties

The Screen property sheet lets you configure how your display will interact with the DOS application associated with the shortcut (see fig. 17.21). A review of some of the relevant options follows:

Part
IV
Ch
17

■ The Usage options specify whether the window housing the DOS application opens full-screen or in a window. After the application has started, you can switch to the other mode by pressing Alt+Enter.

■ You use the Display Toolbar option to specify whether the toolbar appears in the DOS application window.

■ If you choose Restore Settings On Startup, Windows NT will restore a few appropriate screen settings to their last value the next time you run the DOS application, including the toolbar, font type, and font size options.

■ You can improve performance of the DOS application by choosing the Fast ROM Emulation option. When this option is chosen, Windows NT uses its own virtual device drivers to simulate video ROM services required by the DOS application.

■ By choosing the Dynamic Memory Allocation option, memory is dynamically managed by Windows NT if the DOS application uses both text and graphic modes.

FIG. 17.21
The Screen property sheet enables you to configure how your display operates when a DOS application is running.

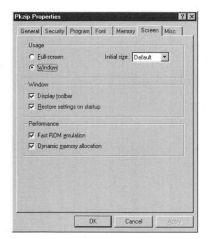

Miscellaneous Properties

The Misc property sheet (see fig. 17.22) shows all the leftover settings not relevant to the other six property sheets. A review of some of the less obvious settings follows:

■ Choosing the Always Suspend option means that the DOS application will not use any Windows NT resources when the application is not in the foreground.

■ QuickEdit lets you use the mouse to mark data in the DOS application window to copy elsewhere. If this option is not specified, you must use the Mark option on the DOS application window toolbar.

■ The Exclusive Mode option specifies that the mouse or other pointing device works only with the DOS application. Other applications will not be able to use the mouse pointer as long as the DOS application is running with this option chosen.

■ Use the Idle Sensitivity slider to determine how sensitive Windows NT is to inactivity in the DOS application. Windows NT recognizes the application is busy by keyboard input. If you specify a particularly high setting, Windows NT will wait less time to decide that the DOS application is idle before it allocates resources to other applications. If you specify a particularly low setting, Windows NT will be more patient waiting for the application to become active before reassigning resources.

FIG. 17.22
You specify screen saver, Windows shortcut key, mouse, and other settings for DOS applications you run in Windows NT on the Misc property sheet.

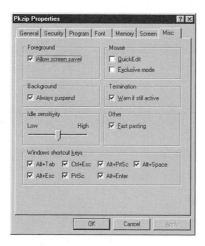

Windows Shortcut Keys   Each of the seven shortcut key combinations shown on the Misc property sheet has a particular function in Windows NT Workstation. For example, Alt+Space opens the Control menu. To reserve any of the shortcut key combinations for use with your DOS applications, check the appropriate box. This way, Windows NT will not respond when you press the combination in your DOS application. Table 17.1 shows the Windows shortcut keys.

Table 17.1 Windows Shortcut Keys

Key/Key Combination	Action
Alt+Tab	Switches you to the next application running in Windows NT. If you press and hold the key combination, a special message box appears displaying the text that appears in the title bar of the next application. By holding down Alt and pressing and releasing Tab, you cycle through all the applications running.
Print Screen	Copies the image of the entire screen to the Clipboard.
Alt+Enter	Toggles an open DOS application between full-screen and window modes.
Alt+Esc	Cycles through all running applications shown on the taskbar, allowing you to switch to one.
Alt+Print Screen	Copies the image of the current window to the Clipboard.
Ctrl+Esc	Opens the Start menu.
Alt+Space	Activates the Control menu in the active window or dialog box.

Customizing the Default Property Sheet

You can still run a DOS application in NT Workstation if you have not set the application's run-time properties. You can do this by opening the Command Prompt window and launching the DOS application. Without you knowing it, however, NT Workstation still uses settings from a property sheet. When you run an application without having created a shortcut, NT Workstation uses the settings in a PIF named _DEFAULT.PIF, which you can examine by viewing the properties of the _default application.

N O T E When you edit the properties of the default PIF, _DEFAULT.PIF, you probably notice that the program file name is _DEFAULT.BAT. This is not a mistake, nor does the file _DEFAULT.BAT exist. The file name is used so that _DEFAULT.PIF can be saved. When an application is run without a PIF—as you learned in this section—the parameters specified in _DEFAULT.PIF are used. NT Workstation substitutes the program file name for the DOS application you're running for _DEFAULT.BAT. ■

To modify the default PIF settings, follow these steps:

1. Right-click the shortcut to _DEFAULT.PIF, which is located in the main Windows NT directory. The environment variable %SystemRoot% can tell you the name of that directory. The Context menu for the shortcut appears.

2. Choose Properties. The Property sheet for the shortcut to _DEFAULT.PIF appears (see fig. 17.23).

FIG. 17.23
This shortcut stores the properties for DOS applications you run without having specified property sheet settings.

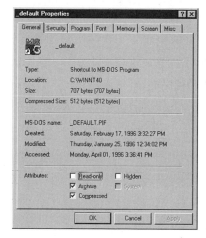

3. Change whatever PIF settings are appropriate.

4. Choose OK.

TROUBLESHOOTING

The mouse pointer does not work properly with my DOS application. There probably is an incompatibility problem with your application and the system mouse pointer. You can turn off the system mouse pointer in the window where your application is running. Switch to the application's window and press Alt+Space to display the Control menu and then choose Hide Mouse Pointer.

Running DOS Applications in Windows NT

There are a few methods you can use to run DOS applications in NT Workstation. The method you choose is based on how stringent the requirements are that the DOS application places on the environment. If the DOS application has few requirements for its environment, such as specific types and amount of memory (extended, expanded) available, you probably can run the application directly from the command prompt. Keep in mind that when a DOS application is run from the command line, any settings specified in CONFIG.NT and AUTOEXEC.NT are used. If the application has strict needs from the environment, you should create a shortcut and modify its property sheets to run the application.

Keep in mind that when you run a DOS application from the command prompt, settings specified in AUTOEXEC.NT and CONFIG.NT are used to initialize the DOS environment. This is because NT Workstation uses the settings specified in _DEFAULT.PIF to run a DOS application without a PIF. The _DEFAULT.PIF points to AUTOEXEC.NT and CONFIG.NT as its initialization files.

TROUBLESHOOTING

When I try to run a DOS application at the command prompt without having set up a shortcut, the application does not start. The first place to check is the AUTOEXEC.NT and CONFIG.NT files. You may have to customize these files with settings required by your application. Because all DOS applications run from the command line use the NT version of AUTOEXEC and CONFIG, you should create custom versions of the files and run the application with a shortcut.

If you are sure that your problem is not with the environment, then NT Workstation may have a problem recognizing the application as a DOS application. To make sure that NT treats your application as a DOS application, use the following syntax on the command line:

> **FORCEDOS** *your application*

where *your application* is the path and file name of the application you want to run.

Running TSRs in NT Workstation

Applications you run in NT Workstation may be dependent on another program being present in memory. This means that to run a particular application, another program must be run first. That initial program loads certain instructions and data required by the main application into the memory of the computer. NT Workstation supports the use of the memory-resident programs, which are also known as *TSRs* (for *terminate-and-stay-resident*). When you launch these applications, typically you see a message on-screen, and then the application seems to complete because the command prompt appears. The reason for this behavior is the design of the program. The program has run, but it is now present in memory, ready for use.

There are two general uses for a TSR in memory. An application may require the TSR to be present, so you must run the TSR before launching the application. Another use for a TSR is as a pop-up program. You may have a favorite calculator, address program, or calendar application that sits in memory until you press the correct key combination, at which time the program pops up on-screen.

Part
IV

Ch
17

Running a TSR with an Application

A DOS application you run may require a specific driver or some other program to be present in memory. The key to achieving this is to run the TSR and your application in the same session of the command interpreter. You need to create a batch file that first runs your TSR and next runs your application. Next, you have to set up a shortcut that runs the batch file in a command prompt window. To do so, you need to understand the use of the CMD.EXE program.

CMD.EXE, which is known as the *command interpreter*, is the program that runs when you choose Command Prompt from the Start menu. Whenever the command prompt appears, you know that CMD.EXE has been launched. So, to run a TSR program, you need to run CMD.EXE and then launch the batch file. You can specify the batch file on the command line of a program item with CMD, or you can create a shortcut that runs CMD, and you specify the batch file as on the Program property sheet.

To set up a TSR to run with an application, follow these steps:

1. Create a batch file. Give the batch file a name associated with the application you want to run. For example, to run the Sidekick application, you might create a file named SK.CMD.

N O T E A *batch file* is a file that lists commands you want to run at once. A batch file has an extension of BAT or CMD, and you can create one using the Edit utility available from the command line. To create a batch file, open a command prompt window, type

> **EDIT** *batch filename*

(where `batch filename` is the name of the batch file you want to create), and press Enter. The Edit utility starts with the file you specified already loaded. ▨

2. Into the batch file, enter the command that launches the TSR required by your application. On a subsequent line, enter the command that launches your application. Be sure to supply the correct path to the program files that launch the TSR and application.

3. Create a shortcut. Specify the following Cmd line:

   CMD /K *batch filename*

   where `batch filename` is the name of the batch file you created in step 1.

N O T E The `/K` parameter tells the command interpreter to stay running after launching the program specified on the command line. This enables the batch file to run immediately and the command window to remain open. ▨

Just because CMD is the program that launches what you may recognize as the DOS prompt, don't think that CMD.EXE is a DOS application. The CMD program is a 32-bit application in NT Workstation that helps build the environment for command-line programs.

Running a Pop-Up TSR

You may have a favorite DOS-based TSR utility that you just can't live without. Create a shortcut for the application. If the application has special requirements, change the shortcut's properties. Next, add the shortcut to the Start menu so that it runs when you start NT Workstation. Whenever you want to use the TSR, switch to the command prompt window and run the TSR. You can specify a shortcut key for the program item that automatically activates the window.

▶ **See** "Customizing the Start Menu," **p. 59**

Working with the Property Sheets for Win16 Applications

After a shortcut is created for a Windows 3.*x* application, you can modify the property sheets for the shortcuts to help the Win16 application run. There are three property sheets associated with the shortcut to any Win16 application (see fig. 17.24). Two of them, General and Security, provide the same information as those for DOS applications. Rather than repeat the information here, refer to the previous sections "General Properties" and "Security Properties" for information about the Win16 application shortcut and how to secure it. This section looks at the options on the Shortcut property sheet.

Part
IV

Ch
17

Win16 Application Property
dialog box

FIG. 17.24
Three property sheets are used to control how Win16 applications interact with Windows NT.

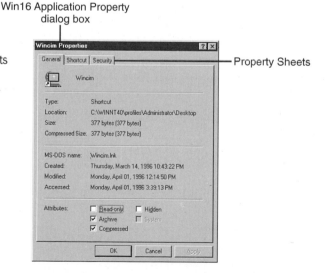

Property Sheets

To change the properties for a Win16 application, follow these steps:

1. Right-click the shortcut to the Win16 application.

2. Choose Properties from the Context menu that appears.

3. Make changes to any of the settings on the three property sheets. To have changes you make take effect without closing the property sheet, choose Apply. To save changes and close the property sheet, choose OK. To close the property sheet with no changes taking effect, choose Cancel.

Shortcut Properties

The Shortcut property sheet for a Win16 application shows the few settings that may need to be tuned for a Windows NT application (see fig. 17.25). For the Change Icon, Run, and Shortcut Key options, refer to "Program Properties" earlier in this chapter. A quick review of the information presented on the property sheet follows:

FIG. 17.25
The Shortcut property sheet for a Win16 application enables you to change the application associated with the shortcut, direct the application to run in its own memory space, and more.

Target indicates the file launched when the shortcut is selected. When you choose Find Target, the folder is opened where the target file is stored (see fig. 17.26).

The Start In means the same as working directory. The Start In directory is the directory that should be made current when the application is launched. This makes it convenient to have the default directory for an application be one where most of the data files for the application are located.

FIG. 17.26
You can open the folder where the target file for a Win16 application shortcut is by choosing Find Target.

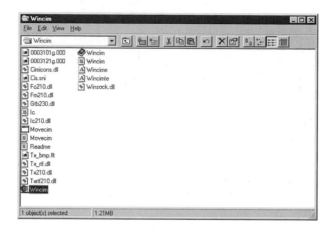

Part
IV
Ch
17

The Start In option also can help solve pathing problems. Most users move applications around their system and sometime have multiple copies of the same application on their system. The Start In directory can point to the original installation directory of an application, helping the application run from anywhere in Windows NT.

Running Win16 Applications in a Separate Memory Space You may find a Win16 application that you run in NT Workstation crashes often. It's likely that the application crashed in Windows 3.*x* as well, and that it also hung the system or caused other applications you were running in Windows 3.*x* to crash. Unfortunately, the default behavior in NT Workstation makes it just as likely that a problematic application will crash other applications. If you recall from the section "A Quick Word about the Architecture" earlier in this chapter, all Win16 applications run in a shared memory space, specifically, one virtual DOS machine. To protect other applications from the errant one (other than discontinuing use of the volatile application), you can specify that the application run in its own memory space. You still can use the application automation tools (OLE, DDE) with applications running in separate memory spaces, so it makes sense to segregate the misbehaving application. To do so, check the Run In Separate Memory Space check box.

If you run a Win16 application that tends to hog processor time, you may want to run that application in its own memory space. In Windows NT's multitasking scheme, such an application could deny processor attention from any other Win16 running in the same memory space. Running the application in its own memory space minimizes the impact of its need for processing time on other applications.

N O T E   If you need to start a Win16 application from the command prompt and you
            want the application to run in its own memory space, use the /SEPARATE
parameter on the command line. For example, to run Microsoft Word for Windows from
the command prompt and run the application in its own memory space, type **START
/SEPARATE WINWORD** and press Enter. ▨

TROUBLESHOOTING

I receive a `"Cannot find DLL"` message when I try to run a Win16 application. This
is usually the result of NT Workstation being installed in a new directory rather than over
an existing Windows system. To solve the problem, try to locate the DLL specified in the
error message. If you cannot find the file anywhere on your system, you may have to
reinstall the application. Install it in NT Workstation. If you can find the DLL, add its
location to the PATH statement in AUTOEXEC.BAT. As an alternative to editing
AUTOEXEC.BAT, you can add the path to the DLL to the list of user environment variables.
Refer to Chapter 12, "Managing Memory, Multitasking, and System Options," for
instruction on working with environment variables.

Running Windows NT and Windows 95 Applications

Not too long ago, there was not a lot to write about applications written for Windows NT. Compared to the number of applications available for Windows 3.1, you could accurately describe the selection of Windows NT-specific applications as scarce. With the increasing popularity of Windows NT, as well as the launch of Windows 95, the introduction of applications for Windows NT has dramatically increased. This doesn't mean that makers of software applications have developed a sudden interest in Windows NT. Microsoft has cleverly established support for Windows NT as a requirement for any Windows 95 applications to qualify for the official Windows 95 logo. Now, any software developer that wants the coveted Windows 95 logo on their product's packaging must ensure that their product works properly in Windows NT. When you consider the huge interest created in Windows 95, you can understand how the quantity of applications built to run in Windows NT has increased so quickly.

Understanding Windows 95 and Windows NT Applications

Here is a quick answer to a question that's probably on your mind: Yes, you can run Windows 95 applications in Windows NT. Read on for more details.

Generally, you can install and run any Windows 95 applications in Windows NT Workstation. This refers to a full range of applications, from those that make some vague reference to Windows 95 on their packaging, like "Tested with Windows 95," to applications that display the real Windows 95 logo. Microsoft established strict requirements for qualifying for the Windows 95 logo, and one of the requirements is directly related to support for Windows NT. The following list summarizes the five major requirements for the Windows 95 logo. The third requirement has the most relevance to this discussion:

- Applications must be built with the Win32 SDK, and a PE (portable executed) executable file must be generated or used by the application.
- Applications must use and support the Windows 95 shell and user interface.
- Applications must be tested and run without issue on Windows NT.
- Applications must use and display long file names.
- Applications should support Plug and Play.

The details of the third requirement also specify that when an attempt is made by the user to use functionality in a Windows 95 application that happens to be running in Windows NT, then that application should gracefully ignore the request. An example of this might be when the application attempts to modify the Start menu or task bar on the Windows 95 desktop.

N O T E For more information about Windows 95 and Windows 95 applications, refer to Que's *Platinum Edition Using Windows 95*. ▪

Figures 17.27 and 17.28 show examples of two Windows 95 applications running under Windows NT Workstation.

FIG. 17.27
Microsoft Excel for Windows 95 runs smoothly and without argument under Windows NT Workstation.

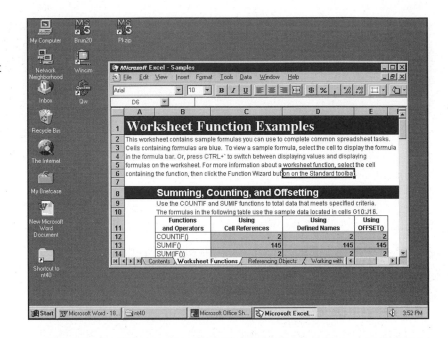

FIG. 17.28
The Dashboard 95 application from Starfish Software appears at home in Windows NT.

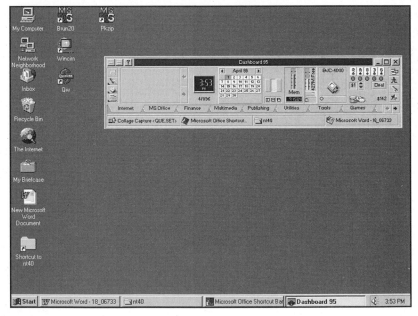

N O T E As much as this chapter is devoted to running Windows NT and Windows 95 applications in Windows NT, you can run these types of applications in an operating system other than Windows 95 and Windows NT. It is possible to run Windows NT and Windows 95 applications in Windows 3.1 using a technology known as *Win32s* from Microsoft. By installing a few files into Windows 3.1, you can add support for running Win32 applications in DOS/Windows. Not all Win32 applications support Win32s, however. Be sure to read the information supplied with the application, or check with the manufacturer. Win32s may also be available from the developer of your Win32 application. You can save hard drive space if your favorite Windows 3.1 application has been released in a Windows 95 version and if you want to maintain your DOS/Windows setup with Windows NT. Using Win32s, you can run the same Win32 application under both Windows 3.1 and Windows NT. ▪

Understanding Win32 Applications

Applications built for either Windows 95 or Windows NT are known as Win32 applications because these applications were built using the Win32 *software development kit* (SDK). A software development kit is a set of libraries and tools that software programmers use to construct software applications. Software developers of operating systems and other specific technologies produce and make SDKs available so that other developers can produce software compatible with their systems. The Win32 SDK provides the software programmer with the tools to build true 32-bit applications. These applications can include threads, which are independent tasks in a general process that an application runs, and applications built with Win32 can preemptively multitask with other Win32 applications. Win32 also lets applications take advantage of new technologies, such as OLE (object linking and embedding) and OpenGL, a new system for presenting two- and three-dimensional graphics.

The use of the Win32 SDK is significant for Windows NT and Windows 95, both 32-bit operating systems. An application built with Win32 can run on both Windows 95 and Windows NT. By using it to develop an application, a programmer knows that his or her application will be compatible with the Windows 95 or Windows NT operating systems.

Launching Windows and Windows 95 Applications

This section provides a quick review of starting applications in Windows NT. After installation of a Win32 application in Windows NT, most likely a choice appears on the Programs menu. There also is a chance that a special utility may be installed for quickly launching the application, such as the case with the Microsoft Office shortcut bar. Also, you can use My Computer or Windows NT Explorer to select the file that executes the application, or you can open the Start menu, choose Run, and then enter or Browse for the file to launch.

Troubleshooting New Applications

As much as you follow instructions perfectly during installation of a new application in Windows NT, there always is a chance that a new application will not run properly after it has been installed. When you run the application for the first time, you might see an on-screen message from the application informing you of a problem, or Windows NT might display a message about a problem. This section helps you troubleshoot some of these issues. You find some practical advice and some references to other chapters in this book. The advice is divided between problems you think are related to the application and problems you think are related to Windows NT. Really, all the problems are *Windows NT-related*, but the error message or condition can probably help you decide which program is the culprit.

Application Problems

The first piece of advice is very general: if you run into any problems when you run an application after it has been installed, check the documentation supplied with the software. A troubleshooting section probably is included. Usually, a table can be found that describes different problems or messages you might encounter with instructions for resolving the problem. Follow the instructions in the documentation.

You also may want to check the system requirements for the application (though you should have done this before you installed the application). Be sure that your system is compatible with software. You may be able to address some of the incompatibility issues, such as by adding more RAM. Other incompatibility problems may take more work, such as changing a critical piece of hardware, like a hard disk controller. Use the following list to start your investigation. If you find you have an incompatibility problem, either address the problem or decide not to use the application.

- *Hard drive space.* Was enough hard disk space available when you installed the application? Check the requirements supplied with the software.
- *RAM.* Do you have the amount of RAM installed in your system required by the application?
- *Hardware.* Is the hardware used in your system compatible with the application—for example, network interface card, display adapter, SCSI controller card, pointing device?
- *Windows NT version.* Does the application require a version of Windows NT Workstation either earlier or later than the version you are presently running? This book is based on version 4.0 of Windows NT Workstation. You may be running version 3.51, 3.1, or even a Beta version. An application also may require that a Windows NT Service Pack be applied.

Windows NT Problems

Table 17.2 describes some common Windows NT problems related to running applications. The chapter that can provide help for the problem also is listed.

Table 17.2   Windows NT Problems with Applications

Problem	Chapter
"Not Enough Memory" messages	Chapter 12, "Managing Memory, Multitasking, and System Options"
"Unable to Find DLL" or other pathing	Chapter 12, "Managing Memory, Multitasking, and System Options"
Problems related to printing with the application or a message describing the requirement for a printer	Chapter 5, "Printing and Setting Up Printers"

continues

Table 17.2 Continued

Problem	Chapter
A message informing you that you may not have proper rights for a particular action the application takes	Chapter 15, "Securing Windows NT Workstation"
A specific Windows NT Service must be running for the application to run properly	Chapter 14, "Managing System Services and Devices"
The application needs access to an unavailable network resource	Chapter 20, "Configuring the Network at Your Workstation"
Very odd behavior, such as bogus messages on the screen or characters input to the system different from what you type, which may indicate you have a computer virus	Chapter 34, "Protecting Your Workstation and Its Data"

From Here...

In this chapter, you learned about the types of applications you can run in Windows NT, which include DOS, Win16, and Win32 applications. You also learned what support Windows NT provides for running these applications. You should be able to run even the most finicky applications in Windows NT. The following chapters can provide you with additional information related to running applications in Windows NT:

■ Chapter 12, "Managing Memory, Multitasking, and System Options."

■ Chapter 14, "Managing System Services and Devices."

CHAPTER 18

Using Windows NT Accessory Applications

by Sue Plumley

If you are upgrading to Windows NT from Windows 3.x or Windows for Workgroups, you will see plenty of familiar faces in the NT environment, including the applications known as the Windows accessories. The Windows accessories are a collection of small but useful applications that perform a variety of different functions, from creating pictures to giving you the time and date. Windows NT includes most of the same accessories you had with Windows and Windows for Workgroups, along with several new accessories. However, despite the identical appearances, the NT accessories have been recompiled into 32-bit versions, which means greater speed and better use of Windows NT's capabilities.

Use Windows WordPad

WordPad is a simple word processing program you can use to create basic documents, such as memos, letters, and fax cover sheets.

Use Chat to communicate with coworkers

Chat enables you to converse with your coworkers over the network; discuss schedules, meetings, work, or after work plans.

Create and Edit drawings with Paint

Paint is the Windows drawing and painting program you can use to create logos, edit art work, and produce fancy headlines for your documents.

The accessories that ship with Windows NT 4 are WordPad, Phone Dialer, Paint, Object Packager, Notepad, HyperTerminal, Clock, ClipBook Viewer, ClipBoard Viewer, Chat, Character Map, Calculator, CD Player, Media Player, Sound Recorder, Volume Control, Freecell, Minesweeper, and Solitaire.

To use any of the accessory applications, open the Start menu, choose Programs, Accessories. All of the accessory applications are listed on the Accessories menu. ■

Using Windows WordPad

WordPad is a basic word-processing application included with Windows NT. Although it doesn't have all of the features of sophisticated, commercial word processors such as Microsoft Word for Windows, it is easy to use and includes enough features to let you create nice-looking documents.

Starting WordPad

To start the Windows WordPad accessory application, choose WordPad from the Accessories menu. WordPad opens to a blank, untitled document.

Alternatively, you can automatically start WordPad by choosing Start, Documents, and the name of the WordPad document you want to open; only the most recently opened documents appear on this list. This launches the WordPad program and auto-loads the document you clicked.

Figure 18.1 shows a blank document in the WordPad screen. By default, WordPad opens to a window; you can enlarge the window or click the Maximize button to enlarge the program window to fill the desktop. The window in the figure has been enlarged to better see the work area.

 TIP   WordPad displays both vertical and horizontal scroll bars in the work area if the entire document cannot display in the window.

Control menu box   Title bar   Menu bar   Ruler   Minimize button Maximize button

FIG. 18.1

The WordPad application is a basic word processing application included with Windows NT.

Toolbar

Formatting toolbar

Cursor (insertion point)

Mouse I-beam

Status bar

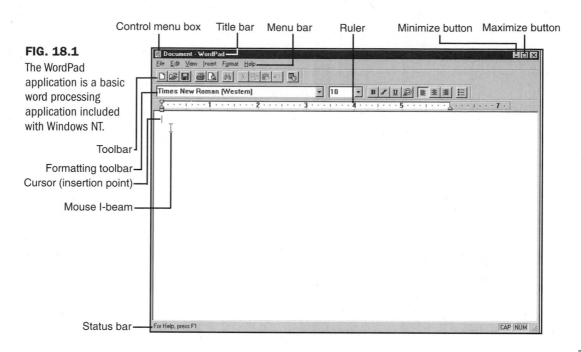

For Help, press F1

Typing Text

You enter text in WordPad as you would in other word processing programs. The blinking cursor in the upper-left corner of the work area is called the *insertion point*, and it indicates your current position in the document.

As you type text in your document, be sure to only press Enter at the end of a paragraph, not at the end of a line. WordPad, like all word processors, automatically wraps the text to the next line (a feature known as *word wrap*) when there is no room left on the current line. This allows WordPad to correctly reformat your document if you later change items such as font size or margins.

Navigating Your Document

To effectively use WordPad, you need to become comfortable with the various commands necessary to move around your WordPad documents. To move the cursor (or insertion point) to a specific location in the document, simply move your mouse pointer (which appears as an I-beam pointer inside the WordPad document window) to the destination and click once. The cursor then moves to that location.

To "pan" the WordPad window up and down or left to right around the document, you can click the scroll bars located on the bottom and right edges of the window. The position of the boxes located inside both of these scroll bars shows your current location relative to the entire document. You can also click and drag these boxes in one direction or the other to move more quickly around the document.

Although mouse movements are commonly used, WordPad also provides some handy keyboard shortcuts for navigating your document, listed in table 18.1.

Table 18.1   Document Navigation Keys

Movement	Keystroke(s)
One character left/right	Left/right-arrow key
One line up/down	Up/down-arrow key
Next/previous word	Ctrl+left/right-arrow key
Beginning of line	Home
End of line	End
Top/bottom of window	Ctrl+Page Up/Down
One screen up/down	Page Up/Page Down
Beginning of document	Ctrl+Home
End of document	Ctrl+End

Saving and Retrieving Your Documents

You can save your WordPad documents to your hard drive or to a floppy disk and then later retrieve the documents for editing, printing, or review.

Saving   Save a document so you can reference it later, if necessary. To save a document, choose File, Save; alternatively, press Ctrl+S. The Save As dialog box appears, as shown in figure 18.2.

Use the Save In drop-down list to choose the appropriate drive and folder. In the File Name text box, enter the name of the file you want to save and choose OK.

FIG. 18.2
The Save As dialog box appears the first time you save a file.

 TIP You can use Windows long file names, if you want, instead of following the traditional 8-character file name with 3-letter extension.

Another option in the Save As dialog box is the Save as Type pull-down list. You can use this option to save your document in a format other than WordPad—such as a DOS text document or rich text format.

N O T E There are several circumstances in which you may need to save your file in a non-WordPad format. One example would be if you share the document with another user who has Microsoft Word for DOS and who can't read a native Windows WordPad file; or if you are editing a text file such as a BAT or CMD batch file that cannot contain any formatting codes and must be saved in text (TXT) format. ■

The File menu contains two options for saving, Save and Save As. The first time you save a document, the Save As dialog box appears. On subsequent saves to the same file using Save, WordPad just overwrites the old version and no dialog box appears. Save As is used later only if you want to make another saved copy of the file with a different name, which creates a separate copy of the file with the new name you specify.

Retrieving Retrieve, or open, a WordPad file when you want to make changes to the file or re-read the document. To retrieve a previously saved file in WordPad, follow these steps:

1. Choose File, Open; or press Ctrl+O.
2. Select the drive from the Look In drop-down list.
3. Select the folder in the window. To open a folder, double-click it; open folders until you find the one that holds the document you want to open.

4. Click the name of the file you want to open, and then choose Open. Alternatively, you can double-click the file name in the window to open it.

N O T E   To view a specific type of file in the Open dialog box, choose the file type from the drop-down list in Files of Type. To view all document types, choose All Documents from the files type list.   ■

Selecting and Editing Document Text

Although small edits in your document are accomplished by moving your insertion point and deleting characters or adding text, editing blocks of text requires that you select the text first. Selected text appears in reverse video on-screen. To select text in your document, do the following:

1. Position your mouse I-beam at either the beginning or end of the block of text you want to select.

2. Click and hold down the left mouse button while you move past the text you want to include in your selection. Text included in the selection appears in reverse type (highlighted). This is known as a *click-and-drag selection*.

3. When you have finished selecting text, release the mouse button. The selection remains in reverse type.

WordPad offers a variety of mouse actions that speed up the process of selecting text. These actions are listed in table 18.2.

Table 18.2   Text Selection Techniques

Selection Area	Action
Any area of text	Click and drag past the area to include in your selection. Another method is to click the beginning of the selection and hold down Shift while clicking the end of the selection.
Single word	Double-click the word.
Single line	Click the white space to the left of the line of text, where your pointer becomes a right-pointing arrow (this area is known as the selection bar).
Multiple lines	Click the left mouse button in the selection bar and drag up or down.

Selection Area	Action
Entire paragraph	Double-click in the selection bar to the left of the paragraph.
Entire document	Press Ctrl and click in the selection bar.

To deselect an area of text, you can either click the left mouse button anywhere in the document or press one of the keyboard arrow keys.

CAUTION

Be careful not to accidentally press any other keys—such as the Enter key or a character or number—when a body of text is selected. If you do, WordPad replaces the *entire selection* with the key(s) you pressed, which could end up removing text you didn't intend to delete. If this occurs, immediately choose Edit, Undo to reverse this action (it may say Undo Typing instead of Undo, depending on what your last action was).

Deleting Text   To delete a block of text, select the text you want to delete, then choose one of the following options:

- Press the Delete or Backspace key.
- Choose Edit, Cut (or press Ctrl+X).
- Choose Edit, Clear (same as Delete).

Moving and Copying Text with the Clipboard   As with deleting text, moving or copying a block of text requires that you first select the text to move or copy. You can use the Windows Clipboard to move or copy text from one place to the other. Think of the Clipboard as a temporary holding area for text and graphics that Windows NT makes available to all applications. The Edit menu of WordPad contains the commands relating to the Windows Clipboard.

To move or copy text using the Windows Clipboard, use the following procedure:

1. Select the block of text you want to move or copy.
2. To move the text block, choose Edit, Cut (or the keyboard equivalent Ctrl+X); to copy, choose Edit, Copy (or the keyboard equivalent Ctrl+C).
3. Position the insertion point at the place in the document where you want the text to be retrieved.

4. Choose <u>E</u>dit, <u>P</u>aste (or the keyboard equivalent Ctrl+V) to retrieve the text block.

CAUTION

The Clipboard holds only one piece of information at a time. It retains the information until the next time an item is cut or copied to the Clipboard. For this reason, you should always choose <u>E</u>dit, <u>P</u>aste immediately after a Cu<u>t</u> or <u>C</u>opy command.

Alternatively, you can use the quicker mouse-oriented technique for moving and copying text in your document; drag-and-drop. To move or copy using the mouse, follow these steps:

1. Select the text to be moved or copied.

2. To move the text, click the selected text and drag it to its new position; a vertical bar moves with the mouse pointer. Place the vertical bar at the point you want to insert the text and release the mouse button. The text appears at the new location.

   To copy the text, press and hold the Ctrl key while dragging the text. When you reach the new location, release the mouse button first, then release the Ctrl key. A copy of the text appears in the new location.

Using Find and Replace   Windows NT WordPad also offers text find-and-replace features that can be useful when you want to search your document or replace multiple occurrences of a particular word or phrase.

Both features are located in WordPad's <u>E</u>dit menu. To search for text, choose <u>E</u>dit, <u>F</u>ind, and the dialog box shown in figure 18.3 appears.

FIG. 18.3
Search for text in the document, matching case, if you like.

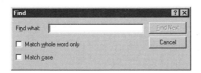

Enter the text you want to search for in the Fi<u>n</u>d What text box. If you want WordPad to match whole words only, click the Match <u>W</u>hole Word Only box. If you want the search to be case-sensitive, click the Match <u>C</u>ase box. Then either choose <u>F</u>ind Next or press Enter. WordPad brings you to the next matching occurrence of the text in the document. To find subsequent matches, click Find Next again (the dialog box doesn't disappear until you choose Cancel). If no matches are found, WordPad notifies you of this.

> **N O T E**   Use the Match Whole Word Only text box in instances where you do not want to find partial words; for example, if you do not choose the Match Whole Word Only option and search for "the", Word finds words such as "their," "therefore," "theorize," "breathe," and so on.

To search for and replace one text string with another, choose Edit, Replace; alternatively, press Ctrl+H. WordPad displays the Replace dialog box that looks similar to the Find dialog box; but the Replace dialog box provides a text box in which you can enter a replace string as well as a search string. After entering this information, choose Find Next to be brought to the next occurrence of the search string. You can either choose Replace to replace just this occurrence, or Replace All to replace this and all remaining occurrences of the text string in your document.

> **CAUTION**
>
> Be *very* sure before choosing Replace All, as there are often times when other unexpected occurrences of a phrase occur in your document which you didn't intend to replace. The safest (but longer) way is to go to each occurrence using Find Next and then choose Replace for those that should be replaced. Alternatively, save your document prior to running a search and replace task, in case you want to abandon the changes and revert back to the saved document.

Formatting Documents

As a word processing application, WordPad gives you a number of features with which to control the appearance of your documents. These features fall into one of the following three categories:

- *Character formatting*. Features that allow you to control character-oriented features, such as type style and type size.

- *Paragraph formatting*. Features that allow you to control paragraph-oriented features, such as justification of text and column alignments.

■ *Page formatting.* Features that allow you to control page-oriented features, such as headers and footers and margin sizes.

Let's take a look at each of these areas and how we use them in WordPad.

Character Formatting You apply character formatting to one or more characters of text, to words, sentences, paragraphs, and so on. There are two ways to format text:

■ For text which you are about to type, set up character formatting the way you want, then type the text that will have the attributes you specified. When you are done typing the text, change the character formatting back to a previous style or use a completely new style.

■ For text that has already been typed in, select the text to which you want to apply character formatting, then make the character formatting changes for the highlighted text.

 TIP Use the keyboard shortcuts to quickly apply attributes: Ctrl+B to boldface text or Ctrl+I to italicize text.

To format text characters, follow these steps:

1. Choose Format, Font. The Font dialog box appears (see fig. 18.4).
2. You can choose to change the following, in the Font dialog box:

    Font. Typeface of the text.

    Font Style. Attributes of the text.

    Size. Point size of the text.

    Effects. Color, Strikeout, or Underline the text.

3. A preview of some text with the font attributes you have selected is shown in the Sample area. Verify that the changes you have made are satisfactory, then click OK to have the changes take effect.

N O T E You can quickly apply font, size, and bold, italic or underline attributes to text using the Formatting toolbar. Use the drop-down lists and select a font or size, or click the attribute button to choose the formatting you want to apply. ■

FIG. 18.4
WordPad allows you to use all of the fonts currently installed in Windows NT.

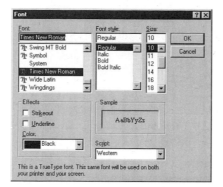

 TROUBLESHOOTING

I selected some text and went into the Font dialog box to change the attributes, but some of the check boxes are grayed. You have selected an area of text that has more than one set of type style setting, such as bold or italic, in it. You can select a smaller area which contains text with the same formatting attributes already set. Alternatively, you can remove all applied styles to the selected text by clicking each grayed box twice; the first click applies the style and the second click removes the style formatting.

I chose a font attribute that isn't printing on my printer. This may have occurred either because your printer is not capable of printing graphics or the particular font chosen, or because the font you have selected does not support the attribute you selected. For best results, use a printer capable of printing graphics and use only Windows TrueType fonts, denoted with a (TT) next to the font name in the Font dialog box.

Paragraph Formatting   *Paragraph formatting* commands, as the name implies, are those that apply to paragraphs of text. Paragraph formatting includes features such as alignment and indentation. By default, WordPad gives you paragraph formatting that is left-aligned (ragged-right margin) with no paragraph indentations.

Paragraph Alignment   One example of a paragraph formatting change you might want to make is alignment. There are three types of alignment available to you—left, right, and center. You can quickly format text by using the alignment buttons on the Formatting toolbar.

Part
IV

Ch
18

As with the other commands, paragraph alignment can be changed for a paragraph you are about to type or for one that already exists. To change alignment, click the alignment button on the Formatting toolbar that corresponds to the alignment you want for the text.

Figure 18.5 shows examples of each of the three types of paragraph alignment, as well as the alignment buttons on the Formatting toolbar.

FIG. 18.5

The three paragraph alignment types in WordPad give you control over your paragraph's appearance.

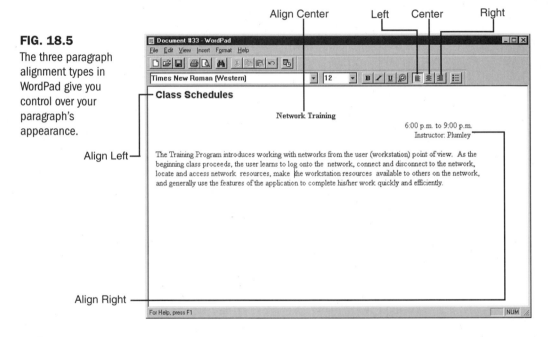

 TIP   You also can change paragraph alignment in the Paragraph dialog box, as shown in figure 18.6.

Indentation   You also can indent your paragraphs; that is, increase the margin for a paragraph so that it is narrower than the other text in your document. This is used for various purposes, including direct quotes.

To set the indentation for a paragraph of text:

1. Select the text for which you want to change the indentation.

2. Choose Format, Paragraph. The Paragraph dialog box appears (see fig. 18.6).

FIG. 18.6

Set indents for the left, right, or first line of the paragraph.

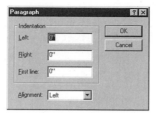

3. Set any or all of the following indentations:

   Left. Indents the left edge of the paragraph (all lines of text) by the amount you set. The measurement is in inches.

   Right. Indents the right edge of the paragraph by the amount, in inches, that you set.

   First Line. Indents only the first line of the paragraph, from the left edge, by the amount, in inches, that you set.

4. Choose OK to close the dialog box.

To set indents on a new paragraph, change the settings as in step 3, type the paragraph, and then change the indents back to zero in the Paragraph dialog box.

Page Formatting   Page formatting includes page size, orientation, margins, and tabs. As with character and paragraph formatting, WordPad makes certain assumptions about the layout of your page. The default page formatting in WordPad is 1.25-inch left and right margins, 1-inch top and bottom margins, left-tab settings every .5 inches, and portrait orientation. In the following sections you learn how to change each of these settings.

Setting Page Margins   One of the most common changes made to a document is the size of the margins. Page margins are the borders between the edge of the page and the text on the page on the top, bottom, left, and right.

N O T E   Your printer may require a minimum amount of margin area; most laser printers, for example, require at least .25-inch for all four margins. Check your printer documentation if you are unsure. ■

Part

IV

Ch

18

To change the margins of your WordPad document, follow these steps:

1. Choose File, Page Setup. The Page Setup dialog box appears (shown in fig. 18.7).

2. In the Margins area, enter the values (in inches) you want for each of the margins (Left, Right, Top, and Bottom) in the respective boxes.

3. Choose OK to close the dialog box or you can change other settings while the dialog box is open.

FIG. 18.7

Set the margins for the current document.

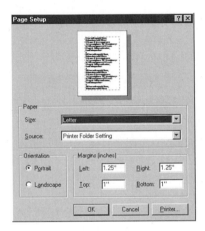

Setting Page Size and Orientation   You set your page size and orientation in the Page Setup dialog box. When setting page size, you might choose an envelope size—such as a commercial envelope #10 or a Monarch envelope—or you might want to change the page size to legal and then back to letter.

> **N O T E** Before changing the paper size, make sure the printer you're using can print in sizes other than 8 1/2 x 11 inches. ▪

You also can set page orientation to either portrait (tall) or landscape (long) depending on what you're printing.

To set page size and orientation, follow these steps:

1. Choose File, Page Setup. The Page Setup dialog box appears (refer to fig. 18.7).

2. To set page size, in the Paper area, display the Size drop-down list box and choose the size paper or envelope you're using.

3. To set orientation, choose either Portrait or Landscape in the Orientation area.

4. Choose OK to close the dialog box and apply the changes to the current document.

 T I P You can only view changes in page size, margins, and orientation in Print Preview. To see the page in print preview, choose File, Print Preview.

Setting Tabs   Tab stops control where the cursor goes when you press the Tab key. WordPad has its tabs preset to every 1/2 inch across the page. WordPad's preset tabs are *left tabs*, which means text is left-aligned at the tab stop.

The tab settings are controlled through the Format, Tab menu command. Figure 18.8 shows the Tabs dialog box in which you can set your own tab stops for the current document.

FIG. 18.8

The Tabs dialog box allows you to set up to 12 tab stops across the page.

To change the tab settings of your document, you can do the following:

1. Choose Format, Tabs. The Tabs dialog box appears.

2. For each tab stop you want to create across the page, enter a number in the Tab Stop Position text box.

3. Choose Set to add the tab stop to the list. Then enter the next tab stop measurement; click Set again.

 T I P To clear one tab stop from the list, select the tab stop measurement and choose Clear; choose Clear All to clear all tabs from the box.

4. Choose OK to close the dialog box and set tabs for the current document.

N O T E You also can click the mouse pointer on the ruler to set a tab and you can adjust the tab placement by dragging the tab to a new location on the ruler. To remove a tab from the ruler, drag the tab down and off the ruler with the mouse pointer. ▩

Printing Documents

Printing-related functions are found in the File menu. The choices related to printing are Print and Print Preview

To print your document, follow these steps:

1. Choose File, Print; alternatively, press Ctrl+P. The Print dialog box appears (see fig. 18.9).

FIG. 18.9
Use the Print option if the printer you want to print from is a local printer or a network printer you are already connected to.

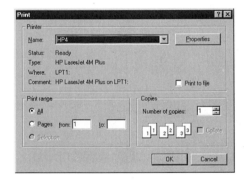

2. The current Windows NT default printer is selected automatically, and appears in the Printer area. To choose a printer other than the default, click the Name down arrow to view the available printer choices.

3. Set the rest of the dialog box as follows:

   Print Range area. Choose to print All pages or a range of pages. To specify a page range, enter the first page in the From text box and the last page number in the To text box. If you've selected text in the document, you can print just the selected text by choosing the Selection option.

   Copies area. Enter the number of copies you want to print and choose whether to Collate the multiple copies.

   Print to File. Choose this check box if you want to print the document to a file instead of a printer.

Also, if you need to change a setting specific to the printer, such as the form type being printed on (letter or legal) or the page orientation (portrait or landscape), choose <u>P</u>roperties and make those changes. ■

4. Click OK or press Enter to print your document.

   ▶ **See** "Understanding the Windows NT Printing Process," **p. 114**

Exiting WordPad

To exit Windows NT WordPad, use one of the following methods:

- ■ Choose <u>F</u>ile, E<u>x</u>it.
- ■ Click the WordPad Control menu box (in the upper left-hand corner of the window) and click <u>C</u>lose; alternatively, press Alt+F4 while the WordPad window is active.
- ■ Double-click the WordPad Control-menu box.
- ■ Click the Close (X) button in the title bar.

If you didn't save your latest changes, WordPad asks if you want to save prior to exiting. Choose <u>Y</u>es to save the changes, <u>N</u>o to close the document without saving the changes, or Cancel to return to the document.

Using Chat

Chat is an application you can use to communicate with others on the network. Similar to using a telephone, Chat enables you to "dial" someone up and have a conversation with them in real time. Although Chat enables communications over the network, the program uses telephone terms, such as dial, hang up, ring, and so on.

Chat installs with Windows NT, Windows for Workgroups, and Windows 95 applications. ■

You also can customize Chat by changing colors, setting preferences, and turning the sound on or off.

Making and Answering Calls

Using Chat, you specify the computer you want to call. That computer notifies the user to pick up. When the other user opens the Chat window, you both can enter and answer each other's messages. When you're finished with the communications, you both hang up and close the Chat program.

 Chat includes the Cut, Copy, and Paste commands that you can use to add or copy text from other Windows applications to your messages.

Making a Call   To make a call, you must know the name of the computer you want to contact.

To make a call, follow these steps:

1. Choose Start, Programs, Accessories, Chat. The Chat window appears (see fig. 18.10).

FIG. 18.10
Use the Chat window to communicate with others; enlarge the window if you need more room.

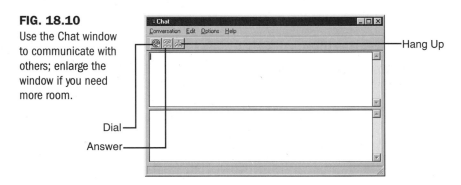

Hang Up

Dial

Answer

2. Choose Conversation, Dial; alternatively, click the Dial tool button. The Select Computer dialog box appears (see fig. 18.11).

3. If you do not see the computer with which you want to communicate in the Select Computer list, do one of the following:

   Double-click the domain name to display workstations in that domain.

   Double-click te workgroup name to display workstations in the workgroup.

   Enter a path to the computer you want to dial in the Computer text box.

4. Select the computer you want to chat with and choose OK. Chat notifies the other computer; when the beeping stops on your computer, you can enter your message in the top half of the Chat window. The recipient's answer appears in the lower half of the window.

FIG. 18.11
All computers in your workgroup appear in the Select Computer list.

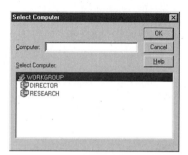

TIP The computer name to which you are connected appears in the title bar of your Chat window; your computer's name appears in the title bar of the recipient's Chat window.

5. When you're finished with your conversation, choose Conversation, Hang Up; alternatively, click the Hang Up button. The other user is notified that you have discontinued the call and they can close their Chat window. Close your Chat window when you're finished making calls by clicking the Close (X) button in the title bar.

Answering a Call   When someone calls you on the Chat line, your computer beeps consistently to notify you of the call. Additionally, the Chat button appears on the taskbar, blinking dark and light to attract your attention.

Click the Chat button on the taskbar to open the Chat window. Click the Answer tool button to let the sender know you're there; alternatively, choose Conversation, Answer. After you answer, the caller can enter the message (see fig. 18.12). Enter your answer in the top half of the Chat window.

When you're finished with your conversation, you can hang up by clicking the Hang Up tool button.

FIG. 18.12
Use Chat for immediate solutions to everyday work questions.

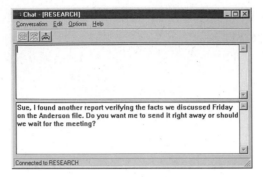

Customizing Chat

You can customize the Chat program by displaying certain elements in the Chat window and by setting preferences such as font and color. If you work in the Chat window a lot, you'll want to be comfortable there.

Displaying Screen Elements   You can display or hide the toolbar, status bar, and turn the sound on and off in Chat. To display or hide these elements, choose Options, Toolbar, Status Bar, and/or Sound. An item with a check mark preceding it means the element is displaying; no check mark means the element is hidden.

Changing Colors   You can change the color of the upper half of the Chat screen. The color you choose also appears on your half of the screen in the recipient's Chat window.

Choose Options, Background Color. The Color Palette appears. Choose the color you want to apply to the background of the screen and choose OK

Changing Fonts   Change the font of the message text you enter; font changes appear in your half of the window in the recipient's Chat window as well as in your own.

Choose Options, Font. The Font dialog box appears (see fig. 18.13). Choose the font, style, and size and choose OK when you're done.

FIG. 18.13
Change fonts for your
messages to make
them easier to read
or more attractive.

Using Paint

Paint is a Windows accessory program that enables you to create simple or elaborate drawings that you can use in other Windows applications, such as logos, maps, illustrations, and so on. Paint has its own set of tools for you to use in your drawings.

> **NOTE** Paint no longer allows you to save in the PCX file format; you can save only bitmapped files in Windows NT 4.0. ■

To start Paint, choose Start, Programs, Accessories, Paint. Figure 18.14 shows the Paint screen.

 TIP To find out what any tool on the Tool Box does, click the tool and view the description in the status bar.

Part
IV

Ch
18

Drawing Lines

When you first open Paint, your mouse pointer appears as a pencil you can use to draw with. Use the Pencil to draw freeform lines, curved lines, and so on. Additionally, you can use the Line and/or Curve tools for creating lines. Figure 18.15 shows the types of lines you can draw with the three line tools and points out the tools on the Tool Box. To use a line tool, click the tool with your mouse; the mouse pointer changes shape.

FIG. 18.14
Use Paint to create art for your documents.

Drawing tools

Line size box

Mouse "pencil"

Drawing area

Palette

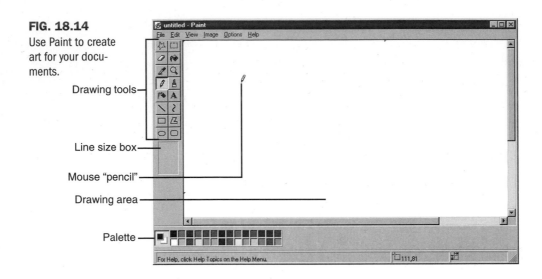

Curve tool   Drawn with Pencil tool   Drawn with Line tool

FIG. 18.15
The different line tools create different line types.

Pencil tool

Line tool

Drawn with Curve tool

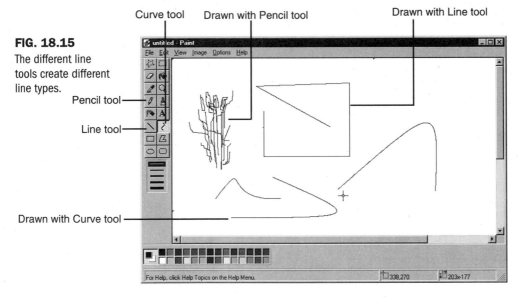

To draw a line using the Pencil tool, press and hold the mouse button while moving the "pencil" across the screen.

To draw a line with the Line tool, click the tool where you want to start the line and drag it to the point you want the line to stop; release the mouse button.

To draw a curve, draw a line and then release the mouse button to define the beginning and ending of the curve. Then press and hold the mouse button again and drag it to define the curve. As you move the mouse, the curve follows the curve tool. When the curve is the way you want it, double-click the mouse button to end the curve; alternatively, release the mouse button and click the Curve tool in the Tool Box before drawing another curve.

 TIP If you draw a line you're unhappy with, choose Edit, Undo and try it again.

Drawing Shapes

You can choose to draw a rectangle, oval, polygon, or rounded rectangle using the four shape tools at the bottom of the Tool Box.

When you click a shape tool, three options appear below the Tool Box—transparent, opaque, and white fill. Figure 18.16 shows several shapes drawn and the shape tools and options used.

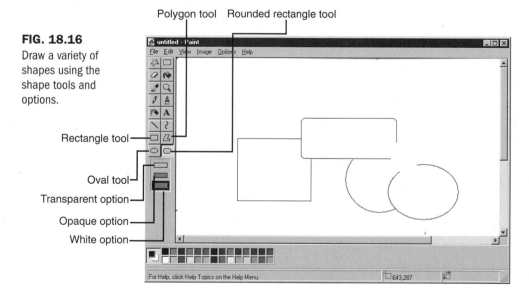

FIG. 18.16
Draw a variety of shapes using the shape tools and options.

Polygon tool   Rounded rectangle tool

Rectangle tool

Oval tool

Transparent option

Opaque option

White option

N O T E To draw a polygon, click the polygon tool and drag it to form the first side of the shape; the tool draws a line. Continue to click and drag the tool to form the sides of the shape. When you're ready to fill in the last side of the polygon, double-click the tool and Paint fills in the last side for you.

Using Color

You assign colors to lines and shapes before you draw them in Paint using the color palette at the bottom of the drawing area. Figure 18.17 shows the palette.

FIG. 18.17
Use the palette to specify line and shape color.

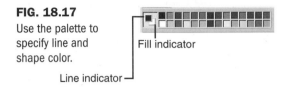

Fill indicator

Line indicator

To assign a line color, click a color in the palette with your left mouse button. The line indicator changes to the selected color. To assign a fill color, click the color in the palette with the right mouse button; the fill indicator changes color. The selected colors remain until you choose other colors.

Using the Paint Tools

Paint includes three tools you can use to apply color—the Brush, Fill with Color, and Airbrush. Use the Brush tool to apply narrow or wide strokes to the drawing. Use the Airbrush to apply a deckled, or sprayed on, effect and use the Fill with Color to fill a shape quickly with a color. Figure 18.18 shows examples of each paint tool and the tools in the Tool Box.

FIG. 18.18
Create different effects using the paint tools.

Fill with color tool

Airbrush tool

Brush strokes defined

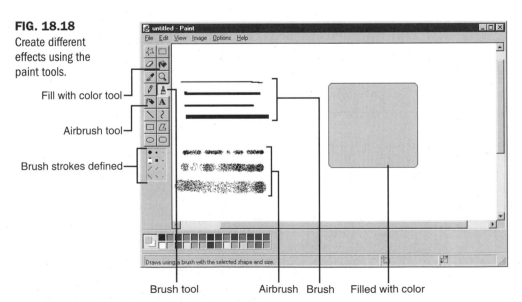

Brush tool   Airbrush Brush   Filled with color

TIP You can choose a paint tool and then a line color in the palette to apply to the items you create with the paint tools.

Adding Text

You can add text to any drawing using the text tool. You can then select the text and format it.

To add text to a drawing, follow these steps:

1. Click the text tool ("A") in the Tool Box and drag it in your drawing to create a box in which to type your text (see fig. 18.19).

FIG. 18.19
Enter the text in the text box you create.

Text tool

Use double-headed arrow to resize text box

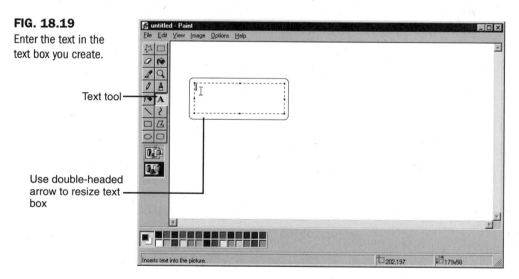

2. Type the text in the text box, pressing Enter at the end of each line.
3. When you use the text tool, the Text toolbar appears. Select the text you want to format and choose the font drop-down list box or the Size drop-down list box; select the font or size you want to change the text to. You also can use the Bold, Italic, or Underline buttons to format the text.

Editing Your Drawing

You can select items in a drawing to move them around on the page and you can delete items, erase parts of items, and copy and paste items.

Part
IV

Ch
18

To use the eraser, select the eraser tool and then select an eraser option (see fig. 18.20).

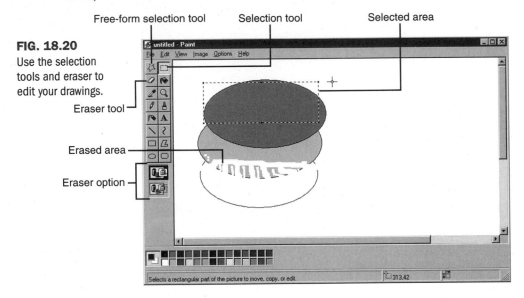

Free-form selection tool   Selection tool   Selected area

FIG. 18.20
Use the selection
tools and eraser to
edit your drawings.

Eraser tool

Erased area

Eraser option

After selecting an item or multiple items, you can copy and paste them to another location or another drawing. To copy and paste selected items, choose Edit, Copy and then choose Edit, Paste.

TROUBLESHOOTING

When I copy my drawing and paste it into another document, the whole page copies, not just the selected part. I end up with a lot of white space around the drawing. Is there anything I can do to make the image area smaller? Yes, choose Image, Attributes; or press Ctrl+E. In the Attributes dialog box, enter the Width and Height of the image area you want for your drawing; for example, 2 inches by 2 inches. Choose OK to close the dialog box and the image area appears on screen, surrounded by small black handles on the corners and sides. You can now select and copy this image area.

Saving and Printing the Drawing

You save and print a Paint drawing the same way you save and print most any accessory document.

To save the drawing, choose File, Save As. In the Save As dialog box, choose a drive and folder in which to save your document. In File Name, enter a name for the drawing. Choose the Save button to complete the process.

To print the drawing, choose File, Print. In the Print dialog box, choose the printer you want to print to, enter the number of copies, and choose the print range. Choose OK to print the drawing.

NOTE   You can open a drawing you've previously saved by choosing File, Open and selecting the file from the list of files in the Open dialog box. ■

Exiting Paint

You can exit the Paint program in any of the following ways:

- Choose File, Exit
- Press Alt+F4
- Click the Close (X) button
- Choose Close from the Control Menu
- Double-click the Control Menu

If you have not saved your drawing, Paint displays a message asking if you want to save the changes. Choose Yes to save, No to close without saving the drawing, or Cancel to return to the drawing.

From Here...

This chapter introduced you to and showed you how to use three of the NT accessories: WordPad, Chat, and Paint. For information about using other NT utilities, see these chapters:

- Chapter 30, "Using HyperTerminal," shows you how to connect to other computers using NT's HyperTerminal accessory and your modem.
- Chapter 32, "Using the Event Viewer," explains how to view the security, system, and audit logs recorded by NT to track problems, errors, and security breaches.

Part
IV

Ch
18

Networking with Windows NT

CHAPTER 19

Understanding Windows NT Network Services

by John Enck

One of the most unique aspects of Windows NT networking is how Windows NT separates client/server and peer-to-peer services from the underlying network protocol. Under Windows NT, you can choose the protocol you want to use in your network—NetBEUI, IPX, or TCP/IP—without worrying how it will affect Windows NT services for file sharing, printer sharing, and program-to-program communications. This flexibility allows you to construct and administer powerful networks that can address the needs of your company without being compromised by the demands of your existing client or server computers. ■

Learn the protocol suites supported by Windows NT

This chapter explains which protocols are supported and discusses their origins and architectures.

How to choose which protocol suite(s) to use

Learn how to pick the best protocol(s) for your network environment, so that you don't run all the protocols at once.

How to control which network services operate over which protocol suites

Learn how to enable or disable support for network services, such as file and print sharing, over your protocols of choice.

Configure and use Windows NT file sharing

Access files on other systems and share files and directories stored on your local hard drives.

Configure and use Windows NT printer sharing

You can access printers attached to other systems and share printers connected to your own system.

Achieving this flexibility does, however, require complexity. Windows NT supports so many options for networking protocols and services that it can be difficult to tell which protocols go with which services and vice versa. With this in mind, this chapter will explore how to configure and use Windows NT networking protocols and services in both a native Microsoft network and in a Novell NetWare environment. ■

Understanding NetBIOS/NetBEUI

In order to appreciate the advantages of the Windows NT network architecture, we need to look back at the original networking model used by IBM, Microsoft, and others. This model was created in 1984 when IBM and Sytek released a Local Area Network (LAN) message interface system named the Network Basic Input/Output System, better known today as NetBIOS. NetBIOS is a generalized program-to-program communication facility that enables peer-to-peer and client/server communications between PCs operating in a LAN environment.

NetBIOS facilitates communication through three key services:

■ *Name service.* Each PC using NetBIOS is assigned a logical name (for example, MKT1, SALES, KIRK, and so on), and other PCs use that name to communicate with that PC. PCs learn about each other's names by listening to announcements PCs make when they join the LAN (for example, "MKT1 now available for service") or by broadcasting a discovery request for a name (for example, "KIRK, are you there?"). Each PC keeps track of the names of other PCs in a local, dynamic table. No centralized name servers are required (or supported).

■ *Session service.* A PC can establish a session with another PC by "calling" it by name. Once the target PC agrees to communicate with the requesting PC, the two PCs can exchange messages with one another until one of them "hangs up." Session service is a connection-oriented service, so while the two PCs are communicating with one another, NetBIOS provides message sequencing and message acknowledgments to insure that all messages sent are properly received.

■ *Datagram services.* Datagram service is a connectionless service that does not require a PC to establish a session with another PC in order to send messages, and does not guarantee the receipt of any messages sent. Datagram services can be used to deliver broadcast or informational messages. Application-level session controls and acknowledgments can also be placed on top of datagram services to make them more reliable.

In addition to these three core services, NetBIOS provides a limited number of status and control functions. For example, these functions can be used to cancel a NetBIOS request, get the current status of the NetBIOS interface, or start a NetBIOS-level trace.

When NetBIOS was first released, the term NetBIOS encompassed both protocol-level and service-level functions. As the industry moved toward using well-defined computing models that separate protocols from services (among other things), the NetBIOS protocol and service aspects were formally separated, and the term NetBIOS Extended User Interface (NetBEUI) was adopted to define the protocol-level functions.

Microsoft pioneered the usage of the term NetBEUI and included support for the NetBIOS/NetBEUI combination in its DOS-based LAN Manager product, in its Windows for Workgroups (WFW) offering, in its Windows 95 offering and, of course, in its Windows NT Workstation and Server products. Unfortunately, while Microsoft clearly distinguishes between the NetBIOS and NetBEUI functions, many other vendors continue to use the term NetBIOS to refer to both protocol and service functions.

Using Server Message Blocks (SMB)

As noted, NetBIOS provides a generalized interface for program-to-program communications. NetBIOS does not, however, provide specific services to facilitate file, print, and other user-related services in a peer-to-peer or client/server LAN. That task falls on the shoulders of *Server Message Blocks* (*SMB*).

Like NetBIOS, SMB is an interface system. But where NetBIOS is a generalized interface system, SMB is a specific interface system that enables file sharing, print sharing, and user-based messaging. Some of the specific services supported by SMB include:

- *Connection Related Services.* Start/end connection.
- *File Related Services.* Includes the following:

  Get disk attributes

  Create/delete directory

  Search for file name(s)

  Create/delete/rename file

  Read/write file

  Lock/unlock file area

  Open/commit/close file

  Get/set file attributes

- *Print Related Services.* Includes open/close spool file, write to spool file, and query print queue.
- *User Related Services.* Includes the following:

  Discover home system for user name

  Send message to user

  Broadcast message to all users

  Receive user message(s)

In the Windows NT environment, SMB functions are integrated into the operating system. For example, when you use File Manager to connect to a network drive (or you issue a NET USE command), you are invoking SMB functions. Also note that NetBIOS and SMB often work together. For example, when you connect to a network drive, you rely on NetBIOS services to find the name of the system sponsoring the directory you need, but you actually connect to and access that network drive using SMB services.

Limitations of SMB/NetBIOS/NetBEUI Architecture

As successful as the SMB/NetBIOS/NetBEUI architecture has been, it is not without its limitations. In particular:

- As previously discussed, NetBIOS uses system names to enable and manage end-to-end connections. Under NetBIOS, names are resolved using broadcast-oriented techniques. For example, when a system joins the

LAN, it broadcasts its name, and when a system wants to establish a connection to a system it has not previously heard from, it broadcasts a name discovery message. Unfortunately, broadcasts create overhead in a LAN and can negatively affect overall performance.

- NetBEUI does not use any addresses other than the physical LAN adapter address (a.k.a. the Medium Access Control, or MAC, address). In contrast, protocols like IPX and TCP/IP add a second level of addressing that defines a network address. This second level address allows IPX and TCP/IP to quickly determine if a transmitted message needs to be routed to another physical network (because it has a different network address) or if it can be serviced on the local network. Because NetBEUI does not use a second level address, NetBEUI cannot distinguish between local and non-local messages and is therefore considered a non-routable protocol.

When you combine the NetBIOS limitation with the NetBEUI limitation, you end up with network traffic that is difficult to manage over multiple, interconnected LANs or in a complex LAN/WAN environment. Specifically, you have NetBIOS generating lots of broadcast messages to resolve names, and because NetBEUI does not support network addressing, these broadcasts must be sent to all of the attached LANs. In effect, NetBIOS and NetBEUI aggravate each other's limitations.

Fortunately, Microsoft recognized the limitations of NetBIOS and NetBEUI and included alternate approaches in the network architecture for Windows NT.

Part
V

Ch
19

Choosing a Protocol

One of the most significant advantages of the Windows NT network architecture is that it formally separates the NetBIOS and SMB services from the LAN-level protocol. Under Windows NT you are not forced to run NetBIOS and SMB over NetBEUI—you can, in fact, choose the network protocol that makes the most sense for your organization's overall network composition. Because you are no longer forced to use NetBEUI for native Microsoft networking traffic, you are no longer constrained by the NetBEUI limitation.

What LAN-level protocols can you choose from? Microsoft provides three protocols that can be used to carry NetBIOS and SMB traffic:

- *NetBEUI Frames (NBF)*. This is an enhanced version of NetBEUI that supports a larger number of systems than the original NetBEUI protocol. Unfortunately, the enhanced version does not include any network addresses and therefore still suffers from the same internetworking limitation as the original protocol.

- *Internetwork Packet eXchange/Sequenced Packet eXchange (IPX/SPX)*. IPX and SPX are the main protocols used in Novell NetWare networks. IPX is a connectionless protocol with no guaranteed delivery, and SPX is a connection-oriented protocol with guaranteed delivery.

- *Transmission Control Protocol/Internet Protocol (TCP/IP)*. TCP/IP is actually a suite of protocols that includes TCP, IP, the User Datagram Protocol (UDP), and several other service protocols. TCP is a connection-oriented protocol with guaranteed delivery, and UDP is a connectionless protocol with no guarantees. Both TCP and UDP rely on IP to resolve network addresses and facilitate the end-to-end delivery of messages.

Microsoft also includes the Data Link Control (DLC) protocol, AppleTalk protocol, the Streams Environment, and the Point-to-Point Tunneling Protocol (PPTP) with Windows NT Workstation and Windows NT Server. DLC, AppleTalk, and the Streams Environment are special purpose products that cannot be used to carry NetBIOS and SMB traffic. DLC is used for IBM host traffic and network printer connectivity. AppleTalk is used for connectivity to Apple computers. The Streams Environment is available as a special interface for network programmers. To be useful, DLC, AppleTalk, and the Streams Environment require additional software not included with Windows NT. PPTP, on the other hand, is used in conjunction with Remote Access Service (RAS) to carry LAN traffic over a wide-area link.

As previously noted, TCP/IP and IPX implement network addresses; therefore, they are both considered routable protocols that can easily be integrated into multi-LAN environments and large wide area networks. This makes either protocol a superior choice to NetBEUI for most applications.

Unfortunately, the standard implementations of TCP/IP and IPX do not address the broadcast-intensive nature of NetBIOS. Because NetBIOS operates above the

LAN-layer protocol, it is isolated from the technical details of the underlying protocol, and by the same token, the underlying protocol is isolated from the technical details of NetBIOS. That means that NetBIOS name resolution will, by default, be handled using broadcast techniques regardless of which LAN-layer protocol is in use.

Microsoft did, however, address this problem by creating optional enhancements for the TCP/IP implementation in Windows NT—and only for the TCP/IP implementation. Specifically, Microsoft borrowed an idea (or two) from the way TCP/IP is used in a UNIX environment and implemented two ways of resolving NetBIOS name requests without generating broadcasts:

- You can configure a LMHOSTS file in each Windows NT system. *LMHOSTS* is a simple text file that contains a list of NetBIOS names and the corresponding TCP/IP address for each name. This is similar to the way that UNIX hosts use a HOSTS file to resolve native TCP/IP name-to-address translations. (You should note that Windows NT also supports a HOSTS file for TCP/IP traffic that does not involve NetBIOS.)

- You can implement a *Windows Internet Name Service* (*WINS*) server. A WINS server provides a centralized database that maps NetBIOS names to TCP/IP addresses. When a WINS client wants to know the address for a NetBIOS name, it simply asks a WINS server. This is similar to the way that UNIX hosts use Domain Name System (DNS) or Network Information Service (NIS) name servers. (Windows NT also supports DNS client operations and Windows NT Server can act as a DNS server.)

Part
V
Ch
19

A given Windows NT system can use one of these approaches, both of these approaches, or neither of these approaches (in which case it resorts to using broadcasts for name resolution). Assuming, however, that either of these approaches is in place, the TCP/IP software in a Windows NT system looks for NetBIOS name discovery requests. When it sees such a request, it looks for the name in its local LMHOSTS file, or it sends an inquiry request to a WINS server.

Finally, please note that the Windows NT implementation of TCP/IP also supports a dynamic IP address assignment protocol—the *Dynamic Host Configuration Protocol* (*DHCP*). Although DHCP is not directly related to the NetBIOS or NetBEUI issues, using DHCP in connection with WINS results in a network that is easy to administer and troubleshoot.

▶ **See** "TCP/IP Basics," **p. 640**

Issues to Consider in Choosing a Protocol

Given the variety of protocols you can deploy under the Windows NT networking architecture, the question becomes: "Which protocol suite should I use?" Unfortunately, there is no right answer. In fact, you need to look at the protocol selection issue from two angles:

- What connections are required outside of native Windows NT network services?

- What is the current and projected layout of your network?

Your requirements for non-native Windows NT network connections are a driving force in determining what protocol suites you need to load under Windows NT. Specifically:

- If you need connectivity to a UNIX system, to the Internet, or to other hosts supporting TCP/IP, then you need to install the TCP/IP protocol suite.

- If your Windows NT workstation is going to need to access a NetWare server as a NetWare client, you need to load the IPX protocol suite.

- If you need connections to an IBM mainframe, you need to install the DLC protocol. (Note: As an alternative, you can deploy the Microsoft SNA Server or third-party connectivity solution.)

- If you need connections to an IBM AS/400, you can use either the DLC protocol or the TCP/IP protocol suite. (Note: As in the mainframe case, you can also deploy the Microsoft SNA Server or third-party connectivity solution.)

- If your Windows NT workstation needs to interact with existing Windows for Workgroups or LAN Manager systems, then you need to deploy the NetBEUI protocol suite under Windows NT.

N O T E   As an alternative, you can install the updated WFW and LAN Manager software included with Windows NT Server. This software brings the range of choices available with Windows NT to the WFW and LAN Manager environments. ■

When you look at protocol suites from the second perspective—which takes into account the current and projected layout of your network—you should consider how native Windows NT services for printing, file sharing, and application will be used in your current and future network. Here you must balance speed, ease of administration, and scalability. The factors you should take into consideration are:

- The two fastest and most efficient protocol suites are IPX and NetBEUI. TCP/IP's large, byte-oriented transmission headers really slow it down in comparison to IPX and NetBEUI.

- The two most secure protocol suites are also IPX and NetBEUI. TCP/IP's byte-oriented protocols make it easy to monitor a TCP/IP network and the simple command protocols used by standard TCP/IP utilities (FTP, Telnet, and so on) are easily penetrated (hacked).

- The protocol suite that is best integrated with Windows NT is NetBEUI. The Windows NT network architecture was designed around NetBEUI and then subsequently adapted for use with IPX and TCP/IP.

- The easiest protocol suite to administer and maintain is TCP/IP. Support for DHCP, WINS, DNS, and the Simple Network Management Protocol (SNMP) facilitates centralized management of TCP/IP-based Windows NT network. Neither IPX nor NetBEUI can match these TCP/IP capabilities.

- The protocol suite that scales the best is TCP/IP. A small TCP/IP LAN can easily be expanded into a large wide area network. IPX is a close second in this category. NetBEUI shouldn't even be taken into consideration. (NetBEUI's deficiency in the area of routing prevents it from being scaled.)

Part

V

Ch

19

You must, of course, take both perspectives into account to determine your protocol needs under Windows NT. For example, if you already have a large, IPX-based local and wide area network installed, then IPX is the obvious choice for both native and non-native Windows NT traffic.

The real beauty (from a networking perspective) of the Windows NT environment is that it allows you to deploy multiple protocols on a concurrent basis. With Windows NT, you can run native Windows NT networking services over IPX and run native TCP/IP services (for example, Telnet and FTP) over TCP/IP. Alternatively, you can run native NetWare services over IPX and run native Windows NT networking services over TCP/IP. You can even deploy all three protocol suites—

NetBEUI, IPX, and TCP/IP—and enable native and non-native services over all of them.

The bottom line is that Windows NT allows you to select and run the protocol suites that makes sense for your workstation connectivity needs and for your overall network strategy.

Configuring Windows NT Protocols and Services

Protocol suites are selected and configured through the Network option located in the Control Panel. If you did not configure network options when you installed Windows NT, you are prompted to do so when you access this icon. Assuming the network has previously been configured, the Network dialog box appears.

N O T E   You can also access the Network dialog box by right-clicking the Network Neighborhood icon on the desktop, and then selecting Properties from the shortcut menu.

Figure 19.1 shows an example Network dialog box. The tabs are used to access properties pages for the five major areas of configuration:

- The Adapters properties page defines which network adapters are physically installed in the system (such as a Novell NE2000 Adapter) and how those adapters are configured (such as IRQ assignment, I/O Port setting, and DMA assignment). Note that this properties page only shows physical network adapters; logical interfaces (such as a Remote Access Service—RAS—interface) will not appear here.

- The Protocols properties page defines which protocols or protocol suites (such as, NetBEUI, IPX, and TCP/IP) are supported and how those protocols are configured (such as, network addresses, system addresses, and routing options).

■ The Services properties page defines the services that can be used in conjunction with the protocol sets. For example, this is where you add support for an FTP server or enable your workstation to function as a file and/or print server for other workstations (for example, the "server" service).

■ The Identification properties page defines the logical (NetBIOS) name of the system and the name of the workgroup or domain the workstation belongs to.

■ The Bindings properties page defines the exact associations between services, protocols, and the available network adapter(s). The Bindings dialog allows you to restrict the operation of specific services over specific protocols, and similarly to restrict the operation of specific protocols over specific network adapters. For example, you can allow file and print server services to operate over the NetBEUI protocol and not the TCP/IP protocol. Or you can configure IPX to run over an EtherNet adapter and NetBEUI to run over a token-ring adapter.

FIG. 19.1
The Network dialog box allows you to select and configure each of the five major areas of configuration. By default, the first properties page (Adapters) is presented.

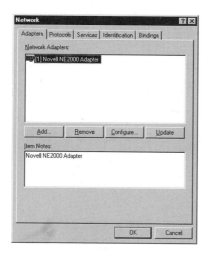

The Adapters Properties Page

Configuration of the physical network adapters is a relatively straightforward process that is explained in detail in Chapter 20, "Configuring the Network at Your Workstation." In brief, you click the Add button in the Adapters properties page to access the list of known network adapters. Once you select an adapter from that list (or select one from a vendor-supplied disk) you are prompted to supply the physical configuration details (such as IRQ, DMA, and I/O Port assignments). These configuration settings can subsequently be changed by selecting the adapter entry and clicking the Properties button.

Less straightforward is the purpose and options for the four remaining properties pages in the Network dialog box. With this in mind, let's take a closer look at these four properties pages.

The Protocols Properties Page

The Protocols properties page allows you to add, remove, and configure individual protocols or protocols suites. Figure 19.2 shows an example Protocols properties page. The current list of protocols is shown in the Network Protocols display area.

As previously discussed in this chapter, the three protocols that can be used for native Windows NT file and print services are NetBEUI, IPX/SPX, and TCP/IP. Four additional protocols—AppleTalk, DLC, PPTP, and Streams—are included with Windows NT for specialized uses. Windows NT installs the NWLink IPX/SPX Compatible Transport by default when you initially set up the network.

FIG. 19.2
The Protocols properties page in the Network dialog box allows you to add and remove protocol support. You can choose as many, or as few, protocols as you need.

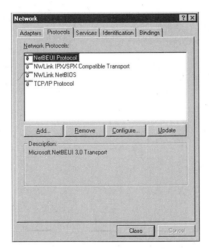

Protocol support can be disabled by highlighting the protocol service in the Network Protocols display area and clicking the Remove button. Note that if you remove the NWLink IPX/SPX Compatible Transport, the NWLink NetBIOS entry is automatically removed. Similarly, if you remove the NWLink NetBIOS entry, the NWLink IPX/SPX Compatible Transport entry is automatically removed.

To add support for a new protocol, click Add. You will receive the Select Network Protocol dialog box, as shown in figure 19.3, which lists the following protocols:

- *AppleTalk Protocol.* This protocol is used by third-party programs to facilitate connectivity to Apple computer networks.

- *DLC Protocol.* This protocol is used by third-party programs for connectivity with IBM mainframes and AS/400 systems.

- *NetBEUI Protocol.* This is one of the three protocols that can be used for native Microsoft networking (Windows NT, Windows 95, Windows for Workgroups, Windows 3.x, and DOS).

- *NWLink IPX/SPX Compatible Transport.* This protocol can be used for both native Microsoft networking and for connectivity to Novell NetWare servers. Note that a second protocol named NWLink NetBIOS is automatically added to your list of Network Protocols when you select this option.

- *PPTP.* This protocol is used to send LAN traffic over a wide area link (via RAS) in a safe and secure manner.

- *Streams Environment.* The Streams Environment provides a general-purpose interface used by third-party protocols.

- *TCP/IP Protocol.* This protocol can be used for native Microsoft networking and for general TCP/IP connectivity to a variety of networks (including the Internet) and computer types (such as, UNIX, Digital VAX, and so on).

Part
V

Ch
19

FIG. 19.3

The Select Network Protocol scroll list enables you to choose what network protocol you want to add support for.

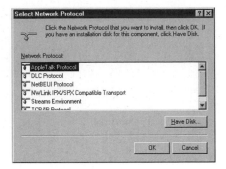

To install a new protocol, select the protocol entry and click the OK button. You are then prompted for your Windows NT product CD so the related software modules can be installed on your local drive.

When you add a new protocol suite, the configuration of that suite is not performed until you click the OK button in the Network Settings dialog box. When you click OK, Windows NT examines your proposed network environment and invokes the configuration dialog boxes required by the new protocols you have added. These dialog boxes allow you to associate the protocol with a specific network adapter board and provide protocol-specific configuration information, if required.

For example, after you add the IPX protocol suite and click OK in the Network Settings dialog box, you will receive a dialog box similar to the one shown in figure 19.4. This configuration dialog box allows you to set the logical address for the network that the workstation belongs to, to tie the protocol to a specific network adapter, and to enable support for specific LAN frame formats.

If you add the TCP/IP protocol, you receive a dialog box similar to the one shown in figure 19.5. Of the three major protocols (NetBEUI/NetBIOS, IPX/SPX, and TCP/IP), TCP/IP is the most complex protocol to configure. At minimum, you must configure a specific IP address for your workstation or enable support for DHCP. Please refer to "Configuring TCP/IP" in Chapter 24 for a detailed explanation of how to set the various TCP/IP properties.

FIG. 19.4

The NWLink IPX/SPX
Properties dialog box
sets the options
associated with the
IPX protocol and the
associated network.

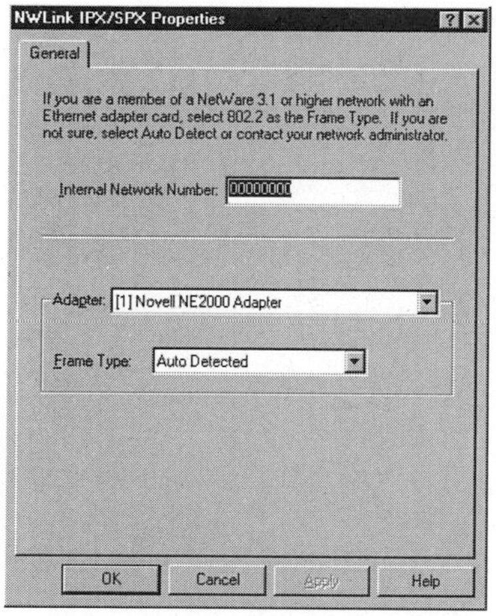

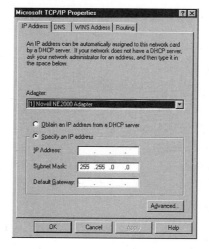

FIG. 19.5

The Microsoft TCP/IP
Properties dialog box
allows you to
configure a wide
range of TCP/IP
options under
Windows NT. During
the initial setup you
must at least specify
a specific IP address
or enable support for
DHCP.

Part

V

Ch

19

Finally, note that the NetBEUI protocol has no configuration settings associated
with it.

After you have specified the required configuration entries for the protocols you
have selected, Windows NT then asks you if you want to restart your system to put
the changes into effect. Virtually none of the changes you make using the Network dialog box go into effect until you restart your system.

N O T E   If you need to change the configuration information associated with the IPX or TCP/IP protocols, simply access the Protocols properties page within the Network dialog box, select the appropriate service entry (for example, NWLink IPX/SPX Compatible Transport or TCP/IP Protocol), and click the Properties button. ▪

The Services Properties Page

The Services properties page is where you configure the networking services you want to operate on top of the protocols you configured using the Protocols properties page. For example, this is where you enable support for your workstation to act as a file and print server for other workstation or enable support for the TCP/IP Simple Network Management Protocol (SNMP). Note that the Services properties page only defines which services are supported—the specific association of individual services with individual protocols is configured using the Bindings tab dialog box.

Windows NT includes a wide variety of network services. Figure 19.6 shows a typical Services tab dialog box. The Network Services display area shows which services are currently installed. By default the Windows NT network installation process installs the following services:

- *Computer Browser.* This service is actually part of the Workstation service and is automatically installed or deleted when the Workstation service is installed or deleted.
- *NetBIOS Interface.* Enables NetBIOS operations. This service must be enabled for native Windows NT networking, regardless of what other protocol is in use.
- *RPC Configuration.* Provides support for distributed, program-to-program communication over a native Microsoft network.
- *Server.* Allows the workstation to offer its local resources (directories and printers) to other systems on the network. In effect, the workstation can become a mini-server in a workgroup environment.
- *Workstation.* Allows the workstation to access native Windows NT networking services. This is a key service if you want the workstation to access network resources.

A Remote Access Service (RAS) entry also will be present if you selected support for remote networking during the initial installation procedure.

FIG. 19.6

The Services properties page allows you to enable or disable specific network services.

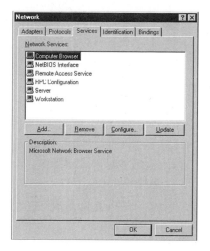

Installed services can be deleted by selecting the entry in the Network Services display area and clicking the Remove button. Note that the Computer Browser entry cannot be deleted by itself; to remove it you must delete the Workstation entry and the Computer Browser entry will be automatically deleted.

To add a new service, press the Add button. You will receive the Select Network Service dialog box, as shown in figure 19.7, which includes the following services:

- *Client Service for NetWare.* Enables connectivity to NetWare file and print servers. This service is not required for native Windows NT networking.

- *Microsoft Peer Web Services.* Installs support for Web, FTP, and Gopher server services.

- *Microsoft TCP/IP Printing.* Provides support for native TCP/IP-based printing (LPD/LPR).

- *NetBIOS Interface.* This is a core service required for native Windows NT networking; it is installed by default.

- *Network Monitor Agent.* Collects information about network usage for the workstation. This information can be examined using the Performance Monitor utility or through more comprehensive management tools like the Microsoft Systems Management Server (SMS).

Part

V

Ch

19

■ *Remote Access Service.* Allows the workstation to access remote servers, and also enables the Internet-oriented PPP and SLIP protocols.

■ *RPC Configuration.* Provides support for distributed, program-to-program communication over a native Microsoft network. This service is normally installed by default.

■ *RPC support for Banyan.* Provides support for distributed, program-to-program communication with workstations implementing the Banyan networking architecture.

■ *SAP Agent.* Provides support for third-party add-on software.

■ *Server.* Allows the workstation to offer its local resources to other systems on the network. The Server service is installed by default.

■ *Simple TCP/IP Services.* Installs a service to support echo, daytime, quote of the day, and several other minor TCP/IP features.

■ *SNMP Service.* Allows the workstation to participate with network management products that support the Simple Network Management Protocol (SNMP).

■ *Workstation.* Allows the workstation to access native Windows NT networking services. This service is installed by default. Note that when you install the Workstation service, its companion service, Computer Browser, is installed as well.

FIG. 19.7

The Select Network Service scroll list enables you to select which network service you want to add.

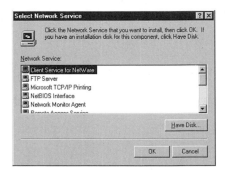

Once you make your selection by clicking the OK button, you are prompted for your Windows NT product CD so the related software modules can be installed on your local drive. If the service you are adding requires additional configuration information, you will be prompted for that information when the service is installed (as opposed to when you close the Network dialog box). For example, if you add support to the SNMP service, you will be prompted for configuration information, as shown in figure 19.8.

FIG. 19.8
The SNMP Properties dialog box allows you to configure the details of the SNMP service. Many network services depend on similar configuration dialogs.

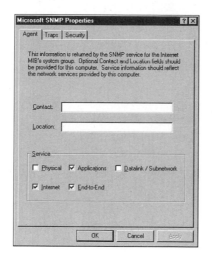

N O T E   If you need to change the configuration information associated with any service, simply access the Services tab in the Network dialog box, select the appropriate service entry (for example, Remote Access Service or SNMP Service), and click Properties.

Part
V

Ch
19

The Identification Properties Page

The Identification properties page in the Network dialog box allows you to view and change the Computer Name and Workgroup/Domain values. Figure 19.9 shows an example Identification tab dialog box. The Computer Name setting assigns the NetBIOS name to your system. This name is used for network traffic coming into and out of your system. In short, this is the name by which the rest of the world will recognize your computer.

FIG. 19.9

The Identification tab dialog box allows you to set the name of the workstation as it will appear on the network, as well as the name of the domain or workgroup the workstation will participate in.

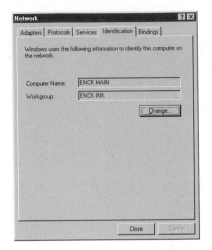

N O T E   The Computer Name value may be used by other software components you install at a later time. Because of this dependency, changing a Computer Name at a later time can often lead to undesirable and particularly frustrating results. The other software components won't be informed of the name change and may cease to function correctly. If at all possible, avoid changing this name after you initially set it up. ▪

The Workgroup value should reflect the name of the domain or workgroup the workstation participates in. There are many differences between domains and workgroups, but the two most significant differences are:

- When you participate in a workgroup, the user authentication process occurs on each system in the workgroup. Other workgroup systems "trust" that each system has performed the authentication. In contrast, all users in a domain are authenticated by a central server (also known as a *domain controller*). Using a centralized server provides greater control and security.

- Workgroups are informal groupings of systems that elect to share resources with one another. Domains are formal collections of systems that can be centrally controlled and administered. The informal nature of workgroups makes it difficult to implement them as large, enterprise-wide solutions. Domains, on the other hand, can be interconnected to create sizable and sophisticated network solutions.

You cannot simply create a domain by changing the setting in the Network Settings dialog box—only Windows NT Server systems can act as domain servers (controllers) and they must be established and configured before workstations can be associated with the domain. Workgroups, on the other hand, can be created on an ad hoc basis.

N O T E Once of the most common errors in configuring a Windows NT network is to fail to configure the workgroup fields consistently on all systems. The workgroup name must be the same for all systems in the network, or they will not be able to "see" one another. ■

The Bindings Properties Page

The formal association between network services and network protocols as well as the association between network protocols and network adapters is termed "binding." By default, native Windows NT networking services (such as, NetBIOS Interface, Server, and Workstation) are enabled for each native protocol you add (such as, NetBEUI, IPX/SPX, and TCP/IP) and each native protocol is bound to each network adapter. In some cases it may be desirable to alter these default settings. For example, you may want to enable IPX/SPX over an EtherNet card, but disable it over a token-ring card. Or you may want to disable the NetBIOS Interface over an Internet link.

You can view and change the current binding information using the Bindings properties page. Figure 19.10 shows a typical Bindings properties page. The display area contains a hierarchical list of entries; by default only the top-level entries are shown. To view additional entries you can click any entry that has a plus sign (+) on its left-hand side. For example, figure 19.11 shows the fully expanded version of the same properties page shown in figure 19.10.

Part
V

Ch
19

FIG. 19.10
The Bindings properties page allows you to view and change the associations between network services, network protocols, and network adapters.

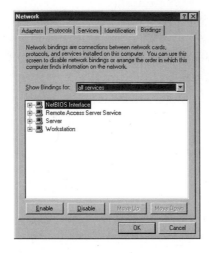

FIG. 19.11
In order to see all of the binding information, you must expand the display information by clicking entries that are preceded by a plus sign ("+").

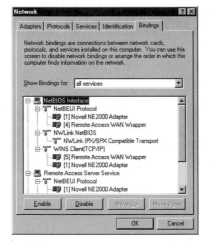

You can view binding information from one of three perspectives:

- *From a services perspective.* This view shows the services as the top-level item and then shows which network protocols are associated with each service and which network adapters are associated with each protocol. This is the default view for the dialog box.

- *From a protocols perspective.* This view shows the protocols as the top-level item and then shows which adapters or lower-level protocols are associated with each protocol entry. An example of this perspective is shown in figure 19.12.

■ *From an adapters perspective.* This view shows the network adapters as the top-level item and then shows which network protocols are associated with each adapter as well as which services are associated with each network protocol. The adapters perspective is really a reversed view of the same information shown in the services perspective. Figure 19.13 shows an example of the adapters perspective.

FIG. 19.12
The protocols perspective in the Bindings properties page shows the association between individual protocols and network adapters or lower-level protocols.

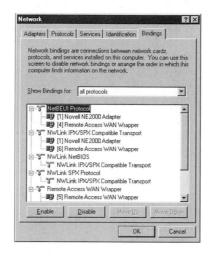

FIG. 19.13
The adapters perspective in the Bindings properties page shows the associations between the network adapters, network protocols, and network services.

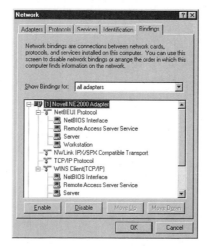

If you are running the native services (NetBIOS Interface, Server, and Work-station) over the three major protocol suites (NetBEUI, IPX, and TCP/IP), the bindings shown in the Bindings dialog box using the services perspective should appear similar to the list shown here:

```
NetBIOS Interface
    NetBEUI Protocol
        Network adapter (e.g., Novell NE2000)
    NWLink NetBIOS
        NWLink IPX/SPX Compatible Transport
    WINS Client (TCP/IP)
        Network adapter (e.g., Novell NE2000)
Server
    NetBEUI Protocol
        Network adapter (e.g., Novell NE2000)
    NWLink IPX/SPX Compatible Transport
    NWLink NetBIOS
        NWLink IPX/SPX Compatible Transport
    WINS Client (TCP/IP)
        Network adapter (e.g., Novell NE2000)
Workstation
    NetBEUI Protocol
        Network adapter (e.g., Novell NE2000)
    NWLink NetBIOS
        NWLink IPX/SPX Compatible Transport
    WINS Client (TCP/IP)
        Network adapter (e.g., Novell NE2000)
```

If you have Remote Access Service (RAS) installed, you should also see RAS "wrapper" entries at the same level where you see the network adapter(s). RAS will have its own top-level entry.

The bindings show the available paths traffic can take in and out of the work-station. For example, the top-level NetBIOS Interface entry and the top-level Workstation entry indicate that the system can send and receive native Windows NT network traffic (NetBIOS and SMB) over the three major protocols. Similarly, the top-level Server entry indicates that the system can service network requests over the three major protocol suites and can also handle program-to-program traffic using the Novell IPX/SPX protocol suite.

If you want to restrict the traffic coming into and out of your system, you simply select the binding entry associated with the service you want to control and click the Disable button. In response, a "no" indicator will appear to the left of that entry and that binding will no longer be used. By disabling specific binds, you can tightly control how protocols are used on your Windows NT workstation. For example, if your workstation runs IPX and TCP/IP, but you don't want native Windows NT networking services to use TCP/IP, you can disable the "WINS Client (TCP/IP)" entry underneath the NetBIOS Interface, Server, and Workstation services.

N O T E If your Windows NT workstation is connected to the Internet or any other public
TCP/IP network, you should, if possible, disable support for native Windows NT
networking services over TCP/IP. This prevents potential intruders from seeing or
interfering with your native Windows NT traffic. ■

Accessing Microsoft Network Resources

Once you have configured your Windows NT workstation to support the services, protocols, and adapters you need, you're ready for the next step—using the integrated commands and utilities in Windows NT to share and access drives and printers over the network.

The first step toward accessing directories and printers over the network occurs when you log on to your workstation. Specifically, the user name you supply during the logon process is used whenever you attempt to access the resources associated with another system in the network. Your workstation sends your user name to the other system so it can determine what access rights, if any, you have to the resources it offers.

The user name and validation process differs between workgroup and domain environments. In a workgroup environment, the workstation you log on to is responsible for authenticating your user name and password based on a local security file. In a domain environment, the user name and password authentication is handled by the domain controller.

After you have successfully signed on to your workgroup or domain, you can access shared directories and printers through the Network Neighborhood interface. Alternatively, you can issue commands at the command-line prompt or run custom batch files from the command-line environment to access the network resources you need. You'll look at both of these approaches in this chapter, but first you need to explore the architecture of directory sharing.

Accessing Shared Directories

Under the Windows NT network architecture, a server system (Windows NT Workstation, Windows NT Server, Windows 95, or Windows for Workgroups) identifies a specific drive and directory point it wants to offer to the network. Workstations accessing this resource can then potentially access all of the subdirectories under the specified directory, but cannot access any parent directories that might be present above the specified directories. If the server system elects to share the drive at the root directory level, then all of the directories on that drive will potentially be available to workstations on the network.

N O T E   If you are using the native Windows NT partition type (NTFS), access to specific directories and files is further restricted based on your user definition and file/directory access permissions. Therefore, even though you may be able to connect to a drive at the root level, your access to directories and files on that drive may still be restricted.

For example, a drive H might contain the following directory structure:

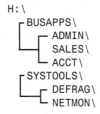

```
H:\
  ┌BUSAPPS\
  │    ┌ ADMIN\
  └────┤  SALES\
       └ ACCT\
  ┌SYSTOOLS\
  │    ┌ DEFRAG\
  └────┤
       └ NETMON\
```

If this example server offers this directory at the root level (H:\), workstations can potentially access all of the information on the disk. If however, the server only offers the H:\BUSAPPS\ directory on the network, then workstations can only potentially access subdirectories below BUSAPPS, and they cannot access any of the information under SYSTOOLS. Finally, if the server only offers the H:\BUSAPPS\SALES directory, then network access is restricted to that specific directory and any subdirectories beneath it.

In reality, a single server will often offer several directories on the networks and restrict access based on the user name of the requesting workstations. By using this approach, the example server might offer both H:\BUSAPPS and H:\BUSAPPS\SALES to the network, but restrict which workstations can access

those resources based on the user names associated with the requesting workstations. Under the Windows NT architecture, a single server can offer as many
views of a disk as it needs to satisfy its business environment.

In addition to restricting access at the user name level, directories can be provided
as read-only resources, read/write resources, or password-protected resources.
Thus, even though you have authorization to access a directory resource, you
might not be able to create files or update information in that directory. If you work
in an environment that includes Windows 95 or Windows for Workgroups systems,
you may find that you are prompted for a password to access the directory, and the
password you provide determines if you gain read-only or read/write access to the
directory resource.

Now take a look at how this architecture comes into play when you use the Windows NT Network Neighborhood interface.

Accessing Shared Drives/Directories from Network Neighborhood To access
shared directories, access the Network Neighborhood interface from your
desktop. When you select this action, Windows NT sends a series of query
messages over the network to determine what systems are present in your
workgroup or domain. The query process can be a time-consuming process, so
don't be surprised if several seconds (or more) elapse before you see the results.

What you see next depends on how your viewing options are set. By default, Windows NT presents a single entry for the network as a whole (Entire Network),
followed by a list of systems participating in the domains and/or workgroups available on the network. Figure 19.14 shows an example Network Neighborhood display of a small workgroup environment.

NOTE You can also access Network Neighborhood information through the Windows
NT Explorer utility. The same information is presented; however, the information
is presented in a manner that is consistent with the Explorer user interface. ▮

Part

V

Ch

19

FIG. 19.14

The Network Neighborhood display shows a list of systems participating in the local workgroup or domain. This figure shows a workgroup that contains three systems (Enck 486p, Enck main, and Enck nt40).

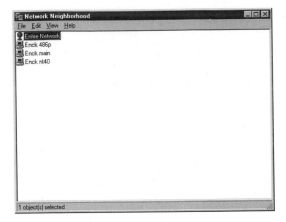

By changing the settings under the View drop-down menu, you can also have the Network Neighborhood items appear as horizontal icons instead of vertical items, or you can include additional detail in the display (for example, the comment field available in Windows 95 and Windows for Workgroups systems). None of these viewing options change the technical content of the display, just the appearance.

From the Network Neighborhood display you can take one of two courses of action. First, you can access the systems that appear on the list to discover what network resources they offer. Second, you can explore the network as a whole to find out what other domains or workgroups are present and then access the systems contained in those workgroups/domains (assuming you have security permission to do so).

N O T E If the system you wish to access is not included on the initial list of systems, you will need to double-click the Entire Network entry to get a list of available networks (such as Microsoft, Novell, and so on). Then double-click the Microsoft Network entry to obtain a list of available workgroups and/or domains. Finally, double-click a specific workgroup or domain entry to see the systems in that workgroup or domain. ∎

Although the Network Neighborhood display contains a list of systems, no shared directories or printer resources are shown. In order to access that level of information, you must double-click the system name. At that point, your Windows NT system will request a list of resources offered by that system. If no additional authorization is required, Windows NT will present a new display window for that system. Figure 19.15 shows the results of requesting listings for two of the systems on the initial Network Neighborhood display (Enck 486p and Enck nt40).

If, on the other hand, additional authorization were required, a password prompt screen would appear. Access to the shared directory would then be determined by the password you provide. Once you supply the password, the connection process completes, and you receive a listing of the logical drive contents, as shown in figure 19.15.

FIG. 19.15

The expanded Network Neighborhood information shows the network drives offered by two systems in the local workgroup/domain. This figure shows that Enck 486p offers a "C" drive and Enck nt40 offers a "C" and "D" drive.

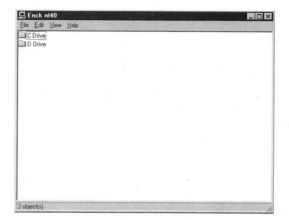

N O T E The Options dialog box under the View drop-down menu item on the Network Neighborhood display allows you to configure Windows NT to open a new display window for each system you explore or to use a single window for all explorations. By default Windows NT uses multiple windows (see fig. 19.15). ■

To access the contents of a shared directory, you can double-click the folder associated with the entry and a new window will appear containing the contents of that folder. For example, figure 19.16 shows the contents of the D drive on system Enck nt40. At that point, you can continue to explore the folders, files, and programs contained in the shared directory as if it were a local folder. Please notice, however, that your ability to change and delete information contained in a shared folder may be limited by the system offering the resource.

FIG. 19.16

Once you double-click a shared directory folder, the contents of that directory are revealed and you can navigate through it like any other desktop folder.

When you are accessing shared directories using the method just described, no drive assignments are given to the shared directories—they are simply network-based elements in your desktop environment. In some cases, however, it is desirable to assign shared directories to drive letters. The most common reason to assign drive letters to shared directories is to accommodate older 8-bit DOS and 16-bit Windows programs that depend on drive letters to access files. Another reason to assign drive letters is to make sure that shared directory connections are re-established when the system re-boots and/or the user logs on.

To map a shared directory to a drive letter, select the shared folder entry in the initial system display window (refer to fig. 19.15) and access the File drop-down menu. On the menu select the Map Network Drive option and a Map Network Drive dialog box similar to the one shown in figure 19.17 appears. This dialog box contains four fields:

■ *Drive*. This field identifies the logical drive letter that will be associated with the shared directories. In other words, this is the drive designation (for example, D:, E:, and so on) you will use to access the information in the shared directory area. By default, Windows NT sets this field to the next drive letter available in your system. You can, however, set it to any unassigned drive letter.

N O T E   Remember that the root level directory on your logical drive corresponds to the directory level configured on the server system. For example, if you mount H:\BUSAPPS\SALES on your J: drive, your J:\ root is locked into the server system's \BUSAPPS\SALES directory—you cannot access higher level directories. ■

■ *Path*. This read-only field identifies the system name of the server and the name of the shared directory resource. In the example in figure 19.17, Enck nt40 is the system name, and D Drive is the name of the shared directory resource. The system name and resource name are described using the notation *system name\resource name*—therefore the example shows a path description of \\Enck nt40\D Drive.

■ *Connect As.* You can optionally use this field to connect to the server system using a different user name. This feature is normally used for cross-domain access.

■ *Reconnect at Logon.* This check box determines if the defined shared folder connection will be re-established when the system re-boots or when the user logs on again.

FIG. 19.17
The Map Network Drive dialog box allows you to associate a drive letter with a shared directory entry and optionally specify that the connection persist after reboots and logout/logons.

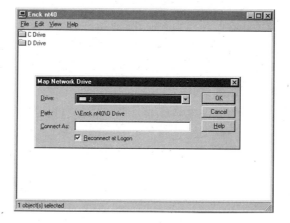

Once you click OK to confirm the values, the shared folder will be assigned a drive letter, and a new window will open revealing the contents of the shared folder. More importantly, the drive connection will also be accessible through the My Computer program. For example, figure 19.18 shows a My Computer view that includes a network connection to drive J.

FIG. 19.18
Once you map a shared directory to a drive letter, the drive appears as an element in the My Computer window. In this case, the J drive represents a mapped network drive.

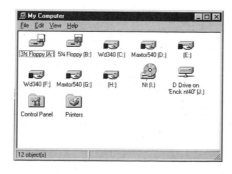

Part
V

Ch
19

Reconnecting Shared Drives/Directories at Logon   If you shut down your desktop when you have open connections to network-based folders (as opposed to mapped network drives), Windows NT will attempt to re-establish those connections when it reinitializes the desktop environment after you log on. Unfortunately, Windows NT cannot always re-establish connections during this process due to timing problems associated with the multi-tasking nature of NT. For example, it may try to open up a network folder window before the Network Neighborhood program has finished identifying all of the systems in the network.

The solution to this problem is to use mapped network drives (as described in the last section) and mark the Reconnect at Logon check box when the drive is mounted. When you take this approach, Windows NT initiates the shared directory connection when it initializes the network instead of when it initializes the desktop environment. The bottom line is that this approach is more predictable and more reliable.

Disconnecting from Shared Drives/Directories   A single Windows NT workstation can concurrently access multiple shared directory resources. Shared directories can also be disconnected and then reconnected at a later time. To disconnect a shared directory that is being accessed in the desktop environment as a folder, all you have to do is close the folder.

To disconnect a shared directory that is being accessed as a mapped network drive, you must open the My Computer view, select the network drive entry, and then access the File drop-down menu. As shown in figure 19.19, the drop-down menu contains a Disconnect option. Just select Disconnect to terminate the mapped network drive connection.

FIG. 19.19
To disconnect a mapped network drive, select that drive in the My Computer window and use the Disconnect option on the File drop-down menu.

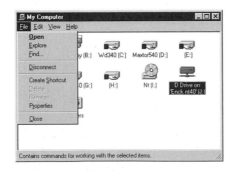

Accessing and Disconnecting Shared Drives/Directories from the Command Line

As previously noted, you can also connect to shared directories from the command-line environment. Specifically, the NET USE command allows you to perform network drive mappings and disconnects. The syntax for the NET USE command is

```
NET USE drive: \\system name\resource password
```

In this syntax, *drive* corresponds to the Drive field in the Map Network Drive dialog box, `\\system name\resource` corresponds to the Path field, and `password` is an optional parameter to specify an access password (if needed). For example, to connect to the shared directory resource previously shown in figure 19.17, you would use the following command:

```
NET USE J: "\\Enck nt40\D Drive"
```

N O T E   If the system name or resource name you want to connect to contains embedded spaces or special characters, you must enclose the parameter in quotes, as shown in the examples in this section. ▪

If you want the drive connection to be re-established the next time your Windows NT workstation starts, you can add the "/PERSISTENT:YES" option to the NET USE command. For example:

```
NET USE J: "\\Enck nt40\D Drive" /PERSISTENT:YES
```

Alternatively, you can specify that a drive connection should not be re-established by using the "/PERSISTENT:NO" option on the NET USE command. For example:

```
NET USE J: "\\Enck nt40\D Drive" /PERSISTENT:NO
```

By default, Windows NT will use the last /PERSISENT setting for all future connections. You can change that setting using the command:

```
NET USE /PERSISTENT:YES
```

or

```
NET USE /PERSISTENT:NO
```

The current setting can be viewed using the NET USE command with no parameters.

Part
V
Ch
19

To disconnect a shared directory, you use the command syntax:

```
NET USE drive: /DELETE
```

For example, the following command disconnects the shared directory that the previous example connected to:

```
NET USE J: /DELETE
```

Additional commands are available to allow you to determine what network resources are available and what resources you are currently using. These commands include:

- `NET VIEW /NETWORK`. Shows the systems currently participating in your domain or workgroup.

- `NET VIEW \\system name`. Shows the resources (if any) sponsored by a specific system.

- `NET USE`. Shows the shared directories and network printers you are currently connected to as well as the status of the /PERSISTENT option.

Accessing Shared Printers

Connecting to a shared printer over the network is conceptually similar to connecting to a shared directory. Like shared directories, your ability to control a network printer (stop, start, pause, and delete documents in the queue) is dependent upon your user name. In most cases, the capability to control a network printer is restricted to administrators and power users.

You can connect to network printers from the Network Neighborhood interface or the command-line environment.

Accessing Shared Printers from Print Manager   Access to network printers is accomplished in much the same way you access shared directories. First, access the Network Neighborhood interface and find the server sponsoring the printer you want to attach to. Double-click that server entry to see a list of resources offered by that server. This list will include shared directories (if any are available) and a Printers folder. Figure 19.20 shows an example server resource list containing both shared directories and a Printers folder. Then double-click the Printers folder to see what printers are available for network access. Figure 19.21 shows an expanded resource list containing a shared printer entry.

FIG. 19.20
The initial list of server resources shows shared directories and a Printers folder that contains shared printer definitions.

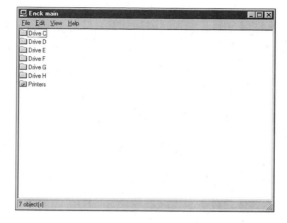

FIG. 19.21
When you double-click the Printer folder in a server's shared resource list, the shared printer definitions appear.

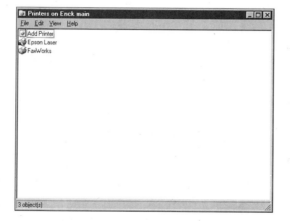

You can connect to a printer on the shared resource list by double-clicking that printer entry. In response, you will receive a dialog box for that printer, as shown in figure 19.22.

The first time you connect to a printer you must install the printer driver so your local workstation applications format output for the printer correctly. To do this, choose Printer, Install in the Printer dialog box. If the printer driver for the printer you are connecting to is not resident on your workstation, the print server will automatically download the correct printer driver, providing the server is a Windows NT system. If the server is not a Windows NT system, you will be prompted for your Windows NT distribution CD so Windows NT can load the corresponding printer driver. If the printer driver is already loaded on your system, the addition of a network printer will proceed.

N O T E   You can also connect to a shared printer using the Add Printer Wizard that appears in the Printers folder. ▪

Once you have successfully downloaded the proper printer driver, a new printer definition is added to the Printers folder in your local system (see fig. 19.23). At that point, you can direct output to the network printer as if it were a local printer.

FIG. 19.22
The completed network printer connection shows how a connected network printer (the Epson Laser shared by ENCK NT40) integrates into the Print Manager as if it were a local printer.

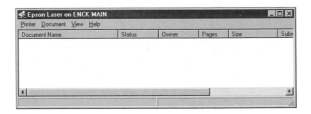

FIG. 19.23
Once you complete the connection to a network printer, the corresponding printer definition is permanently stored in your Printers folder.

Viewing Status Information for a Shared Printer   You can monitor output you send to a network printer by accessing the corresponding printer definition in your Printers folder. This is the same procedure you use to monitor locally attached printers.

Disconnecting from Shared Printers   By default, a network printer connection is maintained as a permanent definition, and the connection will be re-established whenever you restart your Windows NT system. Therefore, in order to disconnect from a network printer, you must actually delete it from your Printers folder.

Accessing and Disconnecting Shared Printers from the Command Line As previously noted, you can also connect to and disconnect from network printers using commands. In order to do this, however, you must have a locally defined printer that uses the correct printer driver and maps to a specific printer port (for example, LPT1, LPT2, and so on). This requirement exists because when you make the connection from the command-line, you associate the network printer to a printer port—a new printer definition is not automatically created.

With this in mind, the command syntax to connect to a network printer is

```
NET USE printer: \\system name\\resource name
```

In this command, *printer*: identifies the port (LPT1:, LPT2:, and so on), *system name* identifies the system sponsoring the printer, and *resource name* is the name assigned to the network printer. For example, the command-line syntax to connect to the network printer "Epson Action Laser" hosted by "Enck nt40" would be

```
NET USE LPT2: "\\Enck nt40\Epson Action Laser"
```

This command assumes that an appropriate printer definition is already in place for LPT2.

N O T E If the system name or resource name you want to connect to contains embedded spaces or special characters, you must enclose the parameter in quotes, as shown in the examples in this section. ▦

To disconnect a network printer, you use the command syntax

```
NET USE printer: /DELETE
```

For example, the following command disconnects the network printer that the previous example connected to:

```
NET USE LPT2: /DELETE
```

As in the case of shared directories, additional commands are available to allow you to determine what network resources are available and what resources you are currently using. These commands include:

Part
V

Ch
19

- `NET VIEW /NETWORK`. Shows the systems currently participating in your domain or workgroup.
- `NET VIEW //system name`. Shows the resources (if any) sponsored by a specific system.
- `NET USE`. Shows the shared directories and network printers you are currently connected to.

Sharing Drives/Directories on Your System

As previously discussed in the "Configuring Windows NT Protocol and Services" section of this chapter, you must install the Server service using the Services tab in the Network dialog box if you want your workstation to provide shared directories or printers to other systems on your network. Assuming that you have installed the Server service, declare the specific directories and printers you want to share using the My Computer interface, the Windows NT Explorer program, or through the Printers folder. For the sake of this discussion, we will focus on directory sharing using the My Computer program interface.

To share a directory, start the My Computer utility and select the drive you want to share. If you want to share the drive at the root directory, you can proceed directly to the next step, otherwise double-click the drive to obtain a new window containing all of the folders in that drive. You can then select the directory (folder) you want to share or you can continue to "drill down" deeper into the directory structure until you locate the key location you want to share.

Windows NT automatically creates administrative resource definitions for the root directory on each logical drive and for the Windows NT directory. The resource names for the root directories are the drive letter followed by a $ (C$, D$, and so on), and the Windows NT directory is assigned a resource name of ADMIN$. You should note that these administrative resource names are not available to other workstations over the networks—they are for internal use only. You must create your own resource definitions.

To create a share definition, access the File drop-down menu and select the Sharing option. The Properties dialog box will appear with the Sharing properties page exposed.

If there is an administrative resource definition or a previous resource definition for the drive and directory you selected, that definition appears in the Sharing tab dialog box, shown in figure 19.24. You can modify previous definitions (but not the administrative resource definition) from this dialog box, but more likely you will click New Share so you can define a new resource. In response, you receive a New Share dialog box, as shown in figure 19.25.

FIG. 19.24

The Sharing properties page shows existing shared directory definitions. This figure shows the administrative definition "C$," which will not accept connections from the network. Non-administrative definitions can also be viewed and altered.

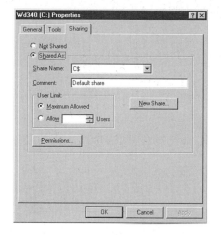

FIG. 19.25

The New Share dialog box is used to describe the name and characteristics of a drive or directory being shared for the first time.

Alternatively, if you select a drive and directory that does not already have a resource definition, the Sharing tab dialog box will be blank. You can then select the Shared As radio button and proceed to complete the dialog box using the same information that goes into the New Share dialog box.

Part

V

Ch

19

The fields in the New Share dialog box allow you define the basic attributes of a shared directory resource:

- *Share Name*. Defines the logical name of the shared directory. This is the name other systems use to access this resource.

- *Comment*. An optional comment for the shared directory. This comment is seen by other systems browsing through the network. Most sites use this field to indicate the physical location of the system, the owner, or some other useful characteristic (such as, "Room 233," "This is Dina's system," "This is the demo Windows 95 system").

- *User Limit*. This area allows you to limit concurrent user access to a specific number of users. Every client system accessing a shared directory consumes CPU and memory resources on your system; therefore, you need to find a tolerable balance between shared access and your workstation performance.

N O T E You can also access the Sharing tab dialog box using the Windows NT Explorer. To do this, select the drive or directory entry you want to share and then choose File, Properties.

Controlling Drive/Directory Access with Share Permissions   The New Share dialog box and the Sharing tab dialog box both feature a Permissions button. When you press this button, the Access Through Share Permissions dialog box appears, as shown in figure 19.26. This window allows you to control which users or user groups can access your shared directory and what type of access they have. For a new share, the user group Everyone is given access—meaning anyone in the network can connect to your shared directory. The Type of Access field located in the bottom of the window then determines if they have read-only, full read/write, or limited update capabilities to the shared directory.

If you want to control access to your shared directory on an individual user or user group basis, delete the Everyone entry (by clicking the Remove button) and then click Add to access the Add Users and Groups dialog box, as shown in figure 19.27. From this dialog box, you control access based on user groups or individual users. By default, user groups are shown—you can view users by clicking the Show Users button. To set permissions, simply add the user or group entry to the permission list area and assign that user or group the desired Type of Access.

FIG. 19.26

The Access Through Share Permissions dialog box allows you to control how users or user groups can access a shared directory. This figure shows a shared directory permission that grants everyone full control (read, write, and delete access).

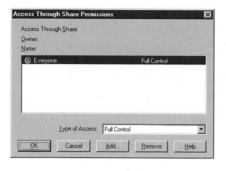

FIG. 19.27

The Add Users and Groups dialog box is used to define permissions for specific user groups or individual users.

N O T E Unless you are in a domain, you are better off using user group definitions, because using individual user definitions requires you to replicate user entries between systems. Although replicating users may not be a problem initially, it can become burdensome as the network grows or when the user community changes. ■

After you define your permission list, click OK to return to the Access Through Share Permissions dialog box, and then click OK again to return to the New Share dialog box. You then click the OK button in the New Share dialog box to return to the Sharing tab dialog box. Then click OK to make the resource you just defined available on the network.

Part

V

Ch

19

How to Stop Sharing Drives/Directories   A *shared directory resource* is a permanent definition that survives workstation restarts. If you want to stop sharing the resource, access the drive/directory using the My Computer program and then select the Sharing option from the File drop-down menu. The current share definition should appear in the Sharing tab dialog box, as shown in figure 19.28. If not, you may have to access the Share Name drop-down list to locate it. Once the sharing definition you want to remove is displayed, click the Remove Share button.

FIG. 19.28
The Sharing properties page allows you to delete a shared drive or directory definition by clicking the Remove Share button.

> **N O T E**   Administrative shared directories (such as, C$, ADMIN$) are automatically created and re-shared when a system is re-started. There is virtually no reason to stop sharing an administrative directory. ▪

Sharing Your Printers

In order to share a local printer on the network, you simply have to mark it as shared and declare a resource name for it. You can perform this action when your create the printer, or you can modify the printer definition at a later time.

To modify an existing printer definition, open the Printers folder and double-click the printer definition to be shared. When the Printer dialog box opens, choose Printer, Sharing. The Printer Sharing properties page appears, as shown in figure 19.29.

FIG. 19.29
The Printer Prope[r]
dialog box allows
to specify that yo[u]
want a local print[er]
shared on the
network. When yo[u]
check the <u>S</u>hare
check box, you m[ust]
also assign a
resource name fo[r]
the printer.

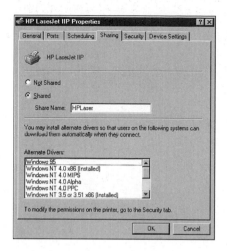

In the Sharing properties page is the <u>S</u>hared checkbox. If you select this check box, the Share Name field becomes available for modification. The Share Name is the resource name for the printer. Other systems see it and select your printer by this name.

After you set the Share Name field, simply click the OK button to make the printer available on the network. If you want to remove this printer from the network at a later time, you use the same procedure; however, you select the Not Shared check box instead.

N O T E You can also access the Printer Sharing properties page by right-clicking the printer definition and selecting the P<u>r</u>operties option. Then click the Sharing tab to access the Sharing properties page. ▪

Setting Permissions for Using the Printer You can set access rights to the printer through the Security properties page on the Printer Properties dialog box. You can access the properties dialog box by right-clicking the printer definition and selecting the P<u>r</u>operties option, or by choosing Printer, P<u>r</u>operties in the Printer dialog box. Once the properties dialog box is displayed, select the Security tab to set or view security information. Figure 19.30 shows the Security properties page. You use the options available in this properties page to set up access permissions for users and/or user groups in a similar manner to how you set permissions for shared directories. Refer to the section "Controlling Drive/ Directory Access with Share Permissions" for more information on this topic.

Part

V

Ch

19

FIG. 19.30
The Security properties page is used to define which users or user groups can access and possibly control the printer via the network.

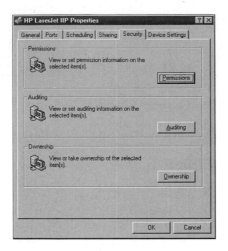

Novell NetWare Integration

The Windows NT Workstation peer-to-peer environment and Windows NT Server client/server environment provide powerful solutions for file and printer sharing, but they are by no means the dominant force in PC LANs—that honor goes to Novell NetWare. NetWare has been the major force in the file and print sharing market for nearly a decade. Therefore, in order for the Windows NT Workstation product to function in today's PC-oriented networks, it must support connectivity to NetWare file and print servers.

In theory, you can approach connecting a Windows NT Workstation to Novell NetWare file and print servers using one of two approaches:

■ You can use the NetWare client software supplied by Microsoft in conjunction with Windows NT.

■ You can use the Novell Windows NT client software.

In reality, Novell did not release support for the Windows NT 4.0 operating system when NT 4.0 was introduced to the market. That means that early 4.0 users have been restricted to using the Microsoft-supplied NetWare client software or older, and often unstable, versions of Novell's NetWare client software.

Fortunately, the Microsoft-supplied client software for NT 4.0 includs new features and functions that make it superior to the client software Microsoft supplied with NT 3.5/3.51. For example, the NT 4.0 client software now supports NetWare 4.x

NetWare Directory Services (NDS) and many of the NetWare APIs used by 16-bit Windows and DOS applications.

Using the Microsoft NetWare Client

The Microsoft NetWare client is included in the Windows NT distribution media and is available for use at no extra cost. Microsoft's NetWare client is currently compatible with NetWare 3.x servers and NetWare 4.x servers (including support for 4.x NetWare Directory Services (NDS)).

In order to install and use Microsoft's NetWare client, your Windows NT network configuration must include support for the IPX protocol suite. The process for selecting and installing the IPX protocol suite is discussed in detail at the beginning of this chapter. You can install this protocol suite prior to, or at the same time, you install the client software.

Assuming the IPX protocol has been installed, access the Network dialog box by activating the Network option in Control Panel. Then click the Services tab to access the list of installed services. If you do not see Client Service for NetWare in the list of services, click Add to obtain the Select Network Service dialog box, as shown in figure 19.31, and select the Client Service for NetWare entry. Then click OK to load the client software into your Windows NT configuration. You are prompted to supply the distribution CD for Windows NT. After the load is complete, click Close to terminate the Network dialog box. You will need to restart your workstation to put the changes into effect.

Part

V

Ch

19

FIG. 19.31
The Client Service for NetWare option can be loaded from the standard Windows NT distribution CD using the Add option in the Services properties page.

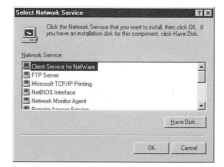

After you restart and log back on your workstation, you receive the Select Preferred Server for NetWare dialog box. This dialog box, shown in figure 19.32, allows you to specify either a Preferred Server (for example, a 3.x NetWare server to be used to authenticate your user name and password) or a Default Tree and Context (for 4.x NetWare environments using NDS). You can also specify that you want a NetWare-based logon script to automatically run when you log on to Windows NT.

TIP The list of preferred server names available for selection is derived from the network. If the server you want to use is not powered on, it will not appear on this list.

FIG. 19.32

The Select Preferred Server for NetWare dialog box allows you to select either the NetWare server or tree and context that will be used for authentication checking when you log on to Windows NT.

At this point, you can select either a NetWare server or default tree and context, or you can defer this selection until later. To select a server, simply choose an entry from the list or enter the name in the Preferred Server field. To select the Default Tree and Context, you must manually enter the correct values (no prompting is available).

When you confirm your entry, your Windows NT system passes your current user name and password to the appropriate NetWare server so it can validate your account. In order for this verification to be successful, your user name and password on your preferred NetWare server must be identical to the user name and password you use on your Windows NT system.

Alternatively, you can leave the Preferred Server and Default Tree and Context fields blank, so authentication is not performed. You can then perform the authentication process through Control Panel or when you attempt to access a NetWare resource.

To control the authentication process through the Control Panel, open the Control Panel and select the Client Service for NetWare (CSNW) option. In response, the Client Service for NetWare dialog box appears (see fig. 19.33), allowing you to identify a Preferred Server or Default Tree and Context. If you change or add any values in this dialog box, they will not go into effect until the next time you log on.

FIG. 19.33

The Client Service for NetWare dialog box allows you to configure NetWare print sharing and logon script options as well as view and change your Preferred Server or Default Tree and Context settings.

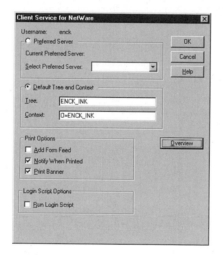

Once you configure a preferred server entry—either through the initial logon sequence or through the Control Panel—that configuration remains in effect until you change it via the Control Panel. If you choose to not specify a Preferred Server or Default Tree and Context, user authentication occurs when you attempt to access a NetWare volume or printer.

Also note that the Client Service for NetWare dialog box contains three options related to print handling and one logon script option:

- *Add Form Feed*. Determines if Windows NT will add a final form feed at the end of the print stream it sends to a NetWare print server.

- *Notify When Printed*. Indicates if you want to receive notification when the print server concludes printing your output.

■ *Print Banner. Specifies* if you want an identifying page printed before your actual output.

■ *Run Login Script.* Indicates if you want your NetWare-based logon script when you log on to NetWare (which is normally handled via the NT logon).

Accessing NetWare Resources via the Microsoft NetWare Client With Microsoft's NetWare client service installed, you can access NetWare file and print services in exactly the same manner you use to access native Microsoft file and print services. For example, if you run Network Neighborhood and double-click the Entire Network entry, you will see a point of entry for the NetWare network, as shown in figure 19.34. You can then double-click the NetWare or Compatible Network entry to view individual servers in that network, as shown in figure 19.35.

FIG. 19.34

When you double-click the Entire Network entry in the Network Neighborhood display, you will be presented with a new window containing multiple network types.

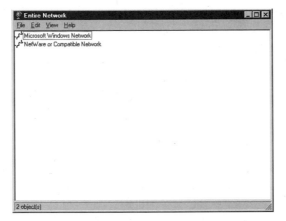

FIG. 19.35

When you double-click the NetWare or Compatible Network entry in the Network Neighborhood display, you will receive a list of available servers and NDS-related information.

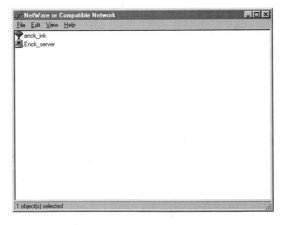

To see the resources available on a NetWare server, double-click the server entry and you will receive a list of supported printers and volumes. You can then access the directories (folders) within a NetWare volume by double-clicking the volume entry. Figure 19.36 shows the resources associated with the server "Enck_server," including the directories available on the SYS volume of that server.

FIG. 19.36
The Enck_server window in this figure shows the printer and volume resources associated with the NetWare server Enck_server. The SYS on Enck_server window shows the three directories (Login, Mail, and Public) available under the SYS volume.

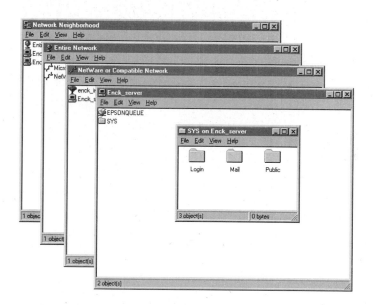

Once you are connected to a NetWare server, you can access folders and files as if they were local folders and files, or you can map NetWare volumes and folders to drive letters. If you map a drive to a NetWare volume you can access all authorized directories as a single network drive. However, you can also map drives to individual directories in that volume, with each directory connection consuming a network drive letter. The procedure for mapping drives is the same procedure used to map drives in a native Microsoft network.

In order to see the directory information or actually connect to a NetWare volume or directory, your user and password must have been previously authenticated by the NetWare server sponsoring the volume. If you did not choose a preferred server, or you attempt to access a server other than your preferred server, you are prompted for user and password information. Simply enter the security information as it pertains to the NetWare server you are attempting to access, and click OK.

Part
V

Ch
19

Access to NetWare-based printers follows the exact same flow as access to Microsoft network-based printers. For example, you can use the Network Neighborhood interface to select a printer from a server shown under the NetWare or Compatible Network entries. Once you are connected to a NetWare printer, you can also reshare that printer with other Microsoft systems as if it were a locally attached printer.

Beyond Microsoft and Novell

As you can see from the topics covered in this chapter, Windows NT provides a powerful and flexible network environment. In situations that require additional networking services—for example, support for the UNIX-oriented Network File System (NFS)—additional third-party software programs can be added, configured, and deployed using the same utilities and procedures that apply to Microsoft and Novell network services. This makes Windows NT an operating system and a network operating system with an open-ended future.

From Here...

In this chapter, you have seen how you can configure and use Microsoft and Novell networking in a LAN environment. For additional information on networking and network related information, you should refer to the following chapters:

- Chapter 20, "Configuring the Network at Your Workstation."
- Chapter 21, "Managing Shared Resources."
- Chapter 23, "Using Dial-Up Networking."
- Chapter 24, "Configuring TCP/IP."
- Chapter 25, "Using Windows NT with the Internet."

Configuring the Network at Your Workstation

by Sue Plumley

When working on a computer that's attached to a network, you may need to adjust hardware settings and configure specific network settings to maintain your connection to the network. Whether you're connected to a Windows NT Server, Novell NetWare, or other network, you may need to make some configuration changes.

You can change, for example, the name of your computer and the domain to which you belong; you also can install adapter card drivers and configure network protocols. You might never need to change any of these settings, but if you install a new or different adapter card, have special needs for logging onto the network, or need to change domains, you can configure for the network from your own workstation. ■

Change computer names

The network uses a computer ID, or name, to refer to each workstation. You can change your computer's name and other identification information.

Change domains

If you're a member of multiple domains, you can switch domains from your workstation to access resources from other computers.

Install and configure an adapter card and driver

Before you can attach to a network, you must configure the network adapter card and driver. This chapter shows you how.

Add and configure a protocol

NT Workstation software provides various protocols—including TCP/IP, NetBEUI, and IPX/SPX-compatible—for communication over the network.

Configuring the Network

You can configure the network and its components—such as adapter cards, protocols, and bindings—in the Network dialog box available from the Control Panel. You must be a member of the Administrators Group for your computer to configure the network from your workstation.

 TIP You can quickly access the Network dialog box by right-clicking the Network Neighborhood and choosing Properties from the shortcut menu.

Additionally, before configuring the network through your workstation, you should find out any specific information you need from your network administrator. For example, if you change your computer's name, the new name must have an account in the domain to which you'll attach; you'll want to confirm your account with the system administrator. Each of the following sections makes note of any information you will need before explaining how to configure the network component.

To open the Network dialog box, follow these steps:

1. Choose Start, Settings, Control Panel.

 2. Open the Network icon by double-clicking the icon. The Network dialog box appears (see fig. 20.1).

FIG. 20.1
Change computer names, protocols, drivers, and so on in the Network dialog box.

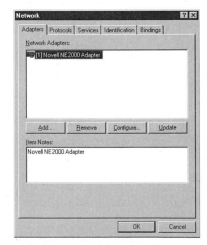

Changing Your Computer's Identification

On the network, your computer is identified by a name and—depending on the type of network—a workgroup or domain name as well. When working on a Novell NetWare network, for example, your computer name only applies to your individual workstation; only your user name is significant to NetWare. When working on a Windows NT Server network, however, the *computer's name* is a unique name that identifies the workstation to the network; the name cannot be the same as any other computer, workgroup, or domain name on the network.

The *workgroup* is a collection of computers grouped together and identified by a group name; workgroups provide convenience and efficiency. You can view workgroups on the network to determine available resources, find files or directories, and so on. A *domain* is a collection of computers on a Windows NT Server network that recognize the same user accounts; domains provide security as well as efficiency. Anyone on the network can join a workgroup, but only those assigned by the system administrator can be members of a domain.

▶ **See** "Managing User Accounts," **p. 388**

Changing Names

You may need to change your computer's name at some point; for example, if another computer or domain is added that is the same as your computer's name or to better identify your workstation and resources.

> **CAUTION**
>
> If you're a member of a Windows NT Server domain, check with your system administrator before changing your computer's name; you may not be able to log on to the domain if you don't check first.

Part

V

Ch

20

To change the name of the computer, follow these steps:

1. In the Network dialog box, choose the Identification tab and choose <u>C</u>hange. The Identification Changes dialog box appears (see fig. 20.2).

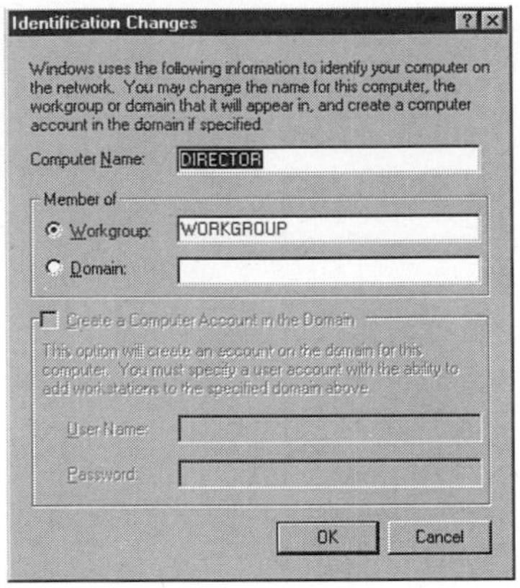

FIG. 20.2
Enter a unique name
to rename your
computer.

2. Enter the computer's new name, typing no more than 15 characters.

   You cannot use any of the following characters:

   : ;" < > * + \ / ? ,

3. Choose OK to close the Computer Name dialog box; choose OK to close the Network dialog box.

TROUBLESHOOTING

I changed my computer's name, and now I can't log onto the domain. What can I do now? You must have an account using the new computer name in the domain before you can log onto the domain. Check with your system administrator to make sure your new computer name is correct and that you have an account on the domain.

Joining a Workgroup or Domain

You can join a workgroup or a Windows NT Server domain from the Network dialog box. To join a workgroup, you must log on as a member of the Administrators group or the Domain Admins global group. Make sure you specify a workgroup name that is not the same as the computer name.

When joining a domain, check with the system administrator to make sure you're using the correct domain name and that you have a user account on that domain.

CAUTION

You cannot easily change the workgroup or domain to which you belong. To change workgroups or domains, you must reinstall Windows NT Server or change the domain or workgroup from the NT Server that authenticates network logons and receives domain security policy.

To join a workgroup or domain, follow these steps:

1. In the Network dialog box, choose the Identification tab and choose Change. The Identification Changes dialog box appears (refer to fig. 20.2).

2. In the Member Of area, choose either Workgroup or Domain. In the text box, enter the exact name of the workgroup or domain.

3. If you choose Domain and you're the domain administrator, enter the User Name and Password for your account. This is only necessary if you have not created an account for the computer in the server manager of the domain controller.

4. Choose OK to close the dialog box. If you joined a domain, a welcome dialog box appears; choose OK to close the box.

TIP You cannot log onto the new domain until you restart Windows.

TROUBLESHOOTING

I entered my workgroup name, but Windows NT displayed a message saying the name entered is not properly formatted. What do I do to format it? Choose OK to close the message box. You do not format the name but you've probably entered a character that doesn't agree with Windows NT workgroup naming conventions. Make sure you follow the naming guidelines and try again.

Adding and Configuring a New Network Adapter

When you choose the Express Setup for Windows NT, Setup checks your network adapter card and installs it for you. The adapter card and software (the card's device driver) enable your computer to communicate over the network. You may find a need to install a new or second adapter card—perhaps your old one stopped working or you wanted a better card for reliability purposes. You can install a new card and configure it using the Network dialog box.

 TIP Windows NT Setup only installs the first network card it comes to; you may have more than one card and need to install the second using the method described here.

Installing the Adapter Card

After physically installing the card to the machine, you must install the card through Windows NT.

To install an adapter card, follow these steps:

1. In the Network dialog box, choose the Adapters tab (see fig. 20.3).

FIG. 20.3
Use the Adapters tab
to add, remove,
configure, or update
an adapter card.

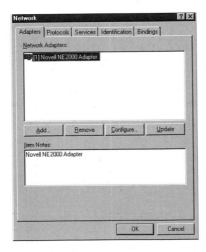

2. Choose <u>A</u>dd. Setup prepares the network card choices, which may take a few minutes, and then displays the Select Network Adapter dialog box (see fig. 20.4).

FIG. 20.4
Choose to add a network adapter card to the list of cards your workstation uses in Windows NT.

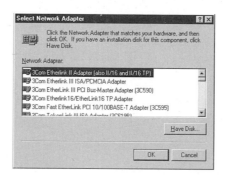

3. From the list box of Network Adapter cards, select the correct card to add to your workstation. If you do not find your card on the list, insert the manufacturer's disk and choose <u>H</u>ave Disk.

4. Choose OK. Setup may ask for a disk or the Windows NT CD; insert the disk or CD and choose OK. Setup copies files to your drive.

5. Follow any other directions on-screen. When finished, choose OK to close the Network dialog box. A reminder appears on-screen; you must restart your computer before the changes take affect.

> **TIP**
> If you have other changes to make in the Network dialog box, such as Protocols or Services, make all changes before restarting the computer—you'll save time.

6. Choose Restart to restart Windows NT.

TROUBLESHOOTING

I have no idea what kind of network card was installed to my computer. Is there any way to find out? You can find out about your network card by checking the documentation that came with the card. If you do not have the documentation, see your system administrator.

Part
V

Ch
20

Installing a Protocol

After installing the adapter card, you must install the software that makes the card work with the system. The software, or *protocol*, enables the card to communicate with the network. The type of protocol you use depends on the type of network you're on. If you do not know the network protocol, ask your system administrator.

The protocol software may be located on a manufacturer's disk that came with the adapter card, or you might find the software on the Windows NT CD.

To install the software, follow these steps:

1. In the Network dialog box, choose the Protocols tab (see fig. 20.5).

FIG. 20.5
Install a new protocol from the Protocols tab.

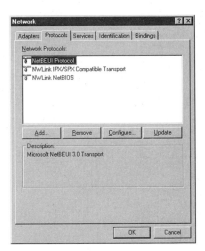

2. Click Add. The Select Network Protocol dialog box appears (see fig. 20.6).

FIG. 20.6
Choose the software, or protocol, you use for the network adapter card.

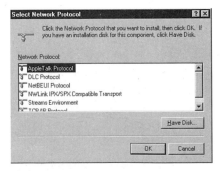

3. From the Network Protocol list box, select the appropriate software for your new adapter card. If your protocol is not listed and you have a manufacturer's disk containing software for the adapter card, choose Have Disk and insert the disk.

4. Choose OK. If Setup asks for a disk or the Windows NT CD, insert the disk or CD and follow directions on-screen.

5. When finished, choose OK in the Network dialog box and restart the computer so the changes can take affect.

Updating a Network Component

If you receive a newer or updated version of an adapter card driver from the manufacturer, you can update the driver in Windows NT in the Network dialog box. An updated driver may contain fixes for previous problems, more efficient software for running the adapter card, or some other improved features or data that make connecting to the network faster, easier, or safer.

To update a network component, follow these steps:

1. In the Protocols or Adapters tab of the Network dialog box, select the component you want to update from either the Network Protocols or the Network Adapters list.

2. Choose Update. Windows NT updates the software or the card. Windows NT may prompt for a manufacturer's disk or the Windows NT CD or disks. Insert the disk or CD and follow directions on-screen.

 ON THE WEB

NE2000 NIC drivers can be found on Novell's Web site at
http://www.novell.com.

Part
V

Ch
20

Removing a Network Component

You can remove protocols or adapter cards from the Network Protocols or Network Adapters list. The software is removed from the list but remains on the hard disk. You remove components in the Network dialog box.

To remove the network component, select the component from the list in either the Adapters or Protocols tab and click <u>R</u>emove. If a dialog box appears, answer any queries to continue removing the component.

TROUBLESHOOTING

I removed some network software that I shouldn't have, and now Windows NT won't let me reinstall it. Is there any way to reinstall the software? Yes, after you remove network software, you must restart your computer before you can reinstall that software. Shut down Windows NT and then start Windows again. Now try to install the software in the Network dialog box.

Configuring the Adapter Card and Protocol

You can configure the adapter card and protocol to set IRQ levels, addresses, frame types, and so on, in the Network dialog box. Table 20.1 explains the components you can configure when dealing with adapter cards and protocols.

Table 20.1   Configuring Components

Component	Description
Adapter Cards	
IRQ Level	Interrupt ReQuest is a line used to gain the system's attention in a timely manner.
I/O Port Address	Input/Output address where data and commands are sent to and from the adapter; an I/O address is exclusive in that it cannot be shared with any other adapter.
Protocols	
Frame Type	A frame is a packet of data that travels on the network; for example, NetWare 4 supports Ethernet frame type 802.2.
Internal Network Number	An 8-digit number that uniquely identifies a NetWare server running in a multinet Windows NT environment.

Adapter Card If you're unsure of the settings for your adapter card, refer to the card's documentation or ask your system administrator. The Windows NT Diagnostics program also can tell you the settings and addresses of hardware on your machine.

To configure your adapter card, follow these steps:

1. In the Adapters tab of the Network dialog box, select the adapter card from the list of Network Adapters.

2. Choose Properties. The adapter's Based Adapter Setup dialog box appears. Figure 20.7 shows the dialog box for a specific network card; your dialog box may look different.

FIG. 20.7
Set an IRQ level and I/O address in the Based Adapter Setup dialog box.

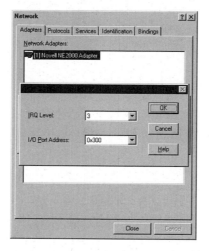

3. Enter any of the configuration settings necessary using table 20.1 as a guide.

4. Choose OK to close the dialog box; choose OK to close the Network dialog box or continue setting options in the dialog box.

Part
V

Ch
20

 TIP If there are other settings in the dialog box that you're unsure of, click Help for more information.

Protocol You can choose the protocol needed from Windows NT supplied protocols, or you can install another protocol. The protocol packages data and sends it back and forth between the computer and the network. When configuring protocol, you select options from the Network dialog box.

To configure network protocol, follow these steps:

1. In the Protocols tab of the Network dialog box, select the protocol in the Network Protocols list box.

2. Click Properties. The protocol's Properties dialog box appears. Figure 20.8 shows one type of protocol configuration dialog box.

FIG. 20.8
Configure the
protocol in your
specific Properties
dialog box.

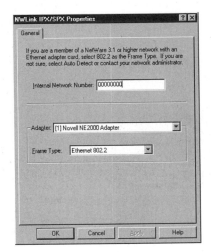

3. In the dialog box, change any options necessary. If you have questions about any options not listed in table 20.1, click the ? button in the protocol's Properties dialog box.

4. Choose OK to close the dialog box and OK again to close the Network dialog box.

Working with Bindings

Bindings are connections between a protocol and the network boards and drivers. Without a bound protocol, the driver cannot communicate with the network and the computer. More than one protocol can be bound to the same driver and board, and the same protocol can be bound to more than one driver on the server, called *layering*.

CAUTION

Unless you are extremely familiar with the requirements of the network and software, you should not reconfigure binding settings. You could sever your network connections.

To view bindings for the network components, follow these steps:

1. In the Network dialog box, click the Bindings tab (see fig. 20.9).

FIG. 20.9
Check to see if any bindings have been disabled.

Disabled binding

Enabled binding

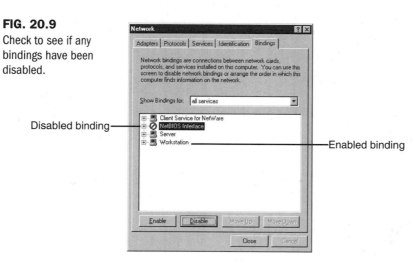

2. In the Show Bindings For drop-down list, choose the type of bindings you want to view.

3. In the Bindings list, any bindings preceded by a red circle have been disabled. You can enable a binding by selecting it and choosing Enable. If you're unsure of a binding for service, protocol, or adapter, ask your system administrator.

4. Choose Close or Cancel to close the dialog box.

Part
V

Ch
20

Adding and Configuring a NetWare Client Service

Services are special features that enable your workstation to operate beyond NT components, such as a NetWare network client, remote access services, or TCP/IP for working with an Internet server.

You can add a Client Service for NetWare that enables your NT computer to attach to a NetWare network and make use of the resources on that network. Microsoft includes a client for you that works well with Novell, as well as an IPX/SPX-compatible protocol you can use.

 TIP You can switch back and forth between a NetWare network and a Windows network after you add the NetWare client. For more information, see the section "Configuring Network Search Order," later in this chapter.

▶ **See** "Configuring TCP/IP," **p. 639**

Adding the Client

The *client* is the service that enables you to connect with the NetWare network. Add the client in the Network dialog box.

To add a Client Service for NetWare, follow these steps:

1. In the Network dialog box, choose the Services tab (see fig. 20.10).

2. To add a service, choose <u>A</u>dd. The Select Network Service dialog box appears (see fig. 20.11).

3. Choose the Client Service for NetWare and choose OK. Windows may prompt you for the NT CD to copy files. When the client is installed, Windows returns to the Network dialog box.

N O T E   If it is not already added to your list of protocols, you must add the NWLink IPX/SPX Compatible Transport protocol. Refer to the section "Installing a Protocol" for more information. ▨

4. To close the Network dialog box, choose Close. NT prompts you to restart your computer for the changes to take place; choose Restart.

FIG. 20.10
A list of installed services appears in the <u>N</u>etwork Services list box.

FIG. 20.11
In the list of <u>N</u>etwork Services, find the service you want to add.

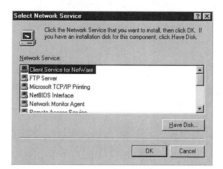

When your computer reboots, you'll be prompted to enter a preferred server. Choose Cancel in this dialog box and choose the server as described in the next section, so NT will remember your choice the next time you log on to the network.

Choosing a Preferred Server

You'll want to choose a preferred server so that NT automatically logs you onto that server when you enter your user name and password at the beginning of each session. You can choose a preferred server, or a default tree and context, in the Client Service for NetWare dialog box.

To choose a preferred server, follow these steps:

1. Open the Control Panel and double-click the CSNW icon to open it.

2. The Client Service for NetWare dialog box appears (see fig. 20.12).

FIG. 20.12

Choose a preferred server for faster and easier logons at the beginning of your session.

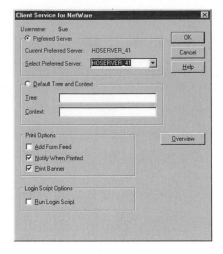

3. In the CSNW dialog box, choose one of the following:

Preferred Server. Use a preferred server if your network is not an NDS (NetWare Directory Services) environment; the preferred server is the one you'll log on to when you connect to Windows NT.

Default Tree and Context. If your network does use NDS, select the default tree and context to specify the position of your computer on the tree.

 T I P Although NetWare enables you to have both a preferred server and a default tree and context, NT only enables you to use one or the other at this time.

4. Choose OK to close the Client Service for NetWare dialog box.

You can now connect to the NetWare network through the Network Neighborhood, as you would connect to any other server or computer attached to your network.

TROUBLESHOOTING

I use login scripts with NetWare. Can I use it with NT? I see the Login Script Options in the CSNW dialog box. No, NT does not support the scripting language used in NetWare login scripts; however, you can set Windows NT logon scripts. A logon script is a batch (BAT or CMD) file that runs each time you log on to the network; the file sets certain conditions and options specific to the user. You can set your logon script in the User Manager; for more information, see Chapter 15, "Securing Windows NT Workstation."

I cannot see my NetWare server in the Network Neighborhood. Have I done something wrong? Probably not. You can check the frame type to see if that's a problem. The frame type is the format of IPX/SPX packets on the network and depends on the NetWare server you're using. If your server is version 3.12 and below, you'll use the 802.3 frame type; if the server is version 4.x, use the 802.2 frame type. Set frame type in the Network dialog box, Protocols tab. Select the protocol and choose Properties. If you're unsure about the frame type, see your system administrator.

My client service for NetWare won't start. Is there anything I can do? Yes, open the Control Panel and double-click the Services icon. In the list of services, find the Client Service for NetWare and make sure it is started. If it is not started, select the service and choose Start. Close the dialog box and check the client again.

Networking with Windows

Unlike networking with NetWare, networking with Windows does not require a client service. Whether you're using Windows NT Server or Windows 95, you can easily attach to the network by adjusting a few settings.

Windows NT networks involve a client and a server, similar to the NetWare network. With NT, an NT Server controls the resources, users, groups, domains, and so on. You can attach to the server on the NT network and use any of the resources you have permission to use. Permissions are controlled by the network administrator.

Windows 95 (and Windows for Workgroups) networks, on the other hand, are peer-to-peer networks, meaning there is no server. Computers are attached to a network and all computers are utilized as workstations. Additionally, all computers can share their resources—printers, files, directories, and so on.

You need the following on your computer to attach to a Windows network:

- *Network adapter*. Installed and configured correctly.
- *Protocol*. Compatible with the NT Server or the other computers on the peer-to-peer network (generally NetBEUI).

Part
V

Ch
20

■ *Identification.* A computer name and workgroup if you're working with Windows 95 or Windows for Workgroups; a computer name and domain name if you're working with Windows NT Server.

■ *Bindings.* Correct bindings for protocols and adapters.

You can refer to the previous sections in this chapter for installing and configuring these elements.

To connect to a Windows network, you use the Network Neighborhood. Double-click the Network Neighborhood icon to display the Network Neighborhood window (see fig. 20.13).

FIG. 20.13
Computers on the Windows network are listed in the window.

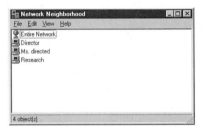

▶ **See** "Sharing Directories and Files," **p. 570**

To access any of the computers on the network, and their resources, simply double-click the computer icon. Figure 20.14 shows a computer's shared drives, folders, and printer.

FIG. 20.14
Use the resources from a server or another computer on the network.

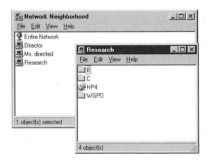

If your computer is a member of both a Microsoft Windows network and a NetWare network, the Windows computers may not appear when you first open the Network Neighborhood. If you do not see the network you want, double-click the Entire Network icon and then double-click the network you want to connect to display the server and/or computers attached to that network.

N O T E The network you attach to at logon and that appears first in the Network Neighborhood depends on the network search order, as described in the next section. ■

TROUBLESHOOTING

I forgot my network password. Is there anything I can do? Yes, you can contact your network administrator and ask him/her to change your password.

I can't see other computers in the Network Neighborhood. What can I do? Double-click the Entire Network icon and see if there are any computers listed in that window; you may be connected to two different networks. Specify the network you want to connect to by double-clicking either Microsoft Network or NetWare Network in the Entire Network window.

You may have switched to a different workgroup. Specify another workgroup in the Identification tab of the Network dialog box. If there's still a problem, check your network cabling, make sure your adapter card is installed and configured, and ask the administrator if the network is up and running.

Configuring Network Search Order

If your computer is connected to more than one kind of network, you can tell Windows NT in which order to search and attach to the network. For example, if you want to attach to the NetWare network first so you can search, retrieve, and print files, you specify that in the Network Access Order dialog box. Windows NT searches for the NetWare network when it starts up and attaches to the network. Additionally, Windows NT discontinues the search after finding the first network.

You can always switch from one network to the other without rebooting your computer. Open theNetwork Neighborhood window and double-click the Entire Network icon. Choose the network you want to attach to from the resulting window. If your user name and password are the same for both networks, you'll have no

Part
V

Ch
20

trouble switching back and forth; if your credentials are not the same for both networks, you'll have to log off of one network and onto the other.

 TIP After connecting to a network, you can log off and log onto another network by choosing Start, Shut Down. Select Close All Programs and Log on as a Different User.

You can change the order of the search and attach in the Network Access Order dialog box. To change the order, follow these steps:

1. In the Network dialog box, choose the Services tab.

2. Click Network Access Order. The Network Access Order dialog box appears (see fig. 20.15).

FIG. 20.15
Select your preference of networks to log onto first.

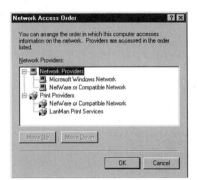

3. In the Network Providers list box, double-click the provider for which you want to change—such as network or print providers—if there are no options listed below the provider.

4. Click the network you want to specify and then click Move Up to move the network up in the list or Move Down to move the network down in the list. The network at the top of the list is the one Windows NT connects to first.

5. Choose OK to close the dialog box; choose OK to close the Network dialog box.

From Here...

In this chapter, you learned to configure network cards and drivers, protocols, and bindings. You may want to see the following chapters for related information:

- Chapter 19, "Understanding Windows NT Network Services," explains the available networking tools and services that come with NT Workstation.
- Chapter 21, "Managing Shared Resources," shows you how to share your directories and files and how to grant permissions for users to access them.
- Chapter 23, "Using Dial-up Networking," shows you how to configure a workstation to attach to a network by modem.

Part
V

Ch
20

Managing Shared Resources

by Sue Plumley

You can share files and directories over the network with anyone you choose. You might want to share directories, for example, containing files with one of your coworkers or share files with all of your coworkers. Some files you might share include spreadsheet, database, accounting, word processing, and so on. Some directories you might share include file and application directories.

In addition to sharing files and directories over the network, you also can stop sharing files and directories at any time. When you stop sharing a directory or file, it's no longer available over the network.

When you designate a directory as shared, the files within that directory are also shared, unless you set file permissions to limit access to your files. When you're the owner of a file or files, you can enable access of those files to anyone on the network or to no one. ■

Share and stop sharing directories and files

Before others on the network can access files and directories on your computer, you must designate those files or directories as shared. You also can stop sharing a file or directory on your machine at any time.

View shared files

NT provides a special icon to represent shared directories and files; you can view shared files on anyone's computer, as long as you have permission.

Set directory and file permissions

After you designate files and directories as shared, you can choose to grant special permissions to individuals and/or groups.

Audit shared files and directories

Track access to any files and directories you designate as shared so you know who uses your resources.

Sharing Directories and Files

You can share directories and the files they contain with others over the network. You can choose with whom you want to share, view shared files, and change sharing properties.

N O T E   For the most part, Windows NT uses the terms *folder* and *directories* interchangeably; when discussing sharing, NT uses the term *directories*. ▨

In addition, you can stop sharing directories at any time to prevent others on the network from viewing and using your directories and files.

Understanding Sharing

To share your directories and files, you must be logged on as a member of the Administrators, Server Operators, or Power Users group. Additionally, you have control over sharing files and directories on remote computers if you're a member of the Administrators group.

▶ **See** "Working with Groups," **p. 389**

Windows NT automatically designates shared resources—directories, drives, printer, and so on—on a workstation, depending on the configuration of the computer. These shared resources are only for administrators, server operators, or backup operators to connect to and use for purposes of managing the network. Only members of the Administrators group can change the sharing properties on these directories including stopping sharing.

As a user, you can select the resource on your workstation and stop sharing it. However, the next time you log on to your computer, the resource automatically changes back to shared. This is so the administrator can always connect to your computer for management, troubleshooting, backing up, and other system tasks.

Sharing and stopping sharing is designated in the Windows Explorer. When you indicate you want to share a directory and its files, Windows NT places an open hand icon beside the directory in the Explorer to indicate it is designated as shared (see fig. 21.1).

FIG. 21.1
Shared directories can be accessed by others on the network.

Shared directories ——

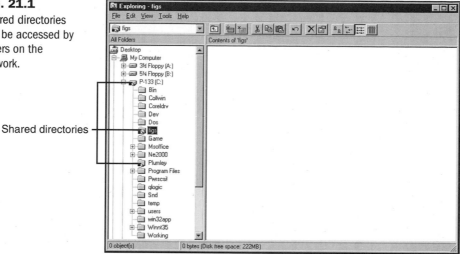

 Drives and directories with a dollar sign in the name, such as ADMIN$, indicate an administrative shared directory. Only members of the Administrators, Server Operators, or Backup Operators groups can access these directories.

Granting Share Rights

You can designate share rights to any directory on your computer. Remember, however, that all files within the directory are also shared, unless you specify permission rights for individual files. For more information, see "Setting Access for Directories and Files" later in this chapter.

N O T E You can only designate share rights to files if the file system used on your computer is NTFS (New Technology File System). You cannot share files in a FAT (File Allocation Table) file system. ■

You indicate shared directories in the Windows Explorer. To open the Explorer and share directories, follow these steps:

1. Choose Start, Programs, Windows NT Explorer to display the Explorer (refer to fig. 21.1).

2. In the directory window (the left window), right-click the directory you want to share to display the shortcut menu.

Part

V

Ch

21

3. Choose S̲haring. The Properties sheet appears; choose the S̲hared As option (see fig. 21.2).

FIG. 21.2

Choose to share a directory and optionally set limits on the share.

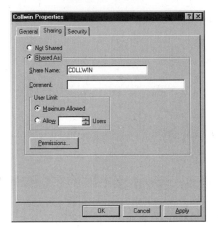

4. In the S̲hare Name text box, enter a new name to call the directory if you don't want to use the default name; Windows NT enters the directory name as the Share name by default.

N O T E The share name can be up to 12 characters long. If you're using the Windows NT file system (NTFS) over the network, 12 characters are fine. However, if MS-DOS computers also connect to and use your shared directories, the share name should conform to MS-DOS naming conventions: an eight-letter name with an optional three-letter extension. ▪

5. Optionally, add a description or note about the directory in the C̲omment text box; other users will see this comment.

6. In the User Limit area of the dialog box, choose one of the following options:

   M̲aximum Allowed. Sets no limit to the number of users who can connect to the shared directory at one time.

   A̲llow. Set a limit by selecting this option and entering the limit you want in the Users text box.

7. Choose OK to close the dialog box and share the directory.

You can set permissions for file access by clicking the Permissions button, explained later in this chapter in the "Setting Access for Directories and Files" section.

TROUBLESHOOTING

I'm logged on as a member of the Administrators group but sharing is not available to me. Is there anything I can do? Yes. Before you can share a directory, the Server service must be running. Normally, the service is automatically started; however if it is not running, you can start the service yourself. To start the Server service, open the Control Panel and open the Services icon. In the Service list, locate Server. In the Status list, make sure the Server is Started. If it is not, select Server and click the Start button. Choose Close to close the Services dialog box.

Viewing Shared Files

You can view any shared files in a shared directory to view file properties, change access attributes, see who has the file open, and to close the file to stop it from being shared.

Viewing Shared Files consists of two steps: viewing the file's properties and viewing the network properties. Included with the file's properties is general information about the file—such as file name, path, size, and so on—and file attributes. *File attributes* are controls you can add to a file to limit access by others.

Included with viewing network properties is general information—such as file name and path, total number of times the file has been opened, and so on. You also can choose to close the file to sharing in the Network Properties dialog box.

Using File Attributes   Set file attributes to control other users' access to your files in a shared directory. On drives formatted to use the Windows NTFS, you need permission to change file attributes. You set file attributes in the file's Properties dialog box.

Table 21.1 describes the file attributes you can set in the file Properties dialog box.

Part

V

Ch

21

Table 21.1 File Attributes

Attribute	Description
Read-Only	Marks files that can be opened and viewed but not changed in any way; changes cannot be saved to the file but the user could save the file under another name
Archive	Marks files as changed since the last backup to ensure the next backup will include it
Compressed	Compresses files and directories; a file moved to another directory takes on the compression attribute of the new directory
Hidden	Hides files so they do not appear in the directory window
System	Identifies files as system files and hides the system file from the directory window

Viewing File Properties   When you view the properties of shared files, the Explorer displays the file type, name, size, path, the DOS name, creation date, the date of the last change to the file, and the last access date. You also can set attributes in the file's Properties dialog box.

To view a shared file's properties, follow these steps:

1. In the Explorer, select the file you want to view.

2. Choose File, Properties. The file's Properties sheet appears (see fig. 21.3). Alternatively, press Alt+Enter on the highlighted file.

3. In the Attributes area, add or remove the attributes you want to use. You will not see the compressed attribute unless your drive has been compressed.

4. Choose OK to close the Properties dialog box.

Changing Share Properties

If you're logged on as a member of the Administrators, Server Operators, or Power Users group, you can change share properties of a directory by changing the number of users, comment information, or permissions. You also can view information about the directory and change the attributes on the directory.

FIG. 21.3

View the properties of the selected file and set attributes.

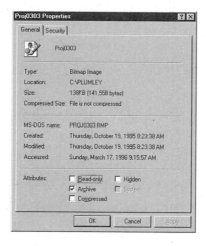

To change share properties, follow these steps:

1. In the Explorer, select the directory whose share properties you want to change.

2. Choose File, Properties. The directory's Properties sheet appears (see fig. 21.4). Make any changes you want in the Attributes area of the General tab.

FIG. 21.4

View details about the directory and modify the attributes.

3. Choose the Sharing tab (see fig. 21.5).

4. You can modify the following properties of the shared directory:

Change the Share Name.

FIG. 21.5
Make changes to the
share settings in the
Sharing tab.

Change or remove the Comment text.

Change the User Limit.

Change Permissions. For more information, see the section "Setting Access for Directories and Files" later in this chapter.

5. Click New Share to set share properties for another directory. Choose OK when finished to return to the directory's Properties sheet.

6. Choose OK when finished to close the directory's Properties sheet.

Stopping Sharing

You can stop sharing directories and the files they contain at any time if you're logged on as a member of the Administrators, Server Operators, or Power Users group.

To stop sharing a directory, follow these steps:

1. In the Explorer, select the drive containing the directories you want to stop sharing.

2. Right-click the directory and choose Sharing from the shortcut menu.

3. In the directory's Properties sheet, choose the Not Shared option.

4. Choose OK to close the Properties sheet.

CAUTION

If you stop sharing a directory that's in use, the users will lose their data.

TROUBLESHOOTING

I chose to stop sharing the ADMIN$ and C$ directories on my computer; I had never chosen to share them. The next time I connected to the network, however, those directories were shared again. Is there any way to get them off of there? No. Any shared directory with a dollar sign in the name is one used for administrative purposes. Only a member of the administrator's group can change attributes on one of these shared directories and only members of the Administrator's, Server Operators, or Power Users group can access these directories. If you choose to stop sharing the directories, the network automatically designates them as shared the next time you connect.

Setting Access for Directories and Files

You can set access for directories and files by granting permissions to other users on the network. *Permissions* are authorizations attached to files and directories that limit user access and the tasks users can perform on the resource in question. A *resource* is any item—file, directory, printer, CD-ROM drive, and so on—shared over a network.

You can set access limits for directories and files using the standard directory and file permissions; additionally, you can set special access permissions when necessary.

You only can set permissions when the drive of the computer is formatted to use the Windows NT file system (NTFS). The File Allocation Table (FAT) drives do not support Windows NT security.

 You can choose to share directories and files only on the NTFS file system; however, you can share directories using the FAT system.

▶ **See** "Windows NT Workstation Features and Capabilities," **p. 17**

Part

V

Ch

21

Understanding Permissions

Permissions are granted to groups on the network instead of to individuals. The Administrators group, for example, has a certain set of permissions, Backup Operators have certain permissions, Users have their own set of permissions, and so on. When you create directories or files, you are the owner of those resources. You control the access to the files or directories you own; therefore, you have the power to grant permissions to the various groups on your network.

The following are some important points to keep in mind about permissions:

- Members of the Users group cannot use a directory or file unless they've been granted permission.

- Members of the Administrators group can take ownership of a file or directory and therefore grant permissions for that resource.

- The permissions assigned to a directory also apply to any subdirectories or files created within that directory; however, file permissions can supersede directory permissions.

- Except for the No Access permission, permissions are cumulative. If, for example, a user is a member of two or more groups, the user inherits each groups' permissions. No access takes precedence in all cases.

Setting Directory Permissions

Setting permissions on a directory defines what certain users can do within the directory. Standard directory permissions you can set on directories include No Access, List, Read, Add, Add & Read, Change, and Full Control.

Permissions Defined   Each permission displays two sets of abbreviations beside the directory; the first set defines the directory permissions, and the second set defines the permissions granted to the files within the directory. The abbreviations for individual permissions are as follows: Read-R, Delete-D, Write-W, Change Permissions-P, Execute-X, and Take Ownership-O.

Table 21.2 shows the permission, abbreviation for directory (first abbreviation) and file (second abbreviation), and a description or the permission.

Table 21.2 Directory Permissions

Permission	Abbreviation	Description
No Access	none/none	Blocks any and all access to a directory and its files
List	RX/not specified	Enables viewing file names and subdirectory names, changing to the directory's subdirectory; doesn't grant access to files
Read	RX/RX	Enables viewing filenames and subdirectory names, changing to the directory's sub-directories, viewing data in files, running applications
Add	WX/not specified	Enables adding files and subdirectories to the directory; doesn't allow access to files
Add & Read	RWX/RX	Enables viewing filenames and subdirectory names, changing to the directory's sub-directories, viewing data in files, running applications, and adding files and subdirectories to the directory
Change	RWXD/RWXD	Enables viewing filenames and subdirectory names, changing to the directory's sub-directories, viewing data in files, running applications, adding files and subdirectories to the directory, changing data in files, deleting the directory and its files
Full Control	All/All	Enables viewing file names and subdirectory names, changing to the directory's sub-directories, viewing data in files, running applications, adding files and subdirectories to the directory, changing data in files, deleting the directory and its files, changing permissions on the directory and its files, and taking ownership of the directory and its files

 TIP A file permission that's not specified means the group cannot use the files unless granted access in another manner, such as individually.

Part
V

Ch

21

Assigning Permissions   You can assign permissions to new users and groups or change the permissions for existing groups in the Directory Permissions dialog box.

To assign permissions to a directory, follow these steps:

1. In the Explorer, select the directory in the directory window.

2. Right-click the directory and choose S̲haring from the shortcut menu. The directory's Properties sheet appears.

3. Choose the Security tab and then choose the P̲ermissions button (see fig. 21.6).

FIG. 21.6

Choose the groups and the permissions you want to assign in the Directory Permissions dialog box.

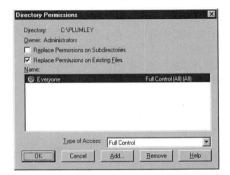

4. Choose either or both of the following check boxes:

   Re̲place Permissions on Subdirectories. Check to apply permissions to all subdirectories; unchecked applies permissions only to the directory and its files.

   Replace Permissions on Existing F̲iles. Check to apply permissions to the files in the directory; clear to apply permissions only to the directory.

5. In the list of N̲ames, select the name of the group you want to apply or change permissions for and select the T̲ype of Access drop-down list box.

6. Select the permission you want to apply to the group and choose OK to close the dialog box. Choose OK to close the Properties sheet.

To remove a user or group from the list, select the name and click the R̲emove button. To add users or groups to the list of names, click the A̲dd button. For more information, see "Auditing Resource Usage" later in this chapter.

Setting Shared Directory Permissions

You can set permissions through a shared directory that resides on a drive that's formatted as NTFS, or FAT. When you set permissions on a shared directory, the permissions are effective only over the network, not within the workstation itself. You must be logged on as a member of the Administrators, Server Operators, or Power Users group to set shared directory permissions.

 TIP Any permissions you set for a shared directory apply to all files and subdirectories in the directory.

To set shared directory permissions, follow these steps:

1. In the Explorer, select the directory for which you want to change or set permissions.

2. Right-click the directory and choose Sharing. The directory's Properties dialog box appears (see fig. 21.7).

FIG. 21.7
Set permissions for shared directories from the directory's Properties sheet.

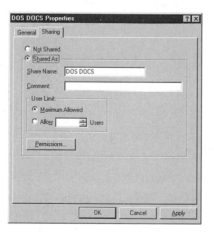

3. Choose the Permissions button. The Access Through Share Permissions dialog box appears (see fig. 21.8).

4. In the Name list, select the group or user whose permissions you want to change.

5. In the Type of Access drop-down list, choose the permission you want to apply to the selected user or group.

Part
V

Ch
21

FIG. 21.8

The Access Through
Share Permissions
dialog box works
just like the Directory
Permissions
dialog box.

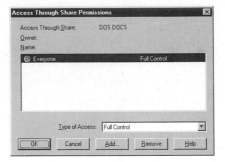

6. Choose OK to close the dialog box.

To remove a user or group from the list, select the name and click Remove. To add
users or groups to the list of names, click Add.

▶ **See** "Auditing Resource Usage," **p. 584**

Setting File Permissions

You set file permissions to grant or limit the access that other network users have
to your files. Files inherit permissions from the directory but you also can add or
remove permissions to individual files.

When setting file permissions, here are a few items to consider:

■ You can only set file permissions if you're using a drive formatted to use the
NTFS.

■ To change file permissions, you must own the file or be granted permission
to change file permissions by the owner.

■ Anyone with Full Control permission on a directory can delete a file in that
directory no matter what file permissions are set.

■ Except for the No Access permission, permissions are cumulative. If, for
example, a user is a member of two or more groups, the user inherits each
groups' permissions.

Permissions Defined   Each permission displays a set of abbreviations beside it
defining the individual permissions. The abbreviations for individual permissions
are as follows: Read-R, Delete-D, Write-W, Change Permissions-P, Execute-X, and
Take Ownership-O.

Table 21.3 shows the permission, abbreviation for the file, and a description of the permission.

Table 21.3 File Permissions

Permission	Abbreviation	Description
No Access	none	Blocks access to the file
Read	RX	Enables viewing the file's data, running the file if it's a program file
Change	RWXD	Enables viewing the file's data, running the file if it's a program file, changing data in the file, deleting the file
Full Control	All	Enables viewing the file's data, running the file if it's a program file, changing data in the file, deleting the file, changing permissions on the file, and taking ownership of the file

Assigning Permissions   You can set and change file permissions only if you're the owner of the file or have been granted permission by the owner to do so.

To assign permissions to a file, follow these steps:

1. In the Explorer, right-click the file you want to assign permissions to and choose Properties from the shortcut menu. The file's Properties sheet appears.

2. Choose the Security tab and the Permissions button. The File Permissions dialog box appears (see fig. 21.9).

FIG. 21.9
Set file permissions for groups and/or users.

Part
V

Ch
21

3. Select the user or group in the list of Names and then choose the permission to grant from the Type of Access drop-down list.

4. Choose OK to close the dialog box.

To remove a user or group from the list, select the name and click Remove button. To add users or groups to the list of names, click Add.

▶ **See** "Auditing Resource Usage," **p. 584**

Auditing Resource Usage

You can audit, or track, the use of files and directories to see which users or groups use which resources. The results of your auditing are recorded in a log that you can view in the Event Viewer. Remember, however, that auditing requires use of memory and other system resources; the more events you audit, the slower your system may become.

 TIP You can audit both successful and unsuccessful actions, but generally, it's the unsuccessful actions you're most concerned with because it is those that cause your trouble.

In addition to auditing activities and events, you can add users and groups to a permission and an auditing list, and you can view and take ownership of files and directories to further manage your workstation.

▶ **See** "Viewing a Log," **p. 930**

Auditing Files and Directories

Select the events, such as read, write, delete, and so on, you want to audit in the Directory or File Auditing dialog box. To audit files and directories, you must be logged on as a member of the Administrator group. Additionally, you must use the NTFS file system to enable setting security auditing options.

To audit a file or directory, follow these steps:

1. In the Explorer, right-click the file(s) or directory you want to audit. Choose Properties from the shortcut menu. The file's or directory's Properties sheet appears.

2. Choose the Security tab and then choose the Auditing button. The File or Directory Auditing dialog box appears (see fig. 21.10).

3. In Name, select the group or user you want to audit.

4. In Events to Audit, select the events you want to track for the specified user or group. Choose either or both Success and Failure to track successful and/or unsuccessful events.

5. Choose OK to close the dialog box.

FIG. 21.10

The Name list displays the currently audited groups and/or users.

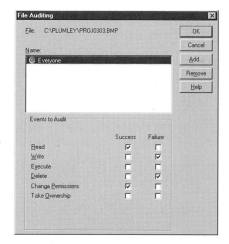

To remove a user or group from the list, select the name and click the Remove button. To add users or groups to the list of names, click the Add button.

To audit a directory, right-click the directory and then choose Properties from the shortcut menu. In the Properties sheet, choose the Security tab and the Auditing tab. In the Directory Auditing dialog box, the options are the same as the File Auditing dialog box except for two additional check boxes:

- *Replace Auditing on Subdirectories*. Choose this checkbox to apply auditing changes to all subdirectories; clear the box to apply auditing changes only to the directory and its files.

- *Replace Auditing on Existing Files*. Check this box to apply auditing changes to the directory and its files; clear the box to apply auditing changes to the directory only.

TROUBLESHOOTING

After I set the auditing options, I get a message saying, `The current Audit`
`Policy does not have auditing turned on.` **What should I do?** Choose OK to
clear the message. Before you can audit files or directories, you must set the audit policy
in the User Manager, an Administrative Tool. In the User Manager, choose Policies, Audit,
and in the Audit Policy dialog box, choose Audit These Events. Select File and Object
Access and then check either or both the Success and Failure check boxes. Choose OK.

▶ **See** "Managing Security Policies," **p. 396**

Adding and Removing Users and Groups

You can add, change, and remove users and groups from the permissions or auditing list in the Directory Permissions dialog box, the Directory Auditing dialog box,
the File Auditing dialog box, and others discussed in this chapter. You also can
search for members of a group and find domains to which a user or member belongs. After adding users and groups to the Name lists, you can assign permissions to them or audit their actions.

To add and remove groups to the list, follow these steps:

1. In any of the Permissions dialog boxes, click Add. The Add Users and
   Groups dialog box appears (see fig. 21.11).

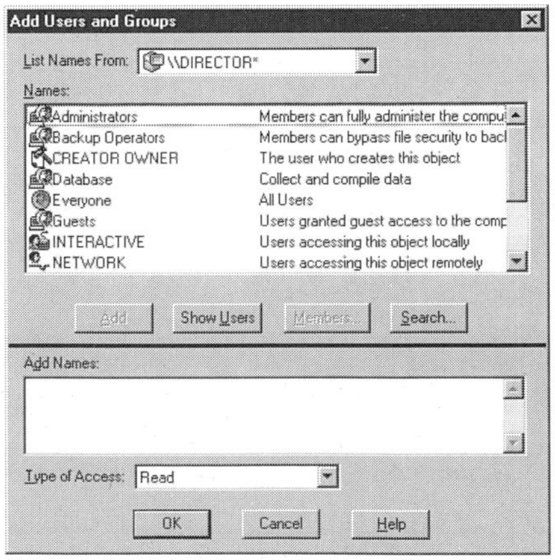

FIG. 21.11
The Add Users and
Groups dialog box
lists various users
and groups to which
you can assign
permissions.

2. In List Names From, choose the computer or the domain from which you want to choose.

 Domains only appear if you're a member of the Windows NT Server network.

3. To display a list of users in addition to the list of groups on the selected computer or domain, click the Show Users button. The list of users appears at the end of the Names list.

4. To view the members of the group, select the group in the Names list and then click the Members button. The Local Group Membership dialog box appears with a list of the members of the specified group (see fig. 21.12). On a Windows NT Server network, however, global groups appear on the list in addition to the local members.

FIG. 21.12
View the individual members of any group.

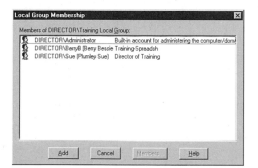

5. In the Membership dialog box, select the specific members and clicking Add; alternatively, select no specific member and click Add to include all members in the Add Users and Groups dialog box list. Windows NT returns to the Add Users and Groups dialog box.

6. To look for a specific user or group on a Windows NT Server network, click Search. In the Find User or Group text box, enter the name of the user or group, specify the domain(s) you want to search, and click Search.

   You can select any found user or group and click Add to add that user or group to the list in the Add Users and Groups dialog box. Windows NT returns to the Add Users and Groups dialog box.

Part
V

Ch
21

T I P In the Add Users and Groups dialog box, you can assign permissions to all users or groups listed in the Add Names list box by choosing the Type of Access drop-down list and selecting the permission.

    7. Choose OK to close the dialog box. All specified users and groups are added to the Name list in the Directory Permissions or Directory Auditing dialog box. Choose OK to close the dialog box.

       ▶ **See** "Working with Groups," **p. 389**

Taking Ownership

You own the files and directories that you create. When you own a resource, you can set permissions and you control how the directories and files are used. Only a member of the Administrators group has the power to take ownership of a file unless you grant permission to another user to take ownership. Additionally, a member of the Administrator's group cannot transfer ownership of any file to anyone else.

You can view your file and directory ownership as well as take ownership. Even though you own a file or directory, periodically view the Owner dialog box to make sure it still belongs to you. To take ownership of another's files or directories, you must be logged on as a member of the Administrator's group.

To view and take ownership, follow these steps:

    1. In the Explorer, right-click the file(s) or directory for which you want to view ownership or take ownership. Choose Properties from the shortcut menu. The file's or directory's Properties sheet appears.

    2. Choose the Security tab and the Ownership button. The Owner dialog box appears (see fig. 21.13).

FIG. 21.13
This file has been taken over by a member of the Administrator's group.

3. To take ownership of the file or directory, click the <u>T</u>ake Ownership button. Windows NT transfers ownership for you and closes the dialog box.

From Here...

In this chapter, you learned to grant access to files and directories on your computer by sharing your resources and setting permissions. For related information, see the following chapters:

■ Chapter 20, "Configuring the Network at Your Workstation," discusses setting up your computer to communicate over the network. Learn about protocols, adapter cards, services, and more.

■ Chapter 32, "Using the Event Viewer," explains how to view the auditing logs you set in this chapter. Track use of your files and directories and then view the results.

Part
V

Ch
21

Going Online with Windows NT Workstation

CHAPTER 22

Installing and Configuring a Modem

by Kathy Ivens

A modem translates computer data (which is digital) into a form that can be handled by the telephone line (which is analog). It sends an analog translation from the computer to the telephone wire (this is called *modulating*). At the other end, a modem takes the analog stream of data from the telephone line and changes it to digital information for the receiving computer (this is called *demodulating*). This process of modulating and demodulating created the shortcut jargon that resulted in the word *modem*. ■

How modems work

Get a good understanding of the inner workings of a modem and how the modem helps you communicate outside of your computer.

Installing a modem with the Modem Wizard

Learn the three-step process to install a modem and how to configure the modem and your location.

Understanding Telephony

Learn how the new Telephony drivers are part of the Windows NT Workstation 4.0 improvements to the performance of serial communications.

Using the Phone Dialer

Phone Dialer is a new application you can use to dial your phone. Learn the many ways this application improves communication.

Understanding Modems and Telephone Communications

When you shop for a modem, you find a mind-boggling variety of brands and features; sorting it all out can be overwhelming. Check the documentation that came with your Windows NT Workstation software to see the list of compatible modems; this will help you make the choice.

 TIP The one choice that is unconnected to compatibility is speed; you make that decision. Go for the fastest modem you can buy without exceeding your budget. In fact, if the next highest speed is slightly over your budget, go for it anyway. Don't let friends and quasi-experts influence you when they ask, "Who do you think you're going to communicate with at 28,800?" Today, you might not dial out and reach lots of 28,800 modems, but the day after tomorrow you probably will. Remember that when two modems connect, they operate at the speed of the slower modem, so it isn't as if your fast modem won't communicate with a computer with a slower modem.

ISDN

An *ISDN (Integrated Services Digital Network) line* is like a telephone line that's been taking vitamins (or steroids). It's built for speed. The line itself is *digital*, meaning you don't need to modulate and demodulate the data stream. That, of course, means you don't need a modem.

ISDN connections are made extremely quickly so that companies currently using open lines to keep remote computers connected will be able to dial, transact, and disconnect almost instantaneously. This means that even though an ISDN line may be more expensive, it's only a cost when it's used.

ISDN lines have to be ordered from your local telephone company, and not all phone companies have the service available. (At the time of this writing, I can say that if you're in the Mid-Atlantic region, the Chicago area, or the Pacific coast, you can probably order the service and have the line installed quickly.)

Instead of a regular modem, you'll need ISDN interface hardware to connect your computer to the ISDN line. And, the computer on the other end must also have ISDN hardware. Several companies are offering ISDN interface hardware, and more companies will join the market as this becomes more popular.

There are currently two types of ISDN service:

■ *BRI (Basic Rate Interface service)*. A copper wire connection capable of maintaining speeds of 64,000 bits per second (bps) or 128Kbps.

NOTE The reason there's a choice of speeds for the BRI ISDN service is that the service is provided over two channels, each of which transmits at 64Kbps. (Actually, there's also a third channel that provides signals to the ISDN hardware at the other end of the transmission). You can configure your ISDN connection so that the two data channels are separate (and each has its own connection port) which enables two different ISDN-connected computers to dial in at 64Kbps. Or, you can configure your ISDN connection so that both channels are used for one connection (attached to a single port) and double the speed with which data is transmitted. ■

■ *PRI (Primary Rate Interface service)*. This service uses fiber optic cable and transmits at speeds up to 1.5 million bps.

Not all telephone companies offer both services, and some aren't offering any ISDN service yet. And, in some communities where telephone companies are offering ISDN service, it's frequently difficult to find anyone to talk to at the telephone company about the choices and the costs.

Also, because the technology is not commonplace yet, the standardization we expect with computer peripherals and their configuration software isn't there. The same thing was true when faster modems first appeared on the market, however, so we can expect hardware vendors to develop and meet standards in the near future.

If you do a lot of data transfer over *POTS (Plain Old Telephone Service)* using a modem, and if ISDN services are available, do an analysis to see if the cost savings in line charges amortize the cost of installing ISDN capabilities—it usually does.

ON THE WEB

Find out if ISDN is available in your area and what it costs from Microsoft's "Get ISDN"
Web page at

> **http://www.microsoft.com/windows/getisdn/**

X.25

At the other end of the technical, state-of-the-art spectrum from ISDN is an X.25
connection. Available either over telephone lines or by cabling, X.25 is an old technology. It's slow (its absolute top speed is 64Kbps but most X.25 connections operate even slower than that) and computer nerds may laugh at it, but it has one thing
that's hard to match—reliability. Data sent over X.25 connection pretty much always arrives at its destination without any errors, without any corruption and without any problem.

One of the reasons an X.25 connection is slow is that all kinds of error checking is
built into its performance. It makes sure that the data that leaves your computer is
exactly the same when it arrives at its destination.

Besides data integrity, there are some other reasons to take a careful look at X.25:

- It's available pretty much everywhere, even in countries that have terrible,
  unreliable telephone services (and in U.S. communities where the local
  telephone company has never heard of ISDN).

- For companies with offices around the world, it's probably the only way to
  ensure that offices in different countries can communicate.

- It's one of the least complicated line protocols. Companies have been known
  to build their own X.25 systems, creating and maintaining everything they
  need without too much difficulty—it's like building your own telephone
  company.

There are two ways to configure X.25 connections:

- *Dial-up*. The X.25 dial-up connection is called a *PAD* (*Packet Assembler-
  Disassembler*). The PAD takes streams of data and converts them to packets.
  It sends the packets to the receiving computer where another PAD turns
  them back into data streams. The PAD exists at a service provider's location

(many companies use SprintNet, but there are probably other X.25 service providers), and the two computers are connected through the service provider.

■ Various configuration options for the computers are necessary, and the result is that there is an inexpensive way to connect two computers over telephone lines. This means that you can have continuous connections between a remote computer and a company server without breaking the budget.

■ *Direct connection.* The X.25 direct connection is established by linking two or more computers with cable (leased-line telephone cable). To do this, each computer must have an X.25 device called a *smart card.* The smart card has a built-in PAD, and this fools the computers into believing they have connected their communication ports to a PAD service provider.

Installing a Modem

Installing a modem is a three-step operation, consisting of:

■ The physical installation

■ The Windows NT 4.0 installation

■ The Windows NT 4.0 configuration process

Attaching the Modem to the Computer

Installing the modem into your computer isn't terribly difficult, but you should take a moment to check the documentation that came with the modem to make sure any dip-switches or jumpers are set accurately for your system and the use you'll make of the modem.

If you have an external modem, you have to connect it to a serial port. Most computers come with two serial ports, although additional serial ports may have been added. You can attach the modem to either serial port.

You must use a modem cable for this, a serial cable not configured specifically for modems will probably not work properly.

There is also a power supply that will need to be plugged into an electrical outlet and you will have to run a telephone cord (usually supplied with the modem) be tween the modem and a wall jack.

If you have an internal modem, you have to open your computer and insert the modem card into an empty slot. Specific instructions are included in the documentation for the modem.

Internal modems become the third serial port, (assuming the computer has two serial ports). COM3 is built into the modem so there is no need for any cable in order to connect to a serial port. You will have to run a telephone cord (usually supplied with the modem) between the modem and the wall jack.

 Most modems (internal and external) have two jacks so you can plug a telephone into the modem and have the use of it when you aren't online. Usually the jacks are marked for line (connect to the wall jack) and phone (connect to your telephone). Some modems have two unmarked jacks and you have to check the documentation to see which is which. And some modems don't care which jack you use for line or telephone—they'll figure it out correctly.

Once the modem is connected to the computer and the telephone line, you can begin the Windows NT installation process.

Using the Windows NT 4.0 Modem Wizard   NT 4.0 has a new feature (new to Windows NT), the Modem Wizard, that makes this quite easy. To install your modem into your operating system, make sure your modem is connected and turned on, then follow these steps:

1. From the Start menu, choose <u>S</u>ettings, <u>C</u>ontrol Panel (or open My Computer, then open Control Panel).

2. Double-click the Modems icon in the Control Panel. This launches the Install New Modem Wizard (see fig. 22.1).

3. If you want the Modem Wizard to detect your modem and install it automatically, choose <u>N</u>ext. This process may take a minute or two.

 If you know your modem is specifically supported and you think it would be faster to find it on the list of modems, select the <u>D</u>on't Detect choice (see the section "Installing a Modem Manually" later in this chapter).

Part VI
Ch 22

FIG. 22.1
The Modem Wizard offers to find and identify your modem to save you the trouble of scrolling through a list of supported modems to find your make and model.

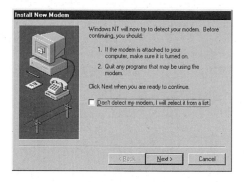

4. The Modem Wizard begins a search to find your modem (see fig. 22.2). It starts with COM1, then moves to COM2, then looks to see if COM3 exists. This may take a little time, depending upon the location of your modem.

FIG. 22.2
The Modem Wizard begins a search through the serial ports to find a modem.

5. If a modem is located, the Modem Wizard begins a dialogue with it to determine the modem make and model (see fig. 22.3).

FIG. 22.3
The Modem Wizard sends queries and reads responses to help identify the modem.

6. Finally, the Modem Wizard displays the make and model of the modem it has found and identified (see fig. 22.4). Depending upon the information displayed, you can take one of the following steps:

FIG. 22.4
The Modem Wizard
found my modem!

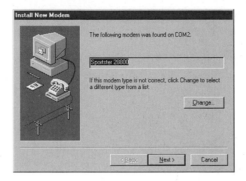

- If the identification is correct, choose Next.
- If the Wizard presents two possible choices, select the correct one, then choose Next.
- If the identification is incorrect, choose Change to see a list of supported modems (see the next section, which explains manual selection of a modem).
- If the Wizard could not find or identify the modem, you will have to take corrective action (covered later in this chapter).

7. The Wizard copies and installs the necessary files to your drive. You may see a message that says you have to restart your computer to use the modem. If you do, choose OK, but do not restart your computer until the modem installation is complete.

8. When the installation process is complete, the Wizard announces that fact. Choose Finish.

If you used the Modem Wizard and everything went perfectly, the Modems Properties dialog box is displayed. Move to the section "Configuring the Modem" for details about configuration properties.

Installing a Modem Manually There are four reasons to install the modem yourself, instead of using the Modem Wizard:

■ You think it would be faster to choose your own modem instead of having the Modem Wizard search for it, and you selected <u>D</u>on't Detect My Modem when the first page of the Wizard was displayed.

■ The Modem Wizard announced it could not find a modem and you're sure all the connections are working.

■ The Modem Wizard selected an incorrect make or model, and you choose <u>C</u>hange instead of <u>N</u>ext on that Wizard page.

■ Your modem is not listed as being supported and you have Windows NT 4.0 drivers from the manufacturers which you have to install.

Follow these steps to install the modem manually:

1. When the list of supported modems is displayed, choose a <u>M</u>anufacturer from the left pane, then scroll through the Mode<u>l</u>s to find the one that matches your modem (see fig. 22.5). If you are installing an unsupported modem and have disks from the manufacturer, choose <u>H</u>ave Disk and follow the instructions for inserting the disk.

FIG. 22.5
All the supported manufacturers and models are listed— scroll through the list to find your modem.

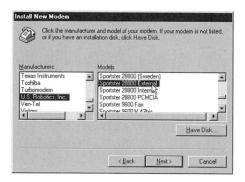

2. You must specify the port the modem is attached to.

   If only one port is available (usually because a mouse is on the other serial port), you can choose <u>A</u>ll Ports and that port will be highlighted.

   Or, choose <u>S</u>elected Port and highlight the appropriate serial port (see fig. 22.6).

   Then choose <u>N</u>ext.

3. The files are copied to your drive. Choose Finish.

FIG. 22.6

Select (highlight) the port to which you've attached the modem.

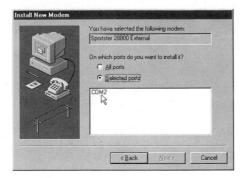

TROUBLESHOOTING

My modem isn't listed and the manufacturer does not have disks for Windows NT 4.0. What do I do? If automatic detection fails or your modem isn't listed when you attempt to select it manually, you have a modem that isn't supported by Windows NT 4.0.

There are two possible solutions to this problem:

- The first solution is obvious—buy another modem.
- The second choice is to try emulation. If there isn't a Windows NT 4.0 driver, the manufacturer may be able to tell you about emulation; in other words, your modem emulates, or acts the same as, another modem. You may have to change some dip switches or jumpers, or enter a specific initialization string in the modem settings, but this choice sometimes works, depending upon how lucky you are.

Configuring the Modem

Once the modem is successfully installed, it needs to be configured. The Modems Properties dialog box displays so you can begin the configuration process (see fig. 22.7).

There are several configuration elements for the modem and you can customize all or some of them to match the expectations of the software you're going to use with the modem.

Configure the General Properties Page   Follow these steps to set the General properties for the modem:

1. Choose Properties to display the modem's Properties dialog box, with the General tab in the foreground (see fig. 22.8).

FIG. 22.7
The Modems Properties dialog box is where you set up the configuration options for using the modem.

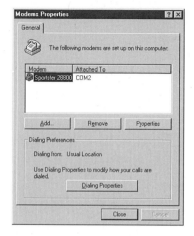

FIG. 22.8
Use the General tab to set volume and speed for the modem.

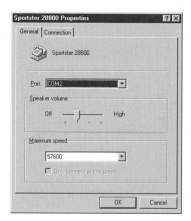

2. Set the Speaker volume higher or lower by moving the slider.

3. Specify a Maximum speed for the transfer of data. Click the arrow to the right of the box to see the available choices of baud rate.

N O T E It never does any harm to set the configuration for a higher speed than the modem's certification. Sometimes it speeds up modem communications.

Avoid the baud rate setting of 14,400, even if your modem is rated at 14,400. Using the 14,400 setting can cause problems in the modem's performance. The modem may hang up upon connecting, not recognize a connection, or exhibit some other bizarre behavior.

If you have a 14,400 modem, set the speed for 19,200 or higher. ▪

Configure the Connection Options   Choose the Connection tab to continue the configuration process (see fig. 22.9), by following these steps:

FIG. 22.9
Configure the
behavior of the
modem while making
a connection.

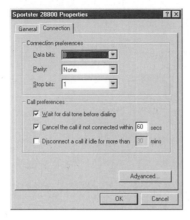

1. Configure the items in the Connection preferences to match those you'll use most often.

TIP The software applications you'll use with your modem will have their own setup programs to specify connection preferences. These settings prevail when you use the application, even if they are not the same as the settings that are established through the Windows NT configuration options.

Connection Preferences

For the technically curious, a brief explanation of the connection preferences items follows:

The serial port to which your modem is connected is an *asynchronous device*. That means data is flowing in both directions without any of it being synchronized. You have to have a way for each end of the connection to indicate what's going on. (It's like using one of the walky-talky gadgets where you can't speak and listen simultaneously and you say "over" when you're finished talking and then listen to the person at the other end.)

In order to communicate properly, both ends of the connection have to agree on these properties. When you dial out, you have to set the connection preferences to match what the *host* (receiving computer) is expecting. It doesn't matter whether you think one method is better or more efficient than the other, your opinion doesn't count—you just have to match what the host is expecting.

All the data that moves through the modem is broken up into packets that contain a specific number of bits (a *bit* is the smallest unit of information a computer handles). Most data is sent as either 7-bit or 8-bit.

The data is sent with a start bit and a stop bit, so the receiving end is told "here comes something," followed by "that's the end of the something." You can configure the number of stop bits that are sent, and while the choices are 1, 1.5, and 2, it's rare to come across a host that is expecting anything greater than 1 stop bit.

Parity is an agreed upon method to handle error checking. The parity choices are:

Even means the sending computer will make sure that the total number of bits is always even. To do this, an additional bit (called a *parity bit*) is added to each stream of data that is sent, and then that parity bit is turned on or off in order to make sure the total number of bits is even. When the host sees the data stream, if an even number of bits is detected, it takes the data. If an odd number of bits is detected, it assumes something got lost during transmission and asks the sending computer to send the data again.

Odd does the same thing as Even, except the goal is to send data with an odd number of on-bits.

Mark always turns on a parity bit regardless of whether this will create an even or odd number of on-bits. This doesn't permit the host to ascertain whether anything was lost during transmission, but it does create a method of letting the host know "here's a parity bit, so you know I've sent you a packet of data."

Space is the same method as Mark, except the parity bit is always turned off.

None does no parity checking. This isn't a disaster-laden choice (in fact, it's a very common choice) because the protocols you can choose to transfer data have error checking of their own. There are a number of protocols available for transferring files, and the software you use will make specific ones available and explain them.

2. Select <u>W</u>ait for Dial Tone if you want the modem to hear a dial tone before it begins to dial out. If you're connected to a regular, normal, telephone line this should be enabled.

3. Choose <u>C</u>ancel the Call and then specify a number of seconds, after which the modem should disconnect if the host doesn't answer.

4. Choose Di̲sconnect a Call and specify a number of seconds; if the connection is idle for an elapsed period longer than the number you specify, then the call will be disconnected. Idle means an absence of data exchange or keyboard (or mouse) activity.

 T I P It's important to configure the modem to disconnect after an idle period if you're dialing in to a host via a long distance connection, or a host that charges for the time online. That way, if you leave the computer to get a cup of coffee and stop to chat with someone, forgetting you're connected, you won't run up a bill the size of the national debt. Some software applications used for these connections will offer the same configuration item, which overrides these settings.

Configure the Advanced Settings   Choose Ad̲vanced from the Connection tab to move to the Advanced Connection Settings properties (see fig. 22.10).

FIG. 22.10
Set the connection environment for the modem.

Most of the configuration decisions for these settings are dependent upon the modem's capabilities (check the documentation) or the host's requirements. Again, the software you use may have some or all of the same options available and whatever you choose will override these settings when the software is active.

Here is a brief overview of the options available:

■ You should choose Use E̲rror Control and C̲ompress data if the modem supports it and if you are connecting to a host that supports these features. If the software you are using provides compression (many Internet software applications do), you may want to turn off the Compress data (which is a hardware compression scheme) because sometimes a double-dose of compression creates a conflict. If you feel your communications sessions are moving slower than they should, experiment by turning off either this Compress Data scheme or the software compression in your application. Then try it the other way around. Go with the one that works best.

- ■ Flow control is a method of handshaking (each modem acknowledges the other's existence, and makes an announcement indicating they're able to communicate). The modem's documentation and the host computer requirements will determine the best choice.

- ■ Modulation type is the communications standard two modems will use if they are having a problem communicating at a high speed. This is the "fallback" position they take. The default is standard. The other choices are dependent upon modem hardware and are generally needed for older, slower modems that don't use today's standards. If the conditions indicate, you can change the Modulation type, but it's a better idea to buy a new modem (or only call computers with modern modems if the problem is on the other end).

- ■ You can use the Extra Settings box to send a command to the modem if there is a reason to do so. Don't use this box for the standard initialization string (which is sent automatically), this is for those rare cases when you need to prepare the modem in some special way for the next communications session.

- ■ Choose Record a Log File if you want to keep a log of events for your communications sessions. You should only enable this feature if you've been having problems. In fact, if the problems are with a particular host, only enable this for sessions with that host. Then you can view the log (MODEMLOG.TXT) to try to ascertain and debug the problems.

Configure the Dialing Properties   When you have finished configuring these modem properties, choose OK to return to the General tab of the original Modems Properties dialog box.

Choose Dialing Properties to configure the way the modem will dial out. The Dialing Properties dialog box displays with the My Locations tab in the foreground (see fig. 22.11).

This properties page is divided into two sections—the top section defines a location and the bottom section sets the configuration for the selected location. In most cases, you'll have only one location but if you're using a portable computer you'll want to define a location for each set of circumstances (working from home, working from other company offices, working from hotels, and so on).

FIG. 22.11
Configure the environment for each location from which you'll be dialing out.

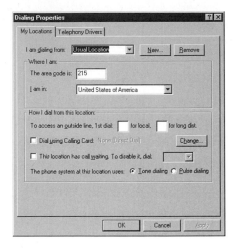

The I am dialing from box defaults to Usual Location and you should start by configuring this default location:

- If you're required to press a telephone key in order To Access an Outside Line, enter the appropriate number (usually a 9) for your phone system. If there's an additional access code (perhaps an 8, or a 0) to permit long distance calls, specify that.

- Dial Using Calling Card is the place to establish the parameters for charging your modem calls. If you use a calling card, enable this selection and choose Change to establish the settings (see fig. 22.12).

FIG. 22.12
You can enter multiple calling card parameters and pick the appropriate one when you're ready to dial.

■ Choose <u>N</u>ew to enter data about a Calling Card. For each Calling Card, enter an identifying name for the Calling Card to <u>u</u>se and then enter your <u>C</u>alling Card Number.

■ Choose <u>A</u>dvanced to establish the dialing rules for dialing when you're using calling cards (see fig. 22.13). Enter the various access phone numbers for using the calling card. You can Copy <u>F</u>rom a previous entry to save keystrokes. Choose Close when you are finished.

FIG. 22.13

Enter the telephone dialing sequences for dialing out under various circumstances.

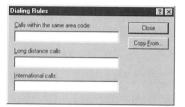

■ This location has call <u>w</u>aiting should be selected if that condition exists. Then specify the correct sequence to dial in the box to disable call waiting. The choices are *70, 70#, and 1170, and you should enter the sequence that the telephone company for this dialing location expects.

■ Select <u>T</u>one Dialing or Pulse Dialing, depending upon the service available at this location.

 If you see a phone with push buttons, don't take it for granted that there's Tone service, especially in offices with older telephone switching equipment. There are telephone instruments with push buttons in Pulse Dialing locations, and each press of a button is translated into a pulse. The way to tell whether or not Tone service is enabled is to press and hold one of the buttons. If the tone persists during the entire time you're holding down the telephone button, Tone service is available. If the tone beeps and stops while you continue to hold down the button, only Pulse service is available.

Once you've completed the configuration of this location, you can configure the next location by choosing <u>N</u>ew from the My Locations tab of the Properties dialog box.

If you only have one location, but you occasionally use the modem to make calls that can be charged to a credit card (especially a company credit card), create a second location. The basic information (area code, accessing outside lines, and so on) will be the same, but the credit card information will already be there.

Understanding Telephony

There's another tab on the Dialing Properties dialog box, entitled Telephony Drivers. The same tab is found on the Telephony Properties dialog box, which is where your Telephony features are configured.

The new Telephony drivers are part of the Windows NT 4.0 improvements to the performance of serial communications. These drivers are the core of Microsoft's new TAPI (Telephony Application Programming Interface).

For users, the most important result of having TAPI is the ability to share a communications port. If you've ever seen the error message "Cannot Initialize Serial Port", you've encountered this problem. Sometimes it happens because you have a communications program running in the background, and you launch another application that wants the modem. More frequently, it's the result of a communications application not releasing (sending an instruction string to close down) the modem and the next application can't connect to it.

TAPI provides standardized methods for software programs that use the serial ports. This does not mean you can make two calls at the same time, but it does mean that programs written for Windows NT 4.0 (which means they use TAPI) will handle the modem properly and you won't get stuck in the middle of a tug of war over the port.

TAPI has a lot more support in it for your serial port; besides that it includes support for:

- PBX services
- PC-based telephony (the telephony hardware is part of the computer)
- LAN services which distribute telephone features across a network
- Voice services to permit voice mail access via your PC (including across a LAN)

UNIMODEM

One of the new concepts for Telephony services is UNIMODEM. This is an architecture used by Windows NT 4.0 that makes use of a single universal modem driver. With UNIMODEM, there's a totally consistent interface to any modem devices on your system. Once you install and configure your modem, all services and software that use the device will find it and use it correctly.

Using Phone Dialer

Windows NT 4.0 includes a phone dialer, a new application you can use to dial your phone. If you want to use this for voice communication, you must have a phone instrument attached to your modem (if you have telephone hardware built into your computer, the phone dialer will interface with it).

To use Phone Dialer:

1. Choose Programs from the Start menu
2. Place your pointer on Accessories.
3. Choose Phone Dialer from the submenu.

The Phone Dialer application launches (see fig. 22.14).

FIG. 22.14
Use the phone dialer
to dial a number
through your
communication port.

4. Enter a number in the Number to dial box (or press the down arrow to see previously dialed numbers and choose one), the choose Dial.

If there are numbers you dial frequently, you can enter them into a speed-dial button. Then all you have to do is click on the entry to dial that number.

You can enter up to eight speed-dial numbers by choosing Speed Dial from the Edit menu. Then use the Edit Speed Dial dialog box to fill in as many buttons as you wish (see fig. 22.15).

FIG. 22.15
The speed dial buttons give you one-click access to numbers you dial frequently.

To enter a new speed dial number:

1. Click on the button you want to use.
2. Enter the name associated with the number in the Name box.
3. Enter the Number to dial.
4. Repeat steps 1 through 3 for each speed dial button you want to configure.
5. Choose Save when you are finished.

You can enter a speed dial number quickly by clicking on a blank button. When the Program Speed Dial dialog box appears (see fig. 22.16), enter a Name and a Number, then choose Save. You can also choose Save and Dial to dial this number immediately.

FIG. 22.16
Just click an empty button and fill in the information for easy storage of speed dial numbers.

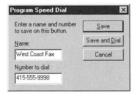

From Here...

Once your modem is installed and running, you can take advantage of all the communications programs that come with Windows NT Workstation 4.0, and any you purchase. For more information on using communications features, read these chapters:

- Chapter 23, "Using Dial-Up Networking."
- Chapter 24, "Configuring TCP/IP."
- Chapter 25, "Using Windows NT with the Internet."
- Chapter 26, "Using Internet Explorer, Internet Mail, and Internet News."
- Chapter 27, "Using Peer Web Services."
- Chapter 29, "Using Windows Messaging."
- Chapter 30, "Using HyperTerminal."

Using Dial-Up Networking

by Kathy Ivens

Dial-Up Networking is a feature that allows you to connect to another computer and work as if you were working on that computer, or to connect to a network that is not part of your local (cabled) network.

In addition to Dial-Up Networking, Windows NT 4.0 also provides Remote Access Service, which permits a workstation to be set up as a host that other computers can dial into.

This means if you have Dial-Up Networking on your home computer and Remote Access Service on your office computer, you could dial in to the office from home and connect to a network server through your office computer.

Or, you could use Dial-Up Networking to create a connection from your office computer to another office computer, or access a company server at a remote location and log on to it. ■

How to install and configure Dial-Up Networking

Learn how to install and configure the hardware and software you'll need in order to connect with other computers via your modem.

Create a phonebook and configure the entries

Learn how to establish protocols, network addresses, and other configuration options for each computer you'll connect to.

Logon to Remote Servers

Learn how to connect to a server that's not part of your cabled LAN.

Customize Dial-Up Networking

Learn about all the customization options, and what they mean to the way you'll use Dial-Up Networking.

Use Remote Access Service to have your workstation act as a host for Dial-Up Networking

Learn how to install and configure Remote Access Service so other computers can dial in to your workstation (and you can dial in to your workstation from home and gain access to the office network).

Dial-Up Networking also provides features for Internet connections.

▶ **See** "Using Windows NT with the Internet," **p. 673** ■

Hardware and Protocols

The hardware you need for Dial-Up Networking (and for Remote Access Service) has to be installed before you begin installing the software. You need one of these peripherals:

- A network adapter card if you're part of a cabled network
- A modem
- An X.25 smart card, if you're on an X.25 network
- An ISDN adapter if you are using an ISDN line

Actually, it's possible to have more than one of the above peripherals on your workstation. For example, you may have a network adapter and also have a modem for dialing out to computers that aren't part of the network.

Understanding the Hardware Terminology

It's probably a good idea to take a brief look at what some of these hardware choices represent, and define some of the terms.

Network Adapters

A network adapter, which is also called a *network interface card* (*NIC*), is a board that is inserted in a computer in order to provide a link to the cable that connects the computer to a network. The type of cable varies, matching the topology choices made by the network administrator. It might be thick or thin cable with a connector, or it might look like telephone cable with a connection that looks like a standard telephone jack and connector.

LAN

A *LAN* (*local area network*) is a network of computers that are connected together by cable and are all in the same physical location.

WAN

WANs (wide area networks) are computers that are indirectly connected. Usually, this means a telephone line. Frequently, WANs are made up of linked LANs.

For example, the LAN in the executive offices of a company may be connected to another LAN that's in a remote warehouse or manufacturing facility. There's a computer at each end that handles the WAN connection between the two, which is accessible by everyone on the LAN. Everyone on each LAN can reach the other LAN through the WAN connection.

Or, the main office of a retail company may have a computer that is accessed by a lot of different computers in the stores. The WAN connection means that transactions in the stores are sent in real-time to the main computer so that inventory and revenue is tracked.

There are numerous combinations and permutations for LAN/WAN setups, but the principles and definitions involved are always the same.

Part
VI

Ch
23

Installing Dial-Up Networking

Once you've made the hardware decisions and installed the resulting peripherals, it's time to install the software.

N O T E If you've upgraded from Windows NT 3.51, and are familiar with Remote Access Service, you should be aware that Dial-Up Networking replaces the dial-out component of RAS. During the installation and configuration of Dial-Up Networking, you'll see dialog boxes and references connected to RAS. This is because the serial port functions and device configuration options are still part of RAS. Also, RAS continues to be the software application you'll use for receiving calls, and information about that is also found in this chapter. ▪

Dial-Up Networking is not installed automatically when you install your Windows NT Workstation 4.0 operating system. In order to add the software, you'll need your original Windows NT media (disks or CD-ROM). Then follow these steps:

1. Open My Computer and double-click the Dial-Up Networking icon. The Dial-Up Networking dialog box displays to ask you if you wish to install the software. Choose Install.

2. The Windows NT Setup dialog box appears and you must enter the location of your Windows NT original media (usually **D:\i386**, where D is the drive letter for your CD-ROM). Press Continue when you have entered the location.

3. The necessary files are transferred to your hard drive (you can watch the progress in the Remote Access Service Setup dialog box).

4. After the files are copied, the Add RAS Device dialog box automatically appears, and any ports that contain devices that can be used for Dial-Up Networking are listed in the RAS Capable <u>D</u>evices box (see fig. 23.1). Select the ports you'll be using for Dial-Up Networking, then choose OK.

FIG. 23.1
The Add RAS Device dialog box displays the ports that are capable of functioning with RAS, along with any attached devices.

CAUTION

If no port is listed, you have to cancel this installation and install the ports from the Control Panel. If ports are listed, but the device you want to use for Dial-Up Networking isn't listed, you can add the device from this dialog box. Choose Install Modem or Install X.25 PAD to install the device.

Configuring Dial-Up Networking

Once the installation program has produced a listing of valid RAS ports and devices, you can begin the configuration process. Before that, however, we should point out that there are three installation procedures available from this dialog box:

■ You can <u>A</u>dd a port, which takes you back through the installation process so you can make a new port available and install a communications device on that port.

■ You can Remove a port to make it unavailable to RAS.

■ You can Clone a modem to copy its setup from one port to another.

To complete the configuration, follow these steps:

1. Select a port, then choose Configure to see the configuration for the port in the Configure Port Usage dialog box (see fig. 23.2).

FIG. 23.2
The default configuration of Dial out only is all you need to use Dial-Up Networking.

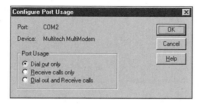

2. Choose OK to return to the Remote Access Setup dialog box, then choose Network.

3. In the Network Configuration dialog box, choose all the protocols you need to connect to other computers (see fig. 23.3).

FIG. 23.3
Install all the protocols you'll need for the various connections you plan to make with Dial-Up Networking.

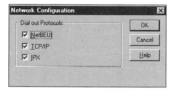

4. Select the protocols you want to be able to use. The available choices are:

■ NetBEUI (Generally Microsoft Networks)

■ TCP/IP (Generally UNIX or Internet)

■ IPX (Novell NetWare networks)

 TIP Multiple protocols are available because there may be a variety of protocols needed by the various host computers you will be accessing.

5. Choose OK to return to the Remote Access Setup dialog box. Then choose Continue. The files are installed and configured to match your choices.

Configuring TCP/IP

If you selected TCP/IP, a unique IP address must be assigned to use when connecting with the server (see fig. 23.4). The network administrator for the host computer will be able to give you the correct IP address.

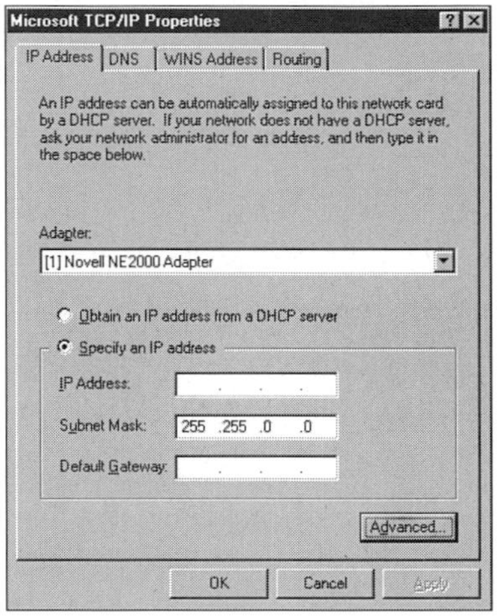

FIG. 23.4
Enter the IP Address to use for the host computer you're dialing into.

If the host computer is using *DHCP (Dynamic Host Configuration Protocol),* you do not have to set the TCP/IP parameters because your TCP/IP connection will be configured by the host when you connect. Without going into a great deal of technical explanation, a DHCP host is one that has been set up to manage IP addresses (instead of accepting one from the client computer that is dialing in). The DHCP host has a mechanism for allocating the TCP/IP parameters, and also has a protocol for communicating this information to the client computer.

At the host end, there are several methods for allocating IP addresses:

- Addresses can be allocated manually by an administrator and then given to client computers as they dial in.

- Addresses can be allocated automatically and the information sent to the client computer. This address is a permanent assignment; whenever that client computer dials in, it gets its IP address.

- Addresses can be allocated dynamically, and as client computers dial in and exit, the address is available for the next client.

The dynamic allocation of addresses is the most common for host computers that serve a large number of dial-in clients that create temporary connections in order to perform some task, then exit. The pool of addresses is available on a "next-up" basis.

Once all the processes are completed, you have to shut down and restart the computer (you see a message to that effect).

Creating the Phonebook

The first time you use Dial-Up Networking (Open My Computer and double-click the Dial-Up Networking icon), a message displays to tell you that the phonebook is empty. The phonebook provides all the information about each remote computer you dial into. Choose OK to begin adding entries to the phonebook. The New Phonebook Entry Wizard launches to walk you through the process of adding and configuring an entry (see fig. 23.5).

FIG. 23.5
The New Phonebook Entry Wizard starts the process of configuring the settings for dialing in to a remote computer.

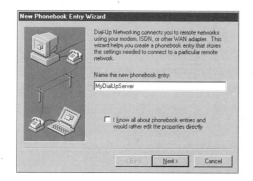

To establish a phonebook entry with the wizard, follow these steps:

1. On the first page, enter a name for this entry in the Name the New Phonebook Entry box. A default name, MyDialUpServer, which you can use if there's only one server you can connect to, is displayed. Otherwise, enter a name that means something to you. Then choose Next.

2. On the Server page (see fig. 23.6), select any conditions that apply to this connection, choosing from these options:

FIG. 23.6
Select any conditions that apply to this connection—you can choose none, one, or as many as you need.

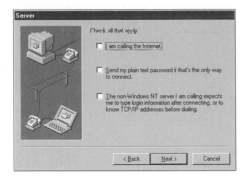

■ I am Calling the Internet, which you can use to dial into your Internet provider (you must have installed TCP/IP to dial into the Internet).

■ Send My Plain Text Password if That's the Only Way to Connect, which you use to dial into a host computer that is expecting to receive a text password.

■ The non-Windows NT Server I am Calling Expects Me to Type Login Information After Connecting, or to Know TCP/IP Addresses Before Dialing, which you use to logon to a host running network software other than NT Server.

3. Choose Next to enter the phone number for the host computer. You can also enter alternate phone numbers, if they exist, so that if the primary number cannot be reached Dial-Up Networking automatically tries the next alternate number. Then choose Next, and choose Finish when the last Wizard page appears to tell you that the process is complete.

N O T E The phone number field for an ISDN connection is handled in a special way if you're dealing with three or more channels in your ISDN line. In order to dial an ISDN connection, you have to specify a telephone number for each channel you're requesting, separating the numbers by a colon. For example, your entry might look like this:

848-9999:848-8888:848-7777

However, to make things simpler, if you have a two-channel ISDN line, you can probably enter only one phone number because most ISDN services automatically use the last number it sees for a single empty channel. Multiple empty channels present a problem, which is why you need to enter two numbers if you have three channels on your line. Incidentally, the numbers can be the same.

On the other hand, to make things more complicated, some ISDN providers require unique numbers for each channel. ■

Adding Phonebook Entries Manually

If you're comfortable with dialing parameters, connection protocols, and all the other settings needed to connect to another computer, you can enter the information manually by selecting the Wizard check box labeled I Know All About Phonebook Entries And Would Rather Edit The Properties Directly.

Manual phonebook entries are accomplished with the New Phonebook Entry dialog box (see fig. 23.7). The information needed on each tab should be self-explanatory (ask the network administrator about any configuration options you can't fill in, such as IP addresses).

FIG. 23.7
Use the New Phonebook Entry dialog box to add host computers to your Dial-Up Networking phonebook—if you're comfortable with communication issues, it's frequently faster than using the wizard.

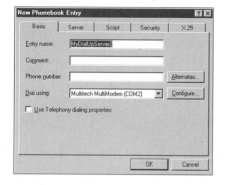

Using Dial-Up Networking

Once you have at least one phonebook entry, you're ready to use Dial-Up Networking. When you double-click the icon in My Computer, the Dial-Up Networking dialog box appears (see fig. 23.8).

FIG. 23.8
When the Dial-Up Networking dialog box appears, click the arrow to the right of the Phonebook Entry to Dial box, and pick the host computer you want to connect to.

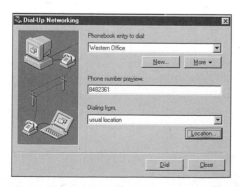

Choose an entry, then choose Dial to begin the connection. If this connection was configured for a password, you'll have to enter one (see fig. 23.9). After you enter your password, select Save Password to bypass this step in the future.

CAUTION

If you choose to save the password and bypass the authentication dialog box, the only way to change your password is to edit the phonebook entry. Move to the Security tab and select Unsave Password. The authentication dialog box reappears the next time you dial out to this connection.

FIG. 23.9
If the connection has been configured to request a password, this authentication dialog box automatically appears.

Customizing Dial-Up Networking

The Dial-Up Networking dialog box has a number of features you can use to manage your phonebook.

Choose New to add another entry to your phonebook. Choose More to perform any of the following tasks:

- Edit Entry and Modem Properties, which brings up the Edit Phonebook Entry dialog box so you can make any necessary changes to the entry's configuration.

- Clone Entry and Modem Properties, which brings up a Phone Entry dialog box with configuration information that duplicates the current entry. This is extremely useful if you want to add an entry that is almost identical to the current one—usually you just have to change the name and/or phone number.

- Delete Entry, which removes the current entry from your phonebook (you are asked to confirm the deletion).

■ Monitor Status, which displays the Dial-Up Networking Monitor dialog box (more information about the Monitor is found in the section "Using the Dial-Up Networking Monitor," later in this chapter).

■ Operator Assisted or Manual Dialing, which toggles this feature off and on. When selected, you have to lift the receiver of the phone instrument attached to the modem and dial an operator directly into the host. When you connect to the host (you usually hear a tone or a squeal), click Connect, then hang up the instrument.

■ User Preferences, which lets you set options for the way you want to use Dial-Up Networking. See the section on Configuring Preferences in this chapter.

■ Logon Preferences, which establishes the options for using Dial-Up Networking when you first log onto Windows NT 4.0.

▶ **See** "Logging On to NT Workstation," **p. 30**

Using Scripts

You can use a script to automate your login to any host (except another NT machine, which does not require any script). A script provides, to the host computer, all the information you normally have to type during the connection process. Most of the time (as in Internet connections), the script is run after you dial in and connect to the host computer.

Windows provides a script file named SWITCH.INF for you to use when you want to configure a script. It is a text file that is really multiple scripts all contained in one file, and there are simple instructions for customizing the script you need. To access it, open it from the \SYSTEM21\RAS subfolder under the folder that holds your Windows NT software.

Your script has six parts to it:

■ Section header (which is the name you give your customized script)

■ Comment lines (for writing notes to explain the customized entries)

■ Commands (the commands or responses that are sent to the host)

- Responses (the responses to your commands that you expect from the host computer)

- Response keywords (the words in a response that specify what to do when the response is received)

- Macros (special functions such as the insertion of a carriage return)

SWITCH.INF supplies samples of each element and explanations of how they are used.

Once you have a script, you can implement it by moving to the Script tab in any Phone Entry dialog box (choose More, Edit Entry, from the Dial-Up Networking window), and choosing Run This Script. The name you assign is the name you give the section header of SWITCH.INF, and Dial-Up Networking searches for the right header and executes the script. You can have as many scripts as you need for all your Dial-Up Networking hosts.

Using the Dial-Up Networking Monitor

You can see the status of a connection while it's in progress by viewing the Dial-Up Networking Monitor. To display the monitor, open the More submenu in the Dial-Up Networking dialog box and choose Monitor Status (or double-click the Dial-Up Networking Monitor icon in the Control Panel).

In addition to the statistics displayed on the Status tab (see fig. 23.10), you can also set preferences for monitoring active connections.

FIG. 23.10
You can view the status of the current connection, including speed, compression information, and any errors that have occurred.

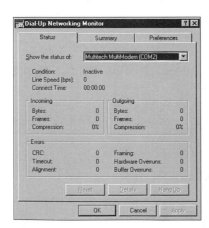

There are two other tabs on the monitor. The Summary tab displays information about the user and network that are connected. The Preferences tab gives you choices about the way you want to monitor connections (see fig. 23.11).

FIG. 23.11
You can configure the options for monitoring a connection and for displaying the status of the connection on your screen.

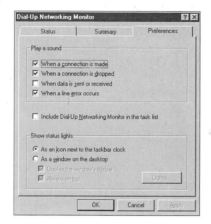

Select or deselect options for monitoring Dial-Up Networking connections by following these guidelines:

1. Choose whether or not you want an audio alert when one of these events occurs:

   ▪ When a Connection is Made

   ▪ When a Connection is Dropped

   ▪ When Data is Sent or Received

   ▪ When a Line Error Occurs

2. Choose whether or not you want to put an icon for Dial-Up Networking on the taskbar.

3. Select the manner in which you want status information to display on your screen:

   ▪ As an Icon Next to the Taskbar Clock

   ▪ As a Window on the Desktop

4. If you choose to place a status window on the desktop, select the configuration for the window by choosing from these options:

   ▪ Display the Window's Titlebar

- Keep the Window Always on <u>T</u>op
- You can click <u>L</u>ights to choose between displaying the status of all devices or just one specific port

Configuring Preferences

To configure the way you want Dial-Up Networking to work for you, open the application and choose <u>M</u>ore, User Preferences. The User Preferences dialog box displays so you can set the options you want when you use Dial-Up Networking.

Dialing Preferences

Use the Dialing tab to have the software autodial a host computer, choosing a different host for each of your locations. For example, if you've established a location for your home, when you launch Dial-Up Networking from that location it will autodial your office computer. For a location you've configured on your office computer, you might create an autodial to a remote server in your organization.

Callback Preferences

Use the Callback tab to create the callback option, which means that when a connection is made and the user is authenticated, the server hangs up the line and then calls the dialing computer back. This is accomplished either by presenting a Callback dialog box and having the client computer enter the telephone number that should be called by the host, or by dialing a preset telephone number. More information about configuring callback options is found in "Managing Users," later in this chapter.

You can opt to skip this feature, invoke it on a call-by-call basis, or choose it as a permanent configuration option.

Appearance Preferences

On the Appearance tab (see fig. 23.12), select whether or not you want specific items to display in the Dial-Up Networking dialog box. The choices are self-explanatory.

FIG. 23.12
You can choose the functions and features you want to see as you work in Dial-Up Networking.

Phonebook Preferences

Use the Phonebook tab to choose a different phonebook when you use Dial-Up Networking. By default, the system phonebook is the designated phonebook, but you can select either a personal phonebook, or another alternate phonebook.

If you choose a personal phonebook, one is created immediately and the contents of the system phonebook are duplicated within it, and you can add more entries as needed. If another user shares your computer with his or her own profile, only the system phonebook is available (or a personal phonebook created by that user) and your personal phonebook remains private. The personal phonebook is stored in the WINDOWSDIRECTORY\SYSTEM32\RAS folder with your logon name as the file name (the system phonebook is stored in the same place with the file name of rasphone).

You can choose an alternate phonebook outside of the \SYSTEM32\RAS subfolder, which is useful for accessing a phonebook on another computer on the network. Choose Browse to find the folder and file you need.

Using Remote Access Service

The other side of Dial-Up Networking is Remote Access Service (RAS), software that runs the host capabilities of a computer when another computer dials in. When your computer is acting as a host it is called an RAS Server.

If you've installed Dial-Up Networking, some of the RAS installation is already accomplished because Dial-Up Networking uses RAS features.

However, for this section assume you haven't installed Dial-Up Networking, and I cover the installation and configuration of RAS. (For many users, it's probable that RAS will be installed on the computer at work and Dial-Up Networking on the computer at home so that telecommuting is in effect).

Installing RAS

RAS is a network service in Windows NT Workstation 4.0 and is installed from the Network icon in the Control Panel. Double-click the Network icon and move to the Services tab, then follow these steps:

1. Choose Add and then choose Remote Access Service from the Network Service box. Choose OK.

2. Enter the path for the Windows NT files (usually **\d:i386**, where d is the drive letter for your CD-ROM) and choose OK.

3. The Remote Access Service files are transferred to your hard drive, and then the Add RAS device dialog box displays a list of RAS capable devices. Choose OK to accept the list, or choose Install Modem, or Install X25 Pad if the list does not include a device attached to the displayed modem.

4. When the Remote Access Setup dialog box appears, choose Configure to configure the port usage. For this exercise, we'll configure this port to receive calls only, then choose OK.

5. When you are returned to the Remote Access Setup dialog box, choose Network to establish network settings for client computers that will dial in. The Network Configuration dialog box appears (see fig. 23.13), and you must set the configuration options for each network protocol you'll need.

FIG. 23.13
If you've configured your RAS ports and devices for receiving calls, you must set the options for allowing client computers to dial in.

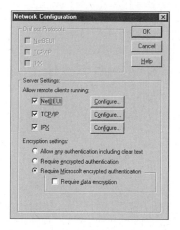

Configuring NetBEUI

For NetBEUI clients, you have to select the level of access you'll permit:

- Choose Entire Network to let clients access the LAN through your workstation.
- Choose This Computer Only, to restrict access to the resources on your workstation.

Configuring TCP/IP

For TCP/IP, the same choices regarding access are available. In addition, you need to configure TCP/IP addresses (see fig. 23.14).

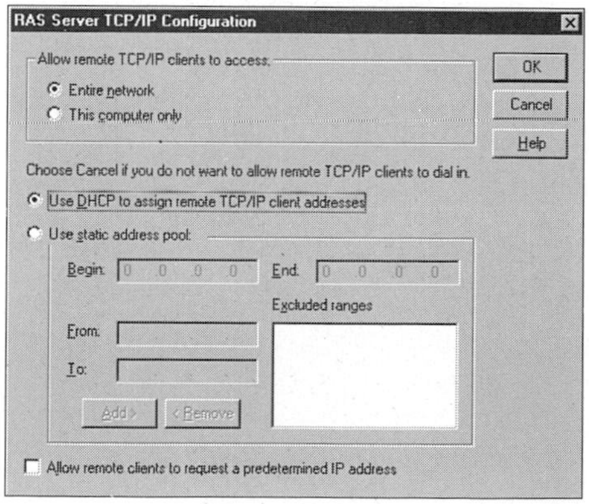

FIG. 23.14
Use the RAS Server TCP/IP Configuration dialog box to set the level of access and to specify IP addresses.

- Choose Use <u>D</u>HCP if you want clients to obtain IP addresses from a dynamic host configuration protocol. Of course, you must have a DHCP server on your network to offer this option.

- Choose Use <u>S</u>tatic Address Pool to have a range of IP addresses available for assignment to clients. Enter the <u>B</u>egin and <u>E</u>nd addresses for the clients.

- To exclude a part of the range, use <u>F</u>rom and <u>T</u>o to enter a beginning and ending address for the subrange you want to exclude. Then choose <u>A</u>dd to add the subrange to the E<u>x</u>cluded Ranges list. You can enter as many excluded ranges as you wish. If you want to remove an excluded range and make it available to clients again, select it in the E<u>x</u>cluded Ranges box, then choose <u>R</u>emove.

- To let clients request a specific address, choose A<u>l</u>low Remote Clients to Request a Predetermined IP Address (predetermined means the address will be part of their configuration for the dial-up entry they use when calling into your workstation).

Configuring IPX

For IPX clients, a level of access choices are available and you must also choose a system for allocating network numbers, and decide how to assign those network numbers to dialed-in clients (see fig. 23.15).

FIG. 23.15
Your computer must provide an IPX network number to dialed-in clients on an IPX network.

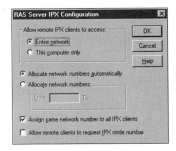

- Choose Allocate Network Numbers <u>A</u>utomatically if you want to assign a network number currently not in use to any RAS client that dials in.

- Choose Allocate Network Numbers if you want to reserve a range of network numbers for dialed-in clients. Specify the first number in the From box and RAS will calculate the number for the To box by determining the number of available ports.

- Choose Assign Same Network Number to All IPX Clients if you want to have all dialed-in clients use the same number. One network number will be added to your routing table. If you deselect this option, a network number will be added to your routing table for each dialed-in RAS client.

- Choose Allow Remote Clients to Request IPX Node Number to let remote clients choose a number other than that provided by the RAS server.

> **CAUTION**
>
> Clients who choose their own node numbers really are choosing existing node numbers and have the same access to your computer or server that the last user of that number had. If security is an issue, you should not select this option.

Encryption Settings

Use the Encryption settings section of the Network Configuration dialog box to establish authentication standards for clients who are dialing in:

- Choose Allow Any Authentication Including Clear Text if you want to permit connections using anything requested by the client. If you have clients dialing in who are using different client software, this is the option you should select.

- Choose Require Encrypted Authentication if you want to insist on encrypted passwords from all clients. Actually, this choice excludes only PAP, and will permit any other authentication requested.

- Choose Require Microsoft Encrypted Authentication to limit authentication to MS-CHAP. You can also select Require data encryption if you want to make sure that all data being sent is encrypted. RAS provides such data encryption capabilities, so this works well if all clients are using RAS.

Complete the Configuration

Once you have completed the protocol configuration, choose OK to return to the Remote Access Setup dialog box. Then choose Continue. The necessary files are transferred to your hard drive and you are returned to the Network dialog box.

When you close the Network dialog box, the bindings are reviewed and stored. You must then shut down and restart the computer in order to have the new settings take effect.

Administering RAS

You can manage the RAS server functions with the RAS Admin tool. It's found in the Administrative Tools program group.

When you first launch Remote Access Admin it shows the current status of RAS (see fig. 23.16).

FIG. 23.16
The Admin window shows that Remote Access Service is running on this workstation for both the local computer and the domain server.

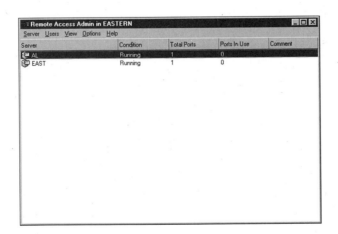

 TIP   If RAS is not running, choose Server, Start Remote Access Service.

There are some RAS functions you can manipulate and manage from the Remote Access Admin window.

Managing Servers

The Server menu provides several management features for RAS:

- You can Start, Stop, Pause, or Continue Remote Access Service.

- You can choose Communication Ports, then select a port to view the Port Status, Disconnect the User attached to the port, Send a Message to the User attached to the port or choose Send to All to send a message to all users on the server.

- You can choose Select Domain or Server to add a server to your RAS service, which means you can use your workstation as an RAS server for another server (clients dialing in reach that server through your computer).

TROUBLESHOOTING

In order to dial in from home and access the network information I need, I have to be able to get to my workstation, then to a server on a remote domain that's part of our WAN. The domain isn't listed on the Select Domain dialog box. How do I make my workstation see a server for that domain? There is no trust relationship between your server and the remote server. The Select Domain dialog box lists only those domains that are trusted by the domain you belong to (the domain you log on to). If you want to be able to access an unlisted domain server, you (or your network administrator) must establish a trust relationship with that domain.

Managing Users

From the Users menu of the RAS Admin window, you can choose Permissions to configure dial-in rights for users (see fig. 23.17).

FIG. 23.17
Only users with network accounts can be managed with Remote Access Admin. You cannot create new user accounts from this application.

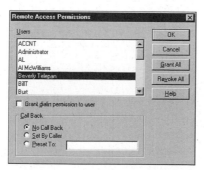

You can give users the right to dial in to your RAS server, which gives them all the permissions you've configured in your RAS software.

- To give all users permission to dial in, choose Grant All.

- Or, you can select individual user names from the Users list box and then choose Grant Dialin Permission to User.

- If you've granted dialin rights to all users and then decide to select only certain users, choose Revoke All and then individually select users for dialin permission.

You can also establish call back rights for each user from this dialog box:

- Choose No Call Back to refuse any request for calling back when this user dials in.

- Choose Set by Caller to have RAS services ask the user for a number to call back.

- Choose Preset To in order to have the server call this user at a specific telephone number, which you must fill in.

 TIP You can set user permissions and call back options for any individual user through the Windows NT User Manager in the Administrative Tools program group. Double-click a user (or select a user and choose User, Properties), then click Dialin on the User Properties dialog box.

You can also manage users who are working on your workstation. Choose Users, Active Users to display a list of users who are currently dialed in. You can select any user and perform any of these actions:

- Choose User Account to see the account details for the user.

- Choose Disconnect User to end the user's dialin session.

- Choose Send Message to send a message to the user (you can also choose Send to All to send a message to all dialed-in users).

The View menu has a Refresh command, and the Options menu offers commands for Low Speed Connections (turns off network browsing for users and permissions to save time), and Save Settings on Exit.

Tips on Working with a Dialed-In Connection

No matter how fast your modem is, or how fast a telephone line is that you're connected to, it's slow when compared to using files on your own computer or on a server to which your computer is attached by cable. However, there are a few rules you can follow that make everything more productive.

Part VI

Ch 23

Don't Run Software Remotely

If you dial in to send or fetch a file, that's a good use of a dial-up connection. However, dialing in to run software from another machine is not generally a good idea, since it's neither productive nor safe.

Accessing and using a database from a remote computer is an exercise in frustration. Your screen changes are slow, and it takes time to send your data back to the remote machine. These slow responses aren't just your problem because most of the time your snail-like processing affects all the cabled-in users of that software. This is not a great way to make friends. Of course, if you have an ISDN line most of the speed problems go away.

It's much more productive to purchase a copy of the software for local use, then upload data or reports to the host machine.

Even client/server packages, which split the processing burden between the workstation and the host/server, aren't good candidates for telephone processing (although for short periods in an emergency it may be a passable system).

Besides that, it can be dangerous to the integrity of data. Telephone lines aren't all that reliable, especially standard telephone lines. Sending data that includes static or extraneous noises can corrupt the data at the other end.

From Here...

This chapter taught you how to connect to the Internet using Dial-Up Networking and how to install and configure Dial-Up Networking. For more information concerning working with the Internet, see the following chapters:

- Chapter 22, "Installing and Configuring a Modem."
- Chapter 24, "Configuring TCP/IP."
- Chapter 25, "Using Windows NT with the Internet."

Configuring TCP/IP

by Kevin Jones

TCP/IP, or Transmission Control Protocol/ Internet Protocol, is the networking protocol of the Internet. It is the most widely supported network protocol, running from large super-computers down to small networks. And because it is the protocol of the Internet, if you want to take your Windows NT workstation for a drive down the Internet, you have to use TCP/IP.

TCP/IP isn't something that you normally inter-act with directly, but because so many services rely on TCP/IP to function, a basic understand-ing of what TCP/IP is and what it provides is extremely useful. ■

The basics of TCP/IP, includ-ing WINS and DHCP

You need to understand all of the bits and pieces of TCP/IP to con-figure and troubleshoot using TCP/IP on your workstation.

How to install and configure TCP/IP on your computer

Getting TCP/IP installed and configured is not trivial. There is a lot of information you need to understand before you begin the process.

Learn about using advanced features of TCP/IP

As your network grows, Windows NT 4.0 provides some useful tools to help maintain your LAN.

How to set up an FTP server on your workstation

You can use the built-in FTP server to share across your intranet, as well as across the Internet. But you should carefully consider all the security issues.

TCP/IP Basics

When you install TCP/IP, you are asked to configure a number of different subsystems. Because these subsystems are interrelated, it is a good idea to have an understanding of all of these services before you begin installing TCP/IP.

The beginnings of TCP/IP can be traced back to the ARPANET. The ARPANET (Advanced Research Projects Agency's Network) began in 1971. Because a standard protocol was needed to support communication between the different computers on the ARPANET, TCP/IP was proposed in 1973. TCP/IP didn't become standardized until 1982, but its appeal was still very limited. It took two events in 1983 to give TCP/IP widespread acceptance. First, the Office of the Secretary of Defense required all Defense Department computers that were connected to long-haul networks to use TCP/IP. Second, the University of California at Berkley released a version of UNIX that contained TCP/IP. Since UNIX was widely used by university computer science departments, the usage of TCP/IP became widespread in computer science research.

TCP/IP is actually a set of complementary protocols. Taken together, they allow information to be divided into small packets and sent across the Internet. These packets may take different routes and arrive in a different order than they were sent. Once all the packets arrive, they are reassembled into the original information. This provides for a robust communications mechanism.

TCP is the protocol used by applications such as FTP (File Transfer Protocol), Telnet, and NFS (Network File System) to package information into packets that will be transported across the Internet. After the packets arrive at their destination, TCP is used on the other end to put them into the correct order.

IP is the protocol that is used to transport the TCP packets across the Internet. The IP protocol assures that the packages eventually get to the correct destination. It does not assure the route that the information will take on its journey from one computer to another.

N O T E The ARPANET, and therefore the Internet, was designed to support military efforts during war. The design was such that if information could not be transported from one machine to another, the information would be rerouted again and again, until it finally reached the correct destination. Fortunately, we never needed to use the networks under such conditions. However, servers do go offline and connections do get broken, but because of TCP/IP, the information will get to its final destination. ▪

TCP/IP Addressing

An IP address consists of four numbers separated by periods. Each number, called a cell, can range from 0 to 255. The addresses are logically divided into different classes, based on the first number. The classes, A–C, are used to provide organizations with ranges of IP addresses.

- ▪ *Class A—Large organizations.* These start with a cell value of 0–126.
- ▪ *Class B—Medium-sized organizations.* They receive IP addresses starting with 128–191.
- ▪ *Class C—Small organizations.* They receive IP addresses starting with 192–223.

You probably noticed that some addresses are not used. These are reserved for special uses. Table 24.1 shows the breakdown of these classes and the number of nodes (or unique IP addresses) available.

Table 24.1 IP Addressing Classes

Address Class	Example	Number of Nodes
A	(100.50.50.50)	16,777,216
B	(175.50.50.50)	65,534
C	(200.50.50.50)	254

A Class A address only specifies the first cell. A Class B address specifies the first two cells. A Class C address specifies the first three cells. So, for example, a company may get a Class C address of 200.50.50.0. This enables it to have 254 unique IP address that it can assign to its users and computers. A Class B address might be specified as 175.50.0.0. This enables the company to have 65,534 unique IP addresses (for example, 175.50.1.1 and 175.50.200.45).

NOTE You may have noticed that not all possible IP addresses are used. Specifically, address 127 is reserved for loopback testing. It should never be sent across a network. Addresses above 223 are reserved for special uses, such as multicast addressing. ■

If a company has a Class A or B address, it may want to divide the network into subnets. TCP/IP has a mechanism that helps make this easy. By using what is called a *subnet mask*, it can separate the IP address in the network ID component and the host ID component. For example, a Class B address of 175.50.200.45 has a network ID of 175.50.0.0, and a host ID of 0.0.200.45. The subnet mask consists of an IP-like address, but the values are either 0 (host) or 255 (network). So the subnet mask for a Class B IP address is 255.255.0.0.

Therefore, if your company had 10 branch offices with 50 computers in each office, you could get 10 Class C IP addresses. However, it would be very maintenance-intensive to have these sites communicate. Alternatively, you could get one Class B address and assign each of the branch offices its own subnet. This makes maintaining sites much easier.

Understanding DHCP

Because each computer in your network needs to have a unique IP address, your system administrator may assign you an IP address. You'll use this value when you configure TCP/IP. However, maintaining a list of who has which IP address is difficult, and providing dedicated IP addresses for computers that are used infrequently can quickly deplete the available IP addresses. To solve this problem, Windows NT supports what is known as *Dynamic Host Configuration Protocol* (*DHCP*). By using this protocol, your computer asks for an IP address when it starts up. The DHCP Server maintains a list of available IP addresses and assigns your computer one of the available IP address. This IP address is "leased" to your computer for a period of time. As this lease period ends, your computer will renew the lease. If your computer was not on the network when the lease expired (plus a little grace period), your computer will request a new IP address when you next connect to the network.

If your network is using DHCP, your system administrator provides you with the IP address of the DHCP Server. You need this address when you configure TCP/IP.

Understanding DNS

Another problem with IP addresses is that users don't remember numbers. People like names much better, so names are typically used when interacting with a user. These names have a specific IP address. When your computer needs to make a request, it must resolve the name the user supplied to an IP address that can be used by the TCP/IP service. To handle this, a Domain Name System (DNS) Server is used. This server keeps a list of computer names and IP address. For example, the name of the Web Server for Macmillan Publishing is **www.mcp.com**. This is much simpler to remember than an IP address.

This DNS Server has its own unique IP address. Your system administrator supplies you with this address, which you use when you configure TCP/IP.

Understanding WINS

Some system services require mapping IP addresses to computer names. Since IP addresses can change, especially when using DHCP or when moving computers between subnets, keeping this mapping correct can be very time-consuming.

To handle this new situation, a *Windows Internet Naming Service* (*WINS*) Server is used. This server is very similar to a DNS Server, but maps IP addresses to NETBIOS/NETBEUI computer names.

Your system administrator tells you whether or not you are using WINS, and if so, gives you the IP address of the WINS Server.

Understanding SNMP

The final protocol you need to know about before you install TCP/IP is *SNMP*, (*Simple Network Management Protocol*). SNMP is a protocol that is used to enable system administrators to monitor and administer computers and gateways on the network. For SNMP to function properly, each computer must run an SNMP agent that monitors your local computer and sends the information to appropriate computer(s) on the network. The system administrator must run another program that accepts the information sent by the agent, and then does whatever is appropriate.

Your system administrator can instruct you to install SNMP software when you install TCP/IP. If so, you need to know the names of the communities (groups of hosts) to which your computer belongs and the addresses of the specific host(s) to which certain information should be sent.

If there are other specific requirements, your system administrator gives you additional information on security and agent configuration, which you need when you configure SNMP.

Installing TCP/IP

To install TCP/IP you must either perform a Custom setup, or, if Windows NT is already installed, you can use the Network item in the Control Panel to install TCP/IP.

Before you begin, however, you need to find out the following information from your system administrator:

- Can you use DHCP to configure your computer? If you can, you have the option of enabling this feature when you install TCP/IP.
- Will your computer be a WINS proxy agent? In other words, will other computers access a WINS Server through your computer?

If you can't use DHCP, you must find out some other information for manually configuring TCP/IP:

- The IP address and subnet mask for your computer. You need one IP address and subnet mask for each network adapter card installed in your computer.
- The IP address of the default local gateway. This may also be called an *IP gateway* or *IP router*.
- Will you be using Domain Name System (DNS)? If so, you need to get the IP address of the DNS Server(s).
- Are there WINS Servers on your network? If there are, you need their addresses, too.

Finally, if you are going to install SNMP, you need to find out the following:

■ All of the Community names for your network.

■ The Trap destination for each community on your network.

■ The IP addresses and computer names for all the SNMP hosts on your network.

For more information on SNMP, see "Configuring SNMP" later in this chapter.

 TIP If you installed Windows NT Workstation by using the Express Setup, TCP/IP was not installed. You must use the Network Control Panel item to add the TCP/IP protocol.

Part
VI

Ch
24

To install TCP/IP follow these steps:

1. From Control Panel, open the Network item by double-clicking it. The Network dialog box appears.

2. Select the Protocols tab (see fig. 24.1).

FIG. 24.1
The Network dialog box appears while installing TCP/IP.

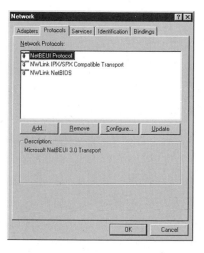

3. Choose Add. The Select Network Protocol dialog box appears.

4. Select TCP/IP Protocol in the Network Protocol list box. Choose OK.

5. The TCP/IP Setup dialog box appears. Choose Yes if you want to have your TCP/IP parameters automatically set by a DHCP server when you restart your computer. Choose No to set your TCP/IP parameters manually.

6. The Windows NT Setup dialog box appears. Type in the full path where the Windows NT setup files are located. Choose OK.

7. Select the Services tab.

8. Choose Add. The Select Network Service dialog box appears.

9. Choose the option you want to install, and then choose OK. The options are detailed in table 24.2. If you install the FTP Server or the SNMP Service, you will be prompted to configure them at this time. See the sections on configuring these options later in the chapter—"Configuring SNMP" and "Configuring FTP Services."

10. The Windows NT Setup dialog box appears. Type in the full path where the Windows NT setup files are located. Choose OK.

11. Repeat steps 9 and 10 for each Service you want to install.

12. Choose OK.

13. Depending on the services you installed, and your particular setup, you may be prompted to restart Windows. If you are, choose Yes. Windows will restart.

TIP If you install Windows NT from a CD-ROM drive and are running an Intel-based computer, the path for the distribution files is \I386 (that is, D:\I386).

Table 24.2 TCP/IP Installation Options

TCP/IP Option	Description
Connectivity Utilities	This option installs both the connectivity utilities (finger, ftp, lpr, tcp, rexec, rsh, telnet, and tftp) and the diagnostic utilities (arp, hostname, ipconfig, lpq, nbtstat, netstat, ping, route, and tracert).
SNMP Utilities	This option installs the SNMP services. These services enable your computer to be administered remotely, using network management tools such as HP Open View or Sun Net Manager.

TCP/IP Option	Description
TCP/IP Network Printing Support	This option installs services to enable you to print to printers attached to UNIX computers (or to TCP/IP printers directly connected to the network), as well as enable UNIX computers to print to printers attached to your computer.
FTP Server Services	This option enables you to provide access to files on your computer using FTP and TCP/IP.
Simple TCP/IP Services	This option installs some common UNIX utilities (Chargen, Daytime, Discard, Echo, and Quote) so that your computer can respond to such request from other computers.

Part VI

Ch 24

Configuring Your TCP/IP Address

If you enabled DHCP, your computer automatically gets its configuration information from the DHCP server. However, if you didn't enable DHCP, you need to configure TCP/IP. You need all of the information your system administrator gave you before you began installing TCP/IP.

> **CAUTION**
>
> In general, you should not manually set any configuration information if DHCP is available. If you began with DHCP enabled and make any changes to the configuration settings, these settings will override the values specified from the DHCP server. This will very likely result not only in your computer behaving strangely, but in someone else's computer on the network also behaving erratically.

The first time you install TCP/IP, if you haven't enabled DHCP, the TCP/IP Configuration dialog box automatically appears. If you need to reconfigure TCP/IP, follow these steps to get to the TCP/IP Configuration dialog box:

1. Open the Network item in Control Panel by double-clicking it, or select it and press Enter. The Network dialog box appears.

2. Choose the Protocols tab.

3. Select TCP/IP Protocol in the Network Protocols list box.

4. Choose Configure. The Microsoft TCP/IP Properties dialog box appears (see fig. 24.2).

FIG. 24.2
The IP Address can be manually set for a Class C subnet without a WINS Server.

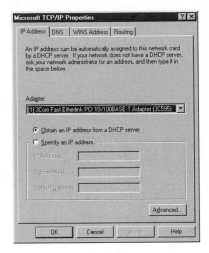

After you have the TCP/IP Configuration dialog box on-screen, follow these steps to configure/reconfigure TCP/IP:

1. Select the IP Address tab.

2. Select the network adapter you are configuring in the Adapter drop-down list box.

3. If you are using DHCP, choose Obtain an IP Address from a DHCP Server. You don't need to type in an IP address or subnet mask. If you aren't using DHCP, choose Specify an IP Address. You must type in the IP Address and Subnet Mask of your computer.

TIP If you aren't enabling DHCP, you must type in the Subnet Mask of your network. Based upon the IP address you just entered, the subnet mask defaults to one of three values— 255.0.0.0, 255.255.0.0, or 255.255.255.0. If this doesn't match the subnet mask your system administrator gave you, call and recheck your IP address and subnet mask values.

4. Enter the <u>D</u>efault Gateway. If this is omitted, your networking will be limited to your local network.

N O T E If you want to configure DNS, see the section "DNS Configuration" later in this chapter. If you want to use WINS to help resolve computer names, see the section "WINS Configuration" later in this chapter. If you want to configure advanced options, see the section "Advanced TCP/IP Configuration" later in this chapter. You might want to do this if you have more than one network adapter in your computer, and these are using TCP/IP for different networks. ■

5. Choose OK, or press Enter.

6. In the Network dialog box, choose OK or press Enter. You must restart your computer to have the new settings take effect.

DNS Configuration

To configure DNS, follow these steps:

1. Choose the DNS tab from the Microsoft TCP/IP Properties dialog box (see "Configuring TCP/IP" earlier in this chapter for instructions on getting to this dialog box). The DNS properties page appears (see fig. 24.3).

FIG. 24.3

You can add DNS Server IP addresses using the DNS properties page.

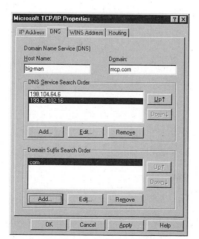

2. By default, the Host Name is the local computer name. You can change this, but should only do so if instructed by your system administrator.

N O T E The host name can be made up of the letters A–Z, the digits 0–9, and the hyphen (-) and period (.). However, Windows NT computer names can contain other characters that are invalid for host names (for example, the underscore (_)). ■

3. You have the option of typing in a Domain Name. This name can use the same characters as a host name. Typically, this is an organizational name followed by an extension. There are a few standard extensions—edu (education), org (organization), mil (military), gov (government), and com (company).

4. Type in the IP address of the DNS Server in the Domain Name Service (DNS) Search Order box. Choose Add to move the IP address you just typed to the list box. The IP address in this list box (which holds a maximum of three addresses), are the DNS servers that your computer will query when it is trying to resolve a domain name to an IP address.

5. To adjust the search order of the DNS Servers, select one of the IP addresses in the list box and then use the up and down buttons—just to the right of the list box—to move the IP address up or down in the list.

6. To remove a DNS Server from the list, select the IP address you want to remove, and then click Remove.

7. To add a domain suffix—a text string that is appended to the host name during domain name resolution—type in the suffix in the Domain Suffix Search Order edit field. Then, click Add. The text string moves to the list box to the right. There can be a maximum of six domain suffixes to try.

8. To adjust the search order, select one of the suffixes and move it up or down in the list box by using the up or down buttons—just to the right of the list box.

9. To remove a suffix, select the suffix you want to remove and then click Remove.

10. To finish configuring DNS, choose OK or press Enter.

WINS Configuration

To configure WINS, follow these steps:

1. Choose the WINS Address tab from the Microsoft TCP/IP Properties dialog box (see "Configuring TCP/IP" earlier in this chapter for instructions on getting to this dialog box). The WINS Address properties page appears (see fig. 24.4).

FIG. 24.4
You can configure WINS functionality using the WINS Address properties page.

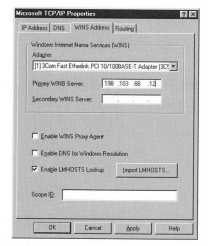

Part
VI

Ch
24

2. Select the network adapter you are configuring in the Adapter drop-down list box.

3. Type in the IP address of the Primary and Secondary (if available) WINS Servers. Your system administrator should have provided you with these IP addresses.

4. If your system administrator has indicated that your computer should be used to help resolve computer names within your network, choose Enable WINS Proxy Agent. Only a few computers in your network should have this feature turned on.

5. If you want to use DNS to resolve computer names for Windows networking applications, choose Enable DNS for Windows Resolution.

6. If your system administrator has specified that you should use an LMHOSTS file to resolve NetBIOS names, choose Enable LMHOSTS Lookup. Then import the LMHOSTS file he specified by choosing Import LMHOSTS.

N O T E Whenever Windows NT tries to resolve a name, it uses the LMHOST file after querying WINS and after trying broadcasts, but before DNS. ▓

7. If you are using NetBIOS over TCP/IP and your system administrator has given you a Scope ID, enter that value. This value is used to enable computers to communicate with each other. Normally, this is left blank.

8. To finish configuring WINS, choose OK.

Advanced TCP/IP Configuration

Setting Advanced TCP/IP configuration information uses a very complex dialog box. This section divides a complex task into two more easily understood tasks— configuring multiple IP address for a single network adapter and configuring multiple IP gateways.

To configure multiple IP addresses, follow these steps:

1. Click Advanced from the IP Address Tab of the Microsoft TCP/IP Properties dialog box (see "Configuring TCP/IP" earlier in this chapter for instructions on getting to this dialog box). The Advanced IP Addressing dialog box appears (see fig. 24.5).

FIG. 24.5
Specify the Default Gateway for one network adapter in the Advanced IP Adressing dialog box.

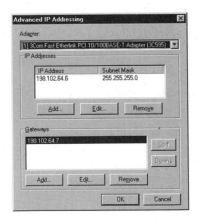

2. Select the adapter you want to configure in the Adapter drop-down list box.

N O T E Any IP address, gateways, and subnet masks that you define are set only for the adapter card you select. ▓

3. If your computer is connected to a network that has multiple IP networks—these are logical, not physical networks—you can define all the IP addresses and subnet masks. Choose <u>A</u>dd and type in the IP address and subnet mask, then choose OK. The new IP address and subnet mask appears in the list box.

4. If you have multiple network cards in your computer, you can define a separate IP address, subnet mask, and gateway(s) for each card. After having selected the card, go back to step 2 and repeat this process for every additional network card for which you need to define new information.

5. To remove an IP address and subnet mask, select the IP address you want to remove from the list box and choose Remo<u>v</u>e.

6. To change an IP address or subnet mask, select the IP address you want to modify from the list box and choose <u>E</u>dit.

7. Choose OK or press Enter to finish configuring multiple IP addresses.

To configure additional default gateways, follow these steps:

1. Click A<u>d</u>vanced from the IP Address Tab of the Microsoft TCP/IP Properties dialog box (see "Configuring TCP/IP" earlier in this chapter for instructions on getting to this dialog box). The Advanced IP Addressing dialog box appears (refer to fig. 24.5).

2. To add additional gateways, choose A<u>d</u>d (in the Gateways group box) and type in the IP address of the additional gateway in the Gateway Address edit field; then choose OK.

3. To adjust the search order priority, select the IP address of the gateway you want to change, and press the up and down buttons to the right of the list box to move the IP address up or down in the list.

4. To remove a gateway address, select the IP address that you want to remove in the list box and choose Re<u>m</u>ove.

5. To change a gateway address, select the IP address that you want to change in the list box and choose Ed<u>i</u>t.

6. Choose OK to finish configuring additional gateways.

Part
VI

Ch
24

Configuring SNMP

When you first install TCP/IP, if you select to also install SNMP, the configuration dialog box automatically appears (go directly to step 4). If you later need to go back and change any of the configuration information, follow these steps:

1. From Control Panel, open the Network item by double-clicking it, or select it and press Enter. The Network dialog box appears.

2. Select the Services tab.

3. Select SNMP Service in the Network Services list box.

4. Choose Configure. The Microsoft SNMP Properties dialog box appears. Select the Traps tab (see fig. 24.6).

FIG. 24.6

You can add the public community name in the Microsoft SNMP Properties dialog box.

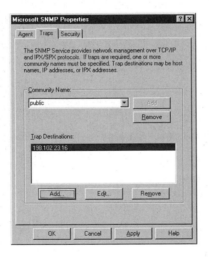

5. To add a community name, type in one of the community names your system administrator has supplied you, in the Community Name edit field. After you type in the name, click Add. Community names are case-sensitive.

6. To remove a community name from the drop down list box, select the name you want to remove and click Remove.

7. To add a trap destination for each community, highlight the community in the list box Send Trap with Community Names. Then choose Add and type in the host name, IP address, or IPX address in the IP Host/Address or IPX Address edit field. Choose OK. The information moves to the list box Trap Destination.

N O T E   A trap destination is the computer that should be notified when an SNMP service gets a request that has an incorrect community name or host name. Because each community name has its own set of trap destinations, make sure that the correct community is highlighted. This trap destination is for the selected community only! ■

8. To remove a trap destination, select the host in the Trap Destination list box and then click Remove.

9. Repeat steps 4–7 for each community your system administrator has supplied.

N O T E   To configure SNMP security, see "Configuring SNMP Security" later in this chapter. To configure an SNMP agent, see "Configuring an SNMP Agent" later in this chapter. ■

10. After finishing your changes, choose OK or press Enter.

 T I P   Even if you don't want to use SNMP, by installing it, you gain the option of using Performance Monitor to monitor performance statistics for TCP/IP services. To do this, you need to use the name **public** as the community came.

▶ **See** "Optimizing Windows NT Workstation Performance," **p. 943**

Configuring SNMP Security   To configure SNMP security, follow these steps:

1. From the Microsoft SNMP Properties dialog box, select the Security tab (see "Configuring SNMP" earlier in this chapter for instructions on how to get to this dialog box). The SNMP Security property page appears (see fig. 24.7).

2. If you want to send a trap when an unauthorized host (or community) tries to request information, select Send Authentication Trap.

3. To add a community name, choose Add... and type in the name of a community your computer will accept requests from in the Community Name edit field. Choose OK.

4. To remove a community that you no longer want to accept requests from, select that community in the list box and click Remove.

5. If you want to accept SNMP packets from any host, select Accept SNMP Packets from Any Host.

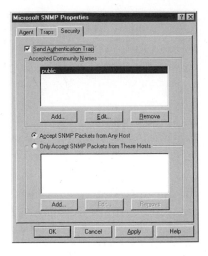

FIG. 24.7
Configure security options in the SNMP Security property page.

6. If you want to restrict the SNMP packets you get from the network to one of a set of hosts, select Only Accept SNMP Packets from These Hosts.

7. If you are restricting SNMP packets, you must specify the host(s) you will accept packets from. To specify a host, choose Add (in the lower group box) and type in the IP address or IPX address of the host you will accept packets from. Choose OK. Repeat this process for each host you will accept SNMP packets from.

8. To remove a host from the list of hosts you will accept SNMP packets from, select the host address in the list box and then click Remove.

9. Choose OK or press Enter when you are finished making changes.

Configuring an SNMP Agent   To configure an SNMP agent, follow these steps:

1. Choose the Agent tab from the Microsoft SNMP Properties dialog box (see "Configuring SNMP" earlier in this chapter for instructions on how to get to this dialog box). The SNMP Agent property page appears, as shown in figure 24.8.

2. Type in your name, or the name of the user of this computer, in the Contact edit field. This name gets displayed by the SNMP management software and so should contain only standard text characters.

3. Type in your location (the location of your computer) in the Location edit field. Again, just use plain text.

4. Select the services that are used on this computer. These are listed in table 24.3.

FIG. 24.8
Configure agent software in the SNMP Agent dialog box.

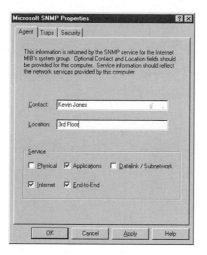

Table 24.3 SNMP Agent Services

SNMP Agent Service	Description
Physical	If your computer manages any physical TCP/IP devices, such as a repeater, select this option.
Datalink/Subnetwork	If your computer manages any TCP/IP subnets or datalinks, such as bridge, select this option.
Internet	If your computer serves as an IP gateway, select this option.
End-to-End	Select this option. This indicates that you are using TCP/IP and you have an IP address.
Applications	Select this option. This indicates that you are using TCP/IP applications, such as e-mail.

Part
VI

Ch
24

5. Choose OK or press Enter. The Network settings dialog box reappears.

6. Choose Close to complete configuring the SNMP Agent.

Setting Up LMHOSTS

Windows NT uses the LMHOSTS file to help resolve computer names that users understand to actual IP addresses. Before DNS and WINS, this was the primary method of resolving names. Now, with DNS and WINS, LMHOSTS files are used less frequently. LMHOSTS files are used primarily to resolve names for remote computers, computers that are not on the local subnet. (A WINS Server can automatically resolve any local computer names.)

Understanding LMHOSTS Files

An LMHOSTS file is simply a text file that contains information that Windows NT can use to resolve computer names to IP addresses. You can use any text editor to modify an LMHOSTS file—it's simply an ASCII text file. However, knowing what to change is the difficult task. If a few simple rules are followed, changing the LMHOSTS file is not difficult. The format of an LMHOSTS file consists of the following pieces:

- Each line corresponds to a single name to address mapping entry.
- Each line begins with the IP address in column one.
- Following the IP address and separated by a space or tab is the computer name.
- Following the computer name can be keywords and comments (see table 24.4).

Table 24.4 LMHOSTS File Keywords

Keyword	Description
#PRE	This keyword causes the entry to be preloaded. It is required for any computers referenced by an #INCLUDE statement.

Keyword	Description
#DOM:*<domain>*	This keyword associated the entry with the specified *<domain>*. This entry must also have the #PRE keyword because this keyword affects the behavior of Logon in a routed TCP/IP environment.
#INCLUDE*<filename>*	This keyword causes the specified file to be parsed as though it were part of this LMHOSTS file. By specifying a file that resides on a network file server, you can have a single, centralized LMHOSTS file for shared usage.
#BEGIN_ALTERNATE	This keyword starts a list of #INCLUDE statements. The list ends with the #END_ALTERNATE keyword. As Windows NT parses this LMHOSTS file, it searches for the file specified in the #INCLUDE files. After it finds one of the specified files, it skips any remaining files. This enables you to have backup copies of the centralized LMHOSTS file on several different file servers.
#END_ALTERNATE	This keyword ends the list of #INCLUDE entries.
\0x*nn*	This character is used to embed nonprinting characters into NetBIOS computer names. This can only be used as the last of the 16 characters that make up a computer name (for example, "ApplicationSrvr\0x03").

The following is an example of an LMHOSTS file:

```
126.48.13.07 MainServer #PRE
126.48.13.58 DomainServer #PRE #DOM:localnet
126.48.13.15 DataServer
#BEGIN_ALTERNATE
#INCLUDE \\MainServer\public\lmhosts
#INCLUDE \\DomainServer\publib\lmhosts
#END_ALTERNATE
126.48.13.14 ApplicationSrvr\0x03 #PRE
```

There are a few things to note about this example:

- MainServer and DomainServer are preloaded using the #PRE keyword. This is required because they are used in the #INCLUDE entries.

- ApplicationSrvr\0x03 is listed at the bottom of the file. This is for performance. When Windows NT needs to resolve a computer name, it reads the

Part

VI

Ch

24

LMHOSTS file one line at a time. Because any preloaded entries don't need to be read again, it is better to put them at the end of the file.

N O T E   When Windows NT preloads the entries with the #PRE keyword in the LMHOSTS file, it only preloads the first 100 #PRE entries. Any additional entries are treated as normal entries and are resolved when the system parses the LMHOSTS file. ■

Using LMHOSTS Files

When one computer on a network (local computer) needs to connect to another computer (remote computer), it tries several ways to locate the remote computer. First, each computer maintains a small cache of computer-name-to-IP-address mappings. If the remote computer isn't listed in its cache, it sends a broadcast across the network asking if the computer it is looking for is available. If the remote computer sees the broadcast, it replies with its IP address. On small networks this works fine. But on larger networks that are divided into subnets, the broadcast is restricted to the subnet of the local computer. If the broadcast fails to find the remoter computer, then the local computer checks its LMHOSTS file. If this fails, an error message appears to the user.

One way to effectively use an LMHOSTS file is to maintain a central LMHOSTS file on a network server. This LMHOSTS file should contain entries for all the computers in the network. By having each computer's local LMHOSTS file #INCLUDE this central LMHOSTS file, each computer can locate any computer in the network.

You should make several copies of this central LMHOSTS file on several different servers. Then, within the #BEGIN_ALTERNATE to #END_ALTERNATE keywords, you should #INCLUDE all of these files. Windows NT tries to find the first #INCLUDEed LMHOSTS file. If it finds it, it skips the others. If it fails (maybe because the server is down), it tries the next file. This continues until it finds a valid file. If it can't, an error message appears.

N O T E   It is important to remember that an LMHOSTS file contains a static computer name to IP address mapping. If you are using DHCP to dynamically assign IP addresses, these two methods don't work well together. Instead, for the computers—

typically servers—that you want to provide references for in a central LMHOSTS file, you must not have those computers use DHCP. Instead, each of those computers must have a manually set IP address. ▇

Finally, while LMHOSTS files are primarily used for locating remote servers for file sharing or printing, Windows NT uses them for one other important purpose. User account security databases and other network-specific services are maintained by domain controllers. There is typically a primary and secondary domain controller. In large networks, it is often the case that a computer in one domain is located on a subnet different than its domain controller. A special keyword in the LMHOSTS file (#DOM:) can identify that a computer is a domain controller (refer to table 24.4). That entry is then maintained in a special cache reserved for domain controllers. This enables a user to log on to a computer even though the computer that maintains the user security database is not on the same subnet.

Using Windows NT FTP Services

By installing the FTP Server on your computer, you can permit other users using TCP/IP to access and transfer files on your computer.

When you install an FTP Server, you must carefully consider the security risks. FTP is tightly coupled with the Windows NT security model. Because of this, if you install FTP Server on an NTFS partition, you have greater protection. You can require that only valid Windows NT users can get FTP access. However, to use FTP, the user name and password must be sent across the network unencrypted. This means it would be possible for someone with physical access to the network to eavesdrop and find the user passwords. Alternatively, you can allow access via the anonymous user option. Users who connect this way only get the user access privileges provided to the Guest user. They will be prompted to supply their e-mail address as their password, but this isn't required.

You must decide on the right approach based on your situation. If you want to allow anyone to have access to the files, use the anonymous login. If you need to restrict access to the files, you must use the Windows NT user login, but this has a potential security risk.

Installing FTP Services

To install FTP Server, follow these steps:

1. From Control Panel, open the Network item by double-clicking it, or select it and press Enter. The Network dialog box appears.

2. Select the Services tab.

3. Click Add. The Select Network Service dialog box appears.

4. Select FTP Server, and then click OK.

5. A message appears describing FTP Security. Choose Yes. The Windows NT Setup dialog box appears.

6. Type in the path of the Windows NT distribution files. Click Continue. The necessary files are installed.

After all the required files have been copied, the FTP Properties dialog box appears (see fig. 24.9). Use this dialog box to configure the FTP service.

FIG. 24.9
The FTP Properties lets you change any settings for FTP.

Configuring FTP Services

When you first install the FTP Server software, the configuration dialog box automatically appears. Later, if you need to change any settings for FTP, follow these steps:

1. Open the Network item in the Control Panel by double-clicking it, or select it and press Enter. The Network dialog box appears.

2. Select the Services tab.

3. Select FTP Server in the Network Services list box.

4. Choose Configure. The FTP Properties dialog box appears.

Once the FTP Properties dialog box is on-screen, follow these steps to configure FTP:

1. Type in the maximum number of simultaneous users you will allow to connect to your computer in the Maximum Connections edit field. The default is 20 simultaneous connections. The maximum limit is 50 connections. A zero (0) indicates that there is no maximum limit.

2. In the Idle Timeout (min) edit field, type in the number of minutes connected users can remain inactive before they are disconnected. The default is 10. The maximum limit is 60 minutes. A value of zero (0) indicates that users will never be disconnected.

3. Type in the initial directory that users are connected to in the Home Directory edit field.

4. Choose whether or not you will allow users to anonymously connect to your computer by choosing Allow Anonymous Connections.

5. If you allow anonymous connections, you must specify which Windows NT user account is used for anonymous users, by entering in the user account in the Username edit field. The default is the Guest account.

6. If you allow anonymous connections, you must specify the password in the Password edit field, for the user account listed in the Username edit field.

7. If you only want to allow anonymous FTP access, choose Allow Only Anonymous Connections. You might do this if you don't want to have users sending unencrypted passwords across the network.

8. Choose OK. You return to the Network Settings dialog box.

9. Choose Close. This completes the configuration of the FTP Server.

Part
VI

Ch
24

Setting FTP Security

If you are allowing other people to have access to files on your computer, you certainly need to be concerned about security. There are three steps you can take in setting your security precautions. First, you must determine whether you will restrict connections to specific users or allow anonymous connections. This was covered in the previous section, "Configuring FTP Services." Second, you can set FTP Security rights for each volume you allow FTP access to. This section covers this aspect of FTP Security. Finally, if you are running the FTP Service on an NTFS volume, you can set additional access rights on a user basis.

TIP Since FTP Security only allows you to set FTP Security on a volume basis, you may want to create a volume for holding only FTP files. Then, any FTP user can only see the files on that volume. You won't have to worry about a user having access to any files on any other drive.

To configure the security features of the FTP Service, follow these steps:

1. Open the FTP Server item in the Control Panel by double-clicking it, or select it and press Enter. The FTP User Sessions dialog box appears.

2. Choose Security. The FTP Server Security dialog box appears (see fig. 24.10).

FIG. 24.10
Configuring the FTP Server Security dialog box allows read access to the C Drive.

3. Select the drive you want to set security access for by using the Partition drop-down list box.

4. Choose Allow Read if you want to allow any connected user to be able to read files on your computer.

5. Choose Allow Write if you want to allow any connected user to be able to write files to your computer.

   Repeat steps 3 through 5 for each partition to which you want to set security access.

6. Choose OK or press Enter. The FTP User Sessions dialog box reappears.

7. Choose OK to finish setting FTP Security options.

TCP/IP Utilities

Windows includes a number of TCP/IP utilities. Some utilities are used to diagnose problems, while others provide connectivity or information. They are listed in table 24.5. To get a complete list of the options for each command, type **command -?** at the command prompt.

N O T E This table is not intended to teach you how to use all of these utilities. Instead, it is intended to show you what is possible. You can find additional information in Windows NT Online help.

Table 24.5   TCP/IP Utilities

Utility	Description
arp	This diagnostic utility enables you to display and modify the address translation tables used by the ARP (Address Resolution Protocol).
finger	This connectivity utility displays information about a user who is connected to a specific system. That system must be running the Finger Service.
ftp	This connectivity utility allows you to connect to a remote FTP Server and transfer files to and from that Server.
hostname	This diagnostic utility simply prints out the name of the current host.
ipconfig	This diagnostic utility displays information about the current TCP/IP configuration. It's particularly useful on machines that are dynamically configured using DHCP.
lpq	This diagnostic utility displays the current status of a print queue on a remote machine that is running an LPD Server.
lpr	This connectivity utility prints a file on a remote machine that is running an LPD Server.
nbtstat	This diagnostic utility displays TCP/IP connections and protocol statistics when using NetBIOS over TCP/IP.
netstat	This diagnostic utility displays TCP/IP connections and protocol statistics.

continues

Table 24.5 Continued

Utility	Description
ping	This diagnostic utility is used to verify connections to one or more remote machines. This is one of the first utilities to try when you are having problems.
rcp	This connectivity utility is used to copy a file from a Windows NT machine to a UNIX machine running rshd (remote shell server), or between two UNIX machines both running rshd. rshd only runs on UNIX machines, so this command can never be used to copy files to a Windows NT machine.
rexec	This connectivity utility is used to execute non-interactive commands on a remote host. Username and password need to be verified. The remote machine must be running the rexecd service.
route	This diagnostic utility is used to manipulate routing tables.
rsh	This connectivity utility is used to execute commands on a remote host. This host must be running the rsh service.
telnet	This connectivity utility starts a terminal emulation session (VT 100, VT 52, or TTY) with a remote host.
tftp	This connectivity utility provides Trivial File Transfer Protocol. It is used to transfer files without user authentication.
tracert	This diagnostic utility is used to determine the route that a packet of data takes from your computer to its destination.

Using Windows NT on the Internet

Up until now, this chapter has focused mostly on TCP/IP and how to get it up and running on your computer. One of the main reasons you've probably done this is to obtain access to the Internet.

If you're in a large corporation, you probably have an MIS staff telling you how to get everything set up properly. They probably have a fair number of rules and regulations on what you can and can't do. If this accurately describes your situation, you may find the rest of this section interesting, but you'll have to follow MIS's rules. You will, however, be better informed when you talk with them and will know what is available.

However, if you are a stand-alone user, a user in a small company, or anyone without the benefit of an MIS staff, this section is definitely for you.

> **N O T E** This section is not intended to provide you with detailed instructions on every possible method of connecting to the Internet. There are whole books written about such topics. Instead, this section gives you an overview of the possibilities. This section covers some of the more common methods of connecting to the Internet and what you need in each case.
>
> This section ends with an overview of the Internet servers (or services) you can run on your Windows NT Workstation computer. It will cover what functionality each server provides, any security risk associated with each server (if any), and what software and/or hardware you'll need. ■

Connecting to the Internet

Windows NT provides a solid foundation for connecting to the Internet. Besides Windows NT, you need to install TCP/IP and have one or more applications that you use to get access to the Internet. If you want to "take up residence" on the Internet, you have to run one or more server applications on your own machine.

Connecting a Single Workstation to the Internet In the simplest scenario, you can simply connect your machine to the Internet for accessing data out on the Net. To make this type of connection, in addition to TCP/IP, you have to have the following:

- RAS (Remote Access Service)
- A modem
- A dial-in account with an Internet Service Provider (using PPP—Point-to-point Protocol—or SLIP—Serial Line Internet Protocol)
- Various Internet tools, such as FTP clients, a Web browser, and e-mail clients

This type of connection works well for accessing data. When you call into your service provider, you most likely get a randomly assigned IP number from a pool of IP addresses your service provider maintains. If you want to run a server on your computer and allow other Internet users to access your computer, things become a bit more involved:

- First, you need to get a domain name. Your Internet provider should be able to supply you with this.

- Second, if you want to run an FTP site or a Web server, you need to get a permanent IP address. This is required so that other computers can reliably find your computer/server.

- Third, unless you only want to provide sporadic access to your server, you want to investigate different methods of connecting to your service provider. Calling up the service and keeping a phone line open 24 hours a day is not a very workable solution.

The most common types of connections are listed in table 24.6. While some of these are appropriate for individual use, the T1 and T3 lines are normally used only by businesses and large organizations, such as university and government sites. Price quotes are estimates only. They will vary depending on where you live and will change over time.

Table 24.6   Internet Connection Types

Connection	Description
PPP dial-in	Connects at modem speed and costs $20–30/month.
SLIP dial-in	Connects at modem speed and costs $20–30/month.
Dedicated SLIP or PPP	Connects at modem speed and costs $200–300/month.
56K line	Connects at 56Kbps and costs $400–600/month. You also have to buy some special equipment.
PPP ISDN	Connects at 128Kbps and costs $70–100/month. You also have to buy some special equipment. Usage charges will also apply.
T1	This dedicated line connects at 1.5 Mbps and costs $1,000–2,000/month. Price also varies depending on the distance.
T3	This dedicated line connects at 45 Mbps and costs $50,000–80,000/month. Price also varies depending on the distance.

Connecting a LAN to the Internet   For smaller networks that are a single subnet in size, you can use a Windows NT machine as an Internet router. This machine needs to have two network adapters installed in it. One adapter is connected to the local LAN. The other adapter would be connected to the Internet. In this situation, IP packets travel from client machines in the network to the Windows NT router and from there, are sent to the Internet.

For larger networks of more than one subnet, the Windows NT router doesn't work. Windows NT does not automatically maintain a TCP/IP router table—a requirement for multiple subnets. Instead, you need to obtain a third-party router that handles this situation. As an additional benefit, the performance of these dedicated routers is better than using Windows NT as a router.

Using Remote Access Service   If you are a dial-up service provider, you need to use RAS. You don't need to use RAS if you are using a leased line to get access to the Internet.

Using RAS enables you to provide access to the Internet in a variety of different situations.

▶ **See** "Using Remote Access Service," **p. 629**

First, you can use RAS if you're dialing into an Internet Service Provider. Second, you can use RAS to enable remote clients to call in and get access to the Internet. Finally, you can use RAS when you are setting up a Windows NT machine to serve as a simple router. See the previous section, "Connecting a LAN to the Internet."

Internet Service Providers   To find an Internet Service Provider in your area, you can look in your phone book. Try looking under *Networking Services*. You can also look in any local computer magazines or newspapers.

The Internet Service Provider should provide certain basic services. These should include:

- TCP/IP addresses and subnet mask
- Internet gateway IP address
- Domain Name Service resolution (DNS Server)

Part
VI

Ch
24

- Mail support (SMTP)
- Access to News (Network News Transfer Protocol—NNTP)

The service provider you find may offer additional services such as registering domain names, Web server access, and so on.

Internet Servers

While the Internet contains a tremendous amount of information, you may have information you want to put out on the Internet. It could be personal information by way of Web pages, company information such as annual reports, or access to the latest version of device drivers your company produces. To make any of these items available to the outside world, you will not only need to connect to the Internet, but you'll also have to run servers on your machines. These servers respond to the requests from other users across the Internet.

FTP Server Windows NT comes with an FTP Server, which can be installed as part of the TCP/IP Protocol. The server enables users to transfer files to and from your computer, depending, of course, on how you set the security options.

> **CAUTION**
>
> Security is always an issue with the Internet. Although you may specify that an FTP user's home directory is D:\FTP\FILES, once users gain access to the drive, they are free to change directories. That means that they have full access to the D drive (NTFS Security can help control this). So, a good rule is to set up a logical drive for FTP files and only put files on there to which you want users to have access.

Gopher Server A Gopher Server is similar to an FTP server. However, the Gopher Server is a little friendlier. The Gopher server provides access to files, directories, other Gopher servers, and aliases—descriptive names for files and directories. This information is displayed in a hierarchical structure and access to the files and directories is more controlled.

Gopher servers can also be configured to search local WAIS servers. See "WAIS Server" later in this chapter.

World Wide Web Server   The explosion of the Internet has been fueled by the World Wide Web. The Web provides a very simple method of allowing users to navigate across the Internet. Instead of interacting with files and directories, users interact with pages of hypertext information. Users are able to move from page to page simply by clicking the hypertext links. Newer pages contain interactive controls such as drop-down menus, edit fields, and radio buttons. By using these controls, users can query databases, input information, and control display options.

ON THE WEB

You can download a free copy of IIS from this site, but you'll need NT Server to use it

   http://www.microsoft.com/

Part

VI

Ch

24

Setting up a Web Server is more involved than setting up an FTP or Gopher Server. To set up these servers, the software simply needs to be installed and configured. The data they make accessible is basically the file system. A Web Server, on the other hand, makes accessible Web pages. The pages are stored on a machine as a text file. This text file uses a very specific format. This format is called *HTML—HyperText Markup Language*. This text file contains text and references to other data or files. These files include images, sound, video, and other pages.

You can access these pages via *Uniform Resource Locators*. These URL's are embedded into Web pages and provide the location of the data and specify the application that is required to properly access the data. For example, the URL for Macmillan Publishing is **www.mcp.com**. So, in a Web browser, you would type in **http://www.mcp.com**. (The **http://** tells the browser that it is a Web page, and the URL tells the browser which page.)

If you are contemplating setting up a Web Server, you need to get additional information on authoring HTML pages and information on the latest enhancements to HTML. By the time this book is in print, new technologies such as Java and JavaScript, as well as Microsoft development tools using OCXs (embedded OLE controls), will provide even more powerful, interactive Web applications.

You have a number of options regarding what Web Server to set up. There are several shareware Web Servers as well as commercial packages from companies such as Netscape, O'Riley, and Microsoft.

WAIS Server   The final server you can install and run on your Windows NT system is a *Wide Area Information Server*. A WAIS Server enables users to search through full-content indexes of sets of files. A WAIS Server really consists of several pieces:

- First, one piece must build and maintain the full-content database.
- Second, a middleman must take the request from the actual WAIS Server and search the index, build a list of results, and return that to the WAIS Server.
- The actual WAIS Server connects with Internet users, accepts their search requests, and returns to them a list of files that meet their search criteria. Users can then select the files, and the WAIS Server returns that information for display on the users' machines.

From Here...

Obviously, there is a lot of additional information you can find about the Internet, Windows NT's support for it, and various Internet applications.

To learn more, refer to these chapters:

- Chapter 15, "Securing Windows NT Workstation," teaches you about user rights.
- Chapter 20, "Configuring the Network at Your Workstation," shows you how to add and configure network adapters and protocols.
- Chapter 23, "Using Dial-Up Networking," teaches you about using RAS to provide remote access to your computer.

CHAPTER 25

Using Windows NT with the Internet

by Paul Sanna

Windows NT Workstation provides a flexible and advanced means of connecting to the Internet, whether you are connecting from a stand-alone computer or from a network. Windows NT has built-in support for TCP/IP dial-up access and PPP or SLIP (all Internet standards). After you are connected to the Internet, you can take advantage of most of its resources using tools built into Windows NT. E-mail, file transfer, Telnet, Web browser, and even newsgroup reading functionality are all built into Windows NT. This chapter provides the details on using Windows NT with the Internet. ■

Understanding the Internet and the Web

Learn about the Internet, including its history, use, and growth today. You also find out about the Web, probably the most compelling aspect of the Internet.

Understanding TCP/IP

TCP/IP is the communication protocol you use to connect to the Internet. If you have heard the term before but never understood what it meant, you can find an explanation of TCP/IP in this chapter.

Choosing an Internet Service Provider

Unless you connect to the Internet via the local area network at a larger office, you need to find an Internet service provider (ISP) to give you access. This chapter shows you where to find an ISP.

Learning how to connect to the Internet

You must follow a few procedures to connect your PC to the Internet. This chapter shows you how to configure Windows NT Workstation to connect to the Internet using Dial-Up Networking, and then how to configure NT to talk to your ISP.

Understanding the Internet

Unless you have been living in a cave in the Himalayas, you have probably heard about the Internet. The Internet is a *network of networks*, a global linkage of millions of computers, containing vast amounts of information, much of it available to anyone with a modem and the right software...for free.

The main functions of the Internet are described in this list:

- *E-mail* (electronic mail). You can send a message to anyone, anywhere in the world (as long as the person has access to the Internet), almost instantaneously and for less than the cost of a regular letter.

- *The World Wide Web* (also known as *the Web, or WWW*). The fastest growing part of the Internet, the Web provides access to files, documents, images, and sounds from thousands of different Web sites using a special programming language called *HyperText Markup Language*, or HTML. This language is used to create hypertext documents that include embedded commands and graphics.

- *UseNet newsgroups.* These *many-to-many* discussion groups feature topics ranging from science, current events, music, computers, alternative issues, and many others. Thousands of newsgroups exist, and the list grows daily.

- *File transfer using file transfer protocol* (FTP). FTP is the Internet protocol for file transfer between computers linked to the Internet.

The Internet is an aggregation of high-speed networks, supported by the National Science Foundation (NSF) and almost 6,000 federal, state, and local systems, as well as university and commercial networks. With more than 30,000,000 users, the Internet has links to networks in Canada, South America, Europe, Australia, and Asia. The network began with about 200 linked computers; today, several million computers are linked all over the world. The Internet is growing so fast that no one can say accurately how big it is today, or how large it will grow tomorrow.

Understanding the World Wide Web

The World Wide Web is the fastest growing and most exciting part of the Internet. The Web was developed in 1989 at CERN (*Centre Européen de Recherche Nucléaire,* which most people call the Particle Physics Research Laboratory) at the University of Bern in Switzerland. Although the rest of the Internet is text oriented, the Web is graphics and sound oriented. Clicking a *hypertext* or *hypermedia link* (a specially encoded text or graphics image) takes you to other documents, called *Web pages*, where you can view images from the Hubble telescope, visit an art museum, watch a video clip of skiers (on a ski resort's page), or hear the haunting theme song from the Fox Network's hit show, *The X Files*—all on your computer.

Unlike other Internet file-retrieval systems, which are hierarchical in nature (you wend your way through descending layers of menus or directories to find what you're looking for), the Web is distributed. It offers links to other parts of the same document or other documents, which are not necessarily at the same Web site as the current document. You travel through the Web using a program called a *graphical browser* (such as Microsoft's Internet Explorer or Netscape's Navigator). For example, you might point and click a phrase on your screen that looks like this:

Macmillan Computer Publishing

You jump directly to the Web page of Macmillan Computer Publishing shown in figure 25.1.

Part
VI

Ch
25

FIG. 25.1
The Macmillan Computer Publishing page, as viewed from Microsoft Internet Explorer. Click elements in the graphic to move to the Web pages for those sites.

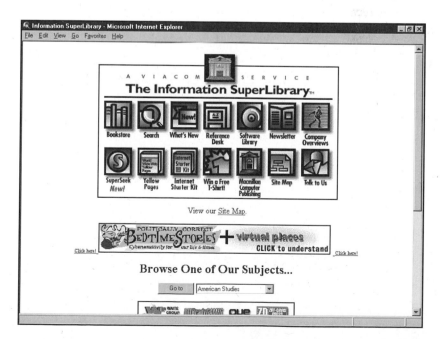

New authoring tools, including Microsoft's Internet Assistant, enable anyone to create his or her own Web page (a kind of advertisement for yourself that anyone on the Web can see).

Understanding TCP/IP

TCP/IP stands for Transmission Control Protocol/Internet Protocol. Every computer on the Internet uses the TCP/IP method to transfer files. As the name indicates, it's actually two protocols. The earliest model was the Internet Protocol, developed in the days of ARPANET (the Advanced Research Projects NETwork, the original Internet, formed in the 1960s) to send data in packets (self-contained units of information) from one computer network to another. The weakness of IP is its inability to deal with poor transmissions. If a packet gets garbled or interrupted, the receiving IP-based machine just tosses it. The TCP protocol makes sure that every packet is delivered to the receiving network in the same order it was sent. A kind of numbering system verifies that the packet received is identical to the one sent. Every network and every computer on the Internet uses TCP/IP to communicate.

Choosing an Internet Service Provider

As the Internet grows by leaps and bounds, more and more businesses, called *Internet service providers* (ISPs), are springing up to provide access. Typically, a local provider offers three or more computers, called *servers*, that are linked directly to the Internet. In turn, the servers provide a dozen or more high-speed modems connected to local telephone lines. In some cities, a new service called Integrated Services Digital Network (ISDN) offers modem speeds of at least 128 kbps. Unless you live in a remote part of the world, finding a service provider is not the problem it was as recently as one year ago. The problem is, what kind of service do you need?

The following list describes some ways to access the Internet:

■ If you attend a college or university, or are employed at a business of any size, you may already have Internet access. See your supervisor, the computer science department, or a network administrator. Make a case for Internet access to your home, or at least for using your organization's access during off-hours.

- Join a commercial online service, such as CompuServe, America Online, or Prodigy. These services handle the connectivity problems for you; all you do is point and click your way to the Net.

- Sign up with a national Internet provider, such as Netcom, PSI Pipeline USA, or IDT. If you live in a rural area or travel a lot, this option may be your best bet. A national provider has access phone numbers in major cities and often has SprintNet or Tymnet access elsewhere.

- Sign up with a local Internet provider. This option is often the most economical way to get on the Net; many services cost as little as $15 to $25 per month. Every major city in the U.S. and around the world has at least one local provider. Look for advertisements in computer magazines, the newspaper, or your classified telephone directory.

Knowing what You Need to Connect to the Internet

By this point in the book, Windows NT's Hardware Wizard has installed and configured your modem, or you have done it yourself. You should be using at least a 14.4 kbps modem, which is about as slow as you want to go on the Internet. After you have chosen your Internet provider, you're ready to set up Windows NT to surf the Net.

Now you need to deal with some more Net jargon: SLIP and PPP. *SLIP* stands for *Serial-Line Internet Protocol*; *PPP* means *Point-to-Point Protocol*. Both are implementations of the TCP/IP Internet protocol over telephone lines. (Unless you access the Net through LAN and Ethernet cabling, you will use telephone lines and SLIP or PPP.)

The two protocols have both technical and practical differences; technically, SLIP is a *network-layer protocol*; PPP is a *link-level protocol*. Practically, this difference means that PPP is faster and more fail-safe than SLIP.

If you have chosen an Internet-only service, you need the following information from your Internet provider:

- The kind of connection provided: SLIP or PPP
- Your username (you can usually choose your own, such as *jsmith*)
- A password—again, you select your own (the most secure passwords have six or more uppercase and lowercase letters and/or numbers)
- The provider's local access phone number
- Your host and domain name
- Your Domain Name Server's IP address (DNS is the method the Internet uses to create unique names for each of the servers on the network)
- Authentication technique (Some ISPs require users to type their login name and password in a *terminal window*—a DOS window that opens when you connect to the service. Other ISPs have automated authentication methods, called PAP or CHAP.)

If your service provider gives you a dedicated IP address to use every time you dial in (in other words, you always log on to the same ISP server), you may also need the following:

- *IP address for you.* This is your computer's unique address.
- *IP subnet mask.* A physical-world analogy might be the apartment number following a street address as a further way of pinpointing a location.
- *Gateway IP address.* This is the address of your ISP's server.

This example shows the setup requirements for an Internet provider:

IP Address:	1.1.1.1
Subnet Mask:	255.0.0.0
Host Name:	Your computer's name (this information was supplied when Windows NT was set up on your computer)
Domain Name:	anynet.com
Dial:	555-0000 (your provider's phone #)
Login:	jsmith
Password:	pAssWoRd (whatever you choose)
Domain Server:	222.222.68.160

Your provider may configure your system for you. At the least, your provider should help you over the phone while you enter the information in the correct Windows NT Dial-Up Network Phonebook dialog boxes (except for your password, which only you and your provider will know).

Configuring Windows NT Dial-Up Networking

To use Windows NT to connect to the Internet, you first must complete two tasks:

- Install Dial-Up Networking
- Install TCP/IP

The installation of Dial-Up Networking is covered in Chapter 19, "Understanding Windows NT Network Services." If you are not sure whether Dial-Up Networking has been installed on your computer, double-click the My Computer icon on the Desktop. If Dial-Up Networking is installed, you see an icon for it (see fig. 25.2).

Part
VI

Ch
25

FIG. 25.2
A view of My Computer, showing Dial-Up Networking installed.

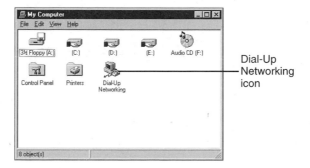

Dial-Up
Networking
icon

Configuring TCP/IP

TCP/IP is covered exclusively in Chapter 24, "Configuring TCP/IP." Consult that chapter to learn how to install TCP/IP. Be sure to follow these few steps, however, to properly connect Windows NT to your ISP with TCP/IP (first install TCP/IP before executing these steps):

1. Open the Start menu and choose Settings, Control Panel. Double-click the Network icon. Choose the Protocol tab and then click TCP/IP Protocol in the Network Protocols list box. Choose Properties and then choose the DNS tab.

2. Type the name of your computer in the Host Name edit box.

3. Type the domain name of your Internet server in the Domain edit box. Obtain this information from your network administrator or your ISP.

4. In the DNS Service Search Order frame, choose the Add button. Enter the primary IP address of your DNS server in the DNS Server box and then choose the Add button. Obtain this information also from your network administrator or ISP.

 TIP If the address you're typing has fewer than three numbers before the period, use the right arrow key to jump to the next area between the periods in the field. If you type three numbers before the period, the cursor automatically moves to the next area.

5. Repeat step 4 to add a secondary IP address that you may get from your network administrator or ISP.

N O T E If your ISP or network administrator provider assigns you a permanent IP address, you can enter that address manually on the IP Address tab. From the Network dialog box, choose Protocols, TCP/IP Protocol, Properties, and then the IP Address tab. Choose the Specify an IP Address option button and enter the assigned address in the IP Address field. You also must type the subnet mask address for your provider in the Subnet Mask field.

When you connect using PPP, you use the permanent IP address rather than one that the Internet service provider dynamically assigns you. When you connect with SLIP, the permanent IP address shows up in the Specify an IP address box to confirm your IP address for your SLIP connection. ■

Creating a Configuration for Your Access Provider

In the preceding sections, you configured Windows NT for TCP/IP connections. Now you need to tell Windows NT about the connection you will be making to your ISP. To do this, you create and configure a new Dial-Up Networking phonebook entry. The phonebook entry contains all the information Windows NT needs to connect to the Internet, or to whatever target you specify in the entry. Follow these steps to create and configure the entry:

1. Open the Start menu and choose Programs, Accessories, and Dial-Up Networking. If this is the first time you have opened Dial-Up Networking, a connection wizard runs to help you enter most of the information necessary for your first dial-up entry. This numbered section helps you supply information to the wizard (see fig. 25.3).

FIG. 25.3
The wizard walks you through the steps of creating a Dial-Up Networking phonebook entry.

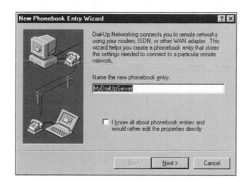

 T I P After you run Dial-Up Networking for the first time, you can access Dial-Up Networking from the My Computer folder on the Desktop.

2. Type the name you will use for this Dial-Up Networking phonebook entry. Make the name relevant to the Internet, such as "My Internet Connection." Because you might also use Dial-Up Networking to connect to your organization's LAN from home, for example, your label for the phonebook entry should be relevant to its use. Choose the Next button.

3. Check the I Am Calling the Internet checkbox and then choose Next.

4. Type the phone number of your ISP and then choose Next. Be sure to type a 1 and area code if they are required to dial from your location. Then choose Next. Windows NT tells you that your phonebook entry is complete. Choose Finish.

5. You arrive in the Dial-Up Networking dialog box (see fig. 25.4).

   You have just a bit more information to provide. If your provider requires you to log on by means of a terminal window (which looks like a DOS window where you type your username and password), you must enable that function. If not, skip to step 6. Choose More and then choose Edit Entry and

Part
VI

Ch
25

Modem Properties. Choose the Script tab and then choose the Pop-Up a Terminal Window option button (see fig. 25.5). Choose OK. You return to the first box of the Dial-Up Networking dialog box.

FIG. 25.4

After supplying a name for your phonebook entry and a phone number, you arrive in the Dial-Up Networking dialog box to supply more information.

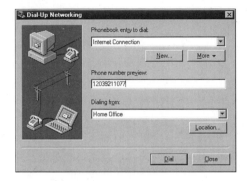

FIG. 25.5

You specify that a pop-up window appears when you connect to your ISP server in order. In the window, you supply your username and password for your ISP account.

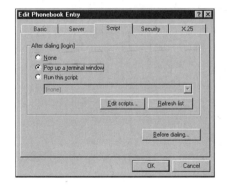

 TIP You can create a custom script that automatically supplies your username and password when you connect to your ISP server. Refer back to Chapter 23, "Using Dial-Up Networking," for help in creating a script or editing the template shipped with Windows NT.

6. Last, you need to specify the type of connection you will be making with this phonebook entry. Choose More and then choose Edit Entry and Modem Properties. Choose the Server tab (see fig. 25.6). From the Network Protocols group, check the TCP/IP option. This option provides quicker connect time after dialing the Internet provider. The NetBEUI and IPX/SPX Compatible options are not relevant to connecting to the Internet. Uncheck them.

In the Dial-Up Server Type drop-down list, select the type of connection: PPP, SLIP, or Windows 3.1. Your Internet provider can tell you which type of account you have. Click OK and then Close.

FIG. 25.6
If you are using a PPP connection, your Server Types dialog box should look like this.

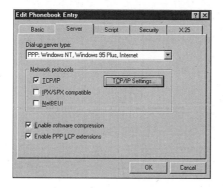

Connecting to Your Internet Provider

You are now ready to dial your Internet provider. Follow these steps:

1. To dial, either double-click the Dial-Up Networking icon in the My Computer folder on the Desktop, or open the Start menu, and then choose Programs, Accessories, Dial-Up Networking.

2. Choose your Internet connection from the Phonebook Entry to Dial drop-down list. If you have just one entry, your Internet connection should be displayed in the list. Choose Dial. You are prompted to supply a username and password. You don't need to enter your username and password here if you have specified that you enter this information in a terminal window that appears after you're connected.

3. After the modem connects and you hear the "hiss," a terminal window appears (see fig. 25.7). Enter your username and password; you should be connected within a few seconds. Choose Done after connection, and the Connection Complete dialog box appears (see fig. 25.8). Choose OK, and you are ready to use whatever Internet software you choose. You should be able to launch your Web browser, Internet mail reader, or other application, and you are ready to go.

Part
VI
Ch
25

FIG. 25.7
Use the After-Dial
Terminal Screen to
enter your user name
and password.

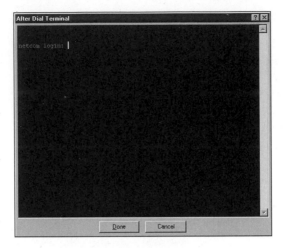

FIG. 25.8
Windows NT informs
you that you are
connected to the
Internet.

Testing Your Connection

To test whether a connection is working, you can use a program that comes with
Windows NT called PING. When executed, PING calls the remote computer you
designate and sends back a response to let you know you're connected. The
program's name comes from submarine sonar, which sends out a *ping* to get an
echo of another hull in the water. To test your connection, follow these steps:

1. After you are connected to your ISP, open a DOS window.

2. At the DOS prompt, type **ping microsoft.com**. If the Microsoft server is
   busy, it may not answer right away. If you do not want to wait for an answer
   from Microsoft, ping your Internet provider's host computer by name by
   typing **ping *host name***. Alternately, you can try to ping by supplying the

host's IP address (such as **ping 128.95.1.4**). After a few milliseconds, the remote host replies:

```
Pinging ftp.microsoft.com [198.105.232.1] with 32 bytes of data:
Reply from 198.105.232.1: bytes=32 time=180ms TTL=18
Reply from 198.105.232.1: bytes=32 time=185ms TTL=18
Reply from 198.105.232.1: bytes=32 time=176ms TTL=18
Reply from 198.105.232.1: bytes=32 time=181ms TTL=18
```

This response tells you that your computer is talking to the server. Unless you have ongoing problems connecting, you will use the PING command only one time.

Connecting to the Internet with a LAN

If your computer is part of a local area network (LAN), connecting to the Internet with Windows NT is as easy as connecting a single user. The main difference is that instead of getting the information you need from an ISP, you obtain it from your network administrator. Windows NT provides seamless integration of Internet and LAN e-mail though a Microsoft API mail driver employing the Microsoft Exchange client. Mail from another computer on the LAN is treated the same as mail from out on the Internet.

To get connected, follow these steps:

1. Open the Start menu and choose Settings, Control Panel. Double-click the Network icon. If you followed the earlier procedures, you now have both Dial-Up Networking and TCP/IP installed. Select the TCP/IP protocol and choose Properties.

2. Select the IP Address tab. If your LAN has a Dynamic Host Configuration Protocol (DHCP) Server, click the button marked Obtain an IP Address Automatically.

3. If your LAN does not have a DHCP server, you need to obtain the IP address from your network administrator. Choose the button marked Specify an IP Address and fill in the address. Use the arrow key to move between the fields separated by periods. Type the Subnet Mask address at this time also.

4. Type the address provided by your network administrator for your network gateway in the Default Gateway box. This address represents the connection point between your LAN and the Internet.

5. Choose Enable DNS. Obtain your Host and Domain names from your network administrator and type them in the spaces provided. For example, your computer might be "Zeus" at IBM. The address would be *zeus.ibm.com*, where *zeus* is the host and *ibm.com* is the domain. If you are part of a smaller organization, you may not have a Domain Name Server of your own but a name provided by your service provider.

6. Still in the DNS property sheet, choose the Add button and type the numeric address of the DNS server your network administrator gives you. If a backup number is provided, choose Add again and type the backup IP address.

7. You're almost done. If your LAN is not using DHCP, or it is running Windows NT Server, you may need to set up the Windows Internet Naming Service, (WINS, pronounced *win-s*). Click the WINS Address tab and follow your network administrator's instructions.

Understanding Internet Services

Now that you have connectivity, you may be wondering what you can do on the Internet. The Internet is a combination communications tool, library, and catalog. Many people think the Internet is the most important source of information available today. More realistic Net surfers have found that, although the Internet has more *data* than anyone can ever begin to comprehend, it doesn't have much *information* (defined as *useful* data). The Net-speak phrase that defines this situation is "a high signal to noise ratio."

Important Services

The following sections take a detailed look at some of the services on the Net.

The World Wide Web   The most exciting development on the Internet recently has been the explosive growth of the Web. Everyone with access to the Internet seems to have a Web page; you can find pages for groups from Microsoft (see fig. 25.9) to The Whole Internet Catalog (see fig. 25.10).

FIG. 25.9

This is the Microsoft Web page.

FIG. 25.10

This is The Whole Internet Catalog, a Web search tool you can use to search for any type of document accessible from the Web.

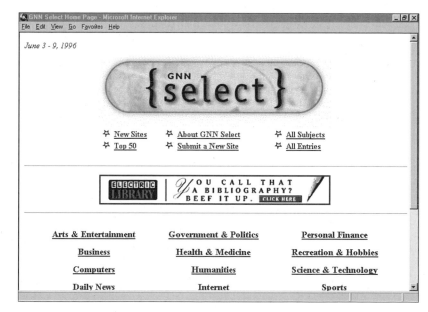

ON THE WEB

All Web pages, or Web sites, are identified by a unique address, called a universal resource locator (URL). The Microsoft page's URL address looks like this

http://www.microsoft.com/

The Whole Internet Catalog page's URL looks like this

http://gnn.com/wic/wics/index.html

All Web addresses begin the same way: http:// (which stands for *HyperText Transfer Protocol*, the Web language). With a Web browser, you also can visit FTP sites (described later in this chapter), which have addresses beginning with ftp://.

CAUTION

Like DOS file names, URLs have *no* spaces. Type the URL—or any Internet address you see—without spaces.

Time magazine has a Web page (see fig. 25.11). Begin with the Time Warner Web page at **http://www.pathfinder.com**.

FIG. 25.11

A view of the *Time* magazine Welcome Web page using the Internet Explorer browser.

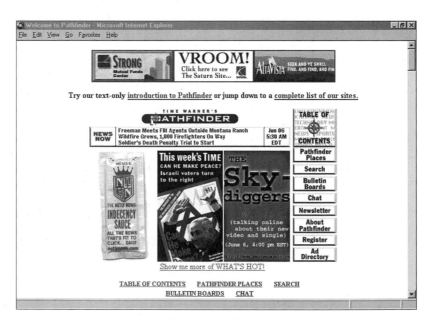

The *Time* magazine site has pictures and articles from its recent issues, a database of past issue contents, and even a BBS for chatting with other *Time* aficionados. The Time Warner page also provides links to other publications like *Sports Illustrated*, *People,* and *Fortune.*

One last note about the Web. Windows NT supplies the Internet Explorer browser with Windows NT. A browser is also provided with Windows 95. You don't *need* to use Internet Explorer, however. You can use any browser you like with Windows. The Netscape Navigator browser is a very capable product, and you can even download a free copy of the browser from the Netscape Web site.

 ON THE WEB

Visit the Netscape Web site at

http://www.netscape.com

E-Mail   The most widely used service the Internet provides is e-mail. With e-mail, you can be in almost instantaneous contact with anyone else on the Internet, no matter where they live or work.

Suppose that you have arranged to meet an associate the next morning in a distant city. It's late at night, your plans have changed, and you need to get in touch with him or her. Send an e-mail message. Most e-mail users check their mail every day.

How do you send an e-mail message? Just as in the outside world, where addresses include numbers, streets, cities, and states, everyone on the Internet has a unique e-mail address that looks like this:

username@anynet.com

Businesses, Internet organizations, and services such as Listserv (a program that keeps track of mailing lists) also have addresses. Your address is composed of your user name (such as jsmith) and your provider's domain. If Jane Smith signs on to America Online for her Internet access, she may have an e-mail address like this one:

jsmith@aol.com

If Joe Smith is already using that login name on AOL, Jane has to pick another one.

The Internet also has *mailing lists*, or e-mail discussion groups, on many topics (such as writing, pets, running a small business, and so on), comprised of members who subscribe to that mailing list.

N O T E   To *subscribe* to a mailing list—in other words, to join the discussion or just read others' postings—you send an e-mail message to the *listserver* who manages that mailing list.

To *send a message* to the members of a mailing list, after you have joined, post a message to the mailing list itself. You respond to messages in the mailing list in the same way you answer an e-mail message from an individual. ■

UseNet Newsgroups   Newsgroups are another important service on the Internet. Whereas e-mail is a one-to-one communication, newsgroups are many-to-many discussions, organized by topics. Over 10,000 newsgroups are currently on the Internet, dealing with every imaginable—and unimaginable—topic. The wildest are the unmoderated alt.* groups (alt is an abbreviation for *alternative*), on topics from **alt.0d** (which seems to be a bunch of test messages) to **alt.zine** (a newsgroup about alternative magazines). You can read messages from a newsgroup to see whether you want to subscribe. After you have subscribed, you can just lurk (Net-surfer's term for reading articles but not posting any) or you can enter into a discussion.

Most newsgroups identify *threads* (series of messages on the same topic) by indenting follow-up messages and by allowing the use of Re to indicate the topic of original posting. Some newsgroups allow you to sort messages by thread so you can follow threads that interest you and avoid those that don't.

When you first log on to the Internet and boot up your news program, the program prompts you to download the current list of newsgroups from the news server. Downloading more than 10,000 newsgroups may take a few minutes, but you need to do it only one time. You can refresh the list from time to time. To read the messages in a newsgroup, select the newsgroup from the list.

FTP   File Transfer Protocol (FTP) is one of the earliest functions of the Internet. FTP enables the movement of files from one computer to another over the Internet. Computers that enable you to dial in to them and download files from them are called FTP servers. Hundreds of FTP servers exist all over the globe, and each server has tens of thousands of files. How do you find what you're looking for?

Archie servers are computers that index the files available on FTP sites. Without going to each FTP site and browsing (a project that can take days and tie up Internet resources), you can go to an Archie server and find files by their names. Of course, if the file is about drug use in ancient Egypt, for example, but is named DR3AEG91.TXT, Archie has no clue what the file contains.

Gopher   Gopher takes over where Archie leaves off. *Gopher servers* are computers on the Internet that maintain lists of files residing on their own computers as well as others. With a *Gopher client* (a menu-based Gopher program you run on your computer) you can search many places on the Internet for the files you need. Gopher also enables you to attach descriptive comments to file names. Another advantage is that many Gopher servers have Web menus; you can use a Web browser, click a file name, and begin downloading a file to your computer.

Another search tool, *Veronica,* enables users to search menu items on Gopher servers. Veronica servers compile databases of Gopher menus and provide information about the files, in addition to the file names and their locations.

WAIS   Suppose that you're looking for as many documents as you can find about drug use in ancient Egypt, but you don't know the names of the files. *WAIS* (Wide Area Information Server) is the most useful search tool for this kind of search. WAIS has an index of keywords contained in all the documents on servers all over the world. Using WAIS, you can type **drugs** and **Egypt** to get information on your topic, even if the file names of the documents containing that information are obscure.

Telnet   Telnet, another Internet protocol, enables users to log in to a remote computer and treat that machine as though it were their own computer. In other words, if you want to get a file located on a machine half-way around the world, you can Telnet to a local computer, use that machine to Telnet to still another, and so on, until you reach your destination. Telnet can save you the cost of a long-distance call. All you need is the name of the local host computer. Recently, Telnet has provided a means for participants in *MUD* (Multiple User Dimension) games to play one another online.

TIP Because you use it to connect to several computers, Telnet is slow and uses a lot of system resources. If you have a better way to access a remote site, use it.

Using Software with the Internet

After all the configuration work you went through to get onto the Internet, it may seem that getting connected was the goal. But the real power of the Internet lies not in the connection, but in what you do after you are there. Windows NT includes a few Internet applications (if you don't like this software, you can find freeware or commercial software for your Internet applications):

- *Telnet* is a Windows NT-based program you use to log on to Internet sites as if your computer were a terminal connected to that computer. This version of Telnet is almost identical to the shareware version available at many sites on the Net; it is minimalist but has a good help file.

- *FTP* is a command-line program, not for the faint of heart, used to download files from remote computers connected to the Internet. A very good freeware Windows-based program is WS_FTP, copyright by John A. Junod, available from your Internet provider or at many FTP sites.

- *A World Wide Web Browser* enables you to cruise quickly around Web sites on the Internet. The top Web browsers are Microsoft's Internet Explorer and Netscape's Navigator. You also need so-called helper programs that enable you to view downloaded graphics and play sound files linked to may Web pages. In some cases, these applications are included with your Web browser. Internet Explorer is included with Windows NT and is covered in Chapter 26, "Using Internet Explorer, Internet Mail, and Internet News."

- *An e-mail tool* helps you read mail you receive across the Internet, as well as send and reply to messages. Windows NT provides an e-mail program for the Internet in its Windows Messaging client. Like Internet Explorer, Windows Messaging provides the standard amenities of any e-mail program but with the advantage of its integration into the operating system. Other top e-mail programs are Eudora, by Qualcomm, available as both a shareware and a commercial program; OS Mail, from Open Systems; and Z-Mail, from

Network Computing Devices, Inc. Last, a new program, Internet Mail, is included with Windows NT. Differing from Windows Messaging, Internet Mail focuses only on Internet mail; it has no links to other mail providers. Internet Mail is covered in Chapter 26, "Using Internet Explorer, Internet Mail, and Internet News."

- *A newsreader* is a tool you use with UseNet newsgroups. Trumpet News Reader is a freeware version, as is WinVN, by Mark Riordan. Also available are NewsXpress and Free Agent. Last, a new product, Internet News from Microsoft, is available free with Windows NT. Internet News is covered in Chapter 26, "Using Internet Explorer, Internet Mail, and Internet News."

Configuring Windows NT Internet Options

Windows NT provides a large number of options for controlling how you use and access the Internet from Windows NT Workstation. You can specify a wide number of options, such as how much storage Windows NT allots to saving images from Web sites you visit (to promote faster retrieval of images on the page when you return). Another option you can choose prevents viewing of Web pages with particularly violent content. Note that the Web browser you use with Windows NT must support the options you choose or these features will be of no use.

To configure the Internet Explorer's interaction with Windows NT, follow these steps:

1. Open the Start menu and choose Settings, Control Panel. Choose the Internet applet. The Internet dialog box appears (see fig. 25.12).

2. Customize how the Internet works by choosing the different tabs and making selections from the options presented. The next seven sections provide details on the options presented under each tab.

3. When you are done, choose OK to save changes and close the dialog box. To save changes but leave the dialog box open, choose Apply. To Cancel any changes made, choose Cancel.

Part
VI

Ch
25

General Options

Options provided on the General dialog box are covered in the following list (see fig. 25.12):

FIG. 25.12

The Internet dialog box contains a number of options for controlling Windows NT's interaction with the Internet.

- *Page Contents.* Deselect any of the checkboxes in the Page Contents frame if you do not want that type of element to appear on Web pages you view. Eliminating elements helps the page load faster. You may still access the page, but small anchors appear in place of those elements. Of course, you lose much of the enjoyment from the Web without access to images, sound, or video.

- *Colors.* You can specify how certain text appears for information you view on the Internet. To specify the color of text and background, check the Use Custom Colors for Text and Background checkbox. Then click the appropriate color box for either test or background and then choose a color from the Color dialog box (see fig. 25.13).

  The Internet also uses colors to demote links to other sites you have viewed and haven't viewed. For example, if a Web site shows a list of other related sites, the addresses of sites you have clicked on the list are shown in one color, and sites you haven't selected are colored differently. To specify the colors used for these two types of site addresses, click the Viewed and the Not yet viewed color boxes and then choose a color from the Color dialog box.

FIG. 25.13
You can choose colors (or create custom ones) for text and background on Internet resources you access in Windows NT.

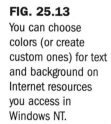
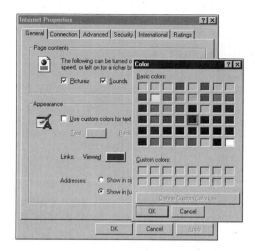

■ *Addresses*. Almost every WWW site provides links to other sites. Depending on the browser you use, as you drag your mouse pointer over the link to another site, the address of that site appears somewhere on-screen, such as the status bar. You can specify whether the full address of the site, for example, **http://www.microsoft.com**, or the short version, such as **www.microsoft.com**, appears by choosing the appropriate option button from the Addresses group.

Connection Options

The Connection tab in the Internet dialog box controls how Windows NT operates when your computer connects to the Internet (see fig. 25.14).

The following list describes the major features found on the Connection dialog box:

■ *Dial Whenever an Internet Connection is Needed*. This handy option enables you to easily access the Internet without having to worry about connecting first. For example, you can open your Web browser and choose a Web site without being concerned about starting Dial-Up Networking first. Windows NT detects that you are attempting to connect to the Internet and automatically attempts to connect to the Internet.

Related to this option is the Dial-Up Networking drop-down list. From the list, you select the Dial-Up Networking phonebook entry to use whenever you access the Internet directly without attempting to connect first. The drop-down list is available only when the Dial Whenever an Internet Connection option is chosen. You also can change the properties of the Dial-Up Networking option you choose or add a new phonebook entry by choosing the Properties and Add buttons.

FIG. 25.14
The Connection dialog box helps you determine how your computer connects to the Internet.

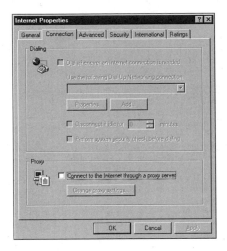

- *Disconnect If Idle.* This option can save you dollars in connect-time. You can specify, in minutes, how long Windows NT should wait for keyboard or mouse activity in your Internet application before automatically disconnecting you.

- *Proxy Servers.* For security reasons, your computer or the network to which it is attached may not connect directly to the Internet. Instead, you use proxy servers, which serve as intermediaries between your computer and the actual network resource you are trying to access, such as a Web site or FTP server. You specify the address of the proxy server you use with Windows NT from the Connection tab.

To configure Windows NT to connect to a proxy server when you are attempting to access an Internet resource, choose the Connect to the Internet through a Proxy Server option, then choose the Change Proxy Settings button. The Proxy Settings dialog box appears (see fig. 25.15).

FIG. 25.15
The Proxy Settings dialog box is where you specify the proxy server for connecting to different types of Internet resources.

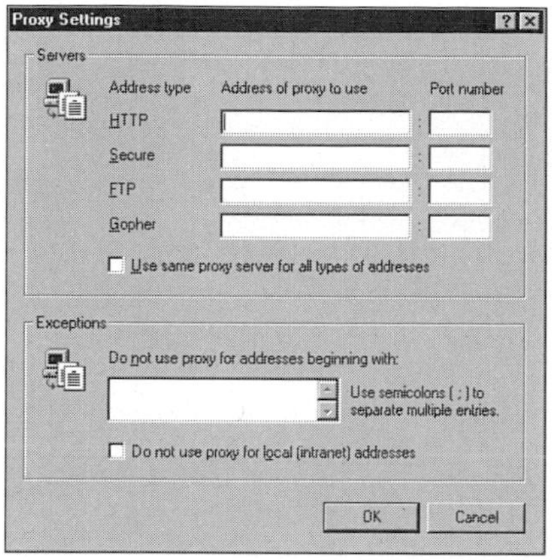

For each type of Internet resource, specify the proxy server address and port number. If a single proxy server is used to access all Internet resources, choose the Use Same Proxy Server for All Types of Addresses option and then enter the address and port number in the fields reserved for HTTP.

You also can enter specific types of addresses that you would not use a proxy server to access. Enter as much of any type of address as you require directly in the Do Not Use Proxy for Addresses Beginning With box. Choose OK to save changes you make in the Proxy Settings dialog box.

Advanced Options

Depending on the amount of graphics and other special elements contained on a Web page, such as audio and video clips, it can take a while for the entire page to appear on your screen. Considering the amount of data that must be sent across the Internet to your PC to display a Web page, performance can be a significant issue. Windows NT enables you to store copies of Web pages you have visited so they load much faster on subsequent visits to that page. Options under the Advanced tab in the Internet dialog box help you control aspects of this feature (see fig. 25.16).

Part
VI

Ch
25

FIG. 25.16

Options in the Advanced dialog box help you configure how your local system stores copies of Web pages you have visited.

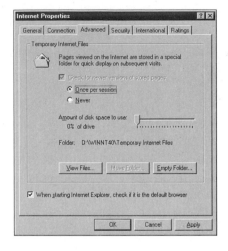

To configure how Windows NT stores and updates Web pages you have viewed, follow these steps:

1. To store images from Web pages you visit, specify how much space to allot to those images on your local hard drive. Drag the slider to the right to increase and left to decrease until the percentage you want to allocate is displayed. If you do not want to store any images on your local system, drag the slider as far to the left as possible.

 T I P If you can spare any room at all, storing images from the Web on your local system makes sense. Performance is significantly better if a page or image is loaded from your local hard drive compared to downloading it from the Web. Considering the cost of access charges, it is probably more economical to upgrade your hard drive to accommodate the Web resources you will be storing.

2. Most sites on the Web are continually evolving. Considering that many of the Web sites are informational in nature, such as the USA Today home page, page content at these sites changes continuously. In addition, rapid advancements in the technology available to developers of Web pages naturally result in frenetic changes in Web site content and appearance. Given these factors, Windows NT gives you the option of automatically updating stored Web pages with pages that have been updated on the Web.

Choose the Check for Newer Versions of Stored Pages check box to automatically update the Web pages stored on your PC with new pages.

3. The Once Per Session and Never option buttons enable you to control when the local versions of Web pages and their images are updated. If you choose Once Per Session, all local versions are checked immediately when you access the Web. Choosing Never means Web pages are not updated until you access the site where the local version originated.

4. You can see the list of pages and images for viewed Web sites that are stored on your system. Seeing the list of Web elements can help you decide which ones you may want to delete to reclaim hard drive space.

To view the list of Web resources you have stored locally, choose the View Files button. An Explorer window appears displaying the list of Web pages and images you have stored on your local system. You can select and then copy, cut, delete, or open any of the resources that appear in the window.

TIP To quickly delete one or more Web resources stored on your computer, select the resource(s) and then choose File, Delete Local Copy.

In addition to viewing the list of Web pages stored locally, you can move the folder where the pages are stored by choosing the Move Folder button. You also can delete all the Web resources stored locally by choosing the Empty Folder button.

▶ **See** "Working with Windows NT Explorer," **p. 163**

Security

The Internet is an open network, and security is an issue for both users of the network and administrators alike. Windows NT provides some security enhancements to protect the data you see and send over the Internet. The options are shown in the Security dialog box (see fig. 25.17).

The following list describes the two sets of options in the Security dialog box:

■ *Open Connection.* Enhancements to a number of Web browsers and services offered by ISPs can help you secure the messages you see and send. Some enhancements can ensure that only the recipient of your message receives it, and that messages you receive over the Internet have not been tampered with in transit. The options in the Safe Connection group in the Security dialog box help you configure some of these options.

It's best to take advantage of any of the options to display warnings or check certificates offered by Windows NT. You can choose both the Warn before Sending Over an Open Connection option and the Warn before Viewing Over an Open Connection option. Also, choose the Always option to check for an open connection regardless of the size of the message you're sending, and be sure to always check security certificates.

FIG. 25.17

The Security dialog box helps you configure security options for your Internet connection.

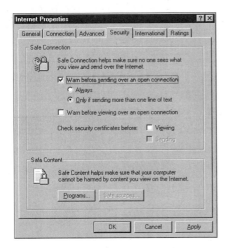

Active Content. Certain Web pages include what is known as *active content.* An example of active content would be a Java application. A Java application is a special Web-page element that is downloaded and then run on your local PC. The active content feature enables Web pages to work interactively with the user.

The Safe Content group at the bottom of the Security dialog box helps secure your system against possibly dangerous active content. When you choose the Programs button, the Programs dialog box appears (see fig. 25.18). From the dialog box, you choose whether to always receive warning when you are about to launch an active content page, whether to let Windows NT decide to warn you, or to receive no warnings. An example of an occasion when you may be warned is when a Java application (also known as a Java applet) is about to be downloaded to your PC.

FIG. 25.18
The options in the Programs dialog box help you determine how to handle Web pages with active content.

International

As a global network, the Internet provides access to information all over the world. As such, you may run into an Internet resource in a language other than your own. In this case, you probably want your keyboard to recognize the characters of the language of the Internet resource you're using. The International dialog box helps you configure your keyboard to work with the different languages you may encounter on the Internet (see fig. 25.19).

FIG. 25.19
You can specify character sets so you can work with Internet resources in languages different from your own.

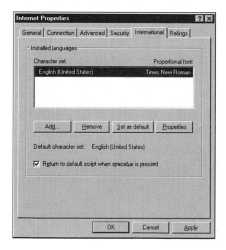

Part
VI

Ch
25

From the International dialog box, you can perform these tasks:

- Add support for a new language by choosing the Add button.

- Change the fonts associated with the language set by choosing the set from the list box and then choosing Properties.

- Delete support for an already installed character set by choosing the character set from the list box and then choosing Remove.

- Choose the default character set used by all Internet resources by choosing the character set from the list box and then choosing Set as default.

Ratings

As more businesses and individuals discover the Internet, the selection of topics for which information is available has also grown. Given the wide range of both users and providers of the Internet, the subject matter of the Internet has become quite diverse. As you may expect, the content offered at a particular Web site may not match the tastes of all users, and some may even call the content on some pages *offensive*. And as you may expect, groups and individuals have demanded that some control be placed over the availability of pages with questionable content.

As a product of this request, Web sites are assigned a particular rating based on their content, much as movies are. Based on a site's rating, you can choose to restrict access to particular sites from your computer. Your decision may be based on a company policy, the wishes of a parent, or your own personal preference. Access to these sites from Windows NT is controlled from the Ratings dialog box (see fig. 25.20).

To use ratings to control access to Internet resources from your computer, follow these steps:

1. From the Ratings dialog box, choose Set Ratings. The first time you choose this option, you are asked to supply a supervisor password. You must supply this password whenever some Rating option is modified. After supplying the new password, the dialog box shown in figure 25.21 appears.

FIG. 25.20
Windows NT lets you take advantage of ratings associated with Web sites.

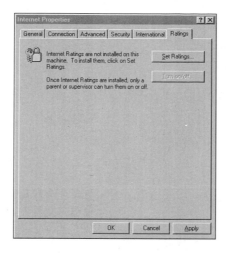

FIG. 25.21
The Internet Ratings dialog box appears after you supply a valid supervisor password.

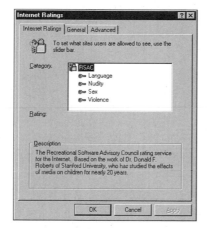

Part

VI

Ch

25

2. The default ratings system used in Windows NT is the Recreational Software Advisory Council (RSAC) rating service. A description of RSAC is at the bottom of the dialog box. Options provided with the ratings system are shown in the Category list box. To use a different ratings system, choose the General tab (see fig. 25.22) and then choose Ratings Systems (see fig. 25.23).

Choose the Add button, and then select the ratings system files to use. Next, choose OK to return to the General dialog box of the Internet Ratings dialog box. Choose the Internet Ratings tab.

FIG. 25.22
You can choose
Internet content
ratings systems to
use with Windows NT
as new systems are
made available.

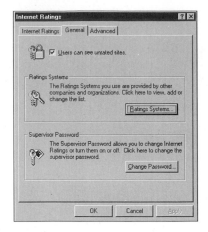

FIG. 25.23
Ratings systems are
stored in special
files, which you load
when you want to
implement a different
ratings system.

3. Specify the type and level of content to which you want to restrict access. Depending on the ratings system you use, different items appear in the Category list box. In the case of the RSAC, content categories like language and violence appear in the list.

Click different categories in the list box, and then use the slider that appears at the bottom of the dialog box to specify the level of the content category to which you will allow access (see fig. 25.24). Web sites will deny your system access if their content is more severe than the level you specified for any one of the categories.

FIG. 25.24
When you choose a content category, a slider appears, enabling you to specify the level of content to which you will allow access from your PC.

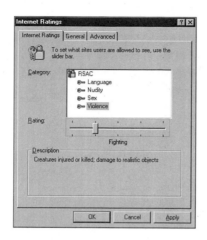

Other Rating Options

A few more options are related to assigning ratings for Internet access:

- You can disable the use of ratings to restrict Internet access. From the Ratings dialog box, choose Turn Off. You need to supply the supervisor password to do so.

- Some sites on the Web may not have ratings. By default, users on your PC *can* visit these sites. To restrict users from seeing Web sites that have not been rated, choose Set Ratings from the Ratings dialog box and select the General tab. Clear the Users Can See Unrated Sites checkbox.

- You can restrict access to Web sites that have a particular rating but still view the sites if you supply the supervisor password at the time you try to access such a site. To set up this option, choose Set Ratings from the Ratings dialog box and select the Advanced tab. Choose the User Can Type in Supervisor Password checkbox.

- Some Web sites act as ratings service bureaus, providing their own ratings to special ratings systems. In this case, you must supply the URL for the site providing the ratings. To do so, you use the Advanced dialog box, which you access by choosing Set Ratings from the Ratings dialog box. You probably should avoid using such a service because performance is usually terrible; this scheme means you must contact and query a secondary Web site for every other Web site you want to access.

Part
VI

Ch
25

From Here...

You should now have a good understanding of the Internet, the services provided by the Internet, and—most importantly—how to set up for and connect to the Internet. The following chapters containing information you may find useful in using the Internet with Windows NT Workstation:

- Chapter 23, "Using Dial-Up Networking."
- Chapter 24, "Configuring TCP/IP."
- Chapter 26, "Using Internet Explorer, Internet Mail, and Internet News."
- Chapter 27, "Using Peer Web Services."

Using Internet Explorer, Internet Mail, and Internet News

by Paul Sanna

During the time between the release of version 4.0 of Windows NT, the current version, and the release of the preceding version, 3.51, interest in the Internet has exploded. Taking advantage of that interest, Windows NT Workstation 4.0 connects easily to the Internet, thanks to built-in TCP/IP and connectivity software. In addition, Microsoft has made available—for free— perhaps the most helpful application for using the Internet: a Web browser. Windows NT includes Internet Explorer 3.0, and you can download Internet Mail 1.0 and Internet News 1.0 in minutes. This chapter introduces you to each of these products. ■

Using Internet Explorer

Internet Explorer 2.0 is Microsoft's full-featured World Wide Web browser. This chapter shows you how to cruise the Web using Internet Explorer. Some of Explorer's unique features include saving the location of your favorite Web sites to a local folder and specifying home and search pages.

Using Internet Mail

Internet Mail is Microsoft's Internet mail reader. This tool provides all the functionality needed to read and write Internet messages. This chapter provides an overview of the tool, which Microsoft is making available for free on its World Wide Web site.

Using Internet News

Internet News is Microsoft's newsreading tool that enables you to read and post messages to the thousands of newsgroups available on the Internet. Internet News includes all the standard functionality you need to work with newsgroups, as well as some interesting new features. This tool will also be available for free on its World Wide Web site.

Using Internet Explorer

Internet Explorer made its debut in August 1995 as part of the Plus Pack for Windows 95. Since then, updates have been available for free on the Internet. Versions of Internet Explorer have also been available for Windows 3.0, Windows NT 3.51, and now for Windows NT 4.0. Having a Web browser bundled with an operating system that ships with built-in TCP/IP support enables you to start cruising the Internet in a snap. All you need is an account on the Internet, and you're all set. Before diving too deep into this chapter, be sure you have connectivity to the Internet from your workstation. To do so, you should have TCP/IP set up on your Workstation and you should have set up a connection to the Internet either with an Internet Service Provider and connection through Dial-Up Networking or via the network to which your workstation is attached.

▶ **See** "Knowing What You Need to Connect to the Internet," **p. 677**

Installing Internet Explorer

Internet Explorer is not installed automatically when you install Windows NT, though you may have Internet Explorer already installed on a machine with Windows NT 4.0. Figure 26.1 shows the Windows NT desktop with the Internet Explorer icon. If you don't see the icon on the Desktop, you probably need to follow the installation procedures that appear after figure 26.1.

 If you haven't installed Internet Explorer version 2.0 but can already access the Web (using another browser or even an earlier version of Internet Explorer), you can download Internet Explorer from Microsoft's Web site. Downloading Internet Explorer guarantees that you get the latest version. To download, using any Web browser, jump to Microsoft's home page at **http://www.microsoft.com** and follow the instructions there to move to the Internet Explorer page and download. If you are asked whether to save the downloaded file to disk or to open the downloaded file immediately, save the file to disk and then run that file. (Internet Explorer should download as a self-extracting file that you can launch independently.) This way, if you have a problem during installation, you can always re-run the file instead of downloading it again.

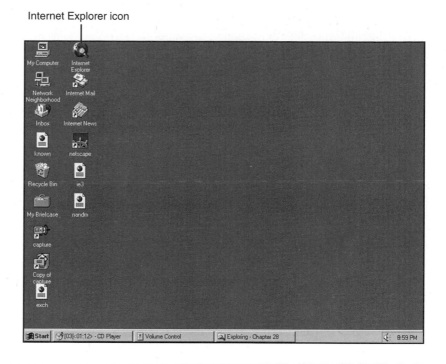

Internet Explorer icon

FIG. 26.1
The icon for Internet Explorer appears on the Desktop after Explorer is installed.

To install Internet Explorer, follow these steps:

1. Open the Start menu and choose Settings, Control Panel.
2. Choose Add/Remove Programs and then choose the Windows NT Setup tab.
3. Choose Accessories from the Components list box, and then choose the Details button.
4. Choose Internet Jumpstart Kit from the list and then choose OK. Next, choose OK from the Add/Remove Programs dialog box. Internet Explorer now installs.

Running Internet Explorer

To launch Internet Explorer, double-click its icon on the Desktop. If a winsock connection has been opened on your PC (by connecting to the Internet before starting Internet Explorer either with another Internet tool or directly from a Dial-Up Networking connection), Internet Explorer attempts to connect to the default home page. If a winsock connection has not been opened, you will be prompted to

Part
VI

Ch
26

attach to the Internet. The default home page is Microsoft's home page. You can change this default to some other page, as described later in this chapter.

Opening a Site on the Web

Every week, hundreds of new Web sites become active on the Internet. Each of these sites has a unique address, and to open one of these sites, you need to supply the site's address. You can use a number of methods to access a specific site on the Web:

- Choose File, Open from the menu, then enter the URL into the Open dialog box. Next, choose OK or press Enter.
- Type the URL directly in the Address drop-down list on the toolbar and press Enter.
- If you have already visited the site during the current session, select it from the Address drop-down list on the toolbar.
- If you have added the Web site to your folder of favorite sites, you can open the site by choosing it from the list on the Favorites menu.

If you visit a particular Web site often, the ultimate convenience is to place a shortcut to that site on the Desktop. Then whenever you want to visit the site, you just select the shortcut on the Desktop. Windows NT connects to the Internet, starts Internet Explorer, and then loads the site referenced by the shortcut. To do this, open the page to which you want to create a shortcut and choose File, Create Shortcut. Internet Explorer displays a message informing you that a shortcut to the page displayed has been created on the Desktop.

Navigating through a Web Site

After you have a Web site opened in Internet Explorer, you can use a variety of options to move through the site. On most Web sites, you find a variety of graphical elements, including links to other Web pages. These links can appear as underlined or colored parts of text, or as pictures. You can tell when your mouse pointer is positioned over a link to another page because the address of the page appears on the status bar (see fig. 26.2).

FIG. 26.2
When the mouse pointer moves over a link to another page, the address of that page appears on the status bar.

Link to another Web page

Address of the page

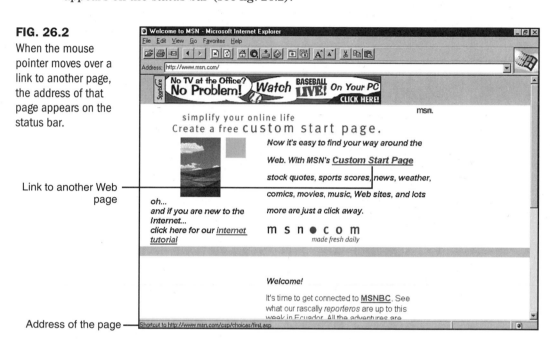

As you browse through different Web sites and the pages in them, you build a history list. The history list shows all the pages you have visited on the Web during the current session. By maintaining the history, you can move quickly to different pages you have already visited. Figure 26.3 shows the navigation tools available to you on the toolbar. Corresponding navigation help is available from the Go menu.

Part
VI

Ch
26

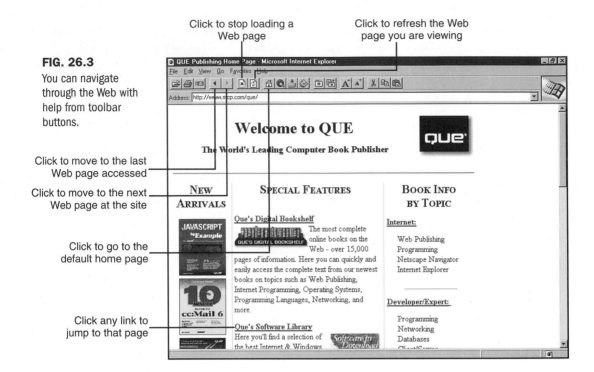

Click to stop loading a
Web page

Click to refresh the Web
page you are viewing

FIG. 26.3
You can navigate
through the Web with
help from toolbar
buttons.

Click to move to the last
Web page accessed

Click to move to the next
Web page at the site

Click to go to the
default home page

Click any link to
jump to that page

Working with Favorite Sites on the Web

Typical Web cruisers have a set of sites they routinely visit. For example, a certain computer book author routinely visits ESPN's home page and Que Publishing's home page, as well as a few news and financial sites. Internet Explorer (like just about every other Web browser) enables you to maintain a list of favorite Web sites, so you can easily go to these pages without entering the URL manually. These steps explain how to add a Web page to your list of favorite sites:

1. Open the page and choose Favorites, Add to Favorites Folder. The Add to Favorites dialog box appears (see fig. 26.4).

2. To add the Web page link to the Favorites folder, choose OK.

3. To store the link elsewhere on your system, choose the Create in button and then either select an existing subfolder of the Favorites folder or create a new folder by choosing the New Folder button. Next, choose OK.

FIG. 26.4
You can add a link to a Web page you visit often to the Favorites folder.

To access a favorite Web site, follow these steps:

1. Choose Favorites from the menu.

2. Choose the Web page from the pages listed at the bottom of the menu.

3. If your Web page does not appear on the list (because there is not enough room to list all your favorites), choose Open Favorites Folder, choose the link to your page, and then press Enter.

Configuring Internet Explorer Options

From the Internet Explorer menu, you can configure a number of options that control how Internet Explorer works. For example, you can specify the level of warnings provided to you by Internet Explorer when you are accessing a site on the Web that might not be secure. You configure the Internet Explorer options from the Options dialog box, which is available from the View menu (see fig. 26.5). In addition, more Internet options are available from the Internet applet in Control Panel.

▶ **See** "Configuring Windows NT Internet Options," **p. 693**

N O T E In the race to have the best Internet tools available, Microsoft provides updates to Internet Explorer, as well as to Internet Mail and Internet News, on a regular and rapid basis. (Netscape, developer of Navigator and other Internet tools, does the same.) You should be aware that downloading updated tools from Microsoft can change some of the options in Control Panel that control how your NT system works with the Internet. For that reason, there is a chance that some of the screens and procedures included in this chapter might not match exactly what you see on your screen. ■

Part
VI

Ch
26

FIG. 26.5

The Options dialog box enables you to configure options for Internet Explorer.

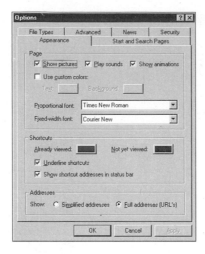

The options on the Start and Search Pages property sheet, shown in figure 26.6, enable you to specify which Web pages are your home page and search page. (A search page enables you to search the entire Web for words or phrases you supply.)

FIG. 26.6

You can specify which Web pages the Internet Explorer should use as your home (start) page and your search page.

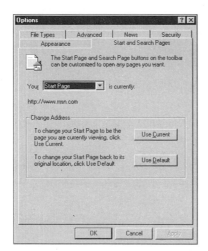

To specify a new home or search page, follow these steps:

1. Open the Web page you want to use and then choose View, Options.

2. Choose the Start and Search Pages tab.

3. Choose Start Page or Search Page from the drop-down list.

4. Choose Use Current, then choose OK.

To switch back to the original home or search page designated by your browser, follow these steps:

1. Choose View, Options.

2. Choose the Start and Search Pages tab.

3. Choose Start Page or Search Page from the drop-down list.

4. Choose Use Default, then choose OK.

 Every day, a Web search service is newly advertised. Some of these services are good and fast, and some are poor and slow. Depending on your Web browser, when you choose Search, services from a good or a bad search provider appear. You want to choose a search tool you can rely on. After you have identified a tool, be sure to update Internet Explorer with that information, as described in this section. Generally, you can tell how good a search provider is by the number of "hits" it return. A hit refers to the occurrence of the word or phrase you searched for in the title of a web document. If you've enter a common term or phrase to search for, and relatively few hits are reported, you probably want to try a different search service and compare the results.

File Types The File Types property sheet enables you to associate different file types with the applications that run them (see fig. 26.7). For example, you associate a Microsoft Excel spreadsheet file type (with an extension of XLS) with Microsoft Excel. Surfing the Internet will, most likely, expose you to even more types of files than ever before, so it's helpful to be able to associate these new file types with the applications they can work with directly from Internet Explorer. Examples of these types of files are images you can edit, sounds you can play, media clips you can view, and database tables you can browse. File types are covered in detail in Chapter 7.

▶ **See** "Understanding File Properties," **p. 181**

Configuring Security Options Internet Explorer provides a few options that help you control whether others can view data you read or send over the Internet. These options are available from the Security tab of the Internet Explorer Options dialog box (see fig. 26.8). The Tell me about Internet Security button brings you to a help screen that describes some of the security capabilities built into Internet Explorer. Options in the Security While Sending frame can help warn you if you

Part
VI
Ch
26

are sending information, such as a credit card number or other personal information, to a site on the Internet that is not secured. If a site is not secure, then information you send to that site may be visible to certain other Internet users.

FIG. 26.7
Using the File Types property sheet, you can associate specific applications with the different types of files you find embedded on Web pages.

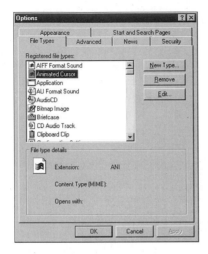

FIG. 26.8
The Security tab helps you ensure that data you see and send over the Internet is secure.

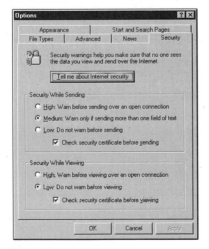

Customizing the Appearance of Internet Explorer

You can change how Internet Explorer appears using these options:

- To view a window showing the HTML code used to display images on-screen, choose <u>V</u>iew, <u>S</u>ource (see fig. 26.9).

N O T E HTML stands for HyperText Markup Language. HTML is the special code that
helps Web browsers and viewers determine how Web pages should appear on
your screen. People who develop Web pages using any number of tools ultimately
develop HTML code. ■

FIG. 26.9

Using Internet
Explorer, you can view
the HTML code
behind any Web
page.

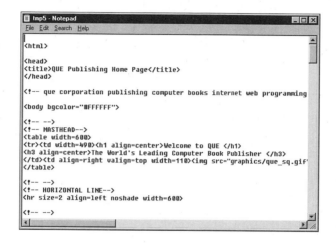

To view the toolbar, choose View, Toolbar. A check mark should appear next
to the Toolbar choice on the menu. To hide the toolbar (hence providing
more screen real estate to view Web pages), choose View, Toolbar to clear
the check next to Toolbar.

To view the status bar, choose View, Status Bar. A check mark should appear
next to the Status Bar choice on the menu. The best reason to keep the
status bar in view is that it displays the URL of any link your mouse pointer
passes over. In addition, the status bar displays important information, such
as the IP address of Internet sites you contact from Internet Explorer.

To hide the status bar, choose View, Status Bar to clear the check next to
Status Bar.

The Appearance tab on the Options dialog box also presents a number of
options for customizing the appearance of Internet Explorer. Choose View,
Options from the menu and then choose the Appearance tab (see fig. 26.10).

In the Page frame, you can specify whether elements such as sound, video

Part VI

Ch 26

FIG. 26.10
The Appearance tab lets you control the font, color, and special elements that appear on Web pages you view.

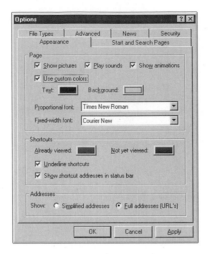

clips, and animated scenes appear when you access Web pages with those elements, and you can also specify the fonts used for text that is formatted in a proportional font and for text that is formatted with a fixed font.

In the Shortcuts frame, you specify how links or shortcuts to other Web pages are formatted. Included is an option to choose the color of the link to another web page (see fig. 26.11).

FIG. 26.11
You can choose any color to represent links you've used and links you haven't used.

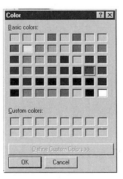

Searching the Web

Internet Explorer helps you search the Web for content you specify. A number of services provide search capabilities for the Web, and Internet Explorer provides a link to a page where you decide which service to use. There is usually a featured search service provider, which is the default service used when you choose search. Links to other search providers are usually provided on the same page. Other Web browsers may provide links to other search programs, or they may provide a link to just one service.

To display the search page, click the Search button on the toolbar or choose Go, Search the Internet from the menu. Figure 26.12 shows the search page accessible from Internet Explorer.

FIG. 26.12
Internet Explorer enables you to choose from a group of search utilities.

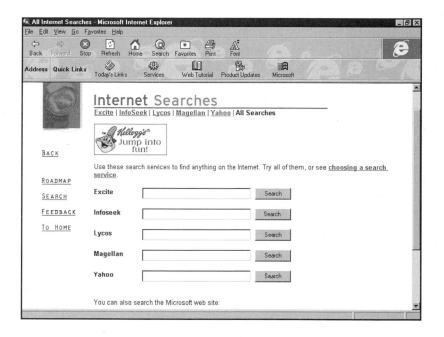

Each search program generally provides the same capabilities. You can get instruction on using the search service from a link on the search page. After the results of your search appear onscreen, you can usually jump directly to the page shown in the results list. Figure 26.13 shows the results of a Web search for the phrase "Windows NT" using the Yahoo service.

Part
VI

Ch
26

FIG. 26.13
A search of the Web using Yahoo finds more than 500 references.

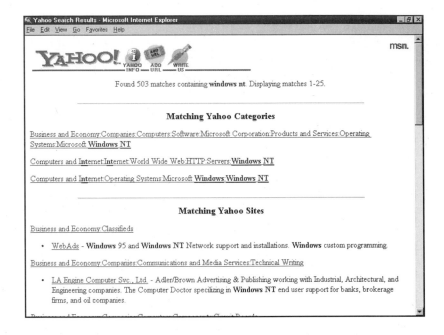

Using Internet Mail and Internet News

Microsoft's involvement in the Internet has evolved steadily and fairly quickly in the past year or so. Near the time of Windows NT 4.0's release, that evolution has not slowed down, so Microsoft has made its Internet tools, such as Internet Explorer, News, and Mail available in different ways. Internet Explorer is shipped with Windows NT, but you also can download it for free from the Web. Internet Mail and Internet News do not ship with Windows NT, but you can download them from the Web, and most likely they will be available in a special Plus Pack for the Internet. Regardless of how you acquire Internet News and Internet Mail, the installation routine remains the same.

Follow the instructions provided with the source for News and Mail to start the installation program. If you download the file from the Internet, you can open the self-extracting file immediately to begin installation, or you can save it to a disk. If you choose the latter, just start the installation by double-clicking the file you download in Windows NT Explorer. If you purchase Internet News and Mail, follow the provided instructions to launch the installation program.

Using Internet Mail

Internet Mail is a new mail reader developed by Microsoft for Windows NT and Windows 95. The program provides basic support for reading and writing Internet mail. Internet Mail differs from Microsoft Windows Messaging (the e-mail tool shipped with Windows NT) in one general but significant way: Internet Mail offers much less functionality. Internet Mail is designed solely for users to read and write mail over the Internet. Unlike Messaging, Internet Mail cannot support incoming or outgoing mail with mail providers other than the Internet. For example, Exchange can support a number of mail providers, such as corporate e-mail systems like Lotus cc:Mail and online services such as Compuserve or the Microsoft Network. Exchange users can read mail from and send mail to mailboxes in those other mail systems. In addition, Messaging includes a number of features that support groups of users in an organization. This section of the chapter, however, focuses on setting up and using Internet Mail.

Setting Up Internet Mail

After Internet Mail is installed, you need to supply your name and e-mail address, plus some other information so Internet Mail can retrieve mail from your Internet mailbox. Internet Mail asks for this information the first time you run it:

1. The Internet Mail Configuration Wizard starts the first time you run Internet Mail (see fig. 26.14). Launch Internet Mail from the Desktop and then choose Next from the first dialog box that appears.

2. In the next dialog box that appears, supply your name and e-mail address (see fig. 26.15). Your name appears in much of the Internet Mail correspondence, so take care when you supply it. Type your e-mail address in the Email Address edit box. You can obtain this information from your Internet service provider (ISP) or your network administrator. After entering the information required, choose the Next button.

   ▶ **See** "Knowing What You Need to Connect to the Internet," **p. 677**

FIG. 26.14

Internet Mail knows the information to ask you the first time you run the program.

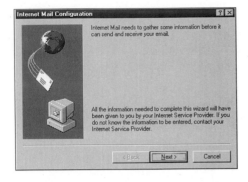

FIG. 26.15

Your name and e-mail address appear in all the messages you send using Internet Mail.

3. The next dialog box that appears also requires information from your ISP or network administrator (see fig. 26.16). Type the name of the server that stores the mail people send you in the Incoming Mail (POP3) Server edit box. Type the name of the server that stores and then routes the messages you send out in the Outgoing Mail (SMTP) Server. Choose the Next button.

FIG. 26.16

Internet Mail needs the name of the servers that handle your incoming and outgoing mail.

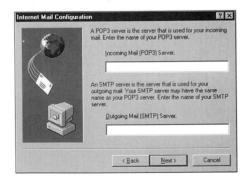

4. For your mail servers to properly identify you, you must supply your e-mail account name and password. Again, with information supplied by your ISP or network administrator, type your e-mail account name in the Email Account dialog box, and type your password in the Password edit box (see fig. 26.17).

FIG. 26.17
Your e-mail account name and password are required to ensure that only you receive mail intended for you.

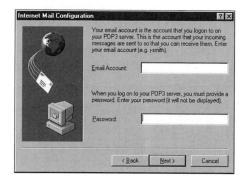

5. E-mail is used in Internet applications other than Internet Mail, such as when you send e-mail from your Web browser or newsreader program. To specify that Internet Mail is used as your default Internet e-mail program, choose the Yes option. If you prefer to use the more powerful Microsoft Exchange e-mail system, which is shipped with Windows NT, choose No (be sure you configure Messaging). Choose Next.

6. In the last dialog box you see, Internet Mail informs you that configuration is complete. Chose Finish to clear the dialog box. After the dialog box disappears, Internet Mail checks your mailbox for the first time.

Part
VI

Ch
26

Recognizing Items in the Internet Mail Window

This section introduces you to the objects you see in the Internet Mail window (see fig. 26.18). Internet Mail provides a few options to help customize the window in which you do all your e-mail work.

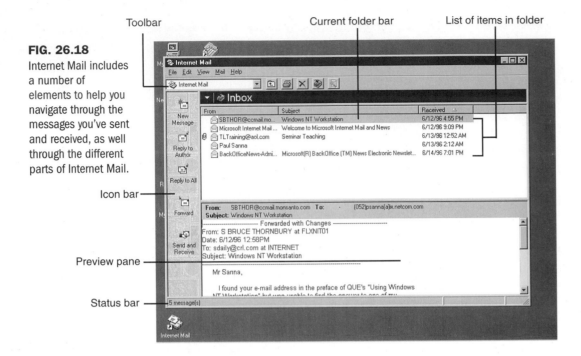

Toolbar   Current folder bar   List of items in folder

FIG. 26.18
Internet Mail includes a number of elements to help you navigate through the messages you've sent and received, as well through the different parts of Internet Mail.

Icon bar

Preview pane

Status bar

Customizing the Internet Mail Window

The following list describes the options for customizing the Internet Mail window:

- *Display or hide the toolbar.* Toggle the display of the toolbar on and off by choosing View, Toolbar from the menu. When the Toolbar choice on the View menu is checked, the toolbar is displayed.

- *Display or hide the status bar.* Toggle the display of the status bar on and off by choosing View, Status Bar from the menu. When the Status Bar choice on the View menu is checked, the status bar is displayed.

- *Display or hide the icon bar.* Toggle the display of the icon bar on and off by choosing View, Icon Bar from the menu. When the Icon Bar choice on the View menu is checked, the icon bar is displayed.

- *Split the screen horizontally or vertically.* You can split the screen into panes displaying the contents of the current folder, such as the Inbox or Outbox, and another pane displaying the items you have selected. Choose View, Preview Pane from the menu and then make the selection you want.

- *Display header information.* You can toggle the display of the header for messages you read in the preview pane. The header is the block of information at the top of any information which includes the sender's address, the message's topic, and your address. To toggle display of the header, choose View, Preview Pane and then Header Information.

- *Change the location of the icon bar.* Move the mouse pointer over any part of the icon bar other than the five icons. The mouse pointer changes to the shape of a hand. Click and drag the icon bar to either side of the window or to the bottom edge of the window.

- *Change the columns in the folder contents pane.* Choose View, Columns from the menu. Choose columns you want to view by selecting them in the Available Columns list box and choosing the Add button. Choose columns you do not want to view by selecting them in the Displayed Columns list box and then choosing Remove button. To change the order of columns displayed, choose a column to move in the Displayed Columns list box and then choose either Move Up or Move Down to reposition it.

Working in the Internet Mail Window

You do all your e-mail work in the Internet Mail window. The following list describes how to complete common tasks, such as sending a new message or replying to mail sent to you:

- *To send and receive mail.* Internet Mail automatically checks your Internet mailbox when you start the program (and you connect to the Internet). If you have been working in Internet mail for a while, you may want to send messages you have composed or check your mailbox again. To do either task, click the Send and Receive button in the icon bar or choose View, Refresh from the menu.

- *To check for new mail.* Choose View, Refresh from the menu.

- *To change the folder.* Click the current folder bar and then from the menu that appears, choose the folder whose contents you want to view (see fig. 26.19). Optionally, you can choose Mail, Go to Folder from the menu.

FIG. 26.19

You can quickly change the folder that appears in the Internet Mail window.

- *To compose a new message.* Choose the New Message button from the icon bar or choose <u>M</u>ail, <u>N</u>ew Message from the menu. Compose the message in the Message window that appears (see fig. 26.20). Then address the message and send it. See the next section, "Working in the Message Window," for help in composing your message.

FIG. 26.20

You use a separate Message window to compose messages.

- *To read a message you have received.* Choose Inbox from the folder bar. To view the message in the preview pane, click the message. To open the message in the Message window, double-click the message or right-click the message and choose <u>O</u>pen from the context menu that appears.

- *To reply to a message you have received.* From the Internet Mail window, select the message to reply to. If you are in the Message window, the message you are viewing is the message you will reply to. From the menu, choose <u>M</u>ail. To reply only to the author of the message, choose Reply to A<u>u</u>thor. To have your reply also sent to any persons on the cc: list, choose Reply to <u>A</u>ll. Compose your message in the Message window, address it, and then send the message (see fig. 26.21). See the following section, "Working in the Message Window," for help in composing your message.

FIG. 26.21
You compose replies to messages you have received in the Message window.

- *To forward a message to someone else.* From the Internet Mail window or the Message window, choose Mail, Forward from the menu. From the Message window, address the message, enter any text you want forwarded with the message, and then send the message.

- *To change the status of messages.* Messages sent to you appear in the Inbox folder. Messages that you haven't read or previewed appear in boldface, and messages you have read appear normal. Sometimes it's helpful to change the status of one, some, or all messages in your Inbox. This is especially helpful if you have access to your Internet mailbox from a number of locations, and you want to mark messages as messages you've read elsewhere. To do so, select the messages whose status you want to change. To select all the messages in your Inbox, choose Edit, Select All from the menu. To change the status of the selected messages to indicate you have read them, choose Edit, Mark as Read from the menu. To change the messages to an unread status, choose Edit, Mark as Unread from the menu.

Part
VI

Ch
26

Working in the Message Window

You will spend a great deal of time composing messages and replies to mail sent to you in the Message window. The Message window appears when you open a message sent to you, or when you choose to compose a message or reply to one. Figure 26.22 shows you how to compose messages and replies.

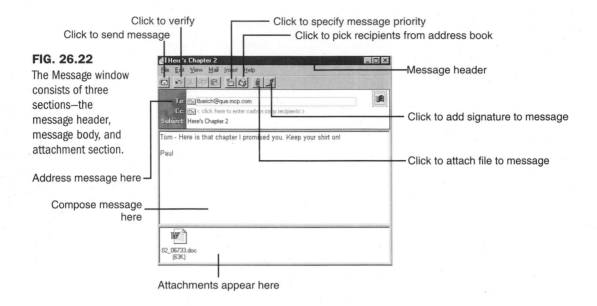

FIG. 26.22
The Message window consists of three sections—the message header, message body, and attachment section.

Click to verify

Click to send message

Click to specify message priority

Click to pick recipients from address book

Message header

Click to add signature to message

Click to attach file to message

Address message here

Compose message here

Attachments appear here

Configuring Internet Mail Options

A number of options are available in Internet Mail to help you specify exactly how you want the utility to operate. This section provides a quick overview of some of the more useful options. The options are presented in six property sheets in the Options dialog box.

To configure Internet Mail options, follow these steps:

1. Choose Mail, Options from the menu. The Options dialog box appears.

2. Customize how the Internet works by choosing the different tabs and making selections from the options presented. The next six sections provide details on the options presented under each tab.

3. When you are done, choose OK to save changes and close the dialog box. To save changes but leave the dialog box open, choose Apply. To cancel any changes made, choose Cancel.

Read Options   The options in the Read property sheet are self-explanatory except for one (see fig. 26.23). As you learned in the preceding section, when you click a message, it appears in the preview pane. Internet Mail marks a message as read if you preview a message for a certain amount of time. The Mark Message as Read option enables you to specify how long a message must remain in the preview pane continuously for its status to change to read.

TIP The Mark Message option can be helpful for people who receive lots of mail. By setting the previewed duration to a low value, a user can browse through messages quickly and have the messages automatically marked as read.

FIG. 26.23
The Read property sheet helps you specify how Internet Mail operates when you read messages.

Send Options   Options in the Send property sheet control how Internet Mail sends messages you compose (see fig. 26.24). Keep in mind these few things about the items presented in the property sheet:

- The Indent the Original Text option can be very helpful when you respond to messages. Because each line of a message you are replying to is preceded with the symbol you specify, you can very easily respond point-by-point to a message you have received. You can clearly identify in the message which comments are yours and which are part of the original message.

- The Advanced Settings button leads to a dialog box where you can configure what happens when you send attachments with messages. From the Advanced Settings dialog box, you specify the character set for messages you send and how the attachments are encoded. You can also determine whether messages are sent when you choose the Send button in the Message window or when you choose Send and Receive.

Part
VI

Ch
26

FIG. 26.24
The Send property sheet contains a number of options that help configure Internet Mail for delivering your messages and responses.

Fonts Options   The Fonts property sheet enables you to specify the typeface, size, and style for three different types of text in Internet Mail messages (see fig. 26.25):

- Text you write when composing a new message
- Text that appears with no formatting
- Text you write when you are replying to a message

To format any of the three types of text, choose the <u>C</u>hange button for the typeface element you want to change and then make selections from the Font dialog box (see fig. 26.26).

FIG. 26.25
Using the Fonts property page, you can specify typeface and style for different types of text that appear in messages you send and receive.

FIG. 26.26
The Font dialog box gives you several options for formatting the different text that appears in Internet Mail.

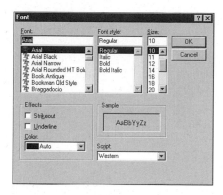

Spelling Options   The Spelling property sheet enables you to configure the use of the spell checker in the message window where you compose messages (see fig. 26.28). All options under the tab are self-explanatory, but one option deserves a bit of attention. Be sure to check the Always Check Spelling before Sending option. Unless you are a perfect speller, it makes sense to avoid embarrassment and check the spelling in your posting (frequently, the problem isn't really with spelling in our memos, but more with typing). This option forces the spell checker to run before a message is sent.

FIG. 26.27
Options in the Spelling property sheet help avoid the embarrassment of typos and sloppy spelling.

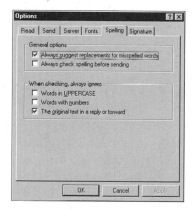

Signature Options   Messages you send naturally show your name as the author. (Remember supplying your name when you set up Internet Mail?) In the body of the message, however, you can edit your name (possibly change it to an organization to which you belong) as well as your e-mail address. Options under the Signature tab can automate some of the signature process for posting messages (see fig. 26.28).

FIG. 26.28
The Signature tab provides options for supplying your name, e-mail address, or other information in mail you create.

If you choose the No Signature option, Internet Mail offers no assistance in providing a signature in your mail. By choosing the Text or File options, you can specify the information you want to appear at the bottom of your mail. You can specify this information in the edit box that appears on the property sheet or in an external file. If you use an external file, you must format the file as simple text so Internet Mail can read it, and you must supply the file's name and location in the edit box.

Using Internet News

As you learned in Chapter 25, "Using Windows NT with the Internet," you use a newsreading program to participate in newsgroup discussions. Microsoft's Internet News program provides you with all the standard features of newsreading programs, like subscribing to news servers, newsgroups, posting messages, attaching files to messages you post or send, and reading messages. This section shows you how to set up Internet News then reviews the product's features and functions.

Setting Up Internet News

The first time you run Internet News, the program leads you through the setup process. Setup is different from the installation process that installs Internet News into Windows NT. Setup tells Internet News about your ISP's news server, your e-mail address, and other information. This list reviews what happens during setup:

1. The first time you use Internet News after installation, the Internet News Configuration Wizard starts up. The first dialog box you see is shown in figure 26.29. Choose Next to move to the next dialog box.

FIG. 26.29
The Configuration Wizard walks you through the setup of Internet News.

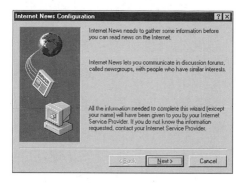

2. The first bit of information you're asked for is your user name and password. If you have already installed Internet Mail, the name and password you supplied to the Mail configuration tool is presented (see fig. 26.30).

FIG. 26.30
You supply the name that will appear in your newsgroup postings, as well as your e-mail address.

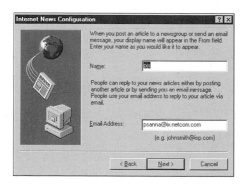

Your name is entered in the Name edit box. This name appears in messages you post to newsgroups. Your e-mail address is entered in the Email Address edit box. You enter your e-mail address because people who read your postings may want to reply to you personally without posting a message in the newsgroup for everyone to read. After entering the information required, choose the Next button.

T I P If you plan to be involved in any *interesting* newsgroup discussions, you may want to choose a clever name that shields your true identity from acquaintances who happen to be participating in the newsgroup. For example, if your name is Homer Simpson, you may not want to supply HOMERSIMP as your name, unless you want readers to recognize you as the author.

3. The next piece of information you provide is probably the most important. Internet News needs the name of the news server you will use. The news server provides to you the newsgroups in which you will be participating. This information is available from your Internet Service Provider (ISP) or your network administrator. The news server may require you to supply your account name and password. In this case, you must enter that information in the dialog box as well (see fig. 26.31). Enter the information and then choose Next.

ON THE WEB

You can log on to Microsoft's news server at

msnews.microsoft.com

FIG. 26.31
Internet News needs to know the name of your default news server.

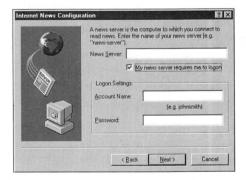

4. Indicate if you want Internet News to act as your default news reader. Choosing Yes means that if you access a newsgroup or posting from any source other than Internet News, such as your Web browser, Internet News launches to help you work. Make your selection and then choose Next.

5. Setup of Internet News is complete. In the last dialog box, choose Finish.

Now that you have supplied information for Internet News to connect to your news server, Internet News tries to make a connection. If logon completes, Internet

News begins download of all the newsgroups on your server (see fig. 26.32). Be patient; downloading may take a few minutes. You are now ready to read postings and respond to comments and questions you read.

FIG. 26.32
Internet News immediately begins downloading newsgroups after you have set up connectivity.

Recognizing Items in the Internet News Window

Before you get to know the features and functionality of Internet News, this section provides a quick review of some of the items you see in the Internet News window. Figure 26.33 points out the most important items in the window.

FIG. 26.33
The Internet News window shows you items in any of the newsgroups to which you subscribe, as well as the text of the item you've selected.

Probably the most important aspect of the information you see in figure 26.33 is the list of postings from Microsoft's newsgroup devoted to applications run in Windows NT. You can identify the newsgroup from the newsgroup bar, which always displays the name of the current newsgroup. In the newsgroup postings pane, you see *headers* for postings in the newsgroup. Instead of seeing the entire message, you see the subject supplied with the original message, as well as some other information. The preview pane shows more of the message. By scrolling through the headers in the newsgroup postings pane, you can read about all the messages posted in the newsgroup.

Subscribing to Newsgroups

After you set up Internet News for the first time or after you add a new news server, you must specify which newsgroups you want to participate in. This process is known as *subscribing*. When you subscribe to a newsgroup, all the messages users post in that newsgroup appear for you in Internet News. By choosing a number of different newsgroups on different news servers, you can participate in discussions on a wide range of topics. Follow these steps to subscribe to newsgroups:

N O T E   This information is presented at this point in the section because as soon as you set up Internet News, newsgroup headings are downloaded to your system. You can immediately specify which newsgroups you want to participate in. ▪

1. Choose News, Newsgroups from the menu or choose the Newsgroups button on the icon bar. The Newsgroups dialog box appears (see fig. 26.34).

2. From the News Server list box on the left side of the dialog box, choose the news server listing the newsgroups from which you want to select. If you have just installed Internet News, it is configured with just one server—the one you specified during setup. After you choose a news server, the list of newsgroups in the middle of the dialog box changes to display newsgroups from the server you chose.

3. To subscribe to a newsgroup, double-click it, or click once on the newsgroup and then choose the Subscribe button. A newspaper icon appears next to any newsgroup you subscribe to (see fig. 26.35). The name of the newsgroup gives you a clue to the content. Some of the newsgroups show a description.

FIG. 26.34
You select newsgroups in which to participate in the Newsgroups dialog box.

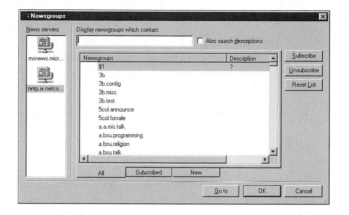

FIG. 26.35
A small icon appears next to newsgroups you have chosen to subscribe to.

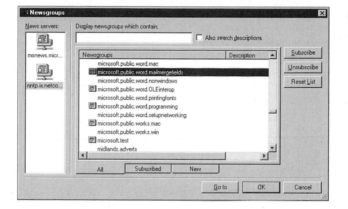

Part
VI

Ch
26

4. To clear the subscription icon from a newsgroup (hence choosing to not subscribe to the group), double-click the newsgroup's name, or click once on the newsgroup and then choose the Unsubscribe button.

5. To see just newsgroups to which you subscribe, choose the Subscribed tab. To see new newsgroups on the selected news server, choose the New tab.

6. After you have completed choosing newsgroups to subscribe to, you have two choices: you can hop right on the newsgroup by clicking the name and choosing the Go To button; or choose OK to return to whatever you were doing in Internet News before you started working with newsgroups.

7. If you choose Go To, Internet News immediately begins downloading postings from the newsgroup you selected.

Adding a News Server

The news server you specified when you set up Internet News is just one of thousands of news servers available. Each news server has its own set of newsgroups in which you can participate. You can generally find the name of news servers in computer magazines, postings on other news servers, and even with new software you receive. Follow these steps to add another news server to the list of servers you have:

1. Choose News, Options from the menu. The Options dialog box appears. Choose the Server tab (see fig. 26.36).

FIG. 26.36

You add new news servers from the Server tab of the Options dialog box.

2. Choose the Add button. The News Server Properties dialog box appears (see fig. 26.37). Type the full name of the news server in the News Server Name box. For example, to add one of Microsoft's news servers, type **msnews.microsoft.com**.

3. To participate in its newsgroups, your news server may require you to log on. This is probably the case if the user ID and password for your new server are different from what you provide to your ISP when Dial-Up Networking connects you to the Internet. If so, choose This Server Requires Me to Logon check box and then supply your user ID in the Account Name edit box, and your password in the Password edit box.

4. To specify a port number, choose the Advanced tab and enter the value. You also can specify the time-out value for the server. The time-out value specifies how long Microsoft should wait for a response from the news server.

FIG. 26.37
Type the name of the news server containing newsgroups to which you want to subscribe in the News Server Properties dialog box.

5. Choose the OK button. The news server is added to the list of servers to which Internet News can connect. Follow the instructions provided earlier in the "Subscribing to Newsgroups" section to specify the newsgroups in which you want to participate that belong to the news server you just added.

Customizing the Internet News Window

A handful of options are available to let you customize the appearance of the Internet News windows:

- *Display or hide the toolbar.* You can toggle the display of the toolbar in the Internet News window by choosing View, Toolbar from the menu. When the Toolbar choice on the View menu is checked, the toolbar is displayed.

- *Display or hide the status bar.* Toggle the display of the status bar on and off by choosing View, Status Bar from the menu. When the Status Bar choice on the View menu is checked, the status bar is displayed.

- *Display or hide the icon bar.* Toggle the display of the icon bar on and off by choosing View, Icon Bar from the menu. When the Icon Bar choice on the View menu is checked, the icon bar is displayed.

- *Split the screen horizontally or vertically.* You can split the screen into panes, one which displays the postings in the currently selected newsgroup, and another that displays the items you have selected. Choose View, Preview Pane from the menu and make the selection you want.

■ *Change the location of the icon bar.* Move the mouse pointer over any part of the icon bar other than the five icons. The mouse pointer changes to the shape of a hand. Click and drag the icon bar to either side of the window or to the bottom edge of the window.

■ *Change the columns in the folder contents pane.* Choose View, Columns from the menu. Choose columns you want to view by selecting them in the Available Columns list box and choosing the Add button. Choose columns you do not want to view by selecting them in the Displayed Columns list box and then choosing the Remove button. To change the order of columns displayed, choose a column to move in the Displayed Columns list box and then choose Move Up or Move Down to reposition the column.

Working with Postings

By this time, you have set up the program to communicate with your default news server, add a new news server, subscribe to newsgroups, and even customize the appearance of Internet News. It's time to start work in Internet News! This list describes some instructions on completing common tasks in Internet News:

■ *To read a posting.* All you do to read a posting is click the header of the posting in the newsgroup posting pane, and the message appears in the preview pane. To read the message in the Message window, double-click the header (see fig. 26.38).

FIG. 26.38
You can read postings more easily in the Message window, which enables you to view messages one at a time.

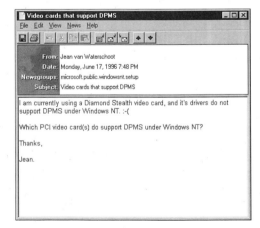

If a plus symbol appears next to a posting, someone has replied directly to that message. Click the plus sign in the newsgroup posting pane to see the header of the response. You may see that the response has a plus symbol as well, which means someone has responded to the response. A minus symbol in front of a posting means that any replies to the posting are in view. No symbol in front of a posting means that the posting has no reply.

■ *To respond to a posting.* If you are reviewing messages in the preview pane, click the message to which you want to respond. If you are reading messages in the Message window, the message you are reading is the message you will respond to.

To respond so that your message appears in the newsgroup, choose News, Reply to News group. To reply to the message via an e-mail message to the author of the posting, choose News, Reply to Author. Write your response in the Message window, then mail your response. See figures 26.39 and 26.40 for help in composing your response in the Message window.

Press the Post button to send
your message to the newsgroup

FIG. 26.39

You can compose responses to postings for the entire newsgroup to read.

Enter response here

Or intersperse your reply in the original posting's text

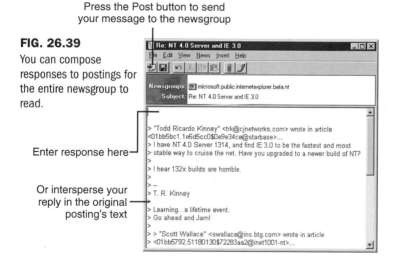

Part
VI

Ch
26

FIG. 26.40
When you reply to the author of a newsgroup posting, the author's e-mail address appears in the Message window.

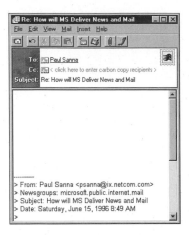

- *To create a new topic.* From the Internet News window or the Message window, choose News, New Message to Newsgroup. In the Message window, type a subject, which will become the header for the message. Then compose your new message and mail it. See figure 26.41 for help.

FIG. 26.41
You create postings to newsgroups in a separate window from the rest of Internet News.

Press the Post button to send your message to the newsgroup

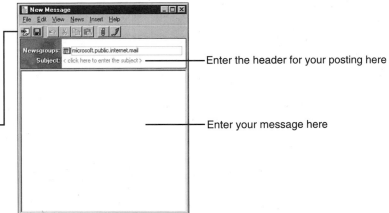

Enter the header for your posting here

Enter your message here

- *To forward a posting to someone via e-mail.* Select the message to post, and then from the Internet News window or the Message window, choose News, Forward from the menu. To send the message as an attachment (which means the recipient doesn't immediately see the forwarded message but must detach to view it), choose <u>N</u>ews, Forward as <u>A</u>ttachment from the menu. Enter the recipient of the message in the Message window, compose any header you want for the message, and then send the message. Figure 26.42 can help you forward a message; Figure 26.43 can help you forward a message as an attachment.

FIG. 26.42

You can forward any posting in a news-group to someone via e-mail.

Press the Send button to mail the message

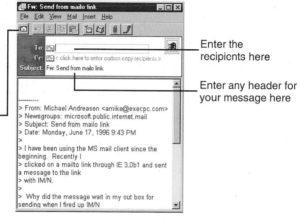

Enter the recipients here

Enter any header for your message here

FIG. 26.43

When you forward a message as an attachment, the attached file appears at the bottom of the Message window, and the recipient must double-click the message to open it.

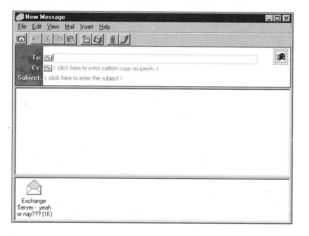

Part

VI

Ch

26

■ *To attach a file to a posting or message.* From the Message window, compose
your message, posting, or reply as you normally would. Next, click the
Attachment button on the toolbar. Select the file to attach. Figure 26.44 points
out the Attachment button.

FIG. 26.44
You can attach any
type of file to a
posting you forward
or a message you
place in a
newsgroup.

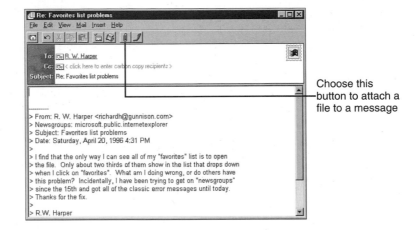

Choose this
button to attach a
file to a message

Understanding Options in the Message Window

The preceding section covered some of the features available in the Message window. This section fills in the gaps, focusing on the rest of the features. Figure 26.45
points out some of the features that help you navigate though newsgroups.

Reply to newsgroup

Reply to author of message you're reading

Forward message you're reading

Read previous message in newsgroup

Read next message in newsgroup

FIG. 26.45
A number of options
in the Internet News
window help you
move through the
messages in a
newsgroup.

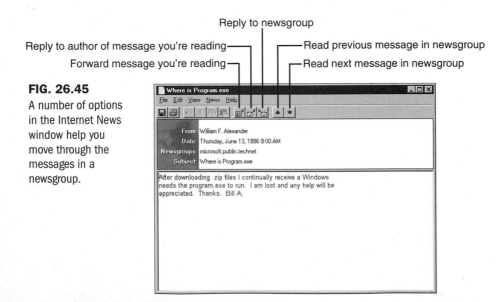

A few more options are available to help you compose messages:

- *Check Spelling.* To check the spelling in your message before you send it, press F7.
- *Check Recipients.* To be sure you have the correct names in the To and CC parts of your message, press Ctrl+K.
- *Maintain Address Book.* To add and delete names from the address book you use to send and forward messages, choose File, Address Book from the menu.

Configuring Internet News

In addition to the preceding options that control navigation and help you compose messages in the Internet News window, a number of options control how the program behaves. For example, you can specify that all postings are marked as read when you leave a newsgroup, or specify how the spell checker works to help edit your postings. These and other options are specified in the Options dialog box, which appears when you choose News, Options from the menu. This section provides an overview of some the useful, relevant options.

Read Options   Options in the Read property sheet determine how often Internet News checks for new messages, if you are notified when new newsgroups appear, plus other aspects of the postings you view in Internet News (see fig. 26.46).

FIG. 26.46
You can specify a number of options related to reading newsgroup postings from the Read property sheet.

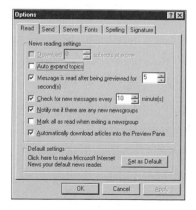

Part
VI

Ch
26

Among the most interesting options are the following:

- *Message is read after you preview it.* Internet News marks a message as read if you view a posting in the preview pane for a certain amount of time. The Message is Read option enables you to specify how long a message must remain in the preview pane for its status to change to read.

- *Download subjects.* When you first subscribe to a newsgroup, downloading all the messages can take a particularly long time, especially for a popular newsgroup. To specify that Internet News stop periodically during download, giving you the opportunity to review some of the postings, specify the number of messages you want to download at one time.

Send Options   Options in the Send property sheet determine the behavior of Internet News when you are posting messages to the newsgroup (see fig. 26.47). The settings can determine whether the original message is copied into the Message window when you are replying to a message, as well as the symbol used to mark lines in the original message (this feature enables you to easily intersperse your comments with the original message).

FIG. 26.47
Using the Send property sheet, you can customize the way Internet News behaves when you are posting messages.

Advanced Send Options   A dialog box with a new set of options appears when you choose the Advanced button on the Send property sheet (see fig. 26.48).

FIG. 26.48
Options in the
Advanced Settings
dialog box help you
deal with large
attachments to your
message.

The options determine, among other things, the format for attachments to messages that you send via e-mail, whether you are replying to or forwarding a message. MIME stands for Multipurpose Internet Mail Extensions. Unfortunately, not all mail readers can understand MIME attachments. Attachments formatted as Unicode, specified by the UUEncode option, require some work as well. A recipient of a message with an attachment in Unicode must acquire a Unicode decoder, available from many locations on the Internet. If you receive a message with a MIME attachment and your e-mail reader cannot handle it, you'll have to ask the sender to resend it in another way.

Other options in the dialog box include helping you break into smaller pieces the larger attachments that you send. If you are downloading one large attachment and you lose the connection, your recipient needs to resume from the start.

Server, Fonts, Spelling, and Signature Options   Options under the Server tab were covered earlier in "Setting Up Internet News." The options you find under the Fonts, Spelling, and Signature tabs for Internet News are the same as the options for Internet Mail except that they apply to the messages you post in newsgroups. Consult the "Configuring Internet Mail Options" section found earlier in this chapter for an explanation of the options in these three property sheets.

Part
VI

Ch
26

From Here...

In this chapter, you learned about Internet Explorer 2.0, and the Internet News and Internet Mail tools. You learned how to use these tools and how to customize their appearance and behavior. Be sure to check Microsoft's Web page for updates to these tools. In addition, the following chapters can provide you with some help in working with the Internet:

- Chapter 24, "Configuring TCP/IP."
- Chapter 25, "Using Windows NT with the Internet."
- Chapter 27, "Using Peer Web Services."

Using Peer Web Services

by Kevin Jones

Peer Web Services allow you to share information on the Internet and intranet. You share this information by creating your own Web, FTP, and Gopher sites on your workstation. These are fully functional servers, but are designed for low volume publishing. ■

Understanding how Peer Web Services work

You learn about the components that comprise the Peer Web Services and what features each component supports. With this knowledge, you will be prepared to publish information on the Internet or on your company's intranet.

Installing Peer Web Services

You learn how to install the Peer Web Services component onto your workstation.

Configuring Peer Web Services

You learn how to configure each of the components of the Peer Web Services. You learn how each component uses security, directories, and server logging.

Securing your Peer Web Services

Learn how to use new key certificates to make your Web site really secure.

Understanding Peer Web Services

Peer Web Services are designed to provide you a way to share information on the Internet or intranet. While these provide many of the same features as stand-alone products, such as Internet Information Server (IIS), they are designed for much lower volume. Because of this, they are ideally suited for sharing information on a corporate intranet.

The information can be shared in any of three ways. First, you can create Web pages and share them using the Web service. Other users on the intranet can then access your Web site using any Web browser, such as Netscape's Navigator or Microsoft's Internet Explorer.

Second, you can simply allow users access to browser-specific directories on your machine using any FTP client. They can use their client software to copy files to or from the FTP-allowed directories.

Third, you can provide access to files using the Gopher service. This is similar to FTP, but provides some additional capabilities, including providing additional file information and links to other computers.

Internet versus Intranet

Throughout this chapter, references are made to the Internet and the intranet. You may be wondering what is the difference between the two. The difference isn't technical, but rather is a difference of usage and implementation.

The Internet is a worldwide network of computers. This network operates using TCP/IP and has several protocols that help share information. These include HTTP (hypertext transfer protocol) for Web browsing and FTP (file transfer protocol) for file sharing.

▶ **See** "Configuring TCP/IP," **p. 639**

An intranet is a private network that uses the same technology (TCP/IP and protocols) used by the Internet. The difference is that users outside of the private network can't access the servers within the intranet. This can be accomplished by a variety of implementation techniques. How this is accomplished isn't important to understanding Peer Web Services. What is important is to understand that this allows you to share confidential information with coworkers, without worrying about information getting outside of your intranet.

Peer Web Services Components

Peer Web Services are comprised of three components—a Web Server, an FTP server, and a Gopher server. There are also management programs—the Internet Service Manager and Key Manager. Together, these programs provide you with the ability to share information on the Internet or intranet. This information can be in the form of Web pages or simply sharing files.

Web Services   The Web service supports sharing HTML files using the HTTP protocol. When a user first connects to the Web service using a Web browser, the Web service responds by sending him the default (or requested) Web page. As the user navigates between pages using the hyperlinks embedded into the Web pages, the Web browser sends a request for each new page.

FTP Services   The FTP service supports sharing any type of file using the FTP protocol. When a user uses an FTP client to access the FTP service, he can view and browse the allowed directories. He can also copy files from the FTP service to his computer. If you have granted users write access, he can copy files from his computer to the FTP server.

Gopher Services   A Gopher service also supports sharing any type of file. However, Gopher adds the ability to create links to other computers, add annotations to file and directories, and add custom menus. This is done by creating tag files. See the section "Creating Gopher Tag Files" later in this chapter.

The Gopher service not only supports all the standard Gopher features, but also supports what are known as Gopher Plus selector strings. This allows the services to return additional information to Gopher clients, such as the administrator's name and e-mail address, file modification dates, and MIME types.

Part
VI

Ch
27

Installing Peer Web Services

Peer Web Services are installed as a networking service. Before you install Peer Web Services, you must first install your network adapter software and, at least, the TCP/IP networking protocol. After you have your network installed and running, you are ready to install the Peer Web Services.

To install the Peer Web Services, follow these steps:

1. From the Start Menu, choose Settings, Control Panel.

2. Select the Network applet and press Enter. The Network dialog box appears (see fig. 27.1).

FIG. 27.1
Use the Network dialog box to install the Peer Web Services.

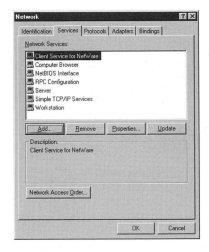

3. Select the Services tab.

4. Choose Add. The Select Network Service dialog box appears (see fig. 27.2).

5. Select Microsoft Peer Web Services and choose OK. The Files Needed dialog box appears.

FIG. 27.2
Select the network service, in this case, Peer Web Services, that you want to install.

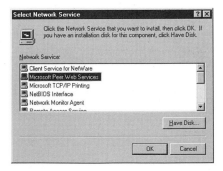

6. Type in the path where the Windows NT installation files can be found. For example, if you are installing from a CD-ROM that is drive D:, you would enter **D:\i386** for Intel-based Windows NT. Choose OK to continue. The Microsoft Peer Web Services dialog box appears.

7. If you are running any applications, you should close them now, before setup begins copying files. After closing any running applications, choose OK to continue. The Microsoft Peer Web Services Setup dialog box appears (see fig. 27.3).

FIG. 27.3
The Peer Web Service options allow you to select which files to install.

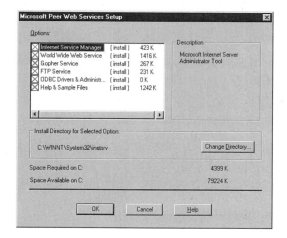

8. Select the portions of the Peer Web Services you want to install in the Options listbox. Those options marked with an "x" will be installed.

9. If you want to install the Peer Web Services into another drive or directory, choose Change Directory. Select the new location to install the Peer Web Services and choose OK to continue.

10. Choose OK to continue. The Publishing Directories dialog box appears (see fig. 27.4).

11. If you want to change the directory that each service publishes to the Internet, type in the new path for each service—World Wide Web, FTP, and Gopher—in the appropriate edit field. Alternately, you can choose Browse to select a new path. Choose OK to continue.

Part
VI
Ch
27

FIG. 27.4
Selecting directories
that will be published
by each Peer Web
Service.

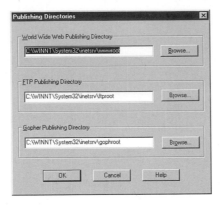

12. If you choose to install the ODBC Drivers, the Install Drivers dialog box will appear. Select the driver(s) you want to install in the Available ODBC Drivers listbox. Choose OK to continue. The driver(s) will now be installed.

13. If the install completes successfully, the dialog box in figure 27.5 appears. Choose OK to finish setup.

14. Choose OK on the Network property page dialog box to complete the install of the Peer Web Services.

FIG. 27.5
Selecting to install all
the Peer Web Service
options.

IUSR_*computername* Account

When you install Peer Web Services, a user account is automatically created that is the default account used for anonymous connections. You can change this default for each service by configuring the Service. See the following sections on configuring the options for each service.

You can change the user rights for the IUSR_*computername* account by using the User Manager. If you are using NTFS volumes, you can set the file permissions the IUSR_*computername* user has for each folder or file by using the Windows NT Explorer.

Configuring Peer Web Services

Each service can be separately configured. You can change such things as the directories used, performance parameters, logging setup, and connection parameters.

Configuring Web Services

There are three basic categories of Web Services you can configure—Service Options, Directories, and Logging.

Configure Web Options   To configure World Wide Web (WWW) Services options, follow these steps:

1. From the Start Menu choose Programs, Microsoft Peer Web Services (Common), and Internet Service Manager.

2. Select the WWW service you want to configure.

3. Choose Properties, Service Properties from the menu. The WWW Service Properties dialog box appears.

4. Choose the Service tab (see fig. 27.6).

5. Enter in the number of seconds without activity that a connection will be kept open before it is disconnected in the Connection Timeout box. The default is 900 seconds, or 15 minutes.

6. Enter in the maximum number of simultaneous connections that you want to allow in the Maximum Connections box. The default is 100,000.

7. Enter in the Username and Password to use when an Anonymous (or Guest) connection is made, in the Username and Password boxes, respectively. By default, the Username is set to IUSR_*computername*.

Part
VI

Ch
27

FIG. 27.6
The default values for
the WWW Service
properties.

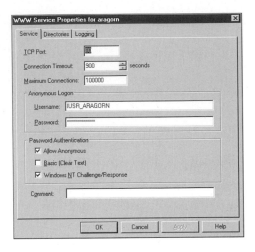

8. Select the types of Password Authentication you want to use. You can select any or all of the following—Allow Anonymous, Basic (Clear Text), and Windows NT Challenge/Response.

9. If you want to have additional information about this service displayed in the Internet Service Manager's Report View, you can add that information in the Comment edit field. For example, you might add a comment about where the machine is located (Kevin's office) or the contents of the Website (Sales and Marketing information).

10. Choose OK to finish setting the options.

Configure Web Directories   To configure WWW Services directories, follow these steps:

1. From the Start Menu, choose Programs, Microsoft Peer Web Services (Common), and Internet Service Manager.

2. Select the WWW service you want to configure.

3. Choose Properties, Service Properties from the menu. The WWW Service Properties dialog box appears.

4. Choose the Directories tab (see fig. 27.7).

FIG. 27.7
The default directories with an additional virtual directory.

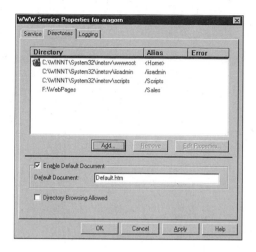

5. To add additional directories, choose Add. To edit the directory properties, select the directory you want to edit in the list box and choose Edit Properties. In either case, the Directories Properties dialog box appears (see fig. 27.8).

6. If you are adding a directory or want to change the directory, type in the path of the Directory edit field or choose Browse to select the directory.

7. If you want this to be the home directory, choose Home Directory. If you want this to be a virtual directory, choose Virtual Directory and type in a name to use as the alias in the Alias edit field.

NOTE Virtual directories don't appear in directory listings in either Web browsers or FTP clients. To access a virtual directory the users must know the virtual directory's alias, and type the URL address in their browser or FTP client. To avoid this, you can create links to the virtual directories in HTML pages, you can create explicit links in tag files so that users can access virtual directories when using Gopher clients, and you can list virtual directories by using directory annotations for FTP clients. ■

8. If the directory you are configuring is specified with a UNC (Universal Naming Convention) name, you need to specify a username and password that will be used when accessing this directory.

Part
VI

Ch
27

9. To set the access rights on the directory, choose any of the following options—Read, Execute, and Require Secure SSL channel.

10. Choose OK to finish setting the directory options.

11. To specify the default document that should be displayed, choose Enable Default Document and type in the file name of that document in the Default Document edit field.

12. If you want the user to be able to get a directory listing of your Website, choose Directory Browsing Allowed.

13. Choose OK to finish setting the WWW Service directory options.

FIG. 27.8
Specifying a virtual
directory for a WWW
Service directory.

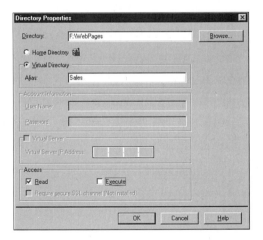

Configuring FTP Services

There are four basic categories of FTP Services you can configure—Service Options, Messages, Directories, and Logging.

Configuring FTP Options   To configure FTP Services options, follow these steps:

1. From the Start Menu, choose Programs, Microsoft Peer Web Services (Common), and Internet Service Manager.

2. Select the FTP service you want to configure.

3. Choose Properties, Service Properties from the menu. The FTP Service Properties dialog box appears.

4. Choose the Service tab (see fig. 27.9).

FIG. 27.9
The default values for the FTP Service properties.

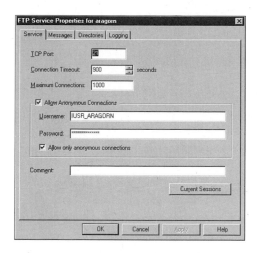

5. Enter in the TCP port number you wish to use. Normally, you should always leave this as the default of 21.

6. Enter in the number of seconds without activity that a connection will be kept open before it is disconnected in the Connection Timeout edit field. The default is 900 seconds, or 15 minutes.

7. Enter in the maximum number of simultaneous connections that you want to allow in the Maximum Connections edit field. The default is 1,000.

8. If you want anonymous access to the FTP site, choose Allow Anonymous Connections.

9. If you allow anonymous access, enter in the username and password to use when an Anonymous (or Guest) connection is made. Enter the username and password in the Username and Password edit fields, respectively. By default, the Username is set to IUSR_*computername*.

10. If you only want to allow anonymous connections, choose Allow only Anonymous Connections.

11. If you want to have additional information about this service displayed in the Internet Service Manager's Report view, you can add that information in the Comment edit field. For example, you might add a comment about where the machine is located (Kevin's office) or the contents of the FTP site (Sales and Marketing information).

12. Choose OK to finish setting the options.

Part
VI

Ch
27

Configuring FTP Messages To configure FTP Services messages, follow these steps:

1. From the Start Menu, choose Programs, Microsoft Peer Web Services (Common), and Internet Service Manager.

2. Select the FTP service you want to configure.

3. Choose Properties, Service Properties from the menu. The FTP Service Properties dialog box appears.

4. Choose the Messages tab (see fig. 27.10).

FIG. 27.10

Setting the messages the user sees when accessing the FTP site.

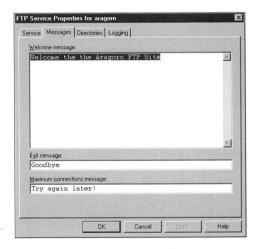

5. Type in the message the user will see when they successfully connect to the FTP site in the Welcome Message edit box. For example, this could be a simple greeting, instructions on where to find files or a What's New message.

6. Type in the message the user will see when they end their connection to the FTP site in the Exit Message edit field.

7. Type in the message the user will see if they can't connect to the FTP site in the Maximum Connection Message edit field. This message will only get displayed if the maximum number of users allowed are already connected to the FTP site. It will not be displayed if there is some error while trying to connect.

8. Choose OK to finish setting the messages.

Configuring FTP Directories   To configure FTP Services directories, follow these steps:

1. From the Start Menu choose Programs, Microsoft Peer Web Services (Common), and Internet Service Manager.

2. Select the FTP service that you want to configure.

3. Choose Properties, Service Properties from the menu. The FTP Service Properties dialog box appears.

4. Choose the Directories tab (see fig. 27.11).

FIG. 27.11
The default values for the FTP Service directories properties.

5. To add additional directories, choose Add. To edit the directory properties, select the directory you want to edit in list box and choose Edit Properties. In either case, the Directories Properties dialog box appears (see fig. 27.12).

7. If you are adding a directory or want to change the directory, type in the path of the Directory edit field or choose Browse to select the directory.

8. If you want this to be the home directory, choose Home Directory. If you want this to be a virtual directory, choose Virtual Directory and type in a name to use as the alias in the Alias edit field.

9. If the directory you are configuring is specified with a UNC (Universal Naming Convention) name, you need to specify a Username and Password that will be used when accessing this directory.

Part
VI

Ch
27

10. To set the access rights on the directory, choose any of the options—Read or Write—in the Access box.

11. Choose OK to finish adding or edit the directory properties.

12. Choose whether you want the FTP directory listing to appear in the MS-DOS or UNIX stype, by selecting either UNIX or MS-DOS in the Directory Listing Style box.

13. Choose OK to finish setting the directory options.

FIG. 27.12
Adding a virtual FTP directory, with only Read access rights.

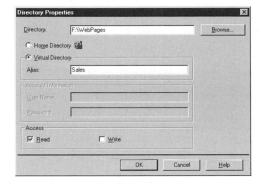

Configuring Gopher Services

There are three basic categories of Gopher Services that you can configure—Service Options, Directories, and Logging.

Configuring Gopher Options   To configure Gopher Services options, follow these steps:

1. From the Start Menu, choose Programs, Microsoft Peer Web Services (Common), and Internet Service Manager.

2. Select the Gopher service that you want to configure.

3. Choose Properties, Service Properties from the menu. The Gopher Service Properties dialog box appears.

4. Choose the Serivce tab (see fig. 27.13).

FIG. 27.13
Configuring the
Gopher Service
options.

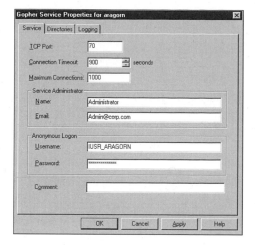

5. Enter in the number of seconds without activity that a connection will be kept open before it is disconnected in the Connection Timeout edit field. The default is 900 seconds, or 15 minutes.

6. Enter in the maximum number of simultaneous connections that you want to allow in the Maximum Connections edit field. The default is 1,000.

7. Enter in the name of the administrator of the Gopher service in the Name edit field. Enter in the e-mail address for the administrator in the Email edit field. This information is provided to users of the gopher service.

8. Enter in the username and password to use when an Anonymous (or Guest) connection is made, in the Username and Password edit fields, respectively. By default, the Username is set to IUSR_*computername*. See the previous section "IUSER *computername* Account."

9. Choose OK to finish setting the options.

Configuring Gopher Directories   To configure Gopher Services directories, follow these steps:

1. From the Start Menu, choose Programs, Microsoft Peer Web Services (Common), and Internet Service Manager.

Part
VI
Ch
27

2. Select the Gopher service you want to configure.

3. Choose Properties, Service Properties from the menu. The Gopher Service Properties dialog box appears.

4. Choose the Directories tab.

5. To add additional directories, choose Add. To edit the directory properties, select the directory you want to edit in list box and choose Edit Properties. In either case, the Directories properties dialog box appears.

6. If you are adding a directory or want to change the directory, type in the path of the Directory edit field or choose Browse to select the directory.

7. If you want this to be the home directory, choose Home Directory. If you want this to be a virtual directory, choose Virtual Directory and type in a name to use as the alias in the Alias edit field (see fig. 27.14).

8. If the directory you are configuring is specified with a UNC (Universal Naming Convention) name, you need to specify a Username and Password that will be used when accessing this directory.

9. Choose OK to finish setting the directory properties.

FIG. 27.14
Specifying a virtual
directory for a
Gopher Service
directory.

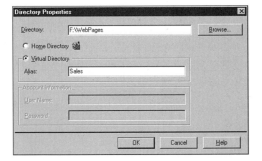

Server Activity Logging

All three of the Peer Web Services can be separately configured to log server activity. This activity includes information such as who accessed the server, when they accessed, and what files or information they accessed. This logging information can be very useful in assessing what content is being used, maintaining security, and monitoring and fine-tuning the server's performance parameter.

Peer Web Service logging is flexible in three areas:

- Generating log files in any of three formats—standard format, European Microsoft Windows NT Academic Centre (EMWAC) format, or National Center for Supercomputing (NCSA) Common Log File format.

- Specifying where the log files get created. This can be on any drive or directory you prefer.

- When new log files get created. This can be on a regularly scheduled basis (daily, weekly, or monthly) or when the log file exceeds a certain size.

Configure Logging Options   To configure the logging options, follow these steps:

1. From the Start menu, choose Programs, Microsoft Peer Web Services (Common), and Internet Service Manager.

2. Select the Peer Web Service (WWW, FTP, or Gopher) you want to configure.

3. Choose Properties, Service Properties from the menu. The Service Properties dialog box appears.

4. Choose the Logging tab (see fig. 27.15). This tab is identical for all the different services.

FIG. 27.15
Specifying automatic file logging for a WWW Service.

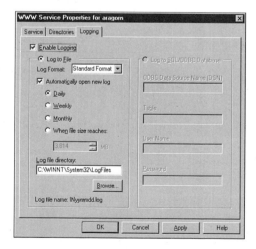

Part

VI

Ch

27

5. To turn logging on, choose Enable Logging.

6. You can either save the log information to a log file or to a database. If you want to log information to a file, choose Log to File. If you are using an ODBC-compliant database, you can log information to a database by choosing Log to SQL/ODBC Database.

7. If you are logging information to a file, you can have a new log file automatically created on a periodic basis. To enable this feature, choose Automatically open new log file. Then select how frequently a log file should be created—Daily, Weekly, Monthly, or When File Size Reaches. If you choose When File Size Reaches, specify the file size limit in the edit field. Finally, you must select what log file format to use. Select the format you want to use in the Log Format drop-down list box.

8. Specify the location of the logfile in the Log File Directory edit field or choose Browse to select a directory.

9. If you are logging information to a database, you need to specify four pieces of information—ODBC Data Source Name, Table, Username, and Password.

10. Choose OK to finish setting the logging options.

Converting Log Files   Although the Peer Web Services only directly generates standard or NCSA format log files, Windows NT comes with a utility that can be used to convert the log file to between the standard, NCSA and EMWAC log file formats. The utility is convlog.exe, located in the Inetpub subdirectory.

The syntax for convlog is:

convlog -s[f|g|w] -t[emwac|ncsa[:GMTOffset]|none] -o[output directory] -f[temp file directory] -h *LogFilename*

See table 27.1 for the meaning of each parameter.

Table 27.1   Log File Conversion Program Parameters

Parameter	Description
-s	Specifies which service log entries to convert. The default is to convert all entries, -sf converts only FTP entries, -sg converts only Gopher entries, and -sw converts only WWW entries.
-t	Specifies the format to convert to. The default is emwac.
-o	Specifies the directory where the output file should be created.
-f	Specifies the directory where temporary files created during the conversion should be stored. The default is to use the directory specified by the TMP environment variable (typically, C:\TEMP).
LogFilename	The name of the log file to be converted.

Log File File Naming Conventions   To be able to reference log files, you need to understand the naming convention used for log files. The name will depend on whether or not you choose to have new log files automatically generated. The file naming convention is:

- INETSV1.LOG if new log files are not automatically generated.
- INETSV*nnn*.LOG if a new log file is created when the file size exceeds the specified maximum. *nnn* is a sequential increasing number. So, for example, the first log file would be INETSV001.LOG, the second would be INETSV002.LOG, and so on.
- IN*mmddyy*.LOG if a new log file is created daily, weekly, or monthly. The *mmddyy* is the month, day, and year. For example, a file created on April 7, 1997 would be IN040797.LOG.

Reading Log Files   A standard log file consists of a comma delimited set of fields. The fields are listed in table 27.2. Any field that doesn't contain data will have a hyphen (-) as a placeholder.

Part
VI

Ch
27

Table 27.2 Log File Fields

Parameter	Examples
Client's IP address	198.24.56.34
Client's username	anonymous, -, kjones
Date	10/12/96
Time	0:00:45, 15:30:23
Service	W3SVC (WWW), MSFTPSVC (FTP), GopherSVC (Gopher)
Computer name	ARAGORN,
IP address of Server	175.45.89.128
Processing time (milliseconds)	500
Bytes received	314
Bytes sent	32049
Service status code	0, 200
Windows NT status code	0
Name of the operation	GET, [376]PASS, file
Target of the operation	logo.gif

A sample line might look like:

198.24.56.34, -, 10/12/96, 15:30:23, W3SVC, ARAGORN, 175.45.89.128, 500, 314, 32049, 200, 0, GET, logo.gif

RegiConfiguring Peer Web Services Entries

This section lists many of the Registry entries that are used by the Peer Web Services, the Internet Service Manager, and the Internet Service Setup program.

The following Registry entries are automatically created when you install the Peer Web Services. Any registry keys not listed here will need to be created.

▶ **See** "Working with the Registry," **p. 893**

AdminEmail	LogFileDirectory
AdminName	LogFileFormat
AllowAnonymous	LogFilePeriod
AllowGuestAccess	LogFileTruncateSize
AnonymousOnly	LogNonAnonymous
AnonymousUserName	LogSqlDataSource
ConnectionTimeOut	LogSqlPassword
EnablePortAttack	LogSqlTableName
ExitMessage	LogSqlUserName
GreetingMessage	LogType
InstallPath	MaxClientsMessage
LogAnonymous	MaxConnections

The following sections list the Registry entries that can't be changed by using one of the management tools, such as Internet Service Manager.

Global Registry Entries   The registry entries in table 27.3 are used to control global aspects of all of the Peer Web Services. These entries are not created by default. If you want to change any of them, you will need to create the registry entry and set its value.

The registry entries are all located in the following Registry path:

HKEY_LOCAL_MACHINE\SYSTEM
 \CurrentControlSet
  \Services
   \InetInfo
    \Parameters

Part

VI

Ch

27

Table 27.3 Global Peer Web Service Registry Entries

Registry Entry	Description
BandwidthLevel	This REG_DWORD entry has a range of 0 - 0xFFFFFFFF and a default value of 0xFFFFFFFF. Specifies the maximum network bandwidth used for Peer Web Services. The value 0xFFFFFFFF means "do not restrict bandwidth."
ListenBackLog	This REG_DWORD entry has range of 1-unlimited and a default of 15. Specifies the maximum number of active connections to hold in the queue waiting for server attention.
LogFileBatchSize	This REG_DWORD entry has a range of 0 - 0xFFFFFFFF and a default value of 64*1024 (64 KB). Specifies the batch size for writing a log file. The server caches the last LogFileBatchSize bytes of data in memory buffers before it dumps the current buffer to disk.
MemoryCacheSize	This REG_DWORD entry has a range of 0 - 0xFFFFFFFF and a default value of 3072000 (3MB). Specifies the amount of memory in bytes to allocate for caching system handles, directory listings, and other values of frequently used data to improve performance of the system. A value of 0 means "do not do any caching."
ObjectCache	This REG_DWORD entry has a range of 0 - 0x7FFFFFFF, 0xFFFFFFFF (seconds) and a default value of 30 seconds. This registry entry controls the Time To Live (TTL) setting. This defines the length of time that objects are held in cached memory. Setting the value to 0xFFFFFFFF disables the object-cache scavenger and allows cached objects to remain in the cache until they are overwritten.

Service Specific Registry Entries   The registry entries in table 27.4 are used to control aspects that are common to all Peer Web Services. However, each entry is set independently for each service. For example, LogonMethod can be set under MSFTPSVC for FTP services, W3SVC for WWW Services, and under GOPHERSVC for Gopher services. These entries in the table are not created by default. If you want to change any of them, you will need to create the registry entry and set its value.

The registry entries are all located in the following Registry path:

HKEY_LOCAL_MACHINE\SYSTEM

\CurrentControlSet

\Services

ServiceName

\Parameters

where *ServiceName* is either W3SVC, FTPSVC, or GopherSVC.

Table 27.4   Peer Web Service Registry Entries for Each Service

Registry Entry	Description
EnableSvcLoc	This REG_DWORD entry has a range of 0 to 1 and a default value of 1. This parameter controls whether or not services register themselves with a service locator. This allows services to be discovered by the Internet Service Manager. If set to 0, the service will not register. If set to 1, it registers the service for service location.
DefaultLogonDomain	This REG_SZ entry specifies the default logon domain that is used to validate a clear text logon when no domain is in the username field. The default value is the name of the local computer.
LogonMethod	This REG_DWORD entry can have a value of 0, 1, or 2 and has a default value of 0. It specifies the logon method for clear-text logons. A value of 0 means users must have the right to log on locally to be given access to the server. A value of 1 means that users must have the right to log on as a batch job. A value of 2 means users will be logged on as network.

WWW Service Registry Keys   The registry entries in table 27.5 are used to control aspects of Web Peer Web Services. As before, the entries in the table are not created by default. If you want to change any of them, you will need to create the registry entry and set its value.

The registry entries are all located in the following Registry path:

> HKEY_LOCAL_MACHINE\SYSTEM
>
> \CurrentControlSet
>
> \Services
>
> \W3SVC
>
> \Parameters

If you examine this Registry path, you will notice additional Registry keys and values. However, the additional Registry keys can be set using one or more management programs and so are not discussed here.

Table 27.5   Log File Fields

Registry Entry	Description	
AcceptByteRanges	REG_DWORD entry can have value of 0 or 1. The default is 1. The value determines whether the HTTP server will process the "Range" header for type "bytes:".	
AccessDeniedMessage	This REG_SZ entry, with a default of " " is the message that is sent back to clients when they have been denied access to the server. This message can be a short HTML document explaining how to gain access or why access was denied.	
DirBrowseControl	This REG_DWORD entry, with a default value of 0x4000001e, specifies both the display attributes of directory browsing and whether the DefaultLoadFile is used. the value used here is arrived at by combining (OR'ing) the values of the attributes listed below.	
	Load Default File	0x40000000
	Directory browsing enabled	0x80000000
	Show Date	0x00000002
	Show Time	0x00000004
	Show Size	0x00000008
	Show Extension	0x00000010
	Display long date	0x00000020

Registry Entry	Description
LogSuccessfulRequests	This REG_DWORD entry with a value of 0 or 1 determines whether or not to record successful activity in the log file. The default of 1 is to log successful activities.
LogErrorRequests	This REG_DWORD entry with a value of 0 or 1 determines whether or not to record errors in the log file. The default value 1, turns error logging on. Zero turns it off.
ScriptTimeout	This REG_DWORD entry has a range of 0x1-0x80000000, and a default value of 0x384. This entry specifies the maximum time the WWW service will wait for a response from CGI scripts.
SecurePort	This REG_DWORD entry has a range of 0x0-0xfa00, and a default value of 0x1bb. This entry specifies the TCP port to use for SSL.
ServerSideIncludesEnabled	This REG_DWORD entry has a value of 0x0 or 0x1, and a default of 0x1. If enabled, 0x1, the use of Include files to permit including repetitive information in files is allowed.
ServerSideIncludesExtension	This REG_SZ entry has a default value of ".stm". It specifies the file extension to use for files that the server will scan for #include statements.

FTP Service Registry Keys   The registry entries in table 27.6 are used to control aspects of FTP Peer Web Services. As before, the entries in the table are not created by default. If you want to change any of them, you will need to create the registry entry and set its value.

The registry entries are all located in the following Registry path:

HKEY_LOCAL_MACHINE\SYSTEM
  \CurrentControlSet
  \Services
  \FTPSVC
  \Parameters

Part
VI

Ch
27

If you examine this Registry path, you will notice additional Registry keys and values. However, the additional information can be set using one or more management programs.

Table 27.6 FTP–Specific Registry Keys

Registry Entry	Description
EnablePortAttack	This REG_DWORD entry has a value of 0 or 1, and a default of 0. This entry is used to prevent a security problem with the FTP protocol specification. The FTP protocol specification allows passive connections to be established based on the port address specified by client. This can allow hackers to execute destructive commands in the FTP service. By default, the FTP service does not allow any connections to port numbers lower than IP_PORT_RESERVED (other than 20).
AccessCheck	This REG_DWORD entry can have any value. This entry is used to check the access rights of incoming user connection. The server impersonates the logged-on user and sets rights according to the rights that the user has for reading and writing to the Registry. If this key does not exist, then read and write permissions are granted. If this key exists, then the user gets the same file read and write rights as he has for this Registry key. This key can be used to help set user access rights when the FTP server is publishing aFAT volume. This is difficult to manage and is not a recommended method of securing an FTP site.
AnnotateDirectories	This REG_DWORD entry has a value of 0 or 1, with 0 being the default. If the value is set to 1, the FTP service will support annotating a directory with custom messages. See the section "Creating FTP Annotation Files" later in this chapter.
LowercaseFiles	This REG_DWORD entry has a value of 0 or 1, with 0 being the default. Administrators can add this value, set to 1, to ensure that the FTP service uses lowercase when comparing file names.

Gopher Service Registry Keys   The registry entries in table 27.7 are used to control aspects of Gopher Peer Web Services. The registry entries are all located in the following Registry path:

> HKEY_LOCAL_MACHINE\SYSTEM
>> \CurrentControlSet
>> \Services
>> \GOPHERSVC
>> \Parameters

If you examine this Registry path, you will notice additional Registry keys and values. However, the additional Registry keys can be set using one or more management programs and so are not discussed here.

Table 27.7   Gopher-Specific Registry Keys

Registry Entry	Description
CheckForWAISDB	This REG_DWORD entry has a value of 0 or 1, with the default being 0. If you have added a WAIS Toolkit, Microsoft does not provide a WAIS Toolkit, this flag is used to specify if search is supported and if the service should check for WAIS Toolkit. If this entry is set to 0, the service does not support searches and will not look for a WAIS Toolkit. If the entry is set to 1, then the service supports searches if Waislook.exe is installed in the system.

Server MIME Mapping Registry Keys   You must configure your server's MultipleInternet Mail Extensions (MIME) mapping if you're publishing files in multiple formats. MIME mapping makes sure that your server returns the file type correctly when returning the file to remote browsers. By default, there are more than 100 MIME mappings installed during setup.

If you need to add additional MIME mappings, you must use the Registry Editor to add MIME mappings under the following Registry path:

> HKEY_LOCAL_MACHINE
>> \SYSTEM

Part
VI

Ch
27

> \CurrentControlSet
>
> \Services
>
> \InetInfo
>
> \Parameters
>
> \MimeMap

A MIME mapping has the following syntax:

> <mime type>,<file name extension>,,<gopher type>

Notice the double comma before the gopher type parameter.

> Example:
>
> text/html,htm,,1
>
> image/jpeg,jpeg,,5

NOTE The file name extension specified as an asterisk (*) is the default MIME type. This is used when a MIME mapping does not exist. For example, to handle a request for the file file.xyz when the file name extension .xyz is not mapped to a MIME type, the server will use the MIME type specified for the asterisk extension. This is used for binary data. Normally, browsers will save such a file to disk. ■

Script Mapping Registry Keys   With Script Mapping (or file name extension mapping), you can map file name extensions to the proper program to run files with those extensions. The following file name extensions are pre-installed:

> .bat or .cmd=C:\WINNT35\System32\cmd.exe /c %s %s
>
> .idc=c:\Inetpub\Server\Httpodbc.dll

You will have to edit the file name extension information in the Windows NT registry, for any other file name extensions.

In the .bat and .cmd example above, the first %s is replaced with URL (that is, E:\Webroot\Scripts\Test.bat). The second %s is replaced with any parameters to the URL (typically a query string. Notice that the second %s is not used if there is an equals sign).

This allows you to reference URLs such as:

■ /scripts/test.bat?This+is+a+search

■ /scripts/bugs.idc?Assign=Johnl

If you need to add additional script mappings, you must use the Registry Editor to add values (of type REG_SZ) to the following Registry path:

HKEY_LOCAL_MACHINE
\SYSTEM
 \CurrentControlSet
 \Services
 \W3SVC
  \Parameters
  \ScriptMap

Each value should be the file name extension you wish to map (for example, .bat) and
the data value should be the command line for the program to run (for example, C:\WINNT35\System32\cmd.exe /c %s %s). You will need to restart the WWW service to enable the new mappings.

Publishing Information with Peer Web Services

Windows NT's Peer Web Services can publish both information and applications. This allows you to publish anything from static Web pages on your Website to interactive applications. You can also use the Peer Web Services to find and extract information from database, as well as insert information into databases.

Understanding Web Publishing

The most popular of the Peer Web Services is the Web Server. This publishes Web Pages. Most Web pages are simple ASCII text files with codes embedded to indicate formatting and hypertext links. These are formatted in HyperText Markup Language (HTML). HTML specifications are changing constantly and you should see the latest HTML specifications (available on the Internet).

While you can use any text editor, such as Notepad, to create and edit your HTML files; you will probably find it easier to use an HTML editor such as Netscape's

Part
VI

Ch
27

Navigator Gold or Internet Assistant for Microsoft Word. You use the HTML editor to create HTML files, which contains references, called hyperlinks, to other Web pages files on your system. Your Web pages can include images and sound. If you include non-HTML files, remote users must have the correct viewing application to view those files.

Once you have created your information in HTML and any other formats, you can copy the files to the default directory for the Web server. This is by default, Inetpub\Wwwroot. Or you can configure the Web Server to use the directory containing your information.

ServerSide Includes ServerSide allows you to modify a Web page by including additional information just before sending the file to a user. This feature is useful for including the same text or graphic on each HTML page, such as a link to the home page.

The format of the include statement is:

<!--#include file="value"-->

The value can be a relative path or a full path, from the home directory of your WWW service.

For example, to include a banner on each Web page that contained a link to your home page, you would need to do the following:

■ Create the file banner.htm that contains the HTML codes for your banner and link. The file would contain HTML code that looks similar to this:

<A HREF="/homepage.htm"><IMG SRC="/images/logo.gif"></A>

■ Use an include file statement where you want the repeated information to appear. For example:

<!--#include file="/banner.htm"-->

■ Name the HTML page using the file name extension .stm (instead of the normal .htm or .html). This tells the Web server that this is an HTML formatted file, but has a ServerSide include.

 TIP Using .stm files may negatively affect performance. Therefore, only use this extension when necessary.

▶ **See** "WWW Service Registry Keys," **p. 771**

Dynamic Web Pages   One of the most dynamic ways to publish information is by creating dynamic Web Pages. These pages can run programs when a user clicks on HTML links or by an embedded HTML form. You can create applications or scripts that communicate with the user in dynamic HTML pages by using programming languages such as C or scripting languages such as Perl.

These interactive programs and scripts can be developed using almost any 32-bit programming language or by using Windows NT batch files. There are two interfaces you can use when you write your applications or script. These are the Common Gateway Interface (CGI) or Microsoft's Internet Server Application Programming Interface (ISAPI). Documentation for CGI can be found on the Internet. Documentation for ISAPI is available from Microsoft via subscription to the Microsoft Developer Network (MSDN).

Common Gateway Interface (CGI) is a specification for passing information among a client Web browser, a Web server, and a CGI application. A CGI application starts when a client Web browser fills out an HTML form or clicks a link in an HTML page on your Web server. The CGI application takes the information the client Web browser supplies and can do almost anything. The results are either returned in an HTML page or posted to a database. CGI applications are sometimes referred to as "scripts" because simple CGI applications are often created with scripting languages, such as Perl.

Microsoft Peer Web Services can use most 32-bit applications that run on Windows NT and conform to the CGI specifications.

ISAPI is a Microsoft extension to its Web servers that serve the same function as CGI. Because the ISAPI extensions are developed as DLLs that are loaded by the Web server at startup, you may find that the ISAPI applications can have better performance and require less overhead (because each request does not start a separate process).

Part
VI

Ch
27

ON THE WEB

For more information on CGI scripting from the NCSA, check out

    http://hoohoo.ncsa.uiuc.edu/cgi/intro.html.

For advanced WEB techniques, check out

    http://www.nas.nasa.gov/NAS/WebWeavers/advanced.html

Using a Database

With the Peer Web Services WWW service and the Open Data Base Connectivity (ODBC) drivers, you can:

- Create Web pages from data in databases.
- Modify information in the database according to user input from a Web page.
- Perform other Structured Query Language (SQL) commands.

The interact occurs as follows:

- Web browsers submit requests to the Internet server by using HTTP.
- Using the Internet Database Connector (IDC), a component of Peer Web Services, interaction with the databases is accomplished. (The Internet Database Connector, Httpodbc.dll, is an ISAPI DLL that uses ODBC to interact with databases.)
- The Internet server responds with an HTML formatted document.

There are two sets of files that control the database interaction. The Internet Database Connector (.idc) files control how the database is accessed. They contain the information needed to connect to the correct ODBC data source and execute the SQL statements. An Internet Database Connector file also contains information about the HTML extension file.

The HTML extension (.htx) file controls how the output Web page is constructed. The HTML extension file is a template for the actual HTML document that will be created and returned to the Web browser. The information obtained by using the IDC is merged with the HTX file to create the output Web page.

Making Files Available with FTP and Gopher

Because of its simple and easy-to-use interface, the World Wide Web has replaced most functions of FTP. However, only the FTP Service is capable of copying files from a client computer to a server computer. If your remote users need this functionality, they must use FTP.

Also, FTP is an extremely easy service to install and maintain. For example, if you already have existing files that you want to make available to remote users, all you have to do is point the FTP service to your files.

Finally, files made available via FTP can be in any format, such as document files, multimedia files, or application files. There is no effort required in converting them to an HTML format.

Creating FTP Annotation Files   Simply pointing remote users at one or more directories may not help them locate the information they need. To help address this shortcoming, FTP can use annotation files. Each directory can contain an annotation file. The annotation file can be used to summarize the information about the directory contents. This summary automatically appears to remote browsers.

With annotation files, you can show FTP users the contents of a particular directory by adding directory descriptions. To create annotation files, follow these steps:

1. In each directory where you want to annotate the information to be displayed to the remote user, create a file called ~ftpsvc~.ckm.

2. Make that file hidden using the Windows NT Explorer.

3. Use the Registry Editor to enable annotated directories. See the section "FTP-Specific Registry Keys" earlier in this chapter.

TROUBLESHOOTING

I've enabled Annotation Files on my FTP Server, but now when I via the FTP directory with a Web browser, I get error messages. You can eliminate such errors by limiting each annotation file to one line.

Creating FTP Special Directories   You can control the root directory displayed to FTP users by adding physical subdirectories to the home directory. These directories cannot be specified by using virtual directories.

First, you can create username directories. You can use FTP username directories to control the root directory presented to remote FTP users. FTP username directories are not created by default during setup. If a user logs on to the FTP server and he has a username that exactly matches a subdirectory in the home directory, that subdirectory is used as his root directory.

Second, you can create an Anonymous directory. This is a directory in the home directory named "Anonymous." If a user logs on using the password Anonymous, the directory name Anonymous is used as the root.

Creating Gopher Tag Files Tag files can be used to supplement the standard gopher display returned to clients with additional information, and to provide links to other computers. The standard information about a file that is returned to a client comes from tag files. Typically, tag files contain:

- Display name
- Host name
- Port number

You can return additional information, such as the server administrator's name and e-mail name, the file's date of creation, and date of last modification, if you are running gopher plus.

You must create tags files for your gopher site with the gdsset utility. To see all of the options for the gdsset command, type **gdsset** at the command line with no parameters.

On FAT file system volumes, the tag file name is the same as the file it describes, with .gtg appended to the file name. For example, if the content file name is readme.txt, then the tag file name would be readme.txt.gtg.

On NTFS volumes, the tag file name is the same as the file it describes with :gtg appended to the file name. For example, if the content file name is readme.txt, then the tag file name would be readme.txt:gtg. Notice that a colon is used, rather than a period.

For tag files that are stored on FAT volumes, editing can be done using most ASCII-based text editors, such as Notepad.exe. The file may need to be unhidden to edit it.

However, tag files stored on NTFS volumes cannot be edited by most text editors. This is because the file is stored in an alternate data stream. Also, you must move the tag file manually when you move the corresponding data files. To move the tag file, first make it visible. Then move the file, and make hidden it again. (You can use Windows NT Explorer to hide and unhide files.)

To create a tag file, you must use the command prompt program gdsset. This can be used to create a tag file for either a file on the server or link to another computer. See table 27.8 for a list of the program options. The syntax for this program is:

gdsset -c -gn -f "description of file" -a "administrator's name" -e e-mail file name -h hostname

Table 27.8   Gdsset Options

Parameter	Description
-c	Use this flag to edit or create a new file.
-gn	The value for n can be any single-digit code from 0 to 9. If you omit this flag, the code for the file type will default to 9, binary.
-a "administrator's name"	The value between the quotation marks is the administrator's name. If you omit this flag, the value defaults to the service administrator's name in the Service dialog box of the Microsoft Internet Service Manager.
-e e-mail	The value is the administrator's e-mail address. If you omit this flag, the value defaults to the service administrator's e-mail name in the Service dialog box of the Microsoft Internet Service Manager.
file name	The value is the name of the tag file you're creating or editing.
-h hostname	The value specifies the name of the computer to link to.

Gdsset automatically hides the tag files you create.

You can display the information stored in a tag file by using the following command:

gdsset -r file name

 T I P To create a batch command to tag a series of similar files (that have the same filetype), use the following syntax:

for %i in (*.txt) do <echo %i && gdsset -c -g0 -f %i %i

Part
VI

Ch
27

Maintaining Security

By using Peer Web Services, you are allowing remote users to connect to your computer. Since you probably don't want to give them complete access to all of your files and programs, you need to implement at least some of the available security features.

Windows NT provides security features that include User Accounts and NTFS volume. There are some Internet protocols that can be implemented to add additional security features.

Security Overview

The Peer Web Services relies on the Windows NT security model. Windows NT implements security features that help you protect your computer and its resources. These are User Accounts and the NTFS file system. You can control access to computer resources by requiring assigned user accounts and passwords. You can then limit the rights of these users' accounts. The Windows NT File System (NTFS) enables you to set permissions to both folders and files located on your computer. You can control access to folders and files in a variety of ways. For example, you can prevent users from copying files to or from a folder or you can prevent users from executing files in certain folders.

In addition to these Windows NT security features, Peer Web Services also supports the Internet standard Secure Sockets Layer (SSL) protocol, which securely encrypts data that is transmitted between clients and servers.

Using User Accounts   Windows NT security requires assigned user accounts. This helps you protect your computer and its resources. Every operation on a Windows NT system identifies who is doing the operation. For example, the user name and password that you log on to Windows NT with, identifies who you are and what you are authorized to do.

Each user's rights is configured in the User Manager program by setting User Rights in the Policies menu. These rights allow a user to perform certain actions on the system. One such right is the *Log on Locally* right. This is required for users to use Internet services if Basic Authentication is being used. If the system is using Windows NT Challenge/Response Authentication, then the *Access this computer from network* right is required for users to use Internet services. Every-one has this right by default.

You can increase security by following these steps:

- Only give the Log on Locally or the Access the computer from this network right to the USR_computername account, the Guests group, or the Everyone group.

- Make all passwords difficult to guess. This is especially true for any account with administrator rights.

- Passwords can be set by using the User Manager utility, or at the system logon prompt.

- To help prevent password attacks, specify how quickly account passwords expire (which forces users to regularly change passwords), and set how many bad logon attempts will be tolerated before locking a user out. You can set these policies by using User Manager.

- Only grant membership to the Administrator group to trusted individuals.

- If you use the predefined Windows NT user accounts Interactive and Net-work, be sure to grant read access to files in your Web site to these user accounts. If you are using Basic Authentication, the requested files must be accessible by the Interactive user for anonymous connections. If you are using Windows NT Challenge/Response authentication protocol, the files must be accessible by the Network user for anonymous connections.

You can restrict Web site access to only users who have a valid Windows NT users name and password. No access is permitted unless a valid user name and pass-word are supplied. If you want to authorize only certain individuals to access your Web site or specific portions controlled by NTFS, password authentication is use-ful. You can enable both anonymous logon access and authenticated access en-abled at the same time.

The user account and password used to authenticate the remote user is the user name that is logged on to the client computer. Because this account must be a valid account on the computer running Peer Web Services, the Windows NT Chal-lenge/Response authentication is very useful in an intranet environment. In such an environment, the client and server computers are in the same, or trusted, domains.

Part
VI

Ch
27

There are two forms of password authentication—Basic and Windows NT Challenge/Response. In Basic authentication, transmissions between the client and server is not encrypted. Intruders could learn user names and passwords because basic authentication sends the client's Windows NT user name and password essentially unencrypted over the networks.

Windows NT Challenge/Response authentication, which currently only works with the Microsoft Internet Explorer, protects the password by securing transmission of the password over the network.

You can enable both basic and Windows NT Challenge/Response authentication. If the Web browser is Internet Explorer, the Windows NT Challenge/Response authentication method is used. Otherwise, it uses basic authentication.

Strangely enough, your FTP site is most secure if you only allow anonymous FTP connections. You can require client authentication for all FTP service connections. However, since the FTP service supports only basic authentication, your site is more secure if you allow only anonymous connections.

> **CAUTION**
>
> FTP sends passwords across the network in clear text. In other words, the password is sent unencryped.

Using NTFS   Any time a file is requested—such as an HTML page—or a resources is requested, such as an Internet Server API (ISAPI)—the request is done on behalf of a Windows NT user. The service uses that user's user name and password in the attempt to fulfill the request. You can control access to files and folders through the Peer Web Services in two ways:

- By setting access permissions in the Windows NT File System (NTFS)
- By setting access permissions in the Internet Service Manager

For the most security, you should locate your files on an NTFS partition. NTFS provides additional security and access control over FAT partitions. Using NTFS, you can restrict access to specific portions of your file system to specific users and services.

Because your data files being published by Peer Web Services are more vulnerable, it is a good idea to apply Access Control Lists (ACLs) to your data files. With

ACLs, you can grant or deny access to the associated file or folder to specific Windows NT user accounts or groups of users. Then, when an Internet service attempts to read or execute a file, the user account offered by the service must have permission, as determined by the ACL associated with the file, to read or execute the file, as determined by the client's user account.

You can use the Windows NT Explorer to configure file and folder ACLs. You have very fine control on what type of access users may have for specific files and directories. For example, some users may have Read-only access, while others may have Read, Change, and Write access. You need to ensure that the IUSR_*computername* and any authenticated accounts are granted or denied appropriate access rights to specific files, folders, and resources.

N O T E The group "Everyone" contains all users and groups, including the IUSR_*computername* account and the Guests group. By default the group Everyone has full control of all files created on an NTFS drive. ■

As a general rule, you should use the settings in table 27.9 when setting access rights.

Table 27.9   Access Rights by File Type

Directory/File Type	Suggested NTFS Access
content	Read access
programs	Read and Execute access
databases	Read and Write access

Network Services

To increase the security for Web site, you want to remove as many methods of connections as possible. One way of doing this is to make sure that you are using only the necessary services on any computer connected to the Internet. It is less likely that an administrative mistake will be made that will leave an opening that could be exploited, the fewer services you have running. To disable any unnecessary services, use the Services application in Control Panel.

You should also use the Bindings feature in the Network application in Control Panel to unbind any unnecessary services from any network adapter cards. You can still use the Server service on your private network by disabling the Server service binding only on network adapter cards connected to the Internet.

Finally, unless it is part of your explicit strategy, don't enable directory browsing on the Directories property sheet. If you enable directory browsing, you are potentially exposing the entire web publishing file structure. In other words, you risk exposing program files or other files to unauthorized access, if it is not properly configured. You should always have a Default.htm page in any directory that you do not want to be browsed. Otherwise, the WWW service will return a web page containing a listing of files in the specified directory (if a default page (Default.htm) is not present).

Secure Sockets Layer

Windows NT provides the security features that help you secure your system from prying eyes. This section discusses the Internet protocols that are used to secure data transmissions to and from your computer. That is, it prevents someone from monitoring the data as it comes and goes from your computer.

Peer Web Services supports a protocol for providing data security. This security protocol, called Secure Sockets Layer (SSL), supports data encryption, server authentication, and message integrity for a TCP/IP connection.

The SSL protocol has been submitted to the W3C working group on security for consideration as a standard security approach for Web browsers and Web servers. SSL provides a security "handshake" that is used to initiate the TCP/IP connection. The client and server use this handshaking to agree on the level of security that they will use. It also fulfills any authentication requirements for the connection. After this initial connection, SSL's only is used to encrypt and decrypt the byte stream being used (for example, HTTP). What this means is that all the information in travel between the client and the server are fully encrypted. This includes any submitted form contents (such as credit card numbers), any HTTP access authorization information (user names and passwords), the URL the client is requesting, and all the data returned from the server.

T I P Encrypt takes time. Therefore, SSL-encrypted transmissions are slower than unencrypted transmissions. To avoid reducing performance across your entire site, you should consider only using SSL for virtual folders that contain highly sensitive or confidential information.

To enable SSL security on your Web server, you will need to do the following:

1. Generate a key pair file and a request file. You can do this using the Key Manager.

2. Request a certificate from a certification authority. The key generated in step 1 is not valid until you obtain a valid key certificate for it. To get a key certificate, send the certificate request file to your key authority service. Until you do so, the key will exist on its host computer, but cannot be used. Verisign is one such certifying authority.

ON THE WEB

Visit Verisign's web site at

www.verising.com

3. Install the certificate on your server.

4. Activate SSL security on a WWW service folder.

There are a few important points to remember when enabling SSL security:

■ You can enable SSL security on the root of your Web site or on one or more virtual folders.

■ Only SSL-enabled clients will be able to browse the SSL-enabled WWW folders.

■ You must use "https://" instead of "http://" in the URL of any documents that reside in an SSL-enabled WWW folder.

Part

VI

Ch

27

From Here...

When you securely use Peer Web Services, there is a lot of interaction between different parts of Windows NT. There are several other chapters that have additional information you may want to read.

- Chapter 15, "Securing Windows NT Workstation," teaches you about the Windows NT security features, such as User Accounts and NTFS permissions.

- Chapter 24, "Configuring TCP/IP," teaches you about TCP/IP and intranets.

- Chapter 31, "Working with the Registry," teaches you about adding and changing Registry entries using the Registry Editors.

CHAPTER 28

Configuring Windows Messaging Services

by Sue Mosher

Microsoft Windows Messaging is essentially an application for sending and receiving messages, though it can also be used to organize documents and other files. You'll find it on your NT desktop as the Inbox icon.

Windows Messaging's messaging tools consist of:

- A place to store the incoming and outgoing messages
- A place to store the addresses you use most often
- Functions for composing and reading messages
- Software to format your messages and deliver them

Organize different information services into profiles

Windows Messaging profiles are stored with your NT user profile.

Set up Windows Messaging to use Microsoft Mail and Internet Mail

You can establish a workgroup postoffice to allow everyone on the network to exchange messages with Microsoft Mail.

Create Personal Folders and Personal Address Book

You can take these with you if you travel, to get access to your mail from everywhere.

Manage additional settings for your Windows Messaging services

Most services can be set up for automatic scheduled connections, to make mail downloads even easier.

N O T E   Windows Messaging uses the same interface and offers many of the same functions as Exchange, Microsoft's client-server messaging and groupware application. However, you cannot connect to an Exchange server with Windows Messaging; you must use the Exchange client. Also, Windows Messaging lacks some of the features of Exchange, notably automatic signatures and rules-based actions for incoming messages. ■

For message storage, Windows Messaging provides Personal Folders, a file where all your messages are kept and organized into folders. You can even store documents and other files in your Personal Folders.

To enter addresses, you'll use the Personal Address Book.

And to actually format and deliver your messages, you'll use one or more information services, such as Microsoft Mail. Some information services also add their own address book to supplement the Personal Address Book.

For each type of message you want to send, you must have an appropriate information service. Two such services are included with NT—Microsoft Mail and Internet Mail.

Microsoft Mail is appropriate for e-mail within your organization, either on your local area network or through a remote dial-up.

While some organizations use Internet Mail for their internal messages, it's most commonly used for communicating with people outside your own office. ■

Understanding Profiles

Windows Messaging keeps the details about your information services, Personal Folders, and Personal Address Book in a profile whose settings are stored in the registry. Before you can use Windows Messaging for messaging, you must have a profile. In fact, everyone using Windows Messaging on a particular machine needs their own profile pointing to their own Microsoft Mail or Internet account, Personal Folders, and Personal Address Book.

TIP If you have more than one profile for yourself, you can set them up to use the same Personal Folders and Personal Address Book. This will let you see the same messages and use the same address list, no matter what profile you're using.

The first time you double-click the Inbox to start Windows Messaging, the Windows Messaging Setup Wizard runs, creating a profile for you automatically. Later in this chapter, you look at the details of the wizard and of setting up services manually.

However, before we move on to the details of configuring services, let's learn more about how these profiles are organized.

Editing an Existing Profile

To work with profiles, use the Mail applet in the Control Panel. The applet opens to the current profile, as seen in figure. 28.1.

FIG. 28.1
This typical profile includes two information services, plus Personal Folders and Personal Address Book.

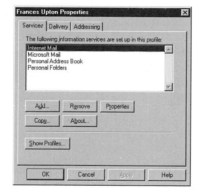

This is where you'll add, remove, and configure information services, using the techniques explored a little later.

To edit a different profile, rather than the current one, follow these steps:

1. In the profile Properties dialog box (see fig. 28.1), choose <u>S</u>how Profiles to get a list of all the profiles that have been established.

2. From the Mail profile list dialog (see fig. 28.2), select the profile you want to edit.

Part
VI

Ch
28

3. Choose P̲roperties to display the list of services for the selected profile.

FIG. 28.2
You may have more
than one profile set
up for Windows
Messaging, perhaps
using a different
combination of
services.

Creating a New Profile

You can create a new profile either with the Windows Messaging Setup Wizard or
by copying an existing profile.

To let the wizard do the job, follow these steps:

1. Start the Mail applet in the Control Panel.

2. In the profile Properties dialog box shown in figure 28.1, choose S̲how
   Profiles.

3. From the Mail dialog box shown in figure 28.2, choose A̲dd to start the
   Windows Messaging Setup Wizard.

To copy all the services from one profile to another, follow these steps:

1. Start the Mail applet in Control Panel.

2. In the profile Properties dialog shown in figure 28.1, choose S̲how Profiles.

3. From the Mail profile list dialog shown in figure 28.2, choose Copy.

4. Enter the name you want to use for the new profile, then choose OK to finish
   creating it.

A new profile created by copying will use the same Personal Folders and Personal
Address Book as the original profile. All you need to do is change the properties of
the copied information services and add or remove services as needed.

TIP If you set Windows Messaging to prompt for a profile, you can also create a profile by choosing New when you see the Choose Profile dialog box.

Switching Between Profiles

If you have established several profiles, you can choose to have Windows Messaging prompt you for a profile or, alternatively, start with a particular profile and no prompt.

Prompting for a Profile   The default is for Windows Messaging to start with no prompt. So if you want to be prompted for a profile, follow these steps:

1. Start the Inbox from your NT desktop.

2. Choose Tools, Options to display the Options dialog box shown in figure 28.3.

3. Choose Prompt For a Profile to Be Used, then choose OK to save the profile setting.

FIG. 28.3

Windows Messaging can either prompt you for a profile or always use a particular profile that you specify.

The next time you start Windows Messaging, you see a Choose Profile dialog box (see fig. 28.4). Select the profile you want to use from the Profile Name list, then choose OK to start Windows Messaging with that profile.

In the Choose Profile dialog box, you can also choose <u>N</u>ew, if you want to create a new profile, or <u>O</u>ptions to make the selected profile the default. The default profile is the one that appears in the Profile <u>N</u>ame list box when you first start Windows Messaging.

FIG. 28.4
If you have more than one Windows Messaging profile, you may want to be able to specify a profile each time you start Windows Messaging.

N O T E   The Choose Profile dialog box is Windows Messaging's only means for specifying a particular profile at startup. There is no command-line argument for starting Windows Messaging with a certain profile. ▨

Using a Profile Without a Prompt   Back on the Options dialog box in figure 28.3, you saw the setting for telling Windows Messaging to prompt for a profile each time it starts. The other available setting is Always <u>U</u>se This Profile. If you use this option, you need to choose which profile you want Windows Messaging to use.

You can also select the startup profile with the Mail applet in Control Panel. Follow these steps:

1. Start the Mail applet in the Control Panel.

2. In the profile Properties dialog box shown in figure 28.1, choose <u>S</u>how Profiles.

3. From the Mail Profile List dialog box shown in figure 28.2, select a profile under When <u>S</u>tarting Microsoft Windows Messaging, Use This Profile.

4. Choose OK to save your startup profile choice.

Gathering Setup Essentials

Before running either the Windows Messaging Setup Wizard or configuring services through the Mail applet in the Control Panel, you must gather basic information about the way you connect to your information services (Microsoft Mail and/or Internet Mail) and about your accounts for those services.

To set up Microsoft Mail, you need to know the following:

- The network path to your Microsoft Mail postoffice
- The name of your Microsoft Mail account and the password

If you don't have this information, your e-mail administrator can provide it.

If this is the first time anyone in your office has used Microsoft Mail, you need to set up a workgroup postoffice and accounts for anyone using Windows Messaging. It only takes a few minutes.

The Internet Mail setup is more complex. If you will be dialing out to an Internet service provider (ISP), you should set up a remote access connection to your ISP before trying to configure Windows Messaging.

▶ **See** "Using Remote Access Service," **p. 629**

In addition, you need the following information about your Internet e-mail account, all of which should be available from your ISP:

- The IP address or name of the server from whom you will download your Internet e-mail. (This needs to be a POP3 server. Ask your ISP to make sure.)
- If a different server handles you're outgoing messages, then you will also need its address.
- Your e-mail address in the format *user@domain*.
- Your e-mail account name and password.

TIP The IP address for the mail server is sometimes different from the IP address used in your remote access connection to the ISP, so make sure you have both.

Using the Windows Messaging Setup Wizard

Using the Windows Messaging Setup Wizard is the easiest way to get started with Windows Messaging. It launches automatically when you start Windows Messaging for the first time (the wizard may be called Microsoft Exchange setup wizards).

N O T E The wizard also runs whenever you create a new profile. If you select its option of manually configuring services, you get a Profile Properties dialog box, similar to that shown in figure 28.1, where you can add or remove services and change their properties. ▧

Before you start the wizard, though, collect the basic information about your Microsoft Mail and/or Internet Mail services, as described in the previous section.

Once you know what you need to set up Windows Messaging, we can walk through the wizard step-by-step:

1. Double-click the Inbox icon on the desktop to start the Windows Messaging Setup Wizard. (It also runs when you add a new profile.)

2. In the first dialog box, shown in figure 28.5, choose Use the Following Information Services.

N O T E If you plan to use neither Microsoft Mail nor Internet Mail, but some other service for Windows Messaging, then choose Manually Configure Information Services. This is also a good choice for experienced users who want to configure all the settings for each service and not just take the defaults that the wizard would use.

Using manual configuration is essentially the same as adding and removing services through the Mail applet in the Control Panel. ▧

3. If you do not plan to use either Microsoft Mail (for internal e-mail) or Internet Mail (for external e-mail and, in some cases, internal), then click that service to deselect it. Otherwise, leave both selected. (For this walk through, assume that you're installing both.)

4. Choose Next to continue.

FIG. 28.5
The Windows Messaging Setup Wizard either configures all the necessary services automatically or allows you to set everything up manually.

5. In the next dialog box, the first for Microsoft Mail, enter the path to the location of your workgroup postoffice, then choose Next to continue.

6. In the second Microsoft Mail dialog box, select your name from the list of users with accounts on the postoffice, then choose Next to continue with the setup for Internet Mail.

7. In the first Internet Mail dialog box, shown in figure 28.6, select your connection to the Internet Mail server from the list or choose New to create a new connection. Then choose Next to continue.

FIG. 28.6
For Internet Mail, you need to use an existing connection profile to connect to your mail server or create a new one.

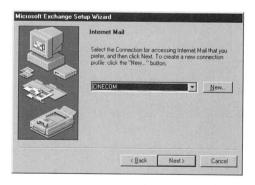

8. Next, under Internet Mail, enter either the name (such as CINECOM.COM) or the IP address (for example, 204.97.70.4) for the Internet Mail server. Then choose Next to continue.

9. In the next Internet Mail dialog, choose Off-line to connect and transfer messages manually or Automatic to have Windows Messaging connect and transfer at regularly scheduled intervals. Choose Next to continue.

Part
VI

Ch
28

10. The next step is to enter your e-mail address and the name you want to appear on messages, using the Internet Mail dialog shown in figure 28.7. For the e-mail address, be sure to use the format *user@domain*. (This is the address that people use to respond to your messages, so be sure to get it right!) Then choose Next to continue.

FIG. 28.7

Enter your e-mail address and the full name that you want to appear on Internet Mail messages.

11. In the last Internet Mail dialog box, enter your mailbox account name and password. The mailbox account may be the same as the *user* portion of your e-mail address in step 10, but it could also be different. Both the account name and password may be case-sensitive. Choose Next to continue.

12. Next, you are asked to enter the path to your Personal Address Book (PAB). Accept the default *only* if you know that you will be the only person using Windows Messaging on this machine and you will never want to access your addresses from any other machine.

The best choice is to use a PAB name that's similar to your Microsoft Mail or Internet Mail login name or is otherwise easy to distinguish from the PABs belonging to other users.

If you think you might be using Windows Messaging from another system at any point, put your PAB on a network drive, not on the local C: drive.

 T I P If you put the PAB in a local folder that you've shared, then you can access it from any point, because it is, in effect, on a network drive.

When you've entered the path to the PAB, choose Next to continue.

13. As with the PAB, you also need to enter a path to your Personal Folders, the file that will be used to store your messages. The same suggestions made for locating and naming the PAB apply here. You'll probably want to use the same name and path as for the PAB, only with a PST extension.

14. Choose Next to continue, then Finish to complete the wizard setup.

 TIP If you have used Windows Messaging previously, then you will already have a Personal Address Book and Personal Folders. Give the wizard the paths to these existing files, rather than creating new ones.

Because the wizard uses default settings for your services, it's always a good idea to check those settings. I review all of them in the next few sections, along with the technique for manually configuring an entire profile or a single new service.

Adding and Configuring Services

Many companies will be developing new services for you to add to Windows Messaging. So, you need to know how to add new services and how to change the settings on the services already in your profile.

Third-party services for Windows Messaging usually come with their own setup programs. You need to perform that setup, then add the service to your Windows Messaging profile (if the setup program didn't do that for you).

Windows Messaging and MAPI

Windows Messaging uses an open interface called MAPI (Messaging Application Programming Interface) that makes it possible to add many different kinds of services. Here are some of those available and where to find them, mainly on the Internet:

Service	Location
Transend MAPI ConnectorWare for cc:Mail	http://www.transendcorp.com/ cware.html
Lotus Notes	Included with Notes 4.0
CompuServe Mail	On CompuServe, type **GO CSMAIL**
AT&T Mail	http://www.att.com/easycommerce/ easylink/new.html#mapi

continues

Part
VI

Ch
28

continued

Service	Location
netApps Internet Series	**http://www.netapps.com/**
Workgroup Internet Gateway	**http://www.demon.co.uk/softalk/**
Netscape Internet Mail	Included with Netscape 2.0 and Transport later
Voice e-mail	**http://www.bonzi.com/**

As of this writing, not all of these services have been tested with Windows NT 4.0.

To add, remove, or alter the services in a profile, run the Mail applet from the Control Panel. If necessary, switch to a different profile as described earlier. (You'll also be working with this same profile Properties dialog box if you chose to manually configure services in Windows Messaging Setup Wizard.)

To add a new service, choose <u>A</u>dd. Windows Messaging displays the Add Services to Profile dialog box, shown in figure 28.8. This dialog box lists all the Windows Messaging services available on your system, including any third-party services

FIG. 28.8
The available information services include not just those shipped with NT, but also third-party plug-ins like Netscape.

you've added. Pick the service you want to add to the profile, then choose OK.

If the service you want is not shown, but you have the setup files for it at another location, then choose Have <u>D</u>isk and install it as you would any other NT application.

▶ **See** "Installing Applications," **p. 424**

N O T E   Usually you can have only one copy of a service in a profile. The exception to this rule is Personal Folders. You can have as many copies of Personal Folders as you like. Each copy represents a separate message storage file. You might want additional Personal Folders files for archiving or for transferring messages between systems. ■

To change the settings for any service, select the service in the Profile Properties dialog box, then choose Properties.

To remove a service from a profile, select it, then choose Remove. Note that this removes the service only from the profile you're currently working with. It does not uninstall it. The service remains available for other profiles to use.

 T I P You can also work with the services for the current profile through the Windows Messaging menus, choosing Tools, Services. If you make changes, exit and log out of Windows Messaging, then log back in to make them effective.

Now that you know how to work with the services in your profile, we can review the settings for the four services that come with NT—Microsoft Mail, Internet Mail, Personal Folders, and Personal Address Book. You'll always access these settings through the profile Properties dialog box.

Adding Microsoft Mail

The Microsoft Mail service is used to connect to a Microsoft Mail postoffice, either a *workgroup postoffice* created with NT, Windows 95, Windows for Workgroups, or a full Microsoft Mail server.

Required Settings

The minimum information you need to set up the Microsoft Mail service is your postoffice location, mailbox name, and password. These are stored on the Connection and Logon tabs in the Microsoft Mail properties dialog box shown in figure 28.9.

Put the network path to the postoffice in the text box labeled Enter the Path to Your Postoffice, or choose Browse to locate the postoffice on your network.

Notice that on the Connection tab you can also pick the method that the Microsoft Mail service will use to connect to the postoffice. Table 28.1 lists your choices.

Part
VI

Ch
28

FIG. 28.9
Microsoft Mail can sense whether you are directly connected to your postoffice and change the way it operates accordingly.

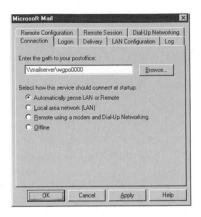

Table 28.1 Microsoft Mail Connection Options

Option	Description
Automatically Sense LAN or Remote	Use either the direct LAN connection or a remote connection, depending on the current state of your system. A good choice if you use your PC both in the office and at home.
Local Area Network	Connect only via the local area network. If the network is not available, you are asked if you want to work offline.
Remote Using a Modem and Dial-Up Networking	Connect only via a Dial-Up Networking or remote access connection. You need to tell Windows Messaging when you want to connect.
Offline	Read and compose messages only. You will not be able to receive or send messages until you switch to a profile using one of the other connection options.

After you've entered the postoffice path, switch to the Logon tab (see fig. 28.10) to enter your mailbox name and password. You can also choose whether you want Windows Messaging to prompt you for a password each time you start Windows Messaging. (If you ever want to change this password, choose Change Mailbox Password.)

FIG. 28.10
Along with the path to your postoffice, your mailbox name and password are the only information required for Microsoft Mail.

N O T E Note that the mailbox name on the Logon tab is different from the name that appears on the list of Microsoft Mail accounts in the Windows Messaging Setup Wizard. Both names are assigned by the postoffice administrator when your account is established. The mailbox name is often a shorthand version of your full name. ▪

Once you've entered the postoffice path, mailbox name, and password, choose OK to close the Microsoft Mail properties dialog box. You're now all set to start Windows Messaging and begin using the Microsoft Mail service.

Delivery and Log Settings

Several other basic settings are contained on the Delivery and Log tabs in the Microsoft Mail properties dialog. See Table 28.2 for the Delivery options.

Table 28.2   Microsoft Mail Delivery Options

Option	Description
Enable Incoming Mail Delivery	Check the postoffice for pending new messages.
Enable Outgoing Mail Delivery	Deliver pending outgoing messages to the postoffice.

continues

Figure 28.2 Continued	
Option	**Description**
Address Types	Select the address types you can use. The choices include Network/Postoffice, plus any connections from your Microsoft Mail server to other types of mail, such as Fax or MHS Mail.
Check for New Mail	Set the interval, in minutes, that Microsoft Mail checks for new mail when you're connected via the local area network.
Immediate Notification	Enable alerts when new mail arrives at the postoffice for you. You can then use Tools, Delivery Now within Windows Messaging to retrieve it. This setting requires NetBIOS, which is installed on NT by default.
Display Global Address List Only	Limit the Microsoft Mail address lists in your Address Book to the Global Address List, which contains all the addresses for your organization. You won't see the individual postoffice address lists.

On the Log tab, you can choose Maintain a Log of Session Events and specify a location where Microsoft Mail will maintain this list. This log can be very useful for troubleshooting and is enabled by default. To view it from within Windows Messaging, choose Tools, Microsoft Mail Tools, View Session Log.

LAN and Remote Configuration Settings

Three additional settings related to your connection to the postoffice are found on the LAN Configuration tab (for times when you're connected via the local area network) and the Remote Configuration tab (for sessions when you dial into the postoffice).

The most important of these is the Use Remote Mail setting. And here we find a big difference between Windows Messaging and the Microsoft Mail application included with previous versions of NT.

The Mail program included a feature called *inbox shadowing* that allowed you to keep incoming messages both on the postoffice and in your message file. With inbox shadowing on, you could read all your incoming mail from any location. This made it a crucial setting for people who needed to access their mail either from different PCs in the same office or from both the office and remote locations.

Windows Messaging does not work the same way. Normally, Windows Messaging transfers messages to and from the postoffice automatically. When it downloads new messages to your Personal Folders, it also deletes them from the postoffice. If you don't want that to happen, then you need to use Remote Mail in Windows Messaging to get your messages, both when you're on the LAN and when you're connecting through remote access.

▶ **See** "Transferring Messages," **p. 847**

Table 28.3 summarizes the Use Remote Mail setting and other settings on the LAN Configuration and Remote Configuration tabs.

Table 28.3   Microsoft Mail LAN and Remote Configuration Settings

Option	Description
Use Remote Mail	Disable automatic delivery of mail. Instead, choose Tools, Remote Mail to download message headers and select which to retrieve and delete. Enable this setting if you need to see incoming messages from more than one location.
Use Local Copy	When you display the address book, use a copy of the postoffice address list stored on the local system rather than the one on the server. Use Tools, Microsoft Mail Tools, Download Address Lists to get a local copy.
Use External Delivery Agent	If you are connecting to a full Microsoft Mail server that is running the EXTERNAL.EXE program to connect to other servers, you can use this option to speed delivery.

Remote Connection Settings

Details of your remote connection to the postoffice are maintained on the Remote Session and Dial-Up Networking tabs.

Here we find another change from the older Microsoft Mail program: Previously, Microsoft provided a separate program, called Microsoft Mail Remote, for dialing into the postoffice, downloading messages, and sending any pending e-mail. Instead of providing a separate program, Windows Messaging integrates these functions into the main application.

However, to get your e-mail remotely with Windows Messaging, you need to be able to make a different kind of connection to your postoffice, a full remote access (also known as Dial-Up Networking) connection. If you formerly used Mail Remote, you will not be able to use the same dial-up for your remote connection in Windows Messaging. You need to check with your network administrator to find out if a remote access dial-up is available to you.

▶ **See** "Using Remote Access Service," **p. 629**

Assume that you have set up your remote access connection to the postoffice, and you want to make it work with Windows Messaging.

The Remote Session tab governs when Windows Messaging will connect remotely and when it will disconnect.

Connect Settings   To check for messages remotely whenever Windows Messaging is started, choose When This Service Is Started.

> **T I P**   Even if you have scheduled sessions, you can always check for mail in Windows Messaging at any time by choosing Tools, Deliver Now or Tools, Remote Mail.

To schedule other connection times, choose Schedule Mail Delivery to bring up the Scheduled Remote Mail Delivery dialog box shown in figure 28.11.

To add a new scheduled connection, follow these steps:

1. From the Scheduled Remote Mail Delivery dialog box (refer to fig. 28.11), choose Add.

2. In the Add Scheduled Session dialog box (see fig. 28.12), select an existing remote access connection from the Use list.

FIG. 28.11
Configure one or more scheduled sessions to check your e-mail automatically from a remote location.

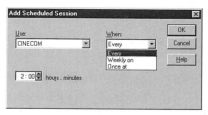

FIG. 28.12
You can schedule remote sessions at daily or weekly intervals, at a specified interval, or for a single date and time.

3. Choose <u>W</u>hen you want to make the connection. For connections at a regular interval, such as every two hours, choose Every. If you want to connect every day at the same time, pick Weekly, then choose the days—perhaps weekdays only. You can also choose Once At to make a connection just once, at a time and date that you provide.

4. Choose OK to close the Add Scheduled Session dialog box and add your new session to the list.

 You can also add, remove, and change the remote connection schedule in Windows Messaging by choosing <u>T</u>ools, Microsoft <u>M</u>ail Tools, <u>S</u>chedule Remote Mail Delivery.

To change the settings for a scheduled session, select it in the Scheduled Remote Mail Delivery dialog box (see fig. 28.11), then choose <u>C</u>hange.

To remove a scheduled session, select it, then choose <u>D</u>elete.

Disconnect Settings   To save on telephone or online charges, you can configure Windows Messaging to disconnect automatically after certain stages of a manual remote session. (These settings do not apply to scheduled sessions, which disconnect automatically after new messages have been retrieved and outgoing e-mail sent.) See Table 28.4 for a list of the disconnect options.

Part
VI

Ch
28

Table 28.4   Microsoft Mail Remote Session Disconnect Options

Option	Description
After Retrieving Mail Headers	Disconnect after you have downloaded headers using Tools, Remote Mail. Does not apply to sessions run with Tools, Delivery Now.
After Sending and Receiving Mail	Disconnect after transferring messages with either Tools, Remote Mail or Tools, Delivery Now.
When You Exit	Keep the remote session connection open once it's established and disconnect only when you exit Windows Messaging.

Dial-Up Networking Settings   Switch to the Dial-Up Networking tab to indicate which remote access connection you want to use and how you want it to operate.

▶ **See** "Using Remote Access Service," **p. 629**

Choose the connection from the Use the Following Dial-Up Networking Connection list. If the you need to add a connection, choose Add. To change an existing connection, choose Edit Entry.

In the Retry box, enter the number of additional times you want Windows Messaging to try to connect if the first attempt fails. The default is 5. To change the time between tries from the default (120 seconds), enter a new time under At (your number) Second Intervals.

Finally, you can choose one of three options for how you want Windows Messaging to monitor your remote connection:

Option	Description
Never Confirm	Does not confirm the remote connection
Confirm On First Session And After Errors	Confirms the first time you connect remotely and if any errors occur
Always Confirm	Confirms the connection every time you use it

Managing a Workgroup Postoffice

If your organization is new to e-mail, you need to set up a *workgroup postoffice* before anyone can install Microsoft Mail as a service in Windows Messaging. A postoffice is a location on a network server where details about your users are stored and messages are kept for delivery to each user.

Installing the Postoffice   Before you install the postoffice, you need to decide where to put it and who will administer it. I recommend that you create a System Administrator account separate from your own mail account. That will make it easier to transfer administration of the postoffice to someone else in the future.

To install a workgroup postoffice, follow these steps:

1. Run the Microsoft Mail Postoffice applet from Control Panel.

2. Choose Create a New Workgroup Postoffice, then choose Next to continue.

3. Under Postoffice Location, enter the name of an existing drive or folder on a network server where you want to create the postoffice. (If you don't have a dedicated server, you can put the postoffice on your own hard drive, then share it with the rest of the network.) Choose Browse if you prefer to browse the network for a good location. Once you've provided a location, choose Next to continue.

4. Confirm the name and location of the new postoffice. Choose Next to continue. Windows Messaging takes a moment or two to create a folder named \WGPO0000 at the location you specified in step 3.

5. The next step is to establish an account for the postoffice administrator, as shown in figure 28.13. When you've entered the details for the administrator account, choose OK.

CAUTION

It is critical that you safeguard the password to the postoffice administrator's account. Without this password, you will not be able to add new users. Your only recourse in the case of a lost password is to delete and re-create the entire postoffice.

There have been many cases where the employee who was responsible for administering the postoffice left the organization without sharing his personal e-mail account password. Don't let this happen to you! Use a separate administrator's account and make sure you keep track of any password changes.

Part VI
Ch
28

FIG. 28.13
Only one account can administer the postoffice. A separate administrator account, not used for regular e-mail, makes it easier to pass this duty from one person to another in the future.

6. You see a final message confirming that the new postoffice has been created reminding you that you must share it with the rest of the network before anyone can use it. Choose OK.

   ▶ **See** "Sharing Directories and Files," **p. 570**

7. If you created the postoffice on your local drive, then use Explorer or My Computer to share it. If the postoffice is on a server, double-check the access rights to make sure that everyone can see it.

Working with User Accounts   The first thing you want to do after creating your postoffice is add some users, so they can start logging into their e-mail accounts with Windows Messaging.

To create a new user, follow these steps:

1. Run the Microsoft Mail Postoffice applet from Control Panel.

2. Choose Administer an Existing Workgroup Postoffice, then choose Next to continue.

3. Specify the Postoffice Location—that is, the folder created when you installed the workgroup postoffice—then choose Next to continue.

4. Enter the Mailbox and Password created for the postoffice administrator. (See fig. 28.13, where these are shown in the Mailbox and Password boxes.) Choose Next to continue.

5. In the Postoffice Manager dialog box shown in figure 28.14, choose Add User.

FIG. 28.14
From the Postoffice
Manager, you can
add, remove, and
edit users and
manage shared
folders.

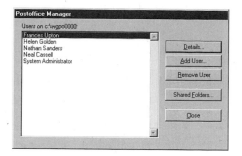

6. In the Add User dialog box (which uses exactly the same fields as the dialog box in figure 28.13), enter a <u>N</u>ame, <u>M</u>ailbox, <u>P</u>assword, and other details about the user.

7. Choose OK to save the new user.

To edit a user—for example, to change a password for someone who's forgotten theirs—follow steps 1–4 to log into the Postoffice Manager. Then select the user and choose <u>D</u>etails to see the name, mailbox, password, and other information about that user account.

To remove a user, follow steps 1–4 to log into the Postoffice Manager. Then select the user and choose <u>R</u>emove User.

N O T E The ability to manage the postoffice with one account while reading Windows Messaging messages with a separate account is one of the big differences between Windows Messaging and Microsoft Mail. With the Mail application included with earlier versions of NT, you were required to run Mail if you wanted to use the postoffice manager functions. With Windows Messaging, postoffice management has been completely separated from the Windows Messaging application itself. ■

Working with Shared Folders   Shared folders are one of the best reasons for having an e-mail system in your organization. They let you post messages to the other people you work with, so you can maintain public bulletin boards, ongoing discussions, and other forums that help you work better as a group.

Only a small amount of maintenance is needed for shared folders, mainly the occasional compression to recover the space that was used by messages that have been deleted.

To manage shared folders, follow these steps:

1. Run the Microsoft Mail Postoffice applet from the Control Panel.

2. Choose Administer an Existing Workgroup Postoffice, then choose Next to continue.

3. Specify the Postoffice Location—that is, the folder created when you installed the workgroup postoffice. Choose Next to continue.

4. Enter the Mailbox and Password created for the postoffice administrator. Choose Next to continue.

5. In the Postoffice Manager dialog box shown in figure 28.14, choose Shared Folders.

6. In the Shared Folders dialog (see fig. 28.15), you can see the status of the folders. If messages have been deleted, the status includes the amount of space that can be recovered (Recoverable Bytes in Folders) by compressing the folders. Choose Compress to recover this space.

FIG. 28.15

The Postoffice Manager gives you a way to check the number and size of any shared folders and compress them if necessary.

7. After compression has been completed, choose Close, then Close again to finish working with the Postoffice Manager.

If you log into Windows Messaging with a profile that uses the Postoffice Manager's account, you can perform two other folder housekeeping tasks:

- Change the permissions on any folder.

- Delete any folder, including those that might be left behind by a user who has been removed from the postoffice.

Adding Internet Mail

If you have an e-mail account with an Internet service provider (ISP), you'll want to install Internet Mail in your profile. The Internet Mail service can also be used with internal postoffices that use the POP3 (Postoffice Protocol version 3) standard.

Required Settings

The Internet Mail service has more mandatory settings than Microsoft Mail, beginning with those on the General tab shown in figure 28.16. All these fields must be filled before you can use Internet Mail. Table 28.5 lists each setting, along with what you need to enter. You should be able to get all this information from your ISP or, if you're connecting to a server inside your organization, from your mail administrator.

FIG. 28.16
To install the Internet Mail service, you need all the details about your e-mail address and mail account.

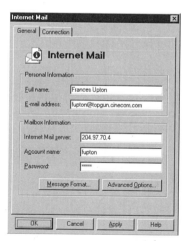

Table 28.5   Internet Mail General Settings

Setting	Description
Full Name	Your name as you want it to appear on the e-mail that you send.
E-Mail Address	Your full e-mail address in the *name@domain* format.
Internet Mail Server	The name or IP address of your mail server. Note that this may not be the same as the server that you use to make a remote access connection to the Internet.
Account Name	Your e-mail account name, which is usually your e-mail address, minus the *@domain* portion.
Password	The password for your e-mail account.

If a server other than that listed under Internet Mail Server processes your outgoing messages, then you need to give the location of that second server. (Again, this is something to ask your ISP about.) To specify a different location for this server, follow these steps:

1. On the General tab of the Internet Mail properties dialog box (see fig. 28.16), choose Advanced Options.

2. In the Advanced Options dialog box, enter the IP address or name of the SMTP (Simple Mail Transfer Protocol) server used to handle outbound messages.

3. Choose OK to close the Advanced Options dialog box.

The final required setting is found on the Connection tab (fig. 28.17). You must indicate how you want Internet Mail to connect to your mail server—via the LAN or with your modem, using a remote access connection.

▶ **See** "Using Remote Access Service," **p. 629**

If you choose Connect Using the Modem, you must specify what remote access connection you want to use. If you want to make a new connection that's not on the list, choose Add Entry to bring up the Add Phone Book Entry dialog box, where you can enter the settings for this connection.

To change the connection settings, choose Edit Entry.

FIG. 28.17
The Internet Mail services offers the option of accessing your mail server via the local area network or with a remote access modem connection.

Choose Login As to display the Login As dialog box, where you can enter your User Name and Password for the chosen connection. Note that these are not necessarily the same as the account name and password for your e-mail account.

Transfer Settings

Internet Mail offers two different ways to work—scheduled or offline. If you are manually configuring Internet Mail, scheduled is the default.

If you choose to work offline, you need to choose either Tools, Delivery Now or Tools, Remote Mail to connect to your mail server. If you work in scheduled mode, Internet Mail connects automatically when you start Windows Messaging and at specified intervals.

To work offline, switch to the Connection tab (see fig. 28.17) and check the box marked Work Off-Line and Use Remote Mail. To work with scheduled connections, uncheck this box.

If you are using scheduled connections, you should choose Schedule and use the Schedule dialog box to tell Windows Messaging how often to connect to your Internet mailbox. The default setting is every 15 minutes. If you have a full-time connection to the Internet (either via your LAN or with an unmetered dial-up), you may want to use one minute for your schedule setting, which forces outgoing messages to be sent almost immediately.

Part
VI

Ch
28

Unlike the Microsoft Mail service, Internet Mail does not provide a way for you to connect at the same time each day. You can, however, set it to connect every 1,440 minutes—in other words, every 24 hours beginning with the time you started Windows Messaging.

Choose Log File to specify a location for a log file and the level of logging you want. This is good for troubleshooting and for getting a sense of how Internet Mail connects. Here are the different choices for logging:

Logging Level	Description
No Logging	No information is written to the log file. This is the default.
Basic	The log file records logon and logoff times, plus error messages.
Troubleshooting	A complete record is kept of all protocol interactions involved in connecting to your Internet mailbox. While this is useful for troubleshooting, it can also produce a very large file, so you should turn it off when you've finished troubleshooting.

Message Format

One more optional setting completes the Internet Mail configuration. This is the message format and is probably the most confusing aspect of sending mail via the Internet.

Several methods have emerged to allow you to send more than just text, in other words, to attach spreadsheets or other files or to send messages with complex formatting. Two of these methods are MIME (Multipurpose Internet Mail Extensions) and UUEncode. Internet Mail can handle both, but certain recipients may be able to handle only one or the other. MIME is set by default, but you can change the default to UUEncode, and still set particular messages to use MIME when you know that the recipients can handle it.

▶ **See** "Sending to the Internet," **p. 845**

To change the default message format, on the General tab, choose Message Format to bring up the Message Format dialog, shown in figure 28.18. To use MIME, check the box marked Use MIME When Sending Messages. To use UUEncode, uncheck that box.

FIG. 28.18
Internet Mail can encode attachments with either the MIME or UUEncode method.

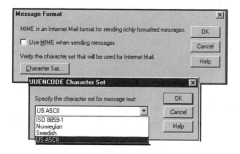

By default, Windows Messaging uses the ISO 8859-1 character set, which supports extended characters that allow you to send and receive messages in a variety of languages. Another frequently used character set is US ASCII, which is used for any plain text messages you send. Windows Messaging also supports the Norwegian and Swedish character sets if you're working primarily in one of those languages.

To change your character set, choose Character Set on the Message Format dialog (see fig. 28.18) and pick the set you want to use from the list.

Using Personal Folders

Personal Folders are unique among the services in Windows Messaging in that you can have more than one instance of them in a profile. You could create a separate Personal Folders file for each project, for example, or for archiving messages for a particular month.

To add a new set of Personal Folders, follow these steps:

1. From the profile's Properties dialog box (refer to fig. 28.1), choose Add.
2. In the Add Service to Profile dialog box (refer to fig. 28.8), select Personal Folders, then choose OK.
3. In the Create/Open Personal Folders File dialog box, specify a folder and filename (with the extension PST), then choose Open to continue.

 TIP If you need access to your Personal Folders from more than one system either on your LAN or from a remote location, then put your Personal Folders on a network server.

4. In the Create Personal Folders dialog box, shown in figure 28.19, give your Personal Folders a <u>N</u>ame. This name appears on the profile's service list and as a top-level folder in the Windows Messaging Viewer.

FIG. 28.19

Additional Personal Folders files provide a way to store project messages and archives.

5. Select the type of encryption for the Personal Folders file from one of these choices:

Encryption Setting	Description
N<u>o</u> Encryption	The PST file cannot be encrypted. You can open it in any word processing program.
Co<u>m</u>pressible Encryption (default)	The PST file can be encrypted, but in a manner that also lets you compress it to save storage space.
<u>B</u>est Encryption	This is the choice for greatest security, but it disables compression.

6. If you want to protect your PST file from other users, enter a password in the <u>P</u>assword and <u>V</u>erify Password boxes.

TIP If you've placed your Personal Folders on a network drive or if other users will be sharing your workstation, then you definitely should password-protect your PST file; otherwise, anyone will be able to open it and read all your messages.

7. To cache the PST password as part of your NT user logon, choose Save This Password in Your Password List.

▶ **See** "Managing User Accounts," **p. 388**

8. Choose OK to save the settings for new Personal Folders file as part of your profile.

To remove a set of Personal Folders from a profile, select the set from the profile's Properties dialog box, then choose Remove.

 TIP When you remove a set of Personal Folders from a profile, the set is not removed from your system. Other profiles can still use it. If you archive messages in separate Personal Folders, you can restore those files as you need them in your main profile, removing them just as easily.

To restore an existing set of Personal Folders to a profile, follow steps 1–3, using the Create/Open Personal Folders File dialog box to locate the existing PST file. (It helps if you gave the PST a meaningful name when you created it.)

Once you've created a Personal Folders file, you can change its display name or password. In the Properties dialog box for the profile, select the Personal Folders you want to work with, then choose Properties to bring up the Personal Folders dialog box shown in figure 28.20.

FIG. 28.20

The properties of the Personal Folders service include the display name for the file, its location, encryption setting, and password.

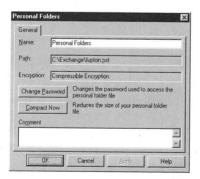

To change the display name, enter the new name in the Name box.

To change the password, choose Change Password.

Enter a descriptive Comment about this file, if you so choose.

Notice that you cannot change the encryption setting, nor can you change the Path, at least not from this dialog box. You must use a different technique to move a set of Personal Folders to a new location. Follow these steps:

1. Choose File, Exit and Log Off to close Windows Messaging if it's currently running.

2. Move the PST file to its new location.

3. Start Windows Messaging again.

4. If the PST file that you moved was your primary Personal Folders file used for storing incoming messages, then you are immediately prompted to indicate the location of this file. Use the Create/Open Personal Folders File dialog box to show Windows Messaging where to find it.

5. If you moved a secondary Personal Folders file, Windows Messaging won't prompt you for the new location until you try to view the messages in it. When it does, just follow step 4, indicating the new location.

6. When you've found the file in step 4 or 5, choose Open to finish setting up the new location.

   ▶ **See** "Message Housekeeping," **p. 869**

Finally, note the Compact Now button. This is used, whether or not you have compression enabled through your encryption setting, to free up space left by deleted items. If you are using compressible encryption, it also compresses the file to shrink it even more.

Configuring the Personal Address Book

The Personal Address Book contains few settings, as you can see in figure 28.21.

To change the display name as you see it in Windows Messaging's Address Book functions, enter a new name in the Name box.

To use a different Personal Address Book, indicate a new file name under Path. If you want to move the Personal Address Book, move it first, then enter the new path here.

FIG. 28.21

The Personal Address Book settings include the display name for the service, the location of the address book file, and the order in which you want names displayed.

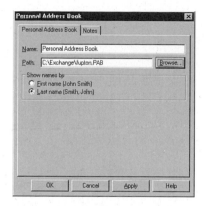

You can also choose whether to display and sort recipients by First Name or Last Name.

For additional settings related to the address book, choose OK to close the Personal Address Book dialog box and return to the profile Properties dialog box (the one that you opened with the Control Panel, Mail). Then switch to the Addressing tab, which is shown in figure 28.22.

FIG. 28.22

The settings for a profile also include how the different address lists are used.

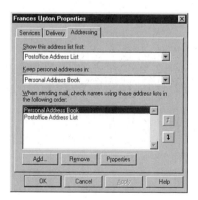

Depending on the services you have installed, you may see additional address lists besides the Personal Address Book. For example, if you are using Microsoft Mail, you have a postoffice address list. If you've installed CompuServe Mail (another third-party Windows Messaging service, like Netscape), you can use the CompuServe Address Book that you may have built with WinCIM.

To determine which of these address books will be listed first when you address a message in Windows Messaging, pick the one you want to see from the Show This Address List First selections.

If you have more than one address book that can hold personal addresses, such as both Personal Address Book and CompuServe Address Book, use Keep Personal Addresses In to select the address book to be used when you add new addresses.

Normally, Windows Messaging looks up names first in your Personal Address Book, then in others that you may have available. You can change this order with the list labeled When Sending Mail, Check Names Using These Address Lists In the Following Order. Use the up and down arrow buttons to rearrange the order.

> **N O T E**   While it may appear from the Addressing dialog box that you can add more than one Personal Address Book, such is not the case. Windows Messaging allows only one Personal Address Book per profile. However, you could have several profiles, each with a different Personal Address Book; maybe one for business, and one for personal use. ▓

Setting Delivery Options

From the Addressing tab, switch to the Delivery tab on the profile Properties dialog box to work with the final group of Windows Messaging settings (see fig. 28.23).

FIG. 28.23
The order of the services listed at the bottom of the Delivery tab determines how Internet messages are sent and how Windows Messaging transfers messages when you choose Tools, Deliver Now Using, All Services.

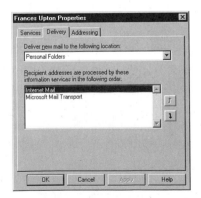

If you have more than one set of Personal Folders in your profile, you can select which one should be used to receive new messages. Make this choice from the list labeled Deliver New Mail to the Following Location.

If you have more than one service capable of delivering mail to the Internet (such as Internet Mail plus Microsoft Mail with an SMTP gateway), pay attention to the order of services listed at the bottom of this dialog. Internet messages are sent via the first service capable of handling them. So, if you want all your Internet messages to go via your ISP, put Internet Mail at the top of the list.

This list also governs the order in which connections are made to your services when you choose Tools, Deliver Now Using, All Services (or press Ctrl+M).

From Here...

You should now be able to install and configure all services included with Windows Messaging, plus add new services as they're introduced.

If you previously used Microsoft Mail with NT, don't forget the changes that Windows Messaging presents—no inbox shadowing, a separate routine for administering the workgroup postoffice, and the need for a remote access connection if you're planning to dial in to get your mail.

For more information related to Windows Messaging and its configuration, see these chapters:

- Chapter 23, "Using Dial-up Networking," will help you set up network services so you can connect to the Microsoft Mail postoffice on your LAN.

- Chapter 25, "Using Windows NT with the Internet," contains the information you need to configure remote connections to a Microsoft Mail postoffice or to your Internet mail server.

- Chapter 28, "Configuring Windows Messaging Services," includes more details on how the Internet works.

- Chapter 29, "Using Windows Messaging," tells you how to send and receive messages using Windows Messaging, and how to use the Personal Folders to store other information.

Part
VI

Ch
28

Using Windows Messaging

by Sue Mosher

In the previous chapter, you followed the steps to set up Windows Messaging with either the Microsoft Mail or Internet Mail service, or both services. Now it's time to put Windows Messaging to work sending and receiving e-mail and storing other kinds of information, such as word processing documents and spreadsheets. ■

Create and send messages

Learn how to start Windows Messaging so you can communicate via e-mail.

Respond to incoming messages

Learn how to use your Inbox and Outbox to manage your message files and send responses.

Manage the address book

Use your Personal Folders file to keep track of messages and other documents.

Configuring the Windows Messaging Viewer

Start Windows Messaging by double-clicking the Inbox icon on your desktop. The Windows Messaging viewer, shown in figure 29.1 appears; open to the Inbox folder so you can see your latest incoming messages.

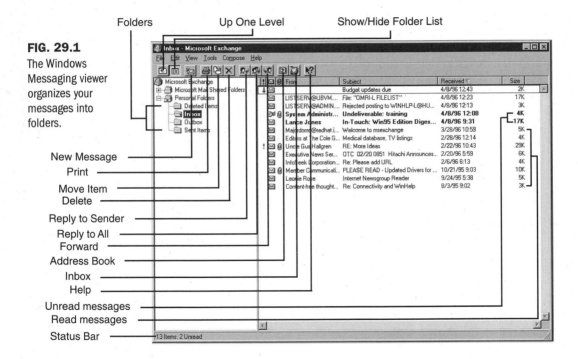

FIG. 29.1
The Windows Messaging viewer organizes your messages into folders.

Messages that you have not yet read are shown in boldface, while those that you have already seen are in the normal font. Table 29.1 summarizes the most common icons in the viewer.

To create a new folder, follow these steps:

1. Select the Personal Folders (or Microsoft Mail Shared Folders) folder set.
2. Choose File, New Folder.
3. Enter the Folder Name, then choose OK to save your new folder.

You can also create folders within other folders. Follow the same steps, only instead of starting with a folder set, start by selecting the folder that you want to be the parent of your new folder.

Sorting Folders   Each folder can sort messages in a different order. The default is set to sort by the date the message was sent (Sent Items folder) or received (other folders), with the most recent messages at the top of the list. You can see this in figure 29.2, where the small downward-pointing arrowhead on the Received column indicates that we are sorting by the received date, latest items first.

To change a folder's sort, click the heading for the column you want to sort by. This will sort the column in ascending order. Click the column heading a second time to sort in descending order. You can also change the sort by choosing View, Sort and selecting Sort Items By Column. Then click Ascending or Descending and choose OK.

Changing the Columns   You can customize the Windows Messaging viewer by changing the columns displayed, the order in which they appear, and their width. As with sorting, the column settings are specific to each folder.

TIP For a project, you might create a new folder that includes both items sent and those you received. In that case, it's a good idea to add new columns to show both the Sent and Received fields and both the To and From fields.

To customize a folder's columns, follow these steps:

1. Choose View, Columns to display the Columns dialog box shown in figure 29.2.

FIG. 29.2
The columns for any
folder can be
rearranged with the
Columns dialog box.

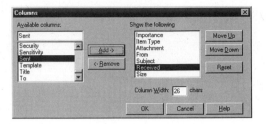

2. In the Show the Following list on the right, click where you want to insert the new column. The new column will appear before the column that you select.

3. In the Available Columns list on the left, select the column you want to add.

4. Choose Add to move the selected column from the left-hand list to the one on the right.

5. Adjust the size of the column, if you like, by typing a new number in the Column Width box.

6. Repeat steps 2-5 until you have the desired columns.

7. If necessary, adjust the position of any column by selecting it in the Show the Following list, then choosing Move Up or Move Down.

8. To remove any unwanted columns, select them in the Show the Following list, then choose Remove.

9. When you've finished working with columns, choose OK to close the Columns dialog box.

 You can return the columns for any folder to their default setup by choosing Reset on the Columns dialog box.

It's easier to adjust the column widths in the Windows Messaging viewer than on the Columns dialog box. To make a column narrower or wider, follow these steps:

1. Position the mouse over the vertical bar to the right of the heading of the column with the width you want to change.

2. When the pointer turns into a double-headed arrow, click and hold the left mouse button.

3. Slide the central bar to the left to make the column narrower or to the right to widen it.

4. Release the left mouse button once the column is the width you want.

Customizing the Toolbar

As with the status bar, you can toggle the toolbar on or off by choosing View, Toolbar. But chances are, you won't want to hide the toolbar. Instead, you want to customize it by adding icons for the Windows Messaging functions you use most.

To customize the toolbar, follow these steps:

1. Choose Tools, Customize Toolbar to display the Customize Toolbar dialog box shown in figure 29.3.

FIG. 29.3
Windows Messaging's customizable toolbar lets you add, remove, and rearrange buttons to suit the way you work.

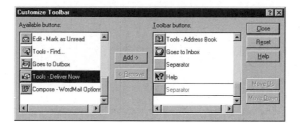

2. In the Toolbar Buttons list on the right, select the position where you want to insert the new button. The new button will appear before the button that you select.

3. In the Available Buttons list on the left, select the button you want to add.

N O T E   The Compose—WordMail Options button shown in figure 29.3 is available only if you have installed the WordMail option for Microsoft Word. WordMail is an enhanced e-mail editor that makes full use of Word's macros, styles, AutoFormat and other features. ▪

4. Choose Add to move the selected button from the left-hand list to the one on the right.

5. Repeat steps 2–4 until you have the desired buttons.

6. If necessary, adjust the position of any button by selecting it in the Toolbar Buttons list, then choosing Move Up or Move Down.

7. Remove any unwanted buttons by selecting them in the Toolbar Buttons list, then choosing Remove.

8. When you've finished customizing the toolbar, choose Close to close the Columns dialog box.

T I P You can return the toolbar to its default setup by choosing Reset on the Customize Toolbar dialog box.

Composing and Sending Messages

Sending a message in Windows Messaging consists of three distinct steps:

1. Creating the message, including the text, any attached files or embedded objects, and one or more recipients

2. Sending the message to the Outbox

3. Transmitting the messages in the Outbox to your information services (Microsoft Mail, Internet Mail, and others) for delivery

It's very important to understand that sending a message is not the same as delivering it. In Windows Messaging, these are two different operations. In this section, you look at composing and sending messages, then cover the steps you need to take to move those messages on to their recipients.

 To compose a message, click the New Message button, choose Compose, New Message or press Ctrl+N. The New Message window shown in figure 29.4 appears. Once you enter a Subject, the title bar for the message window changes from New Message to the subject of the message.

▶ **See** "Customizing the Toolbar," **p. 833**

You can customize the message window's toolbar following exactly the same procedure outlined for customizing the toolbar in the Windows Messaging viewer window. Notice that the message window toolbar includes a range of formatting options. Figure 29.4 depicts a message that uses these different tools.

On the View menu, you find choices for toggling the Toolbar, Formatting Toolbar, and Status Bar on and off.

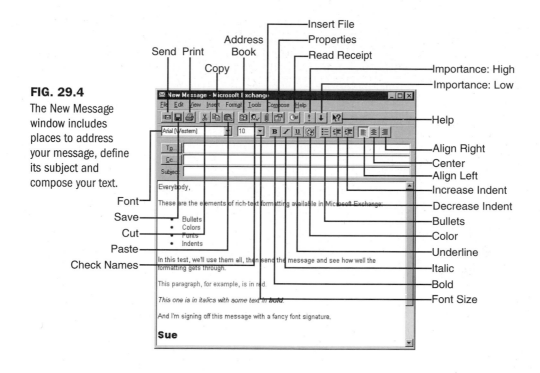

FIG. 29.4
The New Message window includes places to address your message, define its subject and compose your text.

Using the Message Window

Use the To and Cc boxes to address your message, entering the name(s) or address(es) of the recipients. Separate multiple recipient names with semicolons. You can also choose the To or Cc buttons to select from the Address Book, which I cover in detail a little later.

If you want to send a copy without the other recipients knowing about it, you can send a *blind carbon copy*. To activate this feature, choose View, Bcc Box and then enter the recipient's name or address. Once you've opened the Bcc Box, it will appear whenever you open a message window, until you toggle it off by choosing View, Bcc Box again.

In the Subject box, enter the title or subject of the message. Try to make it as informative as possible, so other users can make a quick decision about whether or not to read your message right away. For example, a message to technical support about a problem with your printer would be better off with a subject like Need help with HP LJ4 printer jams rather than just Help.

The large box at the bottom of the message window is where you compose the message itself. You have all the standard Windows text editing tools (cut, copy, paste, and more) available, plus some additional formatting features. You can change fonts, add bold, underlining, italics, or color—even add bullets and change the way your text is indented or aligned.

 To change the default font used for messages, choose Tools, Options and switch to the Send tab. Then choose Font and pick your preferred font from the list.

Not all recipients, however, will be able to see that formatting, so think about who you're sending to before you spend a lot of time dressing up your message. While other Windows Messaging users in your organization will definitely see your formatting, those outside might not. We'll discuss some particular concerns about sending formatted text when we look at sending to the Internet.

If you have the 32-bit version of Microsoft Word or Works or another word processing application with a 32-bit spell check utility, you can spell check your Windows Messaging messages. Choose Tools, Spelling or press F7. To change the way spell check works on your system, choose Tools, Options and switch to the Spelling tab, where you can set general options and determine which words will be ignored by the spell checker.

Once you've addressed and composed your message, click the Send button, choose File, Send or press Ctrl+Enter to send your message. This places it in the Outbox folder. It will be transmitted to the appropriate information service the next time you connect to that service.

▶ **See** "Addressing Messages," **p. 841**

▶ **See** "Sending to the Internet," **p. 845**

Inserting Objects

E-mail really works best when the messages are short. If you can't get your message across in such a small space, it's time to try another tactic. Windows Messaging gives you two—embedded objects and attached files, which I cover in the next section.

Think of embedded objects as fitting the principle of "A picture is worth a thousand words." For example, rather than describing an error to technical support, you could send them a screen snapshot.

Take a snapshot of your screen, then use the Paste button, choose Edit and then Paste, or press Ctrl+V to paste it into a message. Here's how:

1. Copy the entire screen to the clipboard by pressing Print Screen. Or, to copy just the current window, press Alt+PrintScrn.

2. Switch to Windows Messaging.

3. Click the New Message button to start a new message. (You can also choose Compose, New Message or press Ctrl+N.)

4. Click the large box at the bottom of the New Message window.

5. Click the Paste button to copy the screen print into the message. (You can also choose Edit, Paste or press Ctrl+V.)

6. Add your own text explaining the problem, give the message a subject and one or more addresses, then send it.

Pasting a screen print or part of a document from another application is one way to embed an object. You can use a normal paste, as just described, or choose Edit, Paste Special if you want more control over the way in which the information from the object is stored in your message.

For example, in figure 29.5, I've copied a Microsoft Excel chart to the Clipboard and am now using Edit, Paste Special to insert it into a message. You can paste it either as an Excel Chart, which would give the recipient the ability to open it in Excel and see the underlying numbers, or as a Picture—that is, as the chart image only.

 TIP When you're working with Paste Special, you see a choice for Paste Link. Use this only when the source file for the object resides on a network server, where everyone can access it.

FIG. 29.5

When you paste an object into a message, you can use Paste Special to specify how that object should be handled.

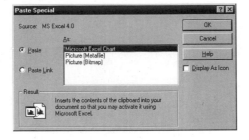

The result of our pasting is shown in figure 29.6. You could have composed this message as a dry list of figures. Or, you could have attached the spreadsheet itself and let the managers open it and draw their own conclusions. This way, with an embedded object, the figures speak for themselves in a graphic fashion.

FIG. 29.6

An embedded object can get your message across more vividly than the equivalent text.

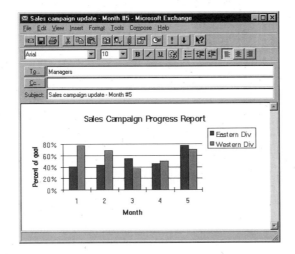

Pasting isn't the only way to embed an object. You can also create an object from scratch or from an existing file by following these steps:

1. Choose Insert, Object to bring up the Insert Object dialog box shown in figure 29.7.

2. If you want to create a new object, choose Create New, then pick an Object Type from the list.

FIG. 29.7
The object types available to you depend on what applications have been installed on your system.

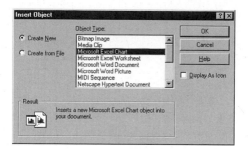

3. To create an object from an existing file, choose Create From File, then browse your system to locate the file.

4. Choose OK to continue.

5. If you chose to create an object from an existing file, that file is pasted as an object into your message or if you chose to create a new object, the toolbars and menu for the object type you selected appear as part of the message window. Create your object using those functions, then click anywhere else in the message to update the object and return to the normal Windows Messaging toolbar and menus.

Attaching Files

Not every message lends itself to the embedded object approach. You wouldn't distribute a 20-page project proposal for comments that way. Instead, you'd attach the file. Your recipients would then be able to open the entire file on their machines, assuming they have a compatible application.

 If you're sending a message to the Internet, you must use attached files rather than embedded objects.

To attach a file, follow these steps:

1. Click the Insert File button or choose Insert, File to display the Insert File dialog box, shown in figure 29.8.

2. Locate the File Name on your system.

FIG. 29.8
Any file on your
system can be
attached to a
Windows Messaging
message.

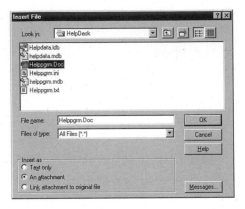

3. Select how you want to insert it. Here are the choices:

Insert As	Description
Text Only	Extracts the text from the file and inserts it into your message.
An Attachment	Inserts the file as an attachment that the message displays as an icon.
Link Attachment to	Inserts a link to the file as an Original File attachment; appropriate only where all recipients can access the file from a network server.

4. Choose OK to close the Insert File dialog and insert the file.

TIP If you're sending exclusively to other Windows Messaging recipients on your LAN, you can also insert Windows Messaging messages using the Messages choice on the Insert File dialog box (refer to fig. 29.8). Alternatively, you can choose Insert, Message from the message window's menu.

Figure 29.9 shows what a message with an attached file looks like. If the file is one of the document types registered on your system, it is shown with the icon for that type of document. Otherwise, it gets a default icon.

▶ **See** "Understanding File Properties," **p. 181**

FIG. 29.9
An attached file is
displayed with both
the filename and an
icon appropriate to
the file type.

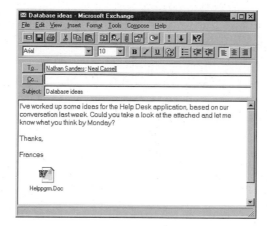

Addressing Messages

The message window (refer to fig. 29.4) includes three places (counting the Bcc
box) to enter the addresses of the people you want to receive your message.
Windows Messaging gives you several different ways to address your message:

- Enter a name or part of a name and let Windows Messaging look it up in the
  address book for you.

- Enter an Internet address in the standard format, name@domain.

- Use the To, Cc or Bcc button to go directly to the address book and pick
  names from there.

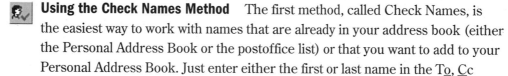

Using the Check Names Method   The first method, called Check Names, is
the easiest way to work with names that are already in your address book (either
the Personal Address Book or the postoffice list) or that you want to add to your
Personal Address Book. Just enter either the first or last name in the To, Cc
or Bcc box.

If you are sending the message to more than one person, separate the names with
semicolons.

When you send the message, Windows Messaging matches the names you
entered with those in your address book. For those with only one match,
Windows Messaging automatically updates your message to include the
person's complete address.

TIP If you want to check the names before you send the message, click the Check Names button, choose Tools, Check Names, or press Ctrl+K.

▶ **See** "Configuring the Personal Address Book," **p. 822**

What if you have two addresses for a recipient, such as an Internet address in your Personal Address Book and a Microsoft Mail address in your postoffice list? In this case, Windows Messaging looks first at one address list, then at the other and uses the first match it finds. The order in which it searches the address list is part of your Windows Messaging profile. To change it, choose Tools, Options and switch to the Addressing tab. Use the up and down arrow keys to change the order Windows Messaging uses to check addresses.

If you have two different addresses for a person in your Personal Address Book or if there are two people with the same name on the postoffice list, Windows Messaging asks you which you want to use by posting a dialog like that shown in figure 29.10.

FIG. 29.10
When there is more than one match for a recipient name, Windows Messaging asks you to choose which to use for this particular message.

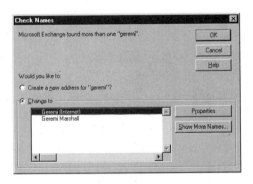

In the Check Names dialog box, select a name from the Change To list, then choose OK to use that name for the message.

You can also choose Create a New Address or Show More Names if none of the addresses shown is the one you want.

Entering Internet Addresses   If you're sending to someone on the Internet who is not already in your address book, enter the name in the To, Cc, or Bcc box in the format name@domain. Internet Explorer puts an address of this type in the To box every time you click an e-mail link on a Web page.

> ▶ **See** "Using Internet Explorer," **p. 708**

This format even works for people on the various online services such as America Online, CompuServe, and The Microsoft Network. Here are some examples of addresses used to reach people who use those services:

Service	Sample Address
America Online	WinMailbag@aol.com
CompuServe	79999.777@compuserve.com
The Microsoft Network	SamMcGee@msn.com

T I P Normal CompuServe addresses look like 79999,777. To send to such an address via Internet Mail, be sure to replace the comma with a period.

 Using the Address Book   To use the address book, click the Address Book button or choose Tools, Address Book, or press Ctrl+Shift+B. You can also choose To, Cc or Bcc. What you get is the Address Book dialog box shown in figure 29.11.

FIG. 29.11
If you prefer to browse the address lists for recipients, you can pick addresses from the Address Book dialog box and move them to the To, Cc, and Bcc boxes.

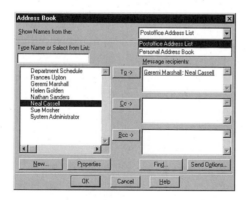

To include an address in your message, select it from the list on the left, then choose To, Cc, or Bcc to place it in the appropriate box. Continue in this fashion until you've selected all the addresses you want, then choose OK to return to the message window.

You can mix and match addresses from different lists, sending a single message to both Microsoft Mail and Internet Mail recipients. To switch lists, pick a different list from the ones in the Show Names list.

Changing Message Properties

Once you've composed and addressed your message, you're ready to send it. To do so, choose File, Send or press Ctrl+Enter. But before you do, you might want to ask for a receipt for this message or give the recipient a clue as to how urgent it is. These are properties that can be set for each message.

 To work with message properties, click the Properties button or choose File, Properties to bring up the Properties dialog box shown in figure 29.12.

FIG. 29.12
Properties for an individual message can override the default message properties in Windows Messaging.

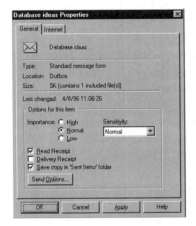

At the top of the dialog box, you can see some basic information about your message, including its size and location. The options that initially appear in the Properties dialog box are defaults, which you can change by choosing Tools, Options and switching to the Send tab, shown in figure 29.13.

To change the message's importance, choose High, Normal or Low. Windows Messaging recipients see a red exclamation point next to messages of high importance, while low importance messages get a blue down arrow. (Recipients using other e-mail software may see something different, depending on the application.) You can also set high or low importance from within the message window by clicking the Importance: High (or Importance: Low) button.

FIG. 29.13
The default message
properties are part of
many options that
can be set for
Windows Messaging.

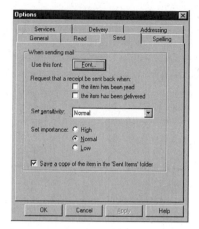

Under Sensitivity, you can choose Normal, Personal, Private, or Confidential. Windows Messaging includes a Sensitivity column that can be used to display this information.

 To be notified when a message has been read by the recipient, choose Read Receipt. (You can also set this from the message window by clicking the Read Receipt button.) Note that not all Internet e-mail servers can return read receipts.

To get a delivery receipt that shows that a message has been successfully transmitted (but not necessarily received and read), choose Delivery Receipt. Both read and delivery receipts are delivered to your Inbox folder.

To keep a copy of the message, choose Save Copy in 'Sent Items' Folder.

When you've finished working with the message Properties dialog box, choose OK.

Sending to the Internet

You have probably noticed the second tab in the message Properties dialog box (refer to fig. 29.12), the Internet tab. Here, you can override the message format settings established for your Internet Mail service when it was installed.

These settings, shown in figure 29.14, come into play when you are either sending an attached file or sending to a recipient in your Personal Address Book who has been configured to use rich text formatting. Sending a message with rich text formatting involves sending an attachment with the formatting information, so it's the same as sending an attached file.

FIG. 29.14
If you're sending a message to Internet recipients, you can set the format for the message.

For example, if your default setting is to use UUEncode but you're sending to someone whom you know can handle MIME messages, you might change the Message Format from UUEncode to MIME.

Unfortunately, the variety of Internet e-mail clients and gateways ensures that there can be no one single way to send Internet messages that will suit all recipients. You probably need to experiment to find out what works best for you and your most frequent correspondents.

▶ **See** "Message Format," **p. 818**

▶ **See** "Adding Internet Mail Addresses," **p. 857**

TROUBLESHOOTING

Some of my Internet recipients say they're getting gibberish at the bottom of my messages instead of attached files.   This sounds like your recipients don't support MIME, so file attachments appear in their encoded format, which, yes, looks like gibberish. If your recipients can handle UUEncode, then switch to that message format, either as your default or for individual messages. If their e-mail software can't handle either UUEncode or MIME, then for them to receive files from you, they need to obtain a utility, such as WinCode, so that the encoded file can be extracted from the message. WinCode's home page is **http://www.global2000.net/users/snappy/snappy/index.html**.

Why do some Internet recipients get = or =20 at the end of every line?   This can happen if you're using ISO 8859-1 as your character set for Internet messages. It's a sign that the receiver's mail gateway can't handle the "soft return" characters that Windows Messaging uses to indicate the end of each line. Try changing the character set to US ASCII.

Why are some people missing all but the first line of my paragraphs?   This is very similar to the previous problem. What's happening is that the recipient isn't able to use the markers that Windows Messaging uses to show where a line should be wrapped. The solution for such recipients is for you to put in a hard return (in other words, to press Enter) at the end of every line of your message.

Transferring Messages

Earlier in this chapter, I noted that sending a message is not the same as delivering it. In this section, you look at the steps needed to move messages from your Outbox to their intended recipients.

First, take a look at the Outbox folder right after you send a message or two. Those messages are listed in italics. If you open a message in the Outbox, perhaps to edit it before it's delivered, you must send it again. Either click the Send button or choose File, Send. If you choose File, Save instead, the message stays in the Outbox, but is not italicized; it won't be sent the next time you transfer mail.

 TIP You can't re-send a message from the Sent Items folder by dragging it to the Outbox folder. Instead, choose Compose, Forward.

Understanding Automatic Versus Manual Transfers

In the previous chapter on configuring Windows Messaging, you explored the connection choices for the Microsoft Mail and Internet Mail services.

The connection settings for your service(s) determine when each transfers messages. For example, if you are connected full-time to the local area network where your Microsoft Mail server resides, then messages are transferred every few minutes, at an interval set by you.

▶ **See** "Adding Microsoft Mail," **p. 803**

▶ **See** "Adding Internet Mail," **p. 815**

Table 29.2 summarizes the types of connection and message transfers possible for each service. Note that for Microsoft Mail, you can enable the Remote Mail feature, even if you're working on a LAN.

Table 29.2   Message Transfer Settings

Service	Connection Type	Transfers Occur
Microsoft Mail	LAN—Full-time connection	When you start Windows Messaging. At the interval specified by the Check for New Mail setting. When you use Deliver Now.
	LAN—Remote Mail connection	When you use Deliver Now or Remote Mail.
	Remote	At scheduled session times. When you use Deliver Now or Remote Mail.
Internet Mail	Scheduled	When you start Windows Messaging. At the interval specified by the Check for New Messages setting. When you use Deliver Now.
	Offline	When you use Deliver Now or Remote Mail.

If you check the Transfers Occur column in Table 29.2, you see that Windows Messaging never delivers your messages at the moment they are sent to the Outbox. Rather, where you have full-time or scheduled connections, messages are automatically delivered at specified intervals. Otherwise, they can be delivered manually at any time by choosing Tools, Deliver Now or Tools, Remote Mail, which you examine in the next section.

Understanding Deliver Now Versus Remote Mail

For manual mail delivery "on demand," Windows Messaging provides two methods: Deliver Now and Remote Mail.

Deliver Now sends everything in your Outbox, downloads all incoming messages from your mail server, and deletes all those new messages from the mail server. Remote Mail gives you more control over message transfers because it enables you to decide which messages to retrieve and which to keep on the server.

▶ **See** "Setting Delivery Options," **p. 824**

To use Deliver Now, choose Tools, Deliver Now, then pick from the list of services. You can also press Ctrl+M to run Deliver Now for all services. Windows Messaging connects to each in turn, in the order specified in the Tools, Options dialog box, on the Delivery tab. This is the same as the Delivery tab you saw when configuring Windows Messaging.

Using Remote Mail

To use Remote Mail, choose Tools, Remote Mail, then pick from the list of services if you have more than one installed. The resulting Remote Mail dialog box is shown in figure 29.15. (The example shows the Remote Mail dialog box for the Internet Mail service, but it looks and works exactly the same for the Microsoft Mail service.)

There are three basic steps to using Remote Mail:

1. Click the Connect button or choose Tools, Connect. Windows Messaging transfers messages from your Outbox, then downloads a list of headers for pending e-mail. These display not just the subject and sender, but also if there are any attachments and how long each item will take to retrieve.

2. Decide what to do with each pending item:

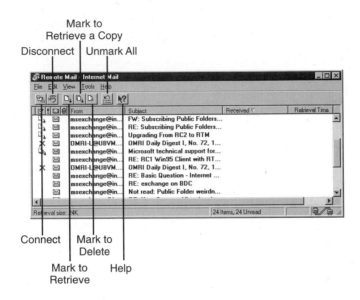

FIG. 29.15
Remote Mail sends all mail in your Outbox, then downloads a list of messages that are pending for you on the server.

 Select the items that you want to retrieve and delete from the server, then click the Mark to Retrieve button, choose Edit, Mark to Retrieve, or press Ctrl+Shift+M.

 Select any items that you want to retrieve, but also leave on the server, then click the Mark to Retrieve a Copy button, choose Edit, Mark to Retrieve a Copy, or press Ctrl+Shift+C.

Select any items that you want to delete from the server, then click the Mark to Delete button, choose Edit, Mark to Delete, or press Ctrl+D.

3. Click the Connect button or choose Tools, Connect to perform all the actions on the headers you marked.

When you've finished the Remote Mail session, either close the window or, if you want to keep the window open but break the network connection, click the Disconnect button or choose Tools, Disconnect.

Working with Incoming Messages

Whether you get new messages via an automatic or scheduled connection or via Delivery Now or Remote Mail, all new messages appear in your Inbox folder.

As you see in this section, Windows Messaging can be configured to notify you when new messages appear. A number of other settings control the way replies are handled. You also look at how to work with messages and attachments outside of Windows Messaging.

Setting Notification Options

When new mail arrives in your Inbox, Windows Messaging can:

- Play a sound
- Briefly change the pointer to an envelope
- Display a notification message
- Any combination of the above

To set these notification options, choose Tools, Options and display the General tab, shown in figure 29.16. Make your choices under When New Mail Arrives, then choose OK.

FIG. 29.16

Options regarding new mail notification are set with the General tab on the Options dialog.

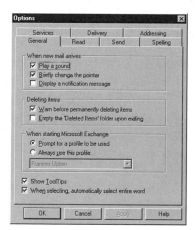

To change the sound used when new mail arrives, follow these steps:

Sounds

1. Choose Start, Control Panel, Sounds.
2. In the Sounds Properties dialog box (see fig. 29.17), select New Mail Notification in the Events list.

FIG. 29.17
Windows Messaging can use any WAV file on your system to alert you to new messages.

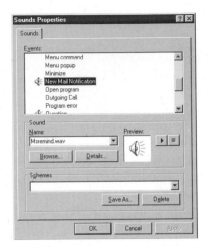

3. Enter the sound file you want to use, either by typing the Name or by choosing Browse to locate it on your system.

4. After you've specified the sound file for New Mail Notification, choose OK to close the Sounds Properties dialog box.

Reading Messages

To read the current message in your Inbox (or any other folder), double-click it, choose File, Open, or press Enter. It opens in a message window similar to that for creating new messages, but without the Formatting toolbar (though you can use View, Formatting Toolbar to see it) and with some new buttons that enable you to work with messages in the Windows Messaging folders (see fig. 29.18).

The toolbar buttons in figure 29.18 represent virtually all the things you might want to do with a message—print it, delete it, move it to another Windows Messaging folder, reply to it, or forward it.

The two arrow buttons are used to browse your messages, without having to close the message window and return to the Windows Messaging viewer. Press the up button to see the previous (next higher) message in the viewer list. Press the down button to display the next (that is, the next lower) message in the list.

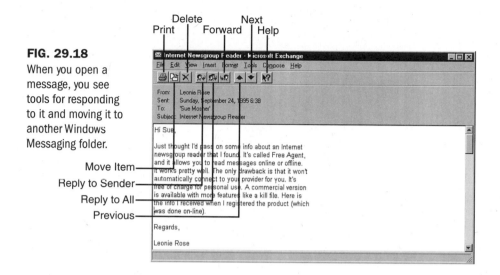

FIG. 29.18
When you open a
message, you see
tools for responding
to it and moving it to
another Windows
Messaging folder.

If the message contains an attachment that appears with a document icon related
to one of your applications, then you can double-click that icon to open the document in the application. Otherwise, you need to save the attachment to your system before you can work with it.

Changing Read Options

Windows Messaging lets you choose what happens when you delete or move a
message that you have open in the message window. To set these and several
other useful options, choose Tools, Options and switch to the Read tab, shown in
figure 29.19.

At the top of the Read tab, you can choose how you want Windows Messaging to
react when you move or delete an open message.

At the bottom of the Read tab, you find key settings for replies and forwarded messages. Choose Font to change the default font used in your message replies.

FIG. 29.19
For settings that affect replies and the way you browse Windows Messaging messages, use the Read tab on the Options dialog box.

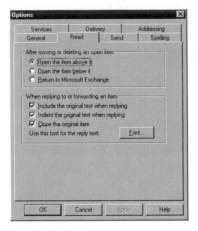

Replying to and Forwarding Messages

You can reply to or forward either a message that you have open in the message window or the currently selected message in the Windows Messaging viewer. The buttons, menu choices, and keystrokes are the same in both places. Table 29.3 lists the different action buttons and their menu and keyboard equivalents.

Table 29.3   Message Reply and Forward Actions

Button	Name	Menu	Keystroke
	Reply to Sender	Compose, Reply to Sender	Ctrl+R
	Reply to All	Compose, Reply to All	Ctrl+Shift+R
	Forward	Compose, Forward	Ctrl+F

When you reply to a message, a new message window appears with the address and subject boxes filled in for you. Depending on your choice from the Options dialog box's Read tab, as discussed in the previous section, you may also see the text of the incoming message.

Forwarding works the same way, except that the address boxes are blank, ready for you to fill in the recipients.

You can add your own text to the reply or forwarded message, just as if it were a new message.

Saving Messages and Attachments

Even though Windows Messaging is capable of storing many megabytes of messages and attachments, there will be times when you want to work with that information outside Windows Messaging.

To save an attachment to your local hard drive (or a network drive), follow these steps:

1. Either open the message with the attachment or select it in the Windows Messaging viewer.

2. Choose File, Save As to get the Save As dialog box shown in figure 29.20.

FIG 29.20
Windows Messaging messages and attachments can be saved to your local drive or a network drive.

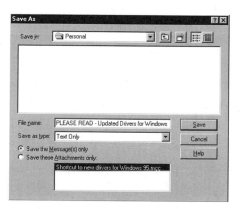

3. Under Save In, choose the folder in which you want to save the attachment(s).

4. Choose Save These Attachments Only.

5. Click any attachments you don't want to save, to deselect them.

6. Choose Save to save the selected attachments.

To save one or more messages, follow these steps:

1. Select the messages you want to save in the Windows Messaging viewer. (Use Ctrl+left mouse click to select multiple messages.)

2. Choose <u>F</u>ile, Save <u>A</u>s.

3. In the Save As dialog box that appears, under Save <u>I</u>n, choose the folder where you want to save the message(s).

4. Either select a file from those in the folder or type in a File <u>N</u>ame.

5. Choose <u>S</u>ave.

6. If you chose an existing file, you are asked whether you want to <u>A</u>ppend To or <u>O</u>verwrite that file.

To save a message that you have open in a message window, choose <u>F</u>ile, Save <u>A</u>s and follow steps 3–6.

When you save an individual message rather than a group of messages, you have several choices under Save As <u>T</u>ype in the Save As dialog box. In addition to Text Only, you see Rich Text Format, which preserves the fonts and other formatting and can be opened by WordPad or Word, and Message Format, which preserves both the formatting and the message attributes, such as the sender. Message Format files use the extension MSG. To open an MSG file, double-click it in Explorer.

Managing Addresses

I talked about the various address lists that you can use, without really getting into the details of where those addresses originate. For the most part, you will be entering new recipients in the Personal Address Book (PAB).

If you're using Microsoft Mail, you'll also use addresses from the postoffice list and, if you're part of a large organization, the global address list. Both of these lists are controlled by your e-mail administrator; you can't add or remove names. However, I show you how to copy a name from the postoffice list to your PAB for faster access.

 To open the Windows Messaging address book, click the Address Book button, choose <u>T</u>ools, <u>A</u>ddress Book, or press Ctrl+Shift+B. You see the Address Book window in figure 29.21.

▶ **See** "Configuring the Personal Address Book," **p. 822**

Delete

Find   New Message

FIG. 29.21
Windows Messaging's
Address Book gives
you access to both
your Personal
Address Book and
address lists
associated with
specific information
services.

New Entry

Properties

Add to Personal
Address Book

Help

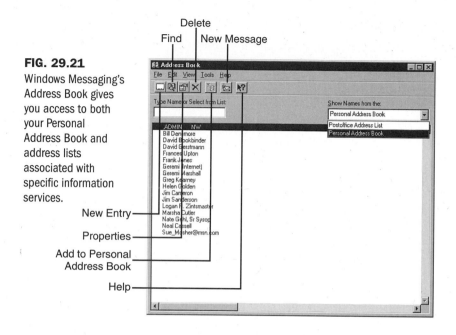

Which list appears under Show Names is governed by the addressing settings for
your profile. To change the initial list, choose Tools, Options, then switch to the
Addressing tab. Change to the list you want under Show This Address List First,
then choose OK to close the Options dialog box.

There are several different ways to add addresses to your PAB:

- Enter an address directly into the PAB, used mainly for Internet Mail
  addresses.
- Copy an address from an incoming or outgoing message.
- Copy an address from another address list, such as the postoffice list.
- Import addresses from another PAB or from a Microsoft Mail message file
  (for example, MSMAIL.MMF).

Adding Internet Mail Addresses

To enter an Internet Mail address directly into the PAB, follow these steps:

1. In the Address Book dialog box (refer to fig. 29.21), click the New Entry
   button or choose File, New Entry.

2. In the New Entry dialog box (see fig. 29.22), select the type of address you
   want to add. This is usually an Internet mail address. (Microsoft Mail addresses are more easily added by copying them from the postoffice list. You
   learn about Personal Distribution Lists in a moment.) Choose OK to continue.

FIG. 29.22
When you add a new
address to your
address book, you
must specify what
type of address it is.

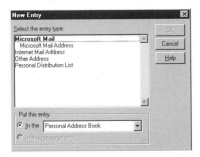

3. In the New Address Properties dialog box shown in figure 29.23, enter the
   Display Name. The display name is the name that you want to appear in the
   Personal Address Book list.

FIG. 29.23
To create a new
Internet address, all
you need to know is
the recipient's e-mail
address.

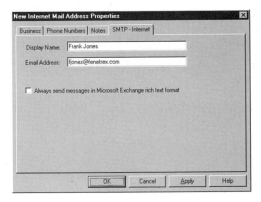

4. Enter the recipient's e-mail address in the name@domain format.

5. If you know that this recipient is also using Windows Messaging or another
   e-mail program that can handle rich text messages with fonts and other
   formatting, then click Always Send Messages in Microsoft Windows Messaging Rich Text Format. Otherwise, leave this box unchecked.

6. Choose OK to save the new entry and return to the Address Book window.

Any message you receive is also a quick and easy source of new addresses. To add an address from an incoming message, follow these steps:

1. Open the message from the Windows Messaging viewer, if it isn't already open.

2. Right-click the address that you want to add to the PAB.

3. From the pop-up menu, choose Add to Personal Address Book.

N O T E   Unlike Microsoft Mail, Windows Messaging does not automatically update your Personal Address Book and add the addresses used in the messages that you send. ▪

Working with Microsoft Mail Addresses

You can add Microsoft Mail addresses to the PAB from incoming messages using the technique just described.

Another way to add Microsoft Mail addresses is to copy them from the postoffice list, using these steps:

1. Use Show Names to switch to the postoffice address list.

2. Select the name you want to add to the PAB.

3. Click the Add to Personal Address List button or choose File, Add to Personal Address List.

If you previously used Microsoft Mail on this system, you may want to import the addresses from the Personal Address Book in your Mail message file. To do this, you need to know the name and location of your MMF file. If it was stored on the local drive, then it's probably C:\WINDOWS\MSMAIL.MMF (or you can check MSMAIL.INI). If it was stored on the server, you can find it in \MMF subfolder under the postoffice folder, but under a file name that doesn't tell you which MMF is whose. You may want to run Mail from another workstation to access the user's account and move the MMF file to a different location on the server, under a more useable file name.

Once you know the location of the MMF file, follow these steps:

1. From the Windows Messaging viewer (not the Address Book window), choose File, Import.

2. In the Specify File to Import dialog box, give the location of your Microsoft Mail message file. It has an MMF extension. When you've entered its location, choose Open to continue.

3. In the Import Mail Data dialog, enter the password for your MMF file.

   Note that you can also import messages from your MMF. If you don't want to do that at this time, click the Import Message box to uncheck it.

4. Choose OK to import the old addresses into your Windows Messaging PAB.

TIP If you frequently need to send to someone for whom you have both Microsoft Mail and Internet Mail addresses, you may want to put both those addresses in your Personal Address Book. That enables you use the Check Names addressing method to pick which one you want to use for any given message.

Rather than read the postoffice list off the network server every time, you may want to keep your own copy locally. (This is especially helpful if you're connecting to the postoffice remotely.) To refresh your local copy of the postoffice list, choose Tools, Microsoft Mail Tools, Download Address Lists.

Importing Other Addresses

You learned about importing Microsoft Mail addresses from your old message file. You can also import addresses from another Windows Messaging Personal Address Book by following these steps:

1. In the Windows Messaging viewer (not the Address Book window), choose File, Import.

2. In the Specify File to Import dialog box, give the location of the Personal Address Book you want to use. It has a PAB extension. When you have entered its location, choose Open to continue.

3. In the Import Mail Data dialog box, choose OK to confirm that you want to import the address book.

Because Windows Messaging does not allow you to share a Personal Address Book with other users (or to have two PABs in one profile), importing is a good way to let other people use the addresses you've collected.

Creating Distribution Lists

There will surely be many cases where you send messages to the same group of people on a regular basis. Maybe you want to send a message to a group of managers that you need to remind to get a report in on time, or maybe you have a collection of people on the Internet that you routinely update with news about your family.

Windows Messaging streamlines the process of sending such messages by allowing you to create personal distribution lists. These are mailing lists that you can access by entering a single address on a message.

To create a personal distribution list, follow these steps:

1. In the Address Book window (refer to fig. 29.21), click the New Entry button or choose File, New Entry.

2. In the New Entry dialog (refer to fig. 29.22), select Personal Distribution List.

3. In the New Personal Distribution List Properties dialog box, enter a Name for the list.

4. Choose Add/Remove Members to display the Edit Members dialog box, shown in figure 29.24.

5. In the Edit Members dialog box, shown in figure 29.24, select the people you want to be on the list in the left column, then choose Members to move the selected names to the right column.

6. If desired, switch to other address lists from the Show Names list, then repeat step 4.

7. To remove a name, select it from the Personal Distribution List box, then press the Delete key to delete it.

8. When you've finished adding and removing names from the list, choose OK twice to save it to your Personal Address Book.

To send a message to a personal distribution list, enter the name of the list in the To, Cc, or Bcc box in the message window.

FIG. 29.24
On a personal distribution list, you can include recipients from both your Personal Address Book and the postoffice list.

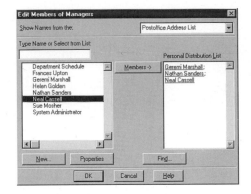

Managing Messages

So far, you've learned about sending and reading messages. What else can you do with the contents of your Windows Messaging folders? You can print them, rearrange them, supplement them with documents from your other Windows applications, and even share them with other users.

In this section, you look at those message management features, plus some tips for message housekeeping.

Importing MS Mail Messages

If you previously used Microsoft Mail on this system, you may want to import the messages from your old Mail message file. To do this, you need to know the name and location of your MMF file. If it was stored on the local drive, then it's probably C:\WINDOWS\MSMAIL.MMF (or you can check MSMAIL.INI). If it was stored on the server, you can find it in \MMF subfolder under the postoffice folder, but under a file name that doesn't tell you which MMF is whose. You may want to run Mail from another workstation to access the user's account and move the MMF file to a different location on the server, under a more useable file name.

Once you know the location of the MMF file, use these steps to import it into Windows Messaging:

1. From the Windows Messaging viewer, choose File, Import.

2. In the Specify File to Import dialog box, specify the location of your

Microsoft Mail message file. It has an MMF extension. When you've entered its location, choose Open to continue.

3. In the Import Mail Data dialog box, enter the password for your MMF file.

   Note that you can also import addresses from your MMF. If you don't want to do that at this time, then click the Import Personal Address Book Entries box to uncheck it.

4. Choose OK to import the old messages into your Windows Messaging PST.

Printing Messages

You can print messages either from the Windows Messaging viewer or from a message window.

To print multiple messages from the Windows Messaging viewer, first select the ones you want to print.

 To print the current message(s) immediately, click the Print button.

▶ **See** "Understanding the Windows NT Printing Process," **p. 114**

To adjust your printer settings before printing the message(s), choose File, Print or press Ctrl+P. In the Print dialog box (see fig. 29.25), you see two Windows Messaging-specific options that supplement the customary Windows NT printer settings.

The first option concerns printing of multiple messages. The default is to print all the items consecutively, without a page break between them. To change that setting, click Start Each Item on a New Page.

The other option deals with attachments. Normally, Windows Messaging does not print a message's file attachments. (Printing attachments would involve opening each file in its associated application, which could take a while.) If you do want attachments to print, then click Print Attachments.

Windows Messaging remembers both of these settings and uses them the next time you print, whether you use the Print button for immediate printing or choose File, Print to go through the Print dialog box.

FIG. 29.25
In addition to the usual NT printer settings, Windows Messaging includes options for printing messages together on a page and for printing attachments.

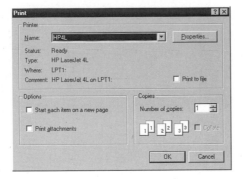

Finding Messages

Once you have more than a few dozen messages, you'll start to appreciate the message Find tool included with Windows Messaging. It lets you search the message details (sender, recipients, and more), the subject box, and the text of the message. You can also specify date ranges, size, and other advanced criteria.

To look for messages, choose Tools, Find. The Find window shown in figure 29.26 depicts a search for messages containing the word "listserv" or the word "subscribe." (Both of these words are related to Internet mailing lists, to which you can subscribe by sending a message to the server managing the list.) Notice how the two words are separated with a semicolon.

FIG. 29.26
In this example of a Find window, you are looking for all messages related to Internet mailing lists that you have subscribed to.

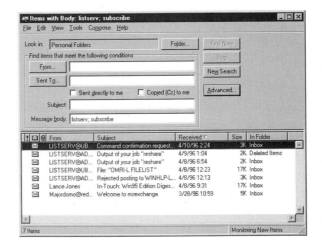

Choose Folder to change the scope of your search, from one folder (with or without its subfolders) to your entire Personal Folders file or all the Microsoft Mail Shared Folders.

Under Find Items That Meet the Following Conditions, you can enter a variety of search criteria:

From (the sender)

Sent To (recipients)

Sent Directly to Me

Copied (Cc) to Me

Subject

Message Body

For additional search criteria, choose Advanced.

Figure 29.27 shows advanced search criteria that you might want to use if you're archiving messages on a monthly basis; this example shows the month of March, 1996.

FIG. 29.27

Use a date range search to gather a group of messages for archiving.

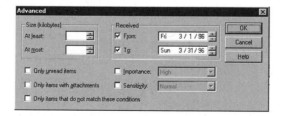

When you've set your search criteria, choose Find Now to run the search. Messages that match your criteria are displayed at the bottom of the Find window. You can do anything with those messages that you could in the Windows Messaging viewer—open, print, move, delete, and so on. For example, if you were looking for items to archive, you could select all the found items, then choose File, Move to put them in a different folder, even into a separate Personal Folders file used just for archiving.

One final Find example will show you how Move works. In figure 29.28, you are looking for all new messages from a particular Internet mailing list.

Under Message Body, you entered text that was copied directly from the signature that appears on each message from that list. (You could also have entered the list sender's address under From.)

After running Find Now, you chose Edit, Select All or Ctrl+A to select all the messages found, then chose File, Move to bring up the Move dialog box that you see on top in figure 29.28. You selected the Windows Messaging List folder, a new folder created within Personal Folders. When you choose OK, all the messages in the Find window are moved to the Windows Messaging List folder.

FIG. 29.28
One handy use of the Find function is to locate a group of items that you want to move to another folder.

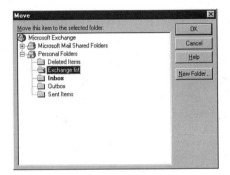

 Another way to move selected messages is to drag them from one folder to another. To copy rather than move, hold down the Ctrl key while you drag.

Find is not a tool that you must put away when you're done with it. If you leave a Find window open, but minimized, it continues to scan for new messages that fit the criteria you specified. And, if that Find window is open when you exit Windows Messaging or shut down NT, then it reopens the next time you start Windows Messaging, ready to begin searching for messages once again.

Storing Documents

So far, you have learned only about Windows Messaging as an e-mail application, but it can do more than that. Consider your Personal Folders as a place to store any kind of information—e-mail messages or documents of any sort.

▶ **See** "Using Personal Folders," **p. 819**

For example, you might create a separate set of Personal Folders to store all the messages and documents related to a new marketing project. Within that information store, you might have a separate folder for logo designs and one for all the project proposal drafts. Still others might contain your budget and feedback from your colleagues. Figure 29.29 shows an example of such a set of folders, including a Word document and several TIF images.

FIG. 29.29
Windows Messaging can store not just messages, but any type of document or other file.

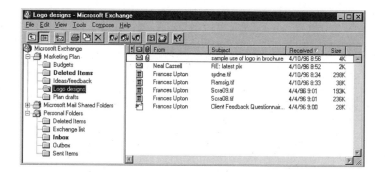

Some of the items stored in the Marketing folders are messages, moved or copied there from Inbox or Sent Items. Others are documents that were originally created in Word, Excel, or other applications. These appear with the same icons that you'd see for documents of those types in Explorer.

To move a document into an Windows Messaging folder, just drag it from Explorer.

▶ **See** "Working with Briefcase," **p. 237**

Put documents in Windows Messaging folders and what do you get? An alternative to Explorer for organizing your files. It comes with an interesting twist: all the documents and messages are held in a single Personal Folders file. If you use Windows Messaging on both a desktop and laptop machine, you find it easy to move this file back and forth with the Briefcase.

Using Shared Folders

If you are using the Microsoft Mail service, you should see an additional set of folders besides your Personal Folders. These are the Microsoft Mail Public Folders, also known as *shared folders*, stored in the postoffice and available for public access, depending on the rights granted by the creator of each folder.

For an example of what you can do with shared folders, look at figure 29.30. A folder named New Health Plan has been created, with two subfolders—Discussion and Plan Documents. We placed messages with file attachments in the Plan Documents folder, which is set for read-only permission, and opened up the Discussion folder for anyone to contribute by giving everyone both read and write access.

FIG. 29.30

Spread the word about your company's new health plan with a shared folder that details the plan's provisions, plus another folder where employees can ask questions and make comments.

Creating a new shared folder is simple. Follow these steps:

1. In the folders list, select either Microsoft Mail Public Folders (if you want a new top-level folder) or one of the existing shared folders (if you want a new subfolder).

2. Choose File, New Folder.

3. In the New Folder dialog, enter a Folder Name, then choose OK to create it.

You get to decide what other Microsoft Mail users can do with your folder; whether they can read or delete messages or add to the messages kept in your folder. Here's how to set these permissions:

1. Select a folder from the Microsoft Mail Public Folders list.

2. Choose File, Properties.

3. Switch to the Permissions tab, shown in figure 29.31.

4. Click Read Permission, Write Permission, and Delete Permission as needed to grant or revoke those access rights.

5. Choose OK to close the folder Properties dialog box and update the folder with the new permissions.

FIG. 29.31
Only the owner of a shared folder can change the permissions granted to other users.

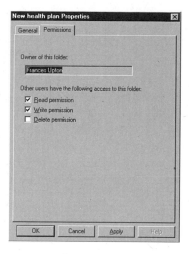

To put an existing message in your new shared folder, use one of these methods:

- Drag the message to the new folder. This will move it.
- Hold down the Ctrl key while you drag the message to the new folder. This will copy it.
- Choose File, Move or File, Copy to move or copy the message.

These methods also work when you have selected more than one message in the Windows Messaging viewer or in a Find window.

To create a new message in a shared folder, follow these steps:

- Click the New Message button to create a new message. (Or, choose Compose, New Message or press Ctrl+N.)
- Enter a Subject and compose the text of your message, attaching any files you need. You do not need to enter any recipients.
- Choose File, Move, then select the destination folder and choose OK to close the message and save it to that folder.

Message Housekeeping

Windows Messaging may have a lot of clever features, but one thing it won't do for you is control the size of your Personal Folders file. This message file can grow and grow and grow. When it does, you definitely see Windows Messaging take longer to start up, especially if you are keeping your Personal Folders file on a network server.

Here are some of the things you can do to keep your Personal Folders trimmed:

- Delete old messages.
- Delete messages with attachments, which tend to be larger than other messages.
- Make sure the Deleted Items folder gets emptied.

 Use Windows Messaging's Find function with an Advanced search using date criteria to locate old messages or using size criteria to find the largest messages, which you might want to delete after saving any attachments.

Items that you delete from various Windows Messaging folders are sent to the Deleted Items folder, giving you a chance to recover them.

Eventually, though, you want these items to disappear completely. Items are deleted permanently when you:

- Delete them from the Deleted Items folder.
- Exit Windows Messaging, with Windows Messaging set up to empty the Deleted Items folder when it closes.

To configure Windows Messaging to empty Deleted Items on exit, choose <u>T</u>ools, <u>O</u>ptions. Then, on the General tab, choose <u>E</u>mpty the 'Deleted Items' Folder upon Exiting.

Note that if you shut down Windows NT without first exiting Windows Messaging, the Deleted Items folder will not be purged, regardless of this setting. You must first exit Windows Messaging, then shut down Windows NT.

Compacting Personal Folders

When you delete items, you won't see an immediate drop in the size of your Personal Folders file. Windows Messaging waits until it has a free moment to compact the file and recover the space freed up by the deleted messages.

To force Windows Messaging to compact Personal Folders, follow these steps:

1. Choose Tools, Options, then switch to the Services tab.

2. Select the Personal Folders service, then choose Properties.

3. In the Personal Folders dialog, choose Compact Now.

4. After compacting is complete, choose OK twice to close the dialogs and return to Windows Messaging.

Repairing the Inbox

It's rare but possible that your Personal Folders file will become damaged. To repair a Personal Folders file, Windows NT provides the Inbox Repair Tool. Follow these steps to use it:

1. Use the Windows NT Explorer to navigate to the \PROGRAM FILES\MICROSOFT Windows Messaging folder.

2. Double-click the SCANPST.EXE file.

TIP You can also locate the SCANPST.EXE file by choosing Start, Find, Files or Folders.

3. In the Inbox Repair Tool dialog box, type the Personal Folders file name into the Enter the Name of the File You Want to Scan box, or choose Browse to locate it on your system.

4. Choose Start to repair the Personal Folders file. After the eight repair functions have completed, you will see a report on any errors found. See figure 29.32 for an example.

5. Choose Repair to actually perform the repair operation and fix the reported errors.

FIG. 29.32

When you fix a Personal Folders file with the Inbox Repair Tool, you can create a backup file before making the repairs.

From Here...

E-mail and information storage are the highlights of Windows Messaging. You should now know how to compose and transmit messages, respond to incoming messages, keep a Personal Address Book, and maintain good order in your message file.

However, that's just the tip of the iceberg for Windows Messaging. The application delivered with Windows NT Workstation is only one version. A different version, called Exchange and distributed with Exchange Server (part of Microsoft BackOffice), adds a whole range of additional features. These include automatic assistants to respond to incoming messages or to move messages into different folders for you.

If you've enjoyed working with Windows Messaging and want to learn more about it in particular and online operations in general, try these chapters:

- Chapter 23, "Using Dial-Up Networking," helps you gain expertise in connecting not just to e-mail services, but to other remote resources that may be available to you.

- Chapter 26, "Using Internet Explorer, Internet Mail, and Internet News," takes you beyond Internet e-mail into the world of information you can access with Windows NT via the Internet.

- Chapter 28, "Configuring Windows Messaging Services," is worth reviewing, to make sure that you've set up Windows Messaging to work exactly the way you want it to.

CHAPTER 30

Using HyperTerminal

by Sue Plumley

Like its siblings Windows and Windows for Workgroups, Windows NT provides an accessory application called HyperTerminal for communicating with other computers using a modem. A modem is a device that allows computers to pass information across a standard telephone line, by turning digital signals into analog tones, and then back again to digital on the receiving end. The other computer might be another PC, a bulletin board system (BBS), or even a mainframe system in a corporation or university.

In order to communicate over a modem, the computers require *communications software* that enables you to control the modem and use its various features. HyperTerminal is such a program. ■

Start HyperTerminal

Start and quit HyperTerminal as you would any program in NT; this chapter shows you how to navigate the menus.

Change and save HyperTerminal settings

Customize HyperTerminal settings for your comfort and ease.

Connect to and disconnect from other computers

Dial up other computers to chat or transfer files. Connecting through HyperTerminal is painless.

Send and receive files

Quickly transfer files between computers using HyperTerminal.

Starting HyperTerminal

When you start HyperTerminal, it prompts you to identify the new connection you plan to make. You can create a new connection by entering the details of the call you're about to make, as described in the next section, or you can cancel the dialog box and open a previously saved connection.

This exercise shows you how to start HyperTerminal; you create a new connection later in the chapter.

1. To start HyperTerminal, choose Start, Programs, Accessories, HyperTerminal.

2. The Connection Description dialog box appears (see fig. 30.1).

FIG. 30.1

Create a new connection or cancel the dialog box.

3. Choose Cancel. The HyperTerminal program window appears (see fig. 30.2).

If this is your first use of HyperTerminal, you may be asked for the default serial port HyperTerminal should use or to verify that a modem is attached to your computer and turned on. Enter the communications (COM) port where your modem is located or check your modem and then click OK. You then see HyperTerminal's main window.

N O T E You must have a modem attached and installed to your computer and turned on before you can use HyperTerminal. To install a modem to your computer, choose the Modems icon in the Control Panel and follow the wizard's directions. ■

FIG. 30.2

The HyperTerminal window provides the tools you need to create connections and make calls with your modem.

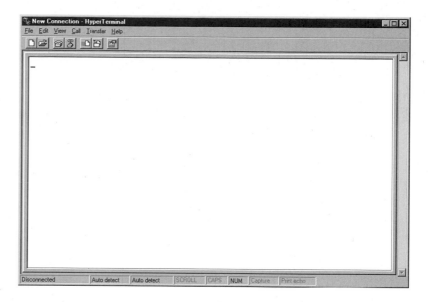

Changing and Saving HyperTerminal Settings

HyperTerminal enables you to connect to other computers via a modem. Before you can connect to another modem, however, you must create what is called a "connection" in HyperTerminal. A connection describes the party to which you will connect. You name the connection and then choose details such as phone number, modem speed, line parity, and so on. After you create a connection by entering the details required, you can save it for future use.

You may be wondering at this point how to know what settings you should choose. To find out the correct settings for a remote computer, you should consult the documentation provided by the organization that runs the remote system, or contact the administrator of the system.

Additionally, you can set options for your location and your own modem as you create a new connection. These settings are saved with this particular connection's file; you can save different settings for different connections.

Creating a New Connection

You'll first need to name the new connection and specify a phone number, area code, and so on. This section begins the process of creating a new connection and the following sections continue the process by showing you how to set options for the connection.

To create a new connection, follow these steps:

1. Choose File, New Connection. The Connection Description dialog box appears (refer to fig. 30.1).

2. In the Name text box, enter a name under which you want to save the connection.

TIP   You can use any characters to name a new connection except for the following: \ / . * ?
" < > | . You also can use spaces within the file name.

3. In the Icon list box, choose an icon to represent the new connection and then choose OK. The Phone Number dialog box appears (see fig. 30.3).

FIG. 30.3
Enter the phone number of the new connection.

4. In the Phone Number text box, enter the number you want to dial. You also can change the country, area code, or the modem or port you'll use to call out on. Choose OK when you're finished. The Connect dialog box appears (see fig. 30.4).

TIP   Choose the Modify button in the Connect dialog box to change any details about the number you are calling, such as phone number, country, area code, and so on.

FIG. 30.4
Set options or edit options in the Connect dialog box.

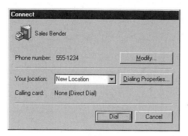

At this point, you can call the remote computer by choosing the Dial button, you can choose the Cancel button, or you can set your location's dialing properties, as described in the next section. If you choose the Cancel button, you're not canceling the creation of the connection; you're simply canceling the dialog box.

N O T E If you choose to create a new connection, open an existing connection, or exit HyperTerminal at any time during the process, HyperTerminal asks if you want to save the connection you're working on. Choose Yes to save or No to abandon any changes. ■

Setting Your Location's Dialing Properties

Dialing properties refer to the options you set for your particular situation. Say, for example, you're in an out-of-town hotel and you need to dial a 9 to dial out of the hotel. You can set that option in the Dialing Properties dialog box.

To set dialing properties, follow these steps:

1. To set dialing properties for your modem, click the Dialing Properties button in the Connect dialog box; alternatively, you can click the Properties button on the Tool Bar. The Dialing Properties sheet appears (see fig. 30.5).

2. In the My Locations tab of the Dialing Properties sheet, confirm the information in the Where I Am area is correct: area code and country.

N O T E If you work on a laptop and travel quite a bit, you might want to create a My Location property sheet for various locations. In the I Am Dialing From area, choose New and then enter a location such as **Home**, **Hotel-Beckley**, or **Office-VA**. Set the options for that location and then add another New location, if you want. ■

Part
VI

Ch
30

FIG. 30.5
Set dialing properties
for your location.

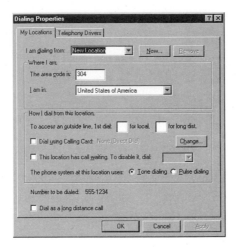

3. In the How I Dial From This Location area, enter the appropriate options as
   follows:

   To Access an Outside Line, 1st Dial. Enter any number required to dial local
   and/or long distance.

   Dial Using Calling Card. Click the Change button to enter the name and
   number of the calling card.

   This Location Has Call Waiting. Check this box, if appropriate, and enter the
   number to dial to disable call waiting while you're on the line.

   Tone/Pulse Dialing. Choose the dialing used by the current phone system.

   Dial as a Long Distance Call. Check this box if a 1 and the area code must be
   dialed to connect to the selected number.

4. Choose OK to return to the Connect dialog box.

You can either choose the Dial button to dial the remote computer or Cancel the
connection; if you choose Cancel, you're not canceling the creation of the connection, only the dialog box.

Configuring Your Modem

You can set options for your own modem, such as speed, parity, speaker volume,
and so on from within HyperTerminal. You also can determine these settings in the
Windows Control Panel, Modems icon.

One particular setting of concern is the speed of your modem. The speed you set for your modem depends on the speed of the remote modem. For example, if you're making a connection between two 14,400 bps/baud modems, you would normally set the speed to either 19,200 or 38,400 instead of 14,400. This is because most modems used today are capable of using some kind of hardware data compression, which substantially increases the effective overall throughput of the modem.

Because most modems auto-negotiate the highest speed at which they can communicate, Windows enables you to set the maximum speed for your modem. This helps ensure that you always make the fastest possible connection. If you set your modem to the highest speed it's capable of, you don't have to worry about the modem to which you're connecting.

> **N O T E** *Baud* is a commonly misunderstood term and often used in place of bits per
> second (bps). Whereas bits per second means just what it says—that is, the
> number of bits per second a modem is capable of transferring—baud refers to the
> number of transitions per second that the modem can make. Although many modems
> use 1 bit per transition, some do not so the two values are not always the same. ■

To set the properties for your modem, follow these steps:

1. Choose File, Properties. The Properties sheet for the new connection appears (see fig. 30.6).

FIG. 30.6
Configure the properties for your own modem.

T I P   In the Phone Number tab, you can choose to modify any of the following existing settings for the connection: icon, country, area code, phone number, or connection.

2. Below the Connect Using selection list, choose the Configure button. Your modem's Properties sheet appears. Figure 30.7 shows a property sheet for a Hayes Accura modem; your property sheets may look different.

FIG. 30.7
Set your modem's speed, parity, and other options in the Phone Number dialog box.

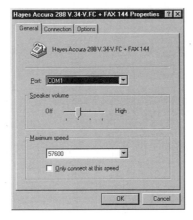

The General tab usually contains a selection for port, speaker volume, and modem speed.

The Connection tab contains data bits, parity, stop bits, and various call preferences, such as whether to wait for a dial tone before dialing.

The Options tab controls such options as dial control and status control.

3. Choose OK when you're finished setting your modem properties.

Configuring Emulation and Other Settings

There are other settings you can choose to make HyperTerminal work more efficiently with the remote modem. You can, for example, set HyperTerminal to emulate the terminal you're calling or you can let Windows automatically detect the terminal setting. You can also control how the text appears on the screen if you're calling a bulletin board, for example, or chatting with someone at the remote site.

The choices you make in the Settings tab depend on the remote computer; if you're unsure of the settings to use, use the Windows defaults or contact the administrator of the remote system for more information. To set emulation and other options, follow these steps:

1. Choose File, Properties to open the Properties sheet for the selected connection. Choose the Settings tab (see fig. 30.8).

FIG. 30.8
Set terminal emulation in the Settings dialog box.

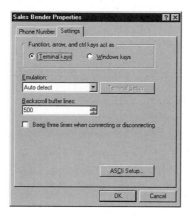

2. In the Function, Arrow, and Ctrl Keys Act As area, choose whether to use Terminal Keys or Windows keys, depending on the remote setup.

3. In the Emulation drop-down list, choose the terminal you want to emulate. If you're unsure of the terminal, choose Auto Detect and let Windows make the decision for you.

N O T E If you choose a terminal from the Emulation list, you can then choose the Terminal Setup button and indicate the terminal modes and character set used by the remote terminal. ▨

4. In the Backscroll Buffer Lines text box, enter the number of lines you want to be able to scroll back and view. Optionally, choose the Beep Three Times When Connecting or Disconnecting check box.

5. Choose the ASCII Setup button. The ASCII Setup dialog box appears (see fig. 30.9).

6. In ASCII Sending, choose from the following options:

Send Line Ends with Line Feeds. Sends a hard return to the remote computer every time you end a line.

FIG. 30.9

Set preferences for the screen; set Echo on/off.

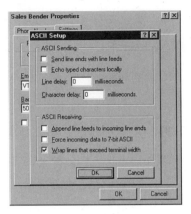

Echo Typed Characters Locally. Displays the text you type on your screen; if deselected, you cannot see what you're typing but the other terminal can.

Line Delay. Sets how long HyperTerminal delays before sending a line of text to the remote computer; enter a number in the text box.

Character Delay. Sets the delay for sending characters you type to the remote computer.

7. In the ASCII Receiving area, choose from the following options:

Append Line Feeds to Incoming Line Ends. Inserts a hard return at the end of every line you receive from the remote computer.

Force Incoming Data to 7-Bit ASCII. Translates 8-bit to 7-bit ASCII.

Wrap Lines That Exceed Terminal Width. Wraps text to the next line if the remote computer sends a line of text that's too wide for your computer screen.

8. Choose OK to close the ASCII Setup dialog box. Choose OK again to close the Properties sheet.

TROUBLESHOOTING

I want to call a bulletin board service but I don't know how. What can I do? Set up a call to a BBS the same as you would any new connection. Enter the name and the number and then modify options if need be.

When viewing a HyperTerminal session, I can see text from the remote computer, but I can't see what I'm typing. In the Settings tab of the connection's Properties sheet, check the box beside the Echo Typed Characters Locally option.

Saving and Retrieving Settings Files

After completing the settings for a new connection, you can save those settings in a file that you can later retrieve, to save time and energy when working with HyperTerminal. When saving your new connection information, you name the file and then choose a specific location in which to store the file. Later, you can open the settings file and immediately dial the remote computer with ease.

Saving Settings Files

By default, HyperTerminal saves the connection setting files in the PROGRAM FILES\WINDOWS NT folder. You can, of course, choose any folder you want to save your settings files in.

To save connection settings to a file, follow these steps:

1. When you're finished creating a connection, choose File, Save As. The Save As dialog box appears.

2. In the Save In drop-down list, choose the folder in which you want to save your settings files.

3. In the File Name text box, enter the name of the file; you can use Windows long file names, if you want.

4. Choose Save.

If you give the setting file the same name as an existing file, you are asked if you want to overwrite the existing file with the new settings file. Choose Yes to overwrite the existing file or No to cancel the save operation. To save the current settings under a different file name (for a remote system that has similar settings requirements but a different phone number), follow the same steps.

Retrieving Settings Files

 To retrieve a settings file, choose <u>F</u>ile, <u>O</u>pen; alternatively, click the Open icon in the toolbar. The Open dialog box appears (see fig. 30.10).

FIG. 30.10
Use the Open dialog box to locate and open a saved settings file.

Choose the folder in which you saved your settings files and select the file name. Choose <u>O</u>pen to retrieve the connection settings. HyperTerminal displays the Connect dialog box from which you can dial the remote computer.

Connecting and Disconnecting

If you open a saved connection settings file, HyperTerminal dials the number automatically for you. You can also call a connection's number at any time during a HyperTerminal setting. You might call a number to chat, to attach to a bulletin board, or to send or receive a file. After you've completed your business with the remote computer, you can disconnect from the call.

Connecting to a Remote Computer

When you connect to a remote computer, HyperTerminal dials the number you specify, paying close attention to any dialing preferences and options you've set.

To connect to a remote computer, you can do one of the following:

- Choose <u>C</u>all, <u>C</u>onnect.
- Click the Connect button on the toolbar.
- Choose the Dial button if you're in the Connect dialog box.

Depending on the remote computer, a variety of things can happen when you reach the party you're calling. A bulletin board service, for example, might answer with a welcome screen or a password screen. Someone who is expecting your call may type some text to welcome you, ask a question, or make a comment.

In answer to questions or queries, you can enter text directly into the Hyper-Terminal screen. Figure 30.11 shows a question entered and an answer from the remote computer.

FIG. 30.11

Enter a message to the remote computer.

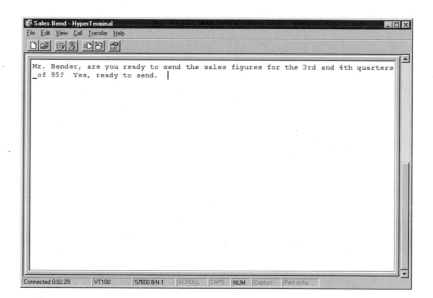

Transferring Files

You can both send and receive files using HyperTerminal. Files do not need to be in any specific format or location.

Receiving   When receiving a file, you can choose to save the file to a folder under a specified file name so you can retrieve the file later.

To receive a file, follow these steps:

1. Choose Transfer, Receive File. The Receive File dialog box appears (see fig. 30.12). The folder to which you save may be different than the one in the figure.

FIG. 30.12

Use the Receive File dialog box to specify details about the file you're about to receive.

2. In the <u>P</u>lace Received File in the Following Folder text box, enter the path to where you want to save the file; alternatively, choose the <u>B</u>rowse button and select the folder from the dialog box.

3. In the <u>U</u>se Receiving Protocol list box, choose the protocol you want to use.

 T I P   The protocol you choose depends on type of file and sender's protocol. If you're unsure, try Zmodem; it's faster and it is the default.

All you have to do is wait for the file. HyperTerminal will automatically receive the file when it is ready. Figure 30.13 shows the dialog box that appears while the file is being received.

FIG. 30.13

This dialog box remains on-screen until the file transfer is complete.

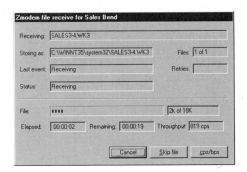

N O T E   If you prefer, you can send a file directly to the printer instead of saving it to your hard disk. Choose <u>T</u>ransfer, Capture to <u>P</u>rinter. HyperTerminal sends the text directly to the printer. ▮

Sending   Sending a file is similar to receiving a file using HyperTerminal.

To send a file, follow these steps:

1. Choose <u>T</u>ransfer, <u>S</u>end File. The Send File dialog box appears (see fig. 30.14).

FIG. 30.14
Send a file to a
remote computer by
specifying the file
name and protocol.

2. In the Filename text box, enter a name; alternatively, click Browse to locate the file on your computer.

3. In the Protocol list, choose the protocol you want to use.

4. When you're ready, choose Send. The Send File dialog box shows the progress of the transfer. Figure 30.15 shows the results of the completed transfer.

FIG. 30.15
When the transfer is
complete, the dialog
box disappears.

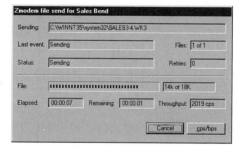

Disconnecting from the Remote

You disconnect from the remote computer when you're finished by doing one of the following:

- Choose Call Disconnect.

- Click the Disconnect tool button on the toolbar.

> **CAUTION**
> Be sure that you disconnect your sessions when finished, especially when using long distance numbers and/or commercial online services that charge for connect time. If you forget to disconnect, you may end up being charged for additional time that you didn't even get to use!

continues

continued

In addition, you should always indicate to the host system that you wish to disconnect (using the host system's disconnect menu option) prior to disconnecting locally in HyperTerminal. This ensures that the host system knows you are no longer logged in—something that isn't always guaranteed if you simply hang up.

Copying and Pasting Information in HyperTerminal

HyperTerminal, like most Windows applications, supports the transfer and sharing of information between programs via the Copy and Paste clipboard functions found in the Edit menu. The clipboard is a Windows transfer area that holds information you want to copy between applications.

If you want to copy information from a HyperTerminal screen to another application, you may do so using the standard Windows Copy and Paste features found in the Edit menu.

To copy and paste information, either to the clipboard in HyperTerminal or to the Host from one of your own applications, follow these steps:

1. Highlight, using click and drag, the information to be copied.
2. Choose Edit, Copy; alternatively, you can press Ctrl+C.
3. Move to the application where you want to retrieve the information using the taskbar.
4. Position the insertion point and choose Edit, Paste function from the destination application's menu to retrieve the text.

   ▶ **See** "Switching Programs with the Taskbar," **p. 63**

Exiting HyperTerminal

When you exit HyperTerminal, the program may display a dialog box asking if you want to save any unsaved connection settings. Choose Yes to save, No to close the program without saving the connection settings, or Cancel to return to HyperTerminal.

To exit HyperTerminal, do one of the following:

- Click the Close (X) button.
- Choose File, Exit.
- Double-click the Control Menu.
- Press Alt+F4.

From Here...

In this chapter, you learned to use HyperTerminal to communicate and transfer files over the phone line. For information about other programs included with NT, see the following chapters:

- Chapter 18, "Using Windows NT Accessory Applications," shows you how to use the WordPad, Paint, and Chat programs that come with NT.
- Chapter 32, "Using the Event Viewer," explains how to view event logs that track such things as security breaches, application problems, and system errors.

Optimizing and Protecting Windows NT Workstation

CHAPTER 31

Working with the Registry

by Kevin Jones

When Windows NT starts up, it needs to know all the information about your system. It needs to know the configuration settings of your hardware; the rights, privileges, and preferences of all users; and information about your installed software. All this information is stored in a database called the *Registry*. This database is critical to getting and keeping your system up and running.

Although you may never need to directly modify the Registry, it is still important to understand what the Registry is and how it works. Not only does this knowledge help you maintain your system, but if you ever need to directly modify the Registry, you'll have the understanding and tools needed to make any necessary changes.

Understand the Registry and its contents

The Registry is a database where all the configuration information about hardware, software, and users is stored. Understanding the structure of the Registry is needed before changes can be safely made.

Modify the Registry with the Registry Editor REGEDIT.EXE

The REGEDIT.EXE registry editor is the primary tool for end-users to use when modifying the Registry.

Modify the Registry with the Registry Editor REGEDT32.EXE

The Regedt32.EXE registry editor is the primary tool for system administrators to use when modifying the Registry.

Know when to modify the Registry directly

Changing the Registry can cause disasterous results. Knowing when and how to safely modify the Registry is very important.

Understanding the Registry

The primary function of the Registry is similar to the function of the INI files found in Windows 3.x (WIN.INI and SYSTEM.INI), as well as CONFIG.SYS and AUTOEXEC.BAT. When Windows NT starts, it gets information from the Registry about the device drivers that it needs to load, hardware installed in your system, and user information. However, the Registry also serves many other functions.

For instance, the Registry also serves as the central clearing house for applications supporting Object Linking and Embedding (OLE). This is where all the OLE-enabled applications store information about themselves—information that other OLE applications may need to know. This kind of information allows you, for example, to edit a Microsoft Excel spreadsheet from within Microsoft Word.

The Registry also is the preferred place for applications to store their own data (for example, the last window position or default font). Before Windows NT, applications stored this kind of information in their own INI files. This resulted in many INI files scattered about on your hard disk. Now, each application can create a section within the Registry where it can neatly and efficiently store its information.

NOTE In a perfect world, INI files would have disappeared in Windows NT. But it is very likely that you are still running one or more old, 16-bit Windows applications. These programs don't use the Registry and still read and write to their own private INI files. But they also expect that WIN.INI, SYSTEM.INI, and other standard INI files are available to them. Windows NT goes to a lot of trouble to make these worlds coexist, but the bottom line is you'll still find INI files on your system. ▨

A Brief History of the Registry

The Registry had its beginnings as the humble Registration Database in Windows 3.1. This database was required so that Windows could make Object Linking and Embedding (OLE) work between applications. Windows needed a central repository where all OLE-enabled applications could store information on the programs and interfaces used to support OLE (for example, displaying, editing, and printing object data).

When Microsoft began engineering Windows NT, they decided to extend the functionality of the Registration Database. Besides just storing information for OLE-enabled applications, Microsoft decided to create a single database to store all the configuration information about the computer—its hardware, software, networking, security, and user profiles. This information collectively is known as the Registry.

N O T E Windows 95 also has a Registry. While this Registry contains the same type of information as the Registry in Windows NT, the files that make up the Registry are different. While there are some other differences—some good and some bad—it's clear that INI files eventually will be completely replaced with the Registry. ▪

Part
VII

Ch
31

Structure of the Registry

The Registry is a hierarchical database—in other words, it is organized in a tree structure. This tree is divided into five main subtrees. These are listed in table 31.1. Each branch or subtree is called a *key*.

Table 31.1 Registry Keys

Key Name	Description
HKEY_CLASSES_ROOT	Contains information on file type associations and Object Linking and Embedding.
HKEY_LOCAL_MACHINE	Contains information about the local computer, including information about hardware, startup options, and system parameters.
HKEY_CURRENT_USER	Contains information about the user currently logged on, including the User Profile, preferences, and network settings.
HKEY_USERS	Contains information about all User Profiles defined on this machine.
HKEY_CURRENT_CONFIG	Contains information about hardware configuration settings.

Each key serves a main function and is further divided into additional keys. These keys also may be further subdivided, and those keys divided again, and so on. Each key has a name unique within its key and may have one or more associated values. Each value has three parts—a name, a data type, and an actual data value. (Each key can have one default value that has no name. All other values must have a name.) For example, the key HKEY_CLASSES_ROOT\.DOC has a default (no name) value of type REG_SZ and an actual value of Word.Document.6.

Table 31.2 lists the five possible data types for Registry values.

Table 31.2   Registry Data Types

Data Type	Description
REG_BINARY	Contains raw binary data.
REG_DWORD	Contains a four-byte value.
REG_EXPAND_SZ	Contains a string (text) that contains a replaceable parameter; for example, in the string notepad.exe %1, the %1 will be replaced with a valid file name.
REG_MULTI_SZ	Contains several strings, separated with a NULL character.
REG_SZ	Contains a text string. This is often used for description values, program names, and so on.

HKEY_LOCAL_MACHINE   The HKEY_LOCAL_MACHINE key contains all the data required to specify the configuration of the local machine. It does not contain data about software programs installed on this computer or information about users defined for this computer. It is divided into five keys—HARDWARE, SAM, SECURITY, SOFTWARE, and SYSTEM.

The HARDWARE key is a dynamic branch of the Registry that is computed each time the computer is booted. It contains information broken down into three more keys—DESCRIPTION, DEVICEMAP, and RESOURCEMAP. Together, these keys contain data that Windows NT requires to boot up your computer to the logon screen. They describe all the hardware in your computer, where additional information about each device is stored within the Registry, and the resources (for example, interrupts, I/O addresses) that each device requires.

TIP Because the HARDWARE key (and all its subkeys) is dynamically created each time the computer is started, it doesn't make sense to try to modify this key. Any changes you make would be overwritten the next time the computer is started.

The SAM key contains data about users and group accounts. Collectively, this data is known as the Security Account Manager database—hence, the key name SAM. The majority of the data in this key is changed by using the User Manager program. This key is also mapped to the key HKEY_LOCAL_MACHINE\ SECURITY\SAM.

The SECURITY key contains security related information, such as user rights, password policy, and local group membership. To change most of the information in this key, use the User Manager program.

The SOFTWARE key contains information about the software installed on this computer. The information is general configuration information and is not user specific. User specific information is stored under HKEY_USERS\SOFTWARE. The SOFTWARE key is further subdivided into Classes, Program Groups, Secure, and description key. Classes is the same key as HKEY_CLASSES_ROOT (see the section "HKEY_CLASSES_ROOT" later in this chapter). The Program Groups key contains information about common programs shared by all users of this local computer. (Information about programs used by specific users are stored under HKEY_CURRENT_USER.) The Secure key provides a secure location where applications can store information that should only be changed by a system administrator. Finally, the description key contains the names and version numbers of the software installed on this computer.

The SYSTEM key contains information needed during the startup of the computer. Similar to the HARDWARE key, the SYSTEM key contains information stored about the computer. (The HARDWARE key contains data computed at startup.) Because this data is critical to getting your computer up and running, multiple copies of the settings are maintained in control sets. These appear as ControlSet00x keys, where "x" is replaced with a number (for example, HKEY_LOCAL_MACHINE\SYSTEM\ControlSet001). These are kept so that if you (or someone like a system administrator) make a change to the Registry that prevents you from starting your computer, you can revert back to an earlier, good configuration.

Part
VII

Ch
31

▶ **See** "What to do When a System Won't Start," **p. 921**

HKEY_CLASSES_ROOT   This key contains the same information that the Registration Database contained under Windows 3.1. This information defines all the file associations and Object Linking and Embedding data. The data is divided into two types of keys: file name extensions and class definitions. The file name extensions map file types to class definitions. For example, the file type key ".DOC" has the value "Word.Document.6." Under the class definitions are all the data needed to perform basic shell and OLE functions. For example, this data is used to enable you to double-click on a Word document in File Manager and have the system launch Word and automatically load the selected document.

This key is actually only required to provide compatibility with Windows 3.1 apps that read and write to the Registration Database. This entire key is actually mapped to HKEY_LOCAL_MACHINE\SOFTWARE\CLASSES.

HKEY_CURRENT_USER   This key contains all the information required for Windows NT to set up the computer for the user logging on to the computer. This includes information like user rights, application preferences, and environment settings. There are seven default keys with HKEY_CURRENT_USER. They are as follows:

- Console
- Control Panel
- Environment
- Keyboard Layout
- Printers
- Program Groups
- Software

TIP You may have noticed that similar types of data appear in different parts of the Registry. You also may have noticed that parts of HKEY_LOCAL_MACHINE and HKEY_CURRENT_USER are the same. In this case, the values in HKEY_CURRENT_USER supersede the values in HKEY_LOCAL_MACHINE. Think of it in this way: HKEY_LOCAL_MACHINE contains the default values that every new user gets; however, as each user changes his preferences, these new values are saved under HKEY_CURRENT_USER.

HKEY_USERS   HKEY_USERS is the key where the data for each user (the user profile) is saved. When a user logs on to the computer, his data is copied from HKEY_USERS*Security ID String* to HKEY_CURRENT_USER. Also, the key HKEY_USERS\.DEFAULT contains the default data for any new users added to the computer.

HKEY_CURRENT_CONFIG   HKEY_CURRENT_CONFIG is a new key that was added with Windows NT 4.0. It contains configuration for the current hardware setup. It is subdivided into two keys, SOFTWARE and SYSTEM.

INI Files and the Registry

As previously described, the Registry fulfills a function similar to the Windows 3.x INI files. If you look in the Windows NT directory of your system, you notice that you still have INI files. These include the standard WIN.INI and SYSTEM.INI files. You may be wondering why you have both the Registry and WIN.INI files. The answer is compatibility. Even though you are running Windows NT, there is still a good chance that you are running at least one old 16-bit, Windows 3.x program, and this program doesn't know anything about the Registry. It is trying to read and write data to WIN.INI and SYSTEM.INI.

What happens when one program writes data to an INI file and another program tries to read the same data from the Registry? To keep all the programs working together, Windows NT can map data contained in an INI file to particular keys in the Registry. This mapping is defined by the data contained under RHKEY_LOCAL_MACHINE\SOFTWARE\MICROSOFT\WINDOWS NT\CURRENT VERSION\INIFILEMAPPING. This Key has subkeys that define particular INI files and particular entries within those INI files. To understand how to interpret the values for these keys, you need to know five symbols used within those keys. These values are listed in table 31.3.

Table 31.3   INI Mapping Symbols

Symbol	Description
!	Write any data to both the Registry and the INI file.
#	When a user logs in, set the Registry value to the value contained in the INI file.
@	Don't read data from the INI file if the data isn't in the Registry.
USR	The INI file data for the entry should be mapped HKEY_CURRENT_USER plus the text value for the key.
SYS	The INI file data for the entry should be mapped HKEY_LOCAL_MACHINE\Software plus the text value for the key.

For example, the value for HKEY_LOCAL_MACHINE\SOFTWARE\ MICROSOFT\WINDOWS NT\CURRENTVERSION\INIFILEMAPPING\ WIN.INI\WINDOWS\BORDERWIDTH is "#USR:Control Panel\Desktop." The # means that the value for the BorderWidth should be reset from the WIN.INI file each time a new user logs in. The USR means that the value for the border width should be stored at HKEY_CURRENT_USER\CONTROL PANEL\DESKTOP\BORDERWIDTH.

Modifying the Registry

Editing the Registry is not recommended by Microsoft. Changing Registry data can result in programs failing to function properly, losing your data, or your computer failing to startup. Even given all these dire warnings, there may be times when you do want—or need—to edit the Registry. Windows NT comes with two tools to help you edit the Registry—both called Registry Editors. You won't see options on the Start Menu for either of these tools. Microsoft doesn't want the uninformed user blindly playing with these tools—that would create a technical support nightmare. However, for the informed user, these tools are available.

N O T E In Windows NT 3.51, there was a registry editor called the Registration Info Editor. This program was used primarily to add file association information—information about how to open and print each particular type of file (that is, *.doc, *.xls, *.txt). This program has been removed from Windows NT 4.0 and has been replaced with the Registry Editor from Windows 95. If you still want to work with this type of information, see the section, "Understanding File Types," in Chapter 4. ■

The Registry Editor REGEDIT.EXE is located in the Windows NT root subdirectory (that is, C:\WINDOWS). This is the same Registry Editor found in Windows 95. It provides an Explorer like view of the Registry, using a single window split into two panes to view the Registry data. This editor is best suited for individual users to make adjustments to their own particular registry settings.

A more "high powered" Registry Editor, REGEDT32.EXE, is located in the Windows NT system subdirectory (that is, C:\WINDOWS\SYSTEM). This Registry Editor uses multiple child windows to view the Registry data, with each major key displayed in its own window. This editor provides some functionality not found in Regedit.exe. For example, REGEDT32 allows loading individual hives, setting user security permissions, and auditing settings. Because of these types of features, this editor is ideal for administrators to use.

> **CAUTION**
>
> When you are using either Registry Editor, you may make a mistake that could stop one of your programs from running correctly, maybe not even running at all. If you aren't so lucky, that mistake could disable your computer and prevent you from connecting to the network or accessing devices attached to your computer. You read it again and again in this chapter—be careful when using the Registry Editor! It is a very good idea to make a backup copy before making any changes.

Part
VII

Ch
31

Using REGEDIT

REGEDIT externally appears to be same Registry Editor that comes with Windows 95 (see fig. 31.1). However, because the way the Registry is stored on the disk is different for Windows NT and Windows 95, and since Windows NT has more security features than Windows 95, the internals of the programs are different. Although the programs appear the same, only about 40 percent of the keys are the same between the Windows 95 and the Windows NT registries.

FIG. 31.1
Use Regedit to view settings for the Console application.

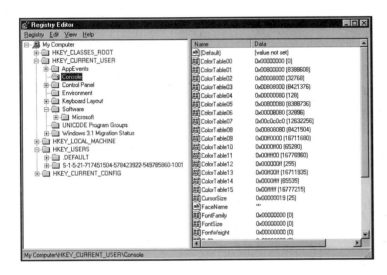

N O T E The Registry for Windows NT is stored as a collection of different files. The Registry for Windows 95 is stored as only two files, SYSTEM.DAT and USER.DAT (with two backups—SYSTEM.DA0 and USER.DA0—of course). ■

▶ **See** "Understanding Hives," **p. 910**

Working with Registration Files

Many applications provide a registration file (*.REG) that contains all the registry keys that the application requires to function properly. Following is a portion of a registration file that comes with Microsoft's Word for Windows. This particular portion contains all the information Word needs to make its wizards function properly:

```
HKEY_CLASSES_ROOT\Word.Wizard = Microsoft Word Wizard
HKEY_CLASSES_ROOT\Word.Wizard\DefaultIcon = winword.exe,4
HKEY_CLASSES_ROOT\Word.Wizard\CLSID = {00020900-0000-0000-C000-
000000000046}
HKEY_CLASSES_ROOT\Word.Wizard\shell = New
HKEY_CLASSES_ROOT\Word.Wizard\shell\New\ddeexec = [FileNew("%1")]
HKEY_CLASSES_ROOT\Word.Wizard\shell\New\ddeexec\Application = WinWord
HKEY_CLASSES_ROOT\Word.Wizard\shell\New\ddeexec\Topic = System
HKEY_CLASSES_ROOT\Word.Wizard\shell\New\command = winword.exe /n
```

With the REGEDIT, you can merge these settings into the Registry. You can also export a portion of the Registry to a registration file. You might do this to make a backup of some registry settings or to copy some settings from one registry to another.

Importing a Registration File   There are instances when you will need to import, or merge, a registration file. Three common instances are:

- When you've installed an application for one user, and then need to update the registry for another user. If the application has provided a registration file, you can log in as the new user and import the file.

- When you need to copy registry settings from one registry to another. You would to this by exporting the necessary settings and then importing that registration file.

- When you want to make a backup copy of the settings before you begin making changes to the Registry. (A smart thing to do.)

To import a registration file, follow these steps:

1. Choose Registry, Import Registry File. The Import Registry File dialog box appears (see fig. 31.2).

2. Browse to the folder that contains the registry file you want to import.

3. Choose Open or press Enter.

4. A message box appears telling you whether or not the file was successfully imported. Choose OK.

FIG. 31.2

Importing the
Registration File for
Word for Windows 7.0

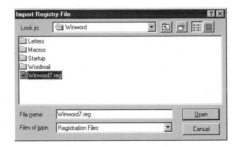

Exporting a Registration File   Exporting registration settings is necessary when you need to copy settings from one registry to another, or when you want to back up a portion of a registry for safety or later use.

To export a portion of the registry, follow these steps.

1. Browse to the key that you want to export and select it. For example, if you want to export the entire HKEY_CLASSES_ROOT key, select that key in the lefthand pane. If you only wanted to export the "txtfile" key (found within the HKEY_CLASSES_ROOT), you would expand the HKEY_CLASSES_ROOT key and select only the "txtfile" key.

2. Choose Registry, Export Registry File. The Export Registry File dialog box appears (see fig. 31.3).

3. Browse to the folder where you would like to store the registry file.

4. Type in the name you want to use for the registry file in the File Name edit field.

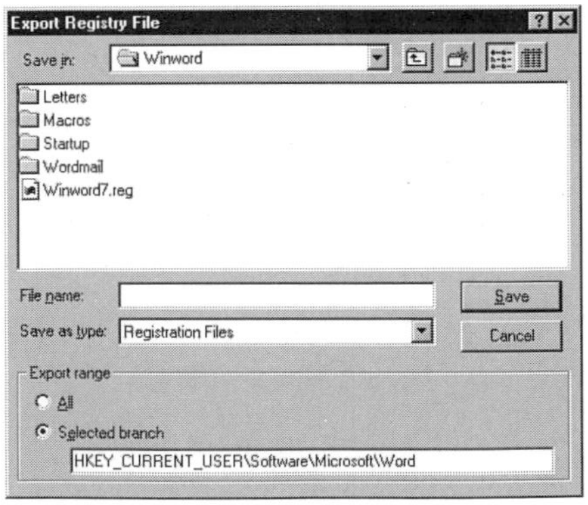

FIG. 31.3

Exporting the Registry
settings for Word for
Windows.

5. You can select to have the entire registry exported by selecting the <u>A</u>ll option in the Export Range group box.

6. Choose <u>S</u>ave or press Enter.

Connecting to a Remote User's Registry

You can connect to a remote user's registry using REGEDIT. This allows you to view their registry to try to diagnose problems, check settings, and make adjustments if necessary. To be able to connect to another user's registry, you need to have proper access permissions.

▶ **See** "Managing Security Policies," **p. 396**

To connect to a remote user's registry, follow these steps:

1. Choose <u>R</u>egistry, <u>C</u>onnect Network Registry. The Connect Network Registry dialog box appears.

2. If you know the computer name that you want to connect to, type the name in the Computer Name edit field.

3. If you don't know the computer name that you want to connect to, choose Browse. The Browse for Computer dialog box appears. Use this dialog to select the computer you want to connect to, and choose OK.

4. Choose OK.

 T I P When you use REGEDIT.EXE to connect to a remote user's Registry, you are connecting to the Registry for the user currently logged on. With REGEDT32.EXE, you can load specific hives. In other words, you could load the registry settings for a user who isn't logged on.

Disconnecting a Remoter User's Registry

After you are finished looking at or working with another user's registry, you can disconnect from his registry. To disconnect, follow these steps:

1. Choose <u>R</u>egistry, <u>D</u>isconnect Network Registry.

2. Choose OK.

Printing the Registry

If you want to make a hard copy of a registry, REGEDIT allows you to print out either the entire registry or specific branches.

If you want to print out the entire registry, follow these steps:

1. Choose Registry, Print. The Print Registry dialog box appears (see fig. 31.4).

2. Select the printer you want to print to in the printer Name drop-down list.

3. Choose All in the Print Range box.

4. Choose OK.

FIG. 31.4
Print out the Registry settings for Word for Windows.

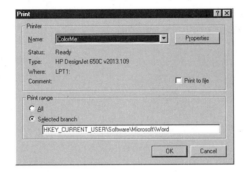

If you want to print out a specific portion of the registry follow these steps:

1. Select the key in the Registry Editor that you want to print. For example, if you wanted to print the "txtfile" key under HKEY_CLASSES_ROOT, expand the HKEY_CLASSES_ROOT key and select the "txtfile" key.

2. Choose Registry, Print. The Print Registry dialog box appears.

3. Select the printer you want to print to in the printer Name drop-down list.

4. Choose Selected Branch in the Print Range box. The edit field contains the name of the key you selected. If the name is wrong, type in the correct name.

5. Choose OK.

Editing the Registry

There are times when you need to change only a specific value or add a single key to the Registry. While this is easy to do with the Registry Editor, please be careful. Making the changes may be easy, but the results can be disastrous.

 TIP The steps listed in the following sections use the menus for REGEDIT to perform the tasks. In Windows NT 4.0, much of the functionality is directly accessible using context menus. So, try directly selecting the key or value and then clicking with the right mouse button. This will bring up a context menu that may have the command you want.

Adding a New Key   To add a new key, follow these steps:

1. Select the registry key in the lefthand pane under where you want to add your new key. For example, if you wanted to add a new file extension, you would selected HKEY_CLASSES_ROOT. However, if you wanted to add a DefaultIcon key for a particular file type, you would select that file type (HKEY_CLASSES_ROOT\wrifile) in the lefthand pane.

2. Choose Edit, New. A cascading submenu appears (see fig. 31.5).

3. Choose Key.

4. The new key appears in the lefthand pane. The name will be New Key # and will already be selected and ready for renaming. Type in the key name you want.

5. Press Enter.

Deleting a Key   To delete a key, follow these steps:

1. Select the Registry key in the lefthand pane that you want to delete.

2. Choose Edit, Delete, or press the Del key.

3. A message box appears, asking you to confirm that you really want to delete the key. Choose OK.

FIG. 31.5
Use the Cascading submenu to add new keys and values.

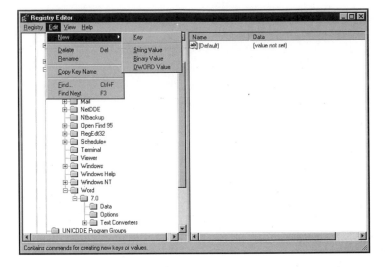

Renaming a Key   To rename a key, follow these steps:

1. Select the registry key in the lefthand pane that you want to rename.

2. The name in the lefthand pane will become selected and ready for renaming. Type in the key name you want.

3. Press Enter.

Adding a New Value   To add a new value, follow these steps:

1. Select the registry key in the lefthand pane under which you want to add the new value.

2. Choose Edit, New. A cascading submenu appears.

3. Choose the type of value you want to add—String Value, Binary Value, DWORD Value.

4. The new value appears in the righthand pane with the name New Value #. The value name will be selected and ready for renaming. Type in the new name you want and press Enter.

The REGEDIT.EXE registry editor only allows you to add three types of values—string, binary, and DWORD. If you want to add either of the additional string types—expandable strings or multi-strings—you'll need to use REGEDT32.EXE.

Deleting a Value   To delete a value, follow these steps:

1. Choose Edit, Delete.
2. A confirmation message box appears, asking you if you really want to delete the value. Choose Yes.

Renaming a Value   To rename a value, follow these steps:

1. The value name will be selected. Type in the new value name.
2. Press Enter.

Changing a Value's Data   To change a value's data, follow these steps:

1. Select the registry key in the lefthand pane that contains the value you want to modify. The righthand pane will display all of the values contained in the selected key.
2. Select the value you want to modify in the righthand pane.
3. Choose Edit, Modify. An "Edit *type*" dialog box appears. This is one of three edit dialogs, one for strings, one for binary data, and one for DWORD data.
4. Type in the new data in the Value Data edit field.
5. Choose OK.

Using REGEDT32

REGEDT32 is the most powerful registry editor available with Windows NT. If you make a mistake using REGEDIT, an application may not work properly or even run. OLE functionality like in-place editing may stop working if you are lucky. If you aren't lucky and you make a mistake using REGEDT32, you may cripple Windows itself or even prevent another user from logging on. Normally, you should use the various administrative tools and Control Panel programs to modify the Registry. However, some applications may not provide tools to modify all their keys, or if you are a developer, you may need to create or modify the keys for your application by hand. When you need to directly modify the Registry, REGEDT32 allows you full and complete access to all the Registry keys.

To run this Registry Editor, follow these steps:

1. From Program Manager, choose File, Run. The Run dialog box appears.

2. Type **regedt32** in the Command Line edit field.

3. Choose OK. The Registry Editor starts.

Understanding the Display

Unlike the simple display of REGEDIT, REGEDT32 has a multiple document interface (MDI). It displays several windows (normally five), where each window displays the contents of one of the five major keys (see fig. 31.6). In much the same way that File Manager displays the contents of a drive (subdirectories and files), this Registry Editor displays the contents of a root key (subkeys and values). You can expand and collapse keys by double-clicking the little folder icons. Icons with a "+" in the folder icon indicate that the key has subkeys. You can also expand and collapse the tree by using the keyboard in the following ways:

- Expand the selected level by choosing Tree, Expand One Level or pressing the + (plus sign) key.

- Expand the entire branch (all the keys underneath the selected key) by choosing Tree, Expand Branch or pressing the * (asterisk) key.

- Expand the entire tree by choosing Tree, Expand All or pressing Ctrl+*.

- Collapse the selected branch by choosing Tree, Collapse Branch or pressing the - (minus) key.

Understanding Hives

The way the Registry is actually stored on your hard disk is as a collection of distinct files. Each of these collections is called a *hive*. The standard hive files are listed in table 31.4. Each hive consists of two files, the actual data and a backup copy (with a LOG extension). In addition, because the system hive is so critical, it has an additional backup copy (with the ALT extension). By default, these files are stored in the SYSTEM32\CONFIG subdirectory of the root Windows subdirectory (that is, C:\WINNT35\SYSTEM32\CONFIG).

FIG. 31.6
You can view Registry data by using the Registry Editor.

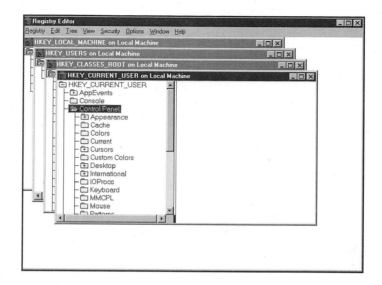

Table 31.4 Standard Hives

Hive	File Names
HKEY_CURRENT_USER	USER####(.LOG) and ADMIN###(.LOG)
HKEY_LOCAL_MACHINE\SAM	SAM(.LOG)
HKEY_LOCAL_MACHINE\SECURITY	SECURITY(.LOG)
HKEY_LOCAL_MACHINE\SOFTWARE	SOFTWARE(.LOG)
HKEY_LOCAL_MACHINE\SYSTEM	SYSTEM(.LOG) and SYSTEM.ALT
HKEY_USERS\DEFAULT	DEFAULT(.LOG)

N O T E LOG files are used to make sure that Registry hives don't get corrupted when hives get updated. To do this, Windows NT writes all changes to the LOG file. Then it marks a part of the Registry to indicate that the Registry is about to get updated. It then performs the update by processing the changes listed in the LOG file. Finally, it unmarks the Registry, indicating that it is done processing the LOG file. If anything happens during the update and your computer crashes, Windows NT can use the LOG file, with its list of changes, to recover the hive when Windows NT restarts. ▪

Part
VII

Ch
31

It is possible to use REGEDT32 to actually load and work with hives of another user and with hives from another computer. You might want to load such a hive if you are making changes to another user's hive because of a change in software or because the other user is having problems running Windows NT.

To load another hive, follow these steps:

1. Choose File, Load Hive.
2. Browse to the drive and subdirectory where the hive you want to load is located.
3. Select the file and choose OK.

After you have worked with the hive, you need to unload it so that it can be loaded by the other user or machine. To unload the hive, choose File, Unload Hive.

Editing the Registry with REGEDT32

REGEDT32 provides a much richer set of controls when you need to edit the Registry. Not only does it allow you to add keys and values, but it allows you to work with all types of values—binary, string, expandable string, DWORD, and multistring. See table 31.5 for descriptions of each data type.

Table 31.5   Registry Data Types

Data Type	Description
Binary (REG_BINARY)	Simple binary data. It is often used to store configuration information for hardware components.
String (REG_SZ)	Text data. It is often used for file names, component descriptions, and so on.
Expandable string (REG_EXPAND_SZ)	Text that contains a variable that will be replaced. For example, many system components add Registry entries that contain %SystemRoot%. When this value is requested by an application, %SystemRoot% is replaced by the actual path of the Windows system files.

Data Type	Description
DWORD (REG_DWORD)	A number 4 bytes long.
Multistring (REG_MULTI_SZ)	Multiple text strings. Each string is separated by a NULL byte (a byte of all zeros). It is often used for device driver information.

Adding a Key   To add a key, follow these steps:

1. Select the primary key you want to add your new key under by clicking the child window's title bar, or choose Window, *primary key name* (for example, HKEY_CLASSES_ROOT).

2. Navigate down the subkey tree until you are at the subkey you want to add your new key under (for example, \AVIFILE\SHELL). Navigate by double-clicking on the key names in the left-hand pane.

3. Choose Edit, Add Key. The Add Key dialog box appears.

4. Enter the key name in the Key Name edit field (for example, **PRINT**). Although there is a field for entering the class of the Registry key, you can ignore this field. This may be used in the future, but for now, it is not used.

5. Choose OK.

Adding a Value   To add a value, follow these steps:

1. Select the primary key you want to add your new value key under by clicking the child window's title bar, or choose Window, *primary key name* (for example, HKEY_CLASSES_ROOT).

2. Navigate down the subkey tree until you are at the subkey you want to add your new value under (for example, \AVIFILE\SHELL\PRINT\COMMAND). Navigate by double-clicking the key names in the left-hand pane.

3. Choose Edit, Add Value. The Add Value dialog box appears (see fig. 31.7).

4. Enter the name of the new value in the Value Name edit field (for example, **PRINT**). Each key may contain one value that does not have a name. This is represented in the display by <No Name>. For example, the <No Name> value for the key HKEY_CLASSES_ROOT\TXTFILE\SHELL\OPEN\COMMAND is notepad.exe %1. This is often used when the key only has one data value.

5. Select the class of the key in the Data Type drop-down list box.

6. Choose OK.

Part
VII

Ch
31

FIG. 31.7
Add a string value to the DDEXEC Registry key.

7. An Editor dialog box (there is one for each data type) appears. Type in the actual data value.

8. Choose OK.

Deleting a Key or Value   To delete a key or value, follow these steps:

1. Select the primary key that contains the key or value you want to delete by clicking the child window's title bar, or choose Window, *primary key name* (for example, HKEY_CLASSES_ROOT).

2. Navigate down the subkey tree until you are at the subkey or value you want to delete (for example, \AVIFILE\SHELL\PRINT). Navigate by double-clicking the key names in the left-hand pane.

3. Select the key or value you want to delete.

4. Choose Edit, Delete, or press the Del key.

5. A prompt appears asking you to confirm that you want to delete the key or value. Choose Yes.

Editing a Value   To edit a value, follow these steps:

1. Select the primary key that contains the value you want to edit by clicking the child window's title bar, or choose Window, *primary key name* (for example, HKEY_CLASSES_ROOT).

2. Navigate down the subkey tree until you are at the subkey that contains the value you want to edit (for example, \AVIFILE\SHELL\PRINT\COMMAND). Navigate by double-clicking the key names in the left-hand pane.

3. Choose Edit, *data type*. The *data type* can be one of four values—Binary, String, DWORD, Multi-String. Although you can edit any value by choosing any data type, it is most useful if you choose the same *data type* command as the value's data type.

4. The *data type* Editor dialog box appears (for example, DWORD Editor). Type in the new data for the value.

5. Choose OK.

Changing the View

The normal default view of REGEDT32 should work fairly well for you. However, if you are working with very low resolution, such as on a laptop (640 × 480), you may find that you want to view only the key pane or the value pane. To change your view between these different views, do one of the following:

- Choose View, Tree and Data to view both the keys and data values.
- Choose View, Tree Only to view only the keys (the lefthand pane).
- Choose View, Data Only to view only the values (the righthand pane).

When you are working in the Tree and Data mode, you can increase the width of either the Tree or Data pane. When you do this, you naturally decrease the width of the other pane. To adjust the widths of the panes, follow these steps:

1. Choose View, Split, or click the separator between the Tree and Data window panes.
2. Move your mouse right to increase the width of the Tree pane, or left to increase the width of the Data pane.
3. When the widths are adjusted the way you want, single-click the left mouse button.

Refreshing REGEDT32 Display The final control you have over the display is when to refresh the contents of display. In other words, the data that is displayed in the Registry Editor is a copy of the Registry's data at the time you started the Registry Editor. It is possible, likely even, that some of the data will have changed since you started. This is especially true if you are working with a Registry on another computer. To update the display so that it displays the most current data, you need to force the Registry Editor to refresh its display. To do this, do one of the following:

- Turn on the automatic refresh by choosing Options, Auto Refresh. If the command already has a check mark beside it, Auto Refresh is already turned on.
- To refresh the entire Registry, choose View, Refresh All or press Shift+F6.
- To refresh just the contents of the active child window, choose View, Refresh Active or press F6.

Part
VII

Ch
31

CAUTION

If you are working with the Registry of a remote computer and have turned on Auto Refresh, it still doesn't show any changes. Auto Refresh only works when you are editing your own local Registry. To make matters worse, Refresh All and Refresh Active are disabled. So if you are working with a remote computer's registry, turn off Auto Refresh and periodically refresh the data yourself.

Using the Security Features of REGEDT32

Although it is very important that you don't carelessly use the Registry Editor—you don't want to cripple your computer or your programs—it is also important that you protect the Registry from changes from other users. There are three basic ways you can help protect the Registry on your computer:

- Protect the actual files themselves using the file security features of Windows NT.

  ▶ **See** "Managing the Boot Process," **p. 405**

- Use the security features available within the Registry Editor to allow users to have access only to certain keys.

- Set up auditing of Registry changes.

The rest of this section discusses the last two preceding options.

 TIP You can take a couple of other easy precautions to protect your registry. First, remove or restrict access to REGEDIT.EXE and especially, REGEDT32.EXE. Second, restrict access to administrators only. No user should need access to your Registry.

Restricting Users from Registry Keys   Much like you can use File Manager to restrict access to files on a user/group basis (if the files are on an NTFS volume), you can use REGEDT32 to restrict access to registry keys on a user/group basis. However, unlike File Manager, even if you are not running on an NTFS volume, the user-based restriction for the Registry will still work. To set user permission for Registry keys, follow these steps:

1. Select the primary key that contains the key you want to restrict access to, by clicking the child window's title bar, or choose <u>W</u>indow, *primary key name* (for example, HKEY_CLASSES_ROOT).

2. Navigate down the subkey tree until you are at the subkey you want to restrict access to (for example, \AVIFILE\SHELL\PRINT). Navigate by double-clicking the key names in the lefthand (tree) pane.

3. Select the key to restrict access to.

4. Choose <u>S</u>ecurity, <u>P</u>ermissions. The Registry Key Permissions dialog box appears (see fig. 31.8).

5. Select the user or group that you want to set the access privileges for. If the user or group isn't shown, choose <u>A</u>dd to add that user or group to the list.

6. Set the type of access by choosing one of the options in the <u>T</u>ype of Access drop-down list box.

7. If the key you are restricting has subkeys and you want your new settings to override whatever settings those subkeys may have had, click the R<u>e</u>place Permission on Existing Subkeys check box.

8. Choose OK.

If you make any restricts to Registry keys, always make sure that Administrators and the System have full access to all keys. Then, if something goes wrong, an Administrator can go back in and reset the changes.

FIG. 31.8
Set Access Permissions on the HKEY_LOCAL_MACHINE Registry Key.

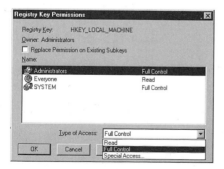

After you make any changes, it is a good idea to turn on auditing changes to those keys you've restricted and test your system, logging on as different users and administrators. This is simply to make sure that the restrictions you've set haven't caused any problems in the normal running of your computer and programs.

N O T E Although REGEDT32 allows permissions to be set on any key, the system automatically assigns permissions to all the hives except for user profile hives. You really shouldn't need to override this behavior. ▦

Auditing Registry Editor Changes   Whenever you need or want to monitor what is changing in your registry—and who is making those changes—you can use the auditing features of the Registry Editor. There are three separate steps that you must do to use auditing:

1. Use the User Manager administrative tool to turn on auditing.

   ▶ **See** "Securing Windows NT Workstation," **p. 379**

2. Use the Registry Editor to set up the auditing parameters for Registry changes.

3. Use the Event Manager to view the audit logs.

To set the auditing parameters using the Registry Editor, follow these steps:

1. Select the primary key that contains the key you want to audit, by clicking the child window's title bar, or choose Window, *primary key name* (for example, HKEY_CLASSES_ROOT).

2. Navigate down the subkey tree until you are at the subkey you want to audit (for example, \AVIFILE\SHELL\PRINT). Navigate by double-clicking the key names in the lefthand (tree) pane.

3. Select the key you want to audit.

4. Choose Security, Auditing. The Registry Key Auditing dialog box appears (see fig. 31.9).

5. Select the user or group that you want to audit. If the user or group isn't shown, choose Add to add that user or group to the list.

6. Set the type of auditing by choosing one or more of the options in the Events to Audit box. See table 31.6 for more details. You can choose to audit either the success or failure, or both. For example, you can choose to audit every time a key is successfully set, every time a failure occurs when trying to set a key, or both events.

7. If the key you are auditing has subkeys and you want to audit those keys also, click the Audit Permission on Existing Subkeys check box.

8. Choose OK.

FIG. 31.9
Set auditing parameters on the HKEY_LOCAL_MACHINE Registry key.

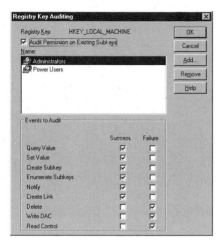

Table 31.6 Auditing Options

Audit Event Type	Description
Query Value	Audit any event that tries to open a key for purposes of reading its value.
Set Value	Audit any event that tries to open a key for purposes of setting its value.
Create Subkey	Audit any event that tries to open a key for purposes of adding a new subkey.
Enumerate Subkeys	Audit any event that tries to open a key for purposes of reading its subkeys.
Notify	Audit any event that tries to open a key for purposes of monitoring when the key will be changed.
Create Link	Audit any event that tries to open a key for purposes of creating a symbolic link.

continues

Table 31.6 Continued

Audit Event Type	Description
Delete	Audit any event that tries to open a key for purposes of deleting the key.
Write DAC	Audit any event that tries to open a key for purposes of finding out who has access to the key.
Read Control	Audit any event that tries to open a key for purposes of determining the owner of the key.

When Should You Modify the Registry?

So far in this chapter, you learned about the Registry and how to use the provided tools to modify it. But you really haven't learned when to modify it. In most cases, you'll probably use tools other than the Registry Editor(s) to make changes—maybe without even realizing that you are changing the Registry. Control Panel applications, the User Manager, and the Windows Setup program all make changes to the Registry. But there are a few times when you need to roll up your sleeves and work directly on the Registry.

Increasing the Size of the Registry

The size of the Registry is limited. The system puts some limits on it so that the Registry can't grow too large and prevent your system from working. The default value for the size of the Registry is set to be 25 percent of the size of the paged pool, which by default is 32M. That makes the default maximum size of the Registry 8M. This means that by default, the Registry cannot grow beyond 8M. Why would it grow? The primary reason for the Registry to grow is when you add new users. But at 8M, the Registry can support about 5,000 users. Unless you are maintaining a very large network, this probably will never be a problem. You also can restrict the Registry from growing very large at all. If you are the only user on your computer, you may want to restrict the size of the Registry to only a few megabytes.

To approximate the current size of your Registry, look in the SYSTEM32/CONFIG subdirectory of the directory where you installed Windows NT (for example, C:\WINNT35\SYSTME32\CONFIG). Total the size of the following files:

- SAM and SAM.LOG
- SECURITY and SECURITY.LOG
- SOFTWARE and SOFTWARE.LOG
- SYSTEM and SYSTEM.LOG
- USER#### and USER####.LOG (for the current user, for example KEVIN000 and KEVIN000.LOG)
- ADMIN### and ADMIN###.LOG (if present)
- DEFAULT and DEFAULT.LOG

While this is not exactly the amount of memory the Registry will take in, it serves as a quick approximation. To set the maximum size of the Registry, follow these steps:

1. Run the Registry Editor, REGEDT32.EXE.
2. Select the HKEY_LOCAL_MACHINE\SYSTEM\CURRENTCONTROLSET\ CONTROL key.
3. Add (or modify if it is already there) the value RegistrySizeLimit. This value should be a REG_DWORD type.
4. Set the value to the maximum size (in megabytes) that you want the Registry to be able to grow to.
5. Exit the Registry Editor by choosing File, Exit.

What to do When a System won't Start

When a system just won't start, you can do a number of things. Hopefully, you've been proactive and have done things like creating an Emergency Repair disk and making regular backups of critical system files. If you have, you have a great leg up. If you haven't, you probably have a lot of work in front of you.

If your system has just failed to start properly, you can force Windows NT to start using the last known good configuration. To do this, follow these steps:

1. Reboot your computer.

2. At the startup prompt, select Windows NT. Press Enter.

3. Immediately press the spacebar.

4. At the Configuration Recovery menu, choose Use Last Known Good Configuration. Press Enter.

This attempts to start your computer using a previously known good configuration.

N O T E   To be considered a good configuration, Windows NT must do two things. First, it must successfully load all startup drivers. Second, a user must have successfully logged on to the computer. After these two events have happened, Windows NT copies the current configuration to the Last Known Good Configuration key in the Registry. ▪

If your computer still fails to load, you may have physical damage to one or more of the Registry hives (the actual files). To solve this type of problem, see the next section.

Restoring Damaged System Files

If you think the Registry is actually damaged—that it isn't a configuration problem—then you will need to restore the damaged files. For this to work, you must have already created backup copies of your Registry.

▶ **See** "Changing the Registry on a Remote System," **p. 923**

N O T E   Windows NT itself maintains a separate backup copy of the system hive, called SYSTEM.ALT. If during startup, Windows NT can't properly load the system hive, it automatically switches and tries to load its backup copy. ▪

The following procedure backs up your Registry files:

1. Boot your computer into another instance of Windows NT, or if Windows NT is installed on a FAT volume, you can boot into MS-DOS.

2. Copy the files in the Windows SYSTEM32/CONFIG subdirectory to another directory. These are your backup copies.

To restore these files, reverse the process by following these steps:

1. Boot your computer into another instance of Windows NT, or if Windows NT is installed on a FAT volume, you can boot into MS-DOS.
2. Copy the backup files to the Windows SYSTEM32/CONFIG subdirectory.
3. Restart your computer, booting into Windows NT.

After you restore these backup files, remember that any changes you made to the Registry between the time that you backed up and restored the files, are lost. For example, if you installed a new program, any Registry keys created by the new program are lost. You will either have to merge the program's registration file (if it has one) into the Registry or reinstall the program. The same goes for any newly installed hardware.

Changing the Registry on a Remote System

If booting into the last known good configuration didn't get your system up and running again, if you don't have backup Registry files, or if restoring the backups didn't fix your problems, you may still be able to fix your problem by using the Registry Editor from another Windows NT system.

For example, if your system won't start into Windows NT because you had to replace some failed hardware (maybe a hard disk controller card), but you can boot into MS-DOS and connect to the network, you can make configuration changes using the Registry Editor on another system.

To load the Registry of a remote computer, follow these steps:

1. Run the Registry Editor.
2. Choose File, Select Computer.
3. Select the computer in the Select Computer list.
4. You can now edit HKEY-USERS and HKEY_LOCAL_MACHINE if you are not a member of the Administrators group. If you are a member, you can edit all keys. This is subject to any access controls that may be in place for the remote registry.

Using REGEDT32 to Find Configuration Problems

Probably one of most useful ways of using the Registry Editor isn't to perform any editing. Rather, you will find that you can quickly look at a lot of configuration data using the Registry Editor. Then you can use another program—a Control Panel program or the User Manager program—to actually make the changes.

When this is coupled with the capability to view the Registry on a remote computer, one user (usually an administrator) can help another user diagnose problems.

For example, if a user had problems running software and environment variable problems were suspected, an administrator could attempt to solve the problem by following these steps:

1. Run the Registry Editor.
2. View the Registry on the remote computer. See "Changing the Registry on a Remote System," earlier in this chapter.
3. View the values of the HKEY_LOCAL_ MACHINE\SYSTEM \CURRENT CONTROL SET\CONTROL\SESSION MANAGER\ENVIRONMENT.
4. If an incorrect value is found, the administrator can immediately fix the problem—remotely.

 TIP Although you can use the Registry Editor to view data when you're looking for conflicts, sometimes the data in the Registry just isn't very helpful. This is especially true when viewing the data for the HKEY_LOCAL_MACHINE\HARDWARE key. Looking at a bunch of bytes just doesn't help. To see this data in a friendlier form, run the Windows NT Diagnostics program. This organizes and displays all the data in an easily understood format.

Customizing Your Windows NT Logon

You can customize the Windows NT logon in two different ways.

First, you may want your computer to automatically log on when it boots up. You might want to do this because the machine is running some service—such as an FTP Internet service—and you want the machine to automatically restart if the power should go out and come back on. To do this, follow these steps:

1. Run the Registry Editor.

2. Select the HKEY_LOCAL_MACHINE\SOFTWARE\MICROSOFT\ WINDOWS NT\CURRENTVERSION\WINLOGON key.

3. Add a value called AutoAdminLogon. This should have a data type of REG_SZ and a data value of 1.

4. Add a value called DefaultPassword. This should have a data type of REG_SZ, and the data value should be set to the password of the user listed in the DefaultUserName value.

Second, you can have Windows NT display a custom logon prompt. You would do this to force the user to press OK to your prompt prior to logging on, maybe for a licensing agreement or disclaimer. To add the custom logon prompt, follow these steps:

1. Run the Registry Editor.

2. Select the HKEY_LOCAL_MACHINE\SOFTWARE\ MICROSOFT\ WINDOWS NT\CURRENTVERSION\WINLOGON key.

3. Add a value called LegalNoticeCaption. This should have a data type of REG_SZ, and the data value should be the text that appears as the caption for the logon prompt.

4. Add a value called LegalNoticeText. This should have a data type of REG_SZ, and the data value should be set to the text of the message for the logon prompt.

Part VII

Ch 31

From Here...

In this chapter you learned about using the two registry editors to directly modify the Register. Because the Registry is central to the operation of the computer, there are several other useful tools.

To learn more, refer to these chapters:

■ Chapter 15, "Securing Windows NT Workstation," teaches you about using Windows NT security features.

■ Chapter 32, "Using the Event Viewer," teaches you about how to determine the conflicting software and hardware.

■ Chapter 35, "Using the Diagnostics Tool," teaches you about how to determine hardware settings.

Using the Event Viewer

by Sue Plumley

When you work on a computer, whether or not you share it with others, problems will eventually surface. Application errors, damaged files, lost data, and so on, may not occur every day, but something will inevitably go wrong. Now, add to that fact other users sharing your resources through a network, and you immediately double or even triple the number of problems that can occur.

In Windows NT Workstation, problems with the system and network—in addition to any other significant occurrences—are recorded as *events*. When an event is crucial to the operation of the system, Windows NT will display a message notifying you of the event; however, for most events, Windows NT simply records them in a log for you to view at your convenience without disturbing you and your work.

Start and stop the Event Viewer

The Event Viewer presents information about your system and displays errors or other problems caused by applications, hardware, and other elements of your system. Use the Event Viewer when you want to identify problems with your computer system.

View an event and its details

When you have a problem with your system, the Event Viewer records the problem and any information about it. Using the Event Viewer, you can easily find those problems.

Modify event logging options

This chapter shows you how to choose which events you want to record and how long you want to keep recorded events, thus enabling you to customize your system to your specific needs.

Archive, save, and view log files

NT enables you to save log files so you can refer to them at any time. Learn to archive and view log files in this chapter.

The event log contains various types of information about your system, applications, and security procedures that you can view, manage, and even generate reports about. With the information about your system presented in the Event Viewer, you can more quickly diagnose and correct any errors or problems that may occur. You view and manage recorded events in the Event Viewer, a tool Windows NT provides in the Administrative Tools group. ■

Understanding the Event Viewer

The Event Viewer enables you to view three logs in which various significant events are recorded. You can select a log to view, set options for what the log records, and save logs to compare them at a later date.

The following are descriptions of the three logs that Windows NT records so you can view them in the Event Viewer:

- *System log.* Records events logged by system components, such as drivers, printers, hardware, and so on.
- *Security log.* Records events that are possible breaches in security, such as unsuccessful attempts to log on to the system.
- *Application log.* Records events logged by software applications, such as file errors, damage to files, and so on.

Starting and Stopping the Viewer

Because the Event Viewer is an administrative tool, you'll find the program in the Administrative Tools group. To start and quit the Event Viewer, follow these steps:

1. From the Desktop, click the Start button and choose Programs, Administrative Tools, Event Viewer. The Event Viewer opens to the System log (see fig. 32.1).

2. To quit the Event Viewer, choose Log, Exit (or press Alt+F4).

FIG. 32.1
The Event Viewer lists information, errors, and data about your system.

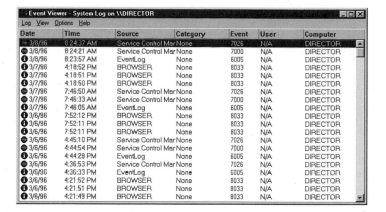

Understanding the Viewer Window

The Event Viewer displays one log at a time and one event within the log on a line. The following is a description of the headings in the Event Viewer:

- *Date*. The date the event took place.
- *Time*. The time the event took place.
- *Source*. The application (driver, system component, program, and so on) that recorded the event.
- *Category*. Classification of the event, such as Logon and Logoff, Policy Change, and so on.
- *Event*. A unique number assigned to the event; often applications support persons will ask for this number when diagnosing a problem.
- *User*. The user logged on and working at the time the event occurred.
- *Computer*. The computer name on which the event occurred.

In addition to the headings in the Event Viewer window, you also can use the icons beside each event to determine the type of event. Following is a list of the event types displayed in the Event Viewer:

Part
VII

Ch
32

Icon	Event Type	Description
	Error	Indicates important problems, such as loss of data or function. Icon looks like a stop sign.
	Warning	Indicates events that may forecast future problems, such as low disk space. The icon is a black exclamation in a yellow circle.
	Information	Indicates successful operations of major services, such as a successful loading of a program. The icon is a white lowercase I in a blue circle.
	Success Audit	Indicates a security access attempt that was successful, such as users logging onto the system. The icon is a padlock.
	Failure Audit	Indicates a security access attempt that failed, such as failed attempts to log on to the system. The icon is a key.

Viewing a Log

When you first open the Event Viewer, it displays the last log you viewed; but you can easily select which of the three logs you prefer to view. After selecting the log, you can choose the events you want to view, sort the events, and look at each individual event's details. Using the Event Viewer features, you can view and manage the events quickly and easily.

Selecting a Log

You can select any of the three logs—System, Security, or Application—to view in the Event Viewer. Choose a log to display the events it contains by choosing Log, and then choose one of the following: System, Security, or Application. The current log's name appears in the title bar, and a check mark appears beside the log's name on the Log menu.

Selecting a Computer

Besides viewing the events on your own computer, you can also view events on other computers, if you have been given rights; you must be logged on as Administrator to access another computer's Event Viewer.

▶ **See** "Working with Groups," **p. 389**

To view another computer's Event Viewer and logs, follow these steps:

1. In the Event Viewer, choose <u>L</u>og, <u>S</u>elect Computer. The Select Computer dialog box appears (see fig. 32.2).

FIG. 32.2
Select a computer from the list, or enter a path to the computer.

2. In the <u>S</u>elect Computer list, select the computer you want to view; if the computer you want does not appear in the list, enter the computer's name in the <u>C</u>omputer text box.

   You must precede the computer name with two backward slashes (\\) so Windows NT knows you're going over the network; for example, **SUE**.

> **TIP** If you're connected to the other computer by modem, select the <u>L</u>ow Speed Connection check box for a more stable connection.

3. Choose OK to connect to the other computer. The computer's Event Viewer appears, and you can manage and view it just like your own.

Viewing Event Details

You can view the details of an event to find out more information about it. In addition to other details, the description of the event will probably be the most helpful you'll find. The text description is created by the source of the event.

To view event details, follow these steps:

1. In the Event Viewer, select the event by clicking it, and then choose View, Detail; alternatively, you can double-click the event in the Viewer or press Enter while the event is highlighted. The Event Detail dialog box appears (see fig. 32.3).

FIG. 32.3
A text description might make it easier to understand the event.

2. The information at the top of the dialog box is the same as in the event log; however, read the text in the Description for more information. You can scroll through the text if necessary.

3. The Data area of the dialog box includes binary data in a hexadecimal format if the Bytes option is selected; to view the data as DWORDS, select the Words option.

 TIP Binary data is primarily used by experienced programmers or technicians familiar with the source application.

4. Choose Previous to view the details for the previous event, or choose Next to view details about the next event in the log.

5. Choose OK when you're finished with the dialog box.

Refreshing the View

When you open the Event Viewer, the log is automatically updated. Additionally, when you choose to view a different log and then return to the original log, the original is updated automatically. However, events that occur while you're viewing the log and event details do not appear in the log until you close it or change logs again.

You can choose to update the events displayed in the Viewer while you're viewing the log, just in case new events occur. Choose View, Refresh, or press the F5 key. New events appear at the top of the Event Viewer window.

Modifying Logging Options

You can set the log size and various options about when to overwrite events within the log so you can always keep the log up-to-date. Additionally, you can change the font used for the event logs.

Changing the Font

You can change the font in which you view the event logs, to make it easier to read for example, by using the Options menu. To change the font, follow these steps:

1. Choose Options, Font. The Font dialog box appears (see fig. 32.4).

2. In the Font drop-down list, choose a different font in which to view the log.

3. In the Font Style list, choose from Regular, Bold, Bold Italic, or Italic, if styles are available; some font types supply only Bold, for example.

4. In the Size list, choose a size for the text in the event log. When you choose a type size, a sample of the selected text appears in the Sample box.

5. When you're happy with the selected type, choose OK to close the dialog box.

FIG. 32.4
Use the Font dialog box to enlarge the text in the log.

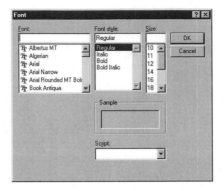

Changing Log Settings

You can change the size of any of the three logs and/or the way in which Windows NT handles the log when it is full.

To change log settings, follow these steps:

1. In the Event Viewer, choose Log, Log Settings. The Event Log Settings dialog box appears (see fig. 32.5).

FIG. 32.5
Change log settings for the System, Security, or Application logs.

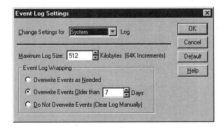

2. In the Change Settings For drop-down list box, choose the log you want to modify.

3. In the Maximum Log Size text box, use the spinner arrow to determine the size (in kilobytes) you want to allot to the selected log. The default maximum log size is 512K, and each click of the spinner arrow adds or subtracts 64K at a time.

Be careful about the maximum size you allot to the logs; the larger the log, the more disk space it takes up.

4. In the Event Log Wrapping area, choose one of the following options:

   Overwrite Events as <u>N</u>eeded. This option ensures that all new events will be written to the log; when the log is full, each new event replaces the oldest event in the log.

   Overwrite Events <u>O</u>lder than n *Days.* Choose this option to specify a number of days to retain the log (from 1 to 365); when the time is up, the new events overwrite the old.

   <u>D</u>o Not Overwrite Events. Choose this option to specify you want to keep all events in the log until you manually clear the log.

 To clear the log manually, choose <u>L</u>og, C<u>l</u>ear All Events.

5. Choose OK to close the Event Log Settings dialog box.

Part
VII

Ch
32

◆ **TROUBLESHOOTING**

I changed some of the options in the Event Log Settings dialog box for each log, and now I want to go back to where it was before. What can I do? In the Event Log Settings dialog box, select the log and then click the De<u>f</u>ault button; select the next log and click the De<u>f</u>ault button again.

I cleared all events from the log before saving it. Is there any way I can get those logged events back? No. After you clear the log, you've lost all events. It's a good idea to save your logs periodically—say, monthly for example—and delete the saved files when you're sure you won't need them again.

Managing Events

You can use some of the Viewer's features to make it easier to find and view events in any of the logs. You can sort events, filter events, and find events.

Sorting Events

You can sort the events in any log by date. Choose to view the most recent files first or the oldest files first. To sort events by date, choose View and either Newest First or Oldest First. The current option displays a check mark next to it in the menu.

Filtering Events

Filtering events means to display only certain types of events. You can, for example, display only errors or only warnings. Additionally, you can sort events by category, date, user, computer, and so on.

To filter events, follow these steps:

1. In the Event Viewer, choose View, Filter Events. The Filter dialog box appears (see fig. 32.6).

FIG. 32.6
Filtering events makes it easier to view the events that might stop work or cause future problems with the workstation.

2. In the View From area of the dialog box, choose from one of the following options:

    First Event. This option shows all events since the first one listed in the log.

    Events On. This option specifies a date and time of the first event you want to view.

3. In the View Through area, choose from one of the following options:

    Last Event. This option shows events through to the last recorded event.

Enter a date and time or use the spinner arrows to change the date and time in the text box.

Events On. This option shows events through to the specified date and time. Enter a date and time, or use the spinner arrows to change the date and time in the text box.

4. In the Types area, deselect any type of event you do not want to display. An X in the check box indicates the option is selected; click it to deselect.

5. Optionally, from the following options enter further criteria for filtering the events in the log:

Source. Enter the application that logged the event, such as a driver or other system component.

Category. Enter the event classification, such as System Event, Object Access, or Account Management.

User. Enter the exact user name.

Computer. Enter the computer's name where the event took place.

Event ID. Enter the specific event's ID number.

6. Choose OK to filter the selected events from the log. Figure 32.7 illustrates a System log with the Information type events filtered out.

FIG. 32.7
Filtering only the information events makes viewing events much easier.

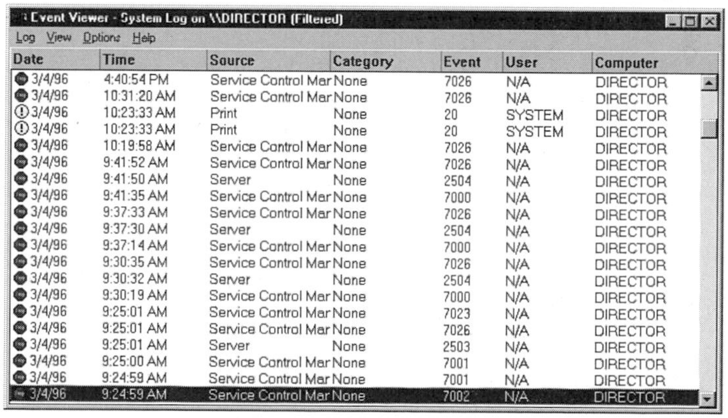

Date	Time	Source	Category	Event	User	Computer
3/4/96	4:40:54 PM	Service Control Mgr	None	7026	N/A	DIRECTOR
3/4/96	10:31:20 AM	Service Control Mgr	None	7026	N/A	DIRECTOR
3/4/96	10:23:33 AM	Print	None	20	SYSTEM	DIRECTOR
3/4/96	10:23:33 AM	Print	None	20	SYSTEM	DIRECTOR
3/4/96	10:19:58 AM	Service Control Mgr	None	7026	N/A	DIRECTOR
3/4/96	9:41:52 AM	Service Control Mgr	None	7026	N/A	DIRECTOR
3/4/96	9:41:50 AM	Server	None	2504	N/A	DIRECTOR
3/4/96	9:41:35 AM	Service Control Mgr	None	7000	N/A	DIRECTOR
3/4/96	9:37:33 AM	Service Control Mgr	None	7026	N/A	DIRECTOR
3/4/96	9:37:30 AM	Server	None	2504	N/A	DIRECTOR
3/4/96	9:37:14 AM	Service Control Mgr	None	7000	N/A	DIRECTOR
3/4/96	9:30:35 AM	Service Control Mgr	None	7026	N/A	DIRECTOR
3/4/96	9:30:32 AM	Server	None	2504	N/A	DIRECTOR
3/4/96	9:30:19 AM	Service Control Mgr	None	7000	N/A	DIRECTOR
3/4/96	9:25:01 AM	Service Control Mgr	None	7023	N/A	DIRECTOR
3/4/96	9:25:01 AM	Service Control Mgr	None	7026	N/A	DIRECTOR
3/4/96	9:25:01 AM	Server	None	2503	N/A	DIRECTOR
3/4/96	9:25:00 AM	Service Control Mgr	None	7001	N/A	DIRECTOR
3/4/96	9:24:59 AM	Service Control Mgr	None	7001	N/A	DIRECTOR
3/4/96	9:24:59 AM	Service Control Mgr	None	7002	N/A	DIRECTOR

TIP To view all events, choose View, All Events, or click Clear from the Filter dialog box.

Part
VII

Ch
32

Finding an Event

You can choose to find specific types of events—such as Warning or Error events—or you can search specific categories or sources of events.

To find specific events or event types, follow these steps:

1. In the Event Viewer, choose View, Find; alternatively, press F3. The Find dialog box appears (see fig. 32.8).

FIG. 32.8
Use the Find dialog box to specify the event for which you search.

2. In the Types area of the Find dialog box, all event types are selected; click an event type to deselect it. Only those events with an X in the check box will be used as search criteria.

3. Optionally, you can narrow the search by completing any or all of the following text boxes:

   Source. Enter the application that logged the event, such as a driver or other system component.

   Category. Enter the event classification, such as System Event, Object Access, or Account Management.

   Event ID. Enter the specific event's ID number.

   Computer. Enter the computer's name where the event took place.

   User. Enter the exact user name.

   Description. Enter all or a portion of the text string in the event's record description.

4. Choose the direction in which to search the log: Up or Down.

5. Choose Find Next. The dialog box closes, and the first event that matches the criteria becomes highlighted in the Event Viewer log.

TIP To quickly find the next event using the same criteria, press F3; the log moves to the next found event.

Archiving Log Files

You can archive event logs to open in the Event Viewer later or to use in other applications. When you save a log file, the entire log is saved except for the binary data for each event; therefore, filtering the log doesn't remove any events from the log.

After archiving the log, you can open it in the Event Viewer and perform any of the management techniques—sorting, filtering, and searching.

Saving the Log

You can save any log to a file, so you can later open it in the Event Viewer or in another application.

To save a log file, follow these steps:

1. In the Event Viewer, choose <u>L</u>og, Sa<u>v</u>e As. The Save As dialog box appears (see fig. 32.9).

FIG. 32.9
Choose a location and a file name for the log to save it for later use.

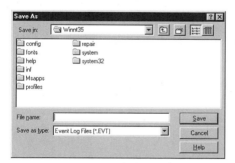

2. In the Save <u>I</u>n drop-down list, choose the drive to which you want to save the event log.

   You can save the file to a network drive by choosing the Network Neighborhood in the Save <u>I</u>n drop-down list or by choosing a mapped drive from the list.

Part
VII

Ch
32

If you save the event logs to the same default drive and folder each time you save a file, you can quickly and easily find it the next time you want to open the file.

3. In the Folders list, choose the folder to which you want to save the event log.

4. In Save as Type, choose to save as one of the following file types:

   Event Log File (EVT). You can open this type of file in the Event Viewer.

   Text Files (TXT). Use this file type to open the log into a word processing program, for example.

   Comma Delim. Text (TXT). Choose this file type to use the log file in a spreadsheet program or table, for example.

5. In the File Name text box, enter an eight-letter file name for the file. You do not need to add the extension; the extension is added automatically.

 When naming event logs, use dates within the name to make events easier to locate.

Viewing an Archived Log

You can view archived logs in the Event Viewer to review the contents, compare events, check for consistent errors, and so on. To view an archived, or saved, log, follow these steps:

1. In the Event Viewer, choose Log, Open. The Open dialog box appears (see fig. 32.10).

FIG. 32.10
Choose the saved log to open and view in the Open dialog box.

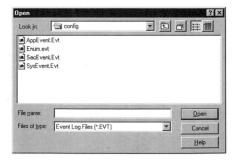

2. Choose the Dri<u>v</u>e and/or <u>D</u>irectory on which the file is stored. Alternatively, click the Net<u>w</u>ork button to connect to the network and access the directory on which the file is stored.

3. In the File <u>N</u>ame list, select the file, or in the File <u>N</u>ame text box, enter the file name.

4. Choose OK to open the event log.

TROUBLESHOOTING

I can't find a log I know I saved. Is there any way besides going through every directory to find it? Yes, choose Start, <u>F</u>ind, <u>F</u>iles or Folders. In the Name & Location tab of the Find dialog box, enter ***.EVT** in the <u>N</u>amed text box. Choose F<u>i</u>nd Now. Windows lists all found files, their names, and the path to each file. Make a note of the path to the file and then close the Find dialog box by choosing <u>F</u>ile, <u>C</u>lose. Now in the Event Viewer, you can open the file for which you search.

From Here...

In this chapter, you learned to open the Event Viewer, view logs, modify logging options, and manage events. You might also want to check out the following chapters:

- Chapter 33, "Optimizing Windows NT Workstation Performance," explains how to use the performance monitor to fine-tune your system.

- Chapter 34, "Protecting Your Workstation and its Data," shows you how to back up your system, protect against viruses, and update your emergency repair disk.

- Chapter 35, "Using the Diagnostics Tool," explains how to view information about your CPU, BIOS, memory, drives, system services, display, and more.

Optimizing Windows NT Workstation Performance

by Kathy Ivens

When you first use Windows NT, the graphical interface, point-and-click procedures, and all the other advantages of the operating system seem wonderful. However, as with all good things, there comes a time when all this power seems routine and you take it for granted. And, following that, you'll probably start to think that some procedures don't seem to be moving as fast as you'd like, or you sometimes feel you'd like a little more responsiveness from your system.

Sometimes, it's not just a matter of tweaking; it's a need to fix problems that have actually developed. You might find that your system really does slow down and become less responsive. As a result, you become less productive. There are a lot of reasons that your system may not perform

Use the Performance Monitor

Design a chart that maps the activity of resources—you choose the resources you want to track.

Keep an eye on system activity

Watch the way your system works to help make decisions about upgrading hardware or changing the way you multitask.

Identify bottlenecks

When performance slows down, learn which resources are causing the bottleneck.

Check configuration changes

Track performance before and after you make changes so you know if the changes you made are doing what you need them to do.

as well as it did at first, and Windows NT provides the capability to give your system periodic tune-ups that can solve those problems. ■

Using the Performance Monitor

To see a detailed view of what's going on in your system, use the Performance Monitor. This is a graphical tool that displays the performance levels of all the system elements.

In the Performance Monitor, each system resource is treated as an object. For example, if you have multiple processors, you see multiple processor objects: there's an object for each physical disk, an object for each running process, running thread, and so on. When you use the Performance Monitor, you are monitoring the objects.

Before we explore the way Performance Monitor works, it's a good idea to define some of the terms you'll run into:

- An *object* is a graphical representation of an element in your system. Icons are objects and usually represent an executable file or a document; for instance, WORD.EXE, or READ.ME. Every element, resource, and device in your system can be represented as an object, and because the Performance Monitor is a graphical program, this is the presentation it uses.

- A *process* is something that's running, or some task being performed, and it's represented as an object in the Performance Monitor. It's using memory and may be using a device or other resource of the computer. When you launch software, that's a process. The services you access in Windows NT—such as the Event Log—are also processes. And some of the system's resources, called *subsystems*, are also processes—the print spooler is a good example.

- *Counters* are the unit of measurement used by the Performance Monitor to display activity. There is a set of counters linked to each object, and the type of activity the counter measures is dependent upon the type of object. There may be counters that measure usage, lengths, or any other measurement that is appropriate for a specific activity.

- *Threads* carry out the instructions needed to run processes. They're the programming codes that make things happen when a process is launched.

Because Windows NT is a multitasking operating system, programmers can take advantage of that environment and multitask the chores that need to be performed as processes run.

Understanding Threads

In the old days, when DOS ruled the world of PCs, programming instructions had to be carried out one at a time, sequentially—do this, then do that. The *"that"* didn't occur until the *"this"* was finished. On your NT system, however, instead of sequential multiple events, you can have simultaneous multiple events. We call an event a thread, and each thread can be tracked by the Performance Monitor.

To help you visualize this, think about using the spell checker in a word processor. You write your document, formatting as you go (each time you format a section of text, the program executes a thread to add the appropriate formatting codes). You then launch the speller, a thread that goes through a series of programmed instructions—looking at each word (a thread), matching what it finds against a pre-determined list of words (another thread), presenting unknown words in a dialog box (yet another thread), and perhaps presenting suggestions (still another thread). Each thread executes, stops executing until you respond, then executes again or launches another section of code to respond to your response (another thread).

Word processors written for multitasking can execute the threads that run the spell checker at the same time the other threads are running. As a result, while you are writing and formatting and saving and printing, the spell check goes on. The spell check thread may be programmed to save the information somewhere until you ask to see it, it may mark the possible problems in some manner (for instance, Microsoft Word for Windows 95 and WordPerfect 7.0 use wavy red lines under the words), and then you can choose whether or not you want to do anything about the potential problem words.

Part
VII

Ch
33

32-bit Software

Generally speaking, buying software specifically written to take advantage of the power of your operating system is a good idea. At best, it enhances productivity. But even if you don't notice the difference, you can feel as if you're on the cutting edge of technology. If software is advertised as being written for a 32-bit environment, it's probably

continues

continued

also written for multithreading. The programmers have split chores into separate threads so you don't have to wait until one thread completes its task to have another, nondependent thread begin.

If you have multiple processors and you purchase software that will respond to that environment (such as Adobe PhotoShop), the speed with which tasks are executed and completed can be rather amazing.

Working with the Performance Monitor Windows

When you use Performance Monitor, there are four different views (windows) available. You can pick the view you want to work in from the View menu:

■ Chart View, which is a way to see what is going on in real-time. You can look at statistics to see why a software package doesn't seem to be performing properly. The chart will show you what is happening while the application runs, checking memory, disk, and so on.

■ Alert View, which lets you know when certain minimum performance criteria aren't being met, or maximum criteria are being exceeded.

■ Log View, which keeps ongoing records that you can examine at any time when you need to learn why performance levels aren't meeting your expectations.

■ Report View, which saves information about specific criteria (selected by you) in an easy-to-examine format.

All four views have the same window, menu bar, toolbar, and status bar (see fig. 33.1).

 TIP Use the Toolbar to switch easily between views instead of using the View menu.

For each window, you can decide on the objects you want to monitor and save those settings to a file. In fact, you can create and save multiple settings files and open the one you need when you feel you should monitor the objects you're tracking in that configuration. Settings files are saved specifically for the current window and you can distinguish between them. In addition, you can save your

Workspace settings, which means the current configuration for each of the windows is saved (useful when all the views are measuring the same type of objects). Once saved, you can Open any settings file through the File menu:

Window Settings	File Extension
Chart	PMC
Alert	PMA
Log	PML
Report	PMR
Workspace	PMW

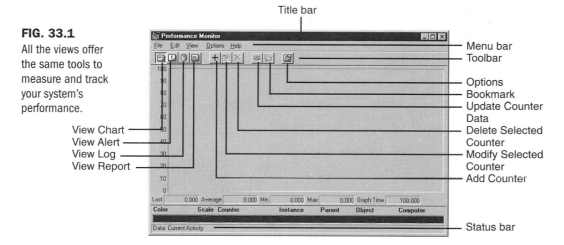

FIG. 33.1
All the views offer the same tools to measure and track your system's performance.

Title bar

Menu bar
Toolbar

Options
Bookmark
Update Counter
Data
Delete Selected
Counter
Modify Selected
Counter
Add Counter

View Chart
View Alert
View Log
View Report

Status bar

Part
VII

Ch
33

When you first invoke the Performance Monitor, there aren't any existing settings files, so you'll be viewing blank windows. The following sections explore the views (windows) in the Performance Monitor.

Creating Charts

Charts are a quick way to view and monitor performance. You can look at a chart and see a graphical representation of your system's activity. This is helpful if you're trying to figure out why you have occasional bottlenecks in the system, or why certain tasks seem to operate very slowly. To create a new chart:

1. Choose File, New Chart. Don't worry that nothing happens to the software window, it's blank, waiting for you to configure it.

2. Choose Edit, Add to Chart, or click the Add to Chart button on the toolbar. The Add to Chart dialog box appears (see fig. 33.2).

FIG. 33.2
Configure the objects you want to chart, including the display options such as color and line style.

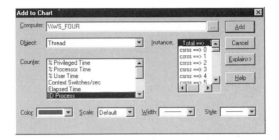

3. Go through each section of the dialog box, selecting the objects you want to monitor.

   Use the Computer list box to specify the computer you want to monitor. By default, your workstation is selected, but if you're on a network you can choose another computer. Click the gray button to the right of the box to see all the computers you can reach.

   Use the Object drop-down list box to select an object to monitor. Click the arrow to the right of the box to see the objects available.

   Use the Counter list box to select a counter (or multiple counters) for the object you've selected. Note that the contents of the Counter box change depending upon your selection in the Object box.

   If you want details on how a counter works, highlight the counter and click Explain. A Counter Definition box appears at the bottom of the window (see fig. 33.3). Use the arrows to scroll through the text of the definition.

FIG. 33.3
Details about the measurements taken for this counter are displayed so you know what it is you're monitoring.

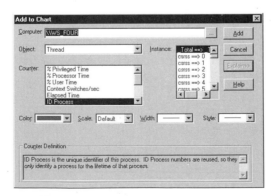

Use the Instance box to select an instance for this counter, if there are multiple instances. The Instance box changes depending upon the Object and Counter you've selected.

NOTE The selections in the Instance box reflect the identification of particular objects and counters.

For example, if you choose PhysicalDisk as the object, you'll see an instance of 0 for the first disk, and you'll also see an Instance of 1 for the second. If you select Paging File as the object, the Instance box displays its path and file name. A port object produces instances for each serial port, and other objects and counters produce more complicated and more numerous instances. ■

Use the Color box to choose a color for the display of the selected counter(s).

Use the Scale box to choose the scale at which you want to display the counter. Think of scale as saying, "I want to see the amount of user time on the processor at the scale of…" and then you can fill in the appropriate scale. The scale can range from .0000001 to 100,000. The smaller the number, the smaller the graph.

Use the Width box to specify the width of the line on the graph. The choices are graphical, not numeric (see fig. 33.4).

FIG. 33.4
Pick the width you'd like to use for the graph of the counter you want to monitor.

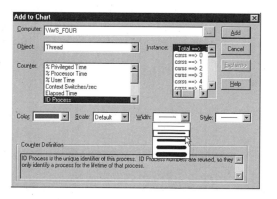

Use the Style box to choose a different style for your graph line. This box is only available if you've selected a thin line. The styles include various types of broken lines, and the thick and decorative lines cannot be displayed as broken lines.

4. As you select each item to monitor, click Add.

5. When you have finished selecting items, click Done (the Cancel button changes to Done when you have configured items) to return to the Chart window.

When you return to the Chart window, the counters you've opted to monitor are displayed with graph lines, while the bottom of your window displays the chart's legend—a list of your choices, along with the configuration settings for each choice (see fig. 33.5).

FIG. 33.5
The activity I chose to monitor is displayed—things are busy because besides running my usual software, I'm running the program that takes this picture.

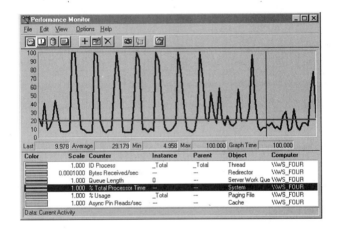

You can change the appearance of your design for this view directly from the legend at the bottom of the Chart window:

■ If you don't like the color or line or scale of any of the other selections you made for a specific counter, select it, then click the Modify Selected Counter button (or just double-click the representation of the line itself at the bottom of the window). An Edit dialog box appears so you can make whatever changes you like.

■ You can delete a counter by selecting and clicking the Delete Selected Counter button (or just press the Delete key).

Changing the Chart Layout and Behavior   While you're in the Chart window, click the Options button to bring up the Chart Options dialog box. This is where you can customize the chart layout (see fig. 33.6).

FIG. 33.6
Use the Chart Options dialog box to modify the way your charts appear or to change the update intervals.

You can change the layout to suit your own taste or to make the chart easier to read—perhaps placing grid marks will make small changes more apparent.

If you want, you can choose to update the data manually, by selecting Manual Update. If you choose Periodic Update, you must specify an Interval (in seconds).

Saving the Chart Configuration   When everything is exactly the way you want it, the right objects and counters are selected, your colors are bright and tasteful, the interval for updates is set, and all the other details are in place, save this configuration.

Choose File, Save Chart Settings, then enter a name for this configuration file. The file extension PMC is added automatically.

 When you configure a chart, don't try to monitor everything in one chart. You can have multiple charts, each of which groups objects and counters logically. Combine objects that have some relationship to each other.

Configuring Alerts

Alerts provide a way to set conditions so that counters that are over or under your specifications have that event logged. Then, you can examine the log in order to diagnose system problems.

You can even configure an Alert to notify you when certain conditions exist. It's a way to tell the Performance Monitor, "Hey, when it gets (or drops) to this level, gimme a yell." You use the Alert window to set the specifications for logging counter numbers and receiving these alerts.

Change to an Alert window by clicking the View Alert button or by choosing View, Alert. To configure Alert settings:

1. Choose File, New Alert Settings to see a blank Alert window.

2. Click the Add Counter button to see the Add to Alert dialog box (see fig. 33.7). The Object, Counter, and Instance choices are the same as those in the Chart window.

FIG. 33.7
Choose the counters you think you need to worry about, or at least keep an eye on.

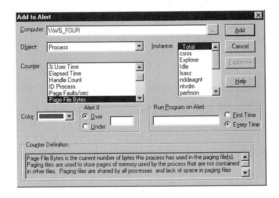

3. For each counter, specify a measurement in the Alert If box, either asking for an alert if the counter is Over or Under a certain measurement.

TIP Remember that the specification you enter in the Alert If box is related to the specific counter you're configuring. For example, if the counter measures percentages, the number you enter means percent.

4. In the Run Program on Alert box, specify the name of a program or batch file you want to run whenever the Alert conditions apply. You can run this alert message program the First Time or Every Time the conditions exist. If you don't want to run a program, leave the Run Program on Alert box blank.

5. Choose Done (the Done button appears when you have added counters) when you have finished selecting counters and thresholds for the Add to Alert window.

6. Save your settings by choosing File, Save Alert Settings. The file is stored with an extension of PMA.

Viewing the Alert Log To see a log of any activity that exceeded or failed to meet the thresholds you configured, choose View, Alert to open the Alert window (see fig. 33.8).

FIG. 33.8
When you see multiple alerts, there's either a serious problem in your system, or you should reconfigure the level at which you asked that an alert be issued.

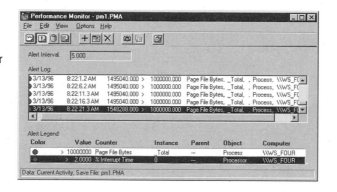

The log that displays shows these elements:

- A colored circle to the left of each listing that matches the color you selected for that counter.

- The date and time the counter failed to meet the threshold you set.

- The value the counter reached, setting off the alert.

- An indication of whether the value is over (>) or under (<) your threshold.

- The threshold you set.

- The name of the counter.

- The computer on which this counter was measured.

The bottom of the window contains the legend for the alert and you can double-click any counter to change the configuration.

You can click the Add Counter button to add additional objects and counters to this Alert configuration.

The log can hold 1,000 alert events. After that number is reached, the oldest alert event is deleted as each new one is added.

Part
VII

Ch
33

TIP If there's an alert while you are working in a different view in the Performance Monitor (perhaps you're working in Chart view), an alert icon will appear in the status bar of your current view window. Each time an alert is logged, a number representing the number of alert events appears next to that alert icon. (If the number moves into double figures, perhaps you should think about leaving the current window and investigating the alert by switching to the Alert view.)

Creating a Log

The purpose of creating a log is to keep information about activity on selected objects so that you can view and analyze the data you've collected. This is a specific log, kept in a specific file, as opposed to the log kept in an Alert window.

To get maximum use from a log, you should set a logging interval that's fairly high (for instance, don't measure every three minutes), and track data over an extended period of time. This gives you plenty of information, collected during varying periods of activity, so you get a bird's eye view of system activity.

To create a log, you need to take two separate steps:

- Create a settings file to specify the objects you want to keep an eye on
- Create a log file to hold the data

Creating the Settings for a Log   Creating a settings file for a log is simply a matter of specifying the objects you want to keep records on:

1. Move to a blank Log window (View, Log) and click the Add Counter button to see the Add To Log dialog box (see fig. 33.9).

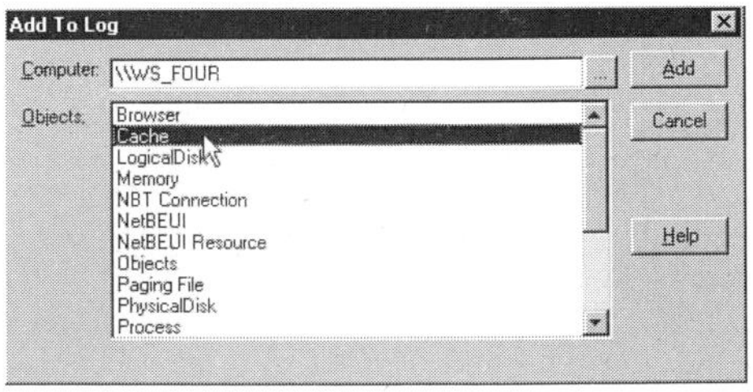

FIG. 33.9
The log maintains data on objects no matter what their use patterns are, so you don't have to specify any conditions for logging.

2. Select each object you want to track, and click <u>A</u>dd. When you have chosen all the objects of interest, click <u>D</u>one.

 TIP Instead of choosing an object and then clicking <u>A</u>dd, you can select multiple objects quickly by holding down the Ctrl key as you click each object you want to track; then choose <u>A</u>dd. If the multiple objects are contiguous, you can select the first object, then press and hold the Shift key and select the last object (or select the first object and drag your mouse to the last object).

3. All the objects you've chosen for your log appear in the Log window. You can delete any object by selecting it and pressing the Delete key, or add another object by clicking the Add <u>C</u>ounter button.

4. Choose <u>F</u>ile, <u>S</u>ave Log Settings and name the file. The file is given an extension of PML.

 TIP You can select objects from multiple computers and place them into this log file. This is a useful approach if you need to analyze the nodes on a peer-to-peer network.

Creating a Log File   Now that you've selected the objects you want to track in your log file, you have to create the log file and specify the conditions for collecting information:

1. Choose <u>O</u>ptions, <u>L</u>og to display the Log Options dialog box (see fig. 33.10).

Part
VII

Ch
33

FIG. 33.10
Use the Log Options dialog box to specify the name of the log file that will collect data and to begin the logging process.

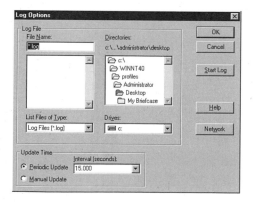

2. Specify the conditions for logging.

   In the File Name box, enter a path and file name for the log.

   In the Update Time section of the dialog box, choose to have automatic Periodic Updates or Manual Updates.

   Choose an Interval for periodic updates, in seconds.

3. If you want to begin the process immediately, click Start Log. If you don't, choose OK.

Whenever you want to start logging, open the Log window and click the Options button, then click Start Log. If you are already logging, the button changes to Stop Log, and you can click it to stop the logging process.

While logging is active, the Performance Monitor Log view shows the name of the log file, it's status, the size of the file, and the logging interval, in addition to the listing of objects being logged.

In addition, the status bar for any of the Performance Monitor views displays a log symbol, along with the size of the log file (which, of course, keeps changing).

Adding Bookmarks   If something interesting, problematic, or significant occurs on your system while logging is active, you should insert a bookmark noting that fact. A bookmark is a comment that's placed into the log file. Then, when you see the time the bookmark was inserted, you can check the same time period to see if anything unusual happened in the system.

For example, if you are logging the status of a serial port, you might want to enter a bookmark if you dial out, in order to see what happened at that moment to the port or any other system resource.

Bookmarks are available only while logging is in process. To add a bookmark into the log:

1. Click the Bookmark button or choose Options, Bookmark.

2. Type in text that reminds you of the circumstances that occurred about which you want to make a notation.

3. Click Add to add the bookmark to the log file.

Now, when you view the log file, you also see all the bookmarks you added.

Creating a Report

Use the Report window to build comprehensive reports that will give you information about the objects and counters you select. The information is easy to view and digest—it's displayed in a column and arranged by object. You can watch the display change as the system chugs along doing its work.

Besides tracking current activity, you have the option to design the report so it displays data from log files you established.

To begin:

1. Move to a Report window by clicking the View Report button on the toolbar, or choosing View, Report.

2. At this point, you need to decide if you want to build a report to see current activity or to view the output of a log file you created in the Log window. To make a choice, choose Options, Data From (see fig. 33.11). For this example, however, you build a report of your own.

FIG. 33.11
Choose to obtain the values of this report from Current Activity or from a Log File you've already established.

3. Begin building the settings by clicking the Add Counter button (or choose Edit, Add to Report).

4. Choose an object from the Object list, then choose a counter for that object from the Counter list box.

5. When you have finished adding the Objects and Counters you want, click Done.

The report appears in your Report window (see fig. 33.12), and you can view it or export it to a spreadsheet program or a database program.

Save the file, which is given an extension of PMR.

Part
VII

Ch
33

FIG. 33.12

I've logged plenty of information about my system, and I can look at more details than I probably know what to do with.

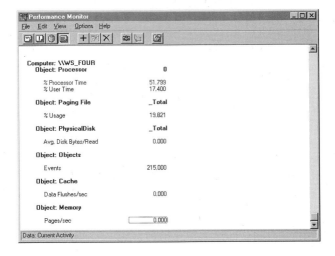

Export the Report   As you build log files and reports, you might want to accumulate them, compare them, or otherwise manipulate the data. One of the best ways to do this is to export the report to an application that provides these capabilities:

1. Choose File, Export Report to bring up the Export As dialog box (see fig. 33.13).

FIG. 33.13

Use the configuration options in the Export As dialog box to format the report for the application type you want to use.

2. In the Column Delimiter section, choose Tab to export the file with tabs as markers between columns if you're planning to use a spreadsheet. Or, choose Comma to export the file with commas as the column delimiter, for use in a database.

3. Enter a file name in the File Name box. If you are using tab delimiting, use the extension TSV. Use CSV as the extension if you are using comma delimiting.

4. Either include the full path or choose a drive and folder from the Dri̲ves and the D̲irectories lists.

5. Choose OK when you are finished. You can open your database or spread-sheet application and load the file into it.

Print the Report   Suppose what you really want to do is just print the report. There's no print option on the menu bar; do you have to export it and load other software to see a printout?

No, you can print it using the Windows NT Print Screen feature. While this involves a little more than just pressing your Print Screen button, it's not onerous.

The way Print Screen works in Windows NT is to create two separate steps. First, the screen that is being printed is really printed to the Clipboard. Then, the report is pasted into the Windows NT Paintbrush program, which you use to print a hard copy (you can also use Paintbrush to clean up, save, and edit the report before sending it to the printer).

This report file is a bitmap image, so you won't be able to edit the data, but you can delete extraneous images.

Use Alt+Print Screen to copy the active window to the Clipboard.

 TIP   If you are working in a full-screen session while you're using the Performance Monitor, just press the Print Screen button to grab the image.

Finding Specific Answers with the Performance Monitor

Sometimes you won't merely want to take a general look at your system and its statistics; there could be a specific problem for which you want a specific answer.

For example, you frequently multitask with the same combination of programs and features—it's a common occurrence for you to have a certain group of open applications. And, at some point, everything slows down. Which program is causing this?

Let's play detective with the help of the Performance Monitor. You should approach this with some logic, and the most logical place to start is to assume that it's a process that's bogging down. Once we know which process is the culprit, you might be able to figure out which resource it's hogging.

The quick way to look at the way the running processes are behaving is to build a special kind of chart called a *histogram*, which displays large blocks instead of thin lines. To build a histogram:

1. Open the Performance Monitor to a blank (new) Chart window.

2. Click the Options button or choose Options, Chart to bring up the Chart Options dialog box; select Histogram from the Gallery section. Then choose OK.

3. Click the Add Counter button, then choose Process from the Object list box. The Instance list box displays every process that is currently running on your system (see fig. 33.14).

FIG. 33.14
Every running process is available for scrutiny—choose all of them or just the ones you think might be causing a problem.

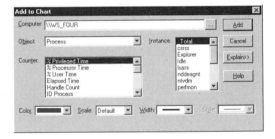

4. Choose the processes you want to examine. You can drag the mouse from the top of the list to the bottom to choose every process. Or, you can click (holding down the Ctrl Key) on each process you think might be the culprit.

TIP You may not be able to distinguish all the processes connected to specific applications. The application name is easy, but there are also system processes that are accessed by those applications and system processes that are always running. So just choose all the processes.

5. Click Add, then choose Done when you are finished selecting Instances.

6. Your histogram appears (see fig. 33.15), and you can match the color of the boxes with the color legend at the bottom of the window to see which process is hogging resources.

FIG. 33.15
The display shows the amount of resources each process is using—by identifying resources that seem to be hogging the system, you might be able to change work habits or settings to speed things up.

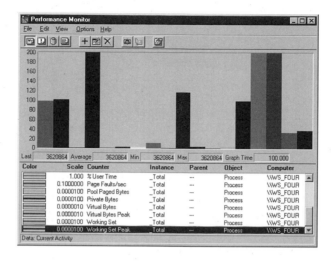

Sometimes the problem isn't curable; the piggy process can't be changed in order to lighten its demands. What you can do, however, is close that application when productivity demands for other applications suggest it. This is a good way to design and plan the way you multitask.

Of course, you always have the option of buying a faster computer or adding RAM to your computer if you want to continue to multitask robust applications.

Fine-Tuning Your System

Once you've gathered reports, looked at the displays in the Performance Monitor, and analyzed what you've seen, there are a few things you can do to tune your system a bit.

Allocating Processor Time

You can change the way Windows NT allocates time on the processor to applications in a multitasking environment. The priorities you set should reflect your own patterns of work; there aren't any absolute rights or wrongs here. To make the changes, follow these steps:

1. Choose Settings from the Start menu, then choose the Control Panel (or open the Control Panel from My Computer).

Part
VII

Ch
33

2. Double-click the System icon to display the System dialog box.

3. Click Tasking to see the Tasking dialog box choices (see fig. 33.16).

FIG. 33.16
You can decide for yourself the way you want processor time distributed to applications.

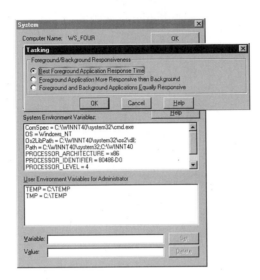

4. You can change the configuration to optimize the way you normally work.

   Choose Best Foreground Application Response Time to ensure that the program running in the foreground gets as much processor time as possible. This is the default option, because the assumption is you are most interested in being productive in the program you're currently using.

   Choose Foreground Application More Responsive than Background to give more processor time to background tasks, but keep the foreground application the recipient of the most processor time. Use this option if your working style is to have important processes running in the background occasionally.

   Choose Foreground and Background Applications Equally Responsive to give applications equal amounts of processor time, regardless of whether they are in the foreground or background. This option works best if you habitually multitask and the background processes continue to work at tasks that are important to your productivity.

5. Choose OK to record your changes.

Optimizing Memory Use

You can also change the way virtual memory is employed if your work habits suggest it. *Virtual memory* is disk-based memory that is used to hold information that applications expect to find in RAM. The operating system swaps data from RAM to virtual memory, and back again as needed, to make sure that every running process gets the memory it needs. The data in virtual memory is held in a file called a *paging file*, named PAGEFILE.SYS.

The more physical memory you have in your computer, the less virtual memory you need, although there's no such thing as adding enough physical memory to eliminate the need for virtual memory—Windows NT is built to expect it and use it.

In order to make the use of the paging file productive and efficient, Windows NT wants a contiguous file so it doesn't have to search the system to find what it needs in the file when it's time to move data back to RAM. Because the size of the file changes constantly, a certain amount of contiguous file space is preallocated on your system. The trick is to make this file big enough to handle all your virtual memory needs without tying up too much disk space.

There are programs that use more memory than other programs. To determine a program's use of memory you can chart the use of memory and paging file through the Performance Monitor.

There are also some common sense assumptions you can make, whether by understanding what a program does or by watching the hard drive indicator (the button that lights up during hard drive access) on your computer.

For the way applications work, if you use a database program that searches for data, manipulates it, returns data to your screen, and saves results, it's safe to assume there's a lot of memory use. If you spend most of your time in database work, you might have to give some consideration to RAM and paging file size.

If there's frequent hard drive access when you aren't saving data to disk yourself, the program is probably forcing the operating system to swap data to the paging file. This means either you should invest in more RAM, or watch out for a paging file that gets incredibly large.

Part
VII

Ch
33

You should look at the virtual memory use in your system and think about whether you should make changes:

1. From the same System dialog box, choose Virtual Memory to display the Virtual Memory dialog box (see fig. 33.17).

FIG. 33.17
The paging file was established using preset considerations depending upon the amount of physical memory in your system and the size of your hard drive—but you can make changes to improve system performance.

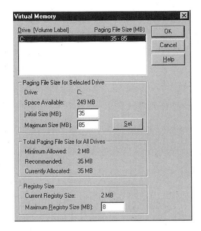

2. You can change the Initial Size or the Maximum Size or both, then click Set to record the changes.

3. Choose OK, and choose OK again when you're returned to the System dialog box. You have to restart the computer to put the changes into effect.

> **CAUTION**
>
> Don't change the paging file unless you know you spend almost all your time using applications that have very low memory needs (reduce the paging file size) or very high memory needs (increase the paging file size). A better solution might be to add more RAM to your system.

You have to be a member of the Administrators group to change the paging file.

Moving the Paging File

If your computer has multiple physical drives, you'll probably be able to speed up the performance of your computer by placing the paging file on the drive that does not contain the NT 4.0 system files. This works because the system files are accessed a great deal and if the frequent access of the paging file is moved to another drive, you're really splitting the work. The fact that one drive is looked to for system files and another for the paging file makes everything happen a little faster.

You can improve on that speed if you have separate controllers for each of the two drives (or if you have a controller that's capable of performing simultaneous reads and writes of the two drives).

Striping also improves the speed of disk action. Blocks of data can be interleaved across multiple drives in a parallel fashion, called *stripe sets*. If you have X amount of data, and three disks operating in parallel, the total data is handled in one-third the time. For example, if you have 12 blocks of data, blocks 1, 4, 7, and 10 are sent to one disk at the same time that blocks 2, 5, 8, and 11 are sent to the second disk, and blocks 3, 6, 9, and 12 are sent to the third.

Understanding Multiple Processors

One way to improve performance on a computer that runs software written to execute parallel threads, is to install additional processors. Now, before you rush out to buy one, you should be aware that it's not quite as easy or as trivial as adding another parallel port.

First of all, you have to be running an operating system that will find the processors and use them. Windows NT 4.0 has that capability, and can handle up to four processors.

Once installed (which we won't cover here), there are some choices to make about how to use the multiple processors productively.

SMP versus AMP

There are two approaches to using multiple processors in a single computer. While Windows NT does not support Asymmetrical Multiprocessing, it's not a bad idea to explain it:

■ *Symmetrical Multiprocessing.* Symmetrical multiprocessing is a strategy in which the load on the processors is split evenly. As processes need the processor, the tasks are distributed to an available processor (one that is either idle or not as busy as another processor). Windows NT 4.0 supports SMP.

- *Asymmetrical Multiprocessing.* Asymmetrical multiprocessing means that the processors are dedicated for specific tasks. You could, for example, assign one processor the role of taking care of all I/O requests from users, and assign another processor the role of executing application software. Windows NT 4.0 does not support AMP.

Optimizing with Hardware Choices

One of the effective ways to improve performance levels is to take a look at the hardware components of your computer, or throughout the network. Because time is money, it's frequently viable to upgrade hardware in order to create a productivity level that raises work output.

The speed of your processor isn't the answer to everything. The speed of the hard drive, the size of the data path, the controllers that manage disk and video, all contribute to the general productivity level of your workstation.

And, it's not just your own Windows NT 4.0 workstation that has to be examined, it's the network. Keep in mind the adage that a network is only as fast as its slowest component. The slowest component, by the way, is frequently the cable.

You also should look at the type of network adapter you're using, perhaps an on-board processor will reduce your particular bottleneck. The bottleneck problems, of course, are a result of a combination of available hardware and application use.

 TIP While technically there isn't supposed to be any problem with mixing NIC brands, I've had experience that proves there can be. It's not always a case of "Ethernet is Ethernet." I've found that NICs handle different tasks in different ways, and when I've mixed them in a large network, the system slows down well below the speed of the slowest component.

From Here...

Keeping an eye on the resources of your system lets you manipulate hardware and software intelligently. For information on related topics, see these chapters:

- Chapter 12, "Managing Memory, Multitasking, and System Options."
- Chapter 35, "Using the Diagnostics Tool."

Part
VII

Ch
33

CHAPTER 34

Protecting Your Workstation and its Data

by Kathy Ivens

Protection is one of those computer issues in which the user must take an active, aggressive role. Your computer's safety is your responsibility. Unlike the frustrations of hardware and software incompatibility, buggy software applications, and other things that drive you nuts, protecting your computer is pretty much under your own control. If the controls you establish work, you're to be congratulated. If there's a disaster that could have been prevented with proper controls, it's probably your fault. ■

Dangers that threaten your computer hardware

Learn about the dangers that lurk in your hardware—viruses, power surges that can damage your hardware, and corrupted files—and how to combat them.

Installing devices to help protect your computer

Learn how to establish a protective working environment by installing virus checkers, backup tools, and other programs.

The Windows NT emergency disk

See how an emergency disk can be your best bet to protect your system from shutting down.

Protecting the Hardware

Hardware gets destroyed or corrupted far more than necessary, and most of the time it's preventable. Certain individual devices in computers (such as hard drives and modems) are more susceptible to damage than other devices, and you have to create an environment that protects them.

Electricity Can Be the Enemy

One of your biggest enemies is your local power company. Another is Mother Nature if you live in an area that has electrical storms. There are, however, some remedies and safeguards you can employ to help offset the potential damage caused by these two entities.

Surge Protectors Whenever the subjects of hardware and electricity come up, I hear users say, "I have a surge suppresser." My answer is, "Big deal, so what?"

Let's talk about surge suppressers by taking a quick overview of the different devices people purchase and what they can do for you (or fail to do for you):

- A cheap, ineffective surge suppresser is only an expensive extension cord. While a weak surge suppresser might provide a bit of protection against a small upward surge in voltage, it's useless against any major invasion of high voltage.

- A good (usually more expensive) surge suppresser will commit suicide in an effort to protect your computer. I've seen good surge protectors destroyed as a result of high voltage, but the computers they were guarding suffered no damage, so they didn't die in vain.

There's no surge suppresser that will protect you from the effects of a direct hit of lightning. No matter how much you spend on the fanciest surge suppresser in the world, it's not going to defend itself or your computer against a million volts.

If you work in an office building with adequate protection against direct lightning hits, the odds are pretty small that the electrical outlet which controls your computer will blow. If you work in a small building or at home, then you need to take precautions.

There's only one real defense against serious lightning strikes—pull the plug out of the wall. If a lightning storm is raging, unplug. If a lightning storm is expected, unplug before you leave for the day.

 TIP Except for storms, it's okay to keep a computer running all the time. Most computers that are never turned off never have CMOS battery problems, their hard drives last longer, and the power supplies rarely need replacement. Just make sure you can hear the fan.

Telephone Lines   It's been my experience that the majority of computer systems destroyed by lightning received the fatal surge through the telephone lines connected to a modem.

I've seen more than a few networks brought to their knees from an electrical hit taken by a modem attached to one of the workstations. The surge went through the modem, through the serial port, to the motherboard, where it found (and fried) the network interface card. The card sent the surge through the network cable, spreading the zap to every card on the system. Some of the cards pushed the surge to their own motherboards.

The fact is that most electric power companies protect their lines. There are lightning arrestors, or other types of protection, at each transformer. Almost no telephone companies in the United States use any form of line protection. Because telephone lines conduct electricity, if one line gets charged with high voltage, it just sizzles and burns whatever is in its path. If you're using surge protectors, be sure to purchase the type that includes protection for telephone lines—one end of the strip has a phone line jack. For real protection, make sure you pull the telephone line out of the wall jack when you're preparing your defense against electrical storms.

Also, telephone system installations should include protection for the lines as soon as they enter the building. Passing the lines through a gas plasma protection device will help to defend them.

While you're protecting your computers by considering surge suppression, remember to protect yourself—stay off the phone during a severe lightning storm. Think of your ear as a modem and your brain as a motherboard.

Part
VII

Ch
34

Line Conditioners   The need for a surge suppresser arises only a few times a year for most people. The number of times voltage rises high enough to damage computer equipment is minuscule compared to the number of times the voltage is low. Most people encounter low voltage at least once a day without knowing it.

A line conditioner is an inexpensive way to regulate the voltage coming into your computer. It takes the power coming out of the wall, measures it for voltage, then pushes voltage up if it's too low, or brings it down if it's a little too high (it can't defend against a real high voltage zap).

Line conditioners are sold by wattage, and a 600W unit (sufficient for most computers) is less than $100.

About Low Voltage   Low voltage (called a *brownout*) destroys electronic equipment. Well before you see lights flicker (a sure sign of a drop in voltage), your hard drive feels the damaging effect of low voltage. Bad spots on a drive, cross-linked files, and even lost clusters can often be blamed on low voltage.

Your computer's power supply can have its life shortened by continuous low voltage, as can the power supply on your printer or scanner or any other peripheral.

Whenever there's a problem with low voltage, there are two entities to blame:

- The local power company
- Computer users

Electric Company Problems   Your local power company generally tries to put out enough power to maintain the optimum of 120V. But there are certain times of the day or certain weather conditions that make this difficult. As a result, most power companies consider anything within six percent of the optimum to be totally acceptable. Don't worry about voltage as long as it's between 105 and 125V.

The truth is that 105V isn't a terrifically safe voltage for computer hard drives, or even for many motor driven devices in homes and buildings. And, 125V can be troublesome for electronic devices. Any further deviation higher or lower becomes a severe problem.

To make matters worse, the electric power company has two other hurdles to leap in its effort to provide 120V to you:

- At certain times of the day, especially around 9 a.m., it's close to impossible to keep the voltage at optimum because copy machines, laser printers, and other power-consuming devices are being turned on all over the area.

- During the summer when it's hot enough for air conditioners to be running constantly, the voltage declines throughout the entire grid that the power company relies on. There's no place to turn for additional power; every member of the grid is in the same predicament. When there's been a strain on the local power company because of storms, there's usually a way to get additional power from another part of the grid, but not when the entire world is running air conditioning.

Using Electricity Efficiently

Other voltage problems occur because users fail to pay attention to common sense, technical specifications, and advice from experts. If you create a situation in which your computer is not getting enough voltage, you have to correct the condition or use a line conditioner to overcome the problems you've created.

Laser printers belong in dedicated outlets. So do copy machines or any other pieces of equipment that pull a lot of amps and need a lot of voltage. You should never put your computer into the same outlet as a laser printer. If you only have one outlet available, put a line conditioner into one plug and attach the computer and monitor to it. Do not plug a laser printer into the line conditioner.

Conditioning All the Lines

If there are low voltage problems all over the office (there are lots of ways to mea-sure voltage, including methods of tracking voltage over a long period and printing the resulting voltage chart), it might be easier and cheaper to put line conditioning onto the source of power—the breaker box. There are intelligent line conditioners that serve this purpose. *Intelligent* means they read the voltage and only correct it if necessary. There are also line conditioners that raise voltage without measuring first, but these dumb line conditioners aren't safe.

Some office buildings have transformers that feed the building or multiple transformers that feed specific parts of the building. And some of these transformers can be adjusted to raise the voltage. This process is called *re-tapping*. It's dangerous. Don't do it. Some electricians think it's a nifty and fast solution, but it's not. The reason it's not a good solution is that it's a permanent solution to a temporary problem, and applying the solution when the problem goes away is dangerous.

For example, if you measure the voltage every day you come to work and see that you're getting 106V out of every wall outlet, it makes sense to think you should push the voltage up about 12 points. That brings you to 118V, still under the 120V optimum, but close enough for your hard drive to stay happy.

Then, on Saturday and Sunday, when the elevators aren't running much, most of the copy machines are turned off and all sorts of other electric gizmos such as coffee pots and popcorn makers aren't pulling on the electrical resources, the voltage coming out of the box is the expected 120V. However, the voltage feeding your running file server is 132V. This can turn the motherboard, hard drive, and all the devices in the computer to toast.

Setting Up an Uninterruptible Power Supply (UPS)

An *Uninterruptible Power Supply* (*UPS*) is a necessity on a network server or a computer used for mission-critical applications. It's almost a necessity for every computer, even if the entire company won't halt if this computer goes down. The danger of corrupted data is an annoyance at best and a revenue risk at worst. Luckily, the price of UPS units has come down to the point that it isn't extravagant to purchase enough UPS units to keep all or most of the computers in any office running when the power fails.

There are two basic types of UPS units:

■ *Always On*, which means that the UPS itself is supplying the power to the computer and charging itself with the power coming from the wall outlet. The computer never sees the power that comes from the wall; it runs totally and completely from the UPS unit. This ensures steady and safe levels of power. However, these units are extremely expensive, need to have fresh batteries installed every couple of years, are very large, and weigh a lot. We generally find these attached to mini-computers or large PC servers that have many users attached, especially where user access is constant (not just weekday work hours).

■ *On When Needed*, which means that the battery kicks in only when the power fails. Actually, these batteries are programmed to kick in when voltage drops sufficiently to scare the UPS into believing the power may be going off, so you never really experience a computer shutdown.

There are two features available with the On When Needed UPS units that you might want to consider:

■ Line conditioning features in addition to battery backup.

■ Software that initiates a shutdown of the system when the battery kicks in. A cable between one of the computer's serial ports and the UPS handles the communications.

Installing the UPS Device

The On When Needed UPS unit is the one generally found attached to PCs, and we'll assume it's the type of UPS you're planning to install on your Windows NT Workstation. We'll also assume you purchased the communication cable (otherwise, it's just a battery and needs no Windows NT configuration).

The physical installation is quite simple—plug the UPS into the wall and plug the computer and monitor into the UPS outlets. Follow the manufacturer's instructions for connecting the cable between the UPS and one of the computer's serial ports. If you're using a serial mouse and an external modem, you'll have to add a serial port to your computer or switch your mouse to a mouse port type.

Part
VII

Ch

34

Configuring the UPS

To tell Windows NT Workstation about the UPS:

1. Choose Settings from the Start menu, then choose Control Panel (or open the Control Panel folder in My Computer or the Explorer).

2. Double-click the UPS icon to display the UPS dialog box (see fig. 34.1). The fields in the dialog box aren't accessible until you select the Uninterruptible Power Supply is Installed On checkbox.

FIG. 34.1

You can configure the UPS for varying levels of features and tasks through the UPS dialog box.

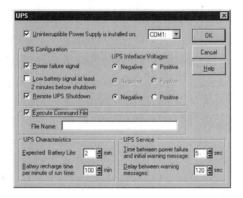

3. Specify the settings that match your UPS features in the UPS Configuration section of the dialog box.

Select the Power Failure Signal check box if your UPS unit has the capability to send a message if the power fails. To your serial port, this message is the same as a clear-to-send (CTS) signal.

Select the Low Battery Signal check box if your UPS unit can issue a warning when the battery power is low. To your serial port, this is like a data-carrier-detect (DCD) cable signal.

Select the Remote UPS Shutdown if you want the UPS software to enable shutdown through a remote computer. While this is generally used for servers, if your workstation is accessible by another computer, you can select this option. To your serial port, this is like a data-terminal-ready (DTR) cable signal.

4. For each item you selected, specify UPS Interface Voltage, either Negative or Positive, so that the serial port can communicate properly. The documentation that was packaged with your UPS system provides this information.

5. Select Execute Command File to have the system execute a command file just before the system is shut down. This is a useful option if you want to make sure certain events occur before shutdown. For example, you might want to logoff a network or close another type of connection.

   The command file is installed or written by you and must have a file name extension of BAT, EXE, or COM.

   The command file must be placed in the \SYSTEM32 directory under the system root directory. For most computers, this means the path is \WINNT\SYSTEM32.

   The command file must complete its program execution in less than 30 seconds in order to ensure it runs before shutdown is complete.

6. Enter the name of the command file in the File Name box.

7. In the Expected Battery Life box, specify the number of minutes that the system can run on battery power. The available range is 2 to 720 minutes.

8. In the Battery Recharge Time box, specify the number of minutes it takes to recharge the battery. This number is the number of recharge minutes needed for each minute of battery run time. The available range is 1 to 250 minutes.

9. In the Time between Power Failure box, specify the number of seconds that should elapse between the failure of power and the first message notifying the user. The available range is 0 to 120 seconds.

 TIP You don't have to set the Time Between Power Failure number to a short interval; it's not necessary to be notified the second the power fails. Most power failures last less than a minute so you just keep working. Besides, the UPS probably beeps.

10. In the Delay Between Warning Messages box, specify the number of seconds that should elapse before the next warning message is sent. The available range is 5 to 300 seconds.

11. Choose OK when you have finished entering data in the dialog box. The system then checks your UPS device to make sure the communication between the serial port and the UPS works.

If, for some reason, you don't want to use the Windows NT management features with your UPS, open the UPS dialog box and deselect the Uninterruptible Power Supply Is Installed On box.

The physical installation and configuration is followed by the startup of UPS services. To accomplish this:

1. Open the Control Panel.

2. Double-click the Services icon to display the Services dialog box (see fig. 34.2), and select UPS in the Service column.

FIG. 34.2
You have to tell the system how you want to launch the UPS services you've installed.

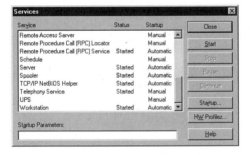

3. Click Startup, then select the method you want to use for starting the service.

Select Automatic to have the service start automatically every time you start your system.

Select Manual to start the service yourself after the system is up and running. To do this, go to the Services dialog box, highlight UPS services, then click Start.

Select Disabled if you don't want the service to start.

Backing Up Your System

No matter how much wonderful, creative, and important work you do on your workstation, if you don't back it up, you've made a statement that it's unimportant and useless.

Backing up is the most important task you perform every day. You never know when your hard drive, or your entire computer, is going to die. Notice the word *when*—it is a matter of *when*, not a matter of *if*. Hard drives die. Some die faster than others, and if you're curious about the normal life expectancy of your hard drive, call the manufacturer. All hard drives have a *MTBF (mean time before failure)* rating, which isn't really a prediction of the date of death, but an indication that the drive isn't going to live forever.

 There are probably more occasions when a backup is used to restore a file deleted in error or totally messed up by a user, than for hard drive failure. Don't think of backing up as merely a hedge against a disastrous failure; it's often useful for lesser traumas.

There are several basic approaches to backing up.

There are hardware/media decisions:

- Back up to disks
- Back up to tape

And there are protocol decisions:

- Incremental backups
- Full backups

Choosing a Backup System

For most office computers, there are three choices for backing up:

- To a network server (if you are on a network), so that your data is backed up when the network is backed up
- To disk
- To a tape backup system

Part
VII

Ch
34

Backing Up to a Server

In many network environments, the application software resides on the server. When users access the software, the resulting data is also saved on the network. Because most networks are backed up regularly, this means your individual work is safe and secure.

However, if you are linked to a network only for printer sharing or e-mail, and your application software is on your local drive, you need to make sure your data is backed up.

The easiest way to accomplish this is to configure your software so that the data is saved directly to the server while you're working. Then, there's no additional user intervention needed to have the server's backup protocols include your data.

If this can't be done, you should create a system for moving your data to the server periodically. Usually, doing this at the end of the day—before the server backup process begins—is the best approach. There are several things you can do to make the whole process easier and more productive:

- Create a personal data directory on both the server and your local drive and save all data from all application software in the local data directory. Then you can just copy that directory to your personal data directory on the server.
- Create data directories for each application on your local drive and then copy all those directories to one personal data directory on the server.

CAUTION

If you copy files from multiple local directories into one target directory, you must be very careful about file naming conventions. You don't want to overwrite one data file with another that has the same name, but was originally stored in a separate directory. The easiest way to avoid trouble with this protocol is to use filename extensions. For example, all the files in the data directory for database reports should end in a specific extension, perhaps DBR, while all your word processing documents have the extension DOC for document or LTR for letters. This way, if you're creating different types of data files for customer SMITH, you won't replace a letter to Smith named SMITH1 with a report on Smith named SMITH1.

■ Create data directories for each application on your local drive and then replicate those data directories on the server and copy each one.

Once you've established a protocol, copying the files is an easy process. You can use Explorer to copy the files, or use a batch file that you create for that purpose. The following sections provide details on each method.

Copying with Explorer

A quick way to copy directories is via the Windows NT Explorer. Before we go through the mouse-clicks or keystrokes for that, however, we should talk about Explorer.

If you moved to Windows NT4 from Windows 3.x or Windows NT 3.51, you've probably noticed that the Explorer is not a newly named version of File Manager. It's a very different animal.

In File Manager it was obvious how to figure out how to look at two drives or two computers—open another window and click the appropriate drive icon from the toolbar.

Doing the same thing in Explorer is a little less obvious, but actually just as easy. In fact you have choices about the way you want to approach this, and we'll walk through the steps needed to copy files in two different ways. You can pick the way that's most comfortable.

Use Two Copies of Explorer   One way is to open another copy of Explorer, then follow these steps:

1. Resize the windows so you can see both of them, making sure that the view of the server includes the target folder and the view of the local drive includes the folder you want to copy (see fig. 34.3).

2. Drag the directory on your local drive to the target directory on the server. When you drag files or directories to a different drive, Windows NT knows you want to perform a copy (dragging from one directory to another on the same drive moves the files instead of copying them, unless you hold down the Ctrl key).

FIG. 34.3

The left pane shows the target folder (Ws4back on the server named Accounting), and the right pane shows my Program Files folder on local Drive C.

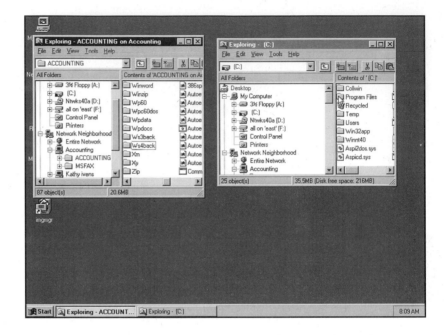

Drag between Panes on a Single Copy of Explorer   Another fast trick is to get used to the idea that the two panes in the Explorer window are independent of each other (unlike File Manager). You can scroll to a drive or folder in the left panel, then chose a different drive or folder in the right panel, and interact (usually copy files) between the two.

1. In the left pane, click the plus sign next to the object representing the server, so you see all the folders.

2. In the left pane, if the local drive is expanded, click the minus sign to eliminate the expanded folder display.

3. Highlight the icon for the local drive, which creates a display of all its folders in the right pane (remember, the server drive is still expanded—it's just probably scrolled up a bit and may be out of sight).

4. If necessary, use the scroll bar in the left pane to move through the display so the target server folder is visible (see fig. 34.4).

5. Drag the directory on your local drive to the target directory on the server.

FIG. 34.4
The Ws4back folder is visible on the left, the Program Files folder is visible on the right—I'm all set.

TIP There are some other choices you might want to experiment with. For example, you can open the Explorer and also open My Computer and move between those windows. Or, you can choose Run from the Start menu and enter **Winfile** in the Open text box to bring up File Manager (it comes with Windows NT) and use multiple windows the way you did with previous versions of Windows.

Completing the Task   Regardless of which approach you use, there are some additional facts to learn and potential problems to consider.

Copying Folders to Folders   The first time you perform this task, a folder (subdirectory) with the same name as your source directory is created in the target folder. Subsequently, be sure you drag the folder to the original target folder; the system then automatically copies the files to the appropriate folder. (If you drag the source folder to the newly created folder, yet another folder is created).

Support for Long File Names   If the server doesn't support long file names, you'll be asked to rename any elements that use those devices. In this case, the folder had a long file name (Program Files) and so did some of the data files in the folder. The Select Filename dialog box walks you through the renaming of any long file

Part
VII

Ch
34

names (see fig. 34.5). You have choices about the way you want to handle each problem file name:

- Enter a <u>N</u>ew name.
- Choose <u>A</u>utomatic to have the system choose a new name.
- <u>S</u>kip the file, don't copy it.

FIG. 34.5

The Select Filename dialog box lets you rename any files that have to be shortened if the target doesn't support long file names.

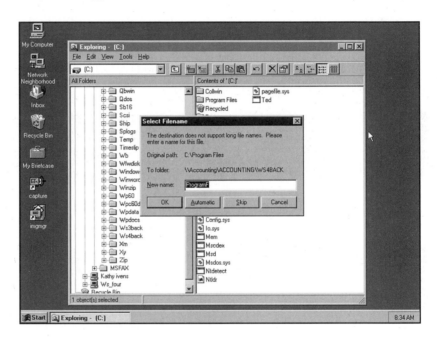

Overwriting Existing Files   For files that already exist in the target directory (many will, since you back up every day), the system asks if you want to overwrite the existing file. Answer <u>Y</u>es. In fact, to make things move faster, answer Yes to <u>A</u>ll so you don't have to confirm each individual file.

Using Right-Click Menus

Instead of dragging directories or files, you can use the menu commands available in the pop-up menus that display when you use the right mouse button:

1. Right-click the folder that contains the files you want to copy to the server.

2. Choose Copy from the pop-up menu.

3. Right-click the target folder.

4. Choose Paste

This quick method doesn't eliminate any need to change long file names, confirm overwriting existing files, and so on.

 T I P When you use the Copy command in this way, you don't see a dialog box asking you to insert the path for the target. This copying system uses the Clipboard approach—the instruction to copy is held in memory, the command is completed when you Paste.

Copying with Batch Files

If you're comfortable working at a command prompt, you can write a batch file that copies the contents of one or more local directories to one or more server directories.

A *batch file* is a text file that contains a series of MS-DOS commands. There is one command on each line, and the file is executed in the order in which the commands are listed. A sample batch file for copying local data to a network server might look like this:

```
COPY C:\WORDPROC\DATA\*.* F:\MYFILES\WORDPROC
COPY C:\DATABASE\DATA\*.* F:\MYFILES\DATABASE
COPY C:\SPREDSHT\DATA\*.* F:\MYFILES\SPREDSHT
EXIT
```

In this example, there are multiple subdirectories on the network to hold my data files by category. If I were placing all my data files into one directory on the server, I would eliminate the subdirectory name at the end of each line.

You can create a batch file in any text editor, and save it with the file extension BAT. Then move to a command prompt and type the file name to launch the batch file.

Incidentally, the EXIT command is in the last line so that the command prompt session will close.

Create a Shortcut for the Backup Batch File

You can also create a shortcut icon to run this batch file from the Desktop. Like many features in Windows NT 4.0 there are a number of ways to accomplish this. You can create the desktop shortcut from the desktop, from Explorer, or from My Computer.

Create a Shortcut from the Desktop   You can create a shortcut right from the desktop by following these steps:

1. Right-click anywhere on the Desktop, then choose New, Shortcut to bring up the Create Shortcut Wizard (see fig. 34.6).

FIG. 34.6
The Shortcut Wizard walks you through all the steps to create a shortcut on the desktop.

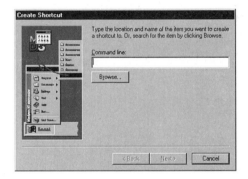

2. In the Create Shortcut dialog box, enter the path and executable file name in the Command Line box. If you don't remember it, choose Browse, and when you find the file, double-click its listing. Then choose Next.

3. Enter a name for the shortcut in the Select a Name box, then choose Next.

4. Select an icon for the shortcut (for some application shortcuts the icon is attached already and you won't see the Select an Icon page), then choose Finish.

Create a Shortcut from Explorer or My Computer   You can use Explorer or My Computer to find a file and then create a shortcut for it, by using these steps:

1. Open Explorer or My Computer and click objects (for Explorer) or double-click objects (My Computer) until you've displayed the executable file for which you need a shortcut.

2. Drag the file to the desktop and the shortcut is automatically created. If the desktop isn't visible, right-click the file, and choose Create Shortcut from the menu.

3. The shortcut is placed in the same location (folder) as the original file, so drag it to the desktop.

Once you have a shortcut, double-click it to launch the program.

Backing Up to Disks   Users who don't want to spend the money for tape backup systems can use disks to back up important files. However, it takes a great deal of will power and dedication to use disk-based backup protocols properly. Sitting in front of a computer, waiting for the system to ask for the next disk, is one of the most incredibly boring tasks in the world.

In fact, it's so boring and time-consuming that there's a very real chance that there will be many days when you just can't face it. And you won't do it. If you neglect to back up frequently, the computer fairies figure it out and they cause your hard drive to crash. Ask anyone you know who has had a hard drive failure if they made a backup immediately before the crash (restrict the question to people who back up to disk). Almost everyone will tell you they hadn't. Don't believe their protestations when they tell you, "I only lost a couple of days work; that's not bad." It *is* bad. In fact, it can be disastrous. It is also unnecessary. Back up all your data. Back up every day. Or, buy a tape backup system.

You have several approaches to choose from if you back up to disk:

- ■ Use Explorer and drag your data directories to the disk.
- ■ Use a utility software application that contains a backup routine.
- ■ Use the MS-DOS BACKUP command from a command prompt. Just follow any prompts to insert disks after you enter the command **BACKUP** *x*: where *x*: is the drive you want to back up (usually C). There are some additional parameters for more advanced features in backup which you can learn about by typing **BACKUP/?**.

The best disk-based backup approach is to eliminate the whole approach and buy a tape system.

Part
VII

Ch
34

Backing Up to Tape

The best, easiest, and most productive backup strategy is that based on tape. There is a large variety of tape backup hardware to choose from, and the prices are extremely reasonable. Some systems, including hardware and software, cost under $100.00. Even if the systems were very expensive because they have additional features you need, they may be worth the price (which can be upwards of $1,000.00 is some cases). You have to ask yourself the question, "What's my data worth to me?" Your data is the most important part of your computer system, so it should be worth more to you than any device or software.

Using Proprietary Tape Backup Software   You can install an application to back up your system, and most of the tape devices on the market come with their own proprietary software.

If the software is compatible with Windows NT 4.0, you can take advantage of the many features available in most of these software packages in order to ensure the integrity of your system. Most tape backup software offers the following features which you need to select during the configuration process:

- Verification of the backup by comparing the tape with the original disk files after the backup is finished. If any files don't match—indicating a possible problem with the copying process—an error log is generated so you can recopy the file or try to ascertain what is wrong with it.

- Unattended backups which you can configure for the middle of the night (don't turn off your computer). This eliminates the need to stop working early in order to have time to back up your data.

- Compression, which enables you to put more bytes on the tape than its original configuration.

Read the documentation that came with your tape system to determine which features are available, and also to understand how they work.

Using the Windows NT Tape Backup Program

Windows NT provides a tape backup program so that you can use a tape unit to back up any file systems you might have on your computers (FAT or NTFS). Not all tape software supports these file systems so the NT program provides backup power for these incompatible applications.

Before you can use the Windows NT tape backup software, you have to install your tape device, load the drivers into the operating system, and configure the backup system.

The physical installation of the tape device is accomplished by following the instructions that came with the unit. It's usually a matter of inserting the device into a bay, securing it with rails and screws, and then connecting the cable to a controller.

Installing the Drivers

Before you can begin using your drive, you need to install the drivers in Windows NT Workstation. If you've installed a tape device that is supported by Windows NT, you need your original Windows NT media (disks or CD-ROM). If your tape device isn't supported by Windows NT, you need a manufacturer's disk containing Windows NT 4.0 drivers (make sure the drivers are specifically for version 4.0). Then follow these steps:

1. Open the Control Panel, then double-click the Tape Devices icon to display the Tape Devices dialog box. The Devices tab should display a message that there are no tape devices found.

2. Click the Drivers tab, then choose Add.

3. In the Select Tape Driver dialog box, scroll through the list to find your tape device (see fig. 34.7). Then choose OK.

Part
VII

Ch
34

FIG. 34.7

If you purchased a drive that is supported by Windows NT, select it from the list.

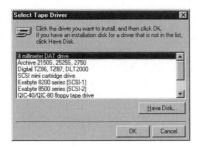

4. If your drive isn't listed, you must have a disk with the appropriate driver. Choose Have Disk.

5. Enter the drive and path for the disk or CD-ROM you're using for this driver, then choose Continue. The appropriate files are copied to your hard drive.

6. When the files are copied, Windows NT will load and start the drivers.

Determining a Backup Philosophy

Once you have the convenience of tape backup, you have a full range of choices about what you want to back up and how. The question of how often should not arise—backing up is a daily task. Here are the common choices:

- Back up your entire drive every day. This is called a *full backup*.
- Back up your entire drive once, then back up only your data every day. This is called a *data-only backup*.
- Back up your drive once a month (or once a week), then back up only the data files that have changed since the last backup. This is called an *incremental backup*.

N O T E Windows NT has developed a set of backup protocols with specific names for each type. They are used for running the backup software and are covered later in this chapter. ■

The more you back up, of course, the longer the backup takes. So what? The beauty of tape is that you don't have to baby-sit it or yawn and fidget as you put disks into a floppy drive.

All the wonderful convenience of tape backup is lost if you buy a tape system that is too small for your drive. If you have to wait for the first tape to fill up, then change tapes, you're missing the point.

 Learn a lesson from those who have "been there"—buy a tape system twice as large as your drive because you might one day install a larger drive or add a second one.

How do you decide which backup plan to use—full, data-only, or incremental? In order to make a decision about anything, including what type of backup to perform, you have to examine the possibilities and ramifications of each choice. The easiest way to do that is to ask the question that seems to be the very basic question in your search for answers: "Why do we back up our computer systems?"

And the answer is, "So that if something happens, we can get back to work quickly."

If you think about it, that means that the purpose of backing up is to restore things as quickly as possible. Follow that logic to its natural conclusion, and you realize the ultimate backup truth: you create a backup protocol to make restoring convenient, not to make backing up convenient.

If you do anything except a full backup, restoring your system is going to be onerous.

If you did data-only backups, you have to reinstall every piece of software on your system, go through the configuration process for each of them, and then restore your data.

If you chose incremental backups, you have a whole mess of tapes that are incremental backups of files that have changed. You have to restore each tape in the proper order to ensure you have the final, correct version of each data file. That could take many hours, if not days.

If you did a total backup, after a disaster you only need to load the backup software on your new drive and then click one button on the toolbar—Restore. Go have a cup of coffee, and when you return, you're back in business. The poor fools who

Part
VII

Ch
34

devised backup schemes that would make backing up each night a quick process will be putting tapes in and taking them out long after you've finished your day's work and headed home for dinner.

Running Windows NT Tape Backup Software

Once you've installed the tape drive and the drivers, it's time to back up your system. Insert a tape in the drive before beginning. Then, follow these steps:

> **CAUTION**
>
> Because Windows NT is a multitasking operating system, it might be tempting to get some work done while the backup is going on. Any file that's open won't be backed up—including software files and drivers and system files. Therefore, it's not a particularly good idea to work during a backup.

1. Choose Programs from the Start menu, then choose Administrative Tools, Backup. The NT Backup Program launches (see fig. 34.8).

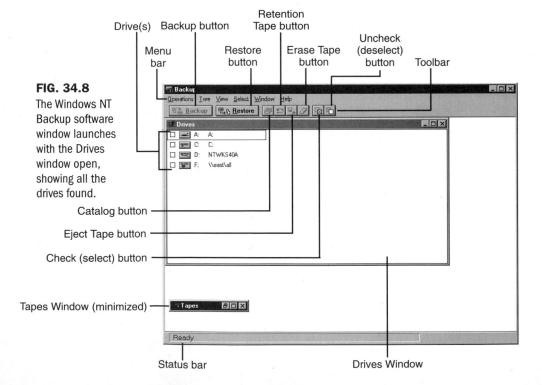

FIG. 34.8
The Windows NT Backup software window launches with the Drives window open, showing all the drives found.

Drive(s) Backup button

Menu bar

Restore button

Retention Tape button

Erase Tape button

Uncheck (deselect) button

Toolbar

Catalog button

Eject Tape button

Check (select) button

Tapes Window (minimized)

Status bar

Drives Window

2. If you want to view the Tape window, double-click the minimized icon. If the tape has a backup on it, you see information about that backup (the drive that was backed up, the date, and more information).

3. Begin your backup according to the type of backup protocol you decide upon.

Full Backup   To perform a full backup:

1. Select the drive(s) you want to back up and click the Check button (or choose Select, Check).

2. Click the Backup button, or choose Operations, Backup.

Partial Backup   To back up specific files or directories:

1. Double-click the drive that contains the files you want to back up. The contents of the drive appear similarly to the way that Explorer presents the drive (see fig. 34.9).

FIG. 34.9
Once you display the directories and files on a drive, you can pick and choose the files and folders you want to back up.

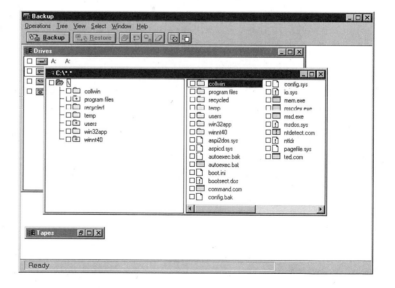

2. Use the options in the Tree menu to expand and collapse the view of the drive.

3. Select the directories or files you want to include in the backup, then click the Check button. If you want to deselect a file, highlight it and click the Uncheck button.

Part
VII

Ch
34

4. Click the Backup button to begin. If the tape fills before the backup is complete, you are prompted to insert another tape.

Setting Backup Options

Once you've selected the drives or files to back up, you can configure options for the way your backup proceeds. When you choose Operations, Backup, the Backup Information dialog box offers a range of options.

Backup Operation Types   NT Backup offers five specific backup types, or protocols, to choose from:

- Normal, which backs up all the selected files and marks the files on the disk to indicate they have been backed up.

- Copy, which backs up all the selected files, but does not mark the disk with any attributes indicating they've been backed up.

- Incremental, which looks at the selected files and only backs up those that have been changed since the last backup. The backed up files are marked with an attribute indicating they were backed up.

- Differential, which looks at the selected files and only backs up those that have been changed since the last backup, but does not mark the files as having been backed up.

- Daily, which looks at the selected files and backs up only those that have been modified or added today. No attributes are marked on the disk to indicate the files were backed up.

 The purpose of the Daily backup type is to let you back up the files you worked on today, the idea being that you might want to take them home to continue your work.

Tape Options   You can configure the manner in which you use tapes by setting the tape options:

- You can append this backup to the tape and place it after the last backup already on the tape.

- You can replace (overwrite) any backup already on the tape with this backup.

- You can enter a name for the tape (I usually use the day of the week and use that tape whenever that day rolls around).

- You can choose whether or not you want to verify the backup by comparing the files on the tape to the original files after the backup is complete.

- You can choose to copy the Windows NT Registry files to the tape (if they arc on the drive being backed up).

> **CAUTION**
>
> Never back up onto the tape that has the last backup. In fact, the safest way to use a tape backup system is to have a unique tape for each day of the week. That way, you have plenty of options for restoring files (in case you accidentally erase an important file).

Logging Options   If you wish, you can have the Windows NT backup software write a log file to the disk following the backup. There are three logging options:

- Don't log.

- Summary log only, in which the major processes are logged, including the time the backup began and a list of any files that couldn't be backed up.

- Full detail log, in which the operations are logged along with the names of every backed-up file and directory.

If you choose to log the backup operation, enter the name of the file to use for logging in the Log File box.

Restoring a Tape Backup

You can restore all or part of the contents of the tape. If you've had a major hardware disaster, you need everything on the tape. But, if you inadvertently deleted a file or overwrote a file and need the original contents, you can restore an individual file.

Before you begin, put the tape you want to restore into the tape drive. Then follow these steps (working with the dialog boxes and choices for tapes is the same as selecting drives):

1. Open the Backup software, then double-click the Tapes icon to open the Tapes window.

Part
VII

Ch
34

2.   Double-click the appropriate tape or backup set to display a catalog of the tape's contents.

3.   To restore the entire tape, select that tape's checkbox. To restore individual files, select the checkbox for each file.

4.   Once you make your selections, click the Restore button.

 TIP If you wish, you can instruct the system to verify the files that are restored to the disk against the files on the tape. Any problems are written to a log file.

Maintaining Tapes

The most important step you can take to keep your backup tapes safe is to get them out of the building. It's not difficult to work out a schedule for this, and it's the only guarantee you have that you'll be back in business in the event of a major calamity. If you have specific tapes for each day of the week, assign a Monday person, a Tuesday person, etc. If your tape backup is performed unattended (either by scheduling it in the middle of the night through the software or by beginning the backup just before you leave for the day), you can establish a schedule that sends the Monday tape off-site on Tuesday, and so on.

If it's onerous to make this scheme work (the hardest part is having people remember to bring the tapes back), then make sure the Friday tape is taken out of the building.

If you can't set up an official office schedule, find a friend who works somewhere else and make a trade deal—"I'll give you mine if you give me yours." Of course, if there is secure or private data on the tape, you have to be selective about your friends. Or, offload that data to a floppy disk and don't back it up to tape.

Physical Tape Maintenance

Depending upon the manufacturer of your tapes and your tape drive, there is probably a cleaning kit available. It's the drive, especially the heads that read/write to tape, that gets cleaned, and this keeps your tapes happy and healthy. Some of these kits are nothing more than special tapes which you insert into the drive. Other cleaning kits involve swabs and liquids for cleaning the unit. Follow the manufacturer's instructions.

It's really dust that's the big enemy here. I've had to repair/clean tape drives at many sites, and I finally figured out that besides cleaning kits, a regular burst of canned air is a great help.

Dust does damage in two ways—it scratches tapes and it prevents the drive from seeing the end of the tape (which is a transparent spot on the tape). The result is that the tape rolls off the end of the spool, making it essentially useless.

Software Tape Maintenance The Windows NT Backup program provides features for taking care of tape maintenance chores. All of the tape maintenance commands are found in the Operations menu:

- Choose Erase Tape to erase the tape. You can choose Quick Erase, which merely deletes the header, or Secure Erase, which deletes the entire tape. The latter choice can take quite a bit of time.

- Choose Retention Tape to have the tape fast-forwarded to the end and then rewind. This eliminates any loose tension in the tape and ensures smooth movement during backups.

- Choose Format Tape to format an unformatted tape. This command is only needed for mini-cartridge tapes.

Protecting Against Viruses

While an NT 4.0 system is not as susceptible to virus infection as Windows 3.x or DOS, rogue programmers are working constantly to figure out a way to do damage. Unfortunately, virus protection is an important computer issue, and you need to be on guard against these damaging programs.

A *virus* is a program that is written to accomplish two objectives:

- Do harm to a computer
- Replicate itself

Viruses attach themselves to executable files in order to carry out both these aims.

When you boot from a disk that has a virus in the boot sector, or you launch a program that has a virus attached, the virus launches. It moves into the system memory where it can have access to all the files in the system. It begins its programmed tasks—damaging files and replicating itself.

There are different ways to program viruses, and they attack computers in different ways:

- *Program viruses*. Infect program files.

 TIP One of the new virus types is the *concept virus*, which attaches to other types of executables, specifically macros. Even though you may not think of a macro as an executable file, it is. It just doesn't show up in Explorer. There are known viruses that attach themselves to Word macros and then spread their damage to documents.

- *Boot viruses*. Recorded by the boot on disks.
- *Stealth viruses*. Programmed for clever methods to hide from virus detection programs.
- *Polymorphic viruses*. Change their aspect in each file they infect, making it difficult to see a pattern in order to identify them.
- *Multipartite viruses*. Infect both program files and boot records.

Practice Safe Computing

To keep viruses away from your computer, you have to avoid letting any questionable files near your computer. Many viruses are spread by software downloads from BBSes that don't check for viruses, or disks that come from an individual rather than a reputable software company.

A smart business protocol is to prohibit users from bringing in disks, or to make an absolute rule that no disk can be placed in a floppy drive without checking it for viruses. This means that people who want to work at home and bring finished work back on a disk have to understand and follow the rules.

Anti-Virus Software

There are lots of virus checkers available, and most of the commercial products are terrific and full-featured. Some anti-virus software is free and can be downloaded from reputable BBSes or services like CompuServe. There are also anti-virus applications distributed as shareware (you pay a fee—usually well under

$100.00—if you decide you want to use the software). If you use a virus checker, make sure it is written to work in Windows NT 4.0. Probably the most popular shareware virus software is from MCAFEE, which can be reached in a variety of ways through your modem:

Internet e-mail: **support@mcafee.com**

Internet FTP: **ftp.mcafee.com**

WWW: **http://www.mcafee.com**

America Online: **MCAFEE**

CompuServe: **GO MCAFEE**

The Microsoft Network: **GO MCAFEE**

Checking for Known Viruses   Most anti-virus software is programmed to look for any of the thousands of known viruses and eradicate any it finds. Because rogue programmers are a busy bunch of animals, new viruses appear all the time. You must keep up with the latest version of your anti-virus software in order to make sure you're covering all the bases.

Checking for Suspicious File Changes   There is also anti-virus software that looks for unusual changes in your system's boot sector or executable file structure. This software species creates a database with specific information about those parts of your system and then checks the current conditions against the expectations derived from the database. If something seems amiss, the software issues a warning of a possible virus.

Checking for Suspicious Behavior   There are certain events that shouldn't occur during your normal computer use. Many anti-virus software programs alert you if something improper seems to be occurring in your system. The alert should trigger an immediate search for viruses unless you know that the event that triggered the alert is an acceptable occurrence.

The suspicious activities that most anti-virus software applications worry about are:

■ *Any attempt to perform a low-level format on a hard disk.* This is not pro-grammed into any software package you're using for office work. In fact, it's a chore usually performed only by the manufacturers of hard drives, although there are some CMOS/BIOS setup programs that let you do it.

Part
VII

Ch
34

■ *Any attempt to write to disk boot records.* There is no reason for any software program to do this. The only common occurrence is during the execution of the FORMAT command, although the MS-DOS BACKUP command also formats a disk if necessary.

■ *Any attempt to write to a program file.* These days, most program files are not self-modifying nor are configuration options usually saved in the program files. However, you may be using some software that changes its basic executable file as a result of your work, so this might be a virus alert that's safe to ignore. If you're not sure, call the software company and see if its program files are self-modifying.

N O T E   Having explained the suspicious activities that virus checkers look for, we should give you a reassuring note. Windows NT is an operating system that takes advantage of the hardware protection capabilities of your processor. That means that when you're operating your computer, all the hardware is protected from software. Without going into a long explanation of how this occurs and why it's important, we'll note that in NT a virus program will be prevented from formatting a hard drive or messing with the boot sector. ■

Configuring Anti-Virus Software

When you install anti-virus software, you usually have several options for its configuration. The most commonly found choices include:

■ Run a virus scan at system startup.

■ Check every executable file when it's launched, and check every disk that is accessed.

■ Run a manually invoked virus scan by launching the anti-virus program.

There are good arguments for and against all of the configuration options, and you should decide upon a scheme that makes you comfortable and matches the way you use your computer. For example, computers that are never turned off won't benefit much from a startup scan. And, users who multitask and constantly open and close software may get extremely annoyed at the delays caused by a virus check every time an executable file is launched. While a manual check is the least invasive, it doesn't do much good if you don't do it regularly. If you're forgetful or lazy about such things, use one of the automatic virus-checking schemes and write off the annoyance as a necessary evil.

Updating the Emergency Repair Disk

During the original setup of your Windows NT Workstation operating system, you had the opportunity to create an *emergency repair disk*. This is a repair disk that you can use if your system becomes corrupt; since it contains the NT System files, the system configuration, and the startup environment of your installation process. If you didn't create an emergency repair disk during the installation of your operating system, you can do it now.

In addition to this disk, the same information is stored on your hard drive in the \WINNT\REPAIR subdirectory. In fact, when you create a repair disk, it is the data in that subdirectory that is written to the disk.

Your original configuration and the system you're using today may not be the same. You may have added or changed devices, changed drive letter assignments, created volume sets, or done any of a number of things that would prevent the Repair feature from working properly.

It's important to update your system repair information occasionally, and it's quite easy to do:

1. Choose <u>R</u>un from the Start menu to display the Run dialog box.
2. In the <u>O</u>pen box, type **rdisk** (the case doesn't matter) to display the Repair Disk Utility dialog box (see fig. 34.10).

Part

VII

Ch

34

FIG. 34.10

Use the Repair Disk Utility to update your emergency disk and the repair information on your hard drive.

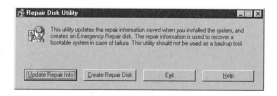

3. Click Update Repair Info to replace existing files in the REPAIR subdirectory with files containing updated information about your system. When this process is finished, you are asked if you want to create a new emergency repair disk.

4. Click Create Repair Disk to create an emergency disk using the information currently contained in the REPAIR subdirectory (in case you didn't create the disk during system setup). This option is appropriate if you haven't changed your computer configuration and can use the original system information that was written to the REPAIR subdirectory.

5. After you make your selection, the system asks you to confirm it, reminding you that the current information will be deleted. Choose OK to continue.

6. When the process is completed, choose Exit to end it.

 TIP Don't use your original emergency disk for the new one, just in case. Insert a new 1.44-inch disk into drive A. You can use a disk that has data you no longer need. The disk is formatted automatically.

From Here...

This chapter taught you how to deal with viruses and corrupt files, and what the dangers of electricity are to your hardware. For further information about protecting your system, see the following chapters:

- Chapter 33, "Optimizing Windows NT Workstation Performance."
- Chapter 35, "Using the Diagnostics Tool."

Using the Diagnostics Tool

by Sam S. Gill

Windows NT 4.0 includes an enhanced version of the diagnostics tool. In addition to its new look, the diagnostics tool contains a wealth of new information about the hardware, the operating system, and the software of the system. All this information is now accessible from one source in an easy-to-read format. In addition to learning how to use Windows NT Diagnostics to access information about your system, you will learn how to use the diagnostics tool to isolate configuration and system problems. As you will see, the diagnostics tool is an invaluable source of information about your system configuration and will become your troubleshooting companion. ■

How to access the diagnostics tool

This chapter will help you understand what the diagnostics tool is, how to use it, and where to find it in Windows NT.

What information is available through the diagnostics tool

The diagnostics tool presents information about many aspects of your Windows NT configuration. In this chapter, you'll learn how to find and then understand information from the diagnostics tool about software, CPU and BIOS, memory, drives, system services and devices, and network connectivity.

Accessing the Diagnostics Tool

You can access the diagnostics tool from the Start menu. Open the Start menu and choose Programs, Administrative Tools, Windows NT Diagnostics.

The Windows NT diagnostics tool appears as a window with multiple tabs (see fig. 35.1). Each tab contains a different category of information about your system setup. When the diagnostics tool appears, it initially presents the Version tab.

FIG. 35.1

The Windows NT diagnostics tool with the Version tab displayed.

There are four command buttons at the bottom of the diagnostics tool window. These buttons provide functionality that is relevant for each tab. The first button, Properties, allows you to obtain more detailed information about items you select.

The Refresh button allows you to refresh the information presented in the window when you suspect that the information is dated.

CAUTION

You will typically use other tools to change values that are being displayed by the diagnostics tool. Changing system values will not automatically update the information being displayed in the diagnostics tool. You should always use refresh.

The third button, Print, allows you to print the information that is being presented in the displayed tab.

The final button, OK, allows you to close the diagnostics tool window.

Two menus appear at the top of the Tool window: File and Help. The File menu allows you to save the information that is being displayed to a file. The Help menu allows you to obtain information about the tool as well as information on how to use it and what items are being displayed.

Viewing Information

In the next several sections, you will be introduced to the detailed information that can be accessed through the various tabs of the tool.

Windows NT Software

The first tab you will see when you open the diagnostics tool is the Version tab. The Version tab displays information about your Windows NT software.

The information being displayed includes the version number of the software being used (such as Windows NT Server, Version 4.0), the Build Number (such as 1234), the processor type for the software (such as x86), and the name and company name of the person who has licensed the software (such as DataWiz).

The important information here is the Build Number. Microsoft releases many revisions of Windows NT. The revisions are uniquely identified by their Build Number. Whenever you encounter a problem that requires assistance from Microsoft, you will need to identify the Build Number as part of your problem report.

CPU and BIOS

To find out information about your CPU and BIOS, click the System tab (see fig. 35.2).

FIG. 35.2

The System tab of the Windows NT Diagnostics window displays information about your CPU and BIOS.

The top part of the window contains information about your system and BIOS. At the top is the information about your system architecture (such as AT/AT Compatible), followed by the information about the Hardware Abstraction Layer (HAL) being used, (for example, PC Compatible EISA/ISA HAL), followed by BIOS information. The BIOS information includes the date, the source, and the version (such as BIOS Date 05/26/95 and Award Modular BIOS v4.50G).

The bottom part of the window contains information about the processors in the system (for example, Processor 0, x86 Family 5 Model 2 Stepping 5 Genuine Intel ˜90MHz) that identifies the processor type (Pentium) and its speed.

A key piece of information in this tab is the HAL identifier. HAL is the layer of Windows NT that a hardware Original Equipment Manufacturer (OEM) will modify in order to adapt Windows NT to the particular hardware environment. It's important for you to learn the source for HAL: is it a generic Microsoft HAL or is it one developed by the OEM? Whenever you run into system configuration problems, the HAL source will let you know who you should call for help—your hardware vendor or Microsoft.

Memory

To view information about memory, you should click the Memory tab (see fig. 35.3). The Memory window contains information that was previously available only in the System icon in the Control Panel. This information includes:

■ The total amount of working memory available to your system in the Physical Memory section. Remember from Chapter 12 that you must have at least 22M of working memory.

■ The size and location of the paging file (PAGEFILE.SYS).

■ The status and amount of memory used by the Kernel.

■ The number of processes, or threads, being managed by Windows NT.

FIG. 35.3
The Memory tab of the Windows NT Diagnostics window displays information about your memory and paging file availability.

The important information in this tab is the amount of memory allocated to your swap file, PAGEFILE.SYS, and its location. In Windows NT, the maximum number of concurrent applications you can run is not limited by the size of physical RAM, but by the size of PAGEFILE.SYS. Since Windows NT uses a virtual memory model with paging, only some of the pages of an application may reside in physical storage during execution while the remaining pages reside on PAGEFILE.SYS. If the size of PAGEFILE.SYS is small, it will limit the number of concurrent applications you can run.

Another important consideration is the location of PAGEFILE.SYS. In Windows NT you are allowed up to 15 different PAGEFILE.SYS segments, one per logical drive. You can enhance the performance of the Virtual Memory Manager (VMM) by defining additional PAGEFILE.SYS segments on other logical drives. VMM will use the additional segments where it can minimize conflicts with other I/O operations.

▶ **See** "Managing Memory in NT Workstation," **p. 300**

Part
VII

Ch
35

Drives on Your Computer

One item of information you will frequently need access to in a Windows NT configuration is what type of drives are available to you and what type are actually recognized by the system. This is especially helpful if you use your system running Windows NT Workstation in a mobile configuration, and the same drives are not available to you if you are not attached to a network, or have an external hard drive or CD-ROM player attached.

To view information about the drives on your computer system, you can choose the Drives tab (see fig. 35.4). The Drives tab gives you the option to view your drive configuration either by type or by letter.

FIG. 35.4

The Drives tab of the Windows NT Diagnostics window displays information about your computer system drives by type.

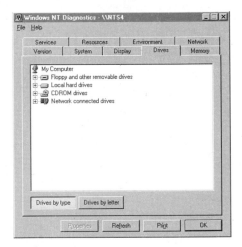

For each drive type you can click the plus (+) to drill down to the drives that belong to each type. When you highlight one of the drives you can get the detailed information on the drive by clicking the Properties command button. The information presented includes the serial number of the drive, the number of bytes per sector, the number of sectors, the number of free, used, and total clusters and bytes on the drive (see fig. 35.5).

As mentioned earlier, you also can view the same information by drive letter rather than drive type (see fig. 36.6).

FIG. 35.5
Detailed information on Drive C, including the number of used and free bytes.

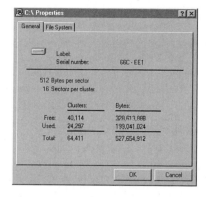

FIG. 35.6
Drive information is displayed by letter type.

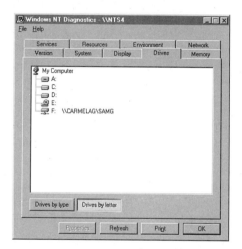

 TIP To change the SCSI drive configuration of your system, you will still need to open the SCSI Adapters icon in the Control Panel.

Your System Services

The health of a Windows NT system is determined by the status of its services and devices.

The Windows NT diagnostics tool provides you with information regarding the status of your system services and devices. In order to access this information you have to select the Services tab. The Services tab provides you with two options as command buttons (see fig. 35.7). You can either view Services or Devices. The default view when you select the Services tab is to view the Services.

FIG. 35.7
When you select the Services tab, you can view the status of services on your system.

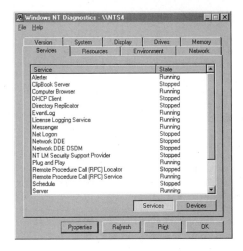

The Services tab presents the status of each system service whether it is running or stopped. When you highlight one of the services such as Network DDE, you can click the Properties button to obtain general information about this service and to find out what other service is dependent on this service (see fig. 35.8).

FIG. 35.8
The service NetDDEDSDM is dependent on NetDDE.

The general information about the service that is displayed includes the path name for where the EXE for the service is located, the start type for the service (Manual or Automatic), the service account name, the error severity, the group, and the service flags for this service. Service flags would indicate such things as whether this service shares a process with other services or whether the service is a kernel device driver.

During Windows NT startup or at any time during normal operation, a service may fail. The failure of a service is recorded in the System Event Log. Once you get a notification of a service failure from the event log, it is now your responsibility to identify the cause of the failure and to remedy the situation. Your first course of action is to track the failure to its source, e.g., a service failed to start because a service that it depends on also failed to start. Using the diagnostics tool, you can backtrack to the original failure. Examples of original failures would be that a service failed to start because it depends on a device that is not available. That is why the statuses of services and devices are displayed in the same tab.

To change the services configuration of your system, you will still need to:

1. Open the Start menu, and choose Settings, Control Panel.

2. Double-click the Services icon.

3. Change the status of a service by using the Start command button for stopped services or the Stop command button for services that are running.

4. Change the setting of a service by clicking the Setting command button (see fig. 35.9). Services can either start automatically or manually.

Most service failures can be traced to device driver failures. The diagnostics tool is a very convenient way to get centralized information about the status of device drivers.

FIG. 35.9
The Services tab also displays information about the status of drivers.

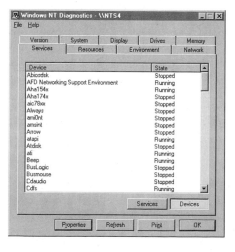

Part

VII

Ch

35

Your Display

You can view information about your display by selecting the Display tab in the Windows NT diagnostics tool (see fig. 35.10). The tab displays information about your adapter and about your driver. The adapter information includes the setting that includes resolution and number of colors ($800 \times 600 \times 256$), the type of monitor (ati compatible), the string, the memory (1M), the chip type (Mach 64), and the DAC type.

FIG. 35.10

The Display tab presents information about your computer display.

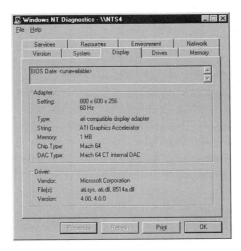

The lower part of the Display tab provides information about the driver being used. The information includes the vendor (e.g., Microsoft Corporation), the file(s) being used, and the version.

Display problems typically occur after system startup, or after you have made changes to the display type. In both cases the system couldn't start using the display type defined. To get the system started, you can always choose to start Windows NT with the default display. Once Windows NT is started, you can start diagnosing your display problems. The diagnostics tool allows you to view the configuration information for your display but not to change it. Display problems may occur as a result of changing the display after the system is shutdown or a failure in your display controller card or device.

▶ **See** "Configuring Your Video Display," **p. 284**

Environment Variables

Many applications running on Windows NT utilize the values of environment variables to determine how they should run. As an example, Microsoft Visual C++ uses an environment variable MSVC to define the path in which Visual C++ is installed. The Environment tab allows you to view information about your environment variables (see fig. 35.11). There are two selections for the environment variables: System and Local user.

When you select System, you get a list of all the environment variables that have been set for the system and their values. The system environment variables are those common to all users of the system. Typically, they are also the ones that are utilized by the services that are started automatically.

FIG. 35.11

The Environment tab displays the values of the System environment variables.

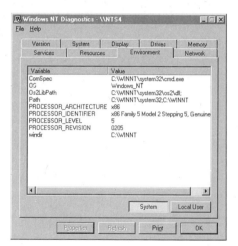

When you select Local User, you get a list of all the environment variables that have been set for the current user's environment. The local user environment variables are those being used by the user that is currently logged on. These environment variables will largely depend on which applications this particular user is authorized to run.

In a typical Windows NT system, you may create a different user profile on your system for different roles you are playing. You may create a developer profile which would be allowed to use many development applications (see fig. 35.12). In addition, you can create a "typical" user profile to test those applications in a "normal" environment. In this scenario, you will have a different set of environment variables for each local user you define.

FIG. 35.12
The Environment tab displays the values of the Local User environment variables.

The values of the environment variables cannot be changed from the diagnostics tool. To modify the environment variables, you have to use the System icon in the Control Panel.

▶ **See** "Working with Environment Variables," **p. 315**

System Resources and Devices

When you install Windows NT or when you add new hardware components to the system, you may run into hardware configuration problems. The Resources tab allows you to view information about your system resources and devices. There are five categories for the resources: IRQ, I/O Port, DMA, Memory, and Devices. For each category, you can select whether you would like to Include Hardware Abstraction Layer (HAL) Resources as well by marking the check box at the top right hand corner.

The first category is IRQ and can be selected by clicking the IRQ command button (see fig. 35.13). You see a list of interrupts, to which device they have been assigned, whether it is a bus interrupt, and if so, the type (such as ISA).

FIG. 35.13

The Resources tab displays the IRQ assignments to the various devices.

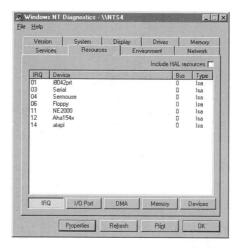

If you mark the Include HAL Resources check box you get a more detailed list that includes the IRQs used by the HAL.

For each IRQ, you can get more details by selecting the Properties command button (see fig. 35.14). The properties provide you with information on the resource owner, the bus type, the bus number, the vector, the affinity mask, and the type.

IRQs are your first source of hardware problems. In particular, watch out for double-defined IRQ: two devices with the same IRQ number. Recall the scenario that was described in the earlier section "Viewing Information about Services," in which a service failure occurred due to a device failure; now you have to trace the device failure to device configuration problems. IRQ is the number-one culprit.

The second category is I/O Port. When you select this category by clicking the I/O Port command button, you get a list of I/O addresses and their assignment (see fig. 35.15). The information includes an I/O address range, the device, the bus number, and the type. Back to the failure scenario: two devices with the same I/O address is your second culprit for device failure.

The third category is DMA. When you select this category by clicking the DMA command button, you get a list of Direct Memory Access (DMA) devices (see fig. 35.16). The information includes the channel number, the I/O port number, the device name, the bus number, and the type.

Part
VII

Ch
35

FIG. 35.14

The properties of the NE2000 IRQ show what type is latched.

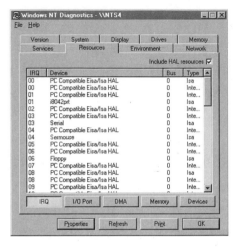

FIG. 35.15

The Resources tab displays the I/O addresses for the various I/O ports.

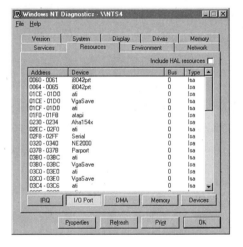

Again, what you want to look out for are devices that have been assigned the same port number. Using Windows NT tools, you will actually not be allowed to assign the same I/O port to different devices. You could, however, create such a situation by making changes in the Registry directly.

CAUTION

You are advised not to make changes to the system configuration by making changes to the values of keys in the Registry. When you change the key value directly, Windows NT does not run any tests to check the validity of your changes. Consequently, your changes may corrupt the whole Windows NT configuration.

FIG. 35.16
The Resources tab displays the address information for all the DMA devices.

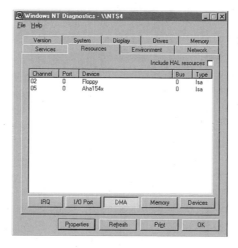

The fourth category is Memory. When you select this category by clicking the Memory command button, you get a list of Memory locations that have been assigned to I/O devices (see fig. 35.17). The information includes a memory address range, an I/O device that memory has been assigned to, the bus number, and the type. After IRQ and I/O port, this is the third culprit in device failure. This failure, however, is much harder to trace. Failures due to improper memory allocations may not manifest themselves in a failure to start, but in inconsistent and random behavior. As an example, if the memory display area is assigned to another device, inconsistent failures will result.

FIG. 35.17
The Resources tab displays the memory address range information for all the I/O devices.

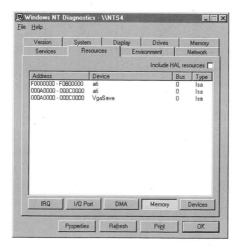

The final category is Devices. When you select this category by clicking the Devices command button, you get a list of Devices (see fig. 35.18).

FIG. 35.18
The Resources tab displays a list of all the devices installed on your computer system.

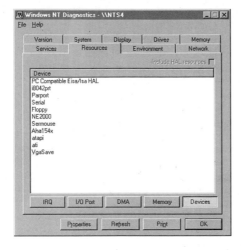

To get more detailed information about each device, you must select the device and then click the Properties command button (see fig. 35.19).

FIG. 35.19
By choosing the Properties command button, you can display the detailed information on the Serial device.

For each device, you get detailed information at the top the resource owner. In addition, for each device the detailed information includes the resource type, the bus number, and the type. In this section, you have seen how you could use the information on system resources and devices.

▶ **See** "Managing System Devices," **p. 371**

Networks

Although great strides have taken place in the installation of Windows NT procedure to overcome network configuration problems, network problems still remain one of the main culprits of Windows NT failures.

The Network tab allows you to view information about your network connections. There are four categories for the Network: General, Transports, Settings, and Statistics.

The first category is General (the default). When you select this category by clicking the General command button, you get a list of network attributes: your access level, the workgroup or domain you belong to, your network version, LAN Root, number of logged on users, to which domain you have been logged on, to which server you have been logged on, and to what account have you logged on (current user) as shown in figure 35.20.

The information in this category is key to determining addressing problems. In a typical situation, you are in explorer and you can't "see" the other members of your domain, or even more frequently, you don't have access to certain resources. The diagnostics tool displays to which domain you have been logged on, which user you have logged on as, and to which groups you belong.

FIG. 35.20

The Network tab displays the general network attributes.

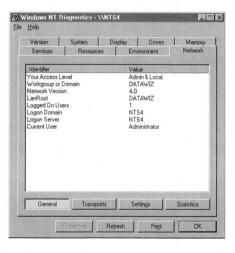

The second category is Transports. When you select this category by clicking the Transports command button, you get a list of network transports (one for each

Part

VII

Ch

35

network card in your computer system): the transport identifier, the network card address, The Virtual Circuit (VC) identifier, and whether (Yes/No) this transport is accessible from a Wide Area Network (WAN).

The transport information tells you which protocol you are using on the system and when using TCP/IP with DHCP which TCP/IP address you have been assigned (see fig. 35.21). Using the wrong protocol or having an improper network address will definitely cause the network to fail.

FIG. 35.21
The Network tab displays the transport information.

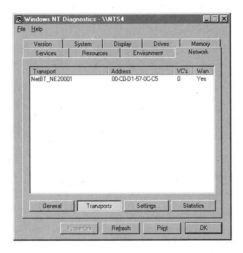

The third category is Settings. When you select this category by clicking the Settings command button, you get a list of network attributes that include such items as: the number of seconds to wait for a character (Character Wait), and the maximum number of network commands in a queue (Network Commands), to name a couple of important ones.

The settings information will help you understand the source of your network failures. If the number of seconds to wait for a character is too low, then in a Wide Area Network (WAN) configuration that may have delays in transfer, you could have a large number of transmission failures.

An example of the importance of identifying the maximum number of network commands in a queue is related to using Windows NT as an application server for many workstations, and in that configuration losing messages (see fig. 35.22). A small queue size is your culprit.

FIG. 35.22
The Network tab displays the network configuration settings.

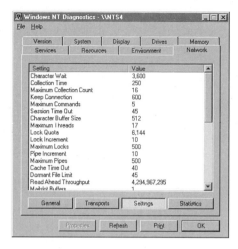

The final category is Statistics. When you select this category by clicking the Statistics command button, you get a list of network measures and their values (see fig. 35.23). The list of attributes includes such items as: the number of bytes received, the number of read operations, and the number of network errors, to name a couple of important ones. The network statistics will assist you in diagnosing any network failures or bottlenecks on your computer system.

One of the key variables you should constantly monitor is the number of network errors. Network errors result from either hardware failure or, as more frequently the case, poor choice of network parameters.

FIG. 35.23
The Network tab displays the network measures and their values.

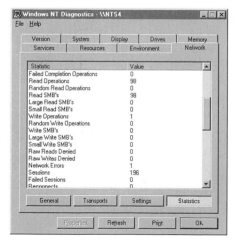

> **N O T E** You will probably find that the Performance Monitor tool is more useful for
> monitoring network statistics. ▪

While the Windows NT diagnostics tool allows you to view network information, it
doesn't allow you to change it. To change network settings you should use the
Network icon in the Control Panel.

▶ **See** "Configuring the Network," **p. 548**

From Here...

The hardest part in fixing any Windows NT system configuration problem is determining what the current system configuration is. In this chapter, you have been
exposed to the details of the information given through the Windows NT diagnostics tool, and you have seen how this information can be used to troubleshoot Windows NT failures. The following chapters can provide you with more information
related to understanding your system:

- Chapter 11, "Changing and Configuring Hardware."
- Chapter 12, "Managing Memory, Multitasking, and System Options."
- Chapter 14, "Managing System Services and Devices."
- Chapter 19, "Understanding Windows NT Network Services."
- Chapter 20, "Configuring the Network at Your Workstation."

Appendixes

Installing Windows NT Workstation

by Paul Sanna

Installing a new operating system is one of the more challenging tasks for any computer user, and Windows NT is no exception. Windows NT supports multiple file systems and other operating systems, forcing you to consider a number of complicated questions before and during installation. For example, what file system do you install? Do you install the same file system on every partition? Can you set up your system to dual-boot with Windows 95? How do you install Windows NT over the network? Preparing you is the goal of this appendix. You find practical guidance on how to answer the prompts that appear as you install Windows NT. It's important that you answer the prompts correctly, because if you change your mind later, you may need to completely reinstall NT. ■

Understanding NT Workstation's hardware requirements

Learn how to audit your system's hardware before installation and the disk partition requirements based on operating systems installed with NT Workstation.

Installing NT Workstation over OS/2 and Windows 95

Get detailed instructions on how to overwrite existing operating systems when installing NT Workstation.

Launching installation

Learn how to customize the NT Workstation installation.

Issues to Address Before Installation

How many times has this happened to you? You acquire new software, open the package, and scan the instructions for installation advice and any other document that looks important. Then you start the installation process, and you find about halfway through that the decision the installation program asked you to make on one of the first few screens was *wrong*. Now you have no way of changing it—short of reinstalling. You'd like to be humble and think that you should have understood the consequences of your decision, but, really, we both know the documentation and on-screen instructions should have done a better job of informing you of the impact and result of your decision. This section is designed to help you avoid this type of problem; you'll learn all the issues to consider before starting installation of NT Workstation.

Hardware Requirements

There are two sets of information you should consider in order to understand whether your hardware will work with NT Workstation. The first is the *Hardware Compatibility List (HCL)*. This document shows by type of hardware what equipment is compatible with Windows NT. The list is updated on a regular basis, certainly with every release of the software. You can usually find updates to the information in the HCL on one of the online information services, such as CompuServe or Microsoft's World Wide Web site. Check the HCL to see that every major component of your system is listed, such as the processor, hard drive, modem, tape drive, and so on. If one of your components is not listed, contact either Microsoft or the manufacturer to see if an updated driver is available.

ON THE WEB

Microsoft's home page on the Internet is at

    http://www.microsoft.com

TIP You may be able to use a hardware device with Windows NT that does not appear on the HCL. Some devices emulate other more widely accepted device models that do appear on the HCL. For example, a particular SCSI controller may not appear on the HCL, though to Windows NT, the device appears to be a SCSI controller with which it is compatible. If there is a particular piece of hardware you want to use on the system running Windows NT and it does not appear on the HCL, you can see if it emulates a device that does show up on the list.

The second set of information you should be concerned about, regarding the hardware you plan to use with NT Workstation, is the minimum hardware requirements. These specifications describe the minimum capacities and classes of hardware that can be used with NT Workstation. Table A.1 shows NT Workstation's minimum hardware requirements.

Table A.1   Minimum Installation Requirements

Item	Requirement
CPU	x86-based system, 486/33 or better, or supported RISC-based platform, such as MIPS R4x00™, DEC AXP, or PowerPC.
RAM	For x86-based systems, 12M minimum/16M recommended, 24–32M realistic. For RISC-based systems, 16M minimum, 24M recommended, 32M realistic.
Hard Disk Storage	108M free space for x86-based systems; 136M for RISC-based systems.
Display	Video adapter and display with at least VGA capabilities.
Disk Drives	For x86-based systems, 3.5-inch floppy drive and CD-ROM. For RISC-based systems, SCSI CD-ROM drive and adapter.

N O T E   Starting with version 4.0, Windows NT no longer supports 386-class processors. ▪

N O T E   The RAM amounts labels as *realistic* in table A.1 come from my own experience. Buy as much RAM as you can reasonably afford. For typical NT Workstation use, you don't have to buy 128M worth of RAM, but one-half the amount is a *very* nice luxury. You will be very happy with 24–32M, as well. ▪

▶ **See** "Where to Get More Information," **p. 1047**

Auditing the Hardware on Your System

The NT Workstation setup program asks you at various times about the hardware installed on your system. You're also asked to supply some settings information, such as the name of your computer, or a network workgroup or Windows NT Server domain to which you want to belong. In order to be prepared for these questions, it's probably a good idea to prepare a list of hardware components and settings on your system before beginning installation:

- Video adapter
- Video display
- Processor type
- Printer model
- Printer alias on network
- CD-ROM adapter
- SCSI controller

- Computer name
- Network user name
- Network password
- Network adapter
- Workgroup name for Microsoft Windows network, or Domain name for NT Server networks

Some of these are only appropriate if your NT Workstation will be attached to a network.

In addition, you should also take inventory of the hardware settings used to configure every device on your computer. From the sound card to hard drive adapter, you should note every relevant hardware setting, IRQ, DMA, and IO Address space, and so on, for every device.

Disk Partition and File System Requirements

You may want to run NT Workstation with another operating system on your computer, such as DOS, Windows 95, or OS/2. If this is the case, you may also want to take advantage of the file system features built into each of the operating systems. In order to manage different file systems on one computer, you may have to create or delete partitions on your hard disk(s). Based on this, there is a simple rule:

> For every file system you want to use on your PC, you will need one partition.

If you want to use the integrated security features built into NT's file system (NTFS) or any other features of NTFS, you'll need one partition formatted with

Part
VIII

App
A

NTFS. If you also want to use DOS on your system, you need another partition formatted with FAT, the DOS operating system's native file system. The reason for this is that DOS cannot recognize data on an NTFS partition. This leads to another important rule:

> The primary partition on your system must be formatted with a file system recognizable by all the operating systems you'll run on that PC.

N O T E The number of file systems present on your system doesn't necessarily indicate the number of operating systems in use. For example, NT Workstation can be installed on a FAT partition. This lets you maintain your DOS system, as well as run NT Workstation. In this case, two operating systems are being used with just one file system.

Now that you know the requirements for disk partitioning with regards to file and operating systems, what do you do? Depending on your preferences, you may have to create a new partition by dividing one. Some options for managing partitions follow:

- *Let the installation do it.* During the installation process, the setup program inspects your system for hard drives and partitions. A list of partitions is presented to you, and you can choose whether to delete one or create a new one. In addition, you can choose whether to format a partition as NTFS, convert a partition to NTFS, or leave a partition unchanged.
- *Do it yourself.* If you know how you want the partitions on your system organized, you can do any of the work required before the NT Workstation setup program is started. If you need a lot of disk management in order to set up your partitions, you may have to back up and restore data, so it's beneficial to take care of this before starting installation.

N O T E To divide one partition into two or more partitions, you'll have to back up all the data on the drive in order to create a new partition. It is impossible in DOS to free up space on one partition in order to create another.

 T I P If you format a partition as FAT during installation, you can convert to NTFS later without having to move all of the files and directories to another location during the process. Use the CONVERT.EXE utility from the command prompt to convert file systems. From the command prompt, type **CONVERT /?** to display help about the utility.

Your work with partitions on your system is dependent on the operating systems and file systems you want present on your system.

▶ **See** "Support for other Operating Systems," **p. 20**

Disk Compression Issues

Windows NT is not compatible with third-party disk compression utilities. Windows NT will have problems installing onto a partition with compressed resources. Before starting setup of Windows NT, you should decompress any compacted resources and eliminate any references to the virtual disk drives that most compression tools use. If any reference to a compression program is made in either AUTOEXEC.BAT or CONFIG.SYS, you should remove the line(s) from the file.

N O T E   The file compression described in the previous chapter should not be confused with the file compression capabilities available on a drive formatted with NTFS, NT's file system. You can find information on NTFS file compression features in Chapter 6, "Working with Folders and Files."

Understanding Your Operating System Options

As you can probably tell by now, when you install NT Workstation, you can preserve the operating system on the computer and choose which operating system to load when you boot the computer. While NT Workstation generally succeeds at installation when DOS is present, there are some gotchas and warnings you should know about, especially when you install with OS/2, Windows 95, and older versions of Windows. Keep in mind that NT Workstation can reliably dual-boot with only one other operating system.

▶ **See** "Changing Boot Options from Control Panel," **p. 412**

Installing with OS/2

If NT Workstation will be installed on a computer that was running OS/2 and DOS, the operating system that was last booted before installation of NT Workstation will be installed as the alternate operating system with Windows NT.

If you have used Boot Manager on the PC where NT Workstation will be installed, there are a few steps you need to take to re-enable it after installation of Windows NT is complete. During installation of Windows NT, the setup program detects the presence of Boot Manager. If Boot Manager is found, you are informed that it will be disabled following completion of installation. To re-enable Boot Manager, start the Disk Administrator tool found in the Administrative Tools program group. Select the Boot Manager partition, and then choose Partition, Mark Active. When you restart your computer, you should have access to Boot Manager.

Installing Windows NT to Dual-Boot with Windows 95

You can install NT Workstation on a system running Windows 95 so that Windows NT dual-boots with Windows 95. Although you probably will have to install into Windows NT most of the applications you've installed in Windows 95, this setup gives you the flexibility to run both powerful operating systems, taking advantage of the best abilities of both.

During installation of Windows NT (from Windows 95, naturally), you must use the **/W** option with the **WINNT** utility, which instructs the installation program to skip the CPU detection phase, as well as the automatic system restart process that occurs at the end of installation. Detailed steps for installing Windows NT to dual-boot with Windows 95 are presented later in this appendix in the section "Running the Installation."

Installing over a Previous Version of Windows 3.x

During the NT Workstation installation process, you can choose whether to install NT Workstation over an existing Windows 3.1 or Windows for Work-groups system. This means that NT Workstation and your existing version of Windows would share the same directory and a number of files. Doing so makes sense, because applications installed into your old version of Windows should run relatively problem-free under Windows NT.

The choice to install over an existing Windows installation also makes sense be-cause the working environment you have in place with the existing version of Win-dows—such as the organization of program groups and the icons in them—can be migrated to your Windows NT configuration. This means you would not have to re-create in NT Workstation the work environment you used in Windows 3.1.

Here is a list of some of the settings that are migrated to your NT Workstation setup from your existing Windows configuration when you install in the same directory as an older version of Windows:

- Program groups and their icons that don't already exist in NT Workstation
- INI file settings for applications you ran in Windows
- Associations set up in File Manager
- Most Control Panel settings

The steps for installing Windows NT over a Windows 3.x installation are presented later in this appendix in the section "Running the Installation."

Installing Windows NT to Dual-Boot with Windows 3.x

You can install Windows NT to dual-boot with an existing version of Windows 3.1 or Windows for Workgroups. You do this by installing Windows NT in a directory different from the one housing your existing Windows 3.x configuration. If you install Windows NT in a different directory, you probably will have to reinstall into Windows NT all the applications you ran with Windows that you want to run in NT. The steps for installing Windows NT to dual-boot with Windows 3.x are presented later in this appendix in the section "Running the Installation."

Installing with an Existing Version of Windows NT

You can upgrade your current Windows NT installation with version 4.0, or you can install the new version of Windows NT to dual-boot with your existing version. In either case, start Windows NT as you normally do, and then launch the installation of the new version from the command prompt. Details of the installation process are covered later in this appendix in the section "Running the Installation."

When you install a new version of Windows NT without upgrading an existing version, you probably will have to reinstall most, if not all, of your applications into your new NT system. In most cases, the installation of a new Windows NT or Windows 95 application is specific to the operating system to which it was installed, so you will be unable to simply point to an already installed application in order to run it.

Running the Installation

By this time, you've learned the information you need to collect about your computer before installing Windows NT; you've learned how to set up file systems on your computer; and you've learned issues about running other operating systems with Windows NT. Now, it's time to look at the installation. Regarding that process, there still are a few more introductory topics to cover. Immediately afterwards, we'll walk through a Windows NT Workstation installation:

■ Use of the WINNT/WINNT32 utilities.

■ Whether you want to create a set of installation boot disks.

■ Whether you are installing over a network.

■ If you are installing Windows NT on a RISC-based system.

Understanding the WINNT/WINNT32 Utilities

WINNT.EXE manages a substantial portion of the installation process, especially the early components. The program has a 32-bit counterpart, WINNT32.EXE, which is used to launch Windows NT installations from existing Windows NT installation. The WINNT basically has two responsibilities:

1. Copy the files that the installation program needs either to your hard disk or to floppy disks that you provide.

2. Launch the installation program.

When you are ready to start installation, you launch the WINNT/WINNT32 utility from the command line. For example, from the command line, you would enter **WINNT32** and press Enter. A number of command line options can help you modify how WINNT behaves. They are explained in table A.2. A detailed explanation for installation follows later in this appendix, and describes exactly when to start WINNT/WINNT32 and how to use it.

Table A.2   WINNT/WINNT32 Command Line Options

Item	Requirement
/s:*sourcepath*	Specifies where the source installation files for Windows are located, where *sourcepath* is a drive and directory location.
/i:*inf_file*	Specifies a custom installation information file, where *inf_file* is the name of the file. Using a custom setup information file lets you customize aspects of the installation, such as not installing certain components, or running unattended, prompt-less installations.
/t:*drive_letter*	Specifies what drive the installation program should use for storing temporary files.
/x	Specifies that the installation program should not attempt to create bootable installation floppy disks.
/b	Skips creation of the bootable installation floppy disks. Instead, the installation setup files are loaded onto your hard disk.
/o	Creates only bootable installation floppy disks. Installation halts after completion of the disks.

Understanding Whether to Create Floppy Disks

During installation, you'll have to decide whether you want Windows NT to create a set of bootable floppy disks to assist with installation. These disks contain the files that the installation program needs before it can run itself from files it installs. If you have spare room on your hard disk (besides the minimum amount required to install Windows NT), approximately 100 MB, you probably can skip the step of creating bootable floppy disks. In this case, the WINNT/WINNT32 program copies the files it needs to your hard disk from either the CD or the network source.

N O T E   Starting with version 4.0, Windows NT can only be installed from the CD. You must have a CD-ROM drive on your system, or installation must be run from a network source where the installation files are stored.

Installing from a Network

In a networked environment, it's likely that a system administrator has prepared a network-accessible location where NT Workstation installation files are loaded. It's convenient for a group of users to install NT Workstation from one location, and it eliminates the need to supply all users with disks. In typical software licensing schemes, only one or a few actual copies of the software are provided to an organization that purchases many licenses. A system such as the one described in this section is used to manage the installation of the software for many users.

The location on the network from which multiple users can install NT Workstation is known as a *sharepoint*. The network administrator creates the sharepoint and loads the NT Workstation installation files there. The steps for installing NT Workstation from a sharepoint are particularly different from the process used to install it from a CD-ROM or disk, so they are provided here.

To install NT Workstation from a sharepoint, follow these steps:

1. Find out from your network administrator where the sharepoint is for the NT Workstation installation. You should be provided with a complete network path, such as SRV1\VOL9:NT351\INSTALL.

2. Connect to the sharepoint. If you are running DOS, connect using your regular network connectivity services. If you are installing onto Windows NT (perhaps upgrading to a new version), connect to the sharepoint using File Manager.

CAUTION

It is possible that the steps for installing NT Workstation from a network sharepoint are very different for your organization than those provided here. Your network administrator has the ability to automate the installation of NT Workstation from a network directory. It is possible that many of the prompts that you normally would see and answer are handled automatically and might not appear on your screen. It is also possible that the entire installation could be run automatically, so you would have nothing to do. Be sure you check with your system administrator before attempting a network installation, especially if you come across NT files on a network.

Special Instructions for RISC-Based Installation

Installation of NT Workstation on a RISC-based system, such as the MIPS R4000 or Dec Alpha AXP, requires some special instruction.

To install NT Workstation on a RISC machine, follow these steps:

1. Ensure that the system partition on the machine is formatted as FAT and is at least 2M in size.

2. Load the NT Workstation CD-ROM into the machine.

3. Restart the computer.

4. Choose Run A Program from the menu. This step could vary based on the machine you are using.

5. At the prompt, type **cd:***platform directory***\\setupldr** and then press Enter. *Platform directory* is the name of the directory on the CD-ROM where NT's files are stored for the platform you're working on.

Walking Through an Installation

Here is the process you'll follow when you install Windows NT on your computer. Based on choices you make during installation, and based on the existing configuration of your computer, your steps might not match exactly the following ones. You'll find the order of events and decisions you'll be forced to make, however, to be very similar.

1. Installation of NT Workstation begins by inserting the installation CD-ROM into the CD drive, or by attaching to the network sharepoint, as described earlier in the "Installing from the Network" section.

2. From the command prompt of your existing operating system, change to the drive and directory where the installation files for Windows NT are located. For Windows NT users, open a command prompt window from Main program group. For Windows 95 users, open the Start menu and then choose Programs, MS-DOS Prompt.

   For example, if you are installing onto a Pentium-based system where the install CD is in the E: drive, set the drive and directory to **E:\\I386**. The documentation supplied with Windows NT can tell you the exact directory name.

3. Using table A.3 as a guide, enter the appropriate **WINNT** command at the prompt and then press Enter. Add the **/B** parameter following the command shown in the table to skip creating the floppy disk.

Table A.3 WINNT Commands for Operating Systems	
O/S	**Command**
Windows NT	WINNT32
DOS, Windows 3.x, Windows for Workgroups	WINNT
Windows 95	WINNT /W

4. The installation program will prompt you for the location of the Windows NT installation files. The path shown on the screen should match the location from which you started the WINNT program.

5. If you skipped the step to create bootable floppy disks, Windows NT will copy installation files to your hard drive and then ask you to press Enter to reboot your system. Do so, and then go to step 6.

6. Label three formatted floppy disks **Setup Boot Disk**, **Setup Disk 2**, and **Setup Disk 3**. Insert the disks as prompted in reverse-numerical order, Setup Disk 3 first and Setup Boot Disk last. After the installation program has copied information onto the Setup Boot Disk, you are prompted to restart your computer. Leave the Setup Boot Disk in the floppy drive; the installation program needs your system to boot from that disk in order to continue. Insert the disks as prompted.

N O T E There have been reports to Microsoft's technical support areas that operating systems like Windows 95 may not restart properly during a Windows NT installation when the floppy disk creation step is skipped. If your system fails to restart, you may want to restart the installation but create the floppy disks. Then, follow the instructions to manually reboot using the bootable floppy disk you created. ▪

7. After your system restarts and the installation program examines your hardware, Windows NT now examines your system for mass storage devices. You are warned that the system may freeze during this process, and you are invited to specify the devices yourself. It's probably worth the risk of your

system halting than having to manually specify mass storage devices, so let the installation program search for devices.

8. Next, you're presented with a list of existing operating systems on your computer. You are invited to install Windows NT to a new directory or to overwrite one of the existing operating systems. Keep in mind that you may only run one other non-Windows NT operating system on your computer besides Windows NT.

9. Following your choice of operating systems, you are prompted to manage the existing disk partitions on your computer. If you completed your homework and read the first section in this appendix, you should be prepared to answer the prompts. If not, read the section "Disk Partition and File System Requirements" to understand the impact of your file system choice.

10. Next, Windows NT copies files to your system in the directory you specified. Following the file copy, the graphical portion of the installation begins. You will be prompted for the following information:

   • The mode of installation you want top use: Typical, Custom, Compact, or Portable. Review these options as they are described on the screen to determine what type of installation you want. It's usually favorable to choose Custom so you can evaluate each option installed on the system.

   • A name for your computer. This name will identify your computer on the network to other computers and other users. If your computer will not run on a network, keep in mind that the name you give will appear in many places in the system, so be sure the name is one you can live with.

   • The password for the Administrator account on the system, which is the account with the greatest rights in the system. The Administrator account creates other accounts for other users of the system (which may in turn create other accounts).

 If you cannot think of an appropriate password immediately, supply *administrator*. Be sure to change the password as soon as you can. Anyone who logs onto Windows NT with the Administrator account has full control over the system and can possibly unknowingly cause great damage.

- Optional components you may want to install, such as Microsoft Exchange, which is Windows NT external messaging system.

- Network information. If you are unclear about any of the answers to prompts that appear, check with a system administrator in your organization.

11. The last steps in installation lead you through setup of the regional components of your configuration, such as local time, and of your display. Upon completion of these, you are asked to reboot your system, and installation is complete.

▶ **See** "Working with Accounts," **p. 380**

Customizing NT Workstation Setup

If you are a system administrator in an organization where a number of users will be installing NT Workstation, a number of tools and strategies can be used to help automate and customize the installation of NT Workstation.

There are three components you can use to help administer the installation of NT Workstation:

- Customize the installation process
- Create an unattended installation system
- Use a utility that copies a model NT system to a networked distribution point and then downloads the workstation system to target computers

Detailed instructions for customizing the installation process and for using the utility that assists in the NT's distribution is available in the Windows NT Resource Kit. The Resource kit is a separate set of manuals and tools that is developed and distributed by Microsoft's publishing arm, Microsoft Press. The process for customizing installation usually means modifying a number of configuration files that Windows NT uses during installation.

The following list includes some aspects of installation that you can customize:

- Which files from a previous version of Windows NT should be deleted
- Which files from a previous version of Windows NT should be saved

- Which files from an existing version of Windows 3.1 or Windows for Workgroups should be used in the Windows NT system
- The default name for the directory to which Windows NT will be installed
- The names of the subdirectories of the main Windows NT directory
- The minimum free disk space allowed to install Windows NT
- The content of program groups created during installation
- Exclusion of certain files during installation
- Exclusion of certain subsystems during installation, such as those that support OS/2, POSIX, Windows, and DOS applications

   ▶ **See** "Online Information Sources," **p. 1048**

Maintaining Windows NT with Service Packs

by Paul Sanna

Microsoft uses service packs to maintain Windows NT Workstation (and Windows NT Server). A *service pack* is an update to one or more NT Workstation files for the purpose of fixing a problem in the software. The service pack usually includes a program that helps automate the application of the service pack. As problems are reported to Microsoft, a decision is made as to whether and when to fix these bugs. When enough bug fixes have collected in the queue, Microsoft creates and releases a service pack.

Service packs are cumulative. This means that a service pack will always include fixes made in previous versions of service packs. This way, you only need to apply the current service pack to get all of the fixes made to the system.

Microsoft does not automatically inform all Windows NT users when a service pack is available. If you track computer industry information sources on a regular basis, such as those described in Appendix C, "Where to Get More Information," you will find out when a service pack is available.

▶ **See** "Getting Drivers and Service Packs," **p. 1048**

The bugs that a service pack addresses are usually listed in the README.TXT file that is distributed with the service pack. Microsoft identifies bugs to users via a seven-character alphanumeric identification number (for example, Q130092). This number is included in the Knowledge Base article that describes the bug. Knowledge Base is a database maintained by Microsoft that tracks known issues—bugs or otherwise—related to its software products. Naturally, there is a Knowledge Base devoted to Windows NT. You can search Knowledge Base free-of-charge (not including connect charges) using most of the online services where Microsoft is present. Examples of some of these services include CompuServe and the Microsoft Network. In addition, the Knowledge Base comes as part of most of Microsoft's subscription information and support services, such as Technet and the Microsoft Developer Network.

Below is an excerpt from the README.TXT file that accompanied Service Pack 1 for NT 3.51. Besides providing other information, the file also listed bugs addressed in the service pack:

```
Q130932: Desktop Remains Active At Logoff
Q130979: User Environment Variables Set Before Default Home Directory
Q131073: Datagram Sends Fail if Route is Not in IPX Cache
Q131241: FTPSVC Orphans Connections, Uses Up Virtual Memory
Q131428: DHCPADMN Reports Error 14 After You Select Local Machine
Q131689: Postscript Jobs Do Not Print Correctly Over SFM and
         AppleTalk
Q132085: Applications Hang When Opening Files when CSNW is Installed
Q132394: Streaming Mode NPMCA.SYS NIC Sleeps on Transmit.
Q132511: Windows NT 3.51 Hangs on Shutdown With Some S3 Based Video
         Cards
Q132722: Server Instability After Reboot Caused by NDIS Driver
         Problem
Q132896: FTP Client Scripts Terminate Without Completing
Q132903: Err Msg Using NetBIOS over TCP/IP (NETBT.SYS): STOP
         0x0000000A
Q133112: NetWkstaSetUid2 API Returns Access Denied ■
```

Acquiring a Windows NT Service Pack

As you know, a service pack will not magically appear in your mailbox. You must acquire a service pack from any one of a number of sources. A description of three places where you can acquire service packs follows. Appendix C covers the different information sources available for Windows NT, including more details on the sources described in this section. In each case, follow the instructions to either download or copy the service pack appropriate to your platform, Intel x86, MIPS, Alpha, or PowerPC.

Part

VIII

App

B

Microsoft Connection on CompuServe

Microsoft's presence on CompuServe includes a forum where you can download Windows NT service packs. To access the forum, type **GO WINNTDL** from any CompuServe prompt.

Microsoft on the Internet

Microsoft has a home page on the Internet that provides links to many pages that have tons of information about Microsoft products and technologies. You can download service packs from Microsoft's Web site.

ON THE WEB

Microsoft's home page on the Internet is at

http://www.microsoft.com

In addition, Microsoft maintains an FTP server for access over the Internet. The server contains patches, drivers, technical documents, NT service packs, and more. Microsoft's server is at **ftp.microsoft.com**. The service packs for NT Workstation can be found in the folder BUSSYS/WINNT/WINNT-PUBLIC/FIXES/USA.

Microsoft Developer Network

The Microsoft Developer Network is a subscription service that provides a quarterly updated CD, packed with information for Windows developers and other Windows professionals. The CD contains technical articles, specifications, full-text books, sample code, conference proceedings, and more. Of the three Levels available, Levels 2 and 3 provide operating systems, including service packs.

▶ **See** "Where to Get More Information," **p. 1047**

Applying a Windows NT Service Pack

The steps for applying a Windows NT service pack depend on the format of the service pack you acquired. The format of the service pack determines both how the service pack was packaged for you to download, and the methods used to apply the pack. It is up to you to determine and then specify which format service pack you need.

One File Service Pack

In the one file format, the service pack is contained in one large, self-extracting file. A *self-extracting file* is actually one or more files compressed into a single file. This single file has a typical executable extension of EXE like other files that you run or execute. When you run the service pack file, however, all of the files compressed into it are extracted into the directory where you ran the file. These files comprise the service pack.

Of the files extracted, you should look for the README.TXT file. This file describes the contents of the service pack. The README.TXT file also tells you what the next step is to apply the service pack. Typically, one of the extracted files is called UPDATE.EXE. This is the file that, when run, installs all of the patches in the service pack to the proper place in your NT Workstation.

TIP This format for service packs is good if you apply the service pack to the same machine where you acquired the service pack. The file will be very large, and it's unlikely it will fit on a floppy disk.

Disk Distribution of Service Pack

Service packs also are available in formats that allow them to be distributed on floppy disk. With this method, you copy or download a set of files rather than just one file. All except for one of the files—README.TXT—will be copied to a single disk. The README.TXT contains the instructions for moving the files to the floppies. A batch file probably is included with the set of files to automate that process. Once the service pack is dispersed among the disks, you run a specific file from the first disk to begin the application of the service pack. The README.TXT file tells you which disk and which file the service pack installation is launched from.

 This format for service packs is appropriate if you apply the service pack to a machine without the capability to acquire the service pack from an online service or a CD. This method also would be appropriate to store the service pack for safe-keeping or for travel.

Where to Get More Information

by Paul Sanna

Online information

Learn about the best places to go online to find out information about Windows NT.

Off-the-shelf information

Find out what resources are available to help you through the rough spots.

The explosive growth of the PC software business has fueled growth in another area: the amount and availability of information about software products. Online sources, such as CompuServe and the World Wide Web are saturated with forums, home pages, lists of related links, and so on, devoted to software. Bookstores usually stock multiple titles covering almost any mainstream software product. Also, with the CD-ROM player as a standard component of any new PC configuration, many users can easily browse the equivalent of reams of printed information on a CD.

Thankfully, this image of a cornucopia of information certainly can be applied to Windows NT Workstation. The shipped documentation adequately covers the basics, but the problems and questions you'll have with NT Workstation most times will extend past the ordinary. It's critical to know where to go for more information. This appendix provides you with information sources about Windows NT Workstation. Just think—with all this information, you may be able to write a book about Windows NT! ▪

Getting Drivers and Service Packs

In addition to getting information, it's likely that you will need to acquire a driver for Windows NT or a service pack. Drivers help Windows NT (and other systems) work with software and hardware. New hardware devices often require drivers to run with NT Workstation, and usually these drivers are available from the information sources described in this appendix. Also, new versions of drivers contain bug fixes and enhancements, so it's important to update your system with these new versions.

Service packs contain updates to Windows NT. The same service pack addresses issues in both the Workstation and Server versions of Windows NT. Released periodically by Microsoft, these packs contain bug fixes and enhancements for NT. Service packs also are available from some of the information sources covered in this appendix.

▶ **See** "Maintaining Windows NT with Service Packs," **p. 1041**

Online Information Sources

Your access to information about Windows NT increases exponentially if you own and use a modem. A number of online services exist that provide a huge amount of technical and practical information about Windows NT. These services, such as CompuServe and The Microsoft Network, give you the capability to do the following:

- Review and download technical articles, reviews, and marketing information about NT Workstation
- Chat online with other NT professionals
- Report problems and leave messages for Microsoft support personnel
- Download drivers, service packs, and utilities

CompuServe

The Microsoft Connection on CompuServe gives you access to most of the services you'll need to get help for NT Workstation (see fig. C.1). You can participate in the NT forum, where you can correspond online with other NT users and with NT support professionals. In addition, you can download bug fixes, service packs, drivers, shareware utilities, and other software. A software library with an associated file finder makes it easy to track down the file you need.

FIG. C.1
The Microsoft Connection on CompuServe is an excellent source for Windows NT Workstation information.

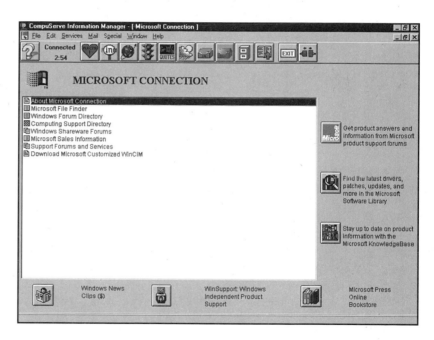

Part
VIII
App
C

If you don't use CompuServe now, you can get connected very easily. You can find CompuServe sign-up kits advertised in almost any computer magazine. If you can't locate CompuServe software kits, you can call CompuServe at 800-848-8199.

To access the Microsoft Connection on CompuServe, type **GO MICROSOFT** at any CompuServe prompt. To access the Windows NT forum directly, type **GO WINNT** at any CompuServe prompt.

The Internet

For those with Internet access, Microsoft's site on the World Wide Web is a good source of information on NT Workstation. This site happens to be one of the only sources of information about NT Workstation that isn't obfuscated with information about NT Server, too. The NT Workstation Web page includes links to both general product information and technical data (see fig. C.2). You can find a product overview of NT Workstation, a comparison of Windows NT to other operating systems, technical briefs, and pages where you can download information.

FIG. C.2

Microsoft provides NT information on the NT Workstation page at Microsoft's World Wide Web site.

ON THE WEB

Microsoft's NT Workstation home page on the Internet is at

http://www.microsoft.com/ntworkstation/

ON THE WEB

Microsoft's home page on the Internet is at

http://www.microsoft.com

Microsoft also maintains an FTP server where you can download patches, service packs, utilities, and documents. You cannot get support from this location, only items to download. Microsoft's FTP server is at **ftp.microsoft.com**.

ON THE WEB

In addition to Microsoft's Web site, there are hundreds of other Web sites devoted to Windows NT. Here is a list of some of my favorites:

> **www.infotech.kumc.edu/winnt** (includes links to numerous Windows NT news groups)
>
> **www.shareware.com/top/MS-WindowsNT-table.html** (most popular Windows NT shareware downloads)
>
> **www.indirect.com/www/ceridgac/ntsite.html** (large index of Windows sites on the Web)

Part VIII

App C

Microsoft Download Service

You can download drivers and patches directly from Microsoft without accessing a particular online service. You can connect to the Microsoft Download service with any communications software. Set your modem to no parity; 8 data bits; 1 stop bit; and dial (206) 936-6735.

Other Online Sources

There are a number of other online services that also can provide you with answers about NT Workstation. They include The Microsoft Network (available with Windows 95), America Online, and Prodigy.

Off-the-Shelf Information

If you cannot use online information services, or if you want to supplement those services with information that is more quickly accessible, then you may be interested in printed or software-based resources. The information services covered in this section includes books, periodicals, and software, such as CD subscription services.

Resource Kits

Microsoft develops and sells the Windows NT Resource Kit. Similar resource kits are also available for Windows 95, Windows 3.1, and Windows for Workgroups. Resource kits pick up where the shipped documentation leaves off. A *resource kit* provides detailed, technical information about many areas of the product it covers. In the case of the Windows NT Resource Kit, you can find troubleshooting information, architectural discussions, network connectivity issues explored, hardware compatibility information, performance monitoring and tuning instruction, and more. Because resource kits tend to focus more on tasks than technology, it's usually very easy to find the information you're looking for. Lastly, most resource kits include software, utilities, and implementation and planning tools.

Developer Network and Technet

Microsoft offers subscriptions to two excellent information services. One is geared toward software developers, while the other is geared toward support and information service professionals.

Developer Network   A Microsoft Developer Network subscription entitles you to quarterly updates in CD format of the Development Library, a newsletter, discounts on Microsoft books, and more. The CD is the most valuable part of the subscription. It includes an update to Knowledge Base (a database of technical articles and NT problem reports), full-text of a number of magazines and books about Windows software development, specifications on Windows and Microsoft technologies (for example, OLE or Telephony), technical articles, and more.

N O T E   You can subscribe to any one of three different levels of the Developer Network. A Level 1 subscriber receives the items described previously. A Level 2 subscriber also receives copies of every Windows operating system (in every available language), Windows 3.11, Windows for Workgroups, Windows NT, and Windows 95, as well as software development kits, device driver kits, and resource kits. Level 3 subscribers also receive Microsoft Backoffice products, including NT Server, SQL Server, Mail/Exchange server, SNA Server, and Systems Management Server. ∎

TechnetMicrosoft   Technet also is a subscription service. You receive 12 double-CD deliveries per year. Each month, one CD contains Knowledge Base, case studies of enterprise solutions using Microsoft products and technologies, technical articles, and more. The other CD contains the latest bug fix patches and drivers for all Microsoft Windows products, including Windows 95, Windows NT, and Windows 3.1. The Technet subscription also includes a newsletter and discount.

Read Readme!

How many of the README files already on your system have you actually read? Whenever you acquire a new piece of software, especially NT Workstation, be sure to read the README file that is shipped with the software. These files are packed with information. A good README file includes warnings about installing the software, hardware compatibility issues, and facts that are either missing or wrong in the shipped documentation.

Read Periodicals

Some of the best information about Windows NT appears in periodicals. These sources are the best place to find breaking NT Workstation news, including Microsoft's plans for the future of Windows NT. A list of the better periodicals probably includes *Information Week* (weekly), *PC Week*, *PC Magazine*, *Windows NT Magazine*, *Computerworld*, *Windows*, and *LAN Times*.❖

Part
VIII

App
C

A Review of the Windows NT GUI

by Paul Sanna

The Windows NT interface

Learn about the graphical details of Windows NT and how to use Windows NT to its fullest.

Using the right tools

Learn how the mouse, control panels, dialog boxes, and menus make it easy to use Windows NT.

Windows NT version 4.0 features the user interface introduced with Windows 95 as perhaps the most prominent aspect of the new release. Though the interface still features windows, icons, and loads of other graphical elements, there is much that is different. There is a new Context menu available by right-clicking any object, and a new hierarchical view for examining the content of your computer. This appendix is designed to introduce you to the new user interface, but it is not intended solely for prior users of Windows. If you've never used Windows, Windows 95, or Windows NT, you'll learn everything you need to know about Microsoft's brand of user interfaces.

This appendix is designed to build upon itself. Concepts and techniques presented later in the appendix are dependent on your understanding concepts and techniques presented earlier. Even so, for some computer users, you may not have to read the entire appendix to be able understand and work with what you see on the Windows NT screen. Table D.1 can help you determine what to read in this appendix. ■

Table D.1 How to Use this Appendix

If You are this Type of User	Read this
You've never used a graphical interface before	Entire appendix
You've used graphical systems before, such as IBM OS/2, or even the DOS shell that became available with version 4.0 of DOS	The sections "Working with Menus," "Working with Windows," and "Working with Windows NT Controls"
You're an experienced Windows 3.x or Windows NT 3.5 user	The sections "Working with Menus" and "Working with Windows NT Controls"
You're an experienced Windows 95 User	Skip this appendix

Presenting the Windows NT Interface

The Windows NT interface is a *graphical user interface* (*GUI*), which means that colorful graphics are used to help you function and perform tasks (see fig. D.1). For example, to start a process such as printing, you might click a button on the screen that looks like a sheet of paper with writing or print on it; or if you need to see more of the letter you are writing, you simply stretch open the area of the screen in which you are writing the letter.

As the user, you play an active role in managing the Windows interface. Just as when you work at your desk, in Windows you can keep open any number of documents at one time. You can move documents you want to focus on to the top of the pile and close folders you are no longer working with. Certainly, the number of tasks you can perform at one time is constrained by how powerful your system is, but the Windows interface makes it easier to multitask.

FIG. D.1

The Windows interface is known as a graphical user interface because of the generous use of pictures, colors, and iconic representations of ideas, concepts, tools, and tasks.

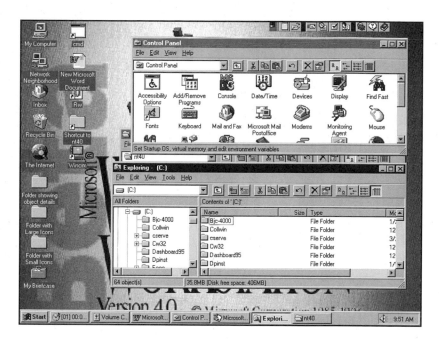

Elements of the Windows NT Interface

The Windows interface is made up of seven major elements. (An experienced Windows user might argue for more or less), but for the sake of this appendix, let's just agree on seven. Figure D.2 shows those main elements, and table D.2 explains their functions.

This section of the appendix is designed to help you become familiar with the important items you see on the screen. In the following sections, you learn more about each of those elements, including how to open and resize windows, use the mouse, move the focus from one object to another, and more.

Part
VIII

App
D

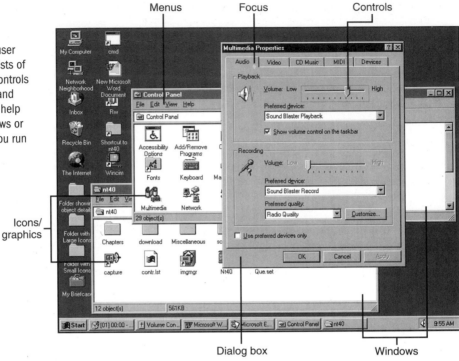

FIG. D.2
The Windows user interface consists of a number of controls that you view and manipulate to help you run Windows or applications you run in Windows.

Menus   Focus   Controls

Icons/graphics

Dialog box   Windows

Table D.2   Major Elements of the Windows NT User Interface

Element	Description
Windows	The most common and most important element of the Windows NT user interface. Every application, tool, and game you run in Windows NT appears in a window. You can open, close, and move windows; change their size; and open windows within other windows. Windows can contain menus, controls such as buttons and list boxes, and other windows.
Dialog box	A type of window. Dialog boxes are used when information is required by Windows NT or a Windows NT application before continuing. Like windows, dialog boxes also can contain controls and sometimes menus.

Element	Description
Controls	The elements in windows that you use to view and manipulate objects on the screen.
Menus	Used to select commands in Windows NT.
Icons/graphics	Represent applications, documents, status of processes, and more.
Focus	Also known as the *selection*; indicates what item on the screen is affected when you type on the keyboard. You need to move the focus on the screen to the control you want to work with.
Mouse pointer	Indicates what object on the screen is affected when you press a button on the mouse.

Understanding the MDI Concept

The windows interface makes use of a concept known as *multiple document interface* (*MDI*). This means that a single application, like Microsoft Excel for Windows 95, can have open multiple windows at once, each housing a different document. These *document windows* all exist within the general Excel *application window* (see fig. D.3). Don't confuse the name *document window* with the type of information contained in the window; even though the individual files you use in Excel are spreadsheets, the windows are still called document windows. The Excel window is known as the *parent window*, and spreadsheet documents open in Excel are known as *child windows*. This concept is used by most Windows applications in which the user creates documents or files.

Part
VIII

App
D

FIG. D.3
Microsoft Excel for
Windows uses the
MDI concept.

Parent window

Child windows

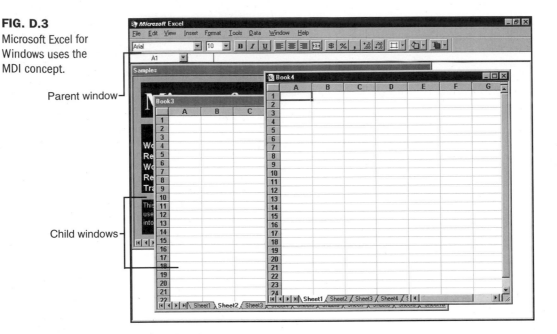

Using the Mouse

Before discussing how to recognize and use elements of the Windows interface, you should understand how to use the tools you have available to work in the interface.

The Windows NT interface makes extensive use of a pointing device. A *pointing device* helps you specify the objects on the screen that you want to work with and perform tasks, such as pressing buttons, selecting text, and more. In most cases, the pointing device used with your computer is a mouse. Other pointing devices are available, such as a drawing tablet, but this appendix (and this book, in general) assumes that your pointing device is a mouse.

NOTE This section presents information about how the mouse works with Windows NT. If you have never used a mouse before, you may want to review the documentation provided with your mouse. Take a moment now to review how the mouse works before proceeding in the appendix. ■

So, what do you do with a mouse in Windows NT? There are six basic tasks you perform with a mouse:

- *Point.* As you move your mouse on the surface of your desk, you should notice a graphic moving on the screen in concert with the movement of the mouse. The picture on your screen is the *mouse pointer*, and the mouse pointer probably is in the shape of an arrow (see fig. D.4). When you move the mouse pointer over a particular object on the screen that you want to work with, you *point* to that object.

FIG. D.4
The mouse pointer usually appears in the shape of an arrowhead.

Mouse pointer —

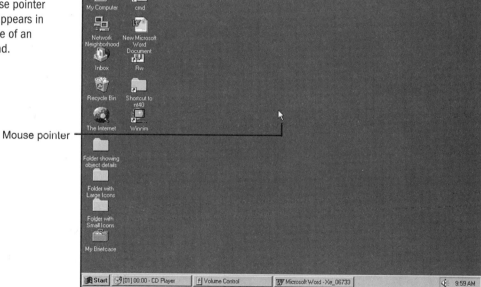

Part
VIII

App
D

- *Click.* Your mouse will have two and perhaps more buttons. These buttons are used to tell Windows that you want to perform some action. Windows applications sit around and wait for the user to do something; clicking the mouse button is one of the events they wait for. To *click*, quickly press down on the primary mouse button and release with your finger.

The vast majority of mice are configured out of the box with the leftmost button as the primary button. If you prefer that the rightmost button be the primary button, such as if you are left-handed, you can swap functionality of the two buttons directly in Windows NT. To do so, open the Control Panel, click once on the Mouse icon, and press Enter. The Buttons property sheet should be active. In the Button configuration frame, you'll see a picture of a mouse, as well as two round buttons, one that says Right-Handed and the other that says Left-Handed. You also see text that describes what operations are assigned to which mouse buttons. Of the two buttons, the one with the center filled in indicates which mouse button—left or right—is the primary button. To change the right- and left-button configuration, click the appropriate one.

- *Point-and-click.* The Windows interface is largely based on your ability to point at something on the screen and then click it. The term *point-and-click* refers to the first two skills discussed in this section. To point and click, you move the mouse pointer over the appropriate object on the screen (point) and then click the primary mouse button.

- *Double-click.* Some operations in Windows NT require you to do more than just point to an object and then click. To launch most applications in Windows, you must *double-click* some object on the screen. To double-click, press down quickly on the primary button on your mouse twice—*click click*! If you don't repeat the click quickly enough, Windows interprets your actions as two clicks, rather than a double-click.

- *Click-and-drag.* There will be many instances in Windows NT when you will want to work with a specific piece of text—such as to underline or delete it— or other types of information, such as a group of cells in a spreadsheet or table. To specify the data you want to work with, you must *highlight* (select) it. When you use the mouse to highlight information in Windows, you use the *click-and-drag* operation. To click-and-drag, click once just before the first element you want to select and hold down the primary button. Move the mouse over the rest of the element you want to specify; notice that the element is highlighted (displayed in reverse colors). When you have high-lighted your entire selection, release the mouse button. The selected text or item stays highlighted.

■ *Drag-and-drop*. There are many instances in Windows NT when you may want to move an object from one position to another. The mouse is typically used to complete this operation, and this operation is known as *drag-and-drop*. To drag and drop, point to an object on the screen, and press and hold down the primary mouse button. Next, while still holding down the button, you move the mouse pointer to point to the new location. Notice on the screen how the object you clicked moves with the mouse pointer. Usually with most applications, the mouse pointer changes to indicate that something is being dragged. When you arrive at the new location, release the mouse button.

N O T E In some applications, you may be forced to execute a click-and-drag before a drag-and-drop operation. An example of this might be one in which you select a range of items in a list box and then drag the list to another location. ■

■ *Right-click*. The new Windows NT user interface takes great advantage of the secondary mouse button. This means that you use the left mouse button for one function and the right mouse button for another. Windows NT requires you to *right-click* to complete a number of operations, such as to display an object's Context menu. This means that you should click using the secondary mouse button.

Part
VIII

App
D

Using the Keyboard

The keyboard also plays a prominent role in the Windows NT interface. Besides being the tool used to enter characters into the computer, Windows NT uses the keyboard for many of the same functions as the mouse. You can move to most controls in windows and dialog boxes using the keyboard, as well as access the menu. In this section, you learn how to use the keyboard to navigate through the Windows NT interface.

Understanding Focus

The key to using the keyboard to move through Windows NT is understanding *focus*. In any windowed application, including Windows NT applications, there will be some visual indication as to which item has been selected. This is also known as *selection*, or *having focus* (or having *the* focus). Depending on the type of controls that appear on the screen, the selection or focus appears differently. In a moment, you see how different controls appear if they are selected. Right now it's important to know what it means to have selection:

> *When an object has focus, any keyboard input affects that object.*

For example, if an icon in a folder has the focus and you press Delete, that icon is deleted. If a check box in a window has the focus and you press the spacebar, an X appears in, or disappears from, the check box.

Recognizing Focus

Different controls indicate they are selected or have the focus in different ways. As you work with Windows NT and Windows NT applications, you'll begin to recognize which object on the screen is selected. Some examples of controls with the focus are provided in this section.

Figure D.5 shows a folder. You can tell the icon for the new Microsoft Word document has the focus because the caption under the icon is highlighted.

FIG. D.5

You can tell the Microsoft Word icon has the focus.

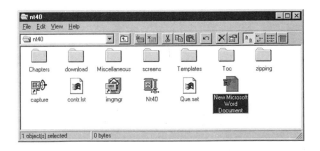

Figure D.6 shows the Date/Time dialog box, which can be accessed from the Control Panel folder. You can tell the Automatically adjust clock for daylight saving changes check box has the focus because of the dotted line that surrounds the text.

You can also look at the <u>A</u>utomatically adjust clock for <u>d</u>aylight saving changes check box in figure D.6 to understand a subtle difference having to do with focus. Controls like a check box can be *selected*, meaning that they are checked or turned on. A check box being selected means that it can show an X in its box, but not necessarily have the focus. You can apply the same concepts to radio buttons, which are covered later in this appendix.

FIG. D.6
When a check box has the focus, such as the Daylight Saving Time check box, a dotted line appears around the control.

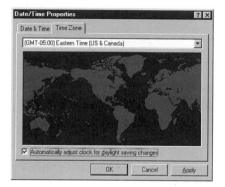

Figure D.7 also shows the Date/Time dialog box. You can tell the Time <u>Z</u>one drop-down list has the focus because the text is highlighted. Compare figure D.6 to D.7 to see how different types of controls in the same dialog box indicate they are selected differently.

FIG. D.7
The Time Zone drop-down list currently is selected.

Part
VIII

App
D

Moving the Focus

There are two methods for using the keyboard to move the focus from one control to another:

- Press Tab until the desired control has the focus
- Press Alt+*accelerator key*

Accelerator Keys   Most controls that appear on the screen have a label. The label usually gives some indication as to the use of the control. You probably also will notice that one character on most labels you see in Windows NT is underscored. For example, in figure D.8, notice that many of the controls in the dialog box have one underscored character in their labels.

FIG. D.8

Most controls have a label that includes an accelerator key.

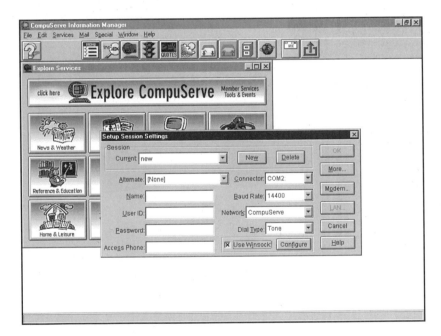

The underscore in any label for a control indicates the accelerator key for the control. By pressing Alt+*accelerator key*, focus moves directly to the control associated with the label. For controls that have their own caption instead of labels, such as a button, the accelerator keys work the same way. The accelerator key is also known as a *hot key*.

Working with Menus

Menus appear in windows and sometimes in dialog boxes in the Windows NT interface. The area at the top of a window or a dialog box where the menu appears is known as the *menu bar*. Most menus in Windows NT and in Windows applications are *pull-down menus*. This means when you select a menu name from the menu bar, the menu appears to be pulled down below your selection (see fig. D.9).

FIG. D.9
Menus in Windows NT and in Windows applications appear to be pulled down beneath the menu bar.

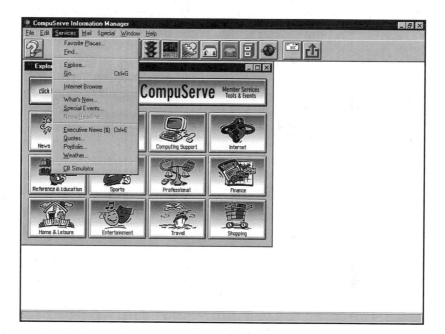

Opening and Closing Menus

You can open and close a menu with either the keyboard or the mouse. A menu remains open until you make a choice from the menu or close the menu by clicking elsewhere on the screen or by pressing Esc.

Like many controls on the screen, menus have accelerator keys, too. Accelerator keys help you open the menu you want. To open a menu using the accelerator key, press Alt+*accelerator key*. To open a menu with the mouse, click its name in the menu bar. Figure D.10 illustrates how to open a menu.

FIG. D.10

You can use either the mouse or the keyboard to open a menu.

Click here to open the File menu

Selecting from a Menu

After a menu is opened, you can select from it. Depending on the menu choice, some task may be launched in your application or perhaps another window or a dialog box appears.

To make a selection from a menu using the mouse, simply click the choice. To make a selection from a menu using the keyboard, use the cursor keys to highlight your selection and press Enter. You'll notice that most menu choices also have accelerator keys. When a menu is opened, all you have to do is press the accelerator key (without the Alt key) to select a choice from an open menu.

 TIP You can also use the cursor keys to move to other menus without closing the menu you have open. With a menu open, you can press the left or right cursor keys to move to and simultaneously open menus adjacent to the menu you have open.

N O T E You might notice that some menu options are followed by the ellipsis symbol. For example, in figure D.9, the ellipsis follows the menu choice Favorite Places. There is a special meaning with the use of an ellipsis. Whenever you see an ellipsis, you know that a dialog box will appear when you make that menu choice. ■

Quick-Key Combinations

In certain menus, you may notice a key combination displayed beside a menu choice (see fig. D.11). This is known as a *quick-key combination* or *shortcut key*. By pressing the quick-key combination, you can make a selection from a menu without displaying the menu. This helps speed up completion of common tasks, such as creating a new document or saving a file. Quick-key combinations vary from application to application, so do not expect the quick-key combination from your word processing program, for example, to work with your to-do list application. Many common tasks such as cut, copy, and paste however, are represented by the same quick-key combinations in every application that uses those operations.

FIG. D.11

Many menu choices have quick-key combinations that allow you to make a menu choice without actually opening a menu.

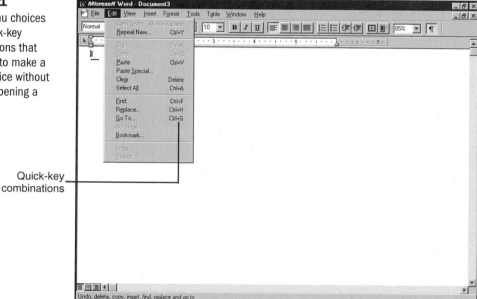

Quick-key combinations

Part
VIII

App
D

Disabled Menu Choices

You may have noticed in figure D.11 that some of the choices on the Edit menu appear gray or *dimmed*, specifically the first choice and a few more. It is common in the Windows NT interface to gray or dim or disable choices or options on-screen that are not appropriate at that time. At the point where it may become appropriate to press a button or click a check box, for example, these options would become active. It is also the case with menu items. In figure D.11, the first choice on the edit menu, Can't Undo, is disabled because the user has taken no action *to undo* with what appears to be a new document. The third and fourth choice, Cut and Copy, are gray because no text has been selected.

Working with Cascading Menus

Some applications you use in Windows NT may use a menu structure more complicated than those seen so far. Rather than the one-dimensional list of choices, some menus require multiple levels. These types of menus are known as *cascading menus*. This is because the menu choices seem to *cascade* from each other, like a waterfall. Figure D.12 shows a demonstration application that uses cascading menus. A right-pointing triangle next to a menu choice indicates a cascading menu is available.

FIG. D.12

The demonstration application shows cascading menus.

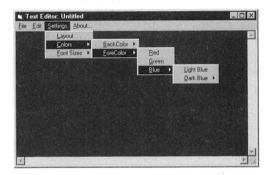

Cascading menus work like other menus. You use the mouse and keyboard to open and make selections from cascading menus.

Cascading menus work differently in Windows NT starting with version 4.0. To display the next level of a menu, all you do is rest the mouse pointer over that menu choice and the submenu appears automatically after a short period of time. The Start menu on the Desktop displays this behavior. When you open the Start menu and move the mouse pointer over the Programs choice, after a short delay, the Programs submenu appears.

Working with Check Menus

Some menu choices can have an on or off state (a *toggle*). When the menu choice is on (*selected*), a check mark appears next to the choice on the menu. When the choice is off (*deselected*), no check mark appears. A typical example of this type of menu is one that toggles on and off the display of the status bar, toolbar, or some other element, or that turns an activity on or off (see fig. D.13).

To check a menu choice, select it as you would any other menu choice. Do the same to deselect a checked menu choice.

FIG. D.13

Some menu choices can have either an on or off state.

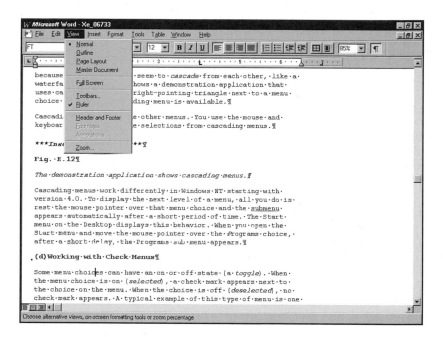

Part

VIII

App

D

Working with Option Menus

A number of menu choices may be grouped and function in a way that only one of the choices in the group can be on at a time. For example, in Microsoft's Word for Windows 95, you can select from the menu what view of your document you want to use: Normal, Outline, Page Layout, or Master Document. Because only one of these options is available at one time, choosing one of the options turns off whatever option was on previously. To indicate which option is on, some graphic element is used in the menu. In the Word for Windows 95 example, a simple dot indicates the current option (see fig. D.13).

Working with Windows

The entire Windows interface is based on the use of windows. Both Windows NT and applications you run in Windows NT present information in windows. Sometimes you may be able to type directly into a window; sometimes a window is filled with controls, such as buttons and list boxes; and sometimes a window will be used just to display information that you can't change.

Applications can present windows in different ways. A word processing program lets you type into a blank document window, and a spreadsheet presents a window as a table. Figure D.14 shows how Windows NT presents information about the hard drives on your system in a window.

FIG. D.14

The Disk Administrator application in Windows NT demonstrates a unique display of information in a window.

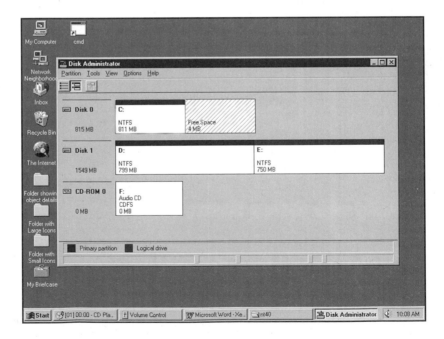

N O T E Generally, in Windows NT only two types of applications do not run in a window: DOS applications that run in full-screen mode, and small applications that run in a dialog box. ■

All windows have a number of standard controls. These controls are used to help size, position, and control the window. Whether you are working with an application or a document window, the controls function in the same manner. Figure D.15 shows the common controls that appear in a window. The sections that follow explain their use.

FIG. D.15
The same controls appear in all windows in the Windows NT interface. Some windows might not display each of the controls, based on the desire of the person who developed the software.

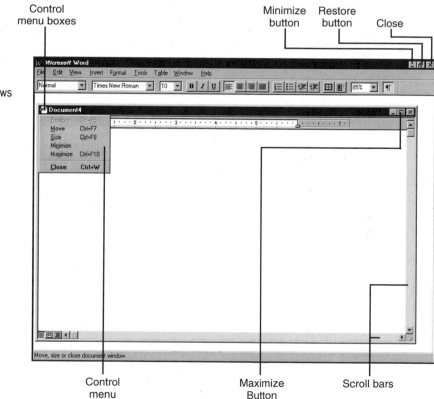

Control menu boxes

Minimize button   Restore button   Close

Control menu

Maximize Button   Scroll bars

Working with the Control Menu

The Control menu provides you with functionality equivalent to using the mouse to resize, minimize, maximize, close, restore, and move a window (see fig. D.16). The Control menu appears when you select the Control-menu icon, which is located in the upper-left corner of a window.

Part

VIII

App

D

If you recall the discussion on MDI earlier in this appendix, you know that a window can appear within another window. For this reason, you might see two control-menu boxes in some applications, one above the other. Because one control-menu box displays the Control menu for the parent window and the other control-menu box displays the Control menu for the document window, you must be sure to open the correct one.

To display the Control menu for any window, click the Control-menu icon. To use the keyboard to open the Control menu for a parent window, press Alt+spacebar. If you are working in an MDI application and two windows are open, press Alt+hyphen once, and then use right and left cursor keys to open the appropriate Control menu. If only one child window is open, just press Alt+hyphen to open its Control menu.

FIG. D.16
The Control menu is used as a keyboard interface to manage the window.

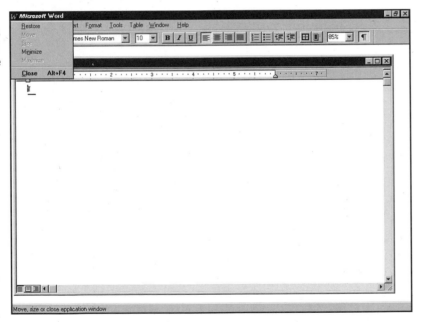

Using the Scroll Bars

To see more of a document, you can either increase the size of the window housing the document, or you can use the scroll bars to move to the area hidden from view. Figure D.17 illustrates how to use the scroll bars.

FIG. D.17
There are a number
of methods for using
the scroll bars.

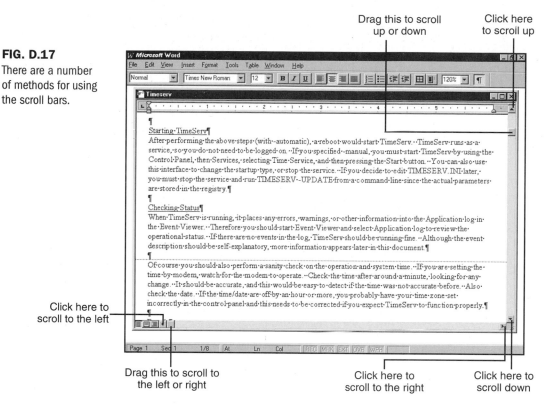

Drag this to scroll
up or down

Click here
to scroll up

Click here to
scroll to the left

Drag this to scroll to
the left or right

Click here to
scroll to the right

Click here to
scroll down

Part
VIII

App
D

Minimizing and Maximizing Windows

Windows can be maximized and minimized. When a window is *maximized*, it fills
up the entire screen (see fig. D.18). When you *minimize* a window, it appears to
close and be replaced by an icon (see fig. D.19).

If the window you want to maximize is a document window—such as a document
you are working with in Word for Windows 95—when you maximize the document
window, it fills only the region of the screen occupied by the application window.
Only an application window, when maximized, fills up all the area of your screen.
Figure D.20 illustrates how to minimize and maximize windows.

FIG. D.18
A maximized window fills up the entire screen or its parent window.

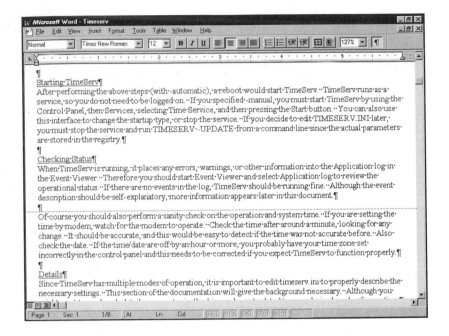

FIG. D.19
A minimized window appears as an icon.

Minimized document windows

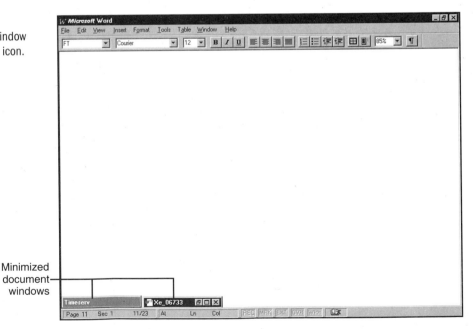

FIG. D.20
You can use the
Control menu or
buttons to minimize
and maximize a
window.

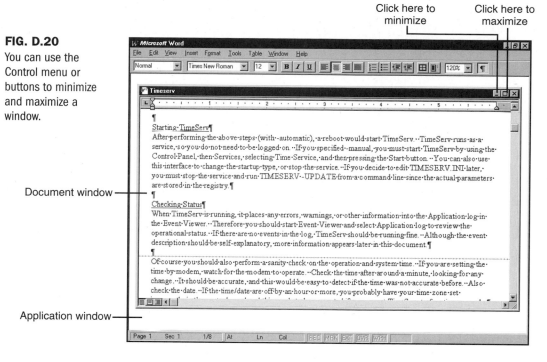

Click here to
minimize

Click here to
maximize

Document window

Application window

Resizing a Window

You can resize a window to increase or decrease its size. The easiest way to resize
a window is to use the mouse. You simply click one border of the window and drag
the border in the direction in which you want to resize the window (see fig. D.21).
If you drag the top or bottom border, you increase or decrease the window's
height. If you drag the right or left border, you widen or narrow the window. If you
drag one of the window's four corners, you can change the window's height and
width at the same time.

Moving a Window

Using the mouse or the keyboard, you can move windows from location to location
on the desktop. To move a window using the mouse, click the title bar of the window and drag the window to a new location. To move a window using the keyboard, choose Move from the Control menu and then use the cursor keys to move
the window. Figure D.22 illustrates how to move a window.

FIG. D.21
Use the mouse to stretch or shrink windows to the size you want.

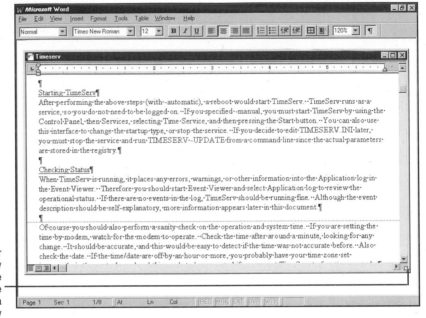

When you shrink or stretch the window by dragging it with the mouse, the mouse pointer changes to a two-headed arrow

 T I P   You cannot move a document window outside of its parent window.

FIG. D.22
You can drag a window to the location you want or you can use the Control menu to help position the window.

Click and drag a window's title bar to move the window

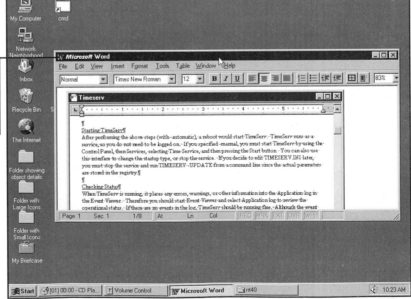

As you try to drag a window to a new location, you might find that it suddenly increases in size and fills the entire screen. This is because you double-clicked the title bar of the window as you tried to move it. When you double-click the title bar of a window, the effect is to maximize the window.

Closing a Window

When you are finished working with a document or an application, you can close the window. If you want to close an application window, you also can choose File, Exit from the application's menu to halt the program and close the window. When you close a document window, the application continues to run, but you no longer can work with the document. If you have not saved the work in the window prior to trying to close it, it is very likely the application will prompt you to save the work first. Here are the different methods available for closing a window:

- Double-click the Control icon
- Choose File, Close
- Choose Close from the document window's Control menu
- Click the close button on the window (see fig. D.23)

Restoring a Window

Windows lets you restore a window to its previous size and position. This is especially helpful if you have minimized a window, or if you have maximized a document window in an application window. You click the Restore button (it looks like a diamond split into top and bottom halves) at the top of a window to restore it (see fig. D.23). You may also choose Restore from a window's Control menu. If a window is minimized, click once on the minimized icon to display the Control menu. Then choose Restore. When a window is maximized, the Maximize button disappears from the set of buttons on the top right of the window, and it is replaced by the Restore button.

FIG. D.23
Buttons are available on most windows to minimize, maximize, restore, and close.

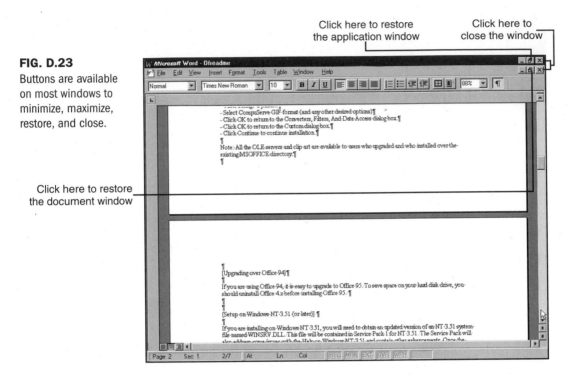

Click here to restore the application window

Click here to close the window

Click here to restore the document window

Working with Windows NT Controls

The tools that help you manage applications in Windows are *controls*. In Windows NT and in applications you run in Windows NT, controls help you see information, select items, specify options, and start processes and tasks. Most Windows applications use a set of approximately nine common controls:

- check box
- command button
- edit box
- radio button
- drop-down list
- list box

- slider control
- spinner control
- tabbed dialog

Software developers, however, can create their own controls. One of the most typical controls found in applications—though not part of the standard Windows NT interface—is the *table control*. The Windows NT interface does not include a grid that software developers can use. For this reason, some applications might employ controls that you may not have seen before. Another example of a common, but not standard, control is the *spinner*. This control is used to enter a value, such as a measurement or an amount. You can enter the value manually, or press either an up or down button to increment or decrement the current value that appears in the control. This section of the appendix reviews the common Windows NT controls, shown in figures D.24 and D.25.

FIG. D.24
The Desktop tool in the Control Panel includes a number of the standard Windows NT controls.

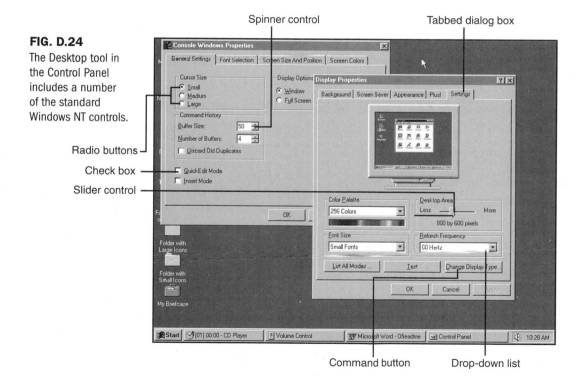

FIG. D.25

A dialog box from Word for Windows 95 also displays a number of standard Windows NT controls.

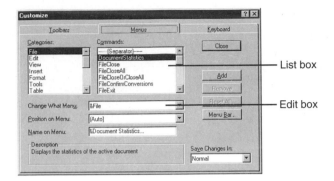

List box

Edit box

Command Buttons

Command buttons are the simplest Windows NT controls to use. The command button has just one use: you click it. Depending on the application in which the button is used, some process may start when you click the button. If the label on the command button is followed by an ellipsis (...), then a dialog box probably appears in response to clicking the button.

Here are the methods available to use a command button:

- Click it
- Press Alt+*accelerator key* if the caption on the button has an accelerator
- Move the focus to the button and press Enter or the spacebar

Edit Boxes

An *edit box* is used to enter and change information. Edit boxes, also known as *text boxes*, can be small—storing as little as one character—or large, storing multiple lines of text. You type in the edit box as you would with any other application. Some special rules affect how you work with text in an edit box. Keep in mind that different Windows applications might break these rules as it suits their needs:

- When you click an edit box, a vertical I-beam cursor appears in the edit box. This indicates the position in the edit box where text will be inserted if you type.
- You can select text in an edit box by using the click-and-drag technique described in the "Using the Mouse" section earlier in this appendix.
- You can select text in an edit box using the keyboard by holding down the Shift key while pressing the left and right cursor keys.

- You can press Home, End, left-arrow, and right-arrow to navigate in an edit box.
- When you press Tab to move the focus to an edit box, the entire content of the edit box becomes highlighted when you arrive at the edit box. Any text highlighted in an edit box—one letter or the entire contents—is immediately replaced by any characters you type.

List Boxes

List boxes are used to present a list of items from which you can select. Some list boxes restrict you from choosing more than one item; other list boxes let you choose multiple items. The latter type of list box is covered later in this section.

You can use the following methods to select an item from a list box:

- Click the item
- Move the focus to the list box and then use the up and down cursor keys to move to your choice

Multi-Select List Boxes Some list boxes allow you to select more than one item at a time. You use special techniques to select multiple items in a list box depending on whether the items you want to select are adjacent. Table D.3 shows you how to make selections in a multi-select list box.

Part

VIII

App

D

Table D.3 Techniques for Selecting Items in Multi-Select List Boxes

Method	Items	Technique
Mouse	Adjacent	Click and drag over the items you want to select, or click once on the first item to select, and then hold the Shift key while you click the last item to select.
Mouse	Non-adjacent	Hold down Ctrl while you click the items you want to select.
Keyboard	Adjacent	Move the focus to the first of the items you want to select. Press and hold down Shift while using the down cursor key to select the other items you want to select.
Keyboard	Non-adjacent	n/a

N O T E   Some applications use a different type of multi-select list box known as the *simple multi-select list box*. This type of list box makes it easy to select multiple non-adjacent items in a list box. You know that you are using a simple extended list box when you can click any item in the list and it becomes highlighted. To select multiple non-adjacent items with the keyboard, move the highlight to the items you want to select and then press the spacebar.   ■

Special List Boxes   Items other than words or phrases might appear in a list box. Some applications show pictures in a list box. Using a list box that contains items other than text is no different than if the list box contains just text; you simply click the item to select, or using the keyboard, you move the focus to the item you want. Microsoft's Word for Windows 95 demonstrates another type of list box. You select which toolbars you want to appear on the screen from a list box that contains check boxes (see fig. D.26).

FIG. D.26
Microsoft's Word for Windows 95 uses check boxes in some of its list boxes.

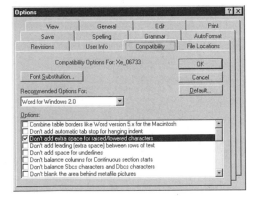

Drop-Down List Boxes

Drop-down list boxes are used to present a smaller list of selections than a list box. Drop-down lists get their name because the list of items drops down when you activate the list. A drop-down list is usually made of two pieces:

■   Edit portion
■   List

The edit portion displays the currently selected item in the list. The rules listed in the "Edit Boxes" section earlier also pertain to the edit portion of a drop-down list.

Certain types of drop-down lists only let you select from the list; you are not allowed to use the edit portion of the control. You can tell a drop-down list that does not allow you to type into the edit portion because the drop-down arrow is attached to the edit portion of the control (see fig. D.27).

Some drop-down lists let you enter a value directly into the edit portion in order to select from the list. Certain drop-down lists will add the value you enter into the edit box to the list if what you type does not exist in the list. You can tell a drop-down list that allows you to type into the edit portion because the drop-down arrow is separated from the edit portion of the control (see fig. D.27).

FIG. D.27
Drop-down lists differ in appearance based on whether you can use the edit portion of the control.

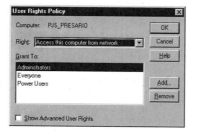

To use the mouse to display the contents of a drop-down list, click the down arrow button. To use the keyboard, move the focus to the drop-down list and press Ctrl+F4.

Radio Buttons

Radio buttons are used to force you to select one option from a group of two or more. Radio buttons, also known as *option buttons*, are always presented in a group; when you select one radio button from the group, all other buttons in the group are deselected. You can use the mouse to click the desired option, or you can use the keyboard to select an option.

Tabbed Dialog Boxes

Although Windows 95 is not the first application to use tabs in a dialog box, the tab control is used predominantly throughout the Windows 95 operating system. The Windows NT version 4.0 interface is the same as that of Windows 95, so it also uses tabbed dialog boxes. If you are unfamiliar with the tabbed dialog box, the control is used to present more information in a dialog box than normally would be possible. Like the tabs found on file folders, the labels on the tabs in a dialog box tell you what information is available. Property sheets demonstrate the tabbed dialog control (see fig. D.28).

FIG. D.28

The property sheets for most objects make use of the tabbed dialog box control.

The tabbed dialog control is easy to use. All you do is click the tab that you want to see. The controls in the dialog box change reflecting the tab you selected. To use the keyboard to select a tab, press the Tab key until the focus moves to the current tab. Next use the left and right cursor keys to select the desired tab.

Spinner Control

The spinner control (see fig. D.29) helps the user select or input a value, very often a numeric value. The spinner control is made up of three components. The edit box portion allows the user to manually enter the value, and the edit control also displays the current value for the control. The up and down buttons increment the value that appears in the edit control portion. Perhaps more of an extravagance than a requirement, the buttons let the user specify a value without touching the keyboard.

FIG. D.29

The Console applet, which helps you customize the window, uses spinner controls to specify the size, buffer, and position of the command prompt window.

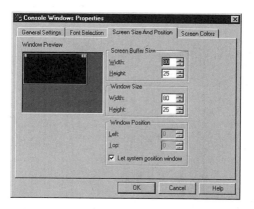

Part
VIII

App
D

Slider Control

Like the spinner control described earlier, the slider control is also used to help the user select a value, but the slider control does so graphically and from a predetermined range of value. Presented either horizontally or graphically, you drag the indicator positioned on the slider in either direction to specify a value. Figure D.30 shows an example of a slider control.

FIG. D.30

The Desktop applet uses a slider to specify how much information is shown on the screen.

What's on the CD

by Brian Underdahl

The CD-ROM that accompanies this book contains a wide variety of useful tools, shareware products, and evaluation versions of software. You'll probably be surprised by the quality and by the diversity of the items. We've tried to assemble the best tools available to help you make more effective use of Windows NT 4.0. You'll find an amazing range of software from screen savers to Internet applications. You'll find disk and file utilities, other useful tools, and a number of fun things, too. In short, the CD-ROM has some of the best Windows NT software you'll find anywhere. ∎

Using the CD-ROM

This appendix lists each of the items on the CD-ROM by name so that it will be easy for you to check out what we've included. Each item listing includes the name of the directory, the filename, a short description, and contact information for the software author. If you wish, you can use the directory and filename information to browse the CD-ROM, but we've provided a much easier way for you to access the files. When you insert the CD-ROM into the drive, a program called Autorun automatically displays a graphical interface to the files on the CD-ROM.

The first time you run the CD-ROM, you may need to run the Setup program to install several interface support files. Later, you'll only need to click the Start button to view the file listings. Simply select a category and you'll see all the files in the category. To see each file's description, select the file in the file listing. Once you've selected a program you'd like to try, you can use the buttons to view the files, install the program, or in some cases, run the program from the CD-ROM.

Important Information about Shareware

Shareware distribution gives users a chance to try software before buying it. If you try a shareware program and continue using it, you are expected to register for it. Individual programs differ on details. Some request registration while others require it. Some specify a maximum trial period, either a set number of days or uses. With registration, you get anything from the simple right to continue using the software to an updated program with a printed manual.

Copyright laws apply to both shareware and commercial software. The software author has not given you the right to continue using their software without registration simply because they have chosen to use shareware distribution.

Software authors use shareware distribution methods for several reasons. One of the most important is that this method enables the authors to keep the cost to you as low as possible. But this system only works if you keep up your end of the bargain. Remember, if you don't register the shareware that you use, there's no incentive for the software authors to produce new shareware products, or even updated versions of existing ones.

So once you've tried out the shareware on the CD-ROM, make one of these choices; register the software you find yourself using, and uninstall any you don't find useful.

N O T E We're constantly on the lookout for top quality software to include with our books. As the largest publisher of computer books, we reach a broad market of computer users. If you are the author of high quality 32-bit Windows shareware, freeware, or evaluation version software and you would like us to consider including your software on a future CD-ROM, please let us know. Send your program name, a brief description of the software and its intended audience, and your complete contact information to

kkloss@que.mcp.com ▨

CD-ROM Contents

One thing you discover when you're assembling an exciting collection of software like this one is that nearly every software author has a new version "just about ready." Given the realities of book publishing, this means that many of the programs on the CD-ROM probably already have newer versions available. In most cases, these newer versions have a few additional features. In a few cases, the newer versions fix problems discovered in the older versions.

If you're happy with the programs on our CD-ROM, there's no reason you can't use the versions we've included (if you register them). Even so, you may want to look on our CD-ROM as a sampler. If you like a program enough to keep using it, you may want to see if a newer version is available. We've included contact information along with each software description to make this much easier for you.

Part
VIII

App
E

Amazing JPEG Screen Saver for Windows 95 and NT v1.25

Filename: AJ95V125.ZIP

Directory: Scrensav

Esm Software's Amazing JPEG Screen Saver for Windows 95 and Windows NT is the perfect product for anyone who loves and collects JPEG images. This screen saver is ideal for displaying corporate logos, family pictures, or any of your favorite images. This program can be configured to load the images progressively, so there is no waiting for screens to appear. First you see a low resolution image pop up on your screen, then watch as the quality improves until you have the high resolution image.

For more information:

> Esm Software
> Ed Milczarek
> P.O. Box 176
> Pierrefonds, Quebec, H9H 4K9, Canada
> **Esm.Software@Netaxis.qc.ca**
> **102762,2715** on CompuServe
> **http://ourworld.compuserve.com/homepages/esmsoftwa**

CD/Spectrum Pro v2.1

Filename:	CDSPRO21.ZIP
Directory:	Funstuff

CD/Spectrum Pro is a shareware CD-Audio Player with Graphical Spectrum Analyzer for Windows 95 and Windows NT 4.0. CD/Spectrum Pro has two independent parts: the CDAudio player and the spectrum analyzer. The CD-Audio player is a full-blown player of audio CDs for your PC. It has many advanced features and complements the spectrum analyzer. The spectrum analyzer graphically depicts the frequency spectra of the CD music in real time. You may use either or both of the components without effect on the other. In other words, if you don't like the CD player, you can close it and use only the spectrum analyzer—or the other way around.

For more information:

> John Hornick
> 203 Bellevue Way NE #474
> Bellevue, WA 98004
> (206) 882-8579
> **http://www.halcyon.com/gator/cdspro.htm**

Catalog Supreme for Windows 95 and NT

Filename: CATSUP.ZIP

Directory: Funstuff

Catalog Supreme for Windows 95 and Windows NT provides you with a simple-to-use, yet functional program that tracks data for computer software, audio recordings, video recordings, and book collections. The program then allows you to sort these records and view them in a simple table format.

For more information:

Wells Software
Chris M Wells
350 4th St.
Elyria, OH 44035
103132,1363 on CompuServe

CleverWatch 4.0.2

Filename: CW40NT.ZIP

Directory: Tools

CleverWatch is an intelligent agent for monitoring and managing Lotus Notes servers. It is designed to detect Notes server problems, notify Notes administrators, and even to automatically take user specified corrective actions. CleverWatch is based on two simple concepts: commands and triggers. *Triggers* specify what should be monitored, and *commands* specify what actions will be taken once a trigger occurs. CleverWatch can detect all types of server crashes, even the hardest Notes crashes like transport protocol communication problems and operating system crashes.

Part
VIII

App
E

For more information:

> CleverSoft, Inc.
> Bill Cronin
> 27 Gorham Rd., Suite #1
> Scarborough, ME 04074
> Phone: (207) 883-3550
> Fax: (207) 883-3369
> **http://www.cleversoft.com**
> **bcronin@cleversoft.com**

Cuneiform OCR v2.0 (CD-Book Bundle/Internet Version)

Filename: CUNE120C.EXE

Directory: Tools

Cuneiform OCR is an extremely accurate, fast, and easy-to-use optical character recognition package. Cuneiform OCR works with all popular Twain-compatible scanners. It also reads faxes from the Exchange Inbox, Fax Group 3, PCX, and TIFF sources. This 15-day evaluation version is the complete working version of the software, and will make your scanner much more useful than it is with the OCR software packaged with the scanner.

For more information:

> Cognitive Technology Corporation
> Yefim Schukin
> 9 El Camino Drive
> Corte Madera, CA 94925
> Phone: (415) 925-2323
> Fax: (415) 461-4010
> **http://www.ocr.com/**
> **ctc@ocr.com**
> **76600,1623** on CompuServe

Curve Fit for Windows 95 v1.1.3

Filename: CFIT95.ZIP

Directory: Tools

Curve Fit is a data analysis tool that allows you to fit X-Y data to a selected curve. Curve types supported are polynomial, log-log polynomial, and semi-log in both X and Y. For the polynomial curve types, you are allowed to select a curve order from 1 to 10. The fit method used is least squares. To help determine how good the fit is for the curve selected, the sum (integral) of the absolute differences (errors) and the coefficient of fit performance are reported. The curve is automatically refitted anytime a change in data or curve type occurs. Two views of the data are supported: listing (List View) and plot (Plot View). Until the application is licensed, you are limited to only seven data points.

For more information:

> Floersch Enterprises
> Richard H. Floersch
> 7307 W. 89th Terrace
> Overland Park, KS 66212
> **http://www.sunflower.org/~dflo/**

DeltaCad v2.1

Filename: DTCAD.ZIP

Directory: Tools

DeltaCad is a powerful, easy-to-learn, CAD (Computer Aided Design) program. It can produce accurately scaled drawings or just pretty pictures to paste into your favorite word processor. DeltaCad can be used for drafting, house plans, decks, business cards, forms, signs, labels, maps, flow charts, home or school projects, and more. DeltaCad is a true 32-bit program compatible with Windows, Windows NT, or Windows 95.

Part
VIII

App
E

For more information:

> Midnight Software, Inc.
> P.O. Box 77352
> Seattle, WA 98177-0352
> Fax: (206) 361-0796
> **102562,1411** on CompuServe

Drag and File Gold v2.03

Filename: DFGOLD.ZIP

Directory: Dskfile

Drag and File Gold File and Archive Manager v2.00 is a very powerful Windows 95/NT file manager. ZIP, GZ, and TAR files appear as folders on a tree with their contents in the file pane. Extracting files is as easy as copying or moving them. It has built-in zipping and unzipping, and virus scanning, and can extract TAR and GZ formats. Drag and File can also zip files with long file and directory names.

For more information:

> Canyon Software
> Attention: Daniel
> 1537 Fourth St., Suite 131
> San Rafael, CA 94901
> **74774,554** on CompuServe

Drag and View for Windows 95 and NT

Filename: DV95.ZIP

Directory: Dskfile

Drag and View for Windows 95/NT v1 enables you to view files with the right mouse button. It views most popular database, word processor, spreadsheet, graphic, and multimedia formats, plus ASCII and HEX formats. It enables you to rotate graphics and save them in other bitmap formats. It plays AVI, MRI, MID, and WAV files. It allows you to edit text files, copy to the Clipboard, print, search, and go to text.

For more information:

Canyon Software
Attention: Daniel
1537 Fourth St., Suite 131
San Rafael, CA 94901
74774,554 on CompuServe

Drag and Zip for Windows 95 and NT

Filename: DZ95.ZIP

Directory: Dskfile

With Drag and Zip, you can zip and unzip files with just a right click of the mouse. It includes built-in zipping, unzipping, extraction of TAR and GZ files, and virus scanning. The program also supports long file names and path names. Drag and Zip links to Mosaic and Netscape, and makes Windows-hosted SFXs. It includes password encryption and multiple disk ZIP files.

For more information:

Canyon Software
Attention: Daniel
1537 Fourth St., Suite 131
San Rafael, CA 94901
74774,554 on CompuServe

Part
VIII

App
E

EXECUTIVE DESK v5.0

Filename: EDESK50.ZIP

Directory: Tools

The EXECUTIVE DESK Information Manager (PIM) program helps you accomplish more using proven time management techniques. It incorporates an address book, to-do lists, follow-up lists, and phone lists into a unique day view for easily organizing your workload. An online help system makes the program easy to use and understand.

For more information:

> Expert's Choice, Inc.
> Harold Gregg
> 4612 Trail West
> Austin, TX 78735
> Phone: (512) 422-1622
> **70034,227** on CompuServe

EasyHelp/Web v2.81a

Filename: EZY281A.EXE

Directory: Internet

EasyHelp/Web is a set of Microsoft Word macros contained in a template called EASYHELP.DOT. These easy-to-use macros can be executed either from the Word toolbar or by using shortcut keys, and enable you to mark up a document with topics and hypertext links and graphics. You can process the marked-up document, then build and view the resulting help file directly from within Word.

EasyHelp/Web also enables you to maintain one document that can be printed out as a hard copy manual or can be viewed as a HELP/HTML file. No complicated footnotes or extra page breaks clutter the document. In fact, the only formatting changes made to the document are colored text, so you can see where the topics and hypertext links are.

For more information:

> Eon Solutions Ltd.
> Jeff Hall
> Eon House, 8 Bottrells Lane
> Chalfont St. Giles, Buckinghamshire, HP8 4EX, ENGLAND
> **eonsol@cix.compulink,co.uk**
> **100130,2471** on CompuServe
> **http://www.eon-solutions.com/**
> **ftp://ftp.u-net.com/com/eon/ezy281.exe**

Ecopad32 v3.50

Filename: ECPD3235.ZIP

Directory: Tools

Ecopad32 V3.50 <ASP> Text Editor for Windows 95 prints up to eight pages of condensed text on one sheet of paper, and supports any printer that is compatible with Windows 95 or Windows NT. The shareware version is fully functional. Ecopad can load and print files up to 32M, and supports two-sided printing.

For more information:

> Azure D'or Software
> David T. Ossorio
> 325 S. Washington Ave., #166
> Kent, WA 98032
> **71533,1573** on CompuServe

Fax-a-Laugh and More!!! (Shareware Version)

Filename: FAXALAF1.ZIP

Directory: Mailfax

Fax-a-Laugh and More!!! creates fax cover sheets, memos, notices, and other forms. It provides the ability to entertain with cartoons, graphics, and illustrations added to the cover page. This program contains a word processor, spell checker, and two databases for ease of use. This program can output documents to your printer or fax modem software. Additional libraries of other artists can be added to the registered version of the program.

For more information:

> The Great Fax Cover Sheet Co.
> Garry Brod
> 6502 Santa Monica Blvd.
> Hollywood, CA 90038
> Phone: (213) 463-7887
> Fax: (213) 463-7237
> **http://www.iwsc.com/greatfax/fal.html**

Part
VIII

App
E

File View for Windows NT (FView) 1.4b

Filename: FVU14B32.ZIP

Directory: Graphics

File View for Windows NT, v1.4 enables you to view files as text, ASCII, or hex dump. It installs as a menu option in Windows File Manager and registers in the Windows Registration Database for both OPEN and PRINT. You can drag-and-drop files to File View, customize the display options to your needs, perform text and hex searches, print, and copy to the Clipboard. The program includes extensive help.

For more information:

> Maze Computer Communications, Inc.
> Jerzy Makowiecki
> 269 Amethyst Way
> Franklin Park, NJ 08823
> Phone: (908) 821-5412
> Fax: (908) 821-5412
> **70152,1501** on CompuServe

Find String for Windows 95 v2.3.1

Filename: FDSTR95.ZIP

Directory: Tools

The Find String application was built to allow application developers, HTML writers, system/network administrators, and others to find a key word or phrase in many lines of many text files quickly and efficiently. It can also be used as stand-alone by developers, HTML writers, and administrators who need to find a piece of information in one or more lines of many files located in multiple directories. Once the text is found, you can launch the editor of your choice to manipulate the data by double-clicking the file or file line. Find String, in addition to launching the editor, can supply the line number to the editor if instructed to do so and can permit command-line parameters if required.

For more information:

> Floersch Enterprises
> Richard H. Floersch
> 7307 W. 89th Terrace
> Overland Park, KS 66212
> **http://www.sunflower.org/~dflo/**

Fnord! Server

Filename: FNORD.ZIP

Directory: Internet

Fnord! is a free Web server released under the GNU license. It includes the source code, and was primarily written as a hobby and learning experience. It is designed for smaller servers and for testing scripts. Fnord is a dynamic package; if you find the program useful, you should access the Fnord Web page for a copy of the most current version.

For more information:

> Brian Morin
> 15 Preserve Drive
> Nashua, NH 03060
> **http://www.wpi.edu/~bmorin/fnord/**

Green Screen Savers v1.3.1.1

Filename: GREENSAV.ZIP

Directory: Scrensav

The Green Screen Savers v1.3.1.1 are Windows 95 and Windows NT applications that display an animated picture (with optional sound) on your screen for a user-selected period of time. The screen then goes completely blank so that Energy Star monitors can enter a power saving mode. This version has improved graphics and works with the Windows 95 Control Panel. Included screen savers are the Jumping Frog, Cricket, Katydid, and Kangaroo Rat Green Savers.

For more information:

> Digital Control Systems
> Royce W. Shofner
> P.O. Box 505
> Hermitage, TN 37076
> Phone: (615) 889-6357
> Fax: (615) 889-9595
> BBS: (615) 889-9595
> **73347,145** on CompuServe

HTML File Merge for Windows 95 v1.1

Filename: HTML95.ZIP

Directory: Internet

The HTML Merge program was built to provide a productivity tool for HTML writers and others to modify existing HTML Web page files more efficiently and with a lot less pain and strain. The program creates a new file for each file you specify in the session file set. Each new file contains information extracted from the specified files and merges that information between optional header/footer markups. The original files are preserved, allowing you to reference them as necessary after the operation. You may define your new HTML markups in the optional header and/or footer files.

Embedded in the header/footer markups, you may define variables. HTML Merge scans the existing file for those variables, extracts the text specified by the variable, and substitutes the extracted text for those variables when it creates the new files. Variables usually define text from the original file that you want retained in the new file under the same or a different format, and usually represent titles, headers, references, links, and images.

For more information:

> Floersch Enterprises
> Richard H. Floersch
> 7307 W. 89th Terrace
> Overland Park, KS 66212
> **http://www.sunflower.org/~dflo/**

HTML Reference Library v2.2

Filename: HTMLIB1.ZIP

Directory: Internet

The HTML Reference Library provides a quick reference to all HTML elements and attributes in current use. This file provides definitions and examples with just a few mouse clicks. New features in this version include coverage for Internet Explorer 3.0, a comparison table showing which features are supported by the major Web browsers, and a color wizard to help you set colors.

For more information:

> Stephen Le Hunte
> **cmlehunt@swansea.ac.uk**

HyperSnap

Filename: HYSNAP.ZIP

Directory: Graphics

This major update to HyperSnap (formerly SnapShot/32) brings professional quality and convenient Windows 95 and NT screen captures to your fingertips. It was designed for ease of use, with powerful and useful features to aid the professional as well as support the needs of the occasional user. You can save your image as a BMP, GIF, or JPEG file. GIFs can optionally be interlaced and include transparent backgrounds, and HyperSnap can create progressive JPEGs, perfect for Web page use. You can choose your color depth for BMP captures, too.

For more information:

> Greg Kochaniak
> 3146 Chestnut St.
> Murrysville, PA 15668
> Phone: (412) 325-4001
> **gregko@kagi.com**
> **http://198.207.242.3/authors/gregko/gregko.htm**

Part
VIII

App
E

Internet Idioms

Filenames: INETXI1.ZIP, for Alpha processors

                      INETXIDM.ZIP, for Intel processors

Directory: Internet

Internet Idioms is part of Ben Goetter's Widgets for Microsoft Exchange collection. This extension patches Exchange to behave more like a traditional Internet mail client. Are you sick of staring at Arial 10 text? Do you miss automated signatures and prefixed replies? Then you'll want to give Internet Idioms a try. Both Intel and Alpha versions are included.

For more information:

> Ben Goetter
> **http://www.angrygraycat.com/goetter/widgets.htm**
> **goetter@halcyon.com**

KopyKat

Filename: KOPYKAT.ZIP

Directory: Tools

KopyKat is a Visual Basic add-in that was created to ease the function of applying the same code to multiple control/event combinations. KopyKat enables you to type in code one time and have the code applied to a specific event for all selected controls in the project at one time. KopyKat displays the available files and controls for the current project. When a new project is opened, KopyKat automatically detects the change and displays the new project.

For more information:

> Terre Wells
> 1901 Winners Circle
> Lawranceville, GA 30243
> Phone: (770) 338-6584
> **102432,357** on CompuServe

MediaChanger 2.52

Filename: MEDIAU1.ZIP

Directory: Funstuff

Media Changer for Windows 95 and NT automatically changes the desktop wallpaper, system sounds, and screen saver each time you run it. You can include Media Changer in your Startup group or folder to have a different system appearance each time you start your PC. It also includes Theme Changer, a freeware application that works with Plus! to change desktop themes automatically.

For more information:

Swoosie Software
Gary Lucero and Mike Henderson
http://www.xmission.com/~myq/swoosie.html
mhenderson@novell.com

MemoPad v1 for Windows 95 and NT

Filename: MEMOPAD.ZIP

Directory: Tools

MemoPad v1 functions as a memo pad that allows for multiple users, making the program ideal for a single user, family of users, and even use in an office or business environment. Added functions of this program include printing of all memos in simple text form or in the form of the on-screen viewed memo. It also allows the computer to be used as big sticky pad.

For more information:

Wells Software
Chris M. Wells
350 4th St.
Elyria, OH 44035
103132,1363 on CompuServe

Part
VIII

App
E

Middle Mouse Button 1.8.3.2

Filename: MBUTTON.ZIP

Directory: Tools

Middle Mouse Button is a Windows 95 and Windows NT application that intercepts the middle mouse button of a three-button mouse and converts a middle button single-click into a default button (normally the left button) double-click. The program dynamically detects if you have selected the Left-Handed Mouse option in the Control Panel. The ergonomics of this action are obvious; one click instead of two rapid clicks causes less wear and tear on both the mouse and the person using the mouse.

For more information:

Digital Control Systems
Royce W. Shofner
P.O. Box 505
Hermitage, TN 37076
Phone: (615) 889-6357
Fax: (615) 889-9595
BBS: (615) 889-9595
73347,145 on CompuServe

MultiVu 2.0

Filename: MULTVU20.ZIP

Directory: Graphics

MultiVu 2.0 is a Windows file viewer. You can browse files up to 2G in size and have up to 20 open files. You can browse contents of ZIP, ARJ, and LZH archives; extract and gather text from multiple files; set bookmarks; and separately control screen and printer fonts. MultiVu 2.0 loads, prints, and searches in the background while browsing open files. It includes multi-user LAN support.

For more information:

> Ivden Technologies
> Phil Grenetz
> 87 Arbor Rd.
> Churchville, PA 18966-1007
> **71221.3602** on CompuServe

NotifyMail 32-Bit v1.0.2

Filename: NMAIL32.EXE

Directory: Mailfax

NotifyMail is an application that listens for a finger connection. When it receives the connection (for the appropriate user), it notifies you of new e-mail. This can be done by having QUALCOMM's Eudora, Pegasus, or any MAPI compliant e-mail client check your mail, displaying a dialog box or playing a sound.

For more information:

> NotifyMail Software
> 5383 Chelsea Ave., #101
> La Jolla, CA 92037-7959
> **http://www.notifymail.com/**

OpalisRobot for Windows NT v2

Filename: OPR_V2.ZIP & ODBC32_V210.ZIP

Directory: Tools

OpalisRobot is a software that automates administration, production, maintenance, and communication tasks on Windows NT systems. You can use OpalisRobot to do things like daily planning of backup or administration tasks, automatic night control of client sites, automation of client/provider communications, and database maintenance. You can use OpalisRobot to easily customize the Windows NT environment.

For more information:

> Opalis
> Laurent Domenech
> 27, Bld Pereire
> 75017 Paris FRANCE
> **71524,27** on CompuServe

Pegasus Mail

Filename: WINPM231.ZIP

Directory: Mailfax

Pegasus Mail is an electronic mail program that can be used in a very wide range of environments, and which is especially well-suited to Internet mail. Individual users with a connection to the Internet via an Internet Service Provider such as PSI or Netcom can use Pegasus Mail to send and retrieve mail. Pegasus Mail is a very comprehensive and powerful system, offering a long list of features and capabilities. You can use Pegasus Mail to automate your mail processing.

For more information:

> Pegasus Mail
> David Harris
> Box 5451
> Dunedin, New Zealand
> **David.Harris@pmail.gen.nz**

Phone Dialer v1 for Windows 95 and NT

Filename: PHONED.ZIP

Directory: Tools

Phone Dialer v1 has the ability to dial calls, save phone numbers in a database, time the phone calls, and calculate an expense for the calls. Also, there is the ability to print the database of phone records. The unregistered version of this program enables the use of 10 records.

For more information:

Wells Software
Chris M. Wells
350 4th St.
Elyria, OH 44035
103132,1363 on CompuServe

PixFolio

Filename: PIXF32.ZIP

Directory: Graphics

PixFolio is a Microsoft Windows program that can view a variety of bitmapped graphics formats and maintain multiple catalogs of images. It supports a broad range of graphics file formats. PixFolio has the ability to build catalogs of images, even those which may reside on different disks. The catalog can then be searched and images can be easily located. The program can also display postage stamp images in a matrix. In addition, you can use PixFolio as a file conversion utility.

For more information:

ACK Software
Allen C. Kempe
298 W. Audubon Drive
Shepherdsville, KY 40165-8836
Phone: (502) 955-7527
allenk@iglou.com
71220,23 on CompuServe
http://www.iglou.com/acksoft/

PolyForm, 60-Day Evaluation

Filename: POLYFORM.ZIP

Directory: Internet

PolyForm is a forms tool that can help make your Web pages interactive. PolyForm enables you to create Web pages with forms, so you can gather and manage information supplied by your Web visitors. For example, with PolyForm users can order products, request information, provide customer feedback, or answer surveys. Each form can be configured separately, so you can collect and store response data as well as recipient information. Information submitted on a form can be sent to specified e-mail addresses, and data can be sent back to the user who fills in the form. PolyForm runs with any Windows Web server that fully supports the Windows Common Gateway Interface (Win-CGI), including WebSite and others.

For more information:

O'Reilly & Associates
Jeannine Cook
101 Morris St.
Sebastopol, CA 95472
Phone: (707) 829-0515
Fax: (707) 829-0104
http://website.ora.com/
http://software.ora.com
jeannine@ora.com

Quick Disk 1.05

Filename: QCKDSK10.ZIP

Directory: Dskfile

Quick Disk is a small Windows utility that adds an icon (a hard disk icon) in the Windows Tray. This enables you to easily get free space information for all your drives. You can choose which types of drives to add in the main window.

For more information:

Benjamin Bourderon
9 Rue Magenta
69100 Villeurbanne FRANCE
100735,2646 on CompuServe
Benjab@msn.com

Random Password Generator v5.0 (Shareware Version)

Filename: PASSGEN.ZIP

Directory: Tools

Random Password Generator v5.0 is a secure method for creating passwords. Random Password Generator randomly selects from a group of numbers, lowercase letters, uppercase letters, and special characters, or any combination thereof and chooses passwords. You have the ability to identify up to one million different passwords, using as many as 25 characters per password. This application randomly selects passwords that have not been previously selected (if desired) and sorts them in order. You can copy selected passwords or save them all as text files. The generator uses numbers, upper and lowercase letters, and special keyboard characters. You can select any combination of these choices to generate passwords. A total of 94 characters are available for the randomizer to select from.

For more information:

Tim Hirtle
102705,2261 on CompuServe

RegFind 0.7

Filename: REGFIND.ZIP

Directory: Tools

RegFind is a utility for searching through a Win32 registry. This utility does not write to the registry and should, therefore, not cause any damage to it. Microsoft has stated that modifications to the registry can render the system unusable. RegFind does not modify the registry in any way. Regfind is a console application; you can run it from a DOS box just like other command line programs. With this program, you can unearth vestiges of obsolete data, such as old host names that are no longer valid. Applications waiting for old hosts to respond only continue after a timeout error is reported. Thus, removing those names from the Registry may allow the application to start faster.

Part
VIII

App
E

For more information:

> Intellisoft, Inc.
> Raju Varghese
> Stockmatt 3
> CH 5316, Leuggern, SWITZERLAND
> **100116,1001** on CompuServe
> **raju@intellisoft.ch**

Rich Text Sentry

Filenames:	RTFGUA1.ZIP, for Alpha processors
	RTFGUARD.ZIP, for Intel processors

Directory: Mailfax

Rich Text Sentry is part of Ben Goetter's Widgets for Microsoft Exchange collection. This extension patches Exchange to prevent you from accidentally sending out rich text messages to recipients running a client other than Exchange. Exchange makes it very easy to send a rich text message to such recipients, and all they see is a huge, unreadable chunk of encoded binary data. If recipients happens to be an Internet mailing list, 5,000 users each receive that chunk. Rich Text Sentry helps guard against such embarrassing accidents.

For more information:

> Ben Goetter
> **http://www.angrygraycat.com/goetter/widgets.htm**
> **goetter@halcyon.com**

RoloDial/MemoPad v1 for Windows 95 and NT

Filename: ROLODIAL.ZIP

Directory: Tools

RoloDial/MemoPad v1 (for Windows 95 and Windows NT) is three programs in one. It includes an address/phone book (with envelope printing), a phone dialer (with rate calculator and automatic phone log), and a sticky pad. RoloDial/ MemoPad is a fully integrated program that ties all program modules together. Multiple users and password protection make this good for home or office. This program is easy to use, set up, and learn.

For more information:

> Wells Software
> Chris M. Wells
> 350 4th St.
> Elyria, OH 44035
> **103132,1363** on CompuServe

Screen Saver Activate for Windows NT

Filename: SSACVT.ZIP

Directory: Scrensav

Screen Saver Activate 1.2.4 for Windows 95 and Windows NT 4.0 provides for convenient activation of the currently selected screen saver with a double mouse click or by a configurable keyboard hot key. It also allows toggling of the screen saver state between enabled/disabled for the current session with a visual indication of the current state. The program provides quick access to the Desktop control panel. If you have password protection enabled for the screen saver, this setting is preserved when Screen Saver Activate launches the screen saver.

For more information:

> Digital Control Systems
> Royce W. Shofner
> P.O. Box 505
> Hermitage, TN 37076
> Phone: (615) 889-6357
> Fax: (615) 889-9595
> BBS: (615) 889-9595
> **73347,145** on CompuServe

Part

VIII

App

E

Search and Replace, Touch for Windows 95, Windows, Windows NT (Shareware Version)

Filename: SR.ZIP

Directory: Tools

Search and Replace for Windows is a fast and easy-to-use search and replace utility that runs on Windows NT and Windows 95. It has been tested on VFAT (Windows 95's file system) and NTFS (Windows NT's optional, more secure file system). This program searches through multiple files and subdirectories for a phrase and can replace it with another phrase. Results are displayed color coded. The program has many options including backup, logging, and a viewer. Search results can be viewed in context, and files can be opened with the associated viewer. The registered version includes a year of e-mailed updates and support.

For more information:

Funduc Software
Mike Funduc
18733 Floral
Livonia, MI 48152
102372,2530 on CompuServe
funduc@sprynet.com

Search Replace for Windows 95 v2.3.1

Filename: FDREPL95.ZIP

Directory: Tools

Search Replace enables you to change a key word or phrase in many lines of many text files quickly and efficiently. Application developers can, for example, wire it into the Microsoft C++ visual work bench by choosing Tools, Options to enrich the editing capability. It can also be used as stand-alone by developers or administrators who need to change a piece of information in one or more lines of many files located in multiple directories.

In today's networking environment, many files can be manipulated on foreign machines. A UNIX file type option is available for those who need to remotely alter text files that conform to the UNIX file standard. UNIX saves files with just a newline (\n), while DOS saves files with a carriage return (\r)+newline(\n) combination. This program enables you to correctly handle UNIX files on your PC.

For more information:

> Floersch Enterprises
> Richard H. Floersch
> 7307 W. 89th Terrace
> Overland Park, KS 66212
> **http://www.sunflower.org/~dflo/**

Serv-U v2.0

> **Filename:**   SERV-U.ZIP
>
> **Directory:**   Internet

Serv-U is a server program or daemon. This FTP server acts as a messenger for file transfer between FTP clients and your computer. Once started, it sits in the background waiting for a client to contact it. After communications are established, it acts out the client's commands. With Serv-U, your PC is turned into an FTP server. This means that others on the computer network to whom you are connected (the Internet, for most people) can access your PC to copy, move, make, and delete files and directories via the FTP protocol.

For more information:

> Rob Beckers
> **rb5@acpub.duke.edu**
> **http://CatSoft.dorm.duke.edu**

SmartDraw 95

> **Filename:**   SDRAW95.ZIP
>
> **Directory:**   Graphics

SmartDraw 95 is the easy-to-use program for Windows 95 that lets anyone draw great looking diagrams, flow charts, flyers, posters, maps, invitations, and other

Part VIII
App E

business graphics. A better value and easier to use than Visio, and more powerful than SnapGrafx, SmartDraw provides drag and drop drawing; lines that automatically stay connected to shapes when they change size or position; rich text editing that automatically places text above, below, or inside shapes; shapes that grow to fit the text; a built-in library of professional-looking design styles that set just the right colors, shadows, and texture for your drawings; a large collection of built-in shape libraries and clip-art (SmartDrawings); and much, much more.

SmartDraw 95 works with the Microsoft Office, Lotus SmartSuite, Corel WordPerfect, and other programs that support OLE. Use SmartDraw for all your everyday drawing needs. You don't have to be an artist to get professional results when you use SmartDraw.

For more information:

> SmartDraw Software
> Paul Stannard
> 9974 Scripps Ranch Blvd., #35
> San Diego, CA 92131
> Phone: (619) 549-0314
> Fax: (619) 549-2830
> **smartdraw@aol.com**

SnagIt/32 v3.01

Filename: SNAG3230.ZIP

Directory: Graphics

SnagIt/32 is an easy-to-use Windows screen capture and print utility for Windows 95 and Windows NT. SnagIt/32 captures your screen, window, or region to the printer, Clipboard, or a variety of file formats, including PCX, JPG, TIF, and BMP. It fully supports Dynamic Data Exchange (DDE) and MAPI for easy integration into your applications. SnagIt/32 supports all Windows video modes and rastering printers.

For more information:

> TechSmith Corporation
> Chris Wheeler
> 3001 Coolidge Road, Suite 400
> East Lansing, MI 44823-6320
> Phone: (517) 333-2100
> Fax: (517) 333-1888
> **c.wheeler@techsmith.com**
> **72662,3267** on CompuServe

Somarsoft ACTSNT v1.7

Filename: ACTSNT.ZIP

Directory: Tools

Somarsoft ACTS sets the PC time via your modem. This is a Windows NT/ Windows 95 program that dials the NIST or USNO time source using a modem, obtains the current time, and uses this time to set the time on your PC. Similar programs designed for DOS do not work under NT because of security issues. Version 1.8 accommodates USNO phone number changes. The unregistered version is fully functional.

For more information:

> Somar Software
> Frank F. Ramos
> P.O. Box 642278
> San Francisco, CA 94164
> Phone: (415) 674-8771
> Fax: (415) 674-8771
> **72202.2574** on CompuServe
> **http://www.somar.com**

StopTime v1.3 for Windows 95 and NT

Filename: STOPTIME.ZIP

Directory: Tools

StopTime v1.3 is a handy clock utility. It enables you to set a timer that beeps when the time has expired, a stop watch, and a functional alarm clock with settings that can be saved. It provides a simple convenient method of resetting the computer's clock and date settings, as well as the ability to display the program settings in the title bar or program icon when run minimized. There is simple phone dialing capability, and the ability to time these calls.

For more information:

Wells Software
Chris M. Wells
350 4th St.
Elyria, OH 44035
103132,1363 on CompuServe

SuperMonitor

Filename: SUPERMON.ZIP

Directory: Tools

SuperMonitor displays your system's resources (such as memory) in windows you can start and stop, thus providing an accurate picture of the resources used. With SuperMonitor, you can easily see how much memory individual programs use, not just the overall picture. The program can display continuous, average, or maximum values in different windows, as well as log in the figures to disk. This shareware version is limited to three minutes of monitoring per window, after which you can start a new monitor window.

For more information:

Tessler's Nifty Tools
Mary Tessler
P.O. Box 1791
San Ramon, CA 94583
71044,542 on CompuServe

T4

Filename: T4_32_E.ZIP

Directory: Funstuff

T4 is a challenging board game for Windows 3.x, Windows NT, or Windows 95. It can be played against the computer or between two human players. It's a game with simple rules, not unlike Othello/Reversi or Four-In-A-Row, but richer and more complex. It has the interesting twist that your opponent can choose which piece you will play. (But revenge is sweet when it's her/his/its turn). The computer opponent plays a fairly decent game, with various skill levels. The package includes a detailed WinHelp file with graphics, and is easy to install.

For more information:

> Dider Frick
> Fbg. du Lac 6
> CH-2000, Neuchatel SWITZERLAND
> **dfrick@dial.eunet.ch**
> **100346,3030** on CompuServe

TaskView v4.2 for Windows 95 and NT

Part VIII

App E

Filename: TVIEW.EXE

Directory: Tools

TaskView is a utility program for Windows 95 and Windows NT that provides the ability to view and manage the active tasks currently operating on the computer. Virtual View capability expands the desktop working area for application programs. It is also particularly useful for terminating programs that are no longer cooperative and setting the priorities of operating tasks.

For more information:

> Reed Consulting
> 2312 Belvedere Drive
> Toledo, OH 43614
> **76237,516** on CompuServe

Tax Assistant v2 for Windows 95 and NT

Filename: TAXASST.ZIP

Directory: Tools

Tax Assistant v2 provides you a simple-to-use, yet functional program that tracks tax data, including personal and business expenses and incomes. The program then totals the amounts for many of the line items in the 1040 form. Basically, it's a simple tax record database. Version 2 adds multiple document interface, undo, and more sophisticated sorting.

For more information:

Wells Software
Chris M. Wells
350 4th St.
Elyria, OH 44035
103132,1363 on CompuServe

Text File Line Break for Windows 95 v1.1

Filename: SBRK95.ZIP

Directory: Dskfile

The Set Text File Line Break program enables you to handle files with long lines by breaking up those lines. You specify a column width, and the program breaks each long line down into multiple lines not exceeding your specified column limit. If a word begins before the specified column but ends after, it is moved to the next line (no hyphenation is attempted). The long line break down continues until a hard line break is encountered. The result is a text file that can be viewed using NOTEPAD.EXE. There are many situations where long line files need to be broken into shorter lines files. This application accomplishes that task in the blink of an eye.

For more information:

Floersch Enterprises
Richard H. Floersch
7307 W. 89th Terrace
Overland Park, KS 66212
http://www.sunflower.org/~dflo/

The Psychedelic Screen Saver Collection v2.5

Filename: PSYCH25.ZIP

Directory: Scrensav

The Psychedelic Screen Saver Collection v2.5 is a collection of screen savers that generate an endless variety of mesmerizing patterns. As the patterns materialize on your screen, the colors shift, undulate, and—generally speaking—look cool. Whether you're into abstract art or mathematics, you'll love these screen savers. Included are 32-bit screen savers for Windows 95 and Windows NT.

For more information:

Michael Irving
3423 175th Ave. NE
Redmond, WA 98052
http://www.halcyon.com/pixel/psych.htm
pixel@halcyon.com

ThumbsPlus v3.0

Filename: THMPLS32.EXE

Directory: Graphics

ThumbsPlus is a graphic file viewer, locator, and organizer that simplifies the process of finding and maintaining graphics, clipart files, fonts, and animations. It displays a small image (thumbnail) of each file. You can use ThumbsPlus to browse, view, edit, crop, launch external editors, and copy images to the Clipboard. You can use drag and drop to organize graphics files by moving them to appropriate directories. ThumbsPlus also creates a slide show from selected graphics, and installs bitmap files as Windows wallpaper. You can print individual graphics files, or the thumbnails themselves, as a catalog. ThumbsPlus can convert to several formats, either one at a time or in batch mode. You can also perform image editing in batch mode. ThumbsPlus also converts metafile graphics to bitmaps (rasterization).

Part
VIII

App
E

For more information:

> Cerious Software, Inc.
> Phillip Crews
> **http://www.cerious.com**
> **pcrews@cerious.com**
> **ftp://ftp.cerious.com**

TimeClock 96 v3 for Windows 95 and NT

Filename: TIMECLOK.ZIP

Directory: Tools

Time Clock 96 v3 for Windows 95 and Windows NT is a super punch clock. It has a simple interface, is easy to learn and use, and yet has comprehensive, powerful features. It tracks employee information in an Access compatible database. Features include automatic time and salary totals, password protection, timecard printing, employee error control, and much more. Let Time Clock 96 save you time and money while making your employee management easier and more effective.

For more information:

> Wells Software
> Chris M. Wells
> 350 4th St.
> Elyria, OH 44035
> **103132,1363** on CompuServe

Touch File Date/Time v1.2.1

Filename: TOUCH95.ZIP

Directory: Tools

The Win95 Touch File Date/Time program enables application developers to set the last modified date and time of selected files to force the compiler to rebuild and or relink their projects. When the application is complete and ready for distribution, the file date/times of the distributed modules can be set to reflect release versions. Application developers can, for example, wire it into the Microsoft C++ visual work bench by choosing Tools, Options to enrich their development environment, or use it as a stand-alone application. The application was designed to handle a huge number of files from multiple directories (more than 100,000 files at a time).

For more information:

> Floersch Enterprises
> Richard H. Floersch
> 7307 W. 89th Terrace
> Overland Park, KS 66212
> **http://www.sunflower.org/~dflo/**

TrueSpeech Batch Converter (Beta Release)

Filename: BATCH.ZIP

Directory: Internet

This conversion utility converts Windows WAV files (8Khz, 16-bit PCM) to the TrueSpeech 8.5 format for use with the TrueSpeech Player or the Windows Sound Recorder. There is no limit to the number or size of the files being converted. WAV files can also be converted and played back with the Windows 95 and Windows NT built-in Sound Recorder; however, Sound Recorder performs only one conversion at a time.

For more information:

> DSP Group, Inc.
> Jon Louis
> 3120 Scott Blvd.
> Santa Clara, CA 95054-3317
> Phone: (408) 986-4300
> Fax: (408) 986-4323
> **Webster@dspg.com**
> **tsplayer@DSPG.com**

TrueSpeech Player 3.10b

Filename: TSPLYNT.EXE

Directory: Internet

The TrueSpeech Player for the Internet offers the highest quality, lowest bandwidth (8.5Kbps) Internet audio available today. It provides real time, streaming audio playback over the Internet, browser independence and bookmarking ability, and the ability to store and listen to your favorite sites directly from the player without needing to first launch your browser. The Windows Sound Recorder can encode WAV files into TrueSpeech, and both Sound Recorder and Media Player can play them back.

For more information:

> DSP Group, Inc.
> Jon Louis
> 3120 Scott Blvd.
> Santa Clara, CA 95054-3317
> Phone: (408) 986-4300
> Fax: (408) 986-4323
> **Webster@dspg.com**
> **tsplayer@DSPG.com**

Turbo Browser for Windows 95 and NT

Filename: TBNTPREV.EXE

Directory: Dskfile

Turbo Browser is designed to provide you with convenient file management and viewing capabilities. The Files and Folders window is similar to that of Windows 95 and Windows NT 4.0 Explorer, along with right-clicking features in Explorer. When you select a file in the Files and Folders window, the file contents automatically appear in the Preview window. By moving up and down the file list, you can easily view additional files. The toolbar icons help you with frequently performed tasks. When you position the cursor over them, you see helpful hints for their functions. A Searchbar is provided to find files quickly.

For more information:

> Pacific Gold Coast Corp.
> Janine Avedisian
> 15 Glen St.
> Glen Cove, NY 11542
> Phone: (516) 759-3011
> Fax: (516) 759-3014
> **74777,3450** on CompuServe

UltraEdit-32 v3.10b

Filename: UEDIT32.ZIP

Directory: Dskfile

UltraEdit-32 Text/Binary Editor 2.11 is a text/hex editor that handles unlimited size files. Features include column edit with column fill, cut, delete, insert sequential number, HEX edit with cut/copy/paste, macros, bookmarks, find and replace, word-wrap, fixup CR/LF, auto indentation, backup file, context sensitive help, line and column display, multiple windows on same file, font selection, Print Preview, go to, drag-and-drop, find in files, and more.

For more information:

> IDM Computer Services
> Ian D. Mead
> 8209 Chestnut Hill Ct.
> West Chester, OH 45069
> Phone: (513) 779-8549
> Fax: (513) 779-8549
> **71613,2654** on CompuServe
> **idm@iglou.com**
> **http://members.aol.com:/idmcompsrv/index.htm**

Part
VIII

App
E

VuePro VuePro-32

Filename: VUEPRO44.EXE

Directory: Graphics

The VuePro 32 program provides you with fast graphic image viewing, excellent image quality, and ease of use. VuePro32 displays all major image file formats, movie files, sound files, and slide show files. ZIP and UUEncoded files are automatically decoded and displayed. The program also enables you to create your own custom screen saver files. VuePro 32 also has a command line interface, which enables other Windows applications to use VuePro 32 to display graphics files or scanned images.

For more information:

> Handy Software
> James R. Wilson
> 101 N. Greenville Ave., Suite 66
> Allen, TX 75002

WebForms v2.1a

Filename: WBFRM.ZIP

Directory: Internet

WebForms v2.1a is a World Wide Web forms generator that automatically creates HTML forms and reads their responses. Responses are sent to your e-mail address. No HTML knowledge or CGI is necessary to use WebForms. It comes with an online help system and tutorial. WebForms is great for taking customer orders, doing surveys, or anything that requires user input on the World Wide Web. It makes doing business on the Web a snap.

For more information:

> Q&D Software Development
> Dave Verscheiser
> 10 B Sentinal Ct.
> Cheatham, NY 07828
> Phone: (201) 635-1824
> **help@q-d.com**

WebImage 1.72

Filename: WI32D.ZIP

Directory: Internet

WebImage is a powerful graphics program that loads images in both full-screen mode and thumbnail mode. When loaded full-screen, images can be panned, zoomed, and edited in the main window. When in thumbnail mode, small thumbnail size images of graphics files appear in the main window. Thumbnails can be selected using the pointer. Double-click a thumbnail to launch it into full-screen viewing mode. The program has transparent GIF, interlaced GIF, and PNG support, and can create imagemaps.

For more information:

> Group 42
> Chris Komnick
> 228 Mill St. #102
> Milford, OH 45150

WebMania! 1.1

Filename: WMNIA.ZIP

Directory: Internet

Part VIII

App E

WebMania! 1.1 is an HTML editor and forms generator that makes Web authoring a breeze and requires little or no HTML or CGI knowledge. Forms responses are sent via e-mail and imported into WebMania's database. It includes support for tables, lists, images, and much more. WebMania! includes up to 60 programmable buttons that you can easily change as HTML standards evolve and as you learn new tags.

For more information:

> Q&D Software Development
> Dave Verscheiser
> 10 B Sentinal Ct.
> Cheatham, NY 07828
> Phone: (201) 635-1824
> **help@q-d.com**

Webodex Organizer

Filename: WDX20B2B.EXE

Directory: Internet

Webodex Organizer is an innovative software product that enables users to store, organize, and access their favorite Internet Web sites, Gopher, FTP, and e-mail addresses. This virtual electronic organizer navigates the Net with your browser and comes packed with the Best of the Net sites.

For more information:

> Novaweb Incorporated Internet Production
> Susan Sweeney
> Suite 200, Cambridge 1, 202 Brownlow Ave.
> Dartmouth, NS, B3B 1T5 CANADA
> Phone: (902) 468-2578
> Fax: (902) 468-9869
> **nip@nova.novaweb.ca**
> **http://novaweb.com/webodex/index.html**

WinImage 2.50

Filename: WIMANT25.ZIP

Directory: Dskfile

WINIMAGE-2.50 enables you to create copies of DMF format disks. You can also open a CD-ROM ISO image file in read-only mode, create a disk image from a floppy disk, extract a file from the image, make an empty image, inject a file into the image file, and put the image on blank disk. This program can read, write, and format DMF format disks.

For more information:

> Gilles Vollant
> 13, Rue Francois Mansart
> F-91540 Mennecy FRANCE
> **100144.2636** on CompuServe

WinZip 6.0a for Windows 95

Filename: WINZIP95.ZIP

Directory: Dskfile

WinZip brings the convenience of Windows to the use of ZIP files. Windows 95, Windows NT, and Windows 3.1 versions are available. Includes PKZIP-compatible built-in zip and unzip, so PKZIP is not needed for basic archive operations, and built-in support for popular Internet file formats: TAR, GZIP, and UNIX compress.

WinZip includes a powerful yet intuitive point-and-click, drag-and-drop interface for viewing, running, extracting, adding, deleting, and testing files in ZIP, LZH, and ARC files, including self-extracting archives. Optional virus scanning support is included.

For more information:

Nico Mak Computing
Nico Mak
115 James P Casey Rd.
Bristol, CT 06010
Phone: (203) 585-5376
Fax: (203) 585-7352
70056.241 on CompuServe
support@winzip.com
www.winzip.com

WrapUP

Filename: WRAPUP.ZIP

Directory: Tools

WrapUp is a program that acts like a Shutdown group to perform actions before you shut down your system. With WrapUp, you can automatically perform actions such as backing up your PC's hard disk(s), logging out of your PC network (LAN), synchronizing your laptop PC's hard disk with your desktop PC's hard disk or vice versa, or any other type of cleanup operation you need to perform.

For more information:

Tessler's Nifty Tools
Mary Tessler
P.O. Box 1791
San Ramon, CA 94583
71044,542 on CompuServe

Index

Check out Que® Books
on the World Wide Web
http://www.mcp.com/que

As the biggest software release in computer history, Windows 95 continues to redefine the computer industry. Click here for the latest info on our Windows 95 books

Make computing quick and easy with these products designed exclusively for new and casual users

Examine the latest releases in word processing, spreadsheets, operating systems, and suites

The Internet, The World Wide Web, CompuServe®, America Online®, Prodigy® —it's a world of ever-changing information. Don't get left behind!

Find out about new additions to our site, new bestsellers and hot topics

In-depth information on high-end topics: find the best reference books for databases, programming, networking, and client/server technologies

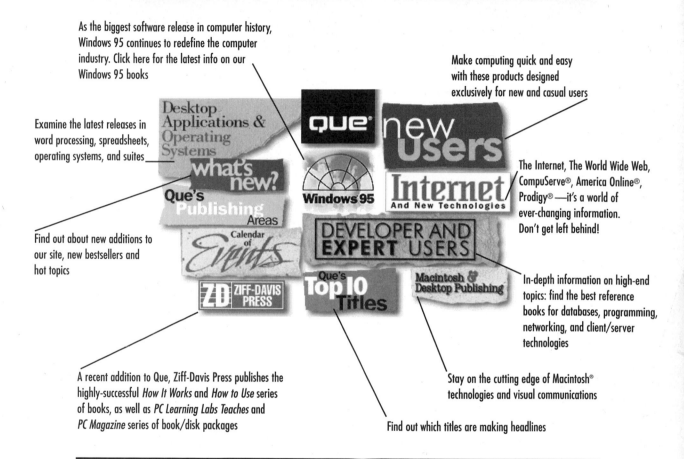

A recent addition to Que, Ziff-Davis Press publishes the highly-successful *How It Works* and *How to Use* series of books, as well as *PC Learning Labs Teaches* and *PC Magazine* series of book/disk packages

Stay on the cutting edge of Macintosh® technologies and visual communications

Find out which titles are making headlines

With 6 separate publishing groups, Que develops products for many specific market segments and areas of computer technology. Explore our Web Site and you'll find information on best-selling titles, newly published titles, upcoming products, authors, and much more.

- Stay informed on the latest industry trends and products available
- Visit our online bookstore for the latest information and editions
- Download software from Que's library of the best shareware and freeware